New Mattheson Studies

Johann Mattheson: engraving (after 1719) by Christian Fritzsch after Wahll (Hamburg, Staatsarchiv)

New Mattheson Studies

Edited by

GEORGE J. BUELOW

Professor of Music, Indiana University

and

HANS JOACHIM MARX

Professor of Musicology, University of Hamburg

CAMBRIDGE UNIVERSITY PRESS

Cambridge

London   New York   New Rochelle

Melbourne   Sydney

Published by the Press Syndicate of the University of Cambridge
The Pitt Building, Trumpington Street, Cambridge CB2 1RP
32 East 57th Street, New York, NY 10022, USA
296 Beaconsfield Parade, Middle Park, Melbourne 3206, Australia

First published 1983

Printed in the United States of America

Library of Congress Cataloging in Publication Data
Main entry under title:
New Mattheson studies.
English and German.
Includes index.
1. Mattheson, Johann, 1681–1764 – Addresses, essays,
lectures. I. Buelow, George J. II. Marx, Hans Joachim,
1935– .
ML55.M327N5   1983   780′.92′4   83–5157
ISBN 0 521 25115 X

Contents

v

Contents

Preface

In 1977 a few American musicologists set out to honor the forthcoming three-hundredth anniversary of Johann Mattheson's birth, to occur in 1981. The impetus came from Professor Ernest Harriss, who had the stimulating and novel suggestion that we should organize a *Festschrift* for Mattheson. *New Mattheson Studies* in effect serves that purpose but also has the greater distinction of demonstrating with its collection of essays the continuing importance and influence of Mattheson's music and writings on musical scholarship after three hundred years.

Once motivated to promote the occasion of the tricentennial, it became apparent that a volume of essays could serve only one aspect of such a major event. Although Mattheson's name has been well known to musicological research since the nineteenth century, only isolated efforts to examine and evaluate the accomplishments of this great German theorist, composer, and philosopher have occurred since the publication of Beekman C. Cannon's major study in 1947. In this realization originated the plan to stimulate new Mattheson research by holding the first International Johann Mattheson Symposium, which the editors of this book organized and implemented. On 26 September 1981 twenty-four musicologists from the United States, England, Europe, and Australia gathered in Wolfenbüttel, Germany, for a three-day symposium held at the magnificent Herzog August Bibliothek. Wolfenbüttel was not inappropriate as the site for such a meeting, for Mattheson, a native of Hamburg, was familiar with the city and its superb ducal library, recording in *Plus ultra* III (p. 575) that he "ehmals in Wolfenbüttel anderthalb hundert musikalischer Schriften angetroffen habe," as well as having attended a performance of a twenty-four-voice composition by Johannes Rosenmüller. This visit to Wolfenbüttel probably took place during the time he attended the *Laurentius-Messe* in neighboring Braunschweig during August

1705 as guest of Duke Anton Ulrich (see *Ehrenpforte*, p. 194). This new volume, then, includes papers presented at the Wolfenbüttel Symposium, but also a number of studies submitted by those authors interested in Mattheson research who could not attend.

During the past five years the editors of the *New Mattheson Studies* have received assistance and encouragement from many friends, colleagues, and institutions. First, our thanks go, in the United States, to Professors Beekman C. Cannon and Ernest Harriss, and in Germany to Professor Paul Raabe, for their advice and concern at various stages of the project. We should like to thank Indiana University and the University of Hamburg for their direct financial aid to the editors. Above all, we are deeply indebted to the Stiftung Volkswagenwerk, Wolfsburg, Germany, for financing the symposium, and the Herzog August Bibliothek, particularly Dr. Sabine Solf and Dr. Hans Haase, director of the Musiksammlung, for making the participants feel so welcome within the unique research facilities of the library. Our thanks also to the English consul general in Hamburg, Mr. K. C. Thom, for wishing to honor Mattheson's lifelong association with the office of the English representative in Hamburg, by giving the members of the symposium an elegant reception on the evening of Mattheson's three-hundredth birthday. Finally, our greatest debt of appreciation goes to Cambridge University Press and its music editor, Rosemary Dooley, for taking on the challenge of publishing the *New Mattheson Studies*.

We hope that the variety and excellence of scholarship found within these pages will suggest to new generations of scholars of eighteenth-century music and German culture in general the enormous significance of Johann Mattheson. If the symposium and this publication stimulate a renewed interest in Mattheson's massive and varied achievements, then those of us who have labored long on these projects will have had ample reward. And in closing this introduction it should not go unrecorded that one additional service was paid to Mattheson in his three-hundredth anniversary year. After decades of inquiries on the part of several individuals regarding his final resting-place in Hamburg's St. Michael's church, and after years of being informed his burial site was lost, Ernest Harriss and the editors of this book were permitted access to the St. Michael's crypt. After a puzzling and momentarily discouraging search, we were able literally to "uncover" his grave plate, buried in two centuries of dust and dirt and an enormous pile of oak cabinetry pieces from a destroyed organ case. By the light of a flashlight we saw revealed for the first time in at least a half century Mattheson's personally composed inscription: "Ruhe Kammer / für Herrn Johann Mattheson / weyland / Grosfürstlicher / Holsteinischer / Legations Rath / und dessen / Ehe Genossin / Zu ewigen Tagen." Discovered just two days before the opening of the Wolfenbüttel symposium and four days before the three-hundredth anniversary of his birthday on 28 September 1981, this fortuitous restoration of Mattheson's grave from the accumulated dirt and neglect of the ages symbolized to us the beginning of a new era for Mattheson scholarship.

January 1983
George J. Buelow, Indiana University
Hans Joachim Marx, University of Hamburg

General abbreviations

AfMw	*Archiv für Musikwissenschaft*
AMl	*Acta musicologica*
AmZ	*Allgemeine musikalische Zeitung*
B-J	*Bach-Jahrbuch*
Cannon, Mattheson	B. C. Cannon, *Johann Mattheson, Spectator in Music* (New Haven, 1947, repr. 1968)
JAMS	*Journal of the American Musicological Society*
JbP	*Jahrbuch der Musikbibliothek Peters*
JMT	*Journal of Music Theory*
Mf	*Die Musikforschung*
MGG	*Die Musik in Geschichte und Gegenwart*
M&L	*Music and Letters*
MQ	*The Musical Quarterly*
MR	*The Music Review*
New Grove	*The New Grove Dictionary of Music and Musicians*
RBM	*Revue belge de musicologie*
RISM	*Répertoire international des sources musicales*
SIMG	*Sammelbände der Internationalen Musik-Gesellschaft*
StA Hbg	Staatsarchiv Hamburg
SP	State Papers, London
ZIMG	*Zeitschrift der Internationalen Musik-Gesellschaft*
ZVHG	*Zeitschrift des Vereins für Hamburgische Geschichte*

Abbreviations for the works of Johann Mattheson

Capellmeister	*Der vollkommene Capellmeister* (1739)
Critica musica I/II	*Critica musica* (1722 and 1725)
Ehrenpforte	*Grundlage einer Ehren-Pforte* (1740)
General-Baß-Schule I	*Große General-Baß-Schule* (1731)
General-Baß-Schule II	*Kleine General-Baß-Schule* (1735)
Göttingischer Ephorus	*Der neue göttingische aber viel schlechter als die alten Lacedämonischen urtheilende Ephorus* (1727)
Händels Lebensbeschreibung	*Georg Friedrich Händels Lebensbeschreibung,* translated by Mattheson (1761)
Melodische Wissenschaft	*Kern melodischer Wissenschafft* (1737)
Mithridat	*Mithridat wider den Gift einer welschen Satyre, genannt La Musica* (1749)
Musicalischer Patriot	*Der musicalische Patriot* (1728)
Orchestre I	*Das neu-eröffnete Orchestre* (1713)
Orchestre II	*Das beschützte Orchestre* (1717)
Orchestre III	*Das forschende Orchestre* (1721)
Organisten-Probe	*Exemplarische Organisten-Probe* (1719)
Panacea I	*Matthesons bewährte Panacea* (1750)
Plus ultra I–IV	*Plus ultra, ein Stückwerk von neuer und mancherley Art,* I (1754), II–III (1755), IV (1756)

Singspiele	*Die neueste Untersuchung der Singspiele* (1744)
Tresespiel	*Philologisches Tresespiel, als ein kleiner Beytrag zur kritischen Geschichte der deutschen Sprache* (1752)

1

The legacy of Johann Mattheson: a retrospective evaluation

BEEKMAN C. CANNON

New Haven, Connecticut

It is a great honor as well as a pleasure to speak tonight on the three-hundredth anniversary of the birth of Johann Mattheson. More than forty years have passed by since I undertook a study of the Mattheson manuscripts, documents, and books constituting his *Nachlaß* left to the Hamburg Stadtbibliothek. My investigations were inspired by the startling disparity between the voluminous, wide-ranging nature of his published works, which I was fortunately able to examine in the Music Library of Yale University and the index of manuscripts contained in Eitner's *Quellen-Lexikon,* and the little serious attention Mattheson as an author, composer, and musician himself had aroused among students and scholars of eighteenth-century music. This symposium, which has brought together such a distinguished international gathering of scholars, has therefore been for me enormously satisfying, for it is positive evidence of the dramatic growth of scholarly curiosity about that extraordinary citizen of Hamburg.

Author, composer, and musician Johann Mattheson certainly was. Today it would not be inappropriate to extend the terms of his intellectual competence by recalling his more than passing interest in the fields of politics, economics and journalism, theology, linguistics and philology. And in justice to his own growing absorption in the meaning of words it seems appropriate to consider for a moment the word "legacy," which is my topic today. The generally accepted meaning of this word now is "a gift to posterity." The word "legacy," or "Vermächtniß" in Mattheson's time, was used more narrowly as a legal term, signifying a gift to a person or institution left in a person's last will or testament. Both the broad and the legal definitions are

Editors' note: Professor Cannon presented this paper, the final event (Öffentlicher Abschlußvortrag) of the International Johann Mattheson Symposium, on 27 September 1981 in the magnificent Augusteerhalle of the Herzog August Bibliothek in Wolfenbüttel.

appropriate for this discussion: In fact Mattheson, before his death, took legal pains to leave not one but several legacies to posterity, and these should provide the substance of any appraisal. But there is still another interpretation of the English word, legacy, that has come down to us from his time and is also fitting for us to bear in mind. It is by Joseph Addison, Mattheson's contemporary, whose writing he admired and sought to emulate. Addison wrote, "Books are the legacies that a great genius leaves to mankind." Undoubtedly Mattheson would have approved of the positive, slightly sententious, character of this statement. It is apposite for us today for two reasons: First, it is only through his books that even a partial appraisal may be made today, and, second, much of Mattheson's genius, his "characteristic disposition," which is what the word "genius" meant to Addison and his contemporaries, is embodied in his books. But not all.

Mattheson's original legacy consisted of three parts: first, his published books and music and, second, a considerable quantity of his music in manuscript. Both of these he left to the Hamburg Stadt-bibliothek. The third, certainly not of less importance to him, was the exceptionally grand organ he donated to the recently completed church of St. Michael. Indeed, with its monumental case surmounted by the donor's portrait, this was a most obvious witness to the personal genius of a man who once admitted to being seized by the fear of God when the organ roared. Together these three elements constituted his carefully formed legacy: music composed and performed by Mattheson the musician, an organ as the most imposing visual and aural evidence of his own material achievement – as well as the symbol of the highest goal of music, the worship of God – and the books to make sure that music is correctly understood, written, and performed to carry out that purpose.

History itself has denied us the opportunity to appraise all but one of these three parts in 1981. Organ and portrait were lost in 1905 when St. Michael's went up in flames, and virtually all of the music Mattheson prized most highly was thought to have met a similar fate in World War II until very recently. Were it still possible to study more than a handful of the music he valued most – that is to say, his operas, cantatas, and serenatas composed for public, official, state, or private occasions, but above all, the oratorios composed for Hamburg Cathedral – how would this affect an appraisal today? Certainly his work as a composer would not measure up in quantity or even in substance to his output as a writer of words. It is also easy to forget the countless hours of time and energy spent as secretary to the British ambassador in Hamburg, represented by hundreds of documents in

2

the Public Record Office in London. Although they may attract little attention today, Mattheson took as much pride in them as he did in his translations of many English literary works, though none of these activities had anything to do with music. Yet, until deafness terminated his work as a composer, composition remained the centerpiece of his efforts.

Mattheson's literary legacy is of course a bounteous storehouse of musical information of many types and in many forms. Accumulated during the most vigorous years of his life, it is as diverse in quality as it is in intrinsic interest. But its sheer bulk, together with the prolixity of the style in which most of it is written, may have constituted a major obstacle to a comprehensive or impartial understanding until recent years. In the past, to be sure, some scholars garnered rich rewards from their excavations; others were so struck by the rudeness of his critical opinions and the force of his personality that they have scarcely penetrated the veneer of his dogmatic style. Few so much as glanced at the music he wrote before it disappeared. Yet throughout his life Mattheson unquestionably thought of himself as a creative practitioner of the art of music – as a composer-musician preoccupied with the nature and goals of music composed, performed, and experienced. He began his literary career to defend and explicate the sacred art by demolishing or reforming all its enemies. Who were they? The targets who inspired his most withering scorn at the outset were numerous. He identified them as the pedantic scholars, musicians, and performers who devoted all their efforts to learned discussion and analysis of antiquated musical theories. He also singled out ill-educated, narrow-minded teachers, parsimonious patrons, and frivolous amateurs. His heroes, on the other hand, were great princes and patrons with enlightened taste and well-filled pockets and, of course, the composers and musicians supported by them. Though these enemies of music fade out in Mattheson's later writing, the latter, despite his own disappointment with the Duke of Schleswig-Holstein, retained their ideal status. Frederick III of Prussia was for him a late recruit to this exclusive company.

Today it is widely held by a number of literary critics that a man's literary style is the mirror of his intellectual makeup. With this in mind it may be interesting to consider the literary style of his early and his later works. Certainly an encounter with his first two *Orchestre* treatises, with their torrential mixture of elements from German, French, English, Latin, and Italian, suggests a mind stuffed with verbal incongruities, often exemplified in macaronic texts. Verbal pretentiousness is of course characteristic of a German literary style that had drawn freely on words from ancient and modern foreign languages for more than a century before Mattheson first set pen to paper. However discordantly this verbal mixture resonates in our ears it is not necessarily an index of intellectual confusion, though it may lead to intellectual inconsistencies. Though Mattheson was clearly interested in the simplification of the German language by the elimination of non-German words, the success of this effort is more visual than actual in his later works.

By the same token, in perusing many of his earlier works, whether a treatise for the *Galant Homme* (a journal for coffee-house readers) or a critical attack on a pompous pedant, one is struck by the extraordinary diversity of the evidence Mattheson uses in support of his arguments. Few men, one is tempted to declare, can have possessed the tireless, voracious curiosity – and gullibility, too – to devour treatises, books, journals, and memoirs ranging from the classical past to ephemeral news reports of the present with such profligate enthusiasm. Few authors have permitted themselves to inundate their readers with so much supplementary evidence, however fascinating, if irrelevant to the pursuit of a particular line of thought. If anything, these characteristics of style and his particular cast of mind are just as marked in his *Vollkommener Capellmeister* of 1739 as in his *Orchestres*, written two or three decades earlier. There is, of course, a shift in the nature of his sources, just as there is in the subjects of his immediate concerns.

In fact, during Mattheson's long career as a writer there is little change in his literary style, his patterns of thought, or his basic spiritual, intellectual, and moral values. He continued to perceive the goals of music from his own brightly colored perspective of a world order reaching back into the past – ultimately to classical antiquity. In his early youth, he tells us, the narrow viewpoint of the conventional citizen of the Lutheran city-state was not for him, but rather the multifaceted world of great affairs, represented or symbolized by the operatic theater. Though his own allegiance to the spiritual order of Lutheranism was never in question, the world that excited his imagination and nourished his thought from the outset was the humanistic, cosmopolitan world presided over by Louis XIV, who for Mattheson was above all others "le premier homme du monde." Hierarchical in all respects, this world represented to him the natural order created by a benign God. Its grand progress, independent of changes wrought by political or military events, led by the banner of empiricism and common sense, is impeded only by the exuberant weeds of ancient ignorance. Since the latter are nourished by the pedantry of antiquated Lutheran musicians, knowledge, through Mattheson's teaching, of all current musical practice and thought elsewhere is the essential antidote. Revolutionary change, however, was foreign to Mattheson's innate conservatism. His position is never in doubt but is nicely expressed in a homely metaphor in an issue of *Critica musica* that appeared in 1724. By this time Mattheson had mapped out his own grand design as a writer, volume by volume for the next fifteen years. Periodically, he asserts, it is necessary for a man to clean house. This process requires neither remodeling, pulling down, nor building a new structure but simply house-cleaning. "To make a house useful," he writes, "cleaning it is not unimportant and must be done thoroughly before one considers new furnishings. Anyone who brings in beautiful tapestries and glittering furnishings before sweeping out all the dirt begins at the wrong end."[1]

As early as 1713 the ultimate goal of this house cleaning is the establishment of affective melodic practice. This remained an immediate goal – not a vision of the future. He does not seem to have encountered directly any of the writing of the early proponents of the *seconda prattica*. He simply took for granted the validity and the long-standing practice of their melodic-rhetorical premises. To be sure, his growing enthusiasm for good melodic writing as the sine qua non of musicianship caused a vast expansion in his thinking by the time he published *Kern melodischer Wissenschafft* in 1737. But his conviction that *scientia melodica* must be grounded upon a thorough knowledge of grammar and rhetoric remained unshaken – if anything, more emphatic. Thus, he may argue that a finely written melody needs only a simple bass, only to remind the reader on the following page that an interesting bass line will contribute more to the beauty of a melody than a dull one, and that proper musical knowledge is based as much upon thorough grounding in the composition of a figured bass as it is upon a thorough knowledge of the art of counterpoint.

As the culmination of his many published offensives in the continuing campaign against ignorance, the *Capellmeister* was therefore designed to provide a comprehensive, detailed summary of all areas of musical knowledge, brought up to date. So far as he is concerned there is nothing radical or visionary in devoting one-third of its

1 "Wiewohl, wenn ein Haus brauchbar seyn soll, ist die Reinigung desselben kein geringes, und muß allerdings vorhergehen, ehe man die *Meubles* zur Hand nimt . . . wer aber zuvor allerhand schöne Tapeten nebst anderm schimmernder Haus-Geräthe hineinbringen, und hernach erst auskehren will, der fängt vom unrechten Ende an." *Critica musica* II, 54.

contents to a detailed discussion of melodic writing: It is simply the musical element most in need of correction. Nor is there any indication of a prophetic awareness of the future direction of musical aspiration and practice. His attitude toward wordless, instrumental music is characteristic. Repeatedly he asserts that instrumental music can never equal, let alone surpass, the expressive power of vocal music. To be sure, he argues, a skillful dramatic composer must be able to express the passions of the soul by instrumental music. Yet he refers the reader to the affective characteristics of dance forms in the context of opera as the appropriate means of achieving this end.

Mattheson was older, perhaps wiser, and vastly more knowledgeable, if not less opinionated, by the completion of his *Vollkommener Capellmeister* in 1739 than he was in 1713. Yet his deep-seated convictions and ideological values all reappear in it, if with sometimes less polemic fire than in the first of the *Orchestres*. The most fundamental of them is the conviction, voiced by Martin Luther, that music is the noblest gift of God to man, next only to theology. Time and again this belief is reiterated in direct quotation or in paraphrase. As an orthodox Lutheran Mattheson must have believed that music in the worship of God should be the most accomplished and expressive that man is able to provide, and that the highest calling of a musician is composing and performing music in the service of God. Undoubtedly he subscribed to the underlying theme of Heinrich Brockes's *Irdisches Vergnügen in Gott* that "since the [natural] world is so beautiful, how glorious must its creator be"[2] and its corollary that man should take the most sensuous pleasure in the pursuit of Christian belief and morality. Again and again Mattheson reminds his readers that the powers of music are an integral part of the natural world provided by a beneficent God. He cites reports of its effect upon animals, its therapeutic powers in the cure of human ailments, and, above all, its natural capacity to move human passions and affections. In his declining years he occupied himself with compiling and discoursing upon the many references to music in the Bible in the further substantiation of his deep-seated convictions. Indeed these books, which were written in his old age and are concerned with what may be termed a theology of music, form a substantial part of his literary legacy.

That music is a natural gift of God provides the foundation for the second of Mattheson's fundamental premises, the promotion and

2 "Da alles auf der Welt so schön, wie herrlich muß der Schöpfer sein." Brockes, *Irdisches Vergnügen in Gott* I, 7.

6

defense of which inspired the most substantial portion of his writing. Since the origin of music is in nature, a true understanding and use of it can be reached only by natural means and not by any artificial or numerical system. Music should not appeal to the eye but only through the ear to the senses, or the passions, which alone communicate pleasure to the soul and to man's reason. This premise lies at the heart of his musical thought. The age-old theoretical controversy about the interval of the fourth provided its primary focus. By no means gifted with a truly original, tightly disciplined mind, he was driven in the defense of his pragmatic position to the study of all the evidence he could find in print or in daily personal experience, and also to efforts to seek out and to demonstrate as composer and teacher what he himself deemed to be the most effective musical means of reaching the passions and affections.

Mattheson's youthful plunge into the enchanting world of opera provided evidence of how this could best be done. Clearly the intensity of this experience, amounting to a kind of personal revelation, remained decisive throughout his life. For it was the operatic high school that taught him the affective powers of the different styles, keys , rhythms, and forms constituting the natural resources of music. It also provided the perspective from which to view music inherited from the past. And it convinced him that the correct use of all these resources depends upon the understanding of the poetic texts to which music is written for the stage or the church. There should of course be no conflict between these areas of musical endeavor. The only difference between them consists in the fact that since religious affections are more profound and diverse than those normally provided in operatic poetry, their musical expression requires a wider range of musical techniques and knowledge.

As presented to the *Galant Homme* in Mattheson's first treatise, the application of these beliefs and their implications were upsetting enough to provoke cries of outrage from those Lutheran musicians whose knowledge of long-standing cosmopolitan musical thought and practice was limited. He would have been disappointed had this not been the case. As with many of his contemporaries, controversy was the necessary fuel for subsequent endeavor, and Mattheson was thus provided with reasons for defending himself as a musician and for justifying intellectually his affective doctrines. In the second and third *Orchestres* his strategy for the defeat of his foes begins to be evident.

First it was necessary to mobilize contemporary musicians favorable to his views and to smoke out the opposition. Second, he had to seek out and present supporting evidence in his intellectual defense from sources as diverse in their position as René Descartes, Athanasius Kircher, and John Locke. As a self-described eclectic he could cite Descartes's doctrines of the passions of the soul while rejecting his doctrine of innate ideas, or Kircher's enthusiasm for the oratorical style while deriding his theories of musical number. Thanks to his diligent researches he could employ the very scholarly weapons of the opposition to overwhelm them by floods of learned references. Reaching beyond the range of scholastic weapons, he next resorts to the form and content of journalism to reach a wider reading public. As his strategy unfolds it begins to resemble the military tactics of his great contemporary, the Duke of Marlborough: to complete the encirclement of a foe already reeling from scholastic and journalistic bombardment with a brilliant cavalry charge. Hence Mattheson's take-over of the musical direction of Hamburg Cathedral – largely, if his own statements can be trusted, at his own expense. For this would provide the means of demonstrating the validity of theatrical church music when composed by a *galant homme* and performed by the best singers and instrumentalists from the Hamburg Opera. By the time of his *Kern melodischer Wissenschafft*, already published and ready for incorporation in his crowning endeavor, *Der vollkommene Capellmeister*, in 1739, his campaigns had been won and the awards were all ready to be made to its leaders in his *Grundlage einer Ehren-Pforte*, published the following year. His foes were all defeated or deceased, except for Jean-Philippe Rameau, who presumably remained happily unconcerned with Mattheson's attacks on his harmonic theories.

It would be hard to deny that if the *Capellmeister* were the only part of Mattheson's literary legacy to survive, we could gain a fair measure of his genius, his characteristic disposition, from it. However complete a summation of his thought this book was intended to be, he himself repeatedly urges its readers to refer to earlier works for a fuller understanding. In particular he refers to the third of the three *Orchestres* and to an article in *Critica musica* entitled "Des fragenden Componist." In the latter, the practical analysis of his own oratorio, *Das Lied des Lammes*, provides a model for how a rational composer should employ the available vocal and instrumental techniques and resources in the composition of an oratorio text.

The choice of this particular oratorio instead of his earlier *Blutrünstiger Kelter-Treter* is at first sight surprising, for he had characterized the latter as a most admirable example of the modern, theatrical style of musical poetry. The former, however, written by Christian

Postel before the turn of the century, was widely known in published form and had already been set to music. Moreover it contained a variety of poetic styles, ranging from outmoded verbal imagery and rhetorical complexity to lyrical simplicity. It therefore provided typical problems for the enlightened composer to solve. The pragmatic quality of Mattheson's approach to model composition is nowhere else as apparent. In one instance he reminds his pupil, Melophile, that since the true aim of music is the expression of the verbal affections, it is completely appropriate to interrupt a four-part fugal exposition by passages in parallel octaves as an expression of scorn; in another, a strictly worked-out double fugue is suitable as a metaphor for disorder rather than order, and in another he advises writing a canon, but not to expect "after all that quill-chewing and toiling to be rewarded for your pains [since] there will probably be not a single one among 2,000 listeners who will notice your finesse."[3] To be sure, his aversion to strict fugal counterpoint is later summed up in a reference to the motets of the imperial Capellmeister (Fux). These, he writes, contain nothing but "a chase undertaken with unsingable, interminable fugues . . . no passions or emotions to be seen for miles, no true melody, no true charm, indeed no meaning to be discovered."[4]

Often crude and picturesque to us, such personal judgments, mingled usually with objective arguments, are the hallmarks of Mattheson's literary legacy. They differ more in degree than in kind from similar obiter dicta by many an eighteenth-century critic of literature and the arts. After all, they were intended for the enlightenment of his own German contemporaries and not for sophisticated readers in European musical centers, where the principles he sought to advance were taken for granted. Thus, his legacy provides a revealing index of the sensitive musical issues between the wider European world – the world of current political, economic, intellectual, and musical affairs, all of which were engrossing to Mattheson – and the provincial German world. His attitude was certainly fashioned less by the limitations of his Lutheran inheritance than by his experience with the international style and conduct of affairs of

3 "Doch hüte dich für wassersüchtigen Modulationen, und machte dir nur, nach allem Federkäuen und saurem Fleiß, keine Rechnung daß dir die Mühe belohnet werde. Unter 2000 Zuhörern wird kaum einer seyn der die Finesse merke." Critica musica II, 28–9.
4 ". . . derjenigen Jagd, welche mit den unsingbaren und unendlichen Fugen angestellet ward . . . Da war keine Leidenschafft oder Gemüths-Bewegung auf viel Meilweges zu sehen; . . . keine rechte Melodie; keine wahre Zierlichkeit, ja gar kein Verstand zu finden." Capellmeister, 222.

patrician Hamburg. During his most vigorous years that great free city was a focus of concern among the leading European powers. Hamburg was as eager to retain its own freedom of action within the context of international intrigue as each of the rival European states, England in particular, was to prevent the predominance of any one of its numbers in political or commercial affairs. There is, I think, an interesting analogy between Hamburg's conduct of affairs and the position Mattheson assumed as musical critic and instructor. Repeatedly in his writing he takes the role of independent arbiter between the rival claims of the most powerful musical styles, the Italian and the French, and warns his readers against the insinuating attractions of the Italian spinners of exuberant melody and the overemphasis on verbal considerations favored by aristocratic French taste.

A pervasive feature of Mattheson's literary legacy is his aim to reach as wide a reading public as possible. As arbiter and critic his constant aim was to instruct first the *galant homme* and later "aller Liebhaber der Music," whom he first addressed in his *Organistenprobe* of 1719, as much as to broaden the intellectual values and perceptions of professional musicians. Though its form is that of a traditional treatise, the contents of the *Capellmeister* can be explained only by the constancy of this objective. In fact there are but few pages in this or any of his books, however practical their purpose or profound their subject, that are not dominated by this aim as much as they are animated by the personal quirks and prejudices of the author. These may be seen as the natural prerogatives of an enlightened musical critic. But criticism was for him inseparable from instruction, and certainly the central motivation of his life was to instruct. This passion animates all of his writing, as it probably did his conversation, which, one suspects, may have taken the form of monologue more frequently than dialogue. And it is as the great teacher of his age who overturned ancient doctrine by new truth that he is extolled in the laudatory verses prefacing his later books.

These are some, but by no means all, of the features of the genius – the characteristic disposition – of Mattheson's surviving legacy. But what meaning does this copious storehouse of fact and fiction, of dogmatic opinion and cantankerous argument, have for us in 1981, 217 years after his death? At a time when extreme individualism is a commonplace in creative endeavor, what relevance is there in John Locke's common bonds of human understanding upon which Mattheson based his elaborate system of musical affections and expatiated upon the techniques of "solid melodic knowledge"? What possible bearing can his principles have for musicians and music lovers of today? Surely they qualify rather too easily for the very terms of opprobrium he used to describe the outmoded pedantries advocated by the enemies of music in his own time. For the scholarly historian, however, infected by the inexhaustible virus of intellectual curiosity, Mattheson's legacy exerts a powerful attraction. For one thing, the range and depth of its contents far exceed those of any of his contemporaries' works. For another, the modern scholar may feel a certain affinity with a man who used with eccentric virtuosity the documentary tools we use, though sometimes with less discrimination.

It is interesting that Mattheson seldom couples the word "scholar" with his own endeavors. Indeed, he seems inclined to associate scholarship with that form of pedantry, inherited from the past, that was dedicated as much to the obfuscation of truth and knowledge as to the preservation of outmoded practice. Yet embedded in the lengthy foreword to his *Capellmeister* he presents an arresting definition of musical scholarship. It is not his own but was appropriated, surprisingly, from a sixteenth-century treatise. In his inimitable phraseology, Mattheson describes its author as "an otherwise ill-disposed witness to the truth of music from whom a true statement occasionally escaped."[5] This ill-disposed witness was Andreas Papius; the statement is culled from his treatise *De consonantibus*, published in Antwerp in 1581. In Mattheson's version it reads as follows:

The mere cognition of the ratio of a tone, a semitone, a comma, or of consonances, etc., will win nobody the name of virtuoso or prince of art. On the contrary, the careful examination of various works produced by great artists according to the laws of nature will do so. By doing this we may understand what this kind of creator has for a soul, and in what way and how one thing more than another (in a particular work) has taken hold of his emotions and disposition: Such knowledge constitutes the highest pinnacle of musical learning and scholarship.[6]

---

5 ". . . einen sonst übel-gesinnten Zeugen . . . , dem doch auch zu seiner Zeit ein wahres Wort entfahren ist."
6 "Die bloße Erkänntniß des Verhalts eines Tons, halben Tons, eines Commatis, der Consonantzen etc. wird keinem den Nahmen eines Virtuosen oder Kunstfürsten zuwege bringen, sondern vielmehr die, nach den Natur-Gesetzen angestellte, genaue Untersuchung der verschiedenen Wercke, welche von grosse Künstlern aus Licht gestellet werden: daraus mögen wir begreiffen was ein jeder Verfasser, nach seiner Art, für einen Geist hat, auf was Weise, und wie weit einer vor dem andern, durch seine besondere Arbeit, sich der menschlichen Gemüther und Neigungen bemeistert, welches der höheste Gipffel musikalischer Wissenschafft ist." *Capellmeister*, Vorrede, 18.

11

Certainly Johann Mattheson's literary legacy provides abundant evidence of his "careful examination" – and, I would add, his judgment according to the laws of nature – of works produced by great artists." His praise for Bach's *Kunst der Fuge* in 1752 is a most obvious but not a rare example. This was the principal means by which he "sought to attain the highest pinnacle of musical learning and scholarship," as described by his predecessor. This goal was coupled, however, with his constant effort to teach and instruct. It is easy to overlook still another dimension of his legacy in our own time when there are such strong pressures on scholars to demonstrate their technical expertise to their fellow scholars. While Mattheson certainly shared this objective, his writings, with all their stylistic and linguistic obscurities and their personal eccentricities, were addressed to a much larger audience: to all readers of books, indeed to all members of what he and his contemporaries characterized as the Republic of Letters.

How then should we evaluate or describe the surviving legacy of Johann Mattheson? To me it is the legacy of a man who, however much he may have prided himself as a composer, exemplified above all else the goals, aspirations and values of a great teacher-scholar.

PART I

Mattheson and his times

2

Hamburg zur Zeit Johann Matthesons: Politik, Wirtschaft und Kultur

HANS WILHELM ECKARDT
Hamburg

Hamburg sei ein "Sonderfall in der Geschichte Deutschlands", stellte der große Historiker Percy Ernst Schramm über seine Vaterstadt fest. Hamburg sei die "allerenglischste Stadt des Kontinents", heißt es in einem vergleichenden Werk zur frühneuzeitlichen Stadtgeschichte[1]. Beiden Äußerungen ist die Aussage gemeinsam, Hamburgs Geschichte sei nicht ohne weiteres mit der anderer deutscher Städte und Gebiete zu vergleichen. Beide Äußerungen lassen sich auch auf Johann Matthesons Biographie und auf die Geschichte seiner Heimatstadt zu seiner Lebenszeit beziehen: Als prominente Person der bürgerlichen Kultur Hamburgs im Kontrast zur höfischen Kultur der deutschen Umwelt nahm er an Hamburgs Sonderrolle ebenso teil wie durch seine diplomatische Tätigkeit für Großbritannien und Holstein-Gottorf[2]. Der starke englische Einfluß in Hamburg zeigt sich an Mattheson geradezu paradigmatisch: Er war nicht nur Sekretär des

Diesen Aufsatz widme ich Rudolf Vierhaus (Göttingen) zum sechzigsten Geburtstag.

1 P. E. Schramm, *Hamburg. Ein Sonderfall in der Geschichte Deutschlands* (Hamburg, 1964); H. Böhme, *Frankfurt und Hamburg. Des Deutschen Reiches Silber- und Goldloch und die allerenglischste Stadt des Kontinents* (Frankfurt aM, 1968), 288. Hamburgs enge Beziehungen zu England sind ein oft herausgestellter Topos, cf. den Vortrag "Beziehungen zu England im Hamburger Kulturbereich", in: G. Grundmann, *Hamburg gestern und heute. Gesammelte Vorträge und Ansprachen zur Architektur, Kunst und Kulturgeschichte der Hansestadt* (Hamburg, 1972), 115–36.

2 Siehe dazu den Aufsatz von F. Fiebig: "Johann Mattheson als Diplomat in Hamburg" in diesem Band. Zum Verständnis des Verhältnisses von Holstein und Dänemark ist hier darauf hinzuweisen, daß ein Teil des Herzogtums Holstein im Besitz des Hauses Gottorf sich befand, ein anderer im Besitz des dänischen Königshauses; beide Fürstenhäuser waren Linien der seit 1460 in Schleswig und Holstein regierenden Oldenburger. Nachdem der Sohn Karl Peter Ulrich des Herzogs Karl Friedrich von Gottorf 1762 als Peter III. russischer Zar geworden war, gelangte der Gottorfer Teil Holsteins 1767–73 im Tauschwege ebenfalls an Dänemark.

britischen Gesandten, sondern auch Ehemann einer Engländerin und Übersetzer und Vermittler englischer Literatur[3].

Um Hamburg zur Zeit Matthesons und damit auch Hamburgs Einfluß auf ihn und seine besondere Rolle in der Geschichte dieser besonderen Stadt verstehen zu können, soll im folgenden versucht werden, ein wenig von dem sozialen und politischen, wirtschaftlichen und kulturellen Umfeld sichtbar zu machen, in dem Mattheson lebte und wirkte. Dazu ist einleitend ein kurzer Blick auf die mittelalterliche und frühneuzeitliche Entwicklung der Stadt vonnöten[4].

I

Aus der Hammaburg, einem um 825 nahe der Mündung der Alster in die Elbe gegründeten Kastell und Handelsplatz, entstand seit 831 das nordeuropäische Missionszentrum des Erzbischofs Ansgar[5]. Nach einem Wikingerüberfall mußte Ansgar 845 in das Bistum Bremen fliehen, das 848 mit dem Erzbistum Hamburg vereinigt wurde. Seitdem hatte Hamburg zwar noch einen Dom, war aber nicht mehr Sitz seines Erzbischofs. Neben der um den Dom liegenden alten Stadt, die nach häufigen kriegerischen Zerstörungen immer wieder aufgebaut wurde, entstand 1188–9 eine vom Holsteiner Grafen Adolf III. und einer Gruppe von Kaufleuten gegründete neue Stadt, die von Kaiser Friedrich Barbarossa mit wichtigen Privilegien (freie Schiffahrt, Befreiung von Zöllen und von der Heerfolge) versehen wurde. Erzbischöfliche Altstadt und gräfliche Neustadt schlossen sich um 1216, ohne ihre jeweiligen Herren zu fragen, zu einem Gemeinwesen zusammen. Anschließend formal ganz unter die

3 Biographische Angaben zu Johann Mattheson beruhen im folgenden auf seinen autobiographischen Ausführungen in der *Ehrenpforte*. Von der Selbstbiographie zehren auch der Artikel in: H. Schröder u.a., *Lexikon der hamburgischen Schriftsteller bis zur Gegenwart*, 8 voll., (Hamburg, 1851–83), hier vol. 5, 1870, 64–80, sowie der Artikel von H. Turnow in: *MGG* 8 (1960), coll. 1795–1815.

4 Als Gesamtdarstellungen der hamburgischen Geschichte sind heranzuziehen: H. Reincke, *Hamburg, ein Abriß der Stadtgeschichte von den Anfängen bis zur Gegenwart* (Bremen,[2] 1926); E. von Lehe, D. Kausche u.a., *Heimatchronik der Freien und Hansestadt Hamburg* (Köln,[2] 1967). Erst nach Abschluß dieses Beitrages erschienen und jetzt vorrangig zu benutzen: H.-D. Loose (Hrg.), *Hamburg. Geschichte der Stadt und ihrer Bewohner*, vol. 1: *Von den Anfängen bis zur Reichsgründung* (Hamburg, 1982), darin für das siebzehnte und achtzehnte Jahrhundert die Beiträge von H.-D. Loose (p. 259–350) und Fr. Kopitzsch (p. 351–414), der überraschenderweise jede Erwähnung Matthesons vermissen läßt.

5 Diese Darstellung der Anfänge des Hamburger Erzbistums ist nicht unumstritten; siehe dazu W. Seegrün, "Das Erzbistum Hamburg–eine Fiktion?" in: *ZVHG* 60 (1974), 1–16, und den Beitrag von Kl. Richter in: Loose, *Hamburg*, 17–100.

Hoheit des Holsteiners geraten, verstand es die Stadt, sich allmählich zielstrebig aus dessen Machtbereich zu lösen und selbst ein umfangreiches Landgebiet am Oberlauf der Alster und am Unterlauf der Elbe zu erwerben, dessen Bewohner Untertanen der Stadt wurden. 1420 wird Hamburg erstmals als Reichsstadt, d.h. nur dem Kaiser unterstehende und zu Gehorsam verpflichtete Stadt, erwähnt, ohne daß dieser Status von Holstein anerkannt wurde.

Im Bündnis mit der zunächst wesentlich bedeutenderen, an der Ostsee gelegenen Reichsstadt Lübeck wurde Hamburg eine der wichtigsten Städte in der Privilegiengemeinschaft der Hanse[6], bis es Lübeck im fünfzehnten Jahrhundert überflügelte und Hauptumschlagplatz des nordeuropäischen Handels wurde. Im Zusammenhang mit der Reformation, der sich Hamburg erst nach einigem Zögern anschloß, gab sich die Stadt die innere politische Verfassung, die zur Zeit von Matthesons Geburt, Kindheit und Jugend, wenn auch keineswegs unangefochten, galt. In Fortführung und Systematisierung mittelalterlicher Ansätze, die in den Rezessen (Einigungen, Verträge) zwischen dem Rat als Obrigkeit und der Gesamtheit derjenigen Einwohner, die das Bürgerrecht besaßen, seit 1410 schriftlich niedergelegt worden waren, erreichten die erbgesessenen Bürger[7] im Langen Rezeß von 1529 erstmals eine geregelte Mitwirkung bei der Gesetzgebung. Danach bedurfte der Rat, dessen Mitglieder lebenslänglich amtierten und der sich bei Vakanzen durch Zuwahl selbst ergänzte, für den Erlaß von Gesetzen – je nach ihrer Bedeutung – der Zustimmung der Erbgesessenen Bürgerschaft oder der als Laienvertretungen in den vier Kirchspielen entstandenen drei Bürgerlichen Kollegien. An ihrer Spitze stand das Kollegium der zwölf Oberalten, das das Kollegium der Achtundvierziger wählte, das wiederum das Kollegium der Hundertvierundvierziger bestimmte[8]. Als der Rezeß von 1563 dem Rat die Finanzhoheit nahm und sie Vertretern der Bürgerschaft, den Kämmereideputierten, gab, hatte Hamburg einen Grad der bürgerlichen Mitverwaltung erreicht, dem andere Städte und Staaten erst nach Jahrhunderten näher kamen.

---

6 Die beste Darstellung der Hansegeschichte: Ph. Dollinger, *Die Hanse* (Stuttgart, [2]1976); für Hamburgs Stellung in der Hanse jetzt: P. Gabrielssons Beitrag in: Loose, *Hamburg*, 101–90.

7 I.e. diejenigen Bürger, die ein Grundstück (Erbe) besaßen.

8 Die beste Zusammenfassung der hamburgischen Verfassungsgeschichte: J. Bolland, *Senat und Bürgerschaft. Über das Verhältnis zwischen Bürger und Stadtregiment im alten Hamburg* (Hamburg,[2] 1977); eine graphische Darstellung des Institutionengefüges bei H. W. Eckardt, *Privilegien und Parlament. Die Auseinandersetzungen um das allgemeine und gleiche Wahlrecht in Hamburg* (Hamburg, 1980), 13 s.

Im Rahmen dieser republikanischen Verfassung verstand es der Rat, der sich auch Senat nannte, im Laufe des siebzehnten Jahrhunderts, seine Machtposition auszubauen und sich, parallel zu den absolutistischen Tendenzen in den Fürstenstaaten[9], als gottgewollte Obrigkeit darzustellen. Dabei konnte er sich auf außenpolitische Erfolge stützen: Im Streit mit dem dänischen König, der seit 1460 zunächst Graf, seit 1474 Herzog von Holstein und damit formal Landesherr der Hamburger war, erstritt der Senat 1618 ein Urteil des Reichskammergerichts, das Hamburgs Reichsunmittelbarkeit, also seinen Status als Reichsstadt, bestätigte. Dänemark bestritt nicht nur die Rechtskraft dieses Urteils, sondern versuchte auch, mit machtpolitischen Repressalien – zu denen die Gründungen der Städte Glückstadt und Altona als Konkurrenten Hamburgs ebenso gehörten wie mehrere militärische Bedrohungen – vollendete Tatsachen zu schaffen. Zwar gelang es den Hamburgern, ihre faktische Selbständigkeit zu bewahren, doch blieb die rechtliche Situation bis 1768 im Schwebezustand[10].

Hamburgs Eigenständigkeit, seine Lage und seine wirtschaftliche Kraft machten es zum Anziehungspunkt für zahlreiche Einwanderer: Seit 1567, endgültig seit 1611 war es Niederlassung der englischen Merchant Adventurers, die – zusammengeschlossen im English Court – individuell allerdings jeweils nur vorübergehend in der Stadt lebten. Dagegen machten die nach der Eroberung Antwerpens durch die Spanier (1585) auf Dauer nach Hamburg kommenden Niederländer zeitweise wohl bis zu einem Viertel der hamburgischen Gesamtbevölkerung aus. Um 1600 fanden aus Portugal vertriebene sephardische Juden Aufnahme in der Stadt, und seit 1640 wanderten in zunehmendem Maße auch deutsche, aschkenasische Juden ein, die Hamburg zusammen mit den Nachbarorten Altona und Wandsbek im Laufe der Zeit zu einer der größten jüdischen Gemeinden in Deutschland machten. Die Aufnahme all dieser Fremden wurde vom Rat und von den am Fernhandel interessierten Großkaufleuten gegen die Widerstände der lutherisch-orthodoxen Geistlichkeit und der von ihr beeinflußten und wirtschaftlich eng ortsbezogen denkenden Krämer und Handwerker durchgesetzt, wobei weniger Toleranzprinzipien als vielmehr ökonomische Interessen ausschlaggebend waren: Die

---

9 Über die allgemeine deutsche Geschichte von der Mitte des siebzehnten bis zur Mitte des achtzehnten Jahrhunderts informiert zuverlässig und problemorientiert: R. Vierhaus, *Deutschland im Zeitalter des Absolutismus, 1648–1763* (Göttingen, 1978).

10 Siehe dazu: H. Reincke, "Hamburgs Aufstieg zur Reichsfreiheit", in: *ZVHG* 47 (1961), 17–34.

fremden Minderheiten brachten ihre wertvollen internationalen Beziehungen mit in die Handels- und Hafenstadt.

Trotz dieser gebotenen Relativierung der hamburgischen Aufnahmebereitschaft bleibt als Faktum bestehen, daß die Stadt in der Zeit blutiger konfessioneller Auseinandersetzungen für viele Menschen zum sicheren Port in einem unsicheren Land wurde[11]. Dies gilt besonders für die Dauer des großen europäischen Krieges, der auf deutschem Boden ausgetragen wurde: Den Dreißigjährigen Krieg[12] überstand die Stadt nicht nur unbeschadet, sondern mit Gewinn. Die rechtzeitig vor Beginn des Krieges fertiggestellten gewaltigen Wallanlagen – deren Verlauf noch heute das Stadtbild prägt – ermöglichten die unangreifbare Neutralität der Stadt, die als Finanz-, Produktions-, Handels- und Verhandlungsplatz allen kriegführenden Parteien nützlich war.

II

Die ökonomische Prosperität und Attraktivität der Stadt drückte sich auch in den wachsenden Bevölkerungszahlen aus: Hatte Hamburg um 1620 noch etwa 38 000 Einwohner, so waren es 1680 um 72 000[13]. Zu den vier alten Kirchspielen (Petri, Jacobi, Katharinen, Nikolai) war als fünftes und volkreichstes, aber politisch zunächst nicht gleichberechtigtes Kirchspiel Michaelis hinzugekommen, das beim Festungsbau als "Neustadt" in die Umwallung einbezogen und anschließend vor allem von den weniger bemittelten Einwohnern besiedelt worden war.

Als Johann Mattheson am 28. September 1681 im Kirchspiel St. Nikolai geboren und einen Tag später getauft wurde[14], stand die politische Gleichberechtigung von St. Michaelis noch aus. Sie gehört

11 Siehe P. E. Schramm, *Gewinn und Verlust. Die Geschichte der Hamburger Senatorenfamilien Jencquel und Luis (16. bis 19. Jahrhundert). Zwei Beispiele für den wirtschaftlichen und sozialen Wandel in Norddeutschland* (Hamburg, 1970).
12 Vor allem für englischsprachige Leser ist nach wie vor die beste Gesamtdarstellung: C. V. Wedgwood, *The Thirty Years War* (London, 1938; deutsche Ausgabe: München, 1967).
13 Cf. H. Mauersberg, *Wirtschafts- und Sozialgeschichte zentraleuropäischer Städte in neuerer Zeit. Dargestellt an den Beispielen von Basel, Frankfurt a. M., Hamburg, Hannover und München* (Göttingen, 1960), 47. Andere Zahlen nennt H. Reincke, "Hamburgs Bevölkerung", in: *Forschungen und Skizzen zur hamburgischen Geschichte* (Hamburg, 1951), p. 167–200, hier 172 ss.: 45 000–54 000 Einwohner für 1620, 50 000–60 000 für 1680. Sowohl Mauersbergs als Reinckes Zahlen beruhen auf Schätzungen.
14 StA Hbg, Taufregister St. Nikolai (Schreibung des Namens: Mattheissen) sowie Genealogische Sammlung 1.

19

in den Zusammenhang der schweren Verfassungskrise, in der sich Hamburg seit 1663 befand und die Anfang der 1680er Jahre einem Höhepunkt zutrieb. Ursache dieser Mattheson Kindheit und Jugend begleitenden Verfassungskämpfe[15] war die Diskrepanz zwischen der rechtlichen und der sozialen Struktur der Hamburger Bevölkerung. Nicht jeder Einwohner Hamburgs war auch Bürger der Stadt, und nicht jeder Bürger hatte die vollen politischen Mitwirkungsrechte[16]. Nur etwa 15–20 Prozent der Einwohner besaßen das Bürgerrecht[17]. Voraussetzungen seines Erwerbs waren der christliche Glaube, die Zahlung eines Bürgergelds und die Leistung des Bürgereids. Das Zugangsrecht zu den Bürgerlichen Kollegien und den Versammlungen der Erbgesessenen Bürgerschaft hatten im wesentlichen jedoch nur diejenigen männlichen Bürger, die lutherischer Konfession waren und ein Grundstück ("Erbe") innerhalb der Stadtmauern ihr Eigen nannten, das in bestimmtem Maße hypothekarisch unbelastet war; in der zweiten Hälfte des siebzehnten Jahrhunderts waren das nur wenige tausend[18]. Hamburgs wirtschaftliche Kraft und die daraus resultierende, sich in dem gewaltigen Festungsbau und der Unterhaltung einer Söldnertruppe und Bürgerwache[19] manifestierende militärische Stärke und Sicherheit beruhte aber nicht allein auf den Leistungen dieser privilegierten Gruppe, sondern auf der Arbeit eines Vielfachen an Bürgern und Einwohnern. Ein knappes Fünftel

15 Den besten Überblick über die Geschichte Hamburgs während der ersten drei Lebensjahrzehnte Mattheson bietet H.-D. Loose, "Hamburg vor dreihundert Jahren. Wirtschaft–Gesellschaft–Politik", in: *300 Jahre Oper in Hamburg 1678–1978* (Hamburg, 1977), 28–35. Außerdem ist heranzuziehen H. Rückleben, *Die Niederwerfung der hamburgischen Ratsgewalt. Kirchliche Bewegungen und bürgerliche Unruhen im ausgehenden 17. Jahrhundert* (Hamburg, 1970). Die "Zwistigkeiten, so der Rath mit den Bürgern hatte", und die damit in Zusammenhang stehenden Verbote der Oper erwähnt Mattheson in der *Ehrenpforte*, 191 s., 196 s.

16 Diese Tatsachen übergeht Schramm, *Hamburg*; hinsichtlich der rechtlichen Abstufungen war Hamburg kein Sonderfall in Deutschland.

17 Da allerdings die Angehörigen eines Bürgers nicht mehr als "Fremde" galten, kann man "nahezu 80 Prozent" der Gesamtbevölkerung als Einwohner bürgerlicher Rechtsstellung bezeichnen: M. Reißmann, *Die hamburgische Kaufmannschaft des 17. Jahrhunderts in sozialgeschichtlicher Sicht* (Hamburg, 1975), 26.

18 Genaue Zahlen fehlen. Für 1809 sind 5187 Erben in den fünf Kirchspielen nachgewiesen: G. Seelig, *Die geschichtliche Entwicklung der hamburgischen Bürgerschaft und die hamburgischen Notabeln* (Hamburg, 1900), 95.

19 Die Bürgerwache bestand aus den zum Militärdienst verpflichteten Bürgern. Jedes Kirchspiel stellte ein Regiment von ca. 2000 Mann, das von einem Ratsherrn im Range eines Obersten kommandiert wurde. Die Untergliederungen wurden von den Bürgerkapitänen befehligt (cf. Telemanns Kapitänsmusiken zu den jährlichen Festmahlen der Offiziere). Jeder Bürger sorgte selbst für seine Ausrüstung und Bewaffnung. Neben der Bürgerwache stand eine Truppe von etwa 2000 Berufssoldaten, die sogenannte Garnison. Siehe dazu: J. Ehlers, *Die Wehrverfassung der Stadt Hamburg im 17. und 18. Jahrhundert* (Boppard, 1966).

der berufstätigen Männer war in kaufmännischen und gut vier Fünftel waren in nichtkaufmännischen Berufen tätig. Diese rund 81 Prozent verteilten sich auf die Handwerker (48%), See- und Fuhrleute (13%), Arbeiter (15%) und die im heute so genannten "Dienstleistungsbereich" Tätigen (5%), wie Juristen, Lehrer, Ärzte, Schreiber, städtische Bedienstete[20]. Nach den Einkommens- und Vermögensverhältnissen verteilten sich diese Berufstätigen mit ihren Familien auf vier Gesellschaftsschichten, deren Grenzen unscharf und vor allem – bei wirtschaftlichem Erfolg bzw. Mißerfolg – nach oben und unten durchlässig waren[21]. Eine dünne Oberschicht (5%) bestand aus reichen Kaufleuten und graduierten Akademikern. Der obere Mittelstand umfaßte wohlhabende Gewerbetreibende wie Goldschmiede, Brauer, Krämer, Schiffer und Makler. Die untere Mittelschicht war die größte Gruppe: vor allem Handwerker, aber auch Gastwirte, Schreiber, Bootsleute – in der Regel ohne Vermögen, aber nicht ohne bescheidenen Besitz. Beide Mittelschichten zusammen dürften etwa 60–5% umfaßt haben. Die besitzlose Unterschicht schließlich bestand aus Gesellen, Arbeitern, Dienstboten, Soldaten etc. (30–5%).

Johann Matthesons Familiengeschichte bietet ein Beispiel für den möglichen sozialen Aufstieg: Sein Großvater war als "Kriegsmann" Mitglied der Unterschicht, sein Vater als Akziseeinnehmer[22] Angehöriger der unteren Mittelschicht, und Johann schaffte als angesehener Künstler, Diplomat und Schriftsteller den Aufstieg in die obere Mittelschicht.

In den politischen Institutionen spiegelte sich die sozioökonomische Gliederung der Bevölkerung nur verzerrt wider. Zwar gab es in Hamburg, anders als in vergleichbaren Städten, kein Patriziat, keine abgeschottete Stadtaristokratie[23], doch wurde es zur

20 Reißmann, *Hamburgische Kaufmannschaft*, 17 ss., 278 ss., 324 ss., 330; cf. Loose, "Hamburg vor dreihundert Jahren", 29.
21 Dies betont Schramm, *Hamburg*, zu Recht, wenn es auch um die Durchlässigkeit zeitweise schlecht bestellt war, was zu den heftigen Verfassungskämpfen führte.
22 *Ehrenpforte*, 187; cf. Schröder, *Lexikon*, vol. 5, 64. Im Hamburgischen Bürgerbuch (StA Hbg) ist der "Zollner Johan Mattheißen" unter dem 11. Mai 1677 verzeichnet; er hat den Bürgereid abgelegt, das Bürgergeld in Höhe von 20 Mark gezahlt und wird zur Stadtverteidigung mit einer Muskete beitragen. Er wird als civis filius bezeichnet, so daß auch sein Vater – des Musikers Großvater – das Bürgerrecht erworben haben müßte. Ein "Kriegsmann" (oder ähnlich) Mattheson läßt sich aber unter den zahlreichen in den Bürgerbüchern verzeichneten Matthesons nicht feststellen, wohl aber "Kröger" (Gastwirt), "Boßmann" (Bootsmann) und andere Berufe.
23 Darin ist Schramm, *Hamburg*, 17 s., zuzustimmen, der sonst dazu neigt, die Hamburger Verhältnisse zu idealisieren; cf. Böhme, *Frankfurt und Hamburg*, 62.

Praxis des Rates, der aus vier Bürgermeistern und vierundzwanzig Ratsherren bestand, sich fast ausschließlich aus Kaufleuten und graduierten Juristen der Oberschicht zu ergänzen. Dabei geriet er seit Anfang der 1660er Jahre in den Verdacht der Vetternwirtschaft. Dazu kam, daß auch die Erbgesessene Bürgerschaft und die Bürgerlichen Kollegien von den wohlhabenden Grundeigentümern der Oberschicht und oberen Mittelschicht beherrscht wurden. Gegen diese Machtverteilung und gegen Nepotismus, Bestechlichkeit und Unfähigkeit im Stadtregiment erhoben sich die mittleren und kleinen Kaufleute und Handwerker, also Teile der Mittelschicht und keineswegs vorwiegend oder gar ausschließlich Angehörige der Unterschicht, des "Pöbels", wie es früher abschätzig hieß[24].

Angeführt von dem Färber und Reeder Cord Jastram und dem Kaufmann Hieronymus Snitger begehrten seit 1672 die sogenannten Subdiakone aus dem Kollegium der Hundertvierundvierziger gegen die mächtigen Oberalten, das vornehmste Bürgerliche Kollegium, auf. Die Tatsache, daß selbst einzelne Ratsmitglieder der Popularpartei mit Sympathie begegneten, zeigt, daß das Mißvergnügen an den herrschenden Verhältnissen kaum auf Neid- oder Haßgefühle der Unteren auf die Oberen zurückzuführen ist, sondern auf Sorge um das Gemeinwesen und auf Streben nach eigenem Einfluß. An den Konventen der Erbgesessenen Bürgerschaft nahmen immer mehr nichterbgesessene Bürger und vereinzelt auch Nichtbürger teil, es wurde nun nach Köpfen, nicht mehr nach Kirchspielen abgestimmt. Die Bürgerschaft nahm sich auch das Recht, ohne Einberufung durch den Rat zusammenzutreten. 1674, 1677 und 1683 erwirkten die Oberalten kaiserliche Hilfe bei der Zurückweisung dieser Entwicklung, doch blieben die kaiserlichen Kommissare und Mandate wirkungslos.

Jastram und Snitger hatten ein Jahrzehnt lang Anhänger gesammelt. 1683 konnten sie, gestützt vor allem auf die untere Mittelschicht, eine fast unumschränkte Herrschaft etablieren. 1685 setzten sie durch, daß St. Michaelis, das volkreichste Kirchspiel, gleichberechtigt zu den Verfassungsorganen zugelassen wurde[25]. Die Popularpartei konnte schließlich nicht nur die Oberalten, sondern auch den Rat überspielen. Bürgermeister Hinrich Meurer wurde – entgegen allen Verfassungsbestimmungen – zur Abdankung gezwungen. Er floh

---

24 Von niederen Bevölkerungskreisen spricht – zumindest mißverständlich – z.B. Rückleben, *Niederwerfung*, 399. Zum folgenden siehe H.-D. Loose, "Die Jastram-Snitgerschen Wirren in der zeitgenössischen Geschichtsschreibung", in *ZVHG* 53 (1967), 1–20.

25 Daher gab es nun fünfzehn Oberalte, aus den Achtundvierzigern wurden die Sechziger, aus den Hundertvierundvierzigern die Hundertachtziger; siehe Eckardt, *Privilegien*, 13.

zum südlichen Nachbarn Hamburgs, dem Herzog von Celle, der wegen finanzieller Forderungen mit der Stadt im Streit lag. Meurer hoffte, mit fürstlicher Hilfe in sein Amt zurückkehren zu können – um die republikanischen Traditionen und Tugenden Hamburgs stand es also bei beiden Parteien recht schlecht.

Im Januar 1686 besetzten cellische Truppen Teile des hamburgischen Landgebiets. Jastram und Snitger konnten diesen Angriff mit eigenen militärischen Mitteln nicht zurückweisen und glaubten, ein Hilfsangebot des dänischen Königs annehmen zu müssen und zu können – sie erkannten nicht, daß das dänische Hilfsangebot alles andere als uneigennützig war, daß der Däne vielmehr eine günstige Gelegenheit gekommen sah, sich die Stadt endgültig botmäßig zu machen, kurz: Die Volksführer bewiesen ihre politische Naivität bei dem Versuch, Teufel mit Beelzebub auszutreiben. Die Bürgerschaft erkannte die Gefahr und öffnete den cellischen Truppen die Tore; ein dänischer Angriff wurde zurückgeschlagen. Jastram und Snitger wurden als Verräter hingerichtet, Meurer konnte als Bürgermeister zurückkehren.

Für wenige Jahre, bis zum Tod des fast diktatorisch regierenden Meurer, konnten Rat und Oberalte ihre Macht wieder ungestört ausüben. In den 1690er Jahren jedoch schuf eine wirtschaftliche, finanzielle und außenpolitische Verschlechterung der hamburgischen Lage – hervorgerufen durch dänische Repressalien und durch die Forderungen des Reiches im Krieg mit Frankreich – eine Situation, in der Skandale im Rat und ein heftiger innerkirchlicher Streit zum Auslöser neuer sozialer und politischer Unruhen werden konnten[26]. Schon 1681 und 1683 hatte ein Streit zwischen dem pietistischen Pastor Anton Reiser von St. Jakobi, der mit seiner Schrift *Theatromania oder die Werke der Finsternis in den öffentlichen Schauspielen* gegen Theater und Oper zu Felde zog und ihr Verbot forderte, und dem Pastor Heinrich Elmenhorst von St. Katharinen, der selbst Libretti für die 1678 in Hamburg gegründete Oper verfaßte, die innerstädtische Unruhe verstärkt. Die theologischen Auseinandersetzungen zwischen Pietismus und lutherischer Orthodoxie führten zu einem polemischen, persönlichen Kampf zwischen einzel-

---

26 Dazu am ausführlichsten Rückleben, *Niederwerfung;* siehe auch Gallois, *Hamburgische Chronik von den ältesten Zeiten bis auf die Jetztzeit,* vol. 3 (Hamburg, 1862), 506 ss. Diese Chronik ist eine Fundgrube für Details der hamburgischen Geschichte. Zur Oper in Hamburg cf. die in Anm. 15 erwähnte Festschrift von 1977 sowie H. J. Marx, "Geschichte der Hamburger Barockoper", *Hamburger Jahrbuch für Musikwissenschaft,* vol. 3: *Studien zur Barockoper* (Hamburg, 1978), 7–34; eod., "Politische und wirtschaftliche Voraussetzungen der Hamburger Barockoper", in: ibid., vol. 5: *Opernsymposium Hamburg 1978* (Laaber, 1981), 81–8.

nen Pastoren; vor allem der Pietist Johann Heinrich Horb von St. Nikolai und der orthodoxe Johann Friedrich Mayer von St. Jakobi verstanden es, große Gefolgschaften von Gläubigen gegeneinander zu mobilisieren. Da der lutherische Glaube die hamburgische Staatsreligion war und kirchliche und städtische Verfassung seit 1529 miteinander eng verzahnt waren, wurde der theologische Streit zum Politikum. Weder das Geistliche Ministerium noch der Senat konnten verhindern, daß Mayers Anhänger 1693 in der – nur noch dem Namen nach Erbgesessenen – Bürgerschaft die Verbannung Horbs durchsetzten. Mißstände in der Verwaltung ließen Mayers kleinbürgerlichen Anhang, der sich seiner Macht soeben bewußt geworden war, nicht zur Ruhe kommen. Zum neuen Volksführer – Jastrams abgeschlagener Kopf steckte noch zur Abschreckung auf dem Millerntor[27] – wurde der Handwerker Balthasar Stielcke. Mayers und Stielckes Agitation führte zu Drohdemonstrationen und Ausschreitungen so heftiger Art, daß sich der Rat 1699 in einem Rezeß der Bürgerschaft unterwerfen mußte: Die Herrschaft der mittleren Bevölkerungsschichten war nach dreizehn Jahren zum zweiten Mal errichtet. Das genügte jedoch nicht, die aufgewühlte Stimmung zu beruhigen. Zwar verließ Mayer Hamburg 1701, doch setzte Pastor Christian Krumbholtz von St. Petri seine Polemik fort und trieb die Konfrontation zwischen Bürgerschaft und Rat auf die Spitze. Anläßlich eines Streits um die Verbrennung mißliebiger Schriften Barthold Feinds (1678–1721)[28], die von Krumbholtz und Stielcke gefordert wurde, enthob die Bürgerschaft bis Februar 1708 sieben Ratsherren ihres Amtes. War dies schon verfassungswidrig, so bedeutete die unter Mißachtung des Selbstergänzungsrechtes des Rates erfolgende Wahl neuer, ihr genehmer Senatoren durch die Bürgerschaft die völlige Auflösung der bisherigen Ordnung; Verfassung und Verwaltung brachen zusammen.

Da dies nicht nur von Kaiser und Reich als Infragestellung der gottgewollten Ordnung überhaupt angesehen wurde, sondern auch zur Vernachlässigung hamburgischer Pflichten gegenüber dem Reich führte und die verworrene Situation wieder einmal dänischen Absichten leichtes Spiel zu bieten schien, griff Kaiser Joseph I. ein. Im Mai 1708 besetzten in seinem Auftrag Truppen des Niedersächsischen Reichskreises (Hannoveraner, Wolfenbüttler, Preußen und Schweden) die Stadt. Eine kaiserliche Kommission unter Leitung

---

27 Gallois, *Chronik*, p. 821, 895.
28 Zu Feind siehe Th. Schrader (Hrg.), *Hamburg vor 200 Jahren* (Hamburg, 1892), 103 ss.

des Grafen Damian Hugo von Schönborn begann, dem funktionsunfähig gewordenen Gemeinwesen wieder eine tragfähige Grundlage zu geben. Das Ergebnis vierjähriger Bemühungen war der Hauptrezeß von 1712, der "keinen Bruch mit der Tradition, sondern letztlich ihre Erfüllung" bedeutete[29], indem er die seit dem Mittelalter während Verfassungsentwicklung Hamburgs aufnahm, zusammenfaßte und in klassisch gewordene Formulierungen goß. Sein erster Artikel bestimmte "als ein ewiges, unveränderliches und unwiderrufliches Fundamentalgesetz", daß das "Kyrion oder das höchste Recht und Gewalt" beim Rat und bei der Erbgesessenen Bürgerschaft "inseparabili nexu conjunctim und zusammen . . . bestehe". Senat und Erbgesessene Bürgerschaft bildeten also gemeinsam die Obrigkeit und waren bei Gesetzgebung und Regierung aufeinander angewiesen und voneinander abhängig. Das Selbstergänzungsrecht der lebenslänglich amtierenden Senatoren wurde bestätigt.

Zu den Konventen der Erbgesessenen Bürgerschaft hatten von nun an folgende männliche Personen lutherischen Glaubens Zutritt:

- die eigentlichen Erbgesessenen, also die Eigentümer eines Grundstücks, für das jetzt bestimmt wurde, daß es einen unbelasteten Wert von mindestens 1000 (innerhalb der Stadtmauern) bzw. 2000 Reichstalern (im Landgebiet) haben mußte;
- die Mitglieder der Bürgerlichen Kollegien;
- die Vorsteher der Ämter (Zünfte);
- die Inhaber von Ehrenämtern in der städtischen Verwaltung, also Richter, Deputierte[30], Offiziere des Bürgermilitärs.

Ausgenommen von diesen Bestimmungen blieben unter anderem "alle, die in fremden Diensten" standen, also auch – hätte er das Bürgerrecht erworben – Johann Mattheson als Sekretär des britischen Gesandten[31]. Zur Konventsteilnahme berechtigt waren 200–350 Per-

---

29 Rückleben, *Niederwerfung*, 359. Der Hauptrezeß ist abgedruckt in N. A. Westphalen, *Geschichte der Haupt-Grundgesetze der Hamburgischen Verfassung*, vol. 1, (Hamburg, 1844), 307–81.

30 Die Bürger wirkten nicht nur über Erbgesessene Bürgerschaft und Bürgerliche Kollegien an der Gesetzgebung, sondern über die Deputationen auch an der Verwaltung mit. Die Deputationen bestanden aus Ratsherren und sachkundigen Bürgern und waren für bestimmte Verwaltungszweige zuständig; die Finanzverwaltung lag ganz in der Hand von Bürgern (Kämmereiverordneten), die jede Ausgabe des Rates genehmigen mußten. Wegen ihrer großen Verwaltungserfahrung hatten also auch diese bürgerlichen Deputierten Zugang zum Konvent der Erbgesessenen Bürgerschaft. Noch heute bestehen bei den hamburgischen Fachbehörden (Ministerien) die beratenden Ausschüsse sachkundiger Bürger.

31 Reglement der Hamburgischen Rahts- und Bürger Conventen, gedruckt bei Westphalen, *Geschichte*, vol. 2, 251–360, hier p. 257. Ausweislich der Bürgerbücher des achtzehnten Jahrhunderts (StA Hbg) hat Mattheson das Bürgerrecht nicht erworben.

sonen[32]: Knapp hundert erbgesessene Bürger konnten ein genügend unbelastetes Grundstück ihr Eigen nennen und waren dadurch qualifiziert, die übrigen waren Inhaber der genannten Funktionen und sicherlich weit überwiegend Erbgesessene, die durch Amt oder Mitgliedschaft in den Bürgerlichen Kollegien die zu hohe hypothekarische Belastung ihres Grundstücks ausglichen. Mit der neuen Regelung wurden also beträchtliche Teile der seit vierzig Jahren aufbegehrenden Mittelschichten von der politischen Mitwirkung ausgeschlossen.

Bis 1859 blieb der Hauptrezeß – von einer kurzen Unterbrechung im Zusammenhang mit dem Napoleonischen Imperialismus abgesehen – in Kraft, galt zumindest zu Lebzeiten Matthesons als Musterbeispiel einer gemischten, d.h. durch aristokratische (Senat) und demokratische (Erbgesessene Bürgerschaft, Bürgerliche Kollegien) Elemente geprägten Verfassung und gab Hamburg die feste Grundlage für eine ruhige Entwicklung im größten Teil des achtzehnten Jahrhunderts.

III

In einer oft nach Revolutionen oder Revolutionsversuchen zu beobachtenden Reaktion begnügte sich auch in Hamburg die Institution, die zugleich Subjekt, Objekt und Forum der Auseinandersetzungen gewesen war, die Erbgesessene Bürgerschaft, von nun an mit einer Statistenrolle: Ihre privilegierten Mitglieder sahen keinen Grund, dem Rat mißtrauisch zu begegnen, man konnte sich endlich wieder ungestört den Geschäften widmen; zwischen 1709 und 1756 waren 193 von 397 Konventen wegen mangelnder Anwesenheit erbgesessener Bürger beschlußunfähig[33].

So konnten die Großkaufleute – die Amsinck und Hudtwalcker, die Jencquel und Voght, die Berenberg und Goßler, um nur einige der Familien zu nennen[34] – die Gunst der Stunde nutzen. Die Verfassung

---

32 Siehe Reincke, *Hamburg*, 134, und Reißmann, *Hamburgische Kaufmannschaft*, 346 ss.

33 Fr. Kopitzsch, "Stadtpolitik zwischen Integration und Repression", in: *Sozialwissenschaftliche Informationen für Unterricht und Schule* 9 (1980), 6–11, hier p. 9.

34 Zur Geschichte der hamburgischen Kaufmannschaft und einzelner Familien siehe Reißmann, *Hamburgische Kaufmannschaft*; Schramm, *Gewinn und Verlust*; eod., *Neun Generationen. Dreihundert Jahre deutscher "Kulturgeschichte" im Lichte der Schicksale einer Hamburger Bürgerfamilie, 1648–1948*, 2 voll. (Göttingen, 1963–4).

26

bot ihnen die Möglichkeit, Rat, Oberaltenkollegium und Käm-
mereideputation zu dominieren und für eine enge Zusammenarbeit
dieser Staatsorgane mit der Commerzdeputation, der 1665 gegründeten Interessenvertretung der Kaufleute und Reeder[35], zu sorgen.
Nach den durch die inneren Unruhen und das recht häufige Auftreten
der Pest bedingten wirtschaftlichen Rückschlägen der letzten Jahrzehnte[36] ging es nun vor allem um die Außen- und Handelspolitik der
Stadt, die durch Hamburgs geographische Lage und seine
wirtschaftlichen Interessen bestimmt wurden. Es ging nun darum, die
in und nach dem Dreißigjährigen Krieg erworbene Stellung als nordeuropäische Handels- und Finanzmetropole wiederzugewinnen und
auszubauen.

Diese zentrale Position als größter deutscher Hafen und – neben
Frankfurt am Main und Leipzig – führender Handelsplatz des Reiches beruhte auf Hamburgs günstiger geographischer Lage an Elbe
und Alster, zwischen Nord- und Ostsee und auf seiner konsequenten
Politik zur Ausnutzung dieser natürlichen Vorteile. Dazu gehörten
die bis ins Mittelalter zurückreichenden Maßnahmen zur militärischen und nautischen Sicherung der Schiffahrt auf der Unterelbe
und in der Elbmündung: Betonnung und Ausbaggerung des Fahr-
wassers, Unterhaltung von Leuchtfeuern und des festen Turms auf
der – bis heute – hamburgischen Insel Neuwerk: mehr als hundert
Kilometer von der Stadt entfernt. Dazu zählte die bereits 1558 gegründete Börse, deren mit finanzieller Unterstützung des Rates mehrmals
erweitertes Gebäude zum bedeutendsten Treffpunkt der Kaufleute in
Nordeuropa wurde. Dazu gehörte vor allem aber auch die hamburgische Währungspolitik[37]: Es war nur zu verständlich, daß Hamburg als Umschlagplatz unter dem zersplitterten und infla-
tionsgefährdeten deutschen Münzwesen besonders litt. Fortschritt-
liche Kaufleute, darunter englische und niederländische, hatten
daher zusammen mit dem Rat die Gründung der Hamburger Bank

---

35 Siehe dazu E. Baasch, *Die Handelskammer zu Hamburg 1665–1915*, vol. 1:
   1665–1814 (Hamburg, 1915).
36 Zur Pest siehe A. Wohlwill, "Hamburg während der Pestjahre 1712–1714", in:
   Jahrbuch der Hamburgischen Wissenschaftlichen Anstalten 10/1892 (Hamburg,
   1893), 289–406; zu den wirtschaftlichen Rückschlägen siehe E. Wiskemann, *Ham-*
   burg und die Welthandelspolitik von den Anfängen bis zur Gegenwart (Hamburg,
   1929), 100, sowie W. Vogel, "Handelskonjunkturen und Wirtschaftskrisen in ihrer
   Auswirkung auf den Seehandel der Hansestädte 1560–1806", in: *Hansische*
   Geschichtsblätter 74 (1956), 50–64, hier p. 59, 63.
37 Siehe zum folgenden: H. Sieveking, "Zum 300. Jahrestag der Gründung der Hamburger Bank", in: *ZVHG* 23 (1919), 52–81; W. Jesse, "Hamburgs Anteil an der
   deutschen Münz- und Geldgeschichte", in: *ZVHG* 38 (1939), 117–44.

Abbildung 1. Stadtplan und Stadtansicht von Hamburg aus dem Jahre
1727 (Staatsarchiv Hamburg)

betrieben, die 1619 nach dem Vorbild Amsterdams errichtet worden
war. Auf der Basis einer Silberdeckung wurde ein dem Handel
dienender Giroverkehr geschaffen; die Verrechnung der Konten erfolgte in hamburgischen Mark Banco, einem Rechengeld, das nie
ausgeprägt wurde. Die Mark Banco hatte einen höheren Wert als das
ausgemünzte, courante (umlaufende) Stadtgeld: die Mark Courant zu

28

16 Schillingen, der Schilling zu 12 Pfennigen. Seit der hamburgischen Münzordnung von 1725–6 wurden 34 Mark Courant aus 233,8 g reinen Silbers geprägt; Courantgeld wurde in ein festes Verhältnis zum Bankgeld gesetzt, es galt ein Agio von 16 Prozent. Der Wert, die Kaufkraft des damaligen Hamburger Geldes im Vergleich zu heutigen Verhältnissen ist nur sehr schwierig zu benennen. Die Angabe, Mattheson habe in seinem zweiten Testament von 1753 der Michaeliskirche zum Orgelbau 40 000 Mark zugedacht und ihr sogar, noch zu Lebzeiten, 44 000 Mark angewiesen, bleibt aber ohne Aussagekraft, wenn man nicht zeitgenössische Vergleichszahlen nennt und eine annähernde Vorstellung von der Kaufkraft gibt. An der Oper hatte Mattheson 1705 eine Besoldung von 300 Talern, beim Gesandten Wich erhielt er zunächst 200, seit 1709 dann 300 Taler jährlich; der Taler entsprach drei Mark. Telemann bekam ein jährliches Gehalt von 1600 Mark, ein Bürgermeister 4000, ein Ratsherr 2000, ein Professor 900–1300, ein Ratsmusikant 80 Mark jährlich. Hinsichtlich der Kaufkraft ist im Vergleich zu 1970 etwa der Multiplikator sechzehn anzusetzen[38].

Gestützt auf die geschilderten und viele andere um- und weitsichtig geschaffenen und genutzten Verkehrs-, Handels- und Währungseinrichtungen vermittelte Hamburg den Handel Nord- und Osteuropas mit Westeuropa und dem Mittelmeerraum[39]. Über die Elbe und ihre Nebenflüsse und über die Kanalverbindungen von Elbe und Oder hatte Hamburg ein Einzugsgebiet, das über Böhmen bis Österreich und Ungarn reichte. Die Beschwerlichkeit des Handelsverkehrs zu Wasser und zu Lande darf allerdings nicht übersehen werden. Ein schwerer Landtransport zwischen Hamburg und Wien dauerte etwa fünf Wochen, von Schlesien nach Hamburg gut vierzehn Tage[40], für eine Reise von Hamburg zu den Besitzungen der Stadt an

---

38 Die Gehaltsangaben nach den Kämmereirechnungen der ersten Hälfte des achtzehnten Jahrhunderts im StA Hbg; siehe E. Kleßmann, *Telemann in Hamburg 1721–1767* (Hamburg, 1980), 43 s. Kaufkraftschätzungen lassen sich angesichts der unterschiedlichen Entwicklung von Ansprüchen, Einkommen und Preisen nur mit großen Vorbehalten anstellen und erlauben allenfalls grobe Vergleiche. Der genannte Multiplikator sechzehn ist einer im StA Hbg zusammengestellten Kaufkrafttabelle entnommen.
39 Für Hamburgs Wirtschaftsgeschichte im siebzehnten und achtzehnten Jahrhundert immer noch unentbehrlich: J. G. Büsch, *Versuch einer Geschichte der hamburgischen Handlung* (Hamburg, 1797).
40 R. Ramcke, *Die Beziehungen zwischen Hamburg und Österreich im 18. Jahrhundert. Kaiserlich-reichsstädtisches Verhältnis im Zeichen von Handels- und Finanzinteressen* (Hamburg, 1969), 8.

der Elbmündung benötigte man drei Tage. Eisgang und Überschwem-
mungen machten der Flußschiffahrt zu schaffen; ärgerlicher, weil
dauernd störend waren die überaus zahlreichen Zollstellen, die jeder
Transport passieren mußte. Allein auf der Elbe zwischen Dresden
und Hamburg waren noch Anfang des neunzehnten Jahrhunderts
dreißig Zölle zu entrichten[41]. Die Hamburger Kaufleute waren
natürlich an Zollerleichterungen lebhaft interessiert und erreichten
im Laufe der Zeit – von 1713 bis 1764 und später – wenigstens in
ihrer eigenen Stadt Ermäßigungen des Durchfuhrzolls für wichtige
Waren[42]. Im übrigen aber hatten die Zollerträge neben den Steuerein-
nahmen eine wesentlich größere Bedeutung für die Staatsfinanzen als
heute, wobei zu bedenken ist, daß manche Zölle – wie z.B. die Akzise
auf Bier, Wein und Vieh – im Grunde eine Verbrauchssteuer waren,
die bei der Einfuhr in die Stadt an den Toren erhoben wurde;
Matthesons Vater war in Hamburg als Akziseeinnehmer tätig.

Das Zollwesen macht deutlich, wie abhängig Hamburg von seiner
Umwelt war, wie wenig es alleine bewirken konnte; als Handelsstadt
war es auf das Wohlwollen vieler anderer Staaten angewiesen. Um
seine inneren Kapazitäten optimal nutzen zu können, bedurfte es der
äußeren Absicherung: Die Außenpolitik hatte den Handelsinteressen
zu dienen; aus dem Primat des Handels folgte das außenpolitische
Ziel: Neutralität im Schutze des Reiches. Damit sollte sowohl dem
Hineingezogenwerden in die europäischen Kriege (Expansionskriege
Frankreichs, holländisch-englische Seekriege, Nordischer Krieg, Tür-
kenkriege) vorgebeugt werden – selbst wenn das Reich beteiligt oder
bedroht war –, als auch Dänemarks Ansprüche mit Reichshilfe
zurückgewiesen werden; Hamburg sei neben (dem von den Türken
bedrohten) Wien und (dem von Frankreich okkupierten) Straßburg
einer der drei Ecksteine des Reiches, argumentierte die Stadt 1690, als
sie Reichshilfe gegen Dänemark brauchte[43]. Von den innerdeutschen
Kriegen in der Mitte des achtzehnten Jahrhunderts (1. und 2.
Schlesischer Krieg, Siebenjähriger Krieg) wollte und mußte Hamburg
sich fernhalten, um es mit keiner Partei zu verderben. Sein mächtig-
ster Nachbar und Kontrolleur der mittleren Elbe war Brandenburg-
Preußen, seine Schutzmacht und sein Stadtherr war der habsbur-
gische Kaiser[44]. Hier wie in den anderen Auseinandersetzungen seit
dem Dreißigjährigen Krieg war Hamburgs Bedeutung als Hafen- und
Handelsstadt, die es durch Neutralität zu schützen galt, gleichzeitig

41 Ibid.   42 Wiskemann, *Welthandelspolitik*, p. 112.   43 Ibid., p. 101.
44 Ibid., 114 s. sowie Ramcke, *Beziehungen*, passim.

Garant dieser Neutralität: Keine Kriegspartei gönnte der anderen den Zugriff auf die Stadt, die damit eine sichere Position im Zentrum des Parallelogramms der Kräfte einnehmen konnte.

Diese Neutralitätspolitik mit Rückversicherung beim Reich war sicherlich eigennützig und zog Kritik und Neid der Konkurrenten auf sich, sie war aber deswegen nicht weniger vernünftig. Sie war nicht nur für Hamburg und seine Bewohner segensreich, sondern für ganz Deutschland von größtem Vorteil: Hamburg hatte als Tor zur Welt eine deutsche Aufgabe; ein Zeitgenosse drückte es mit den Worten aus: "Hamburg ist das große deutsche Magazin[45]."

Ein Großteil des wachsenden Importbedarfs Deutschlands an Tuchen, Seide, Samt, Zucker, Gewürzen und der in Mode kommenden Genußmittel Kaffee, Tee, Schokolade und Tabak wurde durch und über Hamburg befriedigt[46]. Im achtzehnten Jahrhundert bestand die Einfuhr der Stadt – für Eigenbedarf, Weiterverarbeitung oder Umschlag – vor allem aus Getreide, Butter, Käse und Fleisch aus Nordwestdeutschland und den Niederlanden, Wein aus Frankreich und dem Rheinland, Fisch aus Nordeuropa, Hanf und Flachs aus Ost- und Süddeutschland, kolonialfranzösischem Rohzucker, Tuchen aus England, Leinwand aus Schlesien, Metall aus Böhmen und Hölzern aus Skandinavien.

Neben dem europäischen Transithandel war der Eigenexport Hamburgs von beachtlicher Bedeutung: Die Stadt war ein großer Gewerbestandort. Ihre Werften und Kattundruckereien, Strumpfwirkereien, Samt- und Tuchmanufakturen gaben vielen Einwohnern Arbeit und Brot und den Handelsherren weithin begehrte Produkte. Der wohl größte Exporterzeuger Hamburgs im achtzehnten Jahrhundert waren die Zuckersiedereien, in denen um 1800 über 10 000 Personen beschäftigt gewesen sein sollen[47]. Die wichtigsten Ausfuhrartikel der Stadt waren raffinierter Zucker, gefärbte Tuche und Draht sowie Veredelungsprodukte aus Wolle, Fellen und Holz.

Die europäischen Kriege beeinflußten die Hamburger Wirtschaftskonjunktur sowohl positiv als auch negativ[48]. Nachteile ergaben sich z.B. 1741, als die schlesische Leinenzufuhr stockte, oder um 1763, als eine Handelskrise die Folge der während des Siebenjährigen Krieges

45 Chr. L. von Griesheim, *Die Stadt Hamburg in ihrem politischen, oeconomischen und sittlichen Zustande* (Hamburg, 1760), Erste Vorrede, §11.
46 Schramm, *Gewinnn und Verlust*, 11.
47 R. Wiemer, "Industrie und Gewerbe in Hamburg", in: von Lehe u.a., *Heimatchronik*, 559.
48 Vogel, "Handelskonjunkturen", 59–64.

zu sehr vermehrten Handelsbewegungen war. Häufiger jedoch konnten die Hamburger Kaufleute die Gunst der Stunde nutzen, vom kriegsbedingt wachsenden Bedarf profitieren und in fremde, vor allem niederländische Handelsdomänen eindringen. Insgesamt war daher die Bilanz positiv, so daß die Stadt in der ersten Hälfte und in der Mitte des achtzehnten Jahrhunderts zu einem europäischen Handelsplatz erster Ordnung wurde. Sein Einzugsgebiet umfaßte Rußland und Skandinavien, England und Island, die Niederlande, Frankreich und die iberische Halbinsel. Seine bewaffneten Konvoischiffe schützten seine Handelsflotte im Mittelmeer ebenso wie seine Walfangflotte im Nordmeer[49]. An der sogenannten Grönlandfahrt auf Walfang und Robbenschlag bei Spitzbergen beteiligte sich Hamburg seit Mitte des siebzehnten Jahrhunderts und konkurrierte dabei mit Dänemark, England und den Niederlanden.

Auf einem Gebiet jedoch konnten sich Hamburgs europäische Konkurrenten die Stadt vom Leibe halten: im Überseehandel mit Kolonialwaren[50]. Daran waren Hamburgs Kaufleute nur insofern beteiligt, als sie in den europäischen Mutterländern die Waren abholten, die diese aus ihren Kolonien eingeführt hatten; die überseeischen Gebiete selbst blieben den Hamburgern verschlossen. Erst die Loslösung der Vereinigten Staaten von Amerika vom britischen Mutterland öffnete den Hamburger Schiffen den überseeischen Raum – doch das liegt bereits ein Jahrzehnt nach Matthesons Tod. So war Hamburgs Feld im größten Teil des achtzehnten Jahrhunderts zwar noch nicht, wie im neunzehnten Jahrhundert, die Welt, aber doch ganz Europa.

Die Stadt konnte in jeder Beziehung als "kaufmännische Republik"[51] gelten. Dies zeigte sich kurz nach Matthesons Tod, als Hamburg einen politischen Triumph feiern konnte, der die Vorteilhaftigkeit seiner inneren Verfassung mit ihrer kaufmännischen Dominanz und die Richtigkeit seiner zu Sicherheit und Finanzkraft führenden Außen- und Handelspolitik ebenso bestätigte wie die schon oft bewiesene "diplomatische Virtuosität"[52] seiner Kaufleute-Politiker. Um 1765 machte die Commerzdeputation den Rat darauf aufmerksam, daß der dänische Staat einen großen Finanzbedarf habe

49 Wiskemann, *Welthandelspolitik*, 86 s.; E. Baasch, *Hamburgs Convoyschiffahrt und Convoywesen* (Hamburg, 1896).
50 Wiskemann, *Welthandelspolitik*, 105; P. E. Schramm, *Kaufleute zu Haus und über See. Hamburgische Zeugnisse des 17., 18. und 19. Jahrhunderts*(Hamburg, 1949), 19 ss.
51 Böhme, *Frankfurt und Hamburg*, 62.
52 Loose, "Hamburg vor dreihundert Jahren", 28.

und daher vielleicht zu pfandweisen Gebietsabtretungen bereit sei. Es kam zu Verhandlungen, in die auch die rechtlich noch immer offene Frage der hamburgischen Reichsunmittelbarkeit bzw. Zugehörigkeit zum dänischen Holstein einbezogen wurde. Im vertraglichen Ergebnis dieser Verhandlungen, im Gottorfer Vergleich von 1768, erhielt Hamburg gegen hohe finanzielle Leistungen nicht nur territoriale und handelspolitische Vorteile zugesprochen, sondern vor allem die Anerkennung seiner Reichsstandschaft durch Dänemark-Holstein.

Damit blieb – noch bis 1802–3 – nur ein Stachel im Fleisch der hamburgischen Selbständigkeit: der Dom. Seit dem Mittelalter gehörte dessen mitten in der Stadt gelegenes Gebiet zum Erzstift Bremen; der Erzbischof von Bremen war hier nicht nur geistlicher, sondern auch politischer Herr (Landesherr). Als das Erzstift Bremen 1648 säkularisiert, in ein Herzogtum umgewandelt und Schweden zugesprochen wurde, betraf das auch den Dom. Im Nordischen Krieg stieß Dänemark in die schwedischen Herzogtümer Bremen und Verden vor – für Hamburg drohte die Unterelbe auch linksseitig unter dänische Kontrolle zu geraten –, doch wurden diese Gebiete und damit der Dom im Friedensschluß dem Kurfürstentum Hannover zugesprochen. Da Hannover seit 1714 mit Großbritannien in Personalunion verbunden war, ergab sich hier ein neuer Berührungspunkt zwischen Hamburg und England, und Mattheson war bei seiner Tätigkeit am Dom gleichsam auf englischem Gebiet. Das mag heute kurios klingen, war aber nichts Außergewöhnliches in dem territorial zersplitterten und von den europäischen Machtstrukturen durchzogenen Deutschland.

Dänemarks Verzicht auf Bremen und Verden und damit auf die südliche Ausdehnung seiner territorialen Interessen kann durchaus als Ende seiner Hamburgs Selbständigkeit bedrohenden Expansionspolitik gesehen werden und damit als erster Hinweis auf die Möglichkeit der Einigung über Hamburgs Reichsunmittelbarkeit, wie sie wenige Jahre nach Matthesons Tod erfolgte.

IV

So wie die Zeit zwischen Hauptrezeß und Gottorfer Vergleich in wirtschaftlicher und politischer Hinsicht voller vorwärtsdrängender und zukunftsträchtiger Aktivitäten war, so stellt sich dieses Halbjahrhundert auch unter kulturellen Aspekten als lebensvoll und fruchtbringend dar. Dabei war Hamburgs bedeutende wirtschaftliche und politische Rolle geradezu eine der Voraussetzungen seiner kulturellen Bedeutung. Alle großen europäischen Mächte – neben

33

dem Kaiser also Frankreich, Großbritannien-Hannover, Spanien, die Niederlande, Schweden, Dänemark-Holstein, Polen-Sachsen, Brandenburg-Preußen – unterhielten diplomatische Vertretungen in der Stadt[53]. Damit war einmal ein anspruchsvolles Publikum für kulturelle Darbietungen gegeben, zum anderen vermittelten die Mitglieder dieser gebildeten Diplomatengruppe den geistigen Austausch über Grenzen und Entfernungen hinweg und beteiligten sich sogar aktiv und prägend am kulturellen Leben: Mattheson ist dafür ein Beispiel, ein anderes ist Thomas Lediard, der erst Sekretär des dänischen, dann des britischen Gesandten war und von 1727 bis 1732 die Hamburger Oper leitete[54]. Schließlich förderte Hamburgs Stellung als diplomatisches Informationszentrum seine Entwicklung zur Pressestadt, wobei auch hier das benachbarte Altona eine bedeutende Konkurrenz darstellte[55].

Die ersten zeitungsähnlichen Druckwerke waren in Hamburg 1616 erschienen. Zu Matthesons Lebzeiten waren der seit 1673 erscheinende *Hamburgische Relations-Courier* und die mit ihren Vorläufern seit 1710 erscheinende *Staats- und Gelehrtenzeitung des Hamburgischen unpartheyischen Correspondenten* die wichtigsten Blätter. Der *Relations-Courier* erschien bei Thomas von Wiering, einem der bedeutendsten Drucker und Verleger Hamburgs. Bei ihm erschienen die ersten deutschen Ausgaben der Defoe-Romane *Robinson Crusoe* (1720) und – übersetzt von Mattheson – *Moll Flanders* (1723)[56]. Auch Matthesons erste Zeitschrift, *Der Vernünfftler*, wurde "bei seel. Tom. von Wierings Erben bey der Börse" gedruckt. Unter dem Motto "Quidquid agunt homines nostri farrago libelli"[57] erschien diese erste Moralische Wochenschrift in deutscher Sprache

53 Ramcke, *Beziehungen*, 24. Die Diplomaten waren allerdings nicht nur beim Hamburgischen Rat, sondern vor allem beim Niedersächsischen Reichskreis akkreditiert.

54 Dazu zuletzt H. Schwarzwälder, "Der 'deutsche Spion' und Bremen. Thomas Lediard, Sekretär des Gritischen Gesandtern beim Niedersächsischen Kreis in Hamburg und der Gesandte Sir Cyrill Wich", in: *Bremisches Jahrbuch* 57 (1979), 87–123, und H. Chr. Wolff, "Ein Engländer als Direktor der alten Hamburger Oper", in: *Hamburger Jahrbuch für Musikwissenschaft* 3 (1978), 75–83. Lediard war nicht der einzige Diplomat in der Leitung der Oper; siehe dazu die in Anm. 15 genannte Festschrift der Oper, 158.

55 Fr. R. Bertheau, *Kleine Chronologie zur Geschichte des Zeitungswesens in Hamburg von 1616 bis 1913* (Hamburg, 1914); C. Prange, *Die Zeitungen und Zeitschriften des 17. Jahrhunderts in Hamburg und Altona. Ein Beitrag zur Publizisitik der Frühaufklärung* (Hamburg, 1978).

56 W. Kayser, *Drucker und Verleger in Hamburg 1491–1860, Buchhandel in Hamburg* (Hamburg, 1960), 28–43, hier 35.

57 "Was Menschen tun und treiben, gibt uns den Stoff zu schreiben", übersetzt K. Jacoby, *Die ersten moralischen Wochenschriften Hamburgs am Anfange des 18. Jahrhunderts* (Hamburg, 1888), 6.

von Mai 1713 bis Mai 1714. Seine Vorbilder waren die in England herausgegebenen Zeitschriften *The Tattler* (1709–11), *The Spectator* (1711–12) und *The Guardian* (1713), aus denen Matheson in großem Umfang Texte übernahm und für den *Vernünfftler* übersetzte. Da er die Artikel zusätzlich "nach den hamburgischen Sitten so eingerichtet" hat, "daß er anfangs ganz wohl aufgenommen" wurde, scheint diese Methode erfolgreich gewesen zu sein – vielleicht sogar zu erfolgreich: Trotz der im Vergleich zu anderen deutschen Staaten recht milden Zensur wurde der *Vernünfftler* nach dem 100. Stück "gewisser Umstände halber"[58] verboten. Matheson ließ sich durch diesen Rückschlag nicht davon abhalten, auch später journalistisch zu wirken. 1745 arbeitete er an den seit 1732 erscheinenden *Hamburgischen Berichten von neuen Gelehrten Sachen*, herausgegeben von J. P. Kohl, mit[59], und schon in den 1720er Jahren hatte er selbst wieder eigene Zeitschriften herausgegeben: 1722–3 und 1725 *Critica musica*, die erste musikalische Zeitschrift Deutschlands, und 1728 dann *Der musicalische Patriot, welcher seine gründliche Betrachtungen über geist- und weltliche Harmonien, samt dem, was durchgehends davon abhängt, in angenehmer Abwechselung mittheilet, daß Gottes Ehre, das gemeine Beste, und eines jeden Lesers besondere Erbauung dadurch befördert werde*[60].

Mit diesem Zeitschriftentitel bezog sich Matheson auf eine der bekanntesten und verbreitetsten deutschsprachigen Wochenschriften, die wenige Jahre zuvor in Hamburg erschienen war: *Der Patriot*[61]. In einer – damals außerordentlich großen – Auflage von 5000 Exemplaren erschien er zwar nur von 1724 bis 1726, erlebte aber in den folgenden vierzig Jahren vier Neuauflagen. Der Inhalt des *Patrioten* bestand vor allem aus Satiren, Dialogen, Fabeln, Porträts, Erzählungen und – erstmals in Deutschland – echten und fingierten Leserbriefen. Er wollte der Unterhaltung des Lesers ebenso dienen wie der Verbreitung praktischer Vernunft. Er bejahte die relativ modernen, fortgeschrittenen gesellschaftlichen und politischen Verhältnisse in Hamburg, scheute sich aber nicht, die Beseitigung von Mißständen zu fordern. "Suchet der Stadt Bestes" war seine Devise. So galt ein Beitrag der Verbesserung des als vorsintflutlich geschilderten Straßenpflasters, so lobte er die Spendenfreudigkeit der Hamburger zugunsten karitativer Einrichtungen ebenso wie den Zu-

---

58 Zitate aus A. Brandl, *Barthold Heinrich Brockes* (Innsbruck, 1878), 145 s.
59 Bertheau, *Kleine Chronologie*, 29 s.
60 Jacoby, *Wochenschriften*, 45.
61 Das Folgende nach: J. Rathje, "'Der Patriot'. Eine hamburgische Zeitschrift der ersten Hälfte des 18. Jahrhunderts", in: *ZVHG* 65 (1979), 123–43.

stand der Armen- und Waisenfürsorge. Zur Gründung eines Werkhauses, das der Rehabilitierung armer, arbeitswilliger Einwohner dienen sollte, hat der *Patriot* 1726 direkt beigetragen. Besonders in seinen pädagogischen Beiträgen spürt man den Einfluß John Lockes, dessen *Gedanken zur Erziehung* (1693) in Hamburg ihre ersten deutschen Leser fanden[62]. Überhaupt war der *Patriot* vom englischen Einfluß geprägt. Seine Vorbilder waren die englischen Moralischen Wochenschriften, die ja auch durch Matthesons *Vernünfftler* in Hamburg bekannt geworden waren.

Der *Patriot* war geradezu ein Kristallisations- und Ausgangspunkt für die geistige und kulturelle Entwicklung der Stadt in dieser Zeit, er war sowohl Produkt als auch Produzent der Aufklärung in Hamburg. Zu seiner Redaktion gehörten die Schriftsteller und Professoren Michael Richey (1678–1761)[63] und Johann Albert Fabricius (1668–1736), die Ratssyndici Johann Julius Surland (1687–1748) und Johann Klefeker (1698–1775), der Ratsherr und Poet Barthold Heinrich Brockes (1680–1747), der Ratsherr und spätere Bürgermeister Conrad Widow (1686–1754), der spätere Sekretär des Oberalten-Kollegiums Johann Julius Anckelmann (1692–1761) sowie John Thomas (1691–1766), Kaplan am English Court und später Bischof von Salisbury, der Pastor Michael Christoph Brandenburg (ca. 1694–1766), Christian Friedrich Weichmann (1698–1770), Redakteur des *Hollsteinischen unpartheyischen Correspondenten*, und Johann Adolf Hoffmann (1676–1731), ein bekannter Gelehrter. Der Sekretär der englischen Kaufleute in Hamburg, Friedrich von Hagedorn (1708–54), lieferte einzelne Beiträge zum *Patrioten*; ein so unerbittlicher Kritiker wie Lessing nannte Hagedorn 1749 "den größten Dichter unsrer Zeiten"[64].

Der Kreis der Redakteure des *Patrioten* ist identisch mit der sogenannten ersten Patriotischen Gesellschaft in Hamburg, die von 1723 bis 1748 bestand und über die privaten Zirkel um Brockes und Hagedorn und den Freundeskreis um den rationalistischen Religionskritiker Hermann Samuel Reimarus (1694–1768) personell

---

62 H. Noack, "Die geistesgeschichtlichen Grundlagen der patriotischen Gesellschaften", in: *Die Patriotische Gesellschaft zu Hamburg 1765–1965* (Hamburg, s.d.), 9–33, hier 14.

63 Richey, ein Freund Matthesons, verfaßte 1742 die erste Pressegeschichte Hamburgs, veröffentlichte 1743 ein Lexikon der hamburgischen (niedersächsischen) Mundart, trat als Lyriker hervor und versorgte vierzig Jahre lang Telemann mit Texten zu seinen Kantaten und Oratorien.

64 Zitiert nach K. S. Guthke, "Friedrich von Hagedorn und das literarische Leben seiner Zeit im Lichte unveröffentlichter Briefe an Johann Jakob Bodmer", in: *Jahrbuch des Freien Deutschen Hochstifts* (Tübingen, 1966), 1–108, hier 1.

und ideell mit der 1765 gegründeten und bis heute aktiven "Hamburgischen Gesellschaft zur Beförderung der Künste und nützlichen Gewerbe", der sogenannten zweiten Patriotischen Gesellschaft, verbunden ist[65].

Trotz der hohen Meinung Lessings über Hagedorn war nicht er, sondern Brockes das über die Zeiten hinweg wichtigste Mitglied des Kreises um den *Patrioten*. Er kann geradezu als Idealbild des Patrioten gelten, wie der *Patriot* es zeichnete. Schriftstellerisch, beruflich und politisch war er für das allgemeine Wohl tätig. Als Sohn eines erfolgreichen Hamburger Kaufmanns besuchte er die Gelehrtenschule des Johanneums, studierte in Halle und in Wetzlar am Reichskammergericht – auch für Goethe später eine Station –, reiste durch Italien und die Schweiz, Frankreich, England und die Niederlande. 1708 verfaßte er sein erstes Gedicht, 1720 wurde er zum Ratsherrn (Senator) gewählt, übte mehrere hohe Ämter aus, wurde 1735 für sechs Jahre Amtmann in Ritzebüttel, dem hamburgischen Außenposten, der die Elbmündung sicherte. Hier in der ländlichen Abgeschiedenheit, drei Tagesreisen vom Hamburger Rathaus entfernt, konnte er an seinem Hauptwerk, dem *Irdischen Vergnügen in Gott*, weiterarbeiten, einer neuartigen, poetisch-realistischen Naturbeschreibung, mit der Brockes "begann, die Dinge sich näher anzusehen und die deutsche Poesie gewissermaßen in die Natur hinaus spazieren zu führen und mit ihr bekannt zu machen[66]." Diese große Dichtung wurde in den letzten Jahren unter Beteiligung englischer und amerikanischer Germanisten wiederentdeckt[67].

Brockes gehörte auch zu den Freunden und Förderern der Musik in Hamburg. Seine Beziehungen zu Mattheson waren stets gut, Mattheson registrierte jeden Besuch Brockes' "mit sichtlichem Vergnügen" und machte Brockes' Werke in England bekannt[68]. Zusammen mit seinem Vetter, dem in den bürgerlichen Unruhen umstrittenen Schriftsteller Barthold Feind, besuchte Brockes oft die Oper. Deren Leiter Reinhard Keiser (1674–1739) vertonte später als erster Brockes'

65 Siehe J. Rathje, "Geschichte, Wesen und Öffentlichkeitswirkung der Patriotischen Gesellschaft von 1724 in Hamburg", in: *Wolfenbütteler Forschungen* 8 (1980), 51–69; Fr. Kopitzsch, "Die Hamburgische Gesellschaft zur Beförderung der Künste und nützlichen Gewerbe (Patriotische Gesellschaft von 1765) im Zeitalter der Aufklärung", in: ibid., 71–118.
66 F. Wehl, *Hamburgs Literatur im 18. Jahrhundert* (Leipzig, 1856), 206.
67 Siehe H.-D. Loose (Hrg.), *Barthold Heinrich Brockes (1680–1747). Dichter und Ratsherr in Hamburg. Neue Forschungen zu Persönlichkeit und Wirkung* (Hamburg, 1980)
68 Zitat: Schröder, *Lexikon*, vol. 5, 69; cf. *Ehrenpforte*, 198, 204. Zum Verhältnis Mattheson–Brockes: H. P. Fry, "Barthold Heinrich Brockes und die Musik", in: Loose, *Brockes*, 71–104, hier 85 s., 96 s.

1712 erschienenes Passionsoratorium. Auch Händel – der bis 1706 in Hamburg geweilt hatte –, Telemann – der 1721 in die Stadt kam – und Mattheson (1718) vertonten Brockes' Oratorium: ein kaum zu überbietendes Beispiel für Hamburgs fruchtbare kulturelle Mittler-rolle[69].

Bei der 1721 erfolgenden Berufung Telemanns nach Hamburg hatte der Ratsherr Brockes wohl auch maßgeblichen Anteil. Die an Tele-manns Wirken sich entzündende Kritik der Oberalten – sie meinten, daß Telemanns Musik "zur Wollust anreize"[70] – führte schon 1722 zu Überlegungen Telemanns, nach Leipzig zu wechseln; daß ihm der Senat das Bleiben ermöglichte, dürfte auch Brockes zu danken sein[71].

Vielleicht hat die gemeinsame Bekanntschaft mit ihm auch vermit-telnd auf Telemann und Mattheson gewirkt, die zwar schon in Telemanns Frankfurter Zeit miteinander korrespondiert hatten, die sich aber nun "als die beiden musikalischen Großmächte in Ham-burg"[72] zunächst etwas reserviert gegenübertraten; aber schließlich erkannten sie wohl, daß sie im gleichen Sinne tätig waren, indem sie für neue Musik in einem stark von konservativem Unverständnis geprägten Umfeld wirkten. In Hamburg als lutherischer Stadt wurde die Kirchenmusik – damals eine der Hauptformen öffentlicher Musik überhaupt – sehr hoch eingeschätzt, und man ließ sie sich etwas kosten, z.B. besitzt die Stadt seit jener Zeit mit der St. Jacobi-Orgel Arp Schnitgers (1648–1719) eine der wertvollsten Orgeln der Welt. War diese Wertschätzung der musikalischen Kultur also einerseits sehr fruchtbar, so rief sie andererseits, gerade wegen der öffentlichen Bedeutung, oft die Kirche und die von ihr beeinflußten Kollegien auf den Plan, wenn weltliche Musikformen, vor allem die Oper, zum Gegenstand der Musikliebe wurden und allgemeinen Beifall fanden. Mattheson bekam diese kirchliche Kritik, die bis zur zeitweiligen Schließung der Oper reichte, am eigenen Leib zu spüren[73].

Der Einfluß der Kirche auf das geistige Leben manifestierte sich nicht nur im musischen, sondern auch im schulischen Bereich[74]. Die Masse der Hamburger Kinder wurde in Elementarschulen unter-richtet, die von den Kirchen oder von Privatleuten unterhalten wurden. Söhne der Ober- und Mittelschicht besuchten das Johan-neum. Die noch heute bestehende "Gelehrtenschule" war 1529, in

---

69 Ibid., 76 ss.   70 Zitiert nach Kleßmann, *Telemann*, 39.
71 Fry, "Brockes und die Musik", 90.   72 Kleßmann, *Telemann*, 32 s.
73 *Ehrenpforte*, 191 s.; cf. Gallois, *Hamburgische Chronik*, vol. 3, 690 s.
74 Dazu: O. Rüdiger, *Geschichte des hamburgischen Unterrichtswesens* (Hamburg, 1896).

der Reformation, aus dem säkularisierten St. Johanniskloster entstanden. Das Johanneum war eine reine Knabenschule; Mattheson besuchte sie ebenso wie der ein Jahr ältere Brockes[75], Telemann war Kantor der Schule. Die meist fünfzehnjährigen Absolventen des Johanneums konnten anschließend auf das 1613 gegründete Akademische Gymnasium gehen, eine auf den Besuch auswärtiger Universitäten vorbereitende Anstalt, die den Grad des Magister Artium verlieh. Reimarus sowie zwei Mitglieder der ersten Patriotischen Gesellschaft, Richey und Fabricius, waren Professoren des Gymnasiums, Fabricius darüber hinaus 1708–11 Rektor der Gelehrtenschule.

So wie die Kirche als strenger Zensor des Musik- und Theaterlebens, als Schulträger und maßgeblicher Teil der Schulaufsicht, als in die stadtstaatliche Verfassung integrierte und sie mitbestimmende Institution das geistige, gesellschaftliche und politische Leben der Stadt prägte, so dominierten die Kirchen und ihre Türme auch die Silhouette der Stadt. Mit dem von Sonnin und Prey errichteten Neubau der Michaeliskirche (Abbildung 2) – der Altbau war 1750 vom Blitz eingeäschert worden – besaß die Stadt eine der eindrucksvollsten barocken Kirchen Norddeutschlands. Der Orgelausstattung der neuen Michaeliskirche galt Matthesons überaus großzügige Spende von 44 000 Mark. 1762 wurde der Neubau mit einem Festgottesdienst und einem Oratorium Telemanns eingeweiht. Der Bau des Turmes, als "Michel" bis heute Wahrzeichen Hamburgs, wurde allerdings erst 1776 begonnen und 1781 beendet.

Neben den Kirchen waren es die Wallanlagen und die Stadttore, die in die Umwallung einbezogenen Alsterbecken, der Jungfernstieg und die Lombardsbrücke, der Hafen und die Fleete, der Hopfen-, Pferde- und Gänsemarkt, das Rathaus und die Börse, die Gängeviertel der ärmeren Einwohner und die Straßenzüge der wohlhabenderen Bürger (Große Reichenstraße), die das Stadtbild prägten. Innerhalb und außerhalb der Wälle gaben große Alleen Hamburg das Aussehen einer grünen Stadt. Vor den Toren legten sich viele vermögende Hamburger ausgedehnte Gärten und Parks an, wo sie den Sommer verbrachten[76].

75 *Ehrenpforte*, 187; E. Kelter, *Hamburg und sein Johanneum im Wandel der Jahrhunderte 1529–1929* (Hamburg, 1928), 55, 60.
76 Eine zeitgenössische Beschreibung des Stadtbildes bei Griesheim, *Die Stadt Hamburg*, 175 ss. Vom historischen Stadtbild Hamburgs ist nach dem Großen Brand von 1842 und den Zerstörungen im Zweiten Weltkrieg nicht viel übrig geblieben. Zum erhaltenen Rest gehören die kurz vor Matthesons Geburt gebauten Kramer-Amtswohnungen im Schatten der Michaeliskirche; siehe dazu Kl. Bocklitz, "Die Erbauung der Kramer-Amtswohnungen", in: *ZVHG* 56 (1970), 117–20.

Das pflichtmäßige Verhalten Christlicher Gemeinden
in Absicht ihrer Gotteshäuser

in einer Predigt
Am Tage der Einweyhung
der großen und neuen
Hauptkirche zu St. Michaelis in Hamburg
den 19ten Octobr. 1762
vorgestellt
von
Ernst Ludwig Urlich
Pastore- und Scholarchen.

Hamburg, gedruckt und zu bekommen bey Dieterich Anton Harmsen.

Abbildung 2. Titelblatt der gedruckten Predigt, die anläßlich der Einweihung der neuen St. Michaeliskirche in Hamburg gehalten wurde
(Staatsarchiv Hamburg)

Am besten ist es, einen Zeitgenossen Matthesons über seine
Eindrücke in Hamburg und seine Begegnungen mit Hamburgern –
unter ihnen der einundsiebzigjährige Mattheson – berichten zu
lassen. Im Jahr 1753 hielt sich der Journalist und Naturkundler

Christlob Mylius (1722–54) vom 15. Mai bis 2. Juni in Hamburg auf
und führte Tagebuch über seine Beobachtungen und Erlebnisse[77].
Nach seiner Ankunft in der Stadt kehrte er

im schwarzen Adler auf der Mühlenbrücke ein. Hier unter den Fenstern ist
ein Kanal von der Elbe, in welchem ich täglich die Ebbe und Fluth sehen
konnte. Bey der Ebbe trocknete er allemal ganz aus. Diese Stadt ist viel zu
bekannt, als daß ich hier viel davon gedenken sollte. Sie ist ohngefähr halb so
groß als Berlin. Die Häuser sind meistens altväterisch gebauet, und die
meisten die jetzo noch gebaut werden, werden auch nach der alten Art, z.E.
vorne mit Giebeln gebaut. In dem Innern der Stadt sind die Häuser meistens
steinern und ziemlich hoch; doch sind überhaupt die meisten klein und
hölzern. Die meisten Straßen sind sehr enge. Auch sind die Straßen, da sie so
stark gebraucht werden, ziemlich holpricht. In vielen Straßen sind schöne
Bäume, sonderlich Linden. Der Jungfernstieg ist eine lange Lindenallee,
neben welcher das schöne große Bassin ist, welches die Alster macht, die
gleich darauf in der Stadt in die Elbe fällt. Die Alster ist vor Hamburg fast so
breit als die Elbe zu Pirna.
   Die Stadt hat einen schönen Wall und Graben da, wo es nöthig ist. Ersterer
ist ganz mit schönen Lindenalleen besetzt, in welchen man geht und fährt,
doch nicht nach Thorschluß. Die Stadt hat ein ganz ordentlich eingerichtetes
Garnisonregiment von 2000 Mann. Ihre Montur ist ganz roth, jedoch mit
kurzen blauen Aufschlägen. Es sind auch Grenadire dabey. Auch hat die
Stadt eine Compagnie Dragoner von 50 Mann. Ihre Montur ist roth und auf der
Brust und Ermeln blau aufgeschlagen. Ausser diesen wird alle Nächte der
Wall von etlichen 100 Mann Bürgerwache besetzt, welche keine Montur hat
und einen lächerlichen Aufzug macht. Am Müller- oder Altonaer Thore steht
inwendig "Tutissimum Civitatis munimentum concordia". Auswendig
gegen Altona zu steht: "Da nobis pacem, Domine, in diebus nostris", d.i. Gott
behüte uns vor Dänemark!
   Die Börse ist täglich von 12 bis 2 Uhr sehr voll . . . Auf Dressers Kaf-
feehause kommen die besten Kaufleute und Gelehrten täglich um diese Zeit
zusammen, daher ich mich auch daselbst fleissig eingefunden. Unter denen,
welche ich hier kennen gelernt, nenne ich erstlich den Hrn. von Hagedorn,
welcher ein rechtschaffener Mann, ein Menschenfreund und lustiger Com-
pagnon ist. Ich bin fast täglich als Freund mit ihm in Gesellschaft gewesen . . .
   Den 17ten May besah ich den schönen Bau der neuen Michaeliskirche,
welche uns der Baumeister derselben, Hr. Sonin, ein geschickter Mann, selbst
zeigte. An eben diesem Tage gieng ich zuerst auf das Baumhaus an der Elbe,
wo man von oben herunter die Pracht der vielen Schiffe und die Stadt sehen
kann. – Ich bin etlichemal in Altona gewesen. Diese Stadt liegt gleich vor dem
Thore vor Hamburg, und ist nur durch einen Schlagbaum davon unterschieden. Sie ist ganz offen, ziemlich wohl, doch etwas altväterisch nach
der niedersächsischen Art gebaut, und nicht gar groß.

---

77 Das folgende zitiert nach: "Hamburg im Jahre 1753, von Christlob Mylius".
   Mitgeteilt von K. S. Guthke, in: *Hamburgische Geschichts- und Heimatblätter* 9
   (1974), 157–66.

Mylius notiert anschließend Ausflüge zu Fuß, mit dem Wagen und per Schiff, ist begeistert von Hamburgs Umgebung, hat Kontakt zu zahlreichen Personen der guten Gesellschaft, besucht die Stadtbibliothek, das Johanneum und das Akademische Gymnasium, ergötzt sich an den "Vorstellungen der jetzo hier befindlichen italienischen Komödianten", und am

28sten gieng ich zu dem Hrn. Capellmeister Telemann, und besah auch seinen Garten, worin viel fremde und schöne Pflanzen sind. Dieser 70jährige Greis ist noch recht munter und war sehr höflich. Er hat mir zum Andenken meinen Abschied aus Europa componirt.

Zwei Tage später, am 30. Mai,

besuchte ich den Herrn Mattheson, den bekannten Musikgelehrten. Er ist alt, taub, höflich, und sonst noch ziemlich munter. Man muß ihm alles aufschreiben, was man ihm sagen will. Er hat mir auch meinen Abschied aus Eruopa zum Andenken componiret und eine Art einer lateinischen Dedication vorgesetzt.

Den 31sten May am Himmelfahrtstage gieng ich Vormittags in die Jacobikirche und hörte den 83jährigen Pastor Neumeister[78] erzhomiletisch predigen. Er ist noch sehr munter für sein Alter. Die Musik, welche Herr Telemann aufführte, war schön und größtentheils von seiner sehr geschickten Schülerin, der Mademoiselle Schulzin componirt. Vor der Schlußmusik spielte der erste Stadtmusikus bey der Orgel ein schön Solo auf der Violine, wozu ihn der Organist accompagnirte.

Trotz seines für die kurze Aufenthaltszeit recht umfassenden Einblicks in die kulturelle Szene der Stadt huldigt Mylius abschließend einer damals wie heute verbreiteten und unausrottbaren Klischeevorstellung von Hamburg:

Mit der Gelehrsamkeit ist es in Hamburg schlecht beschaffen. Da hört man von nichts als Geld, Waarencourant und Banco, leichten und schweren Gelde und tausend Kleinigkeiten; auch unter den vielen Doctoren und Licentiaten, welche meistens von Herzen unwissend sind. Was noch ja etwas von Universitäten an Verstande mit bringt, das frißt und säuft sich doch hier alles dumm. Weiber, Gärten, Schmäuse und Familienceremonien sind der Gelehrten wie der Kaufleute meiste Beschäftigung.

Mit einem Lob der guten hamburgischen Postverbindungen verläßt Mylius die Stadt.

Mattheson war von dem Besucher als alt und taub, aber "sonst noch ziemlich munter" beschrieben worden. Tatsächlich hatte er ja noch fast elf Jahre zu leben. Als er am 17. April 1764 starb und am 25. April in der Michaeliskirche "bey einer starcken Versammlung von Men-

---

78 Zu dem Geistlichen und Lyriker Erdmann Neumeister (1671–1756) siehe Schröder, *Lexikon*, vol. 5, 494–512.

schen"[79] beigesetzt wurde, stand im *Hamburgischen Correspondenten* vom 27. April:

Der im Jahre 1681 allhie gebohrne, seit 1704 in Königl. Großbritannischen Gesandtschaften über 40, und hernach in Großfürstlich-Hollsteinischen Diensten etliche 20 Jahre gestandene Legationsrath Mattheson hat seinen 83jährigen Lebenslauf am 17ten dieses geendiget. Der von dessen Arbeit gedruckten, theils Staats- und Historischen, theils Moralischen, absonderlich aber Musikalischen Werke sind 88; an Manuscripten aber wol 2 bis 4 mal so viel, die derselbe auf Verlangen, unserm Gymnasio zum Andenken, hinterlassen, nachdem er schon vorher der St. Michaelis-Kirche, bey Lebens-Zeiten, 44 000 Mrk. Hamburger Cour. zum neuen Orgelwerke entrichtet hatte, an welchem jussu Superiorum sein Bildniß mit einer Aufschrift von Richeyischer Feder gesetzt, ihm auch zur Beerdigung ein eignes ausgemauertes Ruhe-Kämmerlein zugetheilet, und seine Leiche darinn, unter einem vollständigen von ihm selbst verfertigten Trauer-Oratorio, am 25sten dieses, beygesetzt worden ist. Wir wissen, außer denen von des, seiner großen Verdienste wegen, unsterblichen ersten Bürgermeisters dieser Republik, Hn. Sillem, zur Trauer-Musik hinterlassenen rührenden Worten, seit dem kein Beyspiel, daß sich jemand selber, auf diese Art, zu Grabe gesungen habe.

Obwohl Geburts- und Todesjahr Matthesons nicht von herausragenden Ereignissen der hamburgischen Geschichte gekennzeichnet werden, ist doch deutlich, daß sich sein dreiundachtzig Jahre währendes Leben von Epoche zu Epoche spannt: Als er geboren wurde, befand sich Hamburg in einer Zeit der Unruhe und des Umbruchs; als er starb, stand die Stadt vor einem der Höhepunkte ihrer Geschichte, kurz vor der Erfüllung ihres jahrhundertelangen Wunsches, eine kaiserlich-freie Reichsstadt zu sein. Im kulturellen Bereich vollzog sich etwa zur Zeit seines Todes ein Personen- und Kulissenwechsel: Telemann – im gleichen Jahr wie Mattheson geboren – starb drei Jahre nach ihm; Hagedorn war 1754, Richey 1761 gestorben. Neues begann mit der zweiten Patriotischen Gesellschaft 1765, mit dem im gleichen Jahr – an der Stelle der abgerissenen Oper – erbauten Schauspielhaus und dem 1767–8 in ihm bestehenden Deutschen Nationaltheater, mit Lessings Ankunft in Hamburg 1767. Die 1760er Jahre waren für Hamburg die Zeit des Endes der Frühaufklärung, die nicht zuletzt von Mattheson geprägt worden war. Er war ein Element des Sonderfalles Hamburg als Vorort der norddeutschen Aufklärung.

Man kann diesen Beitrag nicht besser beschließen und Matthesons hamburgisches Leben nicht besser resümieren als mit seinen eigenen

---

79 StA Hbg, Handschriftensammlung 236: Fr. Chr. Scharppenbarg, *Geschehene Begebenheiten in Hamburg* (1773), 73.

Worten aus der *Ehrenpforte*[80]: "Summa, wie Matthesons äußerstes Bestreben jederzeit gewesen ist, der Kirche, dem Staat und der musikalischen Jugend nach Vermögen zu dienen, der Kirche, nämlich, mit dem klingenden Gottesdienst; dem Staat mit Kopf und Feder; den Lehrbegierigen aber mit Hand, Mund und Druck: so wird er hierinn fortfahren" – denn weder ist Johann Matthesons Wirkung abgeklungen noch ist die Aufklärung am Ziel.

80 *Ehrenpforte*, 217.

3

Johann Mattheson als Diplomat in Hamburg

FOLKERT FIEBIG
Athen

I

Die Gestalt Johann Matthesons wird nur sehr unvollkommen erfaßt, wenn man sie ausschließlich aus seiner Beschäftigung mit Musik zu erschließen versucht. Entscheidend ergänzt wird dieses Bild von Mattheson durch seine Tätigkeit als Sekretär bei dem britischen Gesandten in Hamburg. Diesen Dienst hat er vom 6. Januar 1706[1] an fast fünfzig Jahre lang[2] ausgeübt und der Bericht darüber nimmt in der *Ehrenpforte*[3], dem biographischen Nachschlagwerk über M u s i k e r, einen sehr breiten Raum ein. Auch wenn Mattheson – nach dem bisherigen Stand der Forschung – keine eigenen Arbeiten zu politischen Fragen verfaßt hat, läßt sich allein an den Schilderungen in der *Ehrenpforte* sein politisches Interesse feststellen. Sein eigenhändig verfaßter Lebenslauf schließt mit dem Hinweis auf den Frieden zu Hubertusburg am 15. Februar 1763 zwischen Österreich und Preußen[4].

Uns erscheinen in diesem Zusammenhang folgende Problemkreise wichtig zu sein:

1. Warum hat Mattheson, der erfolgreiche Musiker und Musik-schriftsteller, dieses eher unbedeutend erscheinende Amt als Sekretär des britischen Gesandten angenommen und für so lange Zeit beibehalten?

---

1 *Ehrenpforte*, 195.
2 In der "Weitere Fortsetzung des Mattheson ischen Lebenslaufes" (ab 1759), abgedruckt bei Cannon, *Mattheson*, 219–25, schreibt Mattheson noch 1760 (p. 220) "entzog er [Mattheson] sich doch, nach und nach, den herrschenden Staatsgeschäften". Der Dienst wurde aber tatsächlich schon vorher nicht mehr ausgeübt, siehe dazu unten Abschnitt IV, "Mathesons Tätigkeit".
3 *Ehrenpforte*, Artikel "Mattheson", 187–217 und Anhang 8–33.
4 Cannon, *Mattheson*, 225.

45

2. Inwieweit entspricht sein Aufgabenbereich in diesem Amt seinen intellektuellen Fähigkeiten und Interessen?

3. Wie glaubwürdig sind die zum Teil sehr genau mitgeteilten Daten zu seiner Tätigkeit als Diplomat in der *Ehrenpforte*?

Durch den Vergleich mit anderen Akten seiner diplomatischen Tätigkeit läßt sich insgesamt die Glaubwürdigkeit aller Daten in der *Ehrenpforte*, die für die Biographien zahlreicher Musiker die unentbehrliche Quelle ist, zuverlässig beurteilen.

Bisher gibt es im wesentlichen zwei moderne Biographien über Mattheson, die seine außermusikalische Tätigkeit berücksichtigen[5]. Hans Turnow bezieht sich fast ausschließlich auf die Angaben in der *Ehrenpforte*, während Beekman C. Cannon darüber hinaus die *State Papers* hat untersuchen lassen[6]. Die *State Papers*[7] enthalten neben Verträgen, Abschriften und Übersetzungen von Verträgen sowie Protokollen aus der Amtstätigkeit des britischen Gesandten insbesondere dessen Berichte an die Regierung in London. Sein Amtsbezirk erstreckte sich über Hamburg hinaus auf die anderen Hansestädte Bremen und Lübeck sowie – zumindest unter John von Wich – auf die Fürstentümer Holstein und Mecklenburg. Diese Berichte wurden ziemlich regelmäßig alle zwei bis drei Tage nach London geschickt; sie waren ausschließlich in englischer oder französischer Sprache abgefaßt.

Die von Cannon mitgeteilte Auswertung der *State Papers* können wir in einzelnen Punkten ergänzen. Im Zusammenhang mit den anderen Quellen wie Matthesons *Ehrenpforte* und weiteren Akten des Hamburger Staatsarchivs[8] läßt sich insgesamt das Bild der diplomatischen Tätigkeit Matthesons etwas differenzierter zeichnen.

Wir haben aus den *State Papers* und den Akten des Staatsarchivs Hamburg nicht nur die Stücke untersucht, die von Mattheson in

5 H. Turnow, "Mattheson, Johann", in: *MGG* VIII (1960), coll. 1795–1815, und Cannon, *Mattheson*.

6 Cannon, *Mattheson*, 36, Anm. 85: "Since I have been unable myself to make an examination of this correspondence [*State Papers*] in the London Public Record Office, the above information and all for that which has to do with these letters is taken from a report prepared for me by Mr. Ashley Olmsted".

7 Wir haben die *State Papers* (= SP) durchgesehen für die Zeit vom 2. Januar 1705 (= SP 82/21) bis 30. Oktober 1753 (= SP 82/74). Diese Akten sind verfilmt im Public Record Office, London. Kopien davon finden sich im Staatsarchiv Hamburg (Filmarchiv) unter Nr. S 12510 bis S 12531. An dieser Stelle möchte ich dem Staatsarchiv Hamburg, besonders Herrn Dr. Eckardt, herzlich für die Möglichkeit danken, die Filme einzusehen. Wir veröffentlichen eine Akte aus den *State Papers* im Anhang zu diesem Aufsatz.

8 Verschiedene Akten, den englischen Gesandten und seine Bediensteten betreffend, Geschäftsarchiv Charles Blunt.

eigener Verantwortlichkeit erstellt und daher auch von ihm unterschrieben wurden, sondern haben auch Hinweise auf ihn oder die Tätigkeit des "Sekretärs" aus den anderen Texten ausgewertet.

II

Seit dem 7. November 1704 hatte Mattheson als Nachfolger Georg Friedrich Händels die Erziehung des etwa achtjährigen Cyril Wich übernommen. Er gab dem Sohn des britischen Gesandten in Hamburg Unterricht in Klavier und allgemeiner Musiklehre, wie er insgesamt dessen allgemeine Erziehung als "Hofmeister" beaufsichtigte. Dafür gab Mattheson seine Stellung an der Hamburger Oper als Sänger am 17. Februar 1705 auf, obwohl er dort immerhin jährlich ein Einkommen von ca. 300 Thalern erzielte (ob einschließlich der Kompositionshonorare mit je 50 Thalern, ist nicht klar)[9].

Wir fassen hier nur kurz die Gründe zusammen, die Mattheson bestimmten, das Amt des Sekretärs beim britischen Gesandten in Hamburg zu übernehmen[10]. Es sind dies: Sichere und überdurchschnittlich hohe Einkünfte, die einen gehobenen Lebensstandard ermöglichten, verbunden mit einem gesellschaftlichen Ansehen, das dem eines höheren Standes nahe kam, auf jeden Fall über dem aller Musikerberufe stand. Dazu kam verhältnismäßig viel freie Zeit, die es zuließ, sich mit musikalischen Problemen zu beschäftigen.

So hat Mattheson wahrscheinlich schon 1705, also kurz nachdem er die Erziehung Cyril Wichs übernommen hatte, das Amt des Sekretärs bei dessen Vater ins Auge gefaßt, denn er beginnt in diesem Jahr damit, sich mit englischer Sprache, Geschichte, Recht und Staatskunde zu befassen[11]. Die Erziehung des neunjährigen Cyril kann nicht allein die Beschäftigung mit diesen Bereichen gefordert haben, der Anstoß kommt eher von John Wich, "der mich für mehr Dinge geeignet fand als Spinett zu schlagen oder einen Kontrapunkt zu schreiben"[12]

III
Funktion und Stellung Matthesons

Grundsätzlich ist festzuhalten, daß Mattheson n i c h t im Dienst der britischen Regierung stand, sondern er P r i v a tbediensteter des Ge-

9 *Ehrenpforte*, 193.
10 Siehe dazu die Angaben in der *Ehrenpforte*.   11 *Ehrenpforte*, 195.
12 Brief an Richard Steele vom 26. Dezember 1713. Zitiert nach Cannon, *Mattheson*, 76–7.

47

sandten war. Daher ist es auch nicht verwunderlich, daß in den *State Papers* 1706 keine Mitteilung des Gesandten an seine Regierung zu finden ist, die den neuen Sekretär erwähnt. Die Stellung des Sekretärs bei einem britischen Gesandten war im allgemeinen wohl nicht sehr befriedigend. Wie D. B. Horn schreibt[13], wurden die Privatsekretäre von der Regierung in London generell geradezu als Sicherheitsrisiken angesehen. Da sie, wie Horn ausführt, eine untergeordnete und relativ schlecht bezahlte Tätigkeit übernahmen, hätten sie wenig Anlaß gehabt, diesen Dienst über einen längeren Zeitraum zu versehen. Horn erwähnt Mattheson als eine der ganz wenigen Ausnahmen. Der Gesandte stand sich in Hamburg offenbar finanziell besser als in anderen Orten[14].

Der Sekretär ist üblicherweise niemals Ansprechpartner der Regierung, und der Gesandte kann seinen Posten nur in Ausnahmefällen nach ausdrücklicher, schwer zu erlangender Genehmigung aus London verlassen. Wenn Mattheson aufgrund seiner Stellung als Privatsekretär dennoch am 29. Juli 1741[15] ein Gesuch um Pension an die Regierung nach London schickt, wird darin die durchaus unübliche Entwicklung deutlich, die Mattheson in der Ausfüllung dieses Amtes gemacht hat[16].

Als Sekretär eines ausländischen Gesandten war er von Rechten und Pflichten der Hamburger Bürger ausgenommen und hatte bestimmte Steuer- und Abgabeprivilegien, wie er andererseits aber auch in Hamburg keinen Grund und Boden erwerben konnte[17].

Matthesons Vorgesetzte. Johann Mattheson hat das Amt des Sekretärs offensichtlich am 6. Januar 1706[18] bei dem seit 1702[19] in Hamburg residierenden Geschäftsträger John Wich angetreten. Dieser

---

13 D. B. Horn, *The British Diplomatic Service 1689–1789*, (Oxford, 1961), 38.
14 Siehe dazu Brief Friedrich von Hagedorns vom 17. November 1741, zitiert bei Cannon, *Mattheson*, 35, Anm. 81.
15 29.7.1741 (SP 82/62, p. 103).
16 Es liegen uns keine Angaben darüber vor, ob diese Pension bewilligt wurde oder nicht. Da Mattheson 1742 von James Cope in seinem Amt bestätigt wurde, ist anzunehmen, daß das Gesuch um Pension abgelehnt wurde.
17 Die Häuser, die er besaß, waren auf die Namen von Hamburger Bürgern eingetragen. Siehe dazu Cannon, *Mattheson*, 219–25, besonders 222.
18 *Ehrenpforte*, 195. Die Berichte des Gesandten nach England, wie sie in den *State Papers* gesammelt sind, erwähnen den Amtsantritt Matthesons nicht. Eine gewisse Bestätigung für dieses Datum ergibt sich aber daraus, daß John Wich im Jahre 1705 sämtliche Mitteilungen nach London selbst schreibt, am 8. Januar 1706 aber die Kopie eines Aktenstückes beigefügt ist, die Mattheson geschrieben hat (SP 82/22). Wir haben die State Papers ab dem 2. Januar 1705 durchgesehen.
19 Cannon, *Mattheson*, 35.

starb 1713, sein Sohn Cyril wurde Nachfolger und erhielt 1714 die Ernennung[20]. Im Jahre 1741 wurde Cyril Wich nach Petersburg versetzt[21], James Cope übernahm das Amt in Hamburg. Cope starb am 1. August 1756 in London[22]. Seine Nachfolger erwähnt Mattheson in der *Ehrenpforte* nicht.

Grundsätzliche Aufgaben des Sekretärs. Zu den üblichen Aufgaben eines Sekretärs gehörten die Reinschrift der Gesandtschaftsbriefe und anderer Akten, Aufnahme von Protokollen[23], Ausfertigung von Pässen[24], Übergabe von schriftlichen Mitteilungen des Gesandten an andere Ämter und Personen, wie auch Registrierung und Archivierung der ein- und ausgehenden Schriftstücke[25].

Seit 1714 mußte Mattheson die *Circulars*[26] und die diesen beigefügten Aktenstücke ins Französische übersetzen[27], da Georg I. die englische Sprache nicht beherrschte und doch wohl gelegentlich diese Berichte selber lesen wollte.

Zusammenfassungen und Übersetzungen aus englischen Zeitungen, wie auch Übersetzungen politischer Schriften ins Deutsche gehörten zu seinem Aufgabenbereich, wurden aber extra honoriert[28].

Aufgaben- und Verantwortungsbereich Matthesons über die grundsätzlichen Aufgaben hinaus. Wir wollen nun im folgenden untersuchen, inwieweit Matthesons Aufgaben- und Verantwortungsbereich über die vorher beschriebenen, weniger verantwortlichen unselbständigen Tätigkeiten hinausging.

Da uns eine Dienstanweisung, die Matthesons Rechte und Pflichten grundsätzlich regelt, nicht vorliegt, lassen wir hier eine Übersicht über die Aufgaben des britischen G e s a n d t e n in Hamburg folgen. Damit soll der Aufgabenbereich des Amtes selber abgesteckt und der äußerste Rahmen für Matthesons Tätigkeit gezeigt werden. Er selber spricht sogar davon, daß er am 8. Dezember 1730 für die Abwesenheit seines Vorgesetzten Cyril Wich "seine ordentliche Instructiones ... fast eben des Inhalts [empfing] wie sie die Gesandten

---

20 16.3.1714 (SP 82/31, p. 57).
21 29.7.1741 (SP 82/62, p. 103), ebenso, *Ehrenpforte*, 215.
22 *Ehrenpforte*, Anhang 32.   23 Ibid., 216 (1735).
24 Ibid., Anhang 26, 29.   25 Ibid., 202 (1716).
26 Siehe dazu unten Abschnitt IV, "Berichte an die Regierung".
27 16.11.1714 (SP 82/31, p. 122), Anweisung aus London.
28 Z.B. 1716: "EXTRACT / Der Zeitungen / aus / Gross-Britannien, / So der hiesige / Königliche Ministre, Herr von Wich. mit gestriger Post erhalten, / und hiemit auf dessen Befehl publicirt werden". Titel bei Cannon, *Mattheson*, 162, Nr. 39.

selber haben"[29]. Letztlich läßt sich an der Anweisung für den Gesandten auch das Verhältnis der Tätigkeiten Gesandter–Sekretär beurteilen und damit kann die Stellung Matthesons in diesem Amt und insbesondere bei verschiedenen Vorgesetzten angemessen eingeschätzt werden.

Uns liegen die Anweisungen Georgs II. (König von Großbritannien seit dem 26. Juni 1727) an Cyril Wich vom 28. Mai 1728 vor[30]. Nach jedem Thronwechsel mußten die Gesandten formell in ihrem Amt bestätigt werden. Die Dienstanweisungen wurden ihnen mitgeteilt und erneute Beglaubigungsschreiben für die entsprechenden Regierungen übersandt[31].

Wir gehen davon aus, daß die hier genannten Bestimmungen während der gesamten Amtszeit Matthesons gegolten haben, d.h. mindestens seit 1706[32].

Die Aufgabenbereiche des britischen Gesandten in Hamburg lassen sich wie folgt zusammenfassen[33]:

1. Der Gesandte soll gute Kontakte zu Senat und Magistrat in den Hansestädten Hamburg, Bremen und Lübeck pflegen.

2. Er nimmt hoheitliche Aufgaben über britische Untertanen wahr, fördert die Beachtung und Durchsetzung ihrer Privilegien und Freiheiten ("Immunitys") in Hamburg und setzt sich insbesondere für die Interessen der "Merchant Adventurers" ein[34].

3. Der Gesandte soll regelmäßig Berichte über die Entwicklung des englischen Handels in der Elbmündung nach London schicken[35].

4. Gute Kontakte zu anderen Gesandten in und außerhalb Hamburgs sowie zu den anderen Regierungen sollen dem Gesandten zu gründlichen Informationen verhelfen.

29 *Ehrenpforte*, 213, ähnliche Formulierung erstmalig im Oktober 1719 (*Ehrenpforte*, 205).
30 28.5.1728 (SP 82/45, p. 215–18).
31 Auch bei einer Rangerhöhung des Gesandten, wie z.B. 1719 (Titel eines "Ministers"), 3.11.1719 (SP 82/36, p. 293), wurde eine neue Dienstanweisung gegeben.
32 Titel des Residenten und der Amtsbereich ändern sich in diesen Jahren: der Amtsbereich umfaßte Hamburg, Bremen und Lübeck und wurde offenbar nur für die Amtszeit John Wichs 1709 um die Fürstentümer Holstein und Mecklenburg erweitert.
33 Wir halten uns hier an die Reihenfolge des Originals.
34 Die "Merchant Adventurers" waren ein Zusammenschluß von englischen Kaufleuten in Hamburg mit umfangreichen Handels- und Steuerprivilegien. Es bestand jedoch (zumindest im achtzehnten Jahrhundert) kein Recht auf Aufnahme in diese Gesellschaft, eine einzige Gegenstimme genügte zur Abweisung. Im Interesse der Kaufleute (Konkurrenzfähigkeit) und des Senates (möglichst wenig Einnahmeausfälle) lag es, die Gruppe der Privilegierten möglichst klein zu halten. Siehe H. Hitzigrath, *Die Kompagnie der Merchant Adventurers und die englische Kirchengemeinde in Hamburg 1611–1835* (Hamburg, 1904), 48–52.
35 Diese Anweisung gibt es seit April 1715. Siehe 28.5.1728 (SP 82/45, p. 215–18).

5. Er korrespondiert regelmäßig mit den anderen großbritannischen Vertretern an ausländischen Höfen.

6. Der Gesandte ist verpflichtet, den König bzw. die Staatssekretäre möglichst umfangreich regelmäßig und frühzeitig über alle wichtigen Vorfälle und Absichten anderer Fürsten und Staaten, die ihm bekannt werden, zu informieren.

IV

Wir gliedern unsere Untersuchung entsprechend der vorgenannten Arbeitsbereiche des Gesandten.

Kontakte mit Senat und Magistrat der Städte Hamburg, Bremen und Lübeck. Ein erster Kontakt zwischen dem Gesandten und den jeweiligen Regierungen in seinem Amtsbereich wurde durch die Beglaubigungspapiere hergestellt, die mit den entsprechenden Höflichkeitsformeln übergeben wurden. In Lübeck und Bremen übergab der Gesandte seine Beglaubigungsschreiben persönlich[36], hatte er doch so eine Gelegenheit – bei seinen äußerst seltenen Besuchen in diesen Städten[37] – bestimmte Fragen mit dem Senat zu besprechen. Für Hamburg drücken sich die *State Papers* niemals eindeutig aus[38], es ist anzunehmen, daß – wie es auch in der *Ehrenpforte* heißt[39] – Mattheson selbst das Schreiben überreichte[40]. Diese Aufgabe hatte keine praktische politische Bedeutung, sondern war eher ein ehrenvolles Repräsentationsamt, das Matthesons Bedürfnis nach gesellschaftlichem Ansehen erfüllte[41].

Ob Mattheson einen Vertrag zwischen England und Hamburg über den Heringshandel förmlich unterzeichnet hat[42], konnten wir nicht überprüfen. Nach den Berichten in den *State Papers* hat Wich die Verhandlungen wohl selbst geführt und den Vertrag auch selbst

---

36 20.3.1714 (SP 82/31, p. 61 s.) "personally deliver my Credentialls". Ähnlich 26.7.1715 (SP 82/32, p. 113) und 13.8.1728 (SP 82/45, p. 274 s.).

37 Horn, *British Diplomatic Service*, 25. Briefe von Cyril Wich nach London liegen aus Lübeck, das er wegen seiner dort wohnenden Mutter öfter besuchte, in den *State Papers* häufiger vor als aus Bremen.

38 Die Übergabe des Schreibens wird in den *State Papers* immer als "in den üblichen Formen" beschrieben: 16.3.1714 (SP 82/31, p. 57), ebenso: 6.7.1728 (SP 82/45, p. 248).

39 *Ehrenpforte*, 200, 201, 211.

40 Nur Cope hat 1741 – nach Mattheson – das Beglaubigungsschreiben persönlich überreicht (*Ehrenpforte*, Anhang 19). Mattheson wurde erst 1742 wieder das Amt des Sekretärs übertragen.

41 6.7.1728 (SP 82/45, p. 248 s.).   42 *Ehrenpforte*, 204.

unterschrieben[43]. Wenn Mattheson schreibt, daß er den Vertrag am 8. Februar 1719 "in der Conferentz besiegelt"[44] habe, so ist nicht ausgeschlossen, daß er damit die Paraphierung des Vertrags gemeint hat.

Bei anderen Gelegenheiten zeigt es sich, daß Mattheson keineswegs Briefbote ist, sondern als Vertreter des Gesandten Verhandlungen führt und ein Memorial, eine förmliche diplomatische Note, dem Ersten Bürgermeister Hamburgs übergibt[45].

In der Angelegenheit Charles Blunt, der von der Gesellschaft der Merchant Adventurers trotz der Protektion der Londoner Regierung nicht aufgenommen und daher vom Hamburger Senat wie andere Bürger auch zu Steuern und sonstigen Abgaben herangezogen wird, läßt sich den *State Papers* ein etwas genaueres Bild der Verhandlungsführung Matthesons entnehmen[46].

Wich schickte seinen Sekretär zu dem Senator Stockfleet, dem Verhandlungsführer des Senats, um sich in dieser Angelegenheit über die Behandlung des Charles Blunt zu beschweren, mit der Aufforderung, diese Einwände an die Hamburger Regierung weiterzuleiten. Es handelte sich hier nicht um die Übergabe eines formellen Schreibens, sondern um eine Unterredung, in der Stockfleet auf die Klagen des Sekretärs einging.

Weitere Ansprechpartner Matthesons sind die Stadtsyndici[47]. 1741 wird in den *State Papers* ein Auszug aus den Registern des

43 Da Wich den Vertrag schon vor der endgültigen Zustimmung aus London – das einige Artikel geändert haben wollte – unterzeichnet hatte (unterzeichnen ließ?), folgte ein reger Briefwechsel in dieser Angelegenheit: 10.2.1719 (SP 82/36, p. 49); 14.2.1719 (SP 82/36, p. 57); 17.2.1719 (SP 82/36, p. 59); 3.3.1719 (SP 82/36, p. 71).
44 *Ehrenpforte*, 204.
45 4.8.1729 (SP 82/46, p. 243 ss., Handschrift Matthesons). Übergabe des "Memorial . . . by Sr Cyrill Wich's Secretary to the presiding Burgermaster": 15.10.1729 (SP 82/46, p. 245 s.). Obwohl Cyril Wich neben Mattheson, seinem "Secretarium primarium" (*Musicalischer Patriot*, 103, Abdruck eines Schreibens Wichs vom 24. Februar 1728) zeitweise einen zweiten Sekretär hatte, gehen wir bei diesen wichtigen diplomatischen Aufgaben davon aus, daß sie Mattheson übertragen wurden. Auch in einem Brief vom 4. März 1732 (SP 82/49, p. 49 ss.) spricht Wich von "my Secretary". Hier ist, wie aus anderen Quellen hervorgeht, eindeutig Mattheson gemeint.
46 17.9.1728 (SP 82/45, p. 287–90, Handschrift Matthesons). Hier wird ebenfalls nur von "my Secretary" gesprochen. Aus anderen Akten des Staatsarchives Hamburg geht aber hervor, daß Mattheson sich sehr um diese Angelegenheit gekümmert hat. Diese Auseinandersetzung zog sich bis 1731 hin. Am 2. Januar 1731 (StA Hbg, Geschäftsarchiv Charles Blunt, C1, Briefe an Charles Blunt) schreibt Mattheson an Blunt, daß er auf Nachricht von dem abwesenden Cyril Wich warte und, falls die ausbleiben sollte, "may venture to make a Step *sub spe rati*; and atleast tell these Magistrates, what Letter has been sent in your Behalf".
47 4.3.1732 (SP 82/49, p. 49 ss.).

Hamburger Senats an die Regierung in London (Übersetzung ins Französische, Matthesons Handschrift) übermittelt[48]. Hier heißt es, daß das Angebot des Senats, zusammen mit den Merchant Adventurers bestimmte Probleme zu besprechen, von Syndikus Surland dem Sekretär Mattheson am 9. Juli 1740 schriftlich mitgeteilt wurde, weil dieser in Vertretung des Gesandten eine Antwort auf dessen Memoire vom 27. Juni forderte[49].

Wie weit Mattheson direkt mit dem Bürgermeister Verhandlungen führen konnte, wird aus den Unterlagen nicht klar. Es liegt uns in dieser Hinsicht nur eine Beschwerde Matthesons über einen Senator vor, der ihm das Billett, das den Zugang zum Bürgermeister freigab, nicht unterzeichnen wollte[50].

Nun muß man hierbei natürlich bedenken, daß es sich um einen Brief vom 20. Oktober 1754 handelt und Mattheson aus verschiedenen Gründen, die wir weiter unten erläutern[51], nicht mehr als entscheidungsbefugter Vertreter des Gesandten James Cope angesehen wurde. In einer Abschrift Matthesons liegt in dieser Mappe (Anm. 50) ohne Datumsangabe, aber vor 1747, zwischen den Aktenstücken 18. März 1743 und 20. Oktober 1754 eine von dem Stadtsekretär Dobbeler "ex speciali comm."[52] unterzeichnete Mitteilung vor, daß Bedenken, Mattheson Gehör zu schenken, gegenstandslos seien, auch wenn er "abseiten seiner Vorgesetzten etwas bey Uns[53], oder bey einigen unsres Mittels, vorzustellen haben würde"[54]. Das läßt durchaus auf ziemlich ungehinderten Zutritt zum Bürgermeister schließen.

Hoheitliche Aufgaben über britische Untertanen. Beachtung und Durchsetzung der Privilegien und Freiheiten. Bei dem Vergleich der Angaben in Matthesons *Ehrenpforte* und denen in den *State Papers* haben wir feststellen können, daß die politischen Ereignisse und Daten äußerst korrekt von Mattheson wiedergegeben werden. Er muß

---

48 Extrait des Registres du Senat de Hamburg, Vendredi, Juin 16. 1741 traduit de l'allemand (SP 82/62, p. 72 ss.). In dieser Quelle wird darauf hingewiesen, daß Wich sich in Hannover befand.
49 Ibid.
50 Bitte an den Lic. de Droit und Archivar Schuback, Matthesons guten Bekannten, ein gutes Wort für ihn einzulegen, 20.10.1754 (StA Hbg, Cl. VII Lit. 9b N. 19 Vol. 5a, "Den Englischen Legations Secretaire Mattheson betr.").
51 Siehe unten Abschnitt IV, "Matthesons Tätigkeit".
52 "auf besonderen Befehl". Dobbeler ist am 21. April 1747 gestorben. Das Schreiben muß also vor diesem Datum aufgesetzt worden sein.
53 Damit kann nur der Bürgermeister gemeint sein.
54 StA Hbg, Cl. VII Lit. I. n. 2. f. 4, "Englischer Secretarius Mattheson". Der Name Matthesons nicht ausgeschrieben, sondern nur Abkürzung "J.M." verwendet.

entweder selbst jahrelang Merkbücher geführt haben, oder aber Duplikate der *State Papers* oder ähnliche Akten aus der britischen Gesandtschaft zum Entwurf der *Ehrenpforte* herangezogen haben.

Die größte Abweichung in den Daten liegt uns hinsichtlich einer königlichen Proklamation 1716 vor. Diese Abkündigung wird von Wich am 25. Juni 1716 unterschrieben[55]. Damit wird ein Schlußpunkt unter die Angelegenheiten gesetzt, die in der Woche zuvor mehrfach (seit 19. Juni) erwähnt werden. Mattheson aber berichtet in der *Ehrenpforte*, daß diese Proklamation auf zehn englischen Schiffen am 18. August bekanntgegeben worden sei[56]. Auch wenn dieses Datum nicht auszuschließen ist, erscheint es uns etwas spät. Mattheson kann sich um einen Monat versehen haben. Obwohl in den *State Papers* keine Angabe vorliegt, ist durchaus mit der *Ehrenpforte* anzunehmen, daß Mattheson selber die Abkündigung vornahm. Dieses war mehr eine formelle Aufgabe, die "mit gehörigen Ceremonien, als ein Herold"[57] durchgeführt wurde.

Mattheson veranlaßte auch zivil- und strafrechtliche Maßnahmen der Hamburger Justiz gegenüber britischen Untertanen, da der Gesandtschaft selber eine Rechtshoheit nicht zustand, sie aber andererseits vorher benachrichtigt werden mußte. Im Auftrage Wichs protestiert Mattheson vor dem öffentlichen Notar Thomas Lediard[58] am 31. Juli 1726, um das Erbe von Thomas Bigs[59] für den englischen König zu reklamieren.

Nach den bisherigen Ausführungen erscheint es uns durchaus glaubhaft – die *State Papers* oder andere Akten erwähnen diese Angelegenheit nicht –, daß Mattheson im Jahre 1713 "als Bevollmächtigter"[60] englischen "Schiffs-Hauptleuten" einen Eid abnimmt[61]. Um die Pest nicht weiterzutragen, verpflichten sich die Seeleute, nicht am Ufer der Elbe zu landen. Mit Matthesons Attest

55 25.6.1716 (SP 82/33, p. 185).   56 *Ehrenpforte*, 203.   57 Ibid., p. 203.
58 Thomas Lediard wird von Wich auch als sein Sekretär bezeichnet, 7.6.1728 (StA Hbg Cl. VII Lit. 9b N. 1 Vol. 8 f, "Den Englischen Ministres Bediente . . ."). In dieser nach London übermittelten öffentlichen Urkunde wird er als öffentlicher Notar des Reiches bezeichnet: "Thomas Lediard, Publ. Notary, by Authority of His most sacred Imperial Majesty". Lediard stand wahrscheinlich auch als Rechtsberater im Dienste Wichs. Siehe zu Lediard auch: H. Chr. Wolff, "Ein Engländer als Direktor der alten Hamburger Oper", in: *Hamburger Jahrbuch für Musikwissenschaft* 3 (Studien zur Barockoper) (Hamburg, 1978), 75–83.
59 Bigs war Mitglied der Merchant Adventurers und ohne Leibeserben und ohne Testament gestorben. Die Merchant Adventurers hatten – entgegen großbritannischen Gesetzen – sein Erbe eingezogen. Siehe 31.7.1726 (SP 82/43, p. 165).
60 *Ehrenpforte*, Anhang 12 (zu p. 199).
61 Ibid., 199. John Wich war nach England gereist und Cyril noch nicht im Amt bestätigt.

ließ die dänische Regierung sie passieren und der Handel zwischen Hamburg und England kam nicht zum Erliegen.

Auch die Ausstellung von Pässen und Seegeleitsbriefen, die Mattheson für die Jahre 1748, 1749 und 1751 erwähnt[62], wird zu seinen Aufgaben gehört haben.

Bei einer kurzen Reise Wichs im Oktober 1731 nach Bremen ereignete sich eine gewaltsame Auseinandersetzung zwischen englischen Seeleuten, bei der zwei Engländer getötet und andere verwundet wurden. Mattheson[63] hat ein Gesuch beim Richter eingereicht, und sofort die zuständigen Beamten angewiesen, nach den Mördern zu suchen. Offenbar informierte Mattheson auch den Regierungsvertreter in Altona und die Grafschaft Pinneberg[64].

Auch sonst war es üblich, daß der Sekretär genauso wie der Gesandte selber die Verhaftung unbotmäßiger englischer Matrosen veranlassen konnte. Mattheson beschreibt dieses Verfahren sehr genau in der *Ehrenpforte*[65] an dem Beispiel der schottischen Rebellen, die im Hamburger Hafen Waffen geladen hatten. Diese Angelegenheit ordnet Mattheson zeitlich zwischen zwei andere Angaben mit den Daten 1. September und 21. November und erwähnt, daß er selber dieses Schiff entdeckt und dafür gesorgt habe, daß der Hafenmeister sich Befehl von seinen Vorgesetzten holte, um es zu beschlagnahmen.

Vergleichen wir damit die Angaben in den *State Papers*[66]. Wich hatte danach am 30. Juli 1715 von London den Auftrag bekommen, über alle Schiffe, die in Hamburg beladen würden, genaueste Erkundigungen einzuziehen, ob sie Waffen und Munition an Bord hätten. Wich hat diese Aufgabe – ob zeitweilig oder grundsätzlich, geht nicht aus den Berichten hervor – seinem Sekretär übertragen, denn er schreibt in dem o.a. Brief (Anm. 66), daß "My Secretary has this moment come from aboard the said Ship, and has actually seen in the bottom of the Vessel great heaps of Canon Balls; but time would not permit him to make any further search this night". Auch wenn Wich vorher schreibt[67]: "I [Hervorhebung des Verfassers] have ever since used my best endeavours, to be well inform'd cn this Subject, and have at last discover'd a Ship . . .", dann muß das nicht heißen, daß Wich selber das Schiff entdeckt hat, sondern, daß diese Untersuchung in seiner Verantwortung erfolgte. Der Bericht in der *Ehrenpforte* wird also durch die *State Papers* bestätigt.

---

62 Ibid., Anhang 26, 29.
63 Im Text steht "My Secretary". Der Brief ist von Cyril Wich selbst geschrieben und datiert Bremen, 13. Oktober 1731 (SP 82/48, p. 129).
64 13.10.1731 (SP 82/48, p. 129).   65 *Ehrenpforte*, 201 und Anhang 13 (zu p. 201).
66 22.10.1715 (SP 82/32, 216 s.), Hamburg, Handschrift Matthesons.   67 Ibid.

Auch die Beschreibung der weiteren Maßnahmen entspricht den Angaben in der *Ehrenpforte:* "Upon my desire the Senate arrested the Ship this evening"[68]. Das Verfahren wird ähnlich gewesen sein, wie wenn sich englische Kapitäne über unbotmäßige Matrosen beklagten: Der Gesandte, oder (in seiner Abwesenheit) der Sekretär fertigten ein Schriftstück an den Wasserschaut (Hafenmeister) aus, in dem dieser aufgefordert wurde, bestimmte Leute zu verhaften[69].

Wenn man versucht, die Selbständigkeit Matthesons bei der Regelung dieser Angelegenheiten zu beurteilen, muß man feststellen, daß er – wenn immer möglich – Wich informierte[70]. Bei schwierigen Entscheidungen kam Wich, wenn er in der Nähe erreichbar war, auch selber nach Hamburg zurück[71].

Wich ging Anfang Dezember 1730 nach England[72] und kam offenbar erst Anfang April 1731 nach Hamburg zurück[73]. Es gab für Mattheson in dieser Zeit einige schwierige Probleme zu lösen, die er selber folgendermaßen beschreibt:

Das Jahr 1731. fing sich mit vielen Zwistigkeiten unter den engländischen Kauf- und See-Leuten an, die nach den dahingehörigen Rechten entschieden werden musten. Er [Mattheson] ließ, zu dem Ende, bisweilen 10. und mehr Parteien in einem Tage vor sich kommen; vernahm ihre Klagen und Verantwortungen; hörte Eide ab; ertheilte Befehle; wählte Schiedsmänner; übergab viele Memoralien; hielt öfftere Unterredungen mit Bürgermeistern, Syndicis, Rathmannen und Secretarn[74].

---

68 22.10.1715 (SP 82/32, p. 216 s.), Hamburg, Handschrift Matthesons.
69 Dazu liegen folgende Akten vor, gesammelt unter der Signatur: StA Hbg Cl. VII Lit. I^b N. 1 Vol. 6^c Fasc. 1, "Die vom Englischen H. Envoyé beym Waßer-Schaut gesuchte und erlangte Arrestirung eines . . . [unleserlich] Englischen Matrosen James Johnson betreffend . . . 1733".
(a) 20.9.1733: Dieses Ersuchen um eine Verhaftung ist "Bey Abwesenheit des Königl. Großbrit. H. Abgesandtens" von Mattheson selbst geschrieben und unterschrieben.
(b) 20.2.1739: In der Vernehmung des Wasser-Schauten (vor den Herren Rentzel J.U.L. und Schuback J. U. L.) wird darauf hingewiesen, daß das Verhaftungsersuchen auch – bei Abwesenheit des Gesandten – die Unterschrift des Sekretärs tragen kann.
70 Siehe dazu Bremen, 13.10.1731 (SP 82/48, p. 129): "They write me from Hamburgh" (Wich eigenhändig). Ebenso StA Hbg, Geschäftsarchiv Charles Blunt, C1, Briefe an Charles Blunt, 2. Januar 1731: Brief Matthesons an Blunt, in dem er mitteilt, daß er auf Informationen von Wich aus London wartet.
71 28.7.1739 (SP 82/60, p. 116): "I have been obliged to come to Town sooner, than I expected, on account of severall Disputes, which are lately arisen between our Masters of Ships and their Mariners".
72 Mitteilung in: 1.12.1730 (SP 82/47, p. 223).
73 Für die Zeit vom 22.12.1730 bis 2.4.1731 liegen keine Akten in den *State Papers* vor.
74 *Ehrenpforte*, 213.

In den *State Papers* wird erst im November 1731 und mehrmals 1732 zu diesen Vorgängen Stellung genommen. Die Lage war deshalb so kompliziert, weil die Funktion und die Rechte Matthesons in diesem Amt als Vertreter Wichs sehr verschieden beurteilt wurden.

Es ging darum, daß das Schiff des englischen Untertanen Pott am 22. März 1731 auf Ersuchen eines Hamburger Kaufmanns Hoffmann vom Hamburger Magistrat beschlagnahmt worden war[75]. Normalerweise wurde mit dem britischen Gesandten v o r der Beschlagnahme – da es sich hier um zivilrechtliche Forderungen handelte – Rücksprache genommen und seine Zustimmung eingeholt[76]; in diesem Falle war das nicht geschehen.

W i c h sieht hier alte Rechte verletzt, und sucht auch Rückendeckung in London, um Wiederholungsfälle auszuschließen. Er argumentiert, daß er vorher den Hamburger Magistrat benachrichtigt habe, daß – in seiner Abwesenheit – sein Sekretär dafür sorgen solle, daß Recht über die britischen Handelsleute gesprochen werde und insbesondere darauf zu achten habe, daß die Rechte, derer sich die Engländer seit undenklichen Zeiten erfreuten, nicht verletzt würden[77]. Wie Wich weiter ausführt, hätte der Magistrat zuerst seinen Sekretär über die Gründe für die Beschlagnahme des Schiffes informieren müssen, und nicht, wie es geschehen sei, erst das Schiff zu beschlagnahmen, und erst hinterher Gründe dafür vorzuschieben, die nur darauf abzielten, dies Vorgehen zu rechtfertigen[78]. Pott habe sich über dieses Vorgehen bei "meinem Sekretär" beschwert, und dieser sich an den Senat gewandt mit der Bitte um Abhilfe[79].

Anders hat es der Veranlasser der Beschlagnahme, H o f f m a n n , gesehen. Er hatte Mattheson völlig übergangen, und sich aus dem Grunde nicht – so wird es in den *State Papers* ausgeführt – an den britischen Gesandten gewandt, weil er gewußt habe, daß Wich bis zum Frühling in London war. Da Hoffmann dieses Vorrecht der englischen Handelsleute wohl bekannt war, schreibt er – zitiert bei Wich in den *State Papers* – zunächst am 19. Januar 1731 an Bekannte in Sunderland (Nordengland), die bei ihrem Magistrat eine schriftliche Bitte an den "Hamburger Staat" erwirken sollten wegen Verhaftung Potts und Beschlagnahme seines Schiffes[80].

Die L o n d o n e r R e g i e r u n g sieht eher ausschließlich den Gesandten selber als Geschäftsträger und Mattheson nicht als voll-

---

75 4.3.1732 (SP 82/49, p. 49 ss.).   76 16.11.1731 (SP 82/48, p. 174 ss.).
77 3.6.1732 (SP 82/49, p. 120 ss., Handschrift Matthesons).   78 Ibid.
79 4.3.1732 (SP 82/49, p. 49 ss., Handschrift Matthesons).
80 16.11.1731 (SP 82/48, p. 174 ss.).

gültigen Vertreter. Der englische Staatssekretär Harrington ist der Meinung[81], daß das alte Recht eigentlich nicht so sehr verletzt worden sei, denn das Recht bezöge sich auf die Person des Gesandten, und es sei ja tatsächlich kein Gesandter in Hamburg anwesend gewesen. Die Beurteilung der Funktion und Stellung Matthesons ist natürlich bei allen Parteien durch Interessen bzw. persönliche Freundschaftsverhältnisse beeinflußt. H o f f m a n n wird sich einen Vorteil ausgerechnet haben, wenn er den in Hamburg sofort erreichbaren Mattheson umging, und sich Zustimmung aus der sehr weit entfernten, in Nordengland belegenen Stadt Sunderland holte. Die R e g i e r u n g i n L o n d o n wollte nicht jeden kleinen Vorfall zum Ärger mit Hamburg machen, und stand Sekretären grundsätzlich skeptisch gegenüber[82]. W i c h , der mit Mattheson seit achtzehn Jahren im Amt zusammenarbeitete und ihn seit siebenundzwanzig Jahren kannte, hatte natürlich volles Vertrauen zu Mattheson und betrachtete ihn daher selbstverständlich als denjenigen, der das Amt des Gesandten in seiner Abwesenheit vollgültig ausübte. Er nimmt auch die Stellungnahme Londons nicht unwidersprochen hin[83].

Bericht über die Entwicklung des Handels. Ende Oktober 1719 erbitten die Lords Commissioners of Trade Auskunft über den Heringshandel und Wolleinfuhren in Hamburg bzw. Stade. Es geht wohl darum, die Auswirkungen des im Februar 1719 abgeschlossenen Vertrages über die Einfuhr englischen Herings in Hamburg zu prüfen. Da Wich in der Göhrde ist, wo König Georg sich zur Jagd aufhält, öffnet Mattheson die Briefe und leitet sie dann an Wich weiter. Er sieht es als seine Pflicht an[84], in der Zwischenzeit bereits Informationen einzuholen. Es ging zum einen um die Frage, wieviel britischer Hering jährlich in Hamburg angelandet wird und welche Qualität er im gegenwärtigen Jahr 1719 gehabt habe. Mattheson schreibt nach London zurück, er habe Leute gefragt, die erfahren in solchen Dingen seien. Auch bei der Frage nach Menge und Art der in Stade verzollten englischen und holländischen Wollerzeugnisse beauftragt Mattheson selbständig eine geeignete Person. Um zu zeigen, daß er diese Aufgabe sehr verantwortungsbewußt wahrnimmt, erläutert er, warum diese Person besonders gut dafür geeignet ist[85]. Obwohl er überaus deutlich in diesem Brief darauf hinweist, wie sorgfältig er

81 Whitehall, 16.5.1732, Harrington an Wich (SP 82/49, p. 113 ss.).
82 Cf. oben Abschnitt III.
83 Whitehall, 16.5.1732 (SP 82/49, p. 113 ss.), Antwort von Wich darauf am 3.6.1732 (SP 82/49, p. 120 ss.).
84 27.10.1719 (SP 82/36, p. 284 s., Brief Matthesons nach London).   85 Ibid.

seine Erkundigungen einholt, schreibt er bescheiden, oder – um die Rangordnung gegenüber London wieder herzustellen –, daß seine Angaben *ad interim* (Hervorhebung Mattheson), d.h. bis Wich zurückkommt, den Lords of Trade übermittelt werden mögen. Wich selber werde jeden Punkt der Briefe "more fully and satisfactory"[86] beantworten.

Kontakte zu anderen Gesandten und Regierungen. Während der gesamten Diensttätigkeit als Sekretär lassen sich über die rein geschäftlichen Dinge hinaus persönliche Kontakte Matthesons zu den politisch führenden Persönlichkeiten und ihren Vertretern in Hamburg feststellen.

Auffällig ist, daß es sich sehr häufig um Bekanntschaften oder sogar Freundschaften handelt, die sich zunächst auf dem Gebiet der Musik ergeben haben. Dadurch mögen die politischen Gespräche, die sich teilweise erst in späteren Jahren ergaben, erleichtert worden sein[87].

Hier wären zunächst einmal Matthesons Schüler zu nennen, die später wichtige Funktionen in Regierungsämtern in Hamburg ausübten. Im Jahre 1713 hatte er als Schüler im Generalbaß Herrn von Som, später Syndikus, den Rechtsanwalt Dr. iur. Johann Anton Winckler[88] und dessen Bruder, den Lizentiaten und Sekretär am Dom-Capitel Winckler (gestorben 1747), wie auch Diederico de Dobbeler, später Lizentiat und Stadtsekretär[89]. Matthesons Schulkamerad Barthold Heinrich Brockes war 1720 Ratsherr geworden und 1735 Amtmann in Ritzebüttel. Der Syndikus und spätere Bürgermeister Lucas von Bostel schrieb für Matthesons Komposition zum Petri-Mahl der Ratsherren 1709 die Verse[90].

In Matthesons *Ehrenpforte* sind häufige Reisen in politischen Geschäften nach Quedlinburg vermerkt, wo England versuchte, die Wahl der Prinzessin Maria Elisabeth von Holstein gegenüber Preußen durchzusetzen[91]. Nach langen Auseinandersetzungen seit 1704 wurde diese Prinzessin schließlich 1718 eingesetzt[92]. Mattheson war

---

86 Ibid.
87 Siehe z.B. *Ehrenpforte*, 196: "wozu die Musik des Einführers Stelle vertrat, u. zur Einsicht in Englands Staatsgeschäffte viel halff".
88 Für Johann Anton Winckler komponierte Mattheson 1712 eine Serenade aus Anlaß der Wahl zum Ratssyndikus; siehe Cannon, *Mattheson*, 155, Nr. 24. J. A. Winckler verweigert Mattheson 1754 jedoch den Zutritt zum Bürgermeister. Cf. dazu oben Abschnitt IV, "Kontakte".
89 *Ehrenpforte*, 200.   90 Ibid., 197.   91 Ibid., 195–7.
92 21.6.1718 (SP 82/35, p. 167). Mattheson schreibt in der *Ehrenpforte*, 196–7, daß Maria Elisabeth am 25. September 1710 zum zweiten Male als Äbtissin erwählt und förmlich angenommen worden sei. Wir konnten diesen Vorgang nicht überprüfen,

insofern ein geeigneter Kundschafter und Vermittler, als er die 1704 bis 1718 dort kommissarisch als Äbtissin wirkende Pröbstin Maria Aurora von Königsmarck[93] von einem Konzert 1703 her sehr gut kannte[94]. Mattheson widmete ihr 1713 *Das neu-eröffnete Orchestre*[95].

Mit Glückwunschadressen Matthesons werden die Grafen Schönborn (1708)[96] (Leiter der kaiserlichen Kommission in Hamburg), Metsch (1719)[97] und Fux (das Jahr geht aus der *Ehrenpforte* nicht hervor)[98] in Hamburg empfangen.

"Angenehmen Umgang" pflegt Mattheson mit dem Archivarius adjunctus und späteren Syndikus in Hamburg, Schuback, in den Jahren 1754–5[99].

Dem Syndikus und späteren Bürgermeister Garlieb Sillem widmete er 1712 "Die / Ausbündig – schönen / Eigenschafften / Der . . . / AMERICANIschen / Tobacks – Pflantzen"[100] (Übersetzung aus dem Englischen).

Mit dem holländischen Sekretär[101] und späteren Residenten am Hof des Zaren, Herrn De Bie, hatte Mattheson im Zusammenhang mit der kaiserlichen Kommission in Hamburg 1708 viel zusammengearbeitet[102].

1752 wohnte der holländische Gesandte von Marteville vor der Abreise nach Schweden mit Familie für sieben Wochen bei Mattheson[103], ebenso im Juli 1756 der russische Minister Soltikoff[104].

Dem sächsischen Minister und Feldmarschall[105] Graf Flemming bringt Mattheson 1720 als Subsidienzahlung Englands 60 000 Dukaten nach Leipzig[106]. In der *Ehrenpforte* wird auch diese Summe

---

er ist nicht ausgeschlossen. Die endgültige Einsetzung ins Amt 1718 erwähnt Mattheson in der *Ehrenpforte* nicht.

93 H. Lorenz, *Werdegang von Stift und Stadt Quedlinburg*, vol. 1, (Quedlinburg, 1922), 331–2. Druckfehler: "1728" (p. 331) muß in "1718" verbessert werden. Siehe auch p. 332.

94 *Ehrenpforte*, 191. 1705 vertonte Mattheson einen Text ihrer Schwester: "Le retour du Siècle d'Or". Siehe Cannon, *Mattheson*, 149, Nr. 6.

95 Cannon, *Mattheson*, 157, Nr. 27.   96 Cannon, *Mattheson*, 151–2, Nr. 15.

97 *Ehrenpforte*, 205.   98 Ibid.

99 Brief Matthesons an Schuback 1754 (StA Hbg Cl. VII Lit 9b N. 19 Vol. 5a), "Den Englischen Legations Secretaire Mattheson betr."). Siehe auch *Ehrenpforte*, Anhang 31 (1755).

100 Cannon, *Mattheson*, 154–5, Nr. 23.

101 Am 5.8.1711 (SP 82/28, p. 83) als Sekretär des niederländischen Gesandten erwähnt.

102 *Ehrenpforte*, Anhang 11 (zu p. 195–6).

103 Ibid., Anhang 32.   104 Ibid., Anhang 29.

105 Siehe dazu W. Michael, *Englische Geschichte im 18. Jh.*, (Hamburg, 1896–1955), vol. 5, Anhang 10 und vol. 2/1, 470.

106 20.2.1720 (SP 82/37, p. 17).

genau wiedergegeben, und der Empfang durch Flemming nicht nur als ehrenvoll, sondern auch als freundschaftlich beschrieben[107].

Dem Oberst in einem polnisch-sächsischen Regiment, Freiherr von Löwendahl, widmet Mattheson 1726 die Übersetzung von *The Life of Mary Stewart*[108].

Diese persönlichen Kontakte lassen sich – von der Subsidienzahlung an Flemming abgesehen – nicht auf konkrete politische Auswirkungen hin interpretieren, sie zeigen aber, daß Mattheson vielfältige politische Kontakte hatte, die – nach der Beschreibung in der *Ehrenpforte* – über den rein geschäftsmäßigen Umgang hinausgingen. Sein persönliches Ansehen und seine musikalischen Fähigkeiten machten den Sekretär zu einem von verschiedensten einflußreichen Persönlichkeiten akzeptierten Gesprächspartner.

Kontakte zu Engländern in Deutschland und zu den wichtigen Persönlichkeiten des öffentlichen Lebens in Großbritannien. 1707 lernt Mattheson in Hamburg den vorher inSchweden residierenden und gleichzeitig bei August II. von Polen und Sachsen akkreditierten britischen Gesandten John Robinson kennen[109]. Robinson (1650–1723) wurde später Bevollmächtigter Großbritanniens auf dem Kongreß zu Utrecht (1713), und danach Bischof von Bristol, später von London[110].

Wie die Kontakte mit den anderen Persönlichkeiten des öffentlichen Lebens in Hamburg auch durch die Beschäftigung mit Musik vermittelt wurden (Mattheson schreibt, daß er sich "auf Begehren einiger Herrn Gesandten, mit Orgelspielen ... hören ließ"[111]), so ergibt sich daraus auch 1707 die Freundschaft zu Graf Strafford (1672–1739), dem britischen Gesandten in Berlin[112], der 1711 in den Haag versetzt wird und dann 1713 maßgeblich den Vertrag von Utrecht gestaltet.

Auf den persönlichen Umgang mit Strafford weist Mattheson besonders hin[113] und zählt ihn 1713–14 auch zu den Freunden bei Hofe, die auf Matthesons Wunsch hin tätig werden, um Cyril Wich

107 *Ehrenpforte*, 206.
108 Cannon, *Mattheson*, 184–5, Nr. 98.
109 *Ehrenpforte*, 196, und Anhang 11, betr. p. 196; Cannon, *Mattheson*, 154, Nr. 22.
110 L. Stephen (Ed.), *Dictionary of National Biography* (London, 1885–1901), vol. 17, 23–6. Die Angaben zur politischen Laufbahn Robinsons stimmen in der *Ehrenpforte* und dem *Dictionary* überein.
111 *Ehrenpforte*, 196.
112 Ibid. 196. Siehe auch *Dictionary of National Biography*, vol. 20, 1197–1200. Die Angaben zur politischen Laufbahn stimmen mit denen in der *Ehrenpforte* überein.
113 *Ehrenpforte*, Anhang 12 (zu p. 200).

zum Nachfolger seines Vaters im Amt des britischen Gesandten zu machen[114].

Lord Carteret (1690–1763), der spätere Staatssekretär des Äußeren in England, auch von 1720 bis 1734 Vizekönig in Irland, hörte 1720 "zwo gantzer Stunden"[115] Matthesons musikalischem Vortrag zu.

Die Daten Matthesons zur Biographie der Gesandten haben sich durch andere Quellen bestätigt. Sein persönliches Verhältnis zu ihnen scheint – wie in der *Ehrenpforte* beschrieben – tatsächlich freundschaftlich gewesen zu sein.

Berichte an die Regierung in London. Die *Circulars*[116] wurden normalerweise regelmäßig mit jeder Post, d.h. etwa alle drei bis vier Tage, nach London geschickt. Mündliche Berichte und Briefe von Vertrauensleuten, wie auch von anderen Gesandten aus Deutschland und Nordeuropa, ebenso Informationen aus Zeitungen[117] wurden hinsichtlich ihrer Bedeutung gesichtet und zusammengefaßt zu kürzeren Mitteilungen. Verhältnismäßig selten – am meisten gilt das noch für die Amtszeit John Wichs – werden die Briefe, die der britische Gesandte in Hamburg von Vertrauensleuten bekommen hat, wörtlich abgeschrieben und den *Circulars* beigelegt, vereinzelt auch nur kurze Abschnitte aus Briefen wörtlich in den *Circulars* zitiert.

Um auch hier wieder ein Bild über Matthesons Tätigkeit zu gewinnen, müssen wir uns fragen, welches sein Anteil an diesen Berichten ist. Wir untersuchen im folgenden die Verhältnisse unter den Gesandten John und Cyril Wich, also von Januar 1706 bis Ende August 1741.

Grundsätzlich ist festzustellen, daß die Gesandten die Verantwortung für die *Circulars*, wie sie sich durch ihre Unterschrift ausdrückte, in der Zeit ihrer Anwesenheit in Hamburg nicht an Mattheson abgeben. Diese Korrespondenz, die – natürlich zusammen mit anderen Informationen – in London für politische Entscheidungen ausgewertet wurde, verlangte von dem absendenden Gesandten ein überaus stark ausgeprägtes Verantwortungsgefühl und Beachtung der Vertraulichkeit.

Bei den grundsätzlichen Vorbehalten der britischen Regierungen, die die Sekretäre ihrer Gesandten als Sicherheitsrisiken ansahen, ist es nicht verwunderlich, daß John Wich auch nach dem Dienstantritt Matthesons in Januar 1706 bis zum 5. Juni 1708 a l l e Zirkularbriefe

114 Ibid., 200.   115 Ibid., 206.
116 Z.B. 4.5.1714 (SP 82/31, p. 73 s.): "as usual every Post a Circular of the News of these Parts".
117 Darauf weist Wich am 22.12.1730 (SP 82/47, p. 225) hin.

mit eigener Hand schreibt; der nächste Brief mit Matthesons Handschrift wird auch wieder erst fast zehn Monate später, am 29. März 1709, nach London geschickt. Erst dann findet man Matthesons Handschrift in den *Circulars* regelmäßiger[118]. Seit 1706 aber liegen diesen Berichten ca. fünf oder sechs Mal im Jahr Abschriften Matthesons von verschiedenen Aktenstücken und Berichten[119] bei. Nach Cyril Wichs Amtsantritt finden sich die meisten *Circulars* und deren Anlagen einschließlich der Übersetzungen ins Französische in Matthesons Handschrift; häufig schreibt Cyril Wich auch selber.

Die Unterschrift des Gesandten unter einem *Circular* in Matthesons Handschrift muß nicht unbedingt bedeuten, daß Mattheson nur eine Vorlage ins Reine abschrieb und keinen Anteil am inhaltlichen Entwurf des Briefes hatte.

Um hier Aufschlüsse zu bekommen, haben wir den Stil verschiedener Berichte miteinander verglichen, um aus Unterschieden auf Verfasser zu schließen. Diese Untersuchung blieb jedoch ohne Ergebnis. Weder der Vergleich eines eigenhändigen Briefes von John Wich (30. August 1709)[120] mit einem von ihm nur unterschriebenen (6. Dezember 1709[121]; beide in englischer Sprache) noch die Briefe aus der Übergangszeit zwischen John und Cyril Wich[122] lassen typische Merkmale eines bestimmten Schreibers erkennen.

Rückschlüsse auf das Verhältnis zwischen Cyril Wich und Mattheson beim Entwurf der Zirkularbriefe kann man nur aus zwei Berichten entnehmen. Es sind dies die einzigen Briefe 1706–53 in den *State Papers* von Matthesons Hand, die von seinem Vorgesetzten korrigiert wurden. Der erste Brief ist datiert vom 21. Mai 1715[123], der zweite vom 17. Februar 1719[124].

Wich hat keine inhaltlichen Änderungen vorgenommen, sondern den etwas "geschwollenen" Stil in eine einfachere, präzisere Sprache verbessert. Konkret kann man daraus nur schließen, daß offenbar die letzte Redaktion bei Wich selber lag. Ein Grund dafür, daß an diesen beiden Daten ein im Text korrigierter Brief (1719 ist nur e i n Wort verbessert worden) nach London geschickt wurde, ist uns kaum ersichtlich. Möglicherweise mußte der Brief von 1715, der eine Fülle

---

118 Die folgenden Briefe in Matthesons Handschrift am 9. April 1709 und 3. Mai 1709.
119 Z. B. Bericht aus Dresden, 17.1.1707 (SP 82/23, p. 28).
120 30.8.1709 (SP 82/25, p. 189).   121 6.12.1709 (SP 82/25, p. 299).
122 12.9.1713 (SP 82/31, p. 12), Matthesons Handschrift, Cyril Wichs Unterschrift. Mattheson führte in dieser Zeit mehr oder weniger die Amtsgeschäfte, denn Cyril Wich hatte noch keinerlei Erfahrung und war noch nicht achtzehn Jahre alt. Ebenso Mattheson/Cyril Wich: 24.4.1714 (SP 82/31, p. 71 s.). Cyril Wich eigenhändig: 4.5.1714 (SP 82/31, p. 73 s.), alle in englischer Sprache.
123 21.5.1715 (SP 82/32, p. 19 ss.).   124 17.2.1719 (SP 82/36, p. 59 s.).

von stilistischen Verbesserungen aufweist, aus uns unbekannten Gründen eilig abgeschickt werden, oder aber er ist durch ein Versehen in die Post geraten.

Wenn jedoch die Depeschen des Tages abgefertigt waren, und noch wichtige Nachrichten eintrafen, schickte Mattheson selbst eine eigenständige Nachschrift. Er öffnete also bei Wichs Abwesenheit die Post und entschied, ob die Mitteilung so wichtig war, daß er sie selbst am gleichen Abend noch nach London weiterleiten mußte[125].

Wie wichtig es für die Regierung in London war, daß die Berichte regelmäßig geschickt und von einer vertrauenswürdigen Person abgefaßt worden waren, zeigt sich darin, daß bei Cyril Wichs Krankheit, auch über einen längeren Zeitraum hinweg, Mattheson in London um Entschuldigung nachsuchte, er schickte k e i n e[126] Berichte. Mattheson kannte durchaus die eingehende Post[127] und hätte von daher auch selber die Berichte schreiben können. 1739 schreibt Mattheson anläßlich einer Krankheit Wichs, daß er selbst bei wichtigen Nachrichten London informieren werde[128], am 12. und 19. Mai 1739[129] weist er aber nur auf die immer noch andauernde Krankheit hin. Am 29. Mai 1739 schreibt er zwar selber, gibt aber in indirekter Rede nur wieder, was Cyril Wich ihm zu schreiben aufgetragen hat[130].

Dieses rigide Verhalten im Krankheitsfall von Wich (auch eine Entwicklung 1718–40 ist hier nicht festzustellen) läßt sich unserer Meinung nach nur so erklären, daß diese Briefe formell zur Gesandteneigenschaft gehören, und nur, wenn Wich sich in London eine weite Reise hatte genehmigen lassen und offiziell auch gegenüber London einen Vertreter bestellt hatte, konnte dieser die Berichte schreiben[131]. Mattheson nahm in solchen Fällen diese Aufgabe seit 1713 mehrfach wahr.

---

125 28.7.1722 (SP 82/39, p. 97); 13.7.1723 (SP 82/40, p. 101); 5.11.1726 (SP 82/43, p. 251); 8.11.1726 (SP 82/43, p. 252).
126 13.9.1718 (SP 82/35); 24.12.1728 (SP 82/45); 2.5.1730 (SP 82/47); 6.5.1735 (SP 82/55); 17.1.1736 (SP 82/57); 10.9.1737 (SP 82/58); 29.12.1739 (SP 82/60); 22.3.1740 (SP 82/61); 19.4.1740 (SP 82/61).
127 20.1.1736 (SP 82/57, p. 13). Mattheson entschuldigt Cyril Wich: "he is not yet able to write to MyLord: you will therefore deliver to His Lordship the two inclosed Letters from the Duke of Holstein to Their Majestyes . . ., containing Felicitations on the New Year".
128 5.5.1739 (SP 82/60, p. 89).
129 SP 82/60, p. 90 und 91.   130 29.5.1739 (SP 82/60, p. 95).
131 Wir halten eine sehr vordergründige Erklärung ebenfalls nicht für ausgeschlossen: Wich war nicht immer davon überzeugt, daß er London etwas Wichtiges mitzuteilen hatte, aber er mußte mit jeder Post einen Brief schicken. So waren er und Mattheson vielleicht ganz froh, wenn sie einen Grund hatten, unergiebige Berichte ausfallen zu lassen. Siehe dazu 22.12.1730 (SP 82/47, p. 227).

Bestätigt wird dieser formelle Aspekt, der die Verantwortung der *Circulars* immer an den Gesandten selber bindet, dadurch, daß Wich bei Aufenthalten in der näheren und weiteren Umgebung von Hamburg (sein Gut in Tangstedt, Lübeck oder Bremen, Göhrde) selbst die Berichte schreibt. Auch wenn Mattheson als sein offizieller Vertreter in Hamburg eingesetzt ist, schickt Wich regelmäßig zusätzliche Berichte aus den Orten, in denen er sich gerade aufhält, wie z.B. Paris, das er in einer privaten Angelegenheit besucht hat[132].

Wenn Wich sich in erreichbarer Nähe aufhält, wird er regelmäßig von Mattheson informiert[133]; bei wichtigen Entscheidungen kommt Wich vorzeitig nach Hamburg zurück[134]. Hier ist aber die Aufgabenverteilung schon offen. Mattheson führt die Aufträge an Wich aus London selbständig aus, holt selbst Erkundigungen ein[135] und entscheidet ebenso selbstverständlich, daß ein Brief an Wich, der diesen in der Göhrde nicht mehr erreichen wird, direkt von Hamburg aus nach London geschickt wird[136]. Wenn Cyril Wich in London um die Genehmigung zu einer weiten Reise nachsucht, wird er aufgefordert, einen Vertreter im Amt zu bestellen[137]. Mattheson wird regelmäßig seit 1713 als offizieller Vertreter beider Wichs eingesetzt, worüber sowohl die englische als auch die Hamburger Regierung informiert werden[138]. Hier sind Unterschiede zwischen der Amtszeit von John und der von Cyril Wich festzustellen, nicht jedoch eine Entwicklung zu mehr Selbständigkeit Matthesons im Laufe der Dienstjahre.

John Wich ist auch häufiger verreist[139], er betraut Mattheson aber nur einmal mit diesen Aufgaben, 1713, als "Assistent" seines Sohnes[140]. In Wirklichkeit wird Mattheson die Aufgaben selbst wahrgenommen haben, denn Cyril Wich hatte keinerlei Erfahrung im Amt und war noch keine achtzehn Jahre alt. Mattheson beschreibt übrigens selber seine Stellung als Vertreter John Wichs völlig korrekt in der *Ehrenpforte*[141]: "die Stelle eines Subdelegati zum

132 September 1736 – Januar 1737 ist Wich zur Regelung einer privaten Erbschaftsangelegenheit in Paris. Ebenso vom 5. Juni 1738 – 25. Oktober 1738.
133 z.B. 15.8.1723 (SP 82/40, p. 113): "After having writ the inclosed to Mr. Wich", ebenso 13.10.1731 (SP 82/48, p. 129); 12.7.1737 (SP 82/58, p. 107); 6.7.1739 (SP 82/60, p. 113); 28.7.1739 (SP 82/60, p. 116); 27.7.1740 (SP 82/61, p. 125).
134 5.7.1737 (SP 82/58, p. 105).
135 27.10.1719 (SP 82/36, p. 284 s.); Cf. oben, Abschnitt IV, Bericht.
136 Ausführlicher Bericht an Wich in der Göhrde wird mit Anschreiben und neuer Schlußformel versehen und nach London geschickt . 15.8.1723 (SP 82/40, p. 119–23).
137 24.8.(O.S.)/4.9.(N.S.)1736 (SP 82/57, p. 209 s.).
138 3.6.1732 (SP 82/49, p. 120 ss.).
139 Z.B. Oktober 1709 (SP 82/25, p. 238).
140 26.5.1713 (SP 82/30, p. 170 s.).   141 *Ehrenpforte*, 199.

erstenmahl, Nahmens des jungen Hrn. von Wich" (gesperrt gedruckt von Mattheson).

Die Angaben in der *Ehrenpforte* hinsichtlich der Abwesenheit Cyril Wichs und seiner Vertretung durch Mattheson stimmen mit denen in den *State Papers* überein[142].

In dieser selbständigen Wahrnehmung der Aufgaben Wichs läßt sich nun erstmals die Funktion und Stellung Matthesons konkret belegen. Die Formulierung "will order my Secretary to be very punctual in sending to Mr. de la Faye what ever occurrences of any consequence these parts may afford" erscheint erstmalig am 11. Oktober 1719[143] und wird ähnlich in den folgenden Jahren wiederholt[144].

Mattheson übernimmt hiermit voll verantworlich die Aufgabe, die *Circulars* abzufassen und nach London zu schicken. Damit zeigt sich, daß er durchaus eine Vertrauensstellung im Amt des britischen Gesandten – auch gegenüber der Regierung in London – erreicht hat. Wie selbstverständlich Mattheson als vollwertiger Vertreter von Wich angesehen wird, erhellt aus anderen darüber hinausgehenden Anweisungen.

Mattheson soll sich um alle Angelegenheiten kümmern und tun, was nötig ist, insbesondere dafür zu sorgen, daß alle Rechte und Immunitäten der englischen Handelsleute in Hamburg beachtet werden[145]. Genau wie Wich soll auch Mattheson sich im Notfall Anweisungen aus London holen[146], wie er es auch z.B. im Juni und Juli 1738 tut[147].

Warum die Anweisungen aus London für diese Zeit in den *State Papers* fehlen, ist unklar. Auf Wichs Schreiben vorher sind re-

---

142 Die Reise Wichs im August 1734 (*Ehrenpforte*, 215) läßt sich nach den *State Papers* nicht bestätigen, denn Wich unterschreibt *Circulars* am 10., 17., 20. und 31. August (SP 82/54). Der verhältnismäßig große Zeitabstand zwischen den Briefen ist jedoch ungewöhnlich, daher sind Reisen von wenigen Tagen dazwischen durchaus möglich. Es läßt sich nach den *State Papers* auch nicht jedes Mal ein formeller Auftrag an Mattheson belegen. Cf. 29.6.1729 – Anfang August 1729 Wich verreist (SP 82/46), auch 13.8.1728 (SP 82/45, p. 274 s.). Mattheson erwähnt nicht alle Reisen Wichs, z.B. ist Wich am 22. Oktober 1726 in Bremen (SP 82/43, p. 231) und Mattheson vertritt ihn tatsächlich in verschiedenen Angelegenheiten.

143 11.10.1719 (SP 82/36, p. 275).

144 22.10.1720 (SP 82/37, p. 207 s.); 23.7.1723 (SP 82/40, p. 112); 23.11.1723 (SP 82/40, p. 223); 28.11.1730 (SP 82/47, p. 220); Anfang 1731; Cf. dazu 3.6.1732 (SP 82/49, p. 120 ss.); 11.7.1732 (SP 82/49, p. 143 ss.); 7.9.1736 (SP 82/57, p. 211 ss.); 6.6.1738 (SP 82/59, p. 97 ss.).

145 3.6.1732 (SP 82/49, p. 120); bezieht sich auf Anweisungen Anfang 1731.

146 7.9.1736 (SP 82/57, p. 211 ss.): "upon any particular Emergency, take the Liberty to demand your LordShips Commands for his guidance".

147 SP 82/59, p. 97 ss.

gelmäßig Antworten aus London vorhanden, möglicherweise sind gerade diese Schriftstücke verloren gegangen, oder Mattheson hat sie Wich nach Paris nachgeschickt. Mattheson geht nämlich in seinen Berichten auf Vorgänge in London ein, die aber in den *State Papers* nicht belegt sind[148].

Normalerwiese schickt Mattheson in der Abwesenheit Wichs nur äußerst selten ein *Circular* nach London. Bei Wich wird etwa alle drei Tage ein Bericht abgefertigt, Mattheson schreibt in der Zeit vom 19. November 1720 bis 21. März 1721 nur vier Briefe, ähnlich erscheint vom 23. November bis 17. Dezember 1723 und vom 8. August 1725 bis 8. September 1725 nur e i n Bericht. Keine einzige Mitteilung nach London findet sich vom 22. Dezember 1730 bis 2. April 1731. Das muß aber nicht heißen, daß er seine Pflichten vernachlässigte, es ist eher so zu erklären, daß Mattheson in dieser Zeit mit Wich in London korrespondierte, und dieser die Informationen mündlich weitergab[149]. Damit läß sich auch die einzige Ausnahme erklären: bei Wichs Reise nach Paris 1738 schreibt Mattheson ebenso regelmäßig nach London wie Wich sonst[150].

Es läßt sich also festhalten, daß Nachrichten, die W i c h an seine Regierung weiterleiten konnte, von Mattheson an Wich gereicht und von diesem der Regierung übermittelt wurden. Nur im Ausnahmefall wandte Mattheson sich direkt nach London.

Das läßt sich auch dem Brief vom 15. August 1723 entnehmen, aus dem wir im Anhang zu diesem Aufsatz zwei Seiten im Faksimile veröffentlichen[151]. Dieser Brief ist zunächst an Wich gerichtet, der sich in der Göhrde aufhielt, aber, wie aus dem Begleitschreiben[152] hervorgeht, doch schon auf dem Weg nach Hamburg war und dort am gleichen Tag eintreffen sollte. Daher schickte Mattheson seinen Bericht direkt nach London und änderte nur die Höflichkeitsformel am Schluß von "votre J . . ." (unleserlich) in "Sa Majesté".

Mattheson nimmt seine Aufgabe sehr ernst und verfaßt die Berichte äußerst sorgfältig. Er nennt seine Quellen und beurteilt die Informa-

---

148 23.9.1738 (SP 82/59), Mattheson eigenhändig, auch unterschrieben: "I am sorry of Mr. Tilson's Indisposition". Cf. auch 10.10.1738, Nachschrift (SP 82/59, 166 s.).

149 StA Hbg, Geschäftsarchiv Charles Blunt, C1, Briefe an Charles Blunt. Brief Matthesons an Blunt, 2.1. 1731: "Thô I had a Letter from Sir Cyrill the Post before last Post, yet I had none last Fryday; and consequently no Direction about your Affair". In den anderen Fällen war Wich auch bei Hofe in England, Hannover oder in der Göhrde.

150 1738: 10.6.; 13.6.; 17.6.; 20.6.; 24.6.; usw. bis 17.10. 1738 (SP 82/60).

151 15.8.1723 (SP 82/40, p. 119–23). Dem Public Record Office London sei an dieser Stelle herzlich für die Genehmigung zur Veröffentlichung gedankt.

152 15.8.1723 (SP 82/40, p. 113).

tionen[153]. Auch wenn er selber sich auf mündliche Informationen verläßt, die er aus zweiter Hand über Briefe an Hamburger Kaufleute bekommen hat, teilt er mit, daß er die Originale nicht eingesehen habe. Um Informationen nicht durch seine Formulierung zu verfälschen, zitiert er sie teilweise sogar wörtlich[154]. Er holt selbst Erkundigungen ein und frischt dazu von sich aus den Briefwechsel mit einem Freund auf, der ihn über die Bewegungen der Moskauer Flotte im Baltikum 1723 informieren soll.

So zeigt dieser Brief deutlich, wie selbständig und zuverlässig Mattheson die Vertretung Wichs wahrnimmt.

Matthesons Tätigkeit unter James Cope. Am 29. Juli 1741 bittet Mattheson in Zusammenhang mit der Abberufung Cyril Wichs nach Petersburg den König um eine "kleine Pension" nach sechsunddreißig Jahren "treuen und untadeligen Dienstes", da das Gehör stark nachgelassen habe, er ziemlich alt und ermüdet sei und in ziemlich beschränkten Verhältnissen lebe[155]. Die Pension wird offenbar nicht gewährt, aber fast ein Jahr nach Amtsantritt Copes wird er in seinem Amt bestätigt[156]. Dennoch hat Mattheson die Stellung, wie er sie unter Cyril Wich innehatte, nicht wieder erreicht. Seine Handschrift findet sich in den *State Papers* in den folgenden Jahren äußerst selten, 1747 wird Matthesons Recht, an der Tafel des Gesandten zu speisen, aufgehoben und erst nach wiederholten Gesuchen in Geld abgegolten[157]. 1752 kürzt Cope Matthesons Einkünfte zugunsten des anderen Sekretärs Emanuel Matthias[158] und läßt diesem auch die Nebeneinkünfte aus Zusammenfassung und Übersetzung der Zeitungsartikel zukommen[159].

Bei einer längeren Reise Copes hat Mattheson nur noch indirekt eine Funktion im Amt des Gesandten. Cope teilt am 25. Juni 1751 nach London mit, daß Mattheson sehr gebrechlich geworden und

---

153 Cf. dazu auch 13.9.1718 (SP 82/35, p. 246 s.) und 27.9. 1718 (SP 82/35, p. 258–60). Hier stellt er auch Fragen an den Informanten: "sie erscheinen mir etwas suspekt, da der Minister die Quellen für die Informationen nicht angeben konnte" (Übersetzung des Verfassers).

154 Siehe auch 22.10.1726 (SP 82/43, p. 231 ss.) enthält nur wörtliche Zitate (über vier Seiten lang) aus verschiedenen Briefen, die Mattheson bekommen hat. Er ergänzt nur die Höflichkeitsformel am Schluß.

155 29.7.1741 (SP 82/62, p. 103).

156 Cope trat sein Amt im September 1741 an. Bestallung Matthesons am 14.8.1742 (*Ehrenpforte*, Anhang 21).

157 *Ehrenpforte*, Anhang 25.

158 Handschrift des Emanuel Matthias seit dem 30. März 1742 (vor der Bestätigung Matthesons) in den *State Papers* (SP 82/64).

159 *Ehrenpforte*, Anhang 30 ("Anecdote").

kaum imstande sei, die Amtsgeschäfte zu führen. Daher werde der Privatsekretär Matthias die Korrespondenz erledigen und alle Geschäfte sorgfältig ausführen[160].

1752 wird Mattheson nur noch unter anderen als Berater erwähnt: "alle Freunde und ausländischen Minister wollen meinem Sekretär [Emanuel Matthias] alle mögliche Unterstützung gewähren . . . Der alte Herr Mattheson . . . wird ebenfalls helfen, soweit es ihm möglich ist (und wie es seine Pflicht ist)"[161]. Mattheson beschönigt in der *Ehrenpforte* diese Auffassung Copes, die, wenn man das Alter Matthesons bedenkt (einundsiebzig Jahre), nicht zu hart ist[162].

Wie wir schon oben dargestellt haben[163], werden Matthesons Rechte aus diesem Amt im Laufe der fünfziger Jahre auch bei anderen politischen Geschäftsträgern in Hamburg nicht mehr selbstverständlich anerkannt. Er selber gibt erst 1759 und für die sechziger Jahre zu, daß er sich aus der politischen Tätigkeit zurückgezogen habe[164]. Der Nachfolger Copes, Philip Stanhope (Cope starb 1756), wird in der *Ehrenpforte* nicht erwähnt.

V
Zusammenfassung

Matthesons Interesse, das Amt des Sekretärs beim britischen Gesandten in Hamburg anzutreten, lag zunächst einmal darin, einen gehobenen Lebensstandard zu sichern, angesehen zu sein und dennoch genügend freie Zeit zu behalten, um zu komponieren oder musikalische Schriften zu verfassen.

Ein sehr persönliches Verhältnis zur Familie des Gesandten John Wich wurde durch den Musikunterricht bei dessen Sohn Cyril, dem späteren Gesandten, angebahnt.

Mattheson wuchs unter John Wich immer mehr in verantwortliche Aufgaben eines Sekretärs hinein, nachdem er anfangs ausschließlich Kopien von anderen Schriftstücken erstellte, kann man es als ersten Vertrauensbeweis ansehen, daß Mattheson seit Juni 1708 auch die vertraulichen *Circulars* nach London schrieb, ohne jedoch mit ihrem Entwurf befaßt zu sein.

Sehr guter Kontakt, teilweise sogar persönliche Freundschaften,

---

160 25.6.1751 (SP 82/73, p. 98 s.).
161 7.3.1752 (SP 82/73, p. 257 s.) (Übersetzung des Verfassers).
162 9.3.1752. *Ehrenpforte*, Anhang, 30.
163 Cf. oben, Abschnitt IV, "Kontakte mit Senat".
164 Cannon, *Mattheson*, 220: "Weitere Fortsetzung des Matthesonischen Lebenslaufes".

ergaben sich mit angesehenen und später auch einflußreichen Persönlichkeiten des öffentlichen Lebens in Hamburg und England.

Matthesons musikalische Kenntnisse und Fähigkeiten wurden auch in dem Bekanntenkreis, der sich durch das Amt ergab, sehr geschätzt.

Erstmalig betraute John Wich Mattheson im Jahre 1713 inoffiziell mit der Wahrnehmung der Aufgaben eines Gesandten unter der offiziellen Verantwortlichkeit des jedoch noch unerfahrenen jungen Cyril Wich. Nach dem Tod des Vaters 1713 unterstützt Mattheson über einflußreiche Freunde in London die Nachfolge Cyril Wichs in dem Amt des Gesandten.

Das sehr enge persönliche Verhältnis zwischen Mattheson und Cyril Wich zeigt sich in den Widmungen und Kompositionen Matthesons für Cyril, wie dieser seinen Sekretär ebenso durch Widmungen und öffentliches Lob ehrt.

Von großem Vertrauen zu Mattheson zeugt es, daß Cyril Wich ihm in seiner Abwesenheit regelmäßig die Vertretung im Amt überträgt. Mattheson nimmt hier alle Aufgaben eines Gesandten sehr verantwortungsbewußt wahr. Auch London akzeptiert, daß hier ein Sekretär den Gesandten vertritt – wenn auch die Regierung in London einen graduellen Unterschied nicht übersehen will, den Wich aber, was die praktische Ausübung des Amtes anbelangt, nicht akzeptiert. Trotz seines höheren Alters und der längeren Erfahrung ordnet Mattheson sich Cyril Wich immer unter und ist sicher nicht als Konkurrent Wichs zu sehen, obwohl er gerne selber Gesandter geworden wäre.

Nach der Versetzung Wichs nach Peterburg 1741 erreicht Mattheson diese Selbständigkeit nicht mehr. Möglicherweise hat er das vorausgesehen und reicht ein Gesuch um Pension in London ein, das jedoch offensichtlich abschlägig beschieden wird. Die Aussichten, von dem neuen Gesandten Cope übernommen zu werden, scheinen zunächst völlig offen, und so vermittelt Wich[165] ihm die Ernennung zum "actuellen oder wircklichen Legations-Sekretaire des Herzogs von Holstein".

---

165 Wich teilt ihm die Ernennung am 30. Oktober 1741 mit (*Ehrenpforte*, Anhang 19). Zu Matthesons Tätigkeit beim Herzog von Holstein konnten wir bisher keine Unterlagen ermitteln. In den Findungsbüchern des Landesarchivs Schleswig-Holstein in Gottorf (Schleswig) gab es keine Hinweise. (Cannon schreibt, daß seine Nachforschungen in Kiel erfolglos geblieben seien: Das Landesarchiv ist nicht in Kiel, sondern in Schleswig). Das Magazin ist seit längerer Zeit wegen Baufälligkeit nicht zugänglich.

Cope bestätigt Mattheson 1742 im Amt, hat aber vorher schon einen weiteren Sekretär, Emanuel Matthias, eingestellt, der den immer mehr gebrechlichen Mattheson schnell verdrängt. Cope überträgt ihm kaum noch Aufgaben, und so scheint diese erneute Bestallung eher ein von London empfohlener Ersatz für die Pension zu sein (Lord Carteret, der mit Mattheson gut bekannt war, leitete 1742–4 die Geschäfte des Auswärtigen Amtes in London).

1752 hält Cope ihn kaum noch für fähig, die Oberaufsicht über den Sekretär Matthias während seiner Abwesenheit wahrzunehmen.

Mattheson selber findet sich offenbar erst nach Copes Tod (1756) und endgültig um 1760 damit ab, bei dem britischen Gesandten keine Aufgaben mehr zu haben.

Dieses Amt hat neben Matthesons musikalischer Tätigkeit eine zentrale Stellung in seinem Leben gehabt, auch wenn zunächst eher materielle Gründe ihn bestimmt haven, das Amt anzunehmen, so hat es ihm doch in späterer Zeit viel bedeutet, wie man an dem großen Anteil der politischen Geschehnisse in seiner Biographie der *Ehrenpforte* sehen kann.

Eine eigene Stellungnahme zu politischen Ereignissen ist mit der *Holsteinischen Geschichte* (1744) geplant gewesen, aber – nach unseren Informationen[166] – nicht weit gediehen und von dem Entwurf ist nichts erhalten.

Matthesons sorgfältiger Umgang mit Daten und Fakten, wie es für sein Amt als Sekretär unbedingt erforderlich war, wirkt sich auch in der *Ehrenpforte* aus. Die Angaben haben sich alle als äußerst genau und zuverlässig erwiesen.

Verzeichnis der ungedruckten Quellen

The British Library, London	Department of Manuscripts Sign. 22, 216 ff.
Public Record Office, London	State Papers 82/21 (2.1.1705) bis 82/74 (30.10.1753). Im Hamburger Staatsarchiv (Filmarchiv) S 12510 – S 12531
Staatsarchiv Hamburg	Cl. VII Lit. I. n. 2. f. 4, "Englischer Secretarius Mattheson"
	Cl. VII Lit. I[b] N. 1 Vol. 6[c] Fasc. 1, "Die vom Englischen H. Envoyé beym Waßer-Schaut gesuchte und erlangte Arrestirung eines . . . Englischen Matrosen James Johnson betreffend . . . 1733".

166 Mitteilung des Landesarchivs Schleswig-Holstein in Schleswig vom 30. April 1981.

Cl. VII Lit. 9b N. 1 Vol. 8 f "Den Englischen Ministres Bediente, Kutscher, pretendirte Domestiquen".

Cl. VII Lit. 9b N. 19 Vol. 5a "Den Englischen Legations Secretaire Mattheson betr.".

Geschäftsarchiv Charles Blunt, C1, Briefe an Charles Blunt.

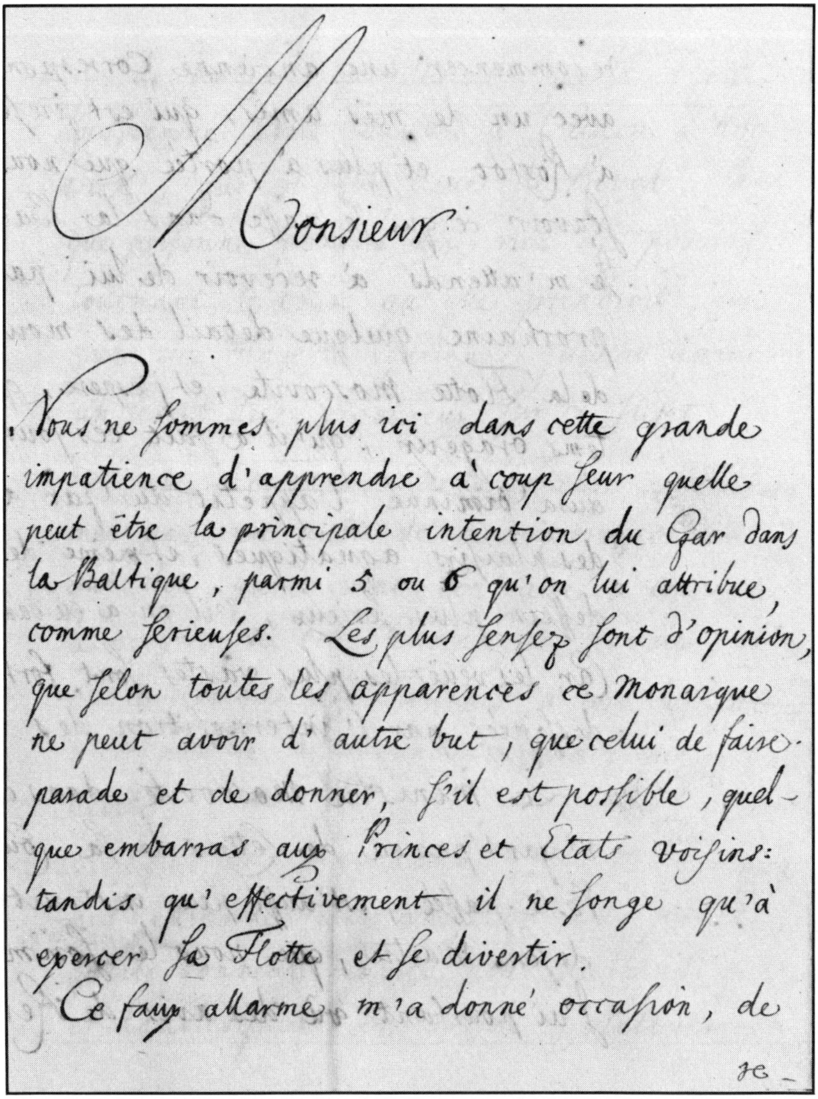

Monsieur

Nous ne sommes plus ici dans cette grande impatience d'apprendre à coup seur quelle peut être la principale intention du Czar dans la Baltique, parmi 5 ou 6 qu'on lui attribue, comme serieuses. Les plus sensez sont d'opinion, que selon toutes les apparences ce monarque ne peut avoir d'autre but, que celui de faire parade et de donner, s'il est possible, quelque embarras aux Princes et Etats voisins: tandis qu'effectivement il ne songe qu'à exercer sa Flotte et se divertir.

Ce faux allarme m'a donné occasion, de

Abbildung 1. London, Public Record Office, State Papers 82/40 vom 15. August 1723 (Autograph Matthesons)

73

peut apprendre de plus certain et de plus important. Sur tout quant aux Galères et Trouppes, qui jusqu'alors ont été dans une parfaite inaction. Je serois bien aise, Monsieur, si ces rapports pouvoient donner quelques lumieres à la Cour, et vous être utiles. Du moins ils feront voir ma bonne volonté et mon attention constante pour le service de Sa Majesté. ⸺

Je suis avec respect

Monsieur

Hambourg. Aoust 15.
1723.

Votre très humble
& obeissant serviteur
Mattheson.

4

Mattheson and the aesthetics of theater

GLORIA FLAHERTY
Bryn Mawr, Pennsylvania

Johann Mattheson was initiated into the world of opera in 1690, when he was merely nine years of age. His musical background was already rather solid, he later liked to write, because he had been "bred in Musik from my Infancy, with somewhat more than common success."[1] The clown's equipment his father bought him during a grave childhoood illness not only cheered him up but also gave him the taste for game playing, make-believe, and acting that remained with him throughout his life.[2] As the young Mattheson fulfilled the various theatrical duties demanded of him in Hamburg, he became increasingly stagestruck. At the age of fifteen, his soprano voice was such that he was sought out for solo female roles.[3] His voice, however, changed the following year, and he played only male parts thereafter. Little by little, Mattheson grew to pride himself on being the kind of performer who combined innate singing ability with histrionic accomplishment. One contemporary observer disagreed, claiming he was "no great singer, for which reason he sang only occasionally; but he was a good actor, a good composer of lessons, and a good player on the harpsichord."[4] Mattheson took such offense at that evaluation of his performing talents that he felt he had to respond. In order to defend himself, he wrote using the third person:

To say that he sang only occasionally is simply ridiculous, when the statement is made of a man who remained on the stage for fifteen years, who nearly always played the chief role and whose natural manner of singing, whose

---

1 In the rough draft of a letter to Richard Steele dated 26 December 1713 and printed in its entirety in Cannon, *Mattheson*, 76–8.
2 *Mithridat*, 136. See also his positive critical assessment of clowns and comic figures in: *Der Vernünfftler* 85 (14 April 1714), sig. Nnn^r−v.
3 *Ehrenpforte*, 190. Cannon, *Mattheson*, discusses the early years in detail, 20–1, 25–6.
4 J. Mainwaring, *Memoirs of the Life of the Late George Frederic Handel* (London, 1760), 31.

gestures and whose actions – all of which are most essential in every opera – aroused in the audience feelings of fear and terror, pity and lament, joy and pleasure.[5]

Performing a convincing death scene onstage before changing and then joining the orchestra as its director seems to have provided Mattheson with a special kind of enjoyment during his early twenties. One such performance also led to a certain amount of physical as well as professional danger. He had written the music for Christian Friedrich Feustking's libretto *Die betrogene Staats-Liebe, oder die unglückliche Cleopatra, Königin von Egypten: Ein musicalisches Trauer-Spiel* in 1704,[6] and during that season he was in the habit of playing Antony, the male lead. His performance was so natural , he wrote later, that the spectators shrieked loudly at the suicide he portrayed ("die Zuschauer, bey der verstellten Selbstentleibung ein lautes Geschrey erhuben").[7] After having died so persuasively during the *Cleopatra* performance of 5 December 1704, Mattheson assumed he would be able to take the directorship of the orchestra away from Handel, his friend and colleague. Handel's outspoken protest during the take-over purportedly led to the famous duel in front of the Theater am Gänsemarkt. Needless to say, most professional actors of that generation were well trained in the aesthetic as well as the gymnastic aspects of fencing. Mattheson himself had begun his fencing lessons as a youngster.[8] Almost sixty years later, he described Handel as "tall, strong, broad shouldered, and physically powerful, hence man enough to defend himself and to be mindful of the sword hanging at his side" ("groß, stark, breit und kräftig vom Leibe, folglich Mannes genug war, sich zu wehren, und des an seiner Seite hän-

5 As quoted by Cannon, p. 27. Unless otherwise noted, the translations are my own. "Daß er nur gelegentlich gesungen haben sollte, ist lächerlich von einem zu sagen, der in 15 Jahren nicht vom Theater gekommen, und fast allemal die Hauptperson vorgestellet, auch sowohl durch ein ungekünsteltes Singen, als durch seine Geberdekunst oder Action, welche in allen Singspielen das Wesentliche ist, bey den Zuschauern bald Furcht und Schrecken, bald Thränen, bald Freude und Vergnügen erwecket hat." *Händels Lebensbeschreibung*, 22.
6 Ed. G. J. Buelow in: *Das Erbe deutscher Musik*, vol. 9 (Mainz, 1975), esp. intro., 7. Biographical information for Feustking (1678–1739) is available in K. Goedeke, *Grundriß zur Geschichte der deutschen Dichtung aus den Quellen*, 2d rev. ed., vol. 3 (Dresden, 1887), 335, and H. Schröder, *Lexikon der hamburgischen Schriftsteller bis zur Gegenwart*, vol. 2 (Hamburg, 1854), 294–5.
7 *Ehrenpforte*, 192. See also his comments in *Singspiele*, 76. Mattheson's frequent inclusion of reminiscences in his theoretical and critical writings stems from his empirical stance and should not be viewed as mere arrogance. As the eighteenth century progressed, it became more and more fashionable for performers to publish their memoirs, diaries, and autobiographies.
8 Schröder, *Lexikon*, vol. 5, 65.

genden Degens eingedenk zu seyn").[9] Neither young man suffered permanent physical injury, and after a few weeks they were once again on friendly terms.

Mattheson took his acting and performing very seriously. Not only the incident with Handel but all of his firsthand experiences with living theater left indelible marks on his critical as well as creative imagination. Their effects are again and again noticeable in his writings.[10] The preface to the second volume of *Critica musica* (1725) reveals how Mattheson perceived his role in improving theatrical standards and in changing public opinion: "I should have enough material to write splendid theatrical anecdotes or an intimate history of opera, but that will have to wait a while, especially since the main purpose of this work has to do with making good musicians rather than good satires, even though the latter would please the greatest number and be not without use" ("Ich hätte Materien genug, schöne *Anecdotes theatrales,* oder eine geheime Opern-Historie zu schreiben; allein, es mag noch eine Weile anstehen: zumal da der Haupt-Zweck dieses Werks mehr dahin gehet, gute *Musicos,* als gute Satyren, zu machen; ob gleich auch diese nicht ohne Nutzen, und dem größesten Hauffen angenehm, seyn würden"). Mattheson stands out at the beginning of the eighteenth century as a sensitive critic, yet resolute defender, of the theatrical arts. During his lifetime, and to a good extent because of his untiring efforts, theater in Germany gained acceptance as an art form and then stature as a cultural force.

In addition to his work specifically in music and theater, Mattheson learned languages, studied philology, read widely in numerous fields, and took full advantage of the cultural resources the wealthy, cosmopolitan city of Hamburg offered. Of the greatest importance for him were the many fine book collections and the societies that cultivated the arts as well as things German. Along with fellow intellectuals who shared such interests, Mattheson contributed to the development of a distinctively German kind of criticism that began to attract attention from thinkers the world over. The methodology

9 *Händels Lebensbeschreibung,* 29–30. See also C. Burney, *An Eighteenth-Century Musical Tour in Central Europe and the Netherlands,* ed. P. A. Scholes (London, 1959), 209–10.

10 W. Braun, *Johann Mattheson und die Aufklärung* (Ph.D. diss., Martin Luther University, Halle-Wittenberg, 1952), 82, reported that Mattheson agreed with Michael Richey (1678–1761) that music belonged to *philosophia effectiva* rather than to *philosophia theoretica.* I disagree with Braun that Mattheson's increasing criticism of theater and the theatrical style after 1720 implied rejection of either, 117–18. On the contrary, the evidence I have been able to gather indicates more interest and more concern.

combined observation and experience with philology and historical learning without ignoring rhetorical concerns that involved basic human psychology. And the constant use of down-to-earth, concrete expressions for abstract ideas helped give the language of German criticism increasing flexibility and sophistication.

I intend to review here Mattheson's utterances on theater, including acting techniques, performance practices, dramatic theory, and theatrical history, in order to show that he was as much an innovator as he was a perpetuator. His efforts to preserve the best of the old theatrical traditions happened to lay the foundation for many new trends. Mattheson may have been hypersensitive to negative remarks about his ability to perform onstage in public, but he remained an honest intellectual who repeatedly gave credit to others, often much younger men, for formulating more succinctly and more meaningfully ideas with which he himself had long grappled.[11]

One idea that Mattheson espoused, cultivated, and almost made into something new was the idea of the *theatrum mundi*. Many pages of *Der musicalische Patriot* (1728) are devoted to explaining the innate theatricality of the whole world ("das theatralische Wesen der gantzen Welt"; p. 109). The word "theatrical" had acquired numerous bad connotations, and with the deft strokes of a dedicated philologist he exposed them and disqualified them. In addition to mentioning its Greek and Latin etymology, he quoted poetry about the world as a stage, cited learned books whose titles incorporated "Theatrum," and discussed the well-defined spaces that in real life were called operating theaters. theaters of war, theaters for anatomical or other scientific demonstration, and so on. Mattheson defined the theatrical as everything that originated with human beings rather than with nature, for example, grammar, logic, rhetoric, music, politics, painting, arithmetic, geometry, and astronomy. He asserted: "Theatrical is nothing other than artificial, something displayed artificially in imitation of nature, that is, something made and to some extent assiduously contrived without, however, appearing either made or contrived" ("Theatralisch ist nichts anders, als künstlich, was künstlicher Weise, in Nachahmung der Natur, zur Schau gestellet wird, i.e., etwas gemachtes, und einigermaßen durch Fleiß erzwungenes, doch so, daß es weder gemacht, noch gezwungen heraus komme oder lasse"; p. 118).

When he observed human activities more intently, he noticed that

11 The most clear-cut example of this involves J. E. Schlegel (1719–49), whose defense of comedy in rhymed verse Mattheson graciously acknowledged and then used to defend opera, even though it had grown out of some of his own earlier writings. This

there always seemed to be something of the theatrical about them. Academic promotions, stock-exchange transactions, military parades, war games, church services, birthdays, anniversaries, and funerals all involved actions, costumes, settings, gestures, modes of behavior, and language different from the norm. Even common actions in everyday life seemed to have about them an element of role playing. As his explorations moved from philology via philosophy toward psychology, he came closer and closer to developing a theory of play. His words about man's natural drive to play games or to create were embedded in the religious but had wide-ranging implications. Years before Justus Möser (1720–94) and Gotthold Ephraim Lessing (1729–81), and decades before Friedrich Schiller (1759–1805) paid attention to such matters, he wrote: "Nature itself propels us to theatrical reality, and everything that is natural belongs there" (". . . daß uns die Natur selbst zum theatralischen Wesen treibet, und alles, was natürlich ist, dahin gehöret"; p. 220).

In *Kern melodischer Wissenschafft* (1737), Mattheson insisted that theater, like the most important things in life, had "always an element of the playful," in the sense of "pretend" or "simulated" ("allemahl etwas spielendes"; p. 22). In *Die neueste Untersuchung der Singspiele* (1744), he explained that the angels were "real, essential, not feigned or imagined actors of the wide theater of the world" ("wirkliche, wesentliche, keine verstellte oder erdichtete Acteurs des weiten Welttheaters"; p. 38); and in *Plus Ultra* (1754–6), he went on to maintain that human beings were their counterparts in the microcosm. His conclusion was, "Everything in the whole world is once and for all theatrical. But theatrical is not therefore simultaneously everything frivolous" ("Alles in der ganzen Welt ist einmal für allemal theatralisch. Aber theatralisch ist darum nicht gleich alles leichtfertig"; p. 432).

Throughout his long life Mattheson persisted in defending theater as a serious, important, and necessary human endeavor. When he published his first treatise on music, *Das neu-eröffnete Orchestre* (1713), operatic theorists were still groping for arguments with which to refute the condemnations of pietistic clergymen and the complaints of neoclassical drama critics. The very idea of opera was at stake, and not just what might strike us as some peripheral, if delightfully amusing, abuses.[12] The thrust of Mattheson's particular defense was that opera was neither a libretto nor a score but rather a

has been discussed in my *Opera in the Development of German Critical Thought* (Princeton, 1978), 90, 138–9.
12 Ibid., 18–27, 37–41.

79

combination of both, or a *confluxum* of arts, as he preferred to call it, performed by human beings on a stage equipped with the latest requisites. Instead of being a mere copy of nature, it was a highly stylized artistic rendition of nature. Again and again he included statements like, "Many an opera appears quite beautiful on the page, but when it is mounted for the theater, it sounds completely different" ("Manche Opera siehet gar schön aus im Buch / allein wenn sie aufs *Theatrum* kommt / klingt es gantz anders"; p. 162). The verbs used are telling: The scenario existed in the printed libretto and could be read, that is, seen, but the music had to be heard in order to be meaningful. He considered music not only a temporal art, but the most freedom-loving and freedom-requiring of all the liberal arts. He did not believe that any purpose could be served by trying to harness it and force it into a preordained rationalistic system. To him, it represented creativity per se. With the following he explained why the creative urge necessitated freedom, an idea that later critics incorporated into the all-important concept of genius: "For through force natural talents are made impotent; man loses his intrinsic spiritual freedom; he becomes grieved, sluggish, lazy, drowsy, and can never again achieve anything worthwhile" ("Denn durch den Zwang werden die Ingenia niedergeschlagen / der Mensch verliehret seine natürliche Gemüths-Freyheit / er wird verdrießlich / träge / faul / schläffrich / und kan nimmer zu was rechts kommen; p. 15).

Mattheson's determination to understand and do justice to performance led to important insights about aesthetic reality and truth as well as about the particular media that constitute the different art forms and genres. One such insight involved the seemingly magical transformation of dead letters, numbers, signs, and notes into something new and different.[13] Another dealt with the inherent temporality and therefore also the transitoriness of any kind of performance.[14] Yet another had to do with spatial dimensions, or the way performers created and controlled the artistic space within which they played.

By the time the *Göttingischer Ephorus* (1727) appeared, Mattheson had learned about articulating clearly the distinctions between recitals, concerts, and stage productions. That was not exactly an easy task. The German language, for all its richness during that period, was

13 *Orchestre* III, 17.
14 *Critica musica* I, 94. The continuing discussion about artificial and natural signs as well as about time and space categories was to become extremely important for Lessing, who then published his own ideas in *Laokoon* (1766). See Flaherty, 217–22.

still developing the kind of syntax and vocabulary that later philosophers and poets took for granted. Mattheson explained that in theater
alone was there the kind of performance that involved portrayal,
representation, and a new make-believe order. And that, he continued, meant opera was essentially a totally different art form from
the cantata. This was his formulation: "In operas, real people act;
cantatas, on the other hand, are mere narratives and observations; that
is quite a big difference, and necessitates a completely different
arrangement and a completely different style in the music as well as
in the poetry."[15]

Mattheson's discussion in *Der musicalische Patriot* stressed the
importance of making the stage production of any given opera seem to
come alive rather than just proceed through time and space. Here he
gave the explanation that resounded throughout the eighteenth century until even Goethe adopted it: "The opera theater is in itself a little
art world, constructed from various building materials on an imposing stage and made with much learning" ("Das Opern-Theatrum an
sich selbst nun ist eine kleine Kunst-Welt, auf einer ansehnlichen
Schau-Bühne von allerhand Bau-Materialien errichtet, und mit vieler
Wissenschafft dazu gemacht"; pp. 117–18). Opera always required
adding, omitting, or changing something so as to re-form the elements
of naked reality into a new and more beautiful artistic order. Mattheson also supported the seminal idea that audiences willingly sus-
pended their disbelief in order to experience that new order:

Theatrical reality consists in the following: the portrayal of an important and
noteworthy matter clearly and vividly through specially chosen words and
delineated executions, as if the actual historical persons (who are not really
present but are introduced speaking and acting), the place and the region, as
well as the deed together with all its ramifications, really appeared before
one's eyes, were heard with one's ears, and were all noticed with one's
rational faculty.[16]

15 "Bey Opern agiern wirckliche Personen; Cantaten hingegen sind nur bloße
    Erzehlungen und Betrachtungen: das ist ein gar großer Unterschied, und erfordert
    eine gantz andre Einrichtung, einen gantz andern Stil, so wol in der Music, als in der
    Poesie." *Ephorus*, 3. In *Melodische Wissenschaft*, 98, however, he wrote that the
    cantata "requires more of artifice than any kind of theatrical music" ("erfordert
    mehr künstliches, als die theatralische Musik überhaupt").
16 "Das theatralische Wesen bestehet darin: Wenn eine wichtige und merckwürdige
    Sache, durch auserlesene Worte und beschriebene Verrichtungen ,so deutlich und
    lebhafft vorgebildet wird, als ob man die rechten, eigentlichen Personen, so zwar
    nicht zugegen, doch aber redend und handelnd eingeführet werden, den Ort und
    die Gegend, die That, samt allen ihren Umständen, wircklich ver Augen sähe, mit
    Ohren hörte, und mit dem Verstande bemerckte" *Musicalischer Patriot*, 117.

Almost a decade later, in *Melodische Wissenschaft*, he explained that "drama" was a Greek word meaning "the kind of performance in which certain persons and deeds are presented true to life" ("eine solche Vorstellung, darin gewisse Personen und Verrichtungen, recht nach dem Leben, aufgeführet werden"; pp. 20–1). The new artistic world order would, however, be believable (that is, probable) to the audience only if each performer knew his role "as if it came forth almost on the spur of the moment, without having been studied or memorized" ("als ob es ohne studiren, oder auswendiglernen, gleichsam aus dem Stegereiff hervorkäme"; p. 21). He insisted that living performers had always been the ones responsible for breathing life into theatrical works and making them memorable. An inferior performance could ruin even the most stageworthy opera. In *Die musikalische Geschmacksprobe* (1744), published together with *Die neueste Untersuchung der Singspiele,* he reminded composers that their "fame, reputation, and usefulness were in the hands of the operatic performers" ("Ruhm, Ansehen und Nutz stehet in den Händen der Operisten"; p. 166). As he wrote in *Critica musica* and elsewhere, the same held true for the performers of all musical pieces.[17]

By no means did Mattheson equate the quality of a production with naturalism of any sort. In *Die neueste Untersuchung der Singspiele* he treated that question in depth. He unequivocally advocated the complete exclusion of anything from common, everyday life. No real animals should be allowed on the stage, nor should there be the kind of violent death scenes that required blood; quiet ones with doleful music, however, were quite acceptable. Certain items from the real world he considered necessary for creating the make-believe order, and he never ignored them. For example, he suggested that composers tell performers dissatisfied with their parts or with some arias that "one would have to hear the entire production on stage with the appropriate costumes, lamps, lights, gentlemen-at-arms, retinue, accompaniment of the entire coast, and harmonizing of the complete orchestra; then it would come out differently" ("man müsse das Ding auf der Schaubühne, mit gehörigen Kleidern, Lampen, Lichtern, Trabanten, Gefolge, Begleitung des ganzen Corpi und Einstimmung, des völligbesetzten Orchesters hören; so werde es schon anders herauskommen"; p. 167). Again and again he mentioned that artificial illumination in addition to the onstage use of candles, lanterns, and

17 *Critica musica* II, 233, 229. See also, for example, *Capellmeister,* 129.

torches helped to represent with a certain degree of verisimilitude the different times of a make-believe day.

When Mattheson referred to quality, he meant the supreme kind of artistry that seduced the rational faculty of the spectators and appealed directly to their emotions so that they instantaneously believed what they were seeing and hearing. Moral axioms and didactic conversations that were not given meaning through personal portrayal ("allerdings durch persönliche Vorstellungen sinnlich und begreiflich gemacht") were to be avoided because they were always more apt to induce yawning ("allemahl fähiger, die Leute zum Gähnen zu bringen"; pp. 4–5). According to him, activity, or three-dimensional portrayal, was essential to operatic representation:

> Furthermore, there is a strong reason why we go to operas, namely, in order to see the artistry with which they are presented. Inasmuch as each of us could otherwise read the printed librettos at home, we also have on that account good cause indeed to love musical plays, because they in their very art of representation allow us the great advantage of clearly distinguishing mediocre singers from superb all-round performers.[18]

The ideal was to have operatic performers who could act as well as sing. With the reverence for language that grew out of his reverence for truth, he tried to give currency to words like *Acteur*, *Operist*, and *Opernspieler*, considering them more appropriate for expressing the ideal than *Sänger* or *Schauspieler*.[19]

Mattheson's treatment of the mannerisms, habits, and practices that diverted attention and prevented the suspension of disbelief reads like a satirist's source-book. In addition to those performers who played sad characters in a happy manner and vice versa, there were those who stuttered or stopped dead in the middle of an aria, those who conversed with each other privately or otherwise paid no attention to the action when they were not performing, and those who held a hopping dance rhythm suitable for a dirge ("eine hüpfende Tanzart

18 "Weiter, da ein starker Bewegungsgrund ist, warum wir in die Opern gehen, nämlich um die Kunst zu sehen, womit sie vorgestellet werden: indem ein jeder sonst die gedruckten Büchlein zu Hause lesen könnte; so hat man in der That auch deswegen gute Ursache, die Singspiele zu lieben, weil sie in der Vorstellungskunst den großen Vortheil an die Hand geben, einen mittelmäßigen Sänger von einem vortrefflichen Acteur sehr weit abzusondern." *Singspiele*, 81.

19 *Singspiele*, 34, 68, 85. See also *Orchestre* I, 161. The standard contemporary dictionaries and encyclopedias, however, continued to define *Acteur* "eine agirende Manns-Person in einem Schauspiele" (a male person acting in a play), J. G. Walther, *Musicalisches Lexicon* (Leipzig, 1732), 8; and J. H. Zedler, *Grosses Vollständiges Universal-Lexikon* (Halle and Leipzig, 1732–54), I, col. 392.

im Klagliede für wahrscheinlich").[20] In order to come alive, the operatic stage required more than just good voices and good looks.

Mattheson, who was interested in all the possible means for synthesizing the components of the stage production of opera, thought that each member of a cast should at least learn what the words of his particular role meant and, ideally, what the entire libretto was about. Encouraging performers to do so was revolutionary in those days when serious onstage rehearsals of cast and orchestra together were mostly, if not totally, unheard of. The situation in spoken theater was equally bad, for actors rarely read the entire play and often depended on the prompter for their own lines. Improvement came gradually and only because of steady complaints from people like Mattheson. As far as opera was concerned, he thought the words of the libretto "must flow from the mouths of the singers so that one might think it was not in their nature to present themselves other than musically" ("müssen aus dem Munde der Singenden so fließen, daß man denken sollte, diese Personen könnten von Natur ihren Vortrag nicht anders, als musikalisch, thun"; p. 79). The reference to nature here actually means effortlessly and convincingly. Mattheson loved to cite as examples performers, himself among them, who were capable of doing that and thereby moving audiences to tears, to gasps, or to shrieks.[21]

Mattheson's training in rhetoric supplied him with many answers to his questions about the aesthetics of theater. His common sense together with his analytical acumen let him make the most of them. Gradually his rhetorical concerns grew into psychological ones. The names of the leading ancient as well as modern authors of handbooks on rhetoric come up often in his writings, as do his attempts to adapt their principles to music.[22] As rhetoric persuades and influences human behavior, he believed, so too does music. In *Der vollkommene Capellmeister* (1739) he suggested that "no one would easily question the close relationship between music and rhetoric. The ancient orators took their best rules from music, considering the gestures as well as the raising and lowering of the voice" (". . . daß nicht leicht

20 *Singspiele*, 106; see also 12, 37, 85–6.
21 Ibid. 15. See also *Capellmeister*, 36.
22 F. Feldmann, "Mattheson und die Rhetorik," in: *Kongress-Bericht Hamburg 1956* (Kassel, 1957), 99–103 H. Kretzschmar, "Allgemeines und Besonderes zur Affektenlehre," in: *JbP* 18 (1912), 64–77, on p. 64–9; H.-H. Unger, *Die Beziehungen zwischen Musik und Rhetorik im 16.–18. Jahrhundert* (Würzburg, 1941), 113–14. A helpful checklist for those interested in literature and acting theory as well as music is G. J. Buelow's "Music, Rhetoric, and the Concept of the Affections: A Selective Bibliography," in: *Notes* 30 (1973), 250–9.

iemand die nahe Verwandschafft zwischen der Ton- und Rede-Kunst in Zweifel ziehen werde. Die alten Redner haben auch ihre besten Regeln aus der Music hergenommen, sowol in Ansehung der Geberden, als in Erhöhung und Erniedrigung der Stimme"; p. 35). Mattheson went on to explain in *Singspiele* that music was a door through which to penetrate the soul itself ("eine Thür, in die Seele selbst hineinzudringen"; p. 29). Its direct appeal to the sense of hearing enabled it to bypass the rational faculty and instantaneously reach the emotions, manipulating them at will. Combined with three-dimensional portrayal in opera, he wrote in *Das neu-eröffnete Orchestre*, music made for an art form of such overpowering effectiveness that it surpassed all others, including painting and sculpture (pp. 167–8). In *Das beschützte Orchestre* (1717) he classified operatic music as belonging to the dramatic or recitative style, which was one suited to the expression of emotions ("ein Styl, welcher die, Gemüths-Bewegungen auszudrücken geschickt ist"; p. 116).

Unlike the many conservative rationalists who got bogged down in analyses of catharsis or of fear and pity without thinking of consulting Aristotle's *Rhetoric*, Mattheson simply used as the cornerstone of his dramatic theory the idea of performers' portraying emotions in order to touch and move the emotions of audiences. Why that was sometimes easier to accomplish than others belonged to the discussion of taste and all its variables. Mattheson's instinctive attraction to seminal ideas led him to ones about the effects of climate, geography, social conditions, and the psychological differences between human beings.[23] In supporting the exegetes of such ideas, like Jean Baptiste Dubos (1670–1742), Barthold Feind (1678–1721), and Johann Ulrich von König (1688–1744), he helped make the way easier for Johann Gottfried Herder (1744–1803) and those who came later.

Mattheson's *Affektenlehre* might have been somewhat old-fashioned insofar as it sought to align certain figures and devices with respective emotions, but it was ultramodern in its advocacy of mood, color, and suggestiveness. His words in *Critica musica* prove that, as well as explaining why he, for one, insisted that performers understand their roles within the context of the whole opera. He wrote: "The emotion is never especially fixed in one or another word; it reigns throughout the discourse, like the soul in the body. It is incorrect, as regards moving the affections, to bind oneself to the words and not to the thoughts" ("Der Affect steckt auch niemals in einem oder andern Worte besonders; er regieret durchgehends in dem

---

23 *Orchestre* I, 81; *Singspiele*, 26–7.

gantzen Vortrage, wie die Seele im Leibe. Es ist unrecht, sich, wegen der Gemüths-Bewegung, an die Werte, und nicht an die Gedancken, zu binden" II, p. 348). Mattheson maintained that such matters were also somehow operative during the creative process of the composer and consequently had to be taken into careful consideration by judges and critics.[24] In so doing, he promulgated the notion of writing reviews about specific performances, a notion that became more and more popular with the public, if not with the performers, as the eighteenth century wore on.[25]

Mattheson's writings also contain frequent allusions to the rhetorical steps of invention, disposition, elaboration, memory, and delivery, or what he termed "Executio (die Ausführung oder Aufführung)" (execution – the performance or representation).[26] Although the performer had relatively little control over the first three, the last two were completely his responsibility. Memorization was simply hard work, but delivery required talent as well as study and discipline. Stage presence and command of what came to be called "körperliche Beredsamkeit," or the rhetoric of body language, were also necessary. Mattheson's study of the classics taught him that the ancients prescribed gestures through certain kinds of musical notations. In *Plus ultra*, for example, he went so far as to contend: "The teachings about the emotions, desires, inclinations, and passions, and also those about the art of gesturing, etc., were in former times included under the heading of music" ("Die Lehren von den Gemüthsbewegungen, Begierden, Neigungen und Leidenschaften, ingleichen von der ganzen Geberdekunst ec. waren in vorigen Zeiten mit unter dem Namen der Musik begriffen"; pp. 395–6).

In matters pertaining to gesture, as in so many others, he advocated a middle course. He opposed the inactivity and dullness of the French style, which he attributed in large part to the inordinate number of solos that necessarily inhibited dramatic movement.[27] Such performances were more like recitals. Again and again he sought to define the basic differences between the form of concerts or recitals and the form of stage representations. Equally objectionable to him were those

---

24 *Melodische Wissenschaft*, 21; *Musicalischer Patriot*, 169.
25 One need only remember that the first seven issues of Lessing's *Hamburgische Dramaturgie* (1767) dealt with one performance – the opening night of the National Theater Enterprise. The attention Lessing gave to it and the care with which he expressed his views were not, however, appreciated by the star performers. When they protested to higher authorities, he was forced to stop and to turn to more theoretical matters. See Flaherty, 224–5.
26 *Orchestre* I, 104.   27 *Critica musica* I, 116n.; *Singspiele*, 66–7.

performers who flailed their arms needlessly, danced around wildly, or moved spastically. He advised them to control their movements and to develop a noble simplicity of gesture, facial expression, and bearing ("in den Geberden, im Gesichte, in den Minen").[28] That advice resembles Hamlet's words to the players, which Lessing and other later writers considered the "golden rule" of acting. For Mattheson, gesticulation was a primordial means of communication that had left vestiges in everyday life as well as in various contemporary rituals and ceremonies, including the bowing, genuflecting, and kneeling of the Christian religion.[29]

In "Von der Geberden-Kunst," the sixth chapter of *Der vollkommene Capellmeister*, he examined the background as well as the artistic implications of nonverbal communication, without which, he maintained, one could accomplish nothing in this world (p. 35). The unconscious movements were of special interest to him because of what they conveyed. All too often it was something unintended. Subsequent theorists were to consider gamblers and children, but Mattheson chose to remain within his own field of expertise and observe musicians, singers, and actors. While admitting that various instruments required certain postures and attitudes, he castigated their players for taking up eccentric ones that bore no relationship whatsoever to the music. Was it beautiful or even tasteful, he asked,

to see before one a dozen violinists who make such physical contortions as to suggest that they have virulent diseases? For a keyboardist to wriggle his jaws, raise and lower his brow, and distort his face to such a degree that children would be terrified? For many players of wind instruments so to mangle or puff up their features (not excluding the lips of the flutist) that even with effort they cannot after half an hour restore them to the correct positions and natural color?[30]

Such movements were not only unseemly, they were also coarsely naturalistic and too revealing. Mattheson, much like the eighteenth-century parent who hired a dancing master to teach his child deportment, thought less about exploring their significance than about modifying them or substituting more decorous ones. In order to do so,

---

28 *Musicalischer Patriot*, 107.   29 Ibid., 132–3.

30 "Wenn er ein Dutzend Geiger vor sich siehet, die keine andre Verdrehungen des Leibes machen, als ob sie böse Kranckheiten hätten? Wenn der Clavierspieler das Maul krümmet, die Stirne auf und nieder ziehet, und sein Antlitz dermaßen verstellet, daß man die Kinder damit erschrecken mögte? Wenn viele bey den WindInstrumenten ihre Gesichts-Züge so zerreißen oder aufblehen (wobey die Lippen zur Querflöte nicht auszuschließen sind) daß sie solche in einer halben Stunde hernach mit Mühe wieder in die rechten Falten und zur natürlichen Farbe bringen können?" *Capellmeister*, 36.

he reviewed ancient writings. Professional pantomimes in antiquity were so good at conveying meaning nonverbally because the players had "at each finger-tip . . . as it were an individual tongue" ("an ieder Finger-Spitze hatten sie gleichsam eine eigne Zunge"; p. 39). Whenever Mattheson recounted the history of acting and the performing arts, he never failed to mention the reaction of audiences. He was especially fond of writing about those who found the gestures of a given performer so convincing that they could be comprehended better than any written or spoken language.[31] Mattheson also enjoyed referring to the love of beauty during antiquity that fostered schools where youngsters were trained in the art of beautiful movement and gesture, or saltation and chironomy.[32] And he suggested reviving the ancient methods and making a new catalogue of gestures: "The organization of such gestures and the arrangement of them in notes was called *orchesis* in Greek and *saltatio* in Latin" ("Solche Geberden anzuordnen und in Noten zu bringen, nannte man auf Griechisch *Orchesin, und Saltationem* auf Lateinisch"; pp. 38–9). Such a catalogue would be especially valuable for performers at the opera because, he wrote, "that is where the trouble really starts" ("da geht der Jammer erst recht an"; p. 36). He thought the French used highly stylized, beautiful gestures as a substitute for musical talent while the Italians, whom he considered inherently more animated, sang beautifully but dissolved all too rapidly into real tears or lapsed into raucous laughter. The Germans were the worst, in his opinion, for they dutifully stood up straight and did not move at all while singing regardless of whatever mimetic cues might be contained in the words. Mattheson's aim was to improve performance practices and make the operatic stage the seat of, and the training-ground for, all kinds of gesture ("der eigentliche Sitz und die rechte hohe Schule für allerhand Geberden"; p. 37). He further helped to prepare the way for the critics of Lessing's generation when he suggested that theater could be a means for transmitting the kind of cultural values and civilized behavior that would ultimately improve the quality of life in the German lands.

Before theater could become what Mattheson envisioned, many changes had to take place. The most urgent ones involved the performers, whom he never ceased to criticize even when writing to support them. He was appalled that society exploited them and then treated them like vagabonds too dishonest and dirty to be buried in

31 *Mithridat*, 135, 138–40.
32 *Die neuangelegte Freuden-Akademie*, 2 vols. (Hamburg, 1751, 1753), II, 112–13.

consecrated ground. Performers, he wrote in *Der musicalische Patriot*, received fewer and generally shabbier benefits than musicians, yet were expected to fulfill many more bourgeois duties. They were worse off than common soldiers (p. 87). In some instances, however, such abusive treatment might have been warranted, for there were those who succumbed to the attractions of profligacy and debauchery, "and as a result often landed in need and misery, especially in old age" ("und darüber offt in Noth und Elend gerathen: absonderlich im Alter"; p. 97). They were the ones, Mattheson explained in *Mithridat wider den Gift einer welschen Satyre, genannt La Musica* (1749), who made solid burghers think, quite erroneously, that music involved no work, but rather dancing, cavorting, eating, and drinking ". . . daß zur Musik keine Arbeit gehöre; sondern lauter Tanzen, Springen, Fressen, Sauffen ec."; p. 112).

Mattheson's attempts to correct such misconceptions always spoke of the numerous demands made on a performer and sometimes alluded to the resultant stress that shortened his or her life. In *Der musicalische Patriot* he wrote most poignantly:

Most of the time an actor truly has more trouble than pleasure from his job. It should not need to be mentioned that he must sing the same song and present the same role ad nauseam. He often becomes so bitter that all zest for life probably vanishes. Those who have never tried it imagine that one is carried along on a tide of unalloyed joy and thinks of nothing else except voluptuousness. Oh, how far off course![33]

Mattheson also worked hard to correct the misconception, originating in ancient Greece, that performers always had something effeminately soft, tender, sensual, and weak about them.[34] Adjectives and adverbs pertaining to the female of the human species were used in German criticism to express utter disapprobation until the shift in values and sensibilities came about in the late eighteenth century. Those words infiltrated Mattheson's critical language too, in spite of the fact that he became one of the staunchest German defenders of women performers.[35] Time and time again he wrote that they, and not the castratos, should be given roles and a chance to cultivate their

33 "Ein Acteur hat wahrhafftig die meiste Zeit vielmehr Verdruß, als Ergetzen, an seiner Verrichtung: denn zu geschweigen, daß er einerley Lied und Vorstellung oft ad nauseam singen und treiben muß, so wird ihm zuweilen das Leben so sauer gemacht, daß ihm die Lust wol vergehen mag. Die es nie versucht haben, stehen in der Einbildung, man schwimme in lauter Freuden, und dencke an nichts, als Wollust. O weit gefehlt!" *Musicalischer Patriot*, 156.
34 *Singspiele*, 14, 22.
35 Ibid., 15–16, 25, 50, 101. See also A. Schering, *Aufführungspraxis alter Musik* (Leipzig, 1931), 170–1.

talents. Although he very well understood the reasons for castratos, he disavowed the continuance of the practice in his own day. Always prepared, however, to defend the performing artist – of whatever age, size, shape, sex, or form – he wrote in 1744: "With the female-sounding voices of the unfortunate castratos, one might, perhaps, find something in the masculine state to take exception about; whether they lead the people astray, however, as is said – that is an unheard-of accusation, about which one still knows nothing here."[36] Believing that such animadversions derived from universal ignorance about castration, he presented in *Mithridat* detailed information on its biblical, mythological, and historical background. He concluded with the question: "How can it be the fault of the poor, unknowing child, in whom no carnal desire or lust has yet manifested itself?" ("Was kann das arme, unwissende Kind dafür, bey welchem noch kein Trieb zum Geize, oder oder zur Wollust sich äußert?" p. 124).

Mattheson considered especially dubious the reasons given for forbidding women to sing in churches. From the beginning of his career, he thought that the divine services were thereby robbed of their best ornament. A head-on confrontation came in the *Critica musica*, where he distinguished the space, time, and other prerequisites of the church from those of the opera house. There he wrote:

As regards women: It is incomprehensible that anyone should want to forbid the fair sex to sing with its own voice the praise of God publicly in the place consecrated to him. One person may say that a woman sings in the opera; so too do men. Another may say she is too pretty; then so must all good-looking faces be excluded from church. If a third says she sings too beautifully, then one has cause indeed to praise God's wonders in the human voice.[37]

Mattheson's subsequent writings offered a wide spectrum of arguments and anecdotes to support the ecclesiastical as well as the

---

36 "Bey den weibermäßigen Stimmen der armen verschnittenen Sänger mögte man noch vielleicht etwas wider das männliche Wesen einzuwenden finden; ob sie aber, wie gesagt wird, das Volk verführen, solches ist eine unerhörte Beschuldigung, von der man hiesiger Orten noch nichts weiß." *Singspiele*, 24. F. Haböck, *Die Kastraten und ihre Gesangkunst: Eine Gesangsphysiologische, Kultur- und Musikhistorische Studie* (Stuttgart, 1927), treated the subject in great detail, but paid very little attention to conditions in the predominantly Protestant cities of northern Germany and even less to open-minded critics like Mattheson.

37 "A propos, vom Frauenzimmer! Es stehet nicht zu begreifen, warum man diesem schönen Geschlechte verbieten will, das Lob Gottes, an dem dazu gewidmeten Orte, öffentlich in seinem Munde zu führen? Sagt einer: Die Person singt in der Opera; so singen ja die Männer auch allda. Sagt der andre: Sie ist zu hübsch; so müssen nur alle artige Gesichter aus der Kirche bleiben. Sagt der dritte: Sie singt gar zu lieblich; so hat man ja Ursache, Gottes Wunder in der Menschen Stimme zu preisen." *Critica musica* II, 320.

secular employment of female singers. He gave biblical citations to prove that women pleased God; he reported how innocent yet musically gifted young nuns were often abducted by ruthless talent scouts; and he came to the defense of the widows whose religiosity made them want to sing during services. The many times Mattheson mentioned his success in hiring women to sing in church shows how proud he was of his pioneering accomplishment.[38] When he wrote *Der vollkommene Capellmeister*, he could not refrain from including a biographical reminiscence that had to do with his efforts on their behalf: "In the beginning, it was demanded that I place them so that no one could see them; ultimately, however, no one could hear or see enough of them" ("Anfangs wurde verlangt, ich sollte sie bey Leibe so stellen, daß sie kein Mensch zu sehen kriegte; zuletzt aber konte man sie nie genug hören und sehen"; p. 482). As a theorist as well as a practical man, Mattheson never underestimated women. In *Die musikalische Geschmacksprobe* he offered the best tribute to womankind. He wrote that composers should continually consult women – whether their wives, mistresses, girlfriends or prima donnas – during the creative process. Women, in his opinion, were among the most sensitive and most articulate critics (p. 164).

The generally abysmal status of performers was of such great concern to Mattheson that he worked hard toward its improvement. In addition to attempting to change public opinion, he concentrated on the performers themselves. He sought to convince them of the honor of their profession and to imbue them with feelings of self-worth and dignity. He wanted them to consider themselves artists rather than artisans, so he wrote again and again that what they were involved in was a liberal art rather than a handicraft ("kein Handwerk sondern eine freie Kunst").[39] The very words they used to describe themselves, like "Musikant," were to be avoided because they were so demeaning and demoralizing. Mattheson encouraged performers to use "Opern-Acteur," which, however, did not pass the linguistic test of time.[40] He thought they lacked roots or a firm sense of their professional history, so he wrote about their ancient Roman predecessors as examples of well-paid, highly honored members of society. He blamed ignorant audiences, who applauded even the very worst performances, for inhibiting the natural development of self-criticism

---

38 *Musicalischer Patriot*, 38, 65, 82. See also Cannon, *Mattheson*, 50–1, and M. Högg, *Die Gesangskunst der Faustina Hasse und das Sängerinnenwesen ihrer Zeit in Deutschland* (Ph.D. diss., University of Berlin, 1931), 13.
39 *Musicalischer Patriot*, 87.
40 *Singspiele*, 16–17; *Musicalischer Patriot*, 106.

in modern performers.[41] His advice to them was to concentrate on the three most important things in order to develop their own judgment, namely, "a powerful expression of that which was to be uttered, a noble simplicity, and charm or grace" ("eine kräfftige Ausdrückung desjenigen, so er hervorbringt, eine edle Einfalt, und die Lieblichkeit oder Anmuth").[42]

Though never sparing his praise of the Italians' exquisite voices and wonderful *Executio*, Mattheson liked to point out that from childhood on they received much more training and encouragement than their colleagues in Germany.[43] German performers did not come from that kind of privileged musical background, but he thought they could make up for it because they were conscientious, reliable, diligent, cooperative, good-natured, and knowledgeable about acting and dancing as well as about singing and playing instruments. All they needed was the proper guidance.[44]

Mattheson's ideas on training performers reflect his profound belief in the interdependence of the operatic arts. In *Der vollkommene Capellmeister* he contended: "Thought concerning this whole science aims at making gesture, words, and sound into a triple cord [braid] and in the last analysis so intricately intertwined that the soul of the auditor is mightily affected" ("Die Meinung mit dieser gantzen Wissenschafft zielet dahin, daß Geberden, Worte und Klang eine dreifache Schnur machen, und zu dem Ende mit einander vollkommen übereinstimmen sollen, daß des Zuhörers Gemüth beweget werde"; p. 37). The fact that opera's collaborators were so uninformed about each other's fields disturbed him greatly. He insisted that that had not been the case in antiquity, for then everyone knew music. He believed that music in his day too was the source of and integrating factor for not only all the arts but also for all the other fields of human endeavor, even philosophy.[45] Mattheson thought the modern situation could be rectified if there were more cooperation and interchange among poets, composers, stage designers, performers, and orchestra players. As late as the *Philologisches Tresespiel* (1752) he was still complaining: "Only very few poets can sing well in the true sense; and similarly, only a few composers are capable of skillfully writing verse. Nevertheless, it would be desirable for mother and daughter, music and poetry, to live together in the same house in fine harmony"

---

41 *Musicalischer Patriot*, 336; also Högg, *Die Gesangskunst der Faustnra Hasse*, 41.
42 *Musicalischer Patriot*, 106.
43 *Orchestre* I, 205; *Critica musica* I, 146, and II, 287–8.
44 *Orchestre* I, 217–18.   45 *Singspiele*, 17–18.

("Die wenigsten Dichter können, im eigentlichen Verstande, gut singen; und auch die wenigsten Notensetzer sind vermögend, geschickte Verse zu machen. Zu wünschen wäre es gleichwohl, daß Mutter und Tochter, Ton- und Dichtkunst, fein harmonisch in einem Hause bey einander wohnten"; p. 56). Music's importance was so obvious to him that he often broke with the critical convention of referring to the sister arts and changed the family relationship. Here he made them mother and daughter, but in earlier writings he viewed them as husband and wife.[46]

Mattheson insisted that it behooved the composer to become involved in training the people who would perform his work. The political as well as aesthetic advantages were well worth the effort and time. Encouraging performers and offering them advice without thoughtless or harsh comment could awaken their loyalty and ensure the devoted cooperation that was so necessary for achieving a stage production of the highest quality. Mattheson held that the genuinely excellent opera composer always had firsthand knowledge about the theatrical arts. Even if the composer could not sing, dance, and act well, his willingness to try taught him a great deal. He learned to recognize the limitations and difficulties of each individual art and to have them constantly before his eyes ("beständig vor Augen").[47] As a result he did not merely pay lip service to them, but he was able to take them into account in practical ways for his own work. In the translation of John Mainwaring's (ca. 1724–1807) biography of Handel, Mattheson noted: "In my opinion, singing and acting have far-reaching importance for the dramatic composer. Hasse knows that very well. He has, I can testify, done both in a praiseworthy way. Keiser also sang extraordinarily beautifully. As a result, both are at a great advantage in composing their melodies" ("Meines Erachtens geht Singen und Agiren sehr weit bey einem dramatischen Komponisten: das weiß Hasse sehr wol, der beydes, me teste, löblich getrieben hat. Keiser sang auch überaus schön: und daher haben beyde in ihren Melodien ein großes voraus"; p. 134). He could not resist writing that Handel, on the other hand, was "kein Sänger, kein Acteur"; p. 134).

Mattheson, who never let his readers forget that he himself was a composer with years of theatrical experience, frequently mentioned his own coaching efforts, especially on behalf of one woman, to whom he apparently sang everything each day for as long as it took her to commit it to memory) ". . . alles so lange vor, bis sie es ins

46 *Critica musica* II, 303, and I, 99.   47 *Melodische Wissenschaft*, 21.

93

Gedächtniß faßte").[48] A perfect Kapellmeister, in his opinion, would be more than willing to volunteer services of that kind. One such historical example was Jean Baptiste Lully (1632–87), whose biography he published in Critica musica (1722). It was to serve as a model of organization and style for all the entries in the Grundlage einer Ehren-Pforte. The fact that it included entire sections (Nos. 18 and 19) on experience in dancing and acting as well as on auditions shows how very important Mattheson considered them. He reported that Lully coached performers in singing, movement, and acting, and even went so far as to use his own money to pay for dancing masters when needed (p. 181). In Der vollkommene Capellmeister he again referred to Lully, this time writing "that he himself instructed all his actors, actresses, and male and female dancers in this art of gesture, that is, in action or portrayal, and in so doing demonstrated that a correct understanding of such matters belongs to the very office and being of the complete Kapellmeister" ". . . daß er alle seine Acteurs, Actricen, Täntzer und Täntzerinnen in dieser Geberden-Kunst, d.i. in der Action selber unterrichtet, und damit gnugsam bezeiget haben, daß es zu dem Amt und Wesen eines vollkommenen Capellmeisters mit gehöre, hierin was rechtes zu verstehen"; p. 37; also Ehrenpforte, 178–80).

Because of his own experience as well as philosophical stance, Mattheson believed in tailoring instruction to the individual performer. There were, however, in addition to the musicological study, historical orientation, and psychological indoctrination, certain basics that all pupils would have to be subjected to. The art of memory was one, and diction was another.[49] Yet another was the familiarity with foreign languages. Voice lessons were an especially important part of the curriculum. Needless to say, he considered the human voice the perfect instrument.[50] In Der vollkommene Capellmeister he advised young pupils to go to church services and participate in congregational singing to have the opportunity "to push the voice to its very limits, which necessarily must happen" ("die Stimme rechtschaffen auszuschreien, welches nothwendig geschehen muß"; p. 96). Another of his methods to expand the lungs, develop breath control, and condition the vocal chords was to dig a hole in a field and, bending down with the mouth close over it, sing and scream

---

48 Händels Lebensbeschreibung, 22; also Capellmeister, 37.
49 Mithridat, 67–8; Tresespiel, 60.
50 Behauptung der himmlischen Musik (Hamburg, 1747), 20.

until exhausted. Learning how to modulate the voice came from constant practice, something he thought was regrettably neglected in the instruction given by local singing teachers. The methods Mattheson suggested derived from his reading about contemporary investigations of the larynx, glottis, epiglottis, and esophagus. He thought scientists should continue to study such anatomical matters as well as some related physiological ones, particularly those having to do with the production of sperm and its effects on the male voice. The results were to be grouped together under the term "phonascia" and be made one of the sciences, or what might now better be called fields of study, required of all performers.[51]

Another such requirement would be *hypocritica*, a science that was "not merely very old, but so ancient that it seems completely new" ("nicht nur sehr alt, sondern so uralt, daß sie gantz neu zu seyn scheinet").[52] As the study of *hypocrisis*, or the art of calculated deception through oratory, dancing, and acting, it taught how to produce, simultaneously, "lively gestures, a face on which the passions of the soul are painted, a posture, a carriage which is convincingly suitable to the person, and a firm voice that is nevertheless versatile enough for its tones to tumble out quickly or come forth with measured slowness" ("lebhaffte Geberden, ein Gesicht, darauf sich die Leidenschafft der Seele abmahlet, eine Stellung, ein Gang, die sich wol zu der Person schicken, eine feste Stimme, die doch dabey geschmeidig ist, so daß ihre Töne entweder geschwind heraus stürtzen, oder mit langsamer Abmessung hervor bringen kann").[53] The word, and its noun agents, *hypocrita* or *Hypokritiker*, evolved out of Mattheson's reading in the history of acting theory, which throughout the ages has repeatedly come up either in rhetorical handbooks or in some relationship to rhetoric. Even though other contemporary theorists, among them Johann Joachim Quantz (1697–1773), thought they were meaningful words and used them regularly, they gained neither the popular nor the academic accep-

---

51 *Capellmeister*, 94–5. Walther, *Musicalisches Lexicon*, 478, treated the topic in the same way as Zedler, *Universal-Lexikon*, vol. 27, col. 2189: "Phonascia: a practice in former times that consisted simply in the artificial changing – now decreasing, now increasing, raising and lowering – of the voice and enunciation while speaking and singing" "Phonascia, war vor Zeiten eine Übung, welche in nichts anders bestünde, denn in einer künstlichen Veränderung, bald Ab- bald Zunehmung, Erhöh- und Erniedrigung der Stimme und Aussprache, im Reden oder Singen". The *phonascus* was a singing master, a music director, or a Kapellmeister.
52 *Capellmeister*, 33.
53 *Musicalischer Patriot*, 107, quoted and translated from an unknown French work.

tance needed to secure absorption into the German language.[54] When Mattheson used them, he did so in order to convey the idea that the performer was someone who portrayed a certain person other than himself ("der eine gewisse andre Person, die er selbst nicht ist, verstellig macht").[55]

Publicly pretending to be someone else has since time immemorial been considered eminently dangerous for society. According to the many Hamburg pastors who time after time referred to the church fathers, such make-believe was reason enough for unequivocally doing away with all theatrical representations in public. Mattheson obviously disagreed in spite of the fact that he thought performers not only automatically related to what they were doing, but also actually felt the emotion they were portraying. In *Critica musica* he wrote: "No one asks so lightly whether or not what is sung is felt, or whether the heart agrees with the voice. How can I then move other people if I myself am not moved by the words that I sing, if I myself do not even understand the words" ("Ob es empfunden werde / was gesungen wird / ob das Herz mit dem Munde übereinstimme / darnach frägt so leicht niemand. Wie kann ich denn andre bewegen / wenn mich die Worte / so ich daher singe / selbst nicht rühren / ja wenn ich sie nicht einmal verstehe" II, p. 15). He admitted that he himself had experienced that kind of emotional empathy when performing the roles of Mutius Scaevola and Antony. As he later reported in *Die neueste Untersuchung der Singspiele*: "Yes, I myself lost my color in so performing, even though I very well knew I was feigning a role" ("Ja, ich selber verlohr die Farbe dabey; ob ich gleich am besten um den Possen wußte"; p. 76). In that same work he went on to state as an accepted fact: "The very best composer and the prettiest of female

---

54 Högg, *Die Gesangskunst der Faustina Hasse*, 44. Walther, *Musicalisches Lexicon*, gives no listings. On the other hand, H. Mendel, *Musikalisches Conversations-Lexikon* (Berlin, 1875), vol. 5, 343, gives the following definition of *Hypokritik*: "According to the categorization of music by Quintilian, acting belongs together with the organic (instrumental) and odic (vocal), that is, the practical components of music, which have to do with its performance and representation" ("Nach der Eintheilung der Musik durch Aristides Quintilianus gehört die H. neben der organischen (Instrumental-) und odischen (Vocal-) Musik zu demjenigen Theil der praktischen Tonkunst, der die Gegenstände, welche die Ausführung und Darstellung betreffen, umfaßt". The word fared no better in English. Compare C. Burney, *A General History of Music from the Earliest Ages to the Present Period* (1789), ed. F. Mercer, 2 vols. (London, 1935), vol. 1, 138: "The term *hypocritic*, which the Greeks likewise called *orchesis*, and the Latins *saltatio*, though it sometimes means dancing, more frequently is used to express gesture, or theatrical action."
55 *Capellmeister*, 37.

singers can arouse no solidly virtuous inclination in the audience if they themselves feel none" ("Der allerbeste Componist, und die allerniedlichste Sängerin können keine tüchtige Tugendregung bey den Zuhörern erwecken, wenn sie selbst keine empfinden"; p. 111).

Being carried away with one's role, however, whether as actor, singer, or musician, was something Mattheson understood but refused to condone as long as the results were either harmful or unpleasant. Especially sad to him was the fact that the death of his hero, Lully, originated during a performance when he was in the heat of action ("in der Hitze der Action").[56] Mattheson anticipated the ideas of Lessing and Denis Diderot (1713–84) insofar as he thought training and hard work would temper complete empathy and prevent the performer from losing his own identity and eventually his mind or life or all three.[57] Because of his support of what we might nowadays classify as a modified type of Method acting, Mattheson, much like those later theorists, rejected treatment of the furies or other kinds of ugliness as being too stark, too potentially dangerous for three-dimensional portrayal.[58]

Nor could a man with Mattheson's background ignore the physical strains as well as the dangers involved in performance. To alleviate them, he advocated total health care and a homegrown kind of preventive medicine. As the eighteenth century progressed, performers gained stature, wealth, and also the attention of physicians who became increasingly interested in their ailments and frequent early deaths.[59] Many of the topics Mattheson discussed were to come up again in later treatises. In *Der vollkommene Capellmeister* he stressed the need for exercise and good posture, which he insisted had

56 *Critica musica* I, 183.
57 J. Eisenschmidt, *Die szenische Darstellung der Opern Händels auf der Londoner Bühne seiner Zeit* (Wolfenbüttel and Berlin, 1940–1), vol. 6, vol. 53–7, overlooks Mattheson's plea for artistic distance. In *The "Affektenlehre" in the Eighteenth Century* (diss., Indiana University, 1955), F. T. Wessel somewhat misleads his readers into believing that Mattheson and those of his generation rather than Plato first discussed the effect of emotional empathy during the various phases of the creative and performing processes; see p. 58–60, 272, 277. H. Lenneberg, on the other hand, fully acknowledges the tradition stemming from antiquity, "Johann Mattheson on Affect and Rhetoric in Music (I)," in: *JMT* 2 (1958), 47–84.
58 *Critica musica* I, 128. I believe Mattheson would have condoned Goethe's internalization of the furies plaguing Orestes in his *Iphigenia auf Tauris* (1779–86), a work conceived under the influence of the late eighteenth-century fashion of musical monodrama and melodrama.
59 *Plus ultra* II, 282. As Haböck, *Die Kastraten*, 12, points out, the most famous eighteenth-century castratos lived well over sixty years. See W. F. Kümmel, *Musik und Medizin: Ihre Wechselbeziehungen in Theorie und Praxis von 800 bis 1800* (Freiburg and Munich, 1977), 101.

beneficial effects on breathing and the voice. Lemon, vinegar, and zwieback he considered better for conditioning and improving the voice than all the medications and drugs taken by even the most notable singers. He thought that much of what they used, tobacco and snuff in particular, was bad for the lungs and all related organs (p. 98).

Being the pragmatic empiricist that he was, he wrote of specific case histories to demonstrate the salubriousness of a moderate diet. There was one successful singer, who, whenever called to perform, eschewed the midday meal in favor of a portion of fennel and a cup of tea. And then there was another who retained his voice into very old age for no other reason than his unusual moderation and abstemiousness in eating and drinking ("die ungemeine Mäßigkeit und Wahl im Essen und Trincken"; p. 95). Heavy foods high in fat content were to be avoided, for they were good only for producing an overstuffed belly ("ein vollgepfropter Bauch"; p. 98). In *Mithridat* he took up the subject once again: "Whoever believes that a singer may eat and drink excessively whatever he pleases does not know what the voice requires in the way of cultivation, or how significant is that which is the very wagon and plough of such artists" [i.e., the tools of that cultivation] ("Wer da meynet, ein Sänger möge wohl fressen und sauffen, der weiß noch nicht was die Stimme für Pflege haben will, und wie viel dasjenige zu bedeuten hat, was solcher Künstler einziger Wagen und Pflug ist"; p. 47). He claimed that no singer could tolerate for very long the kind of stenotic effect that wine had on the throat. On the other hand, he classified beer as healthy, contending that it helped to produce so many good bass voices among the Germans. To support his position on dietary discretion, he also summoned his scholarly background: "Isidore of Seville has mentioned that the choristers of the church fasted on the day before their performance, and, like Daniel and his comrades, nourished themselves otherwise with vegetables. They were therefore mockingly referred to by the heathens as legumes, or bean eaters" ("Isidor hat bemerkt, daß die Kirchensänger, des Tages vor der Musik, gefastet, und sich auch sonst nur, wie Daniel und seine Gesellen, von bloßen Zugemüsen ernähret haben: daher sie von den Heiden, aus Spott, Fabarii, das ist Bonenfresser, genannt worden"; p. 47).

Mattheson must have followed his own prescriptions, for he succeeded in living to a ripe old age. His long life spanned the High Baroque, the Enlightenment, the Rococo, *Empfindsamkeit*, and *Sturm und Drang*. By encouraging the constant interaction of those divergent tendencies, he helped to stimulate the reassessment of styles, attitudes, and tastes that was to produce at the end of the eighteenth century one of Germany's greatest artistic flowerings. It was no mere coincidence that the first national theater, with Lessing as the first officially appointed dramaturgist, was established by a consortium of Hamburg burghers so soon after his death. Nor was it surprising that those burghers were, at least at the beginning of the enterprise, willing to finance a theatrical academy as well as health care and old-age pensions for performing artists. Nor was it surprising that some of the best minds of the later eighteenth century found publishers and an eager reading public in the city where Mattheson had been so active for so long.

5

Zur hamburgischen Gelehrtenrepublik im Zeitalter Matthesons

JÜRGEN RATHJE
Pforzheim

Künste und Wissenschaften in Hamburg erreichen in der ersten Hälfte des achtzehnten Jahrhunderts ihren Höhepunkt. Das geistige Leben der Stadt[1] steht im Zeichen der westeuropäischen Frühaufklärung. Hamburgs Gelehrtenwelt, Literatur und Musik nimmt in Deutschland eine führende Stellung ein. Es ist das Zeitalter Richeys und Reimarus', Brockes' und des *Patrioten*, Telemanns und Matthesons.

Die ersten Jahrzehnte des achtzehnten Jahrhunderts sind zugleich die Zeit Montesquieus und Voltaires – Popes, Addisons und Swifts. Sie gelten als die glücklichsten der französischen Geistesgeschichte. In England bezeichnen sie die Klassik. Es ist die Epoche des philosophischen Optimismus. Geprägt haben diese Generation die Ideen des Thomasius, Leibnizens und Wolffs ebenso wie die pädagogischen Erkenntnisse Fénelons und Lockes.

Oper und Gelehrtenschulen sind die Zentren jener geistigen Aktivitäten, durch welche Hamburg im Zeitalter Matthesons von sich reden macht. Die ältere Tradition kommt den Gelehrtenschulen[2] zu. Das Johanneum wurde bereits 1529 von Johann Bugenhagen gegründet. Es handelt sich dabei um eine anfangs fünf-, später achtklassige Lateinschule. Das in seinen Ursprüngen ebenfalls auf Bugenhagen

---

1 Cf. dazu: F. Wehl, *Hamburgs Literaturleben im achtzehnten Jahrhundert* (Leipzig, 1856); E. Baasch, *Der Einfluß des Handels auf das Geistesleben Hamburgs* (=Pfingstblätter des Hansischen Geschichtsvereins, Blatt V) (Leipzig, 1909); H. Reincke, "Hamburgs Anteil am deutschen Geistesleben der Vergangenheit", in: *Hamburg in seiner wirtschaftlichen und kulturellen Bedeutung für Deutschland* (Hamburg, 1925), 50–84.

2 Dazu: J. A. R. Janssen, *Ausführliche Nachrichten über die sämmtlichen evangelisch-protestantischen Kirchen und Geistlichen der freien und Hansestadt Hamburg und ihres Gebietes, so wie über deren Johanneum, Gymnasium, Bibliothek und die dabei angestellten Männer* (Hamburg, 1826); E. Ph. L. Calmberg, *Geschichte des Johanneums zu Hamburg* (Hamburg, 1829); E. Kelter, *Hamburg und sein Johanneum im Wandel der Jahrhunderte 1529–1929* (Hamburg, 1928).

weisende Akademische Gymnasium, eine Art Selekta des Johanneums, entsteht dagegen seit 1613. Mit seinen sechs Professuren – Logik/Metaphysik, Praktische Philosophie/Beredsamkeit/ Moral, Geschichte/Griechische Sprache, Physik/Poesie, Mathematik, Orientalische Sprachen – war es als Vorbereitungsstufe für das anschließende Studium an einer Universität gedacht. Hamburg selbst besaß keine solche, und das Akademische Gymnasium verlieh auch keine akademischen Grade, konnte aber im Verlaufe seiner Geschichte mit Gelehrten wie Jungius, Lambecius und Placcius aufwarten.

Fünfundsechzig Jahre nach Entstehen dieser zweiten Gelehrtenschule, am 2. Januar 1678, beginnt Deutschlands erste stehende Opernbühne dank der Initiative des im Hamburger Exil lebenden Herzogs Christian Albrecht von Holstein-Gottorf, des Juristen und späteren Ratsherrn Gerhard Schott, des Juristen Peter Lütjen und des Organisten Johann Adam Reincken ihre Tätigkeit. Mit Gründung der Oper erhält die literarische Entwicklung Hamburgs großen Auftrieb. Nicht nur Komponisten von Rang, sondern auch zahlreiche Dichter ruft die Verbindung von Dicht- und Tonkunst auf den Plan, die bis zu Hagedorns Tagen für Hamburgs geistiges Leben bezeichnend bleiben sollte.

In diesem Sinne gehören die Textdichter Christian Heinrich Postel (1658–1705), Christian Friedrich Hunold (1680–1721), Friedrich Christian Feustking (1678–1739), Johann Ulrich von König (1688–1744), Lucas von Bostel (1649–1716), Joachim Beccau (1690–1755) und Barthold Feind (1678–1721) sowohl der Oper als auch der deutschen Literatur an. Ähnliches gilt für den zwar nicht als Librettisten, aber als Kritiker der Oper hervorgetretenen Dichter und späteren Diplomaten Christian Wernicke (1661–1725)[3]. Dieses geistige Klima begünstigt auch das Entstehen von literarischen Freundeskreisen, Gelehrtenzirkeln und gemeinnützigen Gesellschaften.

Der Impuls für solche Gruppenbildungen geht von den Gelehrtenschulen aus. Eine Schlüsselrolle kommt dabei Johann Albert Fabricius zu. Sein Schwiegersohn und Biograph Hermann Samuel Reimarus schreibt das Entstehen dieser Zirkel dem Fabricius eigenen Hang zu gelehrter Geselligkeit zu[4].

---

3 Zur Hamburger Barockoper und ihrer Geschichte: J. Fr. Schütze, *Hamburgische Theater-Geschichte* (Hamburg, 1794); H. Chr. Wolff, *Die Barockoper in Hamburg (1678–1738)*, 2 voll. (Wolfenbüttel, 1957); H. J. Marx, "Geschichte der Hamburger Barockoper. Ein Forschungsbericht", in: *Hamburger Jahrbuch für Musikwissenschaft* 3 (1978), 7–34.

4 *De vita et scriptis Joannis Alberti Fabricii commentarius* (Hamburg, 1737), 83s.

Über drei solcher Gesprächsrunden läßt sich Näheres sagen: die Gelehrtengesellschaft der Bibliotheca Historica, die Teutsch-übende Gesellschaft und die Patriotische Gesellschaft von 1724. Von der erstgenannten Gelehrtengesellschaft[5] zeugt eine von 1715 bis 1729 erscheinende Sammlung[6] historischen Inhalts. Ihre Autoren hatten tausend Bücher zum großen Teil kritisch durchgesehen, deren Titeln Werkanalysen und biographische Notizen zu den Verfassern angefügt und das Ganze in zehn *Centurien* veröffentlicht:

Es haben etliche gute Freunde in Hamburg den Vorsatz gefasset, nach und nach alle Bücher zu recensiren, die zum STUDIO HISTORICO gehören, und ihnen zu Gesichte oder zur sattsamen Kundschafft kommen.
Ihr Hauptwerck ist der Nutzen der studierenden Jugend, und also gehöret dieses Buch eigentlich vor junge Leute, die etwan ein COMPENDIUM HISTORICUM tractiret haben, und sich nunmehro eine Notitiam Librorum zulegen wollen, daraus die Historischen Merckwürdigkeiten genommen werden.
Sie nehmen aber das Wort HISTORIA in einem weitläufftigen Verstande, und also werden in dieser Bibliotheca nicht nur alle Historische, sondern auch alle Geographische, Chronologische, Heraldische und Numismatische Bücher vorkommen.
Ihro Nahmen zu melden, haben die Autores noch zur Zeit nicht nöthig erachtet[7].

Autor dieser Zeilen jedenfalls dürfte Johann Hübner sein, der laut Fabricius auch der Begründer der Bibliotheca Historica ist[8]. Ein Jahr später allerdings wünscht Hübner

auch bekannt zu machen, daß nicht er allein, sondern unterschiedliche gelehrte Leute an der so genannten Bibliotheca Historica arbeiten, und die meisten und besten Artickel von dem Herrn Mich. Richey her kommen[9].

Wie Hübner und Richey, so sind auch die beiden anderen Mitarbeiter Pädagogen: Johann Albert Fabricius und der Kieler Professor Philipp Friedrich Hahn.
Drei Merkmale sind an der Bibliotheca Historica hervorhebenswert: ihr gemeinnütziger Zweck, sodann die Tatsache, daß wir es bei den Autoren – im Sinne Fabricius'[10] – mit einem Gelehr-

---

5 Dazu: J. Scheibe, *Der "Patriot" (1724–1726) und sein Publikum. Untersuchungen über die Verfassergesellschaft und die Leserschaft einer Zeitschrift der frühen Aufklärung* (Göppingen, 1973), 30s.
6 *Hamburgische Bibliotheca Historica, Der Studierenden Jugend zum Besten zusammen getragen*, 10 voll. (Leipzig, 1715–29).
7 Ibid., vol. 1 (Vorrede).
8 J. A. Fabricius, *Vita Joannis Hübnerii, Rectoris Scholae Hamburgensis* (Hamburg, 1731). Dazu: F. L. Hoffmann, "Hamburgische Bibliophilen, Bibliographen und Litteraturhistoriker", in: *Serapeum* 14 (1853), 316 (Anm. 1).
9 *Neue Zeitungen von gelehrten Sachen* (Leipzig, 1716), 126.
10 Reimarus, *De vita Fabricii*.

tenzirkel zu tun haben, der einmal wöchentlich sich zu einer Gesprächsrunde trifft, und schließlich der Personenkreis selbst, seine Neigung zur Gründung weiterer, umfangreicherer Gesellschaften und Freundeskreise:

Eben diese beyden verdienten Männer, Fabricius und Hübner, waren es, welche sich damals mit ihm [Richey] durch das Band einer genaueren Freundschaft in wöchentlichen gelehrten Zusammenkünften vereinigten, bey welcher Gelegenheit im Jahre 1715 der Grund zu der sogenannten deutschübenden Gesellschaft geleget wurde, welche in der Folge durch den Beytritt mehrerer gelehrter und berühmter Mitglieder, eines Anckelmanns, Brockes, Hoffmanns, Klefekers, Surlands, Weichmanns und Widows, verstärkt, und der Anfang der Patriotischen Gesellschaft, einer Gesellschaft, deren Verbindungen und Arbeiten unserm Hamburg wahre Ehre gemacht haben, geworden ist[11].

Der Polyhistor und Polygraph Johann Albert Fabricius ist für seine Zeitgenossen eine international anerkannte Größe. Zahlreich sind die Besuche, die er von in- und ausländischen Freunden erhält. Die größten Gelehrten holen seinen Rat ein. Besonders in England und den Niederlanden steht sein Fachwissen in Ansehen. Entsprechend umfangreich ist seine Korrespondenz. Jean-Pierre Nicéron hat ihn in seine *Mémoires pour servir à l'histoire des hommes illustres dans la République des Lettres*[12] aufgenommen, und der Verleger der französischen Übersetzung seiner *Hydro-Theologie*[13], Pierre Paupie, braucht der Leserschaft den Verfasser nicht erst vorzustellen: "Le nom de Mr. FABRICIUS est si bien connu dans la République des Lettres, qu'il suffit de dire, que l'Ouvrage, que je donne aujourd'hui, est de lui pour en faire l'éloge"[14].

Fabricius' Werk berührt Philosophie und Theologie, mit Sicherheit gehört es der Geschichte der Wissenschaften an, der Altphilologie zumal. Seine *Bibliotheca Latina*, *Bibliotheca Graeca* und *Bibliotheca Latina mediae et infimae aetatis* sind umfassende biographische und bibliographische Materialsammlungen zur gesamten griechischen und lateinischen Literatur des Altertums und des Mittelalters, und zur lateinischen Literatur der Neuzeit[15]. In Methode und literarhistorischer Zielsetzung Peter Lambecius und Daniel Georg Mor-

11 G. Schütze, Vorrede zu vol. 2 von *Michael Richey: Deutsche Gedichte* (herausgegeben von G. Schütze), 3 voll. (Hamburg, 1764–6), XXIIs.
12 40 voll. (Paris, 1727–39), vol. 20, 326ss.
13 *Théologie de l'eau, ou Essai sur la bonté, la sagesse et la puissance de Dieu, manifestées dans la création de l'eau* (Den Haag, 1741), übersetzt von Burnaud.
14 Ibid., Avertissement du Libraire. p. III.
15 *Bibliotheca Latina* .... Erstauflage (Hamburg, 1697); *Bibliotheca Graeca* .... Erstauflage 14 voll. (Hamburg, 1705–28); *Bibliotheca Latina mediae et infimae aetatis*, Erstauflage 6 voll. (Hamburg, 1734–46).

hof verpflichtet[16], diente Fabricius' Werk fortan "nicht nur als Grundlage für die historische und kritische Arbeit der folgenden Generationen, sondern auch als Arsenal fü unsere Klassiker"[17]. Ulrich von Wilamowitz-Moellendorff hält das, was Fabricius bringt, für mehr als Vielwisserei. Die in der *Bibliotheca Graeca* und *Latina* aufgestapelte Wissensmasse sei geradezu unheimlich. Aber er sieht in Fabricius zugleich einen zuverlässigen Berater, der immer an die Bedürfnisse des Benutzers denkt. Alles sei knapp und klar und wohlgeordnet; Fabricius kenne die Bücher und Gelehrten aller Zeiten. Seine besonderen Verdienste bestünden in der Berücksichtigung der Byzantiner, dem dadurch zusammengetragenen Material, der Aufnahme mancher nie oder unzulänglich gedruckten Schriften und in der von ihm besorgten Ausgabe des Sextus Empiricus, die schon durch ihren sprachlichen Index ein Hilfsmittel sei, wie es damals kaum ein anderes gegeben habe[18].

Fabricius' philosophisch-theologisches Werk geht auf französische und englische Versuche zurück, Religion und Naturwissenschaft im Sinne der Frühaufklärung miteinander zu versöhnen. 1714 erscheint seine Übersetzung des *Traité de l'existence de Dieu* von François de Salignac de la Mothe-Fénelon[19] unter dem bezeichnenden Titel *Augenscheinlicher Beweiß / daß ein GOtt sey / Hergenommen aus der Erkänntniß der Natur / und also eingerichtet / daß es auch die Einfältigen begreiffen können*[20]. Es ist das erste Zeugnis physikalischer Theologie aus seiner Hand. Weitere sollten folgen: *Astrotheologie oder Himmlisches Vergnügen in GOTT, bey aufmerksamen Anschauen des Himmels und genauerer Betrachtung der himmlischen Cörper zum augenscheinlichen Beweiß, daß ein GOTT, und derselbige ein Allgütigstes, Allweises, Allmächtiges Wesen sey*[21] von William Derham ist seine nächste Übersetzung. Sie ist, verständlicherweise, Brockes gewidmet, und damals wie heute besonders aktuell durch eine von Fabricius dem Werk hinzugefügte "Nachricht von den Scribenten, die durch Betrachtung der Natur die Menschen zu GOtt zu führen bemühet sind". Es folgt die Übersetzung der Derhamschen *Physico-Theologie*[22]. Schließlich verfaßt er eigene physikalisch-theologische Werke: 1732 eine Feuer-Theologie[23] und,

---

16 C. Bursian, *Geschichte der classischen Philologie in Deutschland* (München und Leipzig, 1883), 360.
17 H. Reincke, "Fabricius, Johann Albert", in: *Neue deutsche Biographie*, vol. 4, 732.
18 "Geschichte der Philologie", in: A. Gercke und E. Norden (Hrsg.): *Einleitung in die Altertumswissenschaft*, vol. 1, 1, p. 41.
19 1. Auflage Paris, 1713, unter dem Titel *Démonstration de l'existence de Dieu*.
20 Hamburg, 1714.   21 Hamburg, 1728.
22 Hamburg, 1730.   23 *Pyrotheologiae sciagraphia . . .* (Hamburg, 1732).

nebst beigefügter Bibliographie zur Geschichte des Seerechts, 1734 die Theologie des Wassers[24].

Wem ist unbekannt, daß Herr D. Fabricius das beste Mittel ergriffen, die Menschen auf die Wercke GOttes aufmercksam zu machen, und die verborgenen Schönheiten derer Geschöpfe in der Absicht zu entdecken, damit zugleich die Güte, Weisheit, Allmacht und Majestät GOTTES offenbaret werde? Durch seine Betrachtung des Feuers hat er die kaltsinnigen und achtlosen Menschen zur Liebe GOTTES angeflammet. Durch eine aufmercksame Betrachtung des Geräusches, und anderer Eigenschaften des Wassers, hat er uns den Mund wässerig gemachet, die Herrlichkeiten derer Geschöpfe genauer einzusehen, und uns zu mehrerer Bewunderung ihres Schöpfers erwecket und aufgemuntert. So hat er auch seinen Lesern Gelegenheit an Hand gegeben, bey bedachtsamen Anschauen des Himmels, ein Himmlisches Vergnügen in Gott zu finden[25].

Fabricius[26] lebte von 1668 bis 1736. 1686 hatte er in seiner Vaterstadt Leipzig Theologie, Philologie und Medizin studiert. Nach Hamburg kommt er 1694 als Famulus und Bibliothekar seines Förderers, des durch den Theater- und den späteren Renovationsstreit bekannten Johann Friedrich Mayer. 1699 promoviert er in Kiel zum Doktor der Theologie und übernimmt in Hamburg am Akademischen Gymnasium die Professur für Moral und Eloquenz, die er bis zu seinem Tode innehat – von 1708 bis 1711 auch das Rektorat des Johanneums. Der vita contemplativa zugetan, schlägt er drei Rufe deutscher Universitäten aus: Greifswald 1701, Gießen 1719, Wittenberg 1726. Fabricius führte ein einfaches und glückliches Familienleben.

Johann Hübner[27] aus Türchau bei Zittau, der zweite Teilnehmer an jener ersten Gelehrtenrunde, war dreiundvierzigjährig im Jahre 1711 als Fabricius' Nachfolger im Rektorat des Johanneums nach Hamburg gekommen. Er war von 1691 bis 1694 Privatdozent in Leipzig gewesen und hatte sich danach als Rektor des Merseburger Gymnasiums durch in mehrere Sprachen übersetzte geschichtliche und

---

24 Hydro-Theologie . . . (Hamburg, 1734).
25 Chr. Kortholt, "Rede, welche zum Gedächtnis des wohlsel. Hrn. D. Jo. Alb. Fabricii, der Moral und Beredsamkeit weltberühmten Profess. des Hamburgischen Gymnasii, in der grösseren Prediger-Gesellschaft zu Leipzig in der Academischen Kirche am 28. Jun. 1736. öffentlich gehalten", in: Reimarus, De vita Fabricii, (Anhang, 12s.).
26 Zu Fabricius: Reimarus, De vita Fabricii, und Reincke in Neue deutsche Biographie, vol. 4, 732–3.
27 Zu Hübner: Calmberg, Geschichts des Johanneums, 211–36; H. Schröder, Lexikon der hamburgischen Schriftsteller bis zur Gegenwart, vol. 3 (Hamburg, 1857), 413–19; H. Kaemmel, in: Allgemeine deutsche Biographie, vol. 13, 267–9; K. Goedeke, Grundriß zur Geschichte der deutschen Dichtung, vol. 3 (Dresden, 1887), 302; Kelter, Hamburg und sein Johanneum, 64–71.

geographische Lehrbücher den Ruf eines großen pädagogischen Neuerers erworben. Unvergessen aber blieb Hübner wegen seiner in über hundert Auflagen erschienenen und zum ersten Mal 1714 veröffentlichten *Zwey und fünfzig auserlesenen Biblischen Historien*[28]. Dieses "erste brauchbare Lehrbuch für den Unterricht in biblischer Geschichte", das in veränderter Gestalt noch bis in die neuere Zeit hinein benutzt wurde[29], erschien zwischen 1726 und 1748 auch auf Lateinisch, Italienisch, Französisch, Schwedisch und Polnisch, zum Teil in mehreren Auflagen. Nennenswerte Achtung als Rektor des Johanneums erwarb Hübner sich dagegen nicht, charakterlicher Mängel wegen hauptsächlich. Dennoch hatte seine Tätigkeit entschieden positive Seiten:

Hübners Bedeutung liegt in seinem Eintreten für pädagogische Reformen im Sinne der Frühaufklärung. Seine Lehrbücher bedeuten entschiedene Abkehr von der einseitigen Lern- und Abfrageschule zugunsten eines zukunftsträchtigeren Arbeitsunterrichtes. Die Aktualität der Hübnerschen Methode, ihre Brauchbarkeit hat 1870 noch Thomas Carlyle bezeugt[30]. Ein Vertreter der Frühaufklärung ist Hübner aber auch durch sein Eintreten für die Förderung der deutschen Sprache. Schon 1696 war in Leipzig sein *Poetisches Handbuch, das ist eine kurzgefaßte Anleitung zur deutschen Poesie* erschienen. Die Förderung der Muttersprache erfährt unter seinem Einfluß auch am Johanneum einen erheblichen Aufschwung. Stilistik und Übungen in deutscher Poesie nehmen in seinem Unterricht einen beträchtlichen Raum ein. An praktischer, zumal rhetorischer Betätigung seiner Schüler liegt ihm. So finden unter seinem Rektorat nach dem Examen jährlich öffentliche Redeübungen, sogenannte *actus oratorii*, statt, in denen neben den klassischen Sprachen auch das Deutsche gepflegt wird. In seiner Hinwendung zur Rhetorik, zur deutschen Sprache und Poesie[31], wird der Einfluß seines Zittauer Lehrers und Rektors Christian Weise deutlich, dessen Andenken er auch während seiner zwanzig Hamburger Jahre in Ehren hielt.

Ein anderer Anhänger der Weiseschen Richtung war Michael Richey[32], das dritte Mitglied des Bibliotheca-Historica-Kreises in

---

28 *aus dem Alten u. Neuen Testamente, der Jugend zum Besten abgefasset* (Leipzig, 1714).
29 Kelter, *Hamburg und sein Johanneum*, 65.   30 Ibid., 66.
31 Hübner ist selber als Dichter hervorgetreten. Siehe Werkverzeichnisse bei Schröder, *Lexikon*, und Goedeke, *Grundriß*.
32 Schütze, Vorreden zu *Richey: Deutsche Gedichte*, voll. 2 und 3; Schröder, *Lexikon*, vol. 6, 262–72; Goedeke, *Grundriß*, vol. 3, 342; M. von Waldberg in *Allgemeine deutsche Biographie*, vol. 28, 436–9.

Hamburg. Kennzeichnend für Richey, eine der einflußreichsten Persönlichkeiten der Frühaufklärung in Hamburg, ist das Eintreten für deutsche Sprache und Literatur, bürgerlichen Gemeinsinn und der *esprit philosophique* als Maßstab allen Urteilens und Handelns.

In welchem Umfang ihm an der Verschönerung der deutschen Sprache und der Emanzipation kulturellen deutschen Selbstbewußtseins gelegen war, zeigen seine *Deutschen Gedichte*[33], seine Aufsätze im *Patrioten*[34] und sein *Idioticon Hamburgense*[35], an dessen zweiter Auflage vom Jahr 1754 auch Johann Mattheson Anteil hatte, und welches das erste niederdeutsche Wörterbuch überhaupt ist[36]. Richey beteiligte sich überdies an den Ausgrabungen des durch die *Cimbrisch-hollsteinischen Antiquitäten-Remarques*[37] bekannten Altertumsforschers Christian Detlev Rhode. Der in Hamburgs Bürgerschaft durch die Reichsexekution von 1708 und den Hauptrezeß 1712 bewirkten Resignation und Staatsverdrossenheit[38] tritt Richey als unermüdlicher Förderer bürgerlichen Selbstbewußtseins entgegen. Sein ganzes Leben ist in diesem frühaufklärerischen Sinne "ein Zusammenhang von patriotischen Gesinnungen und Handlungen"[39] gewesen. Er ist der Panegyrist Hamburgs, aber er schmeichelt Hamburg, gerade w e i l er weiß, daß die Bürgerschaft seiner Zeit meist indolent und beschlußunfähig ist – weil er bürgerliche Betätigung zum Wohl des Gemeinwesens will. Von solch wohlbedachter Schmeichelei zeugen außer Richey-Beiträgen im *Patrioten* vor allem seine, oft von Telemann vertonten, Singgedichte[40]. Richeys Fortschrittlichkeit im Sinne seiner Generation besteht in seinem Eintreten für Selbstkritik, Maß und Vernunft als Richtschnur in allen Lebensbereichen. Bezeichnend für ihn ist dabei der Gedanke

33 Das gilt zumal für deren Inhalte.
34 *Der Patriot*, nach der Originalausgabe Hamburg 1724–6 in drei Textbänden und einem Kommentarband kritisch herausgegeben von W. Martens (Berlin, 1969N); zu Richeys Anteil siehe Scheibe, *Der "Patriot"*, 191–237.
35 Hamburg, 1743.
36 R. A. Th. Krause, "Michael Richey, der Verfasser des ersten niederdeutschen Lexikons", in: *Niedersachsen* 10 (1905), 317–19. Hier besonders p. 318.
37 Hamburg, 1720.
38 Im Zeitraum zwischen dem Hauptrezeß und den Jahren des *Patrioten* ist die Bürgerschaft wegen mangelnden Erscheinens ihrer Mitglieder in der Mahrzahl der Fälle beschlußunfähig. Cf. J. G. Gallois, *Chronik der Stadt Hamburg und ihres Gebiets, von der ersten Gründung bis auf die gegenwärtige Zeit*, vol. 4 (Hamburg, 1863), 1–44. Siehe auch F. Kopitzsch, "Hamburg zwischen Hauptrezeß und Franzosenzeit – Bemerkungen zur Verfassung, Verwaltung und Sozialstruktur", in: W. Rausch (Hrsg.), *Die Städte Mitteleuropas im 17. und 18. Jahrhundert* (Linz, 1981), 181–210, besonders 188s.
39 Schütze, *Richey: Deutsche Gedichte*, vol. 2, p. V.
40 Sie sind in vol. 2 seiner *Deutschen Gedichte* gesammelt.

der Milde, zumal im Zusammenhang mit der Religion. Er neigte der Toleranz zu, nicht dem Zelotentum, war ein "öffentlicher Feind der Heucheley und des Aberglaubens"[41], ohne den christlichen Glauben zu verleugnen.

Michael Richey war Hamburger und lebte von 1678 bis 1761. Am Akademischen Gymnasium hatte er unter Vinzent Placcius und Johann Friedrich Mayer studiert. 1701 bricht er sein 1699 in Wittenberg begonnenes Studium als Magister ab. Von 1704 bis 1713 ist er Rektor im schwedischen Stade, dann Privatmann in Hamburg, wo er 1717 Professor für Geschichte und Griechisch am Akademischen Gymnasium wird und somit Kollege seines Freundes Fabricius. Seine Frau hatte Richey schon 1712 nach sechsjähriger, glücklicher Ehe verloren. Von seinen vier Kindern überlebte ihn keines.

Drei Bereiche kennzeichnen Richeys Einfluß: seine Schüler, seine Gelegenheitsgedichte und die hamburgischen Gelehrtengesellschaften. Die Zahl seiner Schüler war erheblich, zu ihnen gehörten Persönlichkeiten wie Friedrich von Hagedorn, Johann Julius Surland, Johann Albert Heinrich Reimarus und Johann Georg Büsch, der am Ende des Jahrhunderts Richey als einen Menschen bezeichnet, "dessen Asche ich noch verehre", und bekennt: "Nie hat ein Mann meine Hochachtung in höherem Grade besessen, als er die meinige damals"[42]. Richey wurde geliebt. In seiner langen, vierundvierzigjährigen Amtszeit am Akademischen Gymnasium prägte er mehr als eine Generation im Sinne der Prinzipien des *Patrioten*. Man braucht zur Veranschaulichung Richeyschen Einflusses nur die Subskriptionslisten seiner *Deutschen Gedichte* zur Hand zu nehmen: Was im Hamburg jener Tage – von Hermann Samuel Reimarus und Eva König bis zu Johann Melchior Goeze und Telemanns Textdichter Christian Wilhelm Alers – Rang und Namen hatte, ist vertreten. Ebenso nachhaltig ist der Einfluß, den Richey durch die dem Bibliotheca-Historica-Kreis nachfolgenden Gelehrtengesellschaften ausübte:

Ich erinnere Mich mit Vergnügen einer vor 37 Jahren in Hamburg errichteten *Teutsch-übenden Gesellschaft*, die aber, welches zu bedauren, kaum ins vierte Jahr sich aufrecht hielte, und wovon ich nunmehro nur der einzige noch am Leben bin. Diese hatte das Glück und den Vortheil, daß sie von Anbeginn aus Männern von unterschiedenen Nationen bestund, deren Beyträge und Urtheile, in Sachen, den Ursprung und die Rechtschreibung der Wörter betreffend, billiger massen angenommen, erwogen, und zum gewissen Nutzen in der Wahl und Bestätigung des besten angewendet

---

41 Ibid., p. XL.
42 *Ueber den Gang meines Geistes und meiner Thätigkeit* (=*Erfahrungen*, vol. 4) (Hamburg, 1794), 119, 121.

wurden. Also war der grundgelahrte Hr. D. Johann Albert Fabricius ein Meißner, der wolverdiente Hr. Rector Hübner ein Lausitzer, der scharffsinnige Hr. Secretaire Samuel Triewald ein Schwede, der fleissige und beliebte Hr. Johann Ulrich König ein Schwabe. Die übrigen, nehmlich der hochberühmte Hr. Barthold Henrich Brokes, I. V. L. nebst dem Hn. Georg Jacob Hoefft, I. V. D. und mir, waren Nieder-Sachsen[43].

Wöchentliche Sitzungen hält diese Gelehrtenrunde[44] vom 19. Januar 1715 bis zum Herbst 1717 ab. Sie hatte sich Gesetze gegeben, die eine Woche zuvor von Brockes, König, Richey und Fabricius unterzeichnet worden waren. Als Ziel der Teutsch-übenden Gesellschaft sehen diese Gesetze die Hebung der deutschen Sprache und Poesie vor. Sie verlangen aber auch die Mitgliedschaft von sechs Personen. Also tritt ihr im August 1715 der sich in Hamburg aufhaltende schwedische Gouvernementssekretär Samuel Triewald (1688–1743) bei, und im September der Anwalt und spätere Richter am hamburgischen Niedergericht Georg Jakob Hoefft (1686–1719). Als bereits einen Monat darauf Triewald die Gesellschaft verläßt[45], wird im November Johann Hübner aufgenommen, so daß mit ihm, Fabricius und Richey nunmehr drei Mitglieder des Bibliotheca-Historica-Kreises dieser neuen Gelehrtenrunde angehören.

Vor den Augen seiner Freunde von der Teutsch-übenden Gesellschaft entsteht unter anderen Brockes' *Irdisches Vergnügen in Gott*[46]. Besonders anschaulich läßt sich am Beispiel Königs der freundschaftliche Charakter, der verändernde Einfluß und die Lebendigkeit dieser Zusammenkünfte zeigen.

Königs[47] Geschmack und Denkweise sollte diese Gesellschaft erheblich beeinflussen. Noch in seiner Vorrede zu Brockes' Marino-Übersetzung[48] hatte er sich zugunsten Lohensteins geäußert und die Vorbildlichkeit der Opern-Textdichter Postel, Hunold, Feind und

---

43 Richey, *Idioticon Hamburgense*, XII.
44 Cf. Chr. Petersen, "Die Teutsch-übende Gesellschaft in Hamburg", in: *ZVHG* 2 (1847), 533–64, und R. A. Th. Krause, "Die Teutsch-übende Gesellschaft in Hamburg", in: *Niedersachsen* 12 (1907), 186–8.
45 Der Ansicht, Triewald sei im Herbst 1715 von seiner Regierung nach Stockholm zurückgerufen worden und habe d e s h a l b die Gesellschaft verlassen müssen, widerspricht M. Lamm, "Samuel Triewalds lif och diktning", in: *Samlaren* 28 (1907), 112–73, hier 116.
46 9 voll. (Hamburg, 1721–48).
47 Cf. J. Chr. Rost, Vorrede zu *Des Herrn von Königs Gedichte* (Dresden, 1745); Goedeke, *Grundriß*, vol. 3, 336, 346–7; M. Rosenmüller, *Johann Ulrich von König. Ein Beitrag zur Litteraturgeschichte des 18. Jahrhunderts*, phil. Diss. (Leipzig, 1896).
48 B. H. Brockes, *Verteutschter Bethlemitischer Kinder-Mord des Ritters Marino . . . sammt einer Vorrede, Leben des Marino, und einigen Anmerckungen von König* (Hamburg, 1715).

Bressand hervorgehoben. Nun begegnet er in Fabricius und Richey dem Bedürfnis nach Klarheit und Eleganz, in Richey und Hübner überdies dem Streben nach einer Vorherrschaft der Vernunft in der Poesie. Er revidiert seine Leitbilder:

Richey allein kann für eine ganze Menge gelten: denn er schreibt sehr sinnreich, natürlich und wohlfliessend; und wenn man ja hin und wieder einige Wortspiele oder so etwas zu hochsteigendes bey ihm noch izo antrift, so ist es weniger dem Mangel an gutem Geschmack, als der Thorheit des gelehrten Pöbels daselbst zuzuschreiben, dem zu gefallen er manchmal dergleichen einfliessen lassen muss, weil solche Leute sonst glauben, man könne nicht scharfsinnig, oder, wie sie sagen, hoch schreiben, sobald sie verstehen, wass sie lesen. Da er doch sonsten in unsrer Hamburg. deutsch-übenden Gesellschaft, davon Brocks, Er und Ich die Stifter gewesen, allezeit wieder die schwülstige hochtrabende Schreibart gestritten, und in allen dergleichen Meynungen sich beständig auf meine Seite geschlagen, bis sich endlich nach meiner, und eines andern gelehrten Mitglieds Abreise, die Gesellschaft völlig getrennt[49].

Königs Wertschätzung für Richey beruht auf Gegenseitigkeit. Dessen nach einem, übrigens nie aufgeklärten, Mordanschlag auf König[50] entstandenen Verse bezeugen es:

Ein Bley, das klüger war, als sein verfluchter Schütze,
Gieng Deine Brust vorbey, und streifte nur die Hand.
Der Himmel, der den Schuß so gnädig abgewandt,
Zeigt wunderthätig an, was Recht und Unschuld nütze.
Du aber, falscher Neid, was hat dich angetrieben,
Daß dein verdammt Gewehr die edle Hand verletzt,
Die Hand, an deren Kiel sich Phoebus selbst ergetzt?
Du weist nichts mehr, als dieß: Sie hat zu schön geschrieben[51].

Wie die Freunde, so macht sich auch König um diesen Gelehrten-kreis verdient. Er diskutiert mit ihm seine Vita des Marino, rezitiert eigene, beifällig aufgenommene Gelegenheitsgedichte und Epigramme, schlägt ein historisch-kritisches Kompendium aller in Hamburg bislang gespielten Opern auf quellenkundlicher Grundlage vor und verfaßt, "gewissermaßen als Einleitung" dazu eine Rezension der ersten, 1678 am Gänsemarkt aufgeführten Oper *Adam und Eva* von Richter und Theile[52]. Königs Vorschlag wird begrüßt, aber von

---

49 Brief Königs an Johann Jakob Bodmer vom 28. März 1724, zitiert nach Rosenmüller, *Johann Ulrich von König*, 67.
50 Er wurde am 7. März 1715 auf offener Straße verübt und mißglückte. Als Anstifter kamen mehrere persönliche Feinde in Frage.
51 Chr. Fr. Weichmann (Hrsg.), *Poesie der Nieder-Sachsen*, vol. 3 (Hamburg, 1726), 245.
52 Rosenmüller, *Johann Ulrich von König*, 83s. Das Journal der "Teutsch-übenden Gesellschaft" enthält laut Rosenmüller diese Rezension unter Nr. XXXVIII. Er

der Gesellschaft nicht ausgeführt. Mattheson wird diesen Plan später wieder aufgreifen: mit einem chronologischen Verzeichnis der Hamburger Opern im *Musicalischen Patrioten*[53].

Wie gültig das Bündnis zwischen Musik und Literatur auch in diesem Kreise war, zeigt ein an die Freunde gerichtetes Brockes-Gedicht: *Die Laute der Belisa besungen von Belisander*. Diese Verse spielen auf eine tatsächliche Begebenheit an, und ihre Heldin ist niemand anderes als Ilsabe Brockes geborene Lehmann, die der Dichter und spätere Ratsherr 1714 geheiratet hatte:

Die Liebhaber seiner Schriften kennen dieselbe unter dem Nahmen der Belisen; und die Verehrer von Tugend, Artigkeit, Gottesfurcht und Schönheit kennen sie als eine Person, bey der alle diese Stücke mit einer außerordentlichen Geschicklichkeit in der Musik und Französischen Sprache vereiniget[54].

Brockes' Verse über Belisens Lautenspiel sind zugleich eine Verbeugung vor der Musik Georg Friedrich Händels:

So scheints, ob Ihre Hand auf unsichtbare Ahrt
Ein himmlisch Glocken-Spiel mit güld'nen Strickchen zöge,
Und ob die schlanke Hand nicht sprünge, sondern flöge.
Die Sinne folgen Ihr, die Herzen fliehn und stehn,
Nachdem die Fluchten hoch, schnell oder langsam gehn.
Bald singt ein Griff allein, bald rauscht der Töne Menge,
Und macht in Luft und Ohr ein liebliches Gedränge
Von lauten Cirkelchen; bald teilt Sie Mass' und Zeit,
In unbeschreiblicher geschwinder Fertigkeit,
Mit Regel-mässigen unzäligen Manieren.
Oft drohet Sie mit Fleiß, den Wollaut zu verlieren,
In einem falschen Ton; doch zeucht die kluge Hand
Aus einem harten Klang und herben Gegen-Stand
Noch süss're Zärtlichkeit. Will Sie aus Hendels Stücken
Mit einem sanften Satz des Hörers Ohr erquicken:
So greift ein jeder Griff ihm so die Sinnen an,
Daß er den Wunder-Ton nicht g'nug bewundern kann.
Die Saiten weiß Ihr Geist so künstlich auszudehnen,
Daß eine süsse Klag', ein fast verliebtes Sehnen,
Aus todten Sehnen bricht. Gefällt Ihr denn die Eil:
So gleicht an Schnelligkeit kein Sturm, kein Stral, kein Pfeil,
Kein Blitz, kein Wirbel-Wind den wolgemess'nen Sprüngen,
Die Ihrer raschen Hand niemalen mißgelingen.

verweist dabei auf die vormalige Stadtbibliothek (Staatsbibliothek) in Hamburg als Standort. Cf. p. 79.
53 Hamburg, 1728.
54 G. W. Götten, *Das jetztlebende gelehrte Europa, Oder Nachrichten von Den vornehmsten Lebens-Umständen und Schriften jetzt lebender Europäischer Gelehrten*, vol. 1 (Braunschweig, 1735), 35.

> Der Töne Menge bricht, gleichwie ein Strom hervor,
> Und scheint's, man hör' in Ihr den ganzen Musen-Chor.
> . . . .
> Euch, die ihr Sie gehör't, ersuch ich tadelt nicht,
> Ob hätt' ich Ihren Rum nicht hoch genug getrieben!
> Ihr andern, wenn ihr denkt, hier wäre viel erdicht't:
> So hör't Sie erst, dann sprecht, ob ich zu viel geschrieben[55].

Der Freundeskreis bleibt die Antwort nicht lange schuldig. "Als die, vordem hieselbst blühende so genannte Teutsch-übende Gesellschaft, einsmals bey Hrn. Brockes Ihre Zusammenkunft hatte, und zufälliger Weise durch das unvergleichliche Clavier und Lauten-Spiel der Belisa vergnüget wurde: hatte, mit beybehaltenen Reimen, folgenden Einfall zur Antwort an Belisander Richey":

> Wir, die wir Sie gehör't, wir tadeln freylich nicht
> Ob hätt'st du Ihren Rum, aus Gunst, zu hoch getrieben;
> Es hat die Stärke selbst in deinem Lob-Gedicht'
> Ein Wunder solcher Kunst noch viel zu schwach beschrieben[56].

Der Verfasser des *Irdischen Vergnügens in Gott* galt seinen Zeitgenossen als deutscher Dichter von Rang. Er nutzte seinen Einfluß als Ratsherr dazu, Telemann nach Hamburg zu ziehen und trug als solcher im Jahre 1722 nicht unwesentlich zum endgültigen Bleiben seines Freundes bei[57].

Zur Zeit der Teutsch-übenden Gesellschaft hatte der 1680 in Hamburg geborene Barthold Heinrich Brockes[58] Studium und Bildungsreise bereits hinter sich, seine politische Laufbahn aber war noch nicht begonnen. Er hatte in Halle Jura studiert, war danach für kurze Zeit ans Reichskammergericht in Wetzlar gegangen, hatte Deutschland, Italien, die Schweiz, Frankreich und die Niederlande bereist

---

55 *Poesie der Nieder-Sachsen,* vol. 1, 271–2. 56 Ibid., 272.
57 H. P. Fry, "Barthold Heinrich Brockes und die Musik", in: *Barthold Heinrich Brockes (1680–1747), Dichter und Ratsherr in Hamburg. Neue Forschungen zu Persönlichkeit und Werk* (herausgegeben von H.-D. Loose) (Hamburg, 1980), 71–104, besonders 88–90.
58 Cf. J. M. Lappenberg, "Selbstbiographie des Senators Barthold Heinrich Brockes", in: ZVHG 2 (1847), 167–229; A. Brandl, *Barthold Heinrich Brockes* (Innsbruck, 1878). U.-K. Ketelsen, *Die Naturpoesie der norddeutschen Frühaufklärung* (Stuttgart 1974), 25–42; G. Guntermann, *Barthold Heinrich Brockes' "Irdisches Vergnügen in Gott" und die Geschichte seiner Rezeption in der deutschen Germanistik* (Bonn 1980); die Aufsätze von J. Klein, I. M. Kimber, H. P. Fry, G. H. Sutton, G. Guntermann, U.-W. Ketelsen u. das Verzeichnis der Schriften von u. über Brockes (bearbeitet von Fry mit Beiträgen von Guntermann) in: D. Loose, *Barthold Heinrich Brockes.*

und war nach seiner Promotion zum Lizentiaten beider Rechte in Leyden 1704 nach Hamburg zurückgekehrt, wo er zunächst privatisierte. In diese Zeit fällt seine Teilnahme an den Sitzungen der Gesellschaft. Als er 1720 Ratsherr wird, gehört diese allerdings schon der Vergangenheit an, trotz unstreitiger Verdienste:

Allein, da der Mitglieder nur so wenige waren, und in kurtzer Zeit, durch absterben und verreisen, noch weniger wurden, den übrigen aber meistentheils tägliche und mühsälige Ampts-Verrichtungen oblagen; so muste nothwendig, in einer blossen Neben-Arbeit, viel gutes im Entwurffe oder rohen Vorrathe liegen bleiben, und kamen nur etliche, nebenläuffig in der Versammlung verlesene, kleine Aufsätze zur Reife, davon es dem Hn. Hof-Rath Weichmann gefallen, einige seinen Sammlungen der Poesie der Nieder-Sachsen[59] vorzufügen. Wir musten uns also damit zufrieden geben, daß nicht lange hernach, aus denselben Mitgliedern, in die Stelle der erloschenen Grammatischen Gesellschaft, eine Moralische, nehmlich die Patriotische, wieder eintrat, mit welcher es. wegen leichteren und mehren Beytrittes, besser, als mit der Teutsch-übenden, fort wollte, wie davon die am Tage liegenden wolaufgenommenen und schon oft wieder aufgelegten Schriften[60] Zeugniß geben, als worin man, nebst der sittlichen Haupt-Absicht, zum wenigsten durch ein gutes Beispiel, auch der Teutschen Sprache keine Unehre zu machen, bemühet gewesen[61].

Auch die *Patriotische Gesellschaft*[62] – es ist die erste ihres Namens – versteht sich zu wöchentlichen Sitzungen. Die Vorbereitungen zu ihrer Gründung sind bereits im November 1723 im Gang, ihr Sprachrohr, die moralische Wochenschrift *Der Patriot*, erscheint vom 5. Januar 1724 bis zum 28. Dezember 1726, und die Gewohnheit regelmäßiger Sitzungen behält sie bis zu ihrer Auflösung im Jahr 1748 bei. Von Mitgliedern des vorigen Freundeskreises sind wiederum Fabricius, Brockes und Richey dabei. Die deutsche Literatur ist durch zwei neue Namen vertreten: den Journalisten Christian Friedrich Weichmann (1698–1770) und das korrespondierende Mitglied Pastor Michael Christoph Brandenburg (1694–1766) aus Sterley bei Mölln. Noch ein anderer Geistlicher, der Kaplan am English Court John Thomas (1691–1766), gehört dem Kreise an, aber auch der Kunst- und Juwelenhändler Johann Adolf Hoffmann (1676–1731). Auffallend

59 Sie erschien in sechs Bänden (Hamburg, 1721–38).
60 Der *Patriot* erfuhr vier Neuauflagen in Buchform: 1728–9, 1737–8, 1746 und 1765.
61 Richey, *Idioticon Hamburgense*, XIII.
62 Zur Geschichte der Patriotischen Gesellschaft von 1724 cf. II. Hubrig, *Die patriotischen Gesellschaften des 18. Jahrhunderts* (Weinheim, 1957); J. Scheibe, *Der "Patriot"*; J. Rathje, "Geschichte, Wesen und Öffentlichkeitswirkung der Patriotischen Gesellschaft von 1724 in Hamburg", in: *Deutsche patriotische und gemeinnützige Gesellschaften* (herausgegeben von R. Vierhaus) (=Wolfenbütteler Forschungen vol. 8) (München, 1980), 51–69; grundlegend für den *Patrioten* betreffende Fragen ist die Untersuchung von Scheibe.

aber ist, daß an den Aktivitäten dieser Gesellschaft, abgesehen vom Dichter und Ratsherrn Brockes, noch vier weitere Ratspolitiker teilnehmen: der Ratssyndikus Johann Julius Surland (1687–1748), der Ratsherr und spätere Bürgermeister Conrad Widow (1686–1754), Ratssyndikus Johann Klefeker (1698–1775) und der 1727 zum Sekretär beim Kollegium der Oberalten bestellte Anwalt Johann Julius Anckelmann (1692–1761).

Weichmann edierte außer der *Poesie der Nieder-Sachsen* Dichtungen Brockes'[63] und Postels[64]. Hoffmanns in zehn Auflagen erschienenen *Zwey Bücher von der Zufriedenheit*[65] galten dem Freundeskreis als Manifestation zum Ruhm der praktischen Vernunft. Klefekers größtes Verdienst ist seine zwölfbändige *Sammlung der hamburgischen Gesetze und Verfassungen*[66] mit ihren historischen Einleitungen, eine dem Gemeinwohl geltende Leistung im Sinne der Frühaufklärung – für die hamburgische Sozial- und Kulturgeschichte eine Quelle ersten Ranges, deren Wert, so Gottfried Schütze, darin besteht, "daß [wir] uns von unsern Verfassungen nicht mehr dunkle und verwirrte, sondern deutliche und bestimmte Begriffe zu machen vermögend sind"[67]

Außer Widow und Anckelmann treten sämtliche genannten Mitglieder des Kreises auch als Verfasser von Aufsätzen im *Patrioten* hervor, dessen 156 Stücke Satiren, Dialoge, Fabeln, Träume, Porträts, Erzählungen, fingierte und echte Leserbriefe enthalten. Den wöchentlichen Diskussionsergebnissen entsprechend, die sich "aus den Quellen des natürlichen Rechtes und der Sitten-Lehre, imgleichen der Stats- und Haushaltungs-Kunst"[68] herleiten, fällt der Inhalt der Wochenschrift aus: eine – oft amüsante – Unterhaltung einer fiktiven Verfasserfigur, des "alten Patrioten", mit ihren Lesern über Barbarei und Zivilisation.

Die Patriotische Gesellschaft stellt gelehrte Geselligkeit wesentlich in den Dienst des Gemeinwohls. Es geht um die Aktivierung persön-

---

63 *Irdisches Vergnügen in Gott*, voll. 1 und 2 (Hamburg, 1721 und 1727); *Verteutschter Bethlemitischer Kinder-Mord des Ritters Marino*, 3. Auflage (Hamburg, 1727).

64 *Der große Wittekind, in einem Heldengedicht von Christian Henrich Postel . . . Mit einer Vorrede von dessen Leben und Schriften, herausgegeben von C. F. Weichmann* (Hamburg, 1724).

65 *nach Anleitung der Vernunft- und Glaubens-Gründe verfasset* (Hamburg, 1722).

66 *in bürgerlichen, kirchlichen, Kammer-, Handlungs- u. übrigen Polizei-Angelegenheiten u. Geschäften* (Hamburg, 1765–73).

67 G. Schütze, *Register über die sämmtlichen zwölf Theile der Sammlung hamburgischer Gesetze und Verfassungen mit historischen Einleitungen nebst einer Betrachtung über den Inhalt des ganzen Werks* (Hamburg, 1774), 4.

68 M. Richey, "Zuschrift" zu *Der Patriot. Neue und verbesserte Ausgabe, mit vollständigem Register* (Hamburg, 1728–9), vol. 3 (1729), IX–X.

licher Bereitschaft zur Betätigung in öffentlichen Angelegenheiten und die Erlangung der zu diesem Zweck erforderlichen Urteilsfähigkeit:

Es befindet sich in dieser Stadt eine Gesellschaft guter Freunde, die sich einmahl in der Woche mit erbaulichen Unterredungen die Zeit zu vertreiben gewohnt ist. Sie führet zugleich ein besonderes Absehen, gelehrten und artigen Fremden solchen Umgang mit anzubieten, und sodann einem jeden nach seinem Zweck hiesigen Aufenthalt angenehm und nützlich zu machen . . .
Ihr Haupt-Zweck gehet dahin, ohne Anstellung kostbahrer Reisen fremde Länder zu besehen, und durch die verschiedenen Erzehlungen sich eine so lebhafte Vorstellung von denselben zu machen, als wenn sie daselbst persönlich gegenwärtig wären. Sie halten anbey ein ordentliches Protocoll, um aus den bemerckten Verfassungen anderer Völcker wahr zu nehmen, was zu dem Wohlstande des Vaterlandes nützlich ist[69].

Als gemeinnützig gilt den Mitgliedern der Redaktionsgemeinschaft vor allem die im *Patrioten* vorgetragene Kritik an Mißständen i n n e r h a l b der, im übrigen von ihnen bejahten, gesellschaftlichen Verhältnisse der Stadt, deren bürgerliche Ratsverfassung sie lobend hervorheben, um Hamburgs desinteressierte Bürgerschaft zur Wahrnehmung der eigenen Angelegenheiten zu bewegen.

Vier Jahre nach Einstellung der Redaktionsarbeiten, im Jahre 1730, nimmt die Patriotische Gesellschaft den inzwischen als Dresdner Hofdichter allseits gefeierten Johann Ulrich von König anläßlich eines Besuches in Hamburg als Mitglied auf. Weitere Beitritte folgen: Ratsherr Nicolaus Stampeel (1673–1749) und Ratssyndikus Clemens Samuel Lipstorp (1696–1750) im Jahre 1732 und, im darauf folgenden Jahr, Prinz Karl von Bevern (1713–80), der wenig später als Herzog Karl I. zu Braunschweig und Lüneburg von 1735 bis 1780 regieren wird, sowie dessen Hofmeister von Haimburg.

Trotz ursprünglich anonymen Erscheinens des *Patrioten*[70] wirkt die Patriotische Gesellschaft auf die Öffentlichkeit. Das tut sie nicht zuletzt deshalb, weil sie im Rat eine Art Fraktion bildet, die sich lange nach Erscheinen der letzten Nummer der Zeitschrift noch zu Wort meldet[71]. Überdies sollten ihre gemeinnützigen Vorstellungen in politisch-praktischerer Gestalt mit der zweiten Patriotischen Gesellschaft von 1765 wieder aufleben.

---

69 Martens, *Der Patriot*, vol. 3, 72.
70 Erst in der Zuschrift von 1729 nennt Richey die Verfasser.
71 Cf. dazu die Darstellung dieser Fraktion in E. Neumeisters Brief an E. S. Cyprian vom 18. August 1736. Mitgeteilt von Th. Wotschke, ''Erdmann Neumeisters Briefe an Ernst Salomo Cyprian (Schluß)'', in: *ZVHG* 31 (1930), 181.

Der Kreis jener, die der Patriotischen Gesellschaft von 1724 freundschaftlich verbunden waren oder zumindest die dem gemeinen Besten geltenden Überzeugungen der Redaktionsgemeinschaft teilten, dürfte umfangreich gewesen sein. Zu Recht sind von anderer Seite[72] eine Anzahl von Persönlichkeiten ihrem Bekanntenkreis zugerechnet worden: Johann Hübner; der Philologe und Bibliothekar Johann Christian Wolf (1689–1770) und dessen von Fabricius geförderter Bruder Johann Christoph (1683–1739), der Orientalist und Pastor an St. Katharinen; der von Brockes geschätzte Hauslehrer Christian Ludwig von Hagedorns und Wochenschriften-Herausgeber Johann Georg Hamann d. Ä. (1697–1733) sowie Johann Christoph Wolfs und Fabricius' Schüler Hermann Samuel Reimarus (1694–1768), der Verfasser der *Schutzschrift*[73], der außer der Biographie seines Schwiegervaters auch den Katalog zu dessen Bibliothek[74] und aus Hoffmanns Nachlaß die *Neue Erklärung des Buchs Hiob*[75] herausgab sowie Schriften auf Surland und Widow verfaßte[76]. *Patrioten*-Beiträge verfaßten zudem die nicht der Gesellschaft angehörenden Autoren Friedrich von Hagedorn (1708–54) und der seit 1723 amtierende Bürgermeister Johan Anderson (1674–1743) sowie zwei Auswärtige: der Richey-Schüler und Rektor des Lübecker Katharineums Johann Heinrich von Seelen (1688–1762) und der in Basel lebende Dichter Carl Friedrich Drollinger (1688–1742). Der Patriotischen Gesellschaft verbunden war freilich auch Johann Mattheson, der den Mitgliedern der Redaktionsgemeinschaft, seinen "insonders Hochgeehrtesten Herren und Hochgeneigten Gönnern" die *Grosse General-Baß-Schule*[77] widmet und in einem dem Werk vorangestellten Sonett zeigt, daß die für die ältere hamburgische Kulturgeschichte charakteristische Beziehung zwischen Literatur und Musik auch auf diese Gesellschaft anwendbar ist:

72 Scheibe, *Der "Patriot"*, 54.
73 Reimarus arbeitete an dem Manuskript bis zu seinem Tode. Gedruckt wurde es vollständig erst vor einem Jahrzehnt: H. S. Reimarus, *Apologie oder Schutzschrift für die vernünftigen Verehrer Gottes* (herausgegeben von G. Alexander), 2 voll. (Frankfurt, 1972). Weiteres zu Reimarus siehe *Hermann Samuel Reimarus, Handschriften-verzeichnis und Bibliographie* (zusammengestellt und eingeleitet von W. Schmidt-Biggemann) (Göttingen, 1979).
74 *Bibliothecae beati J. A. Fabricii*, 4 voll. (Hamburg, 1738–41).
75 *Joh. Adolph Hofmann's neue Erklärung des Buchs Hiob, mit einer Paraphrase und Vorbericht von Hiob's Person, Buch und dessen Auslegern vermehrt* (Hamburg, 1733).
76 *Pietatis officium memoriae Jo. Jul. Surlandi, J. U. L. et reip. Hamb. Protosyndici praestitum* (Hamburg, 1745); *Vita optime de patria meriti Consulis Conr. Widovii, J. U. L. publice exposita* (Hamburg, 1754).
77 Hamburg, 1731.

117

Es war mein *Patriot*, der musicalisch heisst,
    Vor Jahren kühn genug, sich IHNEN, sonder Fragen,
    (Weil ja bey allen nur ein Hertz, ein Sinn, ein Geist)
Als einem eintzeln Mann, wolmeynend anzutragen;

Itzt aber, da die Welt, was ich nicht durffte sagen,
    Wie viel der Männer sind, ein theures Mit-Glied weis't,
    Mit Nahmen jeden nennt, und nach Verdiensten preis't,
Kann ich es unverblümt auch endlich einmahl wagen:

Ich widme, schönste Zunfft, die niemahls gnug zu loben,
DIR also dieses Buch, voll Lehr- und Wahrheits-Proben
    Von solcher Art Music, die eben nicht gemein.

Was bessers reicht' ich gern, wenn ich was bessers hätte.
Bin ich denn weder Glied noch Kleinod DEINER Kette,
    So werd ich lebenslang doch ihr Gebundner seyn.

Aus den Freundeskreisen und Gelehrtenzirkeln ist offenbar auch
Weichmanns *Poesie der Nieder-Sachsen*[78] hervorgegangen.
Weichmann, der ohnehin schon die Redaktionsarbeit des *Patrioten*
besorgte, läßt die ersten drei Bände der Anthologie von 1721 bis 1726
erscheinen. Ihre dreibändige Fortsetzung besorgt von 1732 bis 1738
der seit 1728 in Hamburg lebende ehemalige Professor der
Kirchengeschichte und der schönen Wissenschaften Johann Peter
Kohl. Ein Blick auf die über siebzig Autoren der Sammlung macht
deutlich, mit welcher Selbstverständlichkeit Textdichter der Oper
und Angehörige der Gelehrten- und Freundeskreise derselben literarischen Tradition zugeordnet werden. Und so finden sich unter den
Verfassern neben dem Opernkritiker Wernicke wieder die Librettisten Postel, Feustking, König, Beccau und Feind. Fabricius und
Richey als Mitglieder des Bibliotheca-Historica-Kreises und der
Teutsch-übenden Gesellschaft sind mit deren Vertretern Brockes,
Hoefft, Triewald sowie König vertreten, der zusammen mit den zuvor
genannten Gesellschaftern Fabricius, Richey und Brockes gemeinsam
mit Brandenburg, Surland und Weichmann zu den Anthologie-Beit-
trägern des *Patriotischen* Freundeskreises gehört. Aber auch *Patrioten*-Sympathisant und -Beiträger Friedrich von Hagedorn ist Autor der *Poesie der Nieder-Sachsen*. Georg Philipp Telemann
(1681–1767) ebenfalls.

Neue Namen kommen hinzu. Die Gelehrtenschulen sind zusätzlich
durch den ab 1732 amtierenden Rektor des Johanneums Johann
Samuel Müller (1701–73) und den von 1719 bis 1743 am Akademi-

---

78 Dazu: A. Schmidt-Temple, *Studien zur Hamburger Lyrik des 18. Jahrhunderts.
(Kantate. Serenata. Oratorium. C. F. Hunold)*, phil. Diss. (München, 1898); R. P.
Bareikis, *The German Anthology from Opitz to the Göttingen Musenalmanach.*
Ph.D. Diss. (Harvard, 1965).

schen Gymnasium wirkenden Konrektor Johann Joachim Neudorf
(169?–1752) vertreten. Zwei Privatgelehrte, der Anthologie-Herausgeber Johann Peter Kohl (1698–1778) und Matthäus Arnold
Wilckens (?–1759), der Sohn des bekannten Archivars, gehören
ebenso zu den Verfassern wie zwei weitere Ratspolitiker: Bürgermeister Garlieb Sillem (1676–1732) und der seit 1734 als Legationssyndikus tätige Johann Richey (1706–38), Michael Richeys Sohn. Auch
vier Hamburger Geistliche, die nicht in unmittelbarem Zusammenhang mit der Oper oder den Gelehrtengesellschaften hervorgetreten sind, befinden sich unter den Dichtern: der Diakon und
spätere Archidiakon an St. Petri Johann Christoph Krüsike
(1682–1745), der Ministeriumskandidat Johann Hartwig Mayer, von
dem nur wenige Lebensdaten bekannt sind, Tobias Heinrich Schubart
(1699–1747), der 1728 Archidiakon an St. Michaelis wurde, und der
von Erdmann Neumeister geförderte spätere Diakon an St. Katharinen
und Dichter der Telemannschen *Landlust* Joachim Johann Daniel
Zimmermann (1710–67). Erwähnenswert als Autor dieser Sammlung
ist auch Jacob Friedrich Lamprecht (1707–44), der den *Hamburgischen Correspondenten* der Jahre 1737 bis 1740 herausgibt und
später Sekretär bei Prinz Heinrich von Preußen wird.

Zwei Lübecker Beiträger sollten wegen ihrer Verbindung zur hamburgischen Gelehrtenrepublik jener Tage nicht übergangen werden:
Johann Heinrich von Seelen und der Hauptpastor von St. Marien,
Senior des Lübecker Geistlichen Ministeriums, Jacob von Melle
(1659–1743), Postels Freund.

Es würde den Rahmen dieser Darstellung sprengen, wollte man sie
auf die in der Anthologie mit abgedruckte Auswahl von Manuskripten aus den Sitzungsprotokollen der Teutsch-übenden
Gesellschaft ausweiten. Eine solche Untersuchung aber, ebenso wie
die Berücksichtigung der Personen, die in der *Poesie der Nieder-
Sachsen* als Adressaten von Gelegenheitsgedichten erscheinen,
würde den Eindruck noch verstärken, daß während der Jahre der
ersten Patriotischen Gesellschaft es der hamburgischen Gelehrtenrepublik gelungen war, ihr Kommunikationsnetz erheblich zu erweitern und daß sie, durch ihr Eintreten für gemeinnützige Aktivitäten, ihre Verbindungen bis zu den politisch maßgebenden
Kreisen der Kaiserlich Freien Reichsstadt ausgedehnt hatte.

Aus solchen Kreisen stammte der Dichter Friedrich von
Hagedorn[79]. Dieser Beiträger des *Patrioten* und der *Poesie der Nieder-*

---

79 Cf. *Friedrichs von Hagedorn poetische Werke* (herausgegeben von J. J. Eschenburg),
vol. 4 (Hamburg, 1800), 1–110; H. Stierling, *Leben und Bildnis Friedrichs von
Hagedorn* (Hamburg 1911); W. Schultze, "Die Brüder Hagedorn", in: *Archiv für*

Sachsen hatte nach einem Rechtsstudium in Jena sich seinerseits um eine Stelle im – dänischen – diplomatischen Dienst bemüht, konnte nachweisbar aber lediglich eine zweijährige, bis 1731 dauernde Anstellung als Privatsekretär des dänischen Gesandten von Söhlenthal in London erhalten, bis er schließlich im Jahre 1733 Sekretär bei der Handelsgesellschaft des English Court in Hamburg wird, dessen Schriftverkehr er übernimmt. Schon bald hat auch Hagedorn einen in unserem Zusammenhang erwähnenswerten Freundeskreis um sich geschart. Büsch erinnert sich:

> Bis vor etwa vierzig Jahren hatte Hamburg eine Anzahl schöner Geister und wiziger Köpfe, die man gewöhnlich um Mittag auf dem Saal des damals Dresserschen Koffe-Hauses beisammen fand. Hagedorn, der sich nicht gern anders, als dort, oder an der Tafel seiner Freunde sprechen lies, fand sich täglich da ein, und so jedermann, dem ein solcher Umgang behagte, mit aller Freiheit, die ein Koffe-Haus giebt[80].

Dieser Kreis setzt dabei auf seine Weise fort, was andere vor ihm begonnen hatten. Die Stadt besaß, wie Hagedorns Biograph Johann Joachim Eschenburg ausführt,

> während der Lebensperiode unsers Dichters eine nicht kleine Anzahl gelehrter und einsichtsvoller Männer, von einem nach Verhältniß der damaligen Zeiten glücklich und vielseitig ausgebildeten Geschmack. Die patriotische Gesellschaft, die im J. 1724 gestiftet wurde, und eigentlich Fortsetzung der ehemaligen deutschübenden Gesellschaft war, trug viel dazu bei, diese Männer einander noch näher zu bringen; und durch geselligen Umgang und feinern Weltbrauch unterschieden sie sich sehr vortheilhaft von den mehr isolirten und selten so traulich vereinten akademischen Gelehrten, bei denen es gewöhnlich auch Kollisionen giebt, die hier bei der Mannichfaltigkeit der Aemter, Pflichten und Lebensweisen wegfielen. Hagedorn fand also den Ton eines geselligen, heitern, und doch belehrenden Umganges unter dieser Klasse von Hamburgs Einwohnern schon gestimmt; er slebst aber trug in der Folge nicht wenig bei, ihn zu veredeln und noch mehr zu beleben[81].

Außer im Dresserschen Kaffeehaus traf man Hagedorn

> mehrere Jahre hindurch jeden Freitag an dem Mittagstische seines vertrautesten Freundes Carpser, wo sich dann die geistvollsten Männer und Reisende jedes, selbst fürstlichen, Standes desto williger einfanden, um seiner Gesellschaft zu genießen. Carpser selbst, dem Hagedorn in seinem

Kulturgeschichte 41(1959), 90–9; G. Stix, *Friedrich von Hagedorn. Menschenbild und Dichtungsauffassung* (Rom 1961); K. S. Guthke, "Friedrich von Hagedorn und das literarische Leben seiner Zeit im Lichte unveröffentlichter Briefe an Johann Jakob Bodmer", in: *Jahrbuch des Freien Deutschen Hochstifts* (1966), 1–108. Schröder, *Lexikon*, vol. 3, 53–64; Goedeke, *Grundriß*, vol. 4, I (3. Auflage), 25–8; K. Wölfel, in: *Neue deutsche Biographie*, vol. 7, 466–7.
80 *Ueber den Gang meines Geistes*, 239.
81 Eschenburg, *Friedrichs-von Hagedorn Werke*, 14.

achten Sinngedichte ein so wahres als schönes Denkmal errichtet hat, war einer der unterhaltendsten und interessantesten Männer. Sein Verdienst als Wundarzt und Gesellschafter wird noch jetzt in Hamburg oft gerühmt, und man hat die alte Benennung der Straße, wo er wohnte, mit dem jetzt ganz gangbaren Namen der Carpserstraße vertauscht[82].

Neben Peter Carpser (1699–1759) begegnet man in Hagedorns Hamburger Freundeskreis auch Personen, die schon in anderem Zusammenhang aufgetreten sind: Brockes, Zimmermann und Matthäus Arnold Wilckens. Aber auch hier erscheinen neue Namen. Neben einem weiteren Arzt, Christoph Lipstorp (1694–1754), gehören zum Hagedornkreis der englische Prediger Murray[83], der Buchhändler und Hagedorn-Verleger Johann Karl Bohn (1712–73), der von Lamprecht geförderte Dichter und spätere Sekretär des Prinzen Georg Ludwig von Holstein-Gottorf Johann Matthias Dreyer (1716–69) sowie zwei Journalisten: der Redakteur der "Gelehrten Sachen" des *Hamburgischen Correspondenten* von 1732 bis 1764, Hagedorns Studienfreund Joachim Friedrich Liscow (1705–?) und der seit 1745 als Chefredakteur des *Correspondenten* tätige Barthold Joachim Zinck (1718–75), der während Brockes' Ritzebütteler Amtmannschaft von 1735 bis 1741 dessen Kinder als Hauslehrer unterrichtete, dann Sekretär und später, bis 1773 Legationsrat an der kurhannöverschen Vertretung in Hamburg war.

Keine gesicherten Aussagen lassen sich über Hagedorns Aktivitäten in dem von Mattheson gegründeten Orden des Guten Geschmacks[84] machen, dessen Kanzler er 1734 war. Genauso wenig ist über den Orden selbst bekannt, zu dem immerhin Persönlichkeiten zählen wie Hagedorns, Carpsers und Liscows Freund, der Anwalt und spätere Großfürstlich Holsteinische Postdirektor Joachim Barthold Borgeest (1701–71) und der Librettist Johann Philipp Praetorius (17?? – ca. 1775), der später als Professor in Trier Jura lehrte.

Ähnlich wie die Frage nach der Verfassung des Ordens und seiner Aktivitäten auf eine Antwort noch wartet, bedarf auch die Realisierung und Weiterentwicklung des im *Patrioten* verkündeten Programms durch den Hagedornkreis[85] einer klärenden Untersuchung.

82 Ibid., 15.   83 Über ihn war nichts in Erfahrung zu bringen.
84 Siehe Schröder, *Lexikon*, vol. 3 55s., und Cannon, *Mattheson*, 69–70, 194. Lebensdaten zu den Ordensmitgliedern Philipp Krieger, Johann Leptho, Heinrich Friedrich Pilgram und Johann Wolff waren nicht zu ermitteln.
85 F. Kopitzsch, "Die Hamburgische Gesellschaft zur Beförderung der Künste und nützlichen Gewerbe (Patriotische Gesellschaft von 1765) im Zeitalter der Aufklärung", in: *Deutsche patriotische und gemeinnützige Gesellschaften* (cf. Anm. 62), 74.

Hagedorn, dessen Freundeskreis weit über Hamburg hinausreichte, wirkte auf die Zeitgenossen vor allem durch seine Lieder und gehört bis heute mit seinem dichterischen Werk zum Kanon der deutschen Literaturgeschichte, in der man – begreiflicherweise – den größten Teil der in diesem Beitrag genannten Namen vergeblich suchen wird. Aber für jene dennoch nicht bedeutungslosen Glieder der hamburgischen Gelehrtenrepublik im Zeitalter Matthesons, denen die Nachwelt vorenthielt, was sie Hagedorn schenkte, gilt möglicherweise dessen "Prophezeiung" vom Jahre 1754:

> Freund, sterb ich einst, so wird ein Bösewicht,
> Der itzt noch schweigt, mir keinen Nachruhm gönnen
> Und über mich und meinen Wert erkennen.
> Es mag geschehn! Den Schnarcher fürcht ich nicht.
> Aus Demut nur will ich ihn dir nicht nennen.
> Sein Tadel ehrt mehr als ein Lobgedicht[86].

86 Fr. von Hagedorn, *Gedichte* (herausgegeben von A. Anger) (Stuttgart, 1968), 180. Zum Nachweis der Lebensdaten Hamburger Autoren siehe, wenn nichts anderes angegeben: H. Schröder, *Lexikon der hamburgischen Schriftsteller bis zur Gegenwart*, 8 voll. (Hamburg, 1851–83).

PART II

Mattheson as composer and writer on music

6

Johann Mattheson's "Inquiring Composer"

BEEKMAN C. CANNON
New Haven, Connecticut

In the fall of 1724, Johann Mattheson published an article entitled Des fragenden Componist as Part V of *Critica musica*, the musical journal he had founded two years earlier.[1] Divided into two so-called hearings constituting the first two issues of the second book of the journal in its complete published form, its full title is "First (and Second) Hearing of the Inquiring Composer on a Certain Passion." In an accompanying footnote Mattheson carefully explains that "because it is deemed necessary to presume that people in many localities may not know what a Passion is, the word means the history of Christ's sufferings, which is musically presented in the oratorio style."[2] Obviously this definition is sufficiently broad to include the traditional "histories" of the Gospels and, at the opposite extreme, poetic paraphrases of them provided by contemporary writers that were used from time to time by Mattheson and his contemporaries.

Mattheson's point of departure in his article is the mosaic text of a Passion by the Hamburg poet Christian Postel as set to music around 1700. Postel's poetic contributions are carefully designed to be inserted at various points within the account of the Passion and crucifixion of Christ contained in the nineteenth chapter of the Gospel of St. John. In accordance with the tradition concerning the original manuscript. Friedrich Chrysander asserted that George Frideric Handel was its

1 *Critica musica / d.i. / Grundrichtige / Untersuch- / und / Beurtheilung, / Vieler, theils vorgefaßten, theils einfältigen / Meinungen, Argumenten und Einwürffe, so in / alten und neuen, gedruckten und ungedruckten, / Musicalischen Schrifften / zu finden / . . . Von Mattheson. Erstes Stück. Hamburg, im May 1722* (-CM when cited in the text of this article).
2 *Des fragenden Componisten / Erstes Verhör / über eine gewiße Passion*. The footnote reads: "Weil man an vielen Orten nicht weiß, was eine Passion in diesem Verstande sey, so habe für nöthig erachtet zu sagen, daß es die Geschichte vom Leiden Christi bedeute, welche, auf oratorische Art, musicalisch vorgestellet wird."

125

composer, in his authoritative biography published in 1919.[3] Though Chrysander was familiar with Mattheson's article, he was apparently unaware of Mattheson's subsequent setting of Postel's text (as *Das Lied des Lammes*) in 1723 and paid no heed to this composer's statement that the earlier composition was made "some twenty or thirty years ago," which implies only that it was composed around 1700. Indeed, Chrysander stated that Handel set Postel's text in 1704 when he, like Mattheson, was serving his musical apprenticeship at the Hamburg opera. On the basis of his attribution this work was subsequently published in a number of editions, and became generally known as Handel's *Passion according to St. John*. In 1964 it was included as authentic in the *Hallische Händel-Ausgabe* by Karl Gustav Fellerer, who, while citing a number of reservations about its authorship, argued that on balance it was an early work of Handel's.[4] This is no longer the opinion of many Handel scholars, among whom Bernd Baselt has summarized a number of convincing reasons against the traditional Chrysander attribution.[5] But if Handel was not the composer, the question remains as to who was the first to set Postel's text to music?

In the absence of any conclusive evidence to date, the identity of the composer of Handel's *St. John Passion* is still a tantalizing question. It is possible, however, to advance strong reasons for disqualifying both Handel and Mattheson. In his "Inquiring Composer" Mattheson contents himself with describing this work as the product of a young composer in his student days, now (in 1724) a "welt-berühmt" man (CM II, 18). Handel was only one of Mattheson's contemporaries, including himself, whom the latter characterized as "world-famous," or as "le premier homme du monde." If it is reasonable to give fair weight to his statement that the work was composed more than twenty years before his own setting of 1723, it is unlikely, to say the least, that either of them would have been commissioned to write it. To be sure, Mattheson was in his own opinion as much of a prodigy as his somewhat younger friend Handel was.[6] Between 1699 and 1704

3 F. Chrysander, *G. F. Händel* (Leipzig, 1919), vol. 1, 90–101.
4 Georg Friedrich Händel, *Passion nach dem Evangelisten Johannes*, ed. K. G. Fellerer, in: *Die hallische Händel-Ausgabe*, Serie I/2 (Kassel, 1964) (-H).
5 B. Baselt, "Händel und Bach: Zur Frage der Passionen", *Bericht über das wissenschaftliche Kolloquium der 24. Handelfestspiele der DDR, Halle, 1976* (Halle, 1977), 58–66. See also W. Braun, "Echtheits- und Datierungsfragen im vokalen Frühwerk G. F. Händels", *Händel-Ehrung der DDR, Halle 1959: Konferenzbericht* (Leipzig, 1961), 61–3.
6 Despite the famous duel between the two men, described by Mattheson in his *Ehrenpforte*, 94–5, they were close friends up to Handel's departure for Italy, and remained in touch throughout Handel's life. See Cannon, *Mattheson*, 31–2.

he seems to have been engrossed in the Hamburg opera, for which he composed four operas, wholly or in part. He fails to acknowledge the composition of any sacred music before 1715, as the newly appointed director of music for the cathedral, and it is hardly credible that he could have resisted listing this *Passion according to St. John* in one or another of the various published catalogs of his achievements as evidence of his youthful if misguided prowess. Handel, on the other hand, was but fifteen years old in 1700, and it is totally inconsistent with his mature creative habits not to have redeployed portions of this music in his later compositions had he been the composer.

As the first modern scholar to call attention to Mattheson's "Des fragenden Componist," Chrysander assumed that the "certain Passion" of the article's title referred to Handel's composition rather than to Postel's so-called *History of Christ's Sufferings*. He appears to have ignored or misread Mattheson's footnote, interpreting the article as an attack on his hero's youthful essay by a contemporary critic jealous of Handel's fame.[7] It is not surprising that many later biographers and Handel scholars were content to rely on this assessment,[8] for a scrupulous reading of "The Inquiring Composer" itself reveals no indication that the author's explicit prescriptions for Postel's text refer directly to a second oratorio on the same text by Mattheson himself. Since the article presents no musical examples to illustrate the author's precepts, Mattheson's readers could hardly be expected to make such an identification either, unless they perused the previous issues of *Critica musica* as carefully as he perhaps expected them to, or were directly acquainted with his *Lied des Lammes*.[9]

Nevertheless, this oratorio by Mattheson is also a setting of Postel's text.[10] Furthermore, it is the specific if unacknowledged model for his remarkable exposition of the aesthetic precepts confronting an enlightened composer of his day. Indeed its existence drastically alters the significance of the "Inquiring Composer," for together oratorio and article provide the inquiring connoisseur and scholar of eighteenth-century music with unique evidence of how an outstanding composer-critic of this epoch applied contemporary aesthetic principles to practical composition.

Das Lied des Lammes, on Postel's Passion text, was composed by

---

7 Chrysander, *Händel*, 90f.

8 K. G. Fellerer in the Foreword to the *St. John Passion* summarizes the main points of criticism of Handel's oratorio in Mattheson's discussion.

9 Johann Mattheson, *Das Lied des Lammes*, ed. B. C. Cannon (Madison, 1971)-M. See also Cannon, *Mattheson*, Crit. Biblio., No. 87.

10 Cannon, *Mattheson*, 45–62, 180–1.

Mattheson the year before he published his "Inquiring Composer," and he directed its performance shortly afterward during Holy Week of 1723 in Hamburg Cathedral. During the eight previous years of his incumbency as director of music there, he had composed some twenty-two works for various Sundays and particular liturgies in the church year, including two other passion oratorios. Thus *Das Lied des Lammes* appeared at the height of his career as a composer of sacred music, and for many reasons he seems to have been particularly proud of it.[11] Neither this work nor any of its companions was published, however, and with the exception of Mattheson's setting of the Brockes Passion, there is no evidence to date that any copies of them were made for contemporary performance outside of Hamburg.[12]

Critica musica, the first monthly musical periodical to be published, made its initial appearance in May 1722. It was clearly Mattheson's intention to employ the new medium of journalism as a means of carrying on and disseminating the arguments advanced in his earlier treatises. It was also to be the vehicle for the continuing exposition of new musical data, ideas, and issues. He establishes in characteristic fashion the tone of this new endeavor in the foreword to the first issue:

The beauty of a garden cannot in itself check the growth of weeds, for the richer the soil the more they will grow. In the wonderful garden of music, I have here and there torn up . . . ancient, deep-rooted, obstinate, thorny, tenacious, disorderly, savage, barbarous brush with all my strength in order to throw it away. I have also frequently thought it would not easily come up again since it must have been reduced to ashes, root and branch, in the fire of reason. But look! no sooner is one spot cleaned up than there appears yet another scandalous annoyance reproducing ancient ignorance in rejuvenated garb (*CM* I, Vortrab, [i]).

Read today in its complete form, *Critica musica* is a varied but homogeneous work designed to bring its readers up to date with a wide variety of musical knowledge through a combination of learned, critical articles and direct news reports. It completes Mattheson's defense in the running battle with his musical opponents initiated in the first of the *Orchestres.* But it also presents crucial arguments to justify the modernization of the traditional contrapuntal devices of sacred music by application of the improvements in modern theatrical style. The locus of this latest offensive is the fifth article, "des Fragenden Componist." Within the context of Mattheson's objectives

11 Ibid., 45f.
12 Ms. of Brockes Passion, Mus. ms. 14,900, Staatsbibliothek Berlin.

stated in the opening pages of the journal and of its contents as a whole, it is difficult to interpret this article as an effort to discredit the talents of the first composer of Postel's Passion. Such an interpretation, indeed, becomes untenable in view of a news item in the tenth issue of the first volume of *Critica musica*, published presumably in February 1723. With its Hamburg dateline it is the only such notice referring to Mattheson's own activities as a composer, it is one of the very few announcements of the contents of subsequent issues, and it provides the direct link between the article itself and the passion oratorio *Das Lied des Lammes*. It reads:

> Meanwhile, sacred music has appeared somewhat more diligently here, and among others the *Autor Criticae*, God be praised, will also direct on 7 March in the Cathedral Church on the occasion of this Anatomie a new and particular Passion, which will include divers *artificia harmonia* such as *Contrapunti doppi, all'ottava, al'a dodecima, Fughe doppie di tre e quattro Soggeti, Canoni overo Fughe legate in Hipodiapente*, and the like; [these] will be freely executed in a modern and melodious style so that the customary dryness of such artifices may scarcely be noticed. The composer has done this, however, not to impute to himself unique knowledge or a great monopoly of such *inventiunculae* – on the contrary, merely to demonstrate (1) that he did not learn to compose only yesterday, (2) that he neither hates nor despises them, and (3) that one may make use of them *magna cum dosi salis melodici*. Indeed, he has been so minded in connection with this task to fashion and set forth at the first opportunity some sixty critical composition-questions, which may be of service to many readers (CM I, 288).

The defensive tone of this news item is striking. In addition to emphasizing his own convictions about the primacy of musical composition, it first of all suggests that Mattheson was smarting from the sting of invective to which he had been subjected, and which, to be sure, he had been returning with interest. Secondly, it constitutes a strong assertion of his prowess and experience as a composer. To be sure, his post provided the opportunity to use opera singers exceptionally freely as soloists in the performance of his oratorios, and considerable local publicity resulted from such a scandalous practice.[13] But his wider reputation in 1724 was probably as one-sided as that of his great contemporary Johann Sebastian Bach, who was known to Mattheson and his contemporaries only as a prodigious performer and a learned composer for the organ. Of all Bach's contemporaries, Mattheson made the most strenuous efforts to acquire

---

13 *Ehrenpforte*, 201–3; Cannon, *Mattheson*, 50. The only oratorio by Mattheson of which a copy appears to have been made for performance outside of Hamburg is his setting of the Brockes Passion, *Der für die Sünde der Welt gemarterte und sterbende Jesus* (Cannon, *Mattheson*, Crit. Biblio., No. 58).

factual information about the lives and works of his musical colleagues in order to present his findings not only in the projected *Ehrenpforte* but from time to time in his other publications. Yet, while praising Bach's organistic talents and, some years later, his phenomenal skill in the learned art of counterpoint,[14] he makes no allusion to Bach as a composer of liturgical music in Weimar or in Leipzig. Despite his own, as he believed prodigious, contributions to sacred music in Hamburg Cathedral, this announcement indicates that they were unknown to his contemporaries, and that he in turn was known only as a theorist and critic.

Another important feature of this announcement, however, is the assertion that the usual dryness of contrapuntal artifices, catalogued so proudly, will be overcome by the modern, melodious style in which they will be clothed. The objective is clear: The tradition and heritage of the antique style is still admirable, but its learned, pedantic limitations will be overcome only by the composer who understands and applies modern melodic knowledge. Here indeed is Mattheson's boldest definition of the central artistic problem facing the Lutheran composer; a successful solution to it is identified as the oratorio he had just completed, *Das Lied des Lammes*. The object of "The Hearings of the Inquiring Composer" in the second book of *Critica musica* is made clear and unequivocal: the questions and the answers contained therein are designed to provide a composer with the practical precepts needed to compose an oratorio poem in a "modern, melodious style."

"The Inquiring Composer" is unique among Mattheson's theoretical works because, as mentioned earlier, it contains no musical illustrations or quotations whatsoever of either exemplary or erroneous settings of a text. After the introduction Melophile, the inquiring composer, asks a total of sixty-three questions on the correct method of composing each section of "a certain Passion" text.[15] Mattheson's responses, of varying length, provide criticisms of the musical deficiencies of the earlier setting and verbal prescriptions of how a composer should set them to music correctly. In this way he demonstrates his convictions that the grammatical, rhetorical, and affective qualities of prose texts (as well, of course, as the structure,

14 *Melodische Wissenschaft*, 147.
15 Postel's poetry was obviously written some time before the composition of the "Handel" St. *John Passion*. Excerpts of the text were first published by Hunold (Menantes) in his *Theatralische, galante und geistliche Gedichte von Menantes* (Hamburg, 1705). See also n.20.

meter, and accentuation of poetic texts) are the decisive factors in musical composition.

At the outset a number of questions arise about Mattheson's choice of this particular Passion text as the basis for a searching analysis by the inquiring composer as well as for his own oratorio. From the introduction and Melophile's opening question it is apparent how strongly he felt the need to explain his decisions. First of all he seeks to forestall criticisms and objections from those familiar with the earlier setting who might question the propriety of making comparisons with the work of a "celebrated composer."

I know full well . . . that I can set forth various points about a *piece* that was made twenty or thirty years ago and, from our knowledge of that time, was well known . . . I do not intend to censure the former efforts of one or another, much less to extract from these excerpts the least blame. . . On the contrary, I wish to show that our art rests upon weak props; that one day should learn from the other, though this does not yet happen, and that one will become most knowledgeable [from observing] even the false steps of great men, and consequently must search for and find stronger foundations and better *Principia*. Next to the glory of God, that is my aim (CM II, 3).

It is surprising that Mattheson's composition on a text previously set to music by a "world-famous" man (and Melophile's professed intention to do likewise) should require such an apologia (CM II, 5). He certainly knew how frequently his predecessors and contemporaries adopted this procedure in composing operas. And only five years earlier, he himself had set to music the much-admired oratorio text by Heinrich Brockes entitled *Der für die Sünde der Welt Gemarterte und sterbende Jesus*, which had also been recently set by three of his leading contemporaries.[16] This had inspired no prefatory apologia – not even a defense of his own musical procedures or of "theatrical church music," such as he was wont to give. Now, however, he sets forth three conditions to justify his action.

The first of these is the purpose for which the composition is undertaken. "If [it] is to expose the mistakes of a world-famous man and to flaunt his errors in order to flatter myself," he writes, "then my conduct cannot be approved of. But if my purpose is for God's honor and not my own, the edification of listeners, and the furtherance of knowledge . . . then one should praise it on all counts" (CM II, 5). To amplify this argument he asserts that "music is rich enough in both melody and its independent harmony for one to make alterations

16 Reinhard Keiser in 1712, Telemann and Handel in 1716.

easily without offense to essentials, and many composers may set the same text in as many different ways.[17] Secondly, many words may have an effect, an in-dwelling expressiveness, missed by the first composer because of faulty emphasis. Thirdly, with respect to the immediate example, many intelligent people have considered that the earlier work should be greatly altered" (*CM* II, 5).

The second of the requisite conditions is the interval of time; twenty to thirty years is adequate to justify a new setting (*CM* II, 11). The third is "occasion." This is explained in such a way as to suggest, without being explicit, that Mattheson composed *Das Lied des Lammes* in order to avoid acceding to requests for a new performance of the earlier score. He argues that examination of the earlier work reveals that many statements were set "contra sana principia melodica," and that it was better to compose the text again than to make the necessary corrections. Finally, "a new composition by a distinguished man might also be expected, and what was good for one man is equally satisfactory for another" (*CM* II, 11–12).

Though the final clause of this statement sounds somewhat equivocal today it reflects perhaps a typical attitude of composers such as Mattheson toward the literary raw materials with which they composed some of the most-admired works. Among the multitude of operas and oratorios composed by his European contemporaries little is known about the relationship between a poet, the opera or oratorio text he writes or compiles, and the composer who sets it to music. In Hamburg, as elsewhere in Europe, there was obviously an enormous demand for textual materials for cantatas, oratorios, and the like, and a large supply of verse turned out by poets and scribblers was available in manuscript or print.

Christian Postel, the author of the poetry for the *St. John Passion* composed by Mattheson and his predecessor, was one of these. Born in 1658 near Hamburg, he studied law at Leipzig, and, after graduating from Rostock in 1683, he made the grand tour of Holland, England, France, and Italy. Thus equipped, he settled down to the life of a typical Hamburg patrician, practicing law and writing poetry. Between 1688 and 1702 he wrote and published no fewer than twenty-eight opera and ballet texts for works performed at the Ham-

17 Mention of the riches of melody inspires a six-page digression on the preeminence of melody over harmony in refutation of a series of specific assertions to the contrary found in Rameau's *Traité de l'harmonie* (Paris, 1722). It is characteristic of Mattheson never to miss an occasion to defend his most passionate convictions about the fundamentals of muscial composition irrespective of the context. CM II, 6f.

burg Opera.[18] Unfortunately no copy of Postel's original text, nor the textbook presumably printed for the first performance of his *St. John Passion*, has come down to us.[19] It is clear, however, that his creative function was restricted to the writing of stanzas commenting or reflecting upon the succession of episodes in the Passion of Christ recounted in the nineteenth chapter of the Gospel according to St. John (the portion assigned to Good Friday) to be inserted at the appropriate places in the unaltered text of the Gospel. In 1705, the year after Postel's death, his literary colleague Hunold (Menantes) wrote in his *Theatralische, galante und geistliche Gedichte:* "The late Licentiate Postel has written divers *Arien* in a Passion made from them, several of which I cannot forbear to extract because they are too little known."[20] The stanzas he printed are the aria texts numbered 8, 35 and 39 in Mattheson's oratorio.[21] Hunold's enthusiasm for the poetic qualities of Postel's stanzas may have influenced Mattheson's choice of text for his passion oratorio, and his severe criticism of the uneven qualities of the poetry, as well as its diverse styles, suggests that the challenges it offered an enlightened composer were more appealing than repugnant.

The same reasons appear to justify his writing of "Des Fragenden Componist." Though neither composer nor title of the earlier work is mentioned by name, a number of musical features are discussed in such explicit detail that the reader can only assume that they refer to an actual work. Frequently these criticisms are made with such strong expressions of disdain, even horror, at the seriousness of the errors committed as to take on a distinctly personal note. But the reader is nevertheless reminded from time to time that they exemplify the errors and ignorance of the past, preserved because of faulty educa-

18 H. Schröder, *Lexikon der hamburgischen Schriftsteller bis zur Gegenwart* (Hamburg, 1851–93), vol. 6, 99f.

19 A photostat copy of the textbook for *Das Lied des Lammes,* formerly in the Hamburg Stadtbibliothek, is in the John Herrick Jackson Music Library, Yale University.

20 Hunold (Menantes), *Theatralische . . . Gedichte,* 34: "Der Seel. Hr. Licentiat Postel hat unterschiedliche Arien in einer vor diesm gemachten Passion verfertiget, dass, weil sie in weniger Händen, ich nicht unterlassen kan, ein paar herause zu ziehen." This is the first edition of Hunold's work, new editions and prints of which appeared during the next several decades issued by various publishers. Though the text is altered in many instances, Postel's stanzas recur in all the editions I have been able to examine.

21 Throughout this article numbered references such as these refer to my edition of Mattheson's oratorio. Because there are many differences between these numbers and those in various editions of the "Handel" *Passion,* I have provided a collation of Mattheson's score and Handel's as published in the *Hallische- Händel-Ausgabe* as an appendix to this article.

tion by the conservative Lutheran cantors and musicians Mattheson was so eager to enlighten. His own solutions are certainly intended to exemplify the dramatic style of the modern, "galant" composer. Again, many prescriptions are so explicitly described that only an obtuse reader, or one who had missed the earlier announcement, would assume that Melophile-Mattheson is not alluding to a work in being. It is thus difficult not to regard Mattheson's article as another example of his arrogance, designed to extol his own abilities as a composer.

The general procedure Mattheson follows in his article is a logical one, and in the context of the whole, even his digressions are elements in a consistent line of argument. As Melophile proceeds from each section of the oratorio text to the next his questions expose the "errors" of various sorts in the earlier musical setting, and provide occasions for Mattheson's prescriptions. As pupil and Master progress, the former occasionally raises questions which have already been answered, thus provoking the latter to increasingly sharp, ironic rejoinders. This form of scrutiny appears to be thorough, but at its conclusion the Master warns Melophile that most of his remarks are "intended [only] to avoid mistakes, with the exception of what has been incidentally interspersed in questions 7, 11, 12, 17, 21, 31, 32, 37, 47, 51 and 52" (CM II, 54). Thus Mattheson, in the role of the rational critic, eagerly and enthusiastically rejects and "sweeps out the accumulated rubbish of the past" and provides both rational, up-to-date principles and practice in their place. Such ruthless demolition of past examples finally prompts Melophile to ask what is to be done when so many errors are encountered "in the works of great, world-famous Masters, whom everyone praises and should praise." Mattheson replies that there is "no better advice than to take refuge in sound reason. . . . No man is so great that one cannot point to mistakes made thirty years or even thirty days . . . ago. No one is so great that there is none greater" (CM II, 18f). This theme of progressive improvement, a doctrine most ardently preached during the period of the Enlightenment, Mattheson had already discussed at some length several years earlier in his *Forschendes Orchestre*.[22]

Postel's Passion text is examined in questions and answers ranging from limited matters of punctuation to broad questions of aesthetic procedure. Despite Mattheson's frequent tendency toward discursiveness and complex verbiage, his mind was an orderly one. The many topics he discusses group themselves under a small number of

22 *Orchestre* III, 83f.

headings, such as the recognition and avoidance of antiquated techniques and stylistic procedures; proper and improper methods of treating matters of punctuation and rhetoric in music; the correct choice of style and techniques in accordance with the specific dramatic situation; and the analysis of the passions contained in the poetic texts, with the proper methods of setting them to music.[23] A mere summary of Mattheson's recommendations would however be misleading if not supported by generous quotations from his writing. It would fail to capture the intensity of his critical sentiments and the flavor of his mode of literary expression, as well as the mixture of the rational, the theological, and the technical arguments he deploys. It would also leave the reader with an inadequate sense of his preoccupation with details as well as with broad aesthetic questions.

Postel's version of the Passion text begins directly with the opening verse of the Gospel for Good Friday (John 19:1). The earlier composer seems to have been content to commence his composition *in medias res*, in accordance with traditional liturgical practice, but the considerable growth and development of the musical passion as a work of art by 1723 makes such an abrupt opening unacceptable to Mattheson. His curt reply to Melophile's pointedly phrased question ("is it a good thing to begin a magnificent piece of church music with a short *recitativo*?") is: "A composer must find such a beginning naked and blunt. He has the right without offending the poet to insert a verse of a hymn or the like as a *ripieno*; for example, the first stanza of *Christus der uns seelig macht*, which explains what has happened to our beloved Savior up to the scourging" (CM II, 12). Since Postel provides no textual introduction to the second part of the oratorio,[24] Melophile is again advised to "take a chorale concerned with the crucifixion and put it at the beginning" (CM II, 44). These recommendations are in accord with Hunold's definition of an oratorio in 1722,[25] though

---

23 A very few questions and answers fall outside these general topics, because they are concerned with the writer's personal taste. An example is Mattheson's objection to the fashion of accompanying arias continuously with ritornellos (CM II, 52, No. LXII).

24 It is to be noted that F. Schroeder in his widely used edition of Handel's *Passion* inserted introductory Sinfonias and four chorales from the later passion oratorio in recognition of this weakness; see *Passion according to Saint John* (Heidelberg, 1956).

25 *Die Allerneueste Art zur Reinen und Galanten Poesie zu gelangen. Allen Edlen und dieser Wissenschaft geneigten Gemüthern, zur vollkommenen Unterricht mit überaus deutlichen Regeln, und angenehmen Exempeln aus Licht gestettet von Menantes* (Hamburg, 1722), 272, XVI: "Sie ist aber kürtzlich also beschaffen, daß ein Biblischer Text mit Arien, unter einander gewechselt werden. Bisweilen thut man auch ein oder ein Paar Gesetze aus einem Choral Gesang dazu." Mattheson,

Mattheson himself had composed a passion in 1721 without including any chorale stanzas whatsoever.[26]

If a stanza of a hymn is appropriate textual material for an introduction to the Gospel narrative, two musical questions arise concerning the proper opening of such an oratorio. Should there be a long introductory *symphony*, and should the chorale itself be set as a fugue (CM II, 12–13)? Mattheson's negative answer to the first question suggests a rapid change in musical taste of which he disapproves. "In my opinion, no," he writes, "though some good composers, because they regard instrumental music as something special, seem to be so much in love with long symphonies or sonatas that they make their exordium as long as an entire sermon. . . . Twenty-four ordinary measures is quite long enough for such a music, which in itself is not short" (CM II, 12–13). (His own "Sonatina" serving as introduction to *Das Lied des Lammes* amounts to only thirteen measures of common time.) Horace's *Ars poetica* supplies a "melopoetic" reason for rejecting the suggestion of a choral fugue:

All beginnings in nature are *uni* and *simple*, plain and simple . . . I have drawn many very melopoetic ideas from *Ars poetica*, especially those which concern the *scientia melodica*. As concerns this particular chorale, neither the text, "Christus der uns seelig macht," nor the melody would be very appropriate for a fugue. For although one could force the melody into a fugue, the words contain merely a narration whose meaning becomes clear only in the fourth line and is therefore much too long for a *thema fugae*. You should there proceed with the plain chorale melody, and so enrich it that devotion will be increased by (1) appropriate changes of the voices, (2) a good full accompaniment, and especially (3) through the progressions of the bass (CM II, 13).

Melophile is persuaded to follow these precepts in fashioning the introductory chorus but, still anxious to show his contrapuntal dexterity, he repeats this question at the opening of the second part of the oratorio. "Now I should like to do something else. What do you think of *contrapunta alla dodecima?*" "That's aiming high," cautions the Master. "In God's name, try out your skill, but don't go too far. Put the cantus firmus in the voices and the counterpoint in the instruments so as not to interfere with the understanding of the words. Bring in some subtle interludes, and take as much care as possible that

Capellmeister, 221: "Denn ein Oratorium ist gleichsam eine geistliche Oper und die göttliche Materie verdient es vielmehr als die menschliche, daß man sie nicht schläfrig ausarbeite. Bey Opern ist alles Schertz; In Kirchen ist alles Ernst, oder sollte es doch seyn."

26 *Der Blut-rünstige Kelter-Treter und von der Erden erhöhete Menschen-Sohn*. See Cannon, *Mattheson*, 175–6.

no one notices the want of freedom" (*CM* II, 45). In Mattheson's settings of these sections of his oratorio the integrity of the chorale melodies is carefully maintained; in the opening chorus the center of musical interest is in the bass line, which generates complex harmonies; in the second section the affective content of the four-part chorale is underlined by dissonant suspensions in the opening phrases of the tenor part, and elsewhere in the other parts, in contrast with the energetic contrapuntal figuration of the strings (M.2 and 33).

Underlying all Mattheson's writing on the art of melodic composition is his concern for the correct "translation" of verbal rhetoric into melodic structure. The repetition of important words or phrases for purposes of oratorical or dramatic emphasis in sermons or ceremonial rhetoric was a prominent element of taste inherited from the previous century. Equivalent musical emphasis was achieved by setting such words to elaborate melismas, as well as by repetition of them. Mattheson is totally unsympathetic to the verbal and musical values these procedures had represented; his encounter with the French style of declamatory recitative during his years at the Hamburg Opera, and his reading and study of contemporary discussions on this subject, led him to regard these practices as contrary to reason and common sense. The earlier passion oratorio reflects many of these stylistic features of the late seventeenth century.[27] Thus it provides a number of examples of various kinds of errors, which the naive questions of Melophile reveal, and consequently a number of opportunities to explain "correct" procedures.

One of Melophile's first questions calls attention to this practice, exemplified by the use of a *passaggio* on the word "geißelt" in the opening recitative of the "Handel" passion. To Mattheson this is a glaring example of the antiquated style, which is inappropriate in a recitative where information is being presented. It is therefore silly and tasteless (*CM* II, 13–14). His advocacy of a declamatory, syllabic style for expository recitative puts him directly at odds with the long-standing German tradition of emphasizing words of affective action by melismas of sinuous shape, exemplified extensively and powerfully in J. S. Bach's *St. John Passion*, composed in the same year as Mattheson's.[28] Mattheson supports his opinion by quoting from one of his favorite sources of French taste, Bonnet's *Histoire de la musique et de ses effets*, (Paris, 1715).[29] Inevitably, when the earlier

---

27 W. Dean, *Handel's Dramatic Oratorios and Masques* (London, 1959), 13f.
28 J. S. Bach, *Passionsmusik nach dem Evangelisten Johannes*, in: *Bach-Gesellschaft*, vol. 12, 54: "Barabbas aber war . . ."
29 Bonnet-Bourdelot, *Histoire de la musique et de ses effets*, vol. 4, 61.

composer, like Bach, underlines the word "gekreuziget" with a brief melisma, he condemns it as "tasteless." (*CM* II, 36).

Mattheson makes a strong distinction, however, between the un-suitability of melismas in recitatives and the effective use in arias. Indeed, when such a word as "geißelt" occurs in an aria text "in which the scourging is being especially meditated upon, a melisma or *neuma* may well be used," he affirms (*CM* II, 13–14). Melophile, who is seldom capable of applying his master's principles consistently, pleads to be allowed to retain the melisma he had in mind for the word "gleichet" in the line "das so Buben gleichet" of the aria "Welche sind des Heilands Erben?" (H.48, M.32) "I intend to make a long run in both voices on this word," he declares, "because of its beautiful diphthong." The Master's reply is, "Oh yes; why not. The word 'gleichet' not only sounds well, but also has an important meaning here." As further justification Mattheson points out the poetic context in which it occurs: "Since humankind is likened to those evil boys, such a word has to be expressed with a run in both voices" (*CM* II, 44).

This line of reasoning would not, however, justify a melisma on the word "schlecht" in the later duet "War das Wasser denn zu schlecht?" (H.62, M.41), as Melophile naively suggests. Mattheson retorts sharply: "Do evil things lend themselves to frills?" (*CM* II, 49) To clarify this point he cites Benedetto Marcello's ironic comments on the contemporary fashion of using coloraturas on all sorts of inappropriate words,[30] and, as further evidence, how sparingly Lully and his successors employ them in their operas, according to Bon-net.[31] Again, a little later, when Melophile suggests that a short coloratura would provide a little "douceur" in the aria meditating on Jesus' cry "I thirst" (H.55) Mattheson takes the occasion to criticize Italian composers for assuming that even in a little aria there must be a *passagio*. "You have learned too much that is wrong and unreasonable from the Italians," he declares. "The word Matten has an *a*. Right! You must have a *coloratur*. But consider whether a man who is faint with thirst (spiritual or physical) should be made to perform to such excesses" (*CM* II, 45–6). In other words dramatic coloraturas may properly be employed in an appropriate affective context, but dramatic sense must not be violated.

Just as inattention to the dramatic situation may lead to the misuse of coloraturas it can also produce errors in the deployment of the

30 Benedetto Marcello, *Il teatro alla moda* (Venice, ca. 1720), 18.
31 Bonnet-Bourdelot, *Histoire de la musique*, vol. 2, 23–4. See *CM* II, 52, No. LXI.

various styles of recitative and arioso. As a dramatist Mattheson contends that there are five different degrees or types of individual statement: (1) the straight narrative style of the Evangelist, (2) the notice placed on the cross by Pilate, (3) the Evangelist's quotation of a prophetic statement, (4) Pilate's and (5) Jesus' words as quoted by the Evangelist. In setting them to music each must be given identity by a different melodic style. The first, as we have seen, should be strictly syllabic, without any decoration, with careful reproduction of the correct inflection and quantitative accent in the music. The second should also be in the conventional recitative style, but a clear distinction should be made through monotony, since the Evangelist presents the words as though he were reading them (*CM* II, 39). The third should be composed in the arioso style but without instruments in order "to differentiate them from the words of God's Son" (*CM* II, 42). Pilate's words should be set in the "obbligat" style of arioso, by which Mattheson means with the use of a melodic basso continuo, but likewise without instrumental accompaniment. Jesus' words, however, should be distinguished from all the others by full instrumental accompaniment. In writing accompanied ariosi for both Pilate and Jesus, his predecessor is clearly at fault. Referring specifically to Jesus' denial of Pilate's authority, Mattheson recommends that Christ's words be accompanied by a serious, majestic symphony to make clear the difference between them (*CM* II, 28), adding that "it is even better, *ob dignitatem personae loquentis*, if the instruments begin with several introductory measures so that Christ's answer will be set off clearly from Pilate's question" (*CM* II, 26).

In addition, Mattheson argues that errors in setting music to words may also spring from inadequate knowledge of punctuation. For example, senseless verbal repetitions may result in improper use of commas and question marks if a composer does not understand their proper function in prose and poetry. The earlier composer's treatment of Pilate's words, wherever they occur, provides recurrent examples of needless repetition. As the words of a commanding or royal personage, they are set in formally designed ariosi to distinguish them from those of less exalted persons, a practice also derived from operatic style. In order to have enough textual material for the melodic phraseology of such ariosi, however, he deemed it necessary copiously to repeat many of Pilate's short statements, such as "Was ich geschrieben habe, hab' ich geschrieben" (H.40). Mattheson regards these repetitions as unnatural for a man as enraged as Pilate is in this case. "God preserve us from such repetitions. . . . He might repeat his decision once or twice, but no more," he declares. Mattheson's own practice, maintained consistently, is to give Pilate's words needed emphasis by setting them in the arioso style, and by repeating his statements twice (*CM* II, 40).

Incorrect knowledge of the use of commas in poetry may be even more severely criticized, Mattheson argues, citing a particularly deplorable example in the first aria of the previous score, "Unsre Bosheit, ohne Zahl" (H.3).

> Unsre Bosheit, ohne Zahl,
> Fühlt der Heiland, der Gerechte,
> Mehr, als selbst der frechen Knechte
>   Peitschen-Streich und Geißel-Quaal.
> Klag', o Mensch, weil dus verschuldet,
> Daß Gott selbst die Geißel duldet.

Here there is a long pause in the vocal part after "der Gerechte" and, at the end of the next line, after "Knechte," presumably in deference to the rhyme.

Mattheson analyzes this situation in detail and sets forth the proper musical procedure most explicitly:

After the first [word, "Gerechte"] there does indeed stand a comma, which might mislead many a person, but without exception no pause is required in the melody at a comma. There are even some, as, Ja, ja, Nein, nein, and the like, which must be leaped over with all diligence in order better to express the passion conveyed in speech. A certain friend makes a distinction between grammatical and rhetorical commas. I don't agree, because all commas belong properly to rhetoric. It is best to introduce the well-known *distinctio inter comma . . . perfectum*, and *comma . . . pendulum*. I plan to do this in my *Vollkommener Capellmeister*, of which much more than the outline is already completed.[32] . . . In melody a *comma perfectum* must have its formal halt, but a *comma pendulum* may be marked at the most by a little pause, a little *suspir*. This must answer the first part of this question.

As to the second, there is not the slightest justification for such an interruption of the text after "Knechte." The order of the words in this stanza is already such as to obscure the meaning for the listener. One way of bringing some sense to the confused construction "would be by inverting the text, for example: 'Unsre Bosheit fühlt er mehr / mehr als selbst die Geißel-Quaal.' Or: 'der Heiland / der Gerechte' with pauses inserted between the words, which would stimulate the listener's thought. And I may proceed in the same manner with the other words, since, for example, the expression 'Gott selbst / selbst Gott' in itself offers a reason for such emphasis" (*CM* II, 16–18).

32 (See *Capellmeister*, 186–7.)

A further occasion for the clarification of his rule regarding commas is provided in the text of the following chorus, "Sei gegrüsset, lieber Juden-König" (H.5, M.6) (see Example 1). In Mattheson's opinion the

Sei ge - grüs - set, lie - ber Ju - den - Kö - nig!

Example 1. *Das Lied des Lammes*, ed. B. C. Cannon, p. 10

comma between the two parts of this brief greeting is a *comma pendulum*, but Melophile points out that the earlier composer repeats the first two words thrice before adding the balance of the sentence. To Mattheson this is clearly incorrect because we "do not know yet who is being hailed, nor in what way he is being welcomed. A little pause between them will make the words clearer," he adds, with his own setting obviously in mind (CM II, 21–2).

It is just as incorrect to insert a comma in the middle of a clause in order to repeat a part of the text, as in the fourth line, "Welche die Felder um Jericho . . ." of the earlier setting of the aria text "Schauet, mein Jesus" (H.9, M.8). "It is more permissible to slip over commas where they are used correctly," Mattheson argues, "than to insert commas where they shouldn't be. This is a daily fault in concerting harmony that violates the rules of melody, which do not suffer the insertion of *incisiones* at points where the meaning of the utterance has not yet been made clear" (CM II, 23). Not even after coloraturas may a rest be inserted to enable the singer to catch his breath. Thus, in composing such an aria text as "Bebet ihr Berge" (M39), which calls for many *passaggi* of "three-flagged notes," Mattheson advised Melophile not to make his melisma "so long the first time that the singer will be in need of breath. If the *Sensus* of the text has been heard once perfectly, you may take more freedom in this respect" (CM II, 48). Mattheson's setting of this aria once again exemplifies this recommendation.

His objections to similar liberties in other portions of the earlier score are even sharper. For example, in the setting of Pilate's reply to the Jews, "Nehmet ihr ihn hin" (H.15), Mattheson censures the interruption and repetition of the text, "denn ich finde, [rest] denn ich finde keine Schuld" with the acid comment: "There is no way of reading this other than to suppose that Pilate stuttered or that something got caught in his throat" (CM II, 24). In the aria "Durch dein Gefängnis" (H.23) the repetition of the last three words of the sixth

141

line, "die Knechtschaft ein," reminds him of senseless repetitions in children's rhymes (*CM* II, 27). On the other hand, repetition is a means of emphasizing words of special significance within the context of a sentence. As a specific instance Melophile calls attention to the phrase "von oben herab" in Jesus' reply to Pilate: "Du hättest keine Macht über mich, wenn sie dir nicht wäre von oben herab gegeben" (M.14). He proposes "to set them off with two rests, and repeat them (so that one may wonder at them) before completing the sentence with 'gegeben.'" Mattheson, however, rejects this procedure "since it leaves the concluding words in the lurch." Instead, he advises Melophile to compose a descending melodic line for them (*CM* II, 26) (Example 2).

mich,   wenn sie dir nicht wä - re von o - ben her-ab ge-ge - ben.

Basso continuo

Example 2. *Das Lied des Lammes*, ed. B. C. Cannon, p. 33

Occasionally verbal meaning and correct rhetorical structure appear to coincide, as in the line "Bedenke doch, o Sünden-Orden!" in the aria text (M.21). Accordingly, Melophile suggests setting off the first two words with a rest, then repeating them as the earlier composer did. But Mattheson replies, "In and of itself a pause [rest] arouses reflection, but you must know what to think and feel about. Therefore first bring the *Sensus* to the understanding, then invert, transpose, and break up the text as much as you want" (*CM* II, 36).

Mattheson's insistence on translating the exact meaning of a text into the proper musical equivalent requires that distinctions between straight questions and rhetorical ones be established. "There are certainly many rhetorical, unreal questions," he writes, "that answer themselves, and thus do not require that the melody be left in *suspenso*." But when Pilate asks Jesus: "Redest du nicht mit mir? Weißt du nicht, das ich Macht habe, dich zu kreuzigen. . . ?" he is speaking directly to him (M.13). "Eventually an answer is obtained, and it is *negative & conditional*. This clearly proves that the concluding words, 'dich loß zu lassen,' are not a formal close; on the contrary they require a pause and a delay, as is customarily the case with questions" – in other words, a semicadence (*CM* II, 25–6).

Respect for the rhetorical integrity of the text in some instances affects fundamental principles of composition, which to Mattheson are discernible through correct assessment of the affective values in a sentence. But conflicts may arise in providing precise representations of words of differing affective content within the same sentence. The kind of error that may result from this situation is exemplified by the previous setting of the first two lines of the aria (M.16):

> Durch dein Gefängniß, Gottes Sohn,
> Muß uns die Freiheit kommen. . .

Like many a seventeenth-century composer confronted with words of such antithetical meanings as "Gefängniß" and "Freiheit," the composer deliberately divides the sentence into two dissimilar musical sections to represent the affective contrast. In such a situation Mattheson remarks that "many a composer would make a mournful violin solo out of this, and with the word 'Gefängniß' introduce especially sad, descending intervals; afterward, with the word 'Freyheit' before him, he would produce another rhythm and think how wonderfully he had extricated himself. Such untimely irruptions are *verborum potius quam sensuum imitationes,* and belong with childish beauties which yet (wonder of wonders) are frequently marveled at by old people." Melophile nevertheless suggests that it would surely be correct "to introduce a merry phrase beginning with the words 'Muß uns die Freyheit' because it concerns freedom." To Mattheson such a procedure would obviously divide and contradict the structure and meaning of the sentence as a whole, and he replies ironically: "Freedom does not extend so widely that it may act against sound reason" (*CM* II, 27).

Solutions to such problems, of course, all depend upon how such an aria should be composed as a whole. In Mattheson's view the answer lies in a correct analysis of the affective content of the text, a topic to which he subsequently devotes considerable attention. Clearly his predecessors, struck by the succession of antithetical words of strong affective content, would seek to represent them successively by contrasting melodic styles. He, on the contrary, recognizes but one dominant affection, which is "joy and consolation over the eternal freedom obtained through Christ [*CM* II, 27] . . . This presents no occasion for alternating *Tempi* since the meter of the verse remains the same throughout. . . . Here is but one affection, though the words

143

are diverse." Accordingly the text may be appropriately set as a duet: "Not only because the words speak in the plural, but also in particular on account of the verbal antitheses, they provide a good opportunity for two *subjecta opposita*. For example, 'Gefängniß – Freyheit, Kerker – Freystatt'" (*CM* II, 28).

To Mattheson correct translation into musical terms of the grammatical and rhetorical features of the statements of each of the protagonists in the drama is obviously of paramount importance. The words of the soldiers, high priests and Jews require especially careful attention. In the first half of the oratorio text there are eight speeches by these groups, each one of which is discussed. The decision as to how each should be composed is dependent upon two interrelated considerations: the affective content and the unfolding dramatic situation. Usually Melophile's questions regarding rhetorical and stylistic matters are inspired by errors or antiquated procedures exemplified in the earlier setting, but here there are few direct references to the choruses in the earlier composition. This does not appear to be because Mattheson's prescriptions correspond to them, for the majority do not.[33] Rather, Mattheson casts Melophile in the role of the ambitious young composer who sees in every choral text the opportunity to display his skill in counterpoint and fugue, the traditional specialities of ecclesiastically trained musicians: Mattheson's discussions, like his own score, reveal his enthusiasm for these choral styles, but also his conviction that they should not be chosen merely because of devotion to "musical science."

The discussion of the first choral text, the soldier's derisive shouts to Jesus, "Sei gegrüsset, lieber Juden-König," illustrates his point of view strikingly (M.6). In answer to Melophile's inquiry as to the affection of this greeting, Mattheson replies, "Ridicule, scorn, laughter, *moquerie*. For this reason the movement [Satz] must not be expressed with highly serious modulation. Whoever fails in this misses the most important point at which *scientia melodica* aims, namely, the affection." His recommendations are specific:

I would use two short *themata*, one for "Sey gegrüsset," with an assumed gravity, the other for "lieber Juden-König," [which] should be designed with little mocking leaps [Example 3]. First I would modulate these irregularities and then introduce a so-called *analysis* thus: "lieber König, sey gegrüsset, lieber Juden-König." Sung swiftly in octaves this will appear spiteful enough, and will be beautiful in its own way (*CM* II, 22).

---

33 See, for example, his comments in answers to questions XXIII–XXVII. Compare also Mattheson's settings of these choruses with those of J. S. Bach.

144

Example 3. *Das Lied des Lammes*, ed. B. C. Cannon, p. 11

Needless to say, these are the ingredients of Mattheson's setting with its alternating fugal passages and refrains in parallel octaves.[34]

Other chorus texts are particularly appropriate for strict instead of free fugal writing. For example, it is quite mistaken to set the priests' bloodthirsty cry "Kreuzige, kreuzige" (H.13, M.10) in slow, mournful harmonies for the simple reason that that in no way correspond with the thoughts of the Jews. "They wish to see Jesus on the cross quickly," declares Mattheson the dramatist, "and to enjoy his suffering. Therefore they make such a confused, insolent, disorderly cry that it may be set only as a wild, passionate fugue. Indeed this is one of the best occasions for a fugue. But we must conceive of a cry in the Jewish sense, not in our own" (CM II, 23). The Jews' outcry, "Weg, weg mit dem, kreuzige ihn," is a similar situation. In identifying two affections, "the first ['Weg, weg'] as swift, and the other ['Kreuzige ihn'] as slow and sad, you are well off the mark," the Master tells Melophile, with reference to the earlier setting (H.29);

It has already been stated that the people and their characters who utter the words must be given first consideration, namely the high priests and learned pedants among the Jews. These people will enjoy seeing Jesus crucified, and they cry out to each other with extreme audacity and vehemence, which passions are so little different from each other that it is most convenient to express them in a double fugue. Here is yet another situation in which a fugue may be justified.

Once again Mattheson's prescription is based precisely on his own setting. "First, take for the first *thema* the words 'Weg, weg,' next, the word 'Kreuzige' with a *melisma*, third, make several ligatures with these words, and fourth, place rests between the 'Weg, weg!' to bring about four *themata*. I well know that such a *Fuga doppia* in this situation will be better than ten *Canones*. Mark also that these few

34 M.6, measures 13–15.

words have two *propositions*, but only one affection: furious rage" (CM II, 34; M.20, H.29).

Example 4. *Das Lied des Lammes*, ed. B. C. Cannon, p. 59

In equating fugues with expressions of confusion and rage, Mattheson distinguishes them from the canonic style which he regards as a learned demonstration of reason and contrapuntal skill. Thus a canon is appropriate to a different affective content, such as the Jews' argumentative retort to Pilate's suggestion that Jesus be released: "Lässest du diesen los, so bist du des Kaisers Freund nicht" (M.18). Melophile is eager to make a canon for this chorus, and Mattheson replies enthusiastically:

If you are really set on it, then go ahead with it. For a canon is to be compared with a syllogism. You might therefore give it a try; but I would never have expected such a question from a true *Melophile*. If it is to be a canon, by all means compose it *hypodiapente*: thus it will look more like a fugue than a canon that is composed in *unisono*. But beware of overflowing modulations and don't expect after all that quill-chewing and toiling to be rewarded for your pains: *Responsura tuo nonquam est par fama labori*. There will probably be not a single one among 2,000 listeners who will notice your finesse, unless he be alerted to it beforehand (CM II, 28–9; M.18, H.25).

This prescription, with its cynically worded conclusion, indicates two attitudes toward learned counterpoint in Mattheson's mind: first, since such knowledge is highly respected by his pedantic fellow musicians, it is highly appropriate to the pedantic scholars who are seeking Christ's death; on the other hand, elaborate musical craftsmanship will be wasted on such a large audience assembled to hear this oratorio.

Mattheson adopts a similarly pragmatic point of view in his analysis of the other speeches by priests, Jews and soldiers. The Jews' declaration "Wir haben ein Gesetze" (M.12, H.17, B.38) is a particularly interesting case because of the parallel settings by both the earlier composer and J. S. Bach. The former's five-part, homophonic

146

chorus emphasizes unanimity of agreement in the face of the law. Bach seems to have regarded this assertion as such an exact counterpart to the Jews' later reference to the law ("Lässest du diesen los") that he contented himself with the same fugue for each chorus. Melophile, with obvious reference to the earlier setting, inquires whether it would not be good "to have all voices burst in simultaneously?" "This could very well be done in another situation," the Master replies,

where only a short outcry is to be expressed, or where the situation is to be treated *praevia deliberatione*. Here, however, we have a true formal *ratiocinatio*, yes, almost a regular syllogism which it is not at all believable that the crowd as a whole, *stante pede, in ore*, has come up with. Therefore it would be much clearer and more reasonable if with each statement or *comma* a single voice takes the lead with the whole chorus repeating the words exactly. Such a procedure can be used in many places, and if it is always observed can have an effect which will not only free this particular piece from mistakes, but will also create an intrinsic beauty – especially if in these exchanges one introduces some *exaggerationes*, repeating, for example, the words "zum Gottes-Sohn" as if in astonishment, etc. (CM II, 24).

His analysis of the Jews' later "Wir haben keinen König" is an extension of this view, for both statements are of the same order. "It is impossible," he argues, "that an orderly syllogism can be produced by many people at once. It is neither credible nor natural for them to coincide. In poetic matters it is one thing, in historical prose speech, quite another. There I may imagine (unanimous) understanding; here not."[35] In other instances, the tendency to resort to a fugue must be resisted, moreover. For example, a fugue would not be at all appropriate for the Jews' "Wir haben keinen König" (M.23, H.34), for the affection is impatience, "and a fugue calls for too many repetitions, while impatience leads to unity . . . Nor do we have here a wild, enraged cry, but only an impatient contradiction" (CM II, 36). Again, the four soldiers' division of Jesus' garments seems to Melophile (as it did to his predecessor) the occasion to set their words in a "clever *contrapunto fugato* so that the notes will be so distributed and syncopated that everyone will be astonished." "Don't be so hasty with counterpoint, fugue, and imitations," Mattheson retorts;

---

35 CM II, 39. Mattheson's reasoning seems clear enough, though his mode of expression is ambiguous. "Eine ordentliche Schluß-Rede kann unmüglich von vielen Personen zugleich hervorgebracht werden. Es ist gar nicht glaublich / noch, naturalich / daß sie zusammen eintreffen sollten. Ein anders ist es in poetischen Sachen; ein anders in ungebundener / historischer Rede. Dort mag ich eine Verabredung erdicten; hier nicht."

Here are four slovenly fellows taking council to determine how to divide the cloak. Is it reasonable for them to do this in syncopated notes, with jerkings and ties, as though cut up, hacked up and torn up? . . . It will be much better to make a four-part recitative which will come out naturally. . . . This is just ordinary speech. Away with all the evils of many pauses and repetitions. *Imitationes verborum sunt scurriles, nisis sensui conveniunt!* (CM II, 41–2)

Matteson's enthusiastic advocacy of the modern theatrical style for music in the service of God permits, in short, few of the stylistic elements traditionally associated with settings of the Gospel text, unless they are appropriate to the affection of the specific text. "I, as a true Melophile," Matteson observes, "am deeply grieved by what you are saying and I truly deplore the fact that there are composers among us who after thirty years certainly would not be able to give an answer when asked about the affection [of a text]" (CM II, 38). Accordingly he takes up each aria in turn in response to Melophile's inquiry as to what its underlying affection is, and how it should be composed. Previous error is not used as a springboard, and there are only a few references to the merits or demerits of his predecessor's settings.

The first aria text (M.4) in the oratorio presents a number of problems with which to reckon, and Matteson provides an exceptionally critical and perceptive analysis of its poetic qualities and form as well as of its affective content. The text is far from being an admirable example of Postel's poetic abilities:

> Unsre Bosheit, ohne Zahl,
> Fühlt der Heiland, der Gerechte,
> Mehr, als selbst der frechen Knechte
>   Peitschen-Streich und Geißel-Quaal.
> Klag', o Mensch, weil dus verschuldet,
> Daß Gott selbst die Geißel duldet
>   Unsre Bosheit etc.

This stanza is prompted by Pilate's scourging of Jesus, and Matteson interprets the principal affection as

the realization that our sins will cause more suffering than the remorse and sorrow naturally inspired by scourging. Therein reposes the affection of these words. That they are truly musical I cannot, for many reasons, say [he adds], though the author was a great, sensitive poet. He knew enough about music to accompany himself at the keyboard. This is not enough, however: Above all things a poet must understand *musica modulatoria*, properly speaking, the practice of singing, and in addition have some understanding of *theoria compositionis*.

This is equally important for singers, too, "many of whom do not understand even the fundamentals of singing." Acknowledging that

148

the first four lines have little charm, he points out that though they contain six distinct ideas their meaning will not be clear until one has reached the end. "Loveliness," he declares, "is lacking if our understanding is delayed as long as it is in this case" (*CM* II, 15). In support of his argument that a poet must understand singing, Mattheson quotes a passage from Bonnet's *Histoire de la musique*: "Pour la douceur des vers il est essential, que le Poète en croye beaucoup le Musicien. Mille mots *excellens* dans la Poèsie qui se recite, deviennent *insupportables* dans celle qui se chante, & c'a été par cet endroit, que RACINE, LA FONTAINE & c. ont echoué à cette dernière, & que si peu *de gens* y ont reussi."[36]

It is obvious that the poetical defects in this aria text do not simplify the composer's task of providing a proper musical setting. A careful examination of it will lead us to perceive, writes Mattheson, "that the precise emotion of remorse contained in this aria will have to be depicted as a depressing of the feelings, as a tragic awareness of our own weakness, with a certain inclination toward goodness and improvement." That the two-part form of the stanza is intended to be composed as a *da capo* aria goes without saying.

The passion of remorse first appears most strongly in the two middle lines, "Klag O Mensch," which must therefore be presented with more pensive melancholy than the *da capo* since the latter contains merely the proposition, whereas the former contain the actual application. An *accompagnement* of transverse flutes and viola da gamba (if they are available) will be very appropriate in this case. In the first part the melody must be properly modest; in the second, a bit sorrowful (*CM* II, 16).

The difficulties of accurately identifying and characterizing the principal affection in this aria, and of achieving its musical counterpart, are again encountered in the text of "Getrost, mein Herz!" (M.25, H.36). Indeed, Melophile prefaces his customary question by remarking, "I don't know what emotion to make out of this stanza, though I have thought long and hard on it" (*CM* II, 37). Making no reference to his predecessor's setting, Mattheson finds the answer by first considering details rather than the sense of the text as a whole. The six-line stanza clearly falls into two equal parts:

> Getrost, mein Herz! hier kannst du Gnad' umfassen,
> Dein Jesus will die Sünder nicht verlassen,
> Und sollt' es auch am Kreuze seyn.
> Wenn du denn nicht die Hülffe kanst erfragen,
> So warte nur: wenn dich das Kreuz wird tragen,
> Stellt er sich in der Mitten ein.

36 Bonnet-Bourdelot, vol. 2, 204.

Mattheson compares this formal profile to "the *strophe & antistrophe* employed in ancient *Tragidis*. A good aria [text] must always have these two pieces, or should customarily have them, since, though little noticed, they provide the foundation of all musical poetry." If the composer looks for the "emphasis," upon which the greatest expression falls, the affection will stare him in the face.

It will not be necessary to tell you, my poor Melophile, how far the *propositio* extends and where the *applicatio* begins. You will notice that in the latter everything is in the *imperativus*: "Warte nur," which identifies the *emphasis*, and also contains the basic affection. Consider! What is the name of the passion which entails waiting? Do you remember what we sing in church: "Die Hoffnung warte der rechten Zeit!"; this hope in the unremitting help of Christ, in the center of the cross, is a very great passion. It consists of courage, longing, and temperate joy, having more of the first two than the last. Also a little fear is involved. Is this not enough material? (CM II, 37)

To convey these qualities of mystical faith in musical terms, Mattheson recommends a line of reasoning with results that are, in fact, totally at odds with his predecessor's musical setting. Whereas the latter constructs his aria upon a *basso ostinato*, Mattheson asserts that

bravery permits no strong accompaniment, for true *courage* must reveal itself *solo*. The bass may thus be plucked with the fingers in the manner of a lute (*gli Bassi pizzicati*) to express a little fear. Longing may be represented by an ardent repetition of the words "Getrost mein Herz, Warte nur, warte nur," and finally, temperate joy by a lively *mouvement*. Thus in my opinion a truly noble monody may be produced (CM II, 37–8).

He follows his own prescription to the letter.

Another aria text that presents affective problems is the moralistic reflection upon the soldiers' division of Jesus' garments:

Du müßt den Rock verliehrn,
Daß wir ihn mögten führn
  Zum Deckel unsrer Sünden-Schuld.
Wir müsten ewig Blösse leiden.
Würd' uns nicht dein Verdienst bekleiden,
  Mit mehr als väterlicher Huld (M.30).

Melophile contends that it contains no special passion, and Mattheson agrees that at first sight there is little to arouse a composer, "for a coat, nakedness, clothing, are in themselves not at all musical. Furthermore, the *propositiones* are mixed up with the *applicationes*." But careful consideration of one's own reactions under such circumstances suggests that thankfulness would indeed be a strong feeling. From this reflection Mattheson concludes that "an eager

150

gratitude is the affection of these words. This is composed of love, friendship, and gratitude . . . leading to heartfelt praise and thanks." In this instance, however, his musical recommendations are far from specific. He contents himself with the remark that "an agreeable, artistic accompaniment will be helpful, and the voice part should express an eager desire" (CM II, 41). To match these requirements he composes this aria for tenor with the accompaniment of a gracefully ornamented part for viola da gamba and viola da braccio in unison.

In contrast to the difficulties exemplified by these two aria texts and "Durch dein Gefängniß," which has been previously discussed, two of Postel's stanzas are obviously conventional and raise problems only of musical execution. These are "Erschüttere mit Krachen" (M.21) and "Bebet ihr Berge" (M.39). The first exemplifies the well-known category of the "rage aria," and Melophile needs no assistance in identifying the affection, the musical style, or the instrumentation to be employed. He asks rather "whether I should tear loose with a fearful *passagio* on the word 'Krachen.'" Mattheson's reply is both practical and rational.

First set the first three lines with suitable liveliness without inserting color-aturas, so that one can tell what the words are supposed to say. Thereafter you may tear loose as much as you like with 'Krachen,' 'Rachen,' and 'Abgrund.' For, though there is nothing easier than to compose such furious arias (if they deserve this name) with many clashes and clatters, there still are many who maintain that the imitation of bestial, brutish, and abominable things in music is something artificial. . . . It is also important to remember, as the poet has not noticed, that an aria does not have to have a *proposition reflexiva*.

He goes on to ask how many listeners will remember the principal questions posed by the text even before the *da capo* unless the composer makes the audience reflect upon it by inversion (CM II, 34–5).

It must be observed that the earlier composer had been guilty of writing an extended coloratura on "Krachen" at the outset. He had also changed meter and tempo, and omitted instrumental parts in the middle section, presumably in deference to the contrasting affection implied by the words "Bedenke doch." Mattheson will have none of this.

The emotion in these words is still the same as before, yet it is not as strong, [for] rage is moderated by an emphatic exposition and realization through which a heaven-crying sin is revealed. Therefore I would permit neither an alteration in the meter nor an instrumental pause, but would introduce a somewhat slower tempo by a little word like *Moderato*, and, instead of strong unison strings, an oboe solo" (CM II, 35–6).

The other text clearly calls for musical tone painting, with the instruments "shivering and trembling," and Melophile wonders whether this should be achieved by using "three-tailed notes". In emphatic agreement the Master points out that terror and fear should be emphasized, "and nothing is more fleeting than millions of guileless notes on a single tone." However, he cautions Melophile not to stick so closely to the meaning of these words "that you would hesitate to put 'earth' higher than 'heaven' by even a single tone, since one might well, in terror, call upon the earth in loftier sounds than upon heaven. In particular, be careful to bring out the last line with greater moderation than the others, since it contains the mournful reason for the horror of all nature" (CM II, 47).

Mattheson's concern that the instrumental accompaniment be carefully chosen for its appropriateness to the affective content of each aria text is evident throughout *Das Lied des Lammes*. This concern is frequently expressed in his instructions to Melophile, but most explicitly in two aria texts of the second part, numbers M.35 and M.37. In the first of these the poet responds to Christ's thirst in impassioned terms:

> Jesu, wornach dürstet dich?
> Da du ja die Matten tränkest;
>   Himmel! ich besinne mich,
> Daß du meiner Angst gedenkest,
>   Und nach Trost, in meiner Noth;
> Durstig bist, biß an den Tod.

As is consistently the case, Mattheson's primary aim is to express the affection of the text. His prescription, phrased somewhat obscurely, commences: "Something beautiful will be made by exaggerating the words and by directing our thoughts in the *proposition* to compassion, but in the *application* to wonderment. An accompaniment *col oboe d'amore e viol di gambe* will not be wrong in this case, though the tone will have to be carefully selected." The accompaniment must never take precedence over the text, however.

First bring the words into good order, then, in the main melody itself, a little *thema* on the instruments that are to precede it will follow of its own accord. I hold this course as much more generally correct than if one concentrates on the accompaniment and only afterward on the main melody, especially when the accompaniment contains nothing very distinctive, as is the case here, where the affections demand more loveliness than strength or vigor [CM II, 45]. . . . If you would have something lively, put it preferably in the middle parts; let the whole be in gentle motion throughout so that the inner, exhausted anxiety of the thirsty Jesus is expressed. It will produce a good harmony, and will not detract from the melody if the aforementioned middle voices are bowed softly on violas da gamba or da braccio (*CM* II, 46).

The text of the following aria springs directly from Christ's final words, "Es ist vollbracht," and the words "Riesen-Stärk" and "Sieges-Pracht" emphasize his triumphant victory:

> O, großes Werk!
> Im Paradieß schon angefangen;
> O, Riesen-Stärk!
> Die Jesum läßt den Sieg erlangen:
> Daß, nach dem Streit, in Sieges-Pracht,
> Er sprechen kann: Es ist vollbracht.

Melophile, anxious to do justice to this meditation on the "grandeur of the Savior's work," suggests that this may be expressed "through wide intervals, and, of course, without the accompaniment." This statement is, at least by implication, a reference to the previous setting, where over a smoothly flowing continuo in eighth notes, wide melodic intervals together with pompous dotted rhythms are the dominant musical features (H.58).

In his response Mattheson does not take issue with the use of wide intervals but is at pains to define the particular affection that the music must express.

The affection here is a joy linked with esteem for the unbelievable kindness of God and the splendid victory of Christ. . . . Accordingly the main point will be established not by [voice] alone but much more by a majestic accompaniment so that the voice may contrive something joyous in its *modulations*, as well as by introducing various *melismas* here and there. But this will not happen through such awkward leaps as many composers use to express joy in imitation of peasants, believing that they cannot be merry without dancing and leaping. Gladness, especially over spiritual grace, is in my opinion not a restless, but much more a peaceful, quiet feeling, and calm without violent lusts; as also in holy writ peace and joy are often joined together. *Exultatio* is one thing, *gaudium* another (*CM* II, 46).

Mattheson expresses this carefully analyzed affection by a flexible combination of the recommended ingredients: sequences of octave leaps in the continuo, sixths in the vocal part, and *violini obbligati* in dotted rhythms in the first section. In the second, these dynamic elements are smoothed out in accordance with his direction that the "conclusion of this aria must have a kinship with the preceding words of Christ, and more earnestness than the rest" (*CM* II, 46–7). Indeed his aria (M.37) concludes with a repetition of the final, unaccompanied, descending melisma of Christ's recitative, transposed from A-flat to the related F minor of the aria (Example 5).

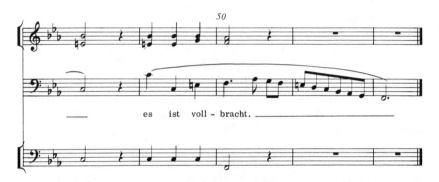

Example 5. *Das Lied des Lammes*, ed. B. C. Cannon, p. 128

The question as to what sorts of poetic texts may be appropriately composed as duets leads to considerable discussion and explanation. This is not surprising considering Mattheson's preoccupation with the correct application of rhetorical rules, his insistence on the precise assessment of the affective content of aria texts, his scorn for outmoded stylistic manners, and his conviction that sacred texts call for a composer's highest skill and craftsmanship. Whereas four of the poetic stanzas are composed as duets in the previous score, Mattheson composed but three, setting the first, "Schauet, mein Jesus," as a *cantabile* solo (m.8, H.9). After a characteristic explanation of the textual affection, Melophile's question concerning the propriety of a duet in this instance elicits only the opinion that the words do not appear particularly appropriate for a duet. "Indeed the *numeri plurales* in the last two lines might just as well call for an entire chorus as

154

for a duet," Mattheson observes (*CM* II, 22–3). Here as in the other three instances it is apparent that affective content is not the only factor in choosing to set a duet.

As we have seen, Mattheson considers the aria text "Durch dein Gefängniß" (M.16) suitable for a duet for the very reasons which caused him to ridicule his predecessor's setting. He makes this assertion "because of the plural numbers prevailing throughout, and the antitheses, which provide good opportunities to introduce and carry through two opposing subjects" (*CM* II, 28). At the same time, because one affection prevails throughout the stanza, one may not alter meter or tempo to emphasize antitheses, as he has pointed out elsewhere (*CM* II, 27). Though he provides no detailed prescription, Mattheson's setting of this duet is one of the most extensive, complex sections in his oratorio. In addition to solo soprano and bass parts, it is written for three independent instrumental parts, flutes, violins, and bassoons with cellos. Each of the most affectively important text phrases is provided with appropriately differentiated melodic phrases, treated in succession at some length. Formal unity is maintained not only by the use of related tonalities but also by the recurrence of the principal melodic subject fugally in vocal and instrumental parts throughout the piece. This is stated at the outset by bassoons and cellos in the tonic key of G minor, answered by the flutes (Example 6). Its animated contour Mattheson applies to the text "muß uns die Freyheit kommen" (Example 7). Slightly altered it is equally applicable to the phrase "die Freystatt aller Frommen" (Example 8). With the omission of the opening upbeat it also provides musical significance to the words "ewig, ewig" (Example 9). Thus this figure links all three phrases together, whereas those dominated by the opposing words "Gefängniß" and "Kerker" are assigned quarter- and eighth-note figures respectively. The duet is thus Mattheson's own skillful application of the style of Agostino Steffani, as may be inferred from his discussion of the stanza "Welche sind des Heilands Erben?" (M.32, H.48).

This aria text is one of the two in question-and-answer form, which leads Melophile to suggest that it be set as a duet:

> Welche sind des Heilands Erben?
>   Lauter böse Krieges-Knecht.
> Must' er denn nur dafür sterben?
>   Nein, dem menschlichen Geschlecht,
> Das so bösen Buben gleichet,
> Hat er sich selbst zur Erbschafft hingereichet.

Example 6. *Das Lied des Lammes*, ed. B. C. Cannon, p. 36

Melophile proposes to have "both voices one after the other presenting each question, and, thereafter, the answers in the same fashion.
Would this not be something new?" he asks. Mattheson's reply,
transparently ironic, is: "It would indeed be something new, but not
good. I can well see that you would put the voices in dialogue together
canonically, by Steffani's method, but that would not work at all well
in this case." He concedes that "such duets in this harmonic form
have their virtues, and may well be used in contrasting or antithetical
expressions. But this species is not at all suited to questions and

156

uns die Frei-heit kom-men, Got - - tes __ Sohn, Muss

dein Ge - fäng - nis, Muss uns die Frei-heit kom-men, Got -

uns die Frei-heit kom-men, Durch

- tes __ Sohn, die

Example 7. *Das Lied des Lammes*, ed. B. C. Cannon, p. 37

Frei-statt all - er From-men, Dein Ker - ker ist die

Ker - ker ist die Frei-statt al - ler From-men, Dein

Frei - - -

Ker - ker ist der

Example 8. *Das Lied des Lammes*, ed. B. C. Cannon, p. 41

157

Example 9. *Das Lied des Lammes,* ed. B. C. Cannon, p. 44

answers." He goes on to recommend his own solution, which is to make a chorus that "may be contrived as a *responsorium,* or an *antiphona moderna.* Let one voice alone commence, and the entire chorus respond. Thus pleasing exchanges can be made if one well captures the affection [of the text], which here is a secret joy over Jesus' inheritance" (*CM* II, 43).

Consideration of this specific problem leads Mattheson to express his thoughts on duets in general.

In a correctly concerted duet the words should be so well arranged that they contain either two conflicting opinions or such a unity of thought as may be revealed through different expressions. Otherwise, if two persons sing the same words throughout, there is little occasion for concerted harmony, unless one allows them to saunter one after the other in the manner of a canon or prefers the French method of singing *à deux* to the Italian one. With questions and answers (as we have here) the circumstances outlined above do not obtain, they are not well suited for concerted duets. There is, to be sure, a certain kind of setting for two voices that consists merely in questions and answers; but that is not the case here. These [latter] settings need no special harmonic complexities but proceed quite plainly and naturally – When, for example, one person asks: *Morirai?* and the other answers: *non morira,* and goes on to ask: *m'amerai?* and the first replies: *dir lo non so,* and so on. In the opera *La forza della virtù* we have such a duet in which one person speaks

158

only two words.[37] Clotilde sings: "Ach! speak, ye lips, answer!" and Fernando asks in embarrassment: "And what?" This had a splendid effect and filled the masses in the parterre with enthusiasm for this tender scene. Concerted duets are indeed more artistic and require more assiduity; but the ones described last are much more naive, natural, and stirring. Thus here too we can see the superiority of a simple, melodious manner for which I shall plead unceasingly, since there is the greatest lack of it, and yet it is what is needed most. If, however, there are no questions and answers, and someone wants to employ this manner [of composition] out of laziness, incapacity, or plain ignorance, thinking that silliness and simplicity are one and the same – then he will certainly expose his baseness and lack of invention (CM II, 43–4).

Two other aria texts provide further occasions for duet settings by both composers. Since they differ in character, Mattheson takes occasion to expand upon this analysis. The first of these (M.41), a seven-line stanza, is a reflection on the significance of the issue of blood and water from Christ's pierced body:

> War das Wasser denn zu schlecht
> Unsre Sünden-Schuld zu baden?
> Mensche, ja, für deinen Schaden
> War nur Göttlichs Blut gerecht.
> So solln, weil ich leb' auf Erden,
> Aus den Augen Quellen werden,
> Die von Blut und Thränen roth.

Since it is in the form of question and answer, Melophile again proposes a duet in the concerted style in emulation of what a "good friend" has done. The earlier setting does indeed follow the model of Steffani, with the voices entering in fugal imitation with each successive clause or sentence of the text (H.62). Here Mattheson strongly affirms the suitability of a duet, but emphatically disapproves of using the kind of concerted procedure in which each voice

proceeds *imitando* or fugally. . . . If a person clearly utters a question, then the other should properly answer it alone. Otherwise there will only be confusion, which hinders the necessary clarity of the discourse. Also, the question may not be inevitably *proprie* but can well be taken as rhetorical. . . . In the answer our so-called Analysis may have a rather good effect. For example: "Mensche, ja, es war zu schlecht" (CM II, 48).

Suiting this suggestion to the words, Mattheson himself transposes word order and repeats phrases in order to emphasize or bring out different textual meanings.

In doubt as to how to compose the concluding aria text (M.43), Melophile asks which emotion should receive attention:

37 *La forza della virtù*, by Reinhard Keiser, performed in Hamburg in 1700.

159

Ich gehe mit ins Grab!
Was frag' ich nach dem Himmel!
Nach allem Welt-Getümmel!
Weil Jesus scheidet ab.
Ich gehe mit ins Grab.

Mattheson answers in considerable detail. Though this text is not in the form of question and answer and is implicitly individualistic, there is no doubt about the propriety of setting it as a duet. Rather his concern is that the composer direct all his attention

to the various *expressiones* to be drawn from the words, notwithstanding the fact that they are not obvious at first sight. . . . These expressions reside in the first three words, where one person might sing: "Ich gehe," and the other rejoin "Ich gehe mit." In such a way may a fully concerted duet be started, especially if one person likewise puts in one voice the question: "Ins Grab?" and the other answers affirmatively: "Ins Grab." In such a fashion, and I would add in no other, may a pleasing fugal duet be forthcoming, even though the poet has hardly intended it. The affection is here doubled, or dual. In the first line one must express longing for Jesus to the very grave itself; in the other, however, a stubborn contempt of the earthly by means of a change in the *mouvement* etc." (CM II, 51–2).

Because of the overriding importance of the opening words, Mattheson is opposed to the use of ritornelli. In any case, "Ritornelli are no longer in fashion," he points out, "for nowadays most arias are accompanied with instruments throughout." Another reason is that "the opening words are also employed at the conclusion: 'Ich gehe mit ins Grab', and a greater longing will be expressed if after the word 'Grab' nothing is added, since this is surely the *ultima rerum*" (CM II, 52–3).

Postel supplied a four-line stanza of farewell to the dead Christ as a conclusion to his Passion text, which Handel set in a five-part homophonic chorus. Bach also used this text for the final chorus of his *St. John Passion*, following it, however, with the chorale stanza, "Ach, Herr, laß dein lieb' Engelein,"[38] traditionally and liturgically associated with the suffering and religious significance of the crucifixion. Mattheson's formula for this situation is an unusual combination of farewell chorus and chorale (M.45). While accepting Postel's stanza he proposes that the melody composed for it be "intertwined" with the chorale melody *O Jesu dessen Schmerzen*.[39] His disquisition on this topic is a particularly striking example of his

38 The third stanza of *Herzlich lieb, hab ich dich*, melody by Bernhardt Schmidt, text by Martin Schalding.
39 The tenth and last stanza of *Als Gottes Lamm und Leue*, by Paul Gerhardt.

rational analysis of the poetic text itself and the requirements of a proper conclusion to a "magnificent" work. It is prompted by Melophile's inquiry about "making a good counterpoint" at this juncture. "Certainly counterpoint," Mattheson replies, adding sarcastically,

you are more interested in such stuff than in the affection, and other circumstances belonging *ad melodicam*. I am surprised that you have not inquired about using a *passagio* on the word "Schlafe" because it has a beautiful *vocalis* and would sound well? First you must consider above all the emotions in these words of love and thankfulness, and arrange your melody accordingly to be tender, flowing and lovely. And if you will make a counterpoint choose *all-ottava*: for the *alla decima* does not produce such good melodies, and *alla dodecima* has already been used. Above all, however, take as a *Canto fermo* a chorale that is suitable to those words. For example, *O Jesu, dessen Schmerzen.* . . . It has *expressiones* which will be better brought out, because the name of him to whom one wishes a tender rest is not to be found in the poetry. . . . Intertwine the two texts with a suitable melodic counterpoint so that they may be clearly understood: accompany them with *Sordinen* (that is, with muted violins and cellos), with transverse flutes, and smoothly blown bassoons, so that the last [part of the work] will be perhaps the best (CM II, 53–4).

Mattheson's final chorus in *Das Lied des Lammes* follows these specifications in an arresting fashion. The integration of Postel's four-line stanza with the eight lines of the chorale provides enough verbal material for an extensive piece of 236 measures, laid out in two sections. The affective content of the poetry is enriched by the *expressiones* of the chorale text, with the phrases of the chorale cantus firmus assigned successively to each of the four choral voices. A four-part orchestral ritornello of thirty measures, with exactly prescribed instrumentation, introduces the melodic materials designed to clothe Postel's verse, and sets off in turn each of the subsections of the piece. Mattheson's concern for the audibility of the text is guaranteed by the transparent contrapuntal style, and the predominance of the chorale text and melody is enhanced by the unusually careful dynamic markings.

Throughout "The Inquiring Composer," *Das Lied des Lammes* proves to be the specific projection of the artistic practice Mattheson advocates. With the evidence of the score at hand, its primary goal is a reasoned defense of his own creative procedures. At the same time it is clearly intended as a practical demonstration of the rhetorical precepts underlying an enlightened, rational theory of musical composition. Together the two documents contain the essential premises upon which their author developed his subsequent moralistic polemics on the paramount significance of what he termed "theatrical church music,"[40] and they form an unacknowledged but essential section of the treatise that is the culmination of his ideas on music, *Der vollkommene Capellmeister*.[41]

A striking feature of Mattheson's musical philosophy is his belief in empiricism and, consequently, in the dominance of practice over theory. That is the cardinal principle running through all his writing, and this lesson in how to compose a passion must thus be recognized as a central pillar of his musical philosophy. Though taking for granted the enduring value of the traditions of polyphony, he repeatedly warns against flaunting them for the sake of vaunting one's learning and insists that they are merely elements of the composer's craft that, like all others, should be subservient to the affective and theatrical requirements of a chosen text. The musical tenets the enlightened theoretical teacher delivers to his students (in the *collegii musici* referred to in the concluding paragraphs of his article, for example) and to his readers are based not upon inherited musical canons (syllogisms, as he describes them) but upon the analysis of the rhetorical and affective content of the text to be set to music.

In its personal arrogance and self-assurance Mattheson's style is typical of that of many other eighteenth-century writers who also took for granted their right and obligation to enlighten their contemporaries. In his assessment of the fruits of this inquiry, Mattheson emphasizes the fact that most of its contents are simply intended to show how to avoid error. "If you think over all these things, Melophile," he writes, "you must not conclude that you have created something beautiful and perfect . . . since most of these remarks are intended only to avoid pitfalls. It is not enough [to learn how] to avoid mistakes. Purity and correctness are not all that constitute good composition." Indeed, in order to produce a good result all errors must first be eliminated. "To make a house useful, cleaning it is not unimportant, and must be done thoroughly before one considers the furnishings." Extending his metaphor of the enlightened householder, he adds: "Anyone who brings in beautiful tapestries and other glittering furnishings before sweeping out all the dirt begins at the wrong end" (CM II, 54–5).

In his continuing struggle to enlighten his readers Mattheson emphasizes in particular French practice, taste, and esteem for music, exemplified preeminently by the achievements of Lully, and by contemporary aesthetic criticism. In attempting to ensure that the requirements of textual clarity, proper accentuation and verbal em-

40 *Melodische Wissenschaft*, 71f.　41 See *Capellmeister*, 176f, 184f.

phasis are carried out, and that textual punctuation in musical settings is correctly evaluated, he seeks to protect his fellow musicians from the excesses of Italian music with its taste for extensive *passaggi.* He wishes also to liberate them from the moribund tradition of learned counterpoint, while encouraging a simplified style of canon and fugue when warranted by the text.

French musical criticism also inspires the strong emphasis he places upon the correct appraisal of the affective content of a text to ensure its proper musical treatment. A reader of this article lacking access to his or his predecessor's score is invariably provided with the textual material under discussion – specific passages from the Gospel and complete citations of Postel's poetry – to enable him to appreciate Mattheson's musical criticisms and recommendations. For it is his firm conviction that the act of musical composition is both a rhetorical and a pragmatic action. As a devout Lutheran he is convinced that no other textual material provides such a wide range of profoundly serious affections and emotions as a dramatic religious subject. By the same token, it is naturally valid to insert Lutheran chorales to round out, supplement, or increase religious understanding.

Taken as a whole, the questions raised by Melophile, but even more the answers they receive, are remarkable for their attention to explicit detail as well as broad principle and for the musical prescriptions for every significant feature of the text. Neither textual inadequacies nor ways to correct them are overlooked, and for each recommendation Mattheson provides a rational explanation. His prescriptions are as accurately carried out in *Das Lied des Lammes* as the faulty solutions resulting from "ignorance and prejudice" are exemplified in the earlier *Passion according to St. John.* However, it must be emphasized that only the many pointed allusions to the earlier work of a certain "celebrated" composer, formerly well known in Hamburg, provide clues to identify it. Not once in the article itself does the author suggest that his own composition exists other than as a hypothetical illustration of the principles it contains. Mattheson thus reveals his own critical position in unequivocal terms: reason united with the senses, focused like a spotlight upon the musico-poetic attitudes of a given text, will prove an infallible guide in composing music for it. There is therefore no need to provide analyses of specific musical solutions to individual details, any more than there is any reason to take into consideration individualistic or subjective taste or inspiration.

In the context of Mattheson's long-range plans of musical enlightenment, "The Inquiring Composer" was the "working paper" for his long-announced goal of a treatise on "essential melodic knowledge" – *Kern melodischer Wissenschafft*, published a dozen years later in 1737.[42] This treatise, somewhat revised to reduce its most contentious qualities, becomes the central one of the three grand parts that constitute Mattheson's most comprehensive musical treatise, *Der vollkommene Capellmeister* of 1739. The culmination of his efforts, this encyclopedic work was designed to bring music, "a beautiful form of knowledge, to the highest perfection,"[43] and it may be fairly described as the summation of his knowledge and thought accumulated over the course of his many years as a composer, theorist, critic, and scholar.

Mattheson's inexhaustible interest in every European musical activity – creative, critical, or financial – about which he was able to learn, accounts for many changes in emphasis and a considerably broader perspective on the essentials of rational musical knowledge than the premises so vigorously argued in "The Inquiring Composer." A number of antiquated procedures for which the earlier St. John Passion was severely censured are not even mentioned, though two of its most important topics are not only retained but also receive considerable attention. The first of these is the importance of understanding where the principal verbal accent and emphasis fall within a clause or sentence, and how to provide correct musical equivalents through the relative duration of tones and the rise and fall in the melodic contours of a recitative. After recommending to the reader the specific passages in "The Inquiring Composer" dealing with that problem,[44] he goes into an extended discussion of the rhetorical and grammatical questions concerned. As illustrations he quotes four different passages from recitatives in the "Handel" Passion, only the first of which elicited attention in his article.[45] Most significantly, he presents as correct solutions rewritten versions of the original musical materials rather than the parallel passages from his own oratorio. The apparent reason for this is that, by his progressive reasoning, the latter no longer qualify as correct.

42 Cannon, *Mattheson*, No. 134.
43 Ibid., No. 138. The comprehensive goal of this book is indicated by its title: *Der / Vollkommene / Capellmeister / Das ist / Gründliche Anzeige / aller derjenigen Sachen, / die einer wissen, können, und vollkommen inne haben muß, / der eine Capelle / mit Ehren und Nutzen vorstehen will*
44 *Capellmeister*, 176: "Worin nun dieser Gehalt und Sing-Accent bestehen, davon hat die musicalische Critic p. 40, 41, und 42 und 43 zulängliche Nachricht gegeben."
45 CM II, 40, "Und machten vier Theil . . ."

The second topic discussed and explained at much greater length than in "The Inquiring Composer" deals with the basic grammatic structures found in prose and poetry, and the paramount importance of knowing the correct musical equivalents and, particularly, of understanding subtle differences in punctuation. As in his earlier work, Mattheson considers the most troublesome of these to be the identification of the *comma pendulum* as opposed to the *comma perfectum*. But the illustrations chosen to clarify this problem are entirely different. Instead of presenting the reader with examples of incorrect writing by any composer, he provides extensive quotations of two vocal melodies from arias in his *Lied des Lammes*, explaining carefully how each provides accurate solutions. These are "Schauet, mein Jesus," No. 8, and "Getrost, mein Herz," No. 25.[46]

Nevertheless, with the explicit evidence of the two existing oratorios at hand, "The Inquiring Composer" provides more vivid evidence of a rationalistic composer's understanding of expressive musical rhetoric than *Der vollkommene Capellmeister* does. Indeed, no other document with such an aesthetic attitude toward artistic creation reveals as sharply the contrast between the attitudes of an "enlightened" composer and the postexistential composer of two centuries later. An individualistic approach to the composition of a theatrical oratorio is as unthinkable to Mattheson as the notion that consideration should be given to any objective criteria of taste or musical techniques would be to the young composer of the 1980s. To be sure, Mattheson's contemporaries were the inheritors of a number of well-established methods, techniques, and styles. If many of these were ancient and thus truly antiquated, it was because of the procrustean bed of ecclesiastical, theoretical pedantry in which they were embedded. By demolishing this traditional superstructure the most time-honored skills of contrapuntal craftsmanship could be rescued and modernized by being adapted to contemporary melodic style and the harmonic procedures associated with it. For here was a language generated in the more recent past on the premise of the *homme universelle*, the educated man in whom reason, harmoniously united with common sense, is a reliable and final arbiter.

Obviously the greatest necessity for Mattheson, the enlightened but devout Lutheran, was to prove to his German colleagues that sacred music could serve its highest ends only by accepting these premises, by incorporating the best of the past with all of the more recent

---

46 *Capellmeister*, 185.

developments exemplified by opera. Informed by rational analysis of the affections and their musical equivalents, intellectually open to the developments and discoveries of modern music, and guided by the empirical philosophy as expounded by John Locke and others, the young composer's path could indeed be smooth and straight.

Appendix

The first two columns below provide a collation of the two *Passions according to St. John* by (I) Mattheson: Johann Mattheson, *Das Lied des Lammes* (Madison, 1971), and (II) Handel: Georg Friedrich Händel, *Passion nach dem Evangelisten Johannes, Die Hallische Händel-Ausgabe,* Serie I/2 (Kassel, 1964). Column (III), *Critica musica,* refers to the paragraph number of Mattheson's article *Des fragenden Componist,* in his *Critica musica* (Hamburg, 1722–5, repr. Amsterdam, 1964), in which each section of the two *Passions* is discussed.

I. Mattheson	II. Handel	III. Critica musica
1. Sonatina	1. Sinfonia	III
2. Chorale, Christus, der uns selig macht		IV
3. Recit., Da nahm Pilatus Jesus	2. Recit.	II, V
4. Aria, Unsre Bosheit	3. Aria	VI–VIII
5. Recit., Und die Kriegsknechte	4. Recit.	IX
6. Tutti, Sei gegrüsset	5. Coro	X, XI
7. Recit., Und gaben ihm	6. Recit.	
Arioso, Sehet, ich führe ihn	7. Ariosos	
Recit., Also ging Jesus heraus	8. Recit.	
8. Aria, Schauet, mein Jesus	9. Duetto	XII–XIV
9. Recit., Und er spricht	10. Recit.	
(Arioso) Sehet welch ein Mensch	11. Arioso	
Recit., Da ihn die Hohenpriester	12. Recit.	
10. Tutti, Kreuzige, kreuzige	13. Coro	XV
11. Recit., Pilatus spricht	14. Recit.	XVI
(Arioso) Nehmet ihr ihn hin	15. Arioso	
Recit., Die Juden antworteten ihm	16. Recit.	
12. Tutti, Wir haben ein Gesetze	17. Coro	XVII

13. Recit., Da Pilatus das Wort höret	18. Recit.	
(Arioso) Redest du nicht	19. Arioso	XVIII–XX XXVIII
Recit., Jesus antwortet	20. Recit.	
14. Accomp., Du hättest keine Macht	21. Aria	XXI, XXII XXVIII
15. Recit., Von dem an trachtet	22. Recit.	
16. Duetto, Durch dein Gefängnis	23. Aria	XXIII–XXVII
17. Recit., Die Juden aber schrieen	24. Recit.	
18. Canon, Lässest du diesen los	25. Coro	XXIX, XXX
19. Recit., Da Pilatus das Wort höret	26. Recit.	
(Arioso) Siehet, das ist euer König	27. Arioso	
Recit., Sie schrieen alle	28. Recit.	
20. Fuga doppio, Weg, weg mit dem	29. Coro	XXXI
21. Aria, Erschüttere mit Krachen	30. Aria	XXXII–XXXIV
22. Recit., Spricht Pilatus zu ihnem	31. Recit.	
(Arioso) Soll ich euren König	32. Arioso	
Recit., Die Hohenpriester antworteten	33. Recit.	
23. Tutti, Wir haben keinen König	34. Coro	XXXV
24. Recit., Da überantwortet er ihn	35. Recit.	XXXVI
25. Arietta, Getrost, mein Herz!	36. Aria	XXXVII, XXXVIII
26. Recit., Pilatus aber schrieb	37. Recit.	XXXIX–XL
27. Tutti, Schreib nicht der Juden König	38. Coro	XLI
28. Recit., Pilatus antwortet	39. Recit.	
Oblig., Was ich geschrieben habe	40. Arioso	XLII
29. Recit., Die Krieges Knechte aber	41. Recit.	XLIII
30. Aria, Du müßt den Rock	42. Aria	XLIV
31. Recit., Den Rock aber war	43. Recit.	

(continued)

Recit., Lasset uns den nicht	44. Coro	XLV
Recit., Auf daβ erfüllet würde	45. Recit.	XLVI
(Arioso) Sie habe meine Kleider	46. Accompagnato	
Recit., Solches taten	47. Recit.	
32. Antiphon, Welche sind des Heilands Erben?	48. Duetto	XLVII, XLVIII
33. Canto Fermo, Es dient zu meinen Freuden		XLIX, L
34. Recit., Es stund aber	49. Recit.	
Adagio, Weib, siehe	50. Arioso	
Recit., Darnach spricht er	51. Recit.	
Adagio, Siehe, das ist deine Mutter	52. Arioso	
Recit. Und von Stund an	53. Recit.	
Adagio, Mich dürstet	54. Arioso	
35. Aria, Jesu, wornach dürstet dich	55. Aria	LI, LII
36. Recit., Da stand ein Gefäβ	56. Recit.	
Accomp., Es ist vollbracht	57. Arioso	
37. Aria, O, groβes Werk!	58. Aria	LIII
38. Recit., Und neigte das Haupt	59. Recit.	
39. Aria, Bebet ihr Berge	60. Aria	LIV–LVI
40. Recit., Die Juden aber	61. Recit.	
41. (Duetto) War das Wasser	62. Duetto	LVII–LIX
42. Recit., Un der das gesehen hat	63. Recit.	
43. Duetto, Ich gehe mit ins Grab	64. Duetto	LX–LXII
44. Recit., Es war aber an der Stätte	65. Recit.	
45. Contrapunto, Schlafe wohl' nach deinen Leiden	66. Coro	LXIII

168

7

Mattheson's arrangement of Handel's *Radamisto* for the Hamburg Opera

WINTON DEAN

Godalming, England

It is well known that soon after Handel established himself as a dramatic composer in London his operas became increasingly popular in Hamburg. Between 1715 and 1734 fifteen of them, including the Venetian *Agrippina*, were staged there, and several remained in the repertory until the closure of the Hamburg Opera in 1738. Apart from Braunschweig, which had connections with the English court after the accession of the Elector of Hanover as King George I, Hamburg saw far more contemporary Handel productions than any other city on the continent. There were obvious reasons for this. As a free city it had close commercial and cultural links with England. The young Handel had spent three impressionable years there, playing in the theater orchestra, learning his trade, and composing his first operas. And several influential friends and colleagues were active in Hamburg, among them Keiser, Mattheson, and Telemann, each of whom was concerned in the introduction of one or more of Handel's London operas.

Although librettos for all these productions survive, most of the scores have been lost. It is clear, however, that they had to be adapted for the Hamburg public. Apart from *Agrippina*, which was given in Italian throughout, they were sung in a mixture of two languages, the regular Hamburg practice: the recitatives and on occasion some of the arias in German, the majority of the arias and set pieces in the original Italian. The librettos printed a German translation, generally in prose, alongside the Italian arias. The degree of rearrangement to which the operas were subjected varied widely. While the recitatives had to be recomposed, some productions retained the original plots and most if not all of Handel's arias and set pieces. Others were changed, sometimes very considerably. The Hamburg public liked not only spectacle, of which there was plenty in the London theatre, but choruses, extra ballets, and if possible comic relief; and they were developing a

169

taste for that Italian curiosity, the pasticcio. There was a tendency to divide the music as evenly as possible between the available singers, regardless of their importance in the plot. This was common in Italy too, but it was very different from Handel's own practice when he adapted old Italian librettos for his operas in London.

As early as 1717 the magic opera *Amadigi*, produced in Hamburg under the title *Oriana*, received three extra characters, including a buffo servant who consoled himself with drink; most of the new music was by Keiser. J. G. Linike added choruses of concubines and comic peasants and extra music for minor characters to *Giulio Cesare*. Telemann in particular was inclined to dilute Handel's most serious and tragic operas with extravagances of this kind. He introduced a scene at the foot of Mount Olympus, with a ballet of Highlanders and their women, into Act I of *Tamerlano*, and a Tartar dance at a most unsuitable moment in Act II. His version of *Ottone* is virtually a pasticcio, with an extra character and additional arias not only by Telemann himself but by various Italian composers. The most extreme case is *Riccardo primo*, where the degree of buffoonery almost approaches that of Telemann's own *Der geduldige Socrates*.[1]

None of this is surprising. Probably no one at that period regarded an old opera as a work of art whose integrity had to be respected in revivals. That is a modern conception. In any case, it would not have been practical in the present instance. All Handel's operas after he left Hamburg were composed according to the Italian *opera seria* convention (admittedly with variations of his own), many of them for the greatest singers in Europe. A central feature of this tradition was that the heroic parts were designed for high voices, sopranos or altos, and sung by castratos or women – often by both in different performances. The Hamburg company was very differently constituted. Castratos did appear there occasionally: Valentino Urbani in 1722, Campioli from 1722 to 1726. (Both sang under Handel in London.) Male parts were sometimes sung by women, for example Julius Caesar by Dominichina Pollone in 1729.[2] But the usual practice was to transpose these heroic parts down an octave for tenors and basses, simply because more of them were available. The implications of this are considered below.

Mattheson's version of *Radamisto*, one of five Handel operas of

---

1 See E. Dahnk-Baroffio, "Händels *Riccardo primo* in Deutschland," in: *50 Jahre Göttinger Händel-Festspiele*, ed. W. Meyerhoff (Kassel, 1970), 150–66.
2 K. Zelm, "Die Sänger der Hamburger Gänsemarkt-Oper," in: *Hamburger Jahrbuch für Musikwissenschaft* 3 (1978), 35–73, on p. 65.

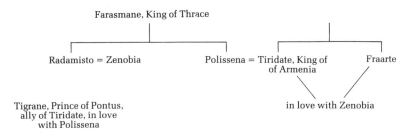

Figure 1. Relationships between the characters in *Radamisto*

which the Hamburg score survives,[3] was produced in January 1722 under the title *Zenobia, oder das Muster rechtschaffener ehelichen Liebe*. It enjoyed considerable success, with at least 30 performances, most of them in the first two seasons; there was a ten-year gap before its last revival in 1736. Before examining Mattheson's treatment of the score, and how it conformed with the work of his Hamburg contemporaries, it is necessary to say something about the opera itself and its early history. *Radamisto*, composed for the first season of the Royal Academy, the most ambitious of all attempts to establish Italian opera in London, is one of Handel's grandest and most heroic operas. There is no light relief at all. The characters, all of royal or princely blood, are torn by the most passionate emotions (Figure 1 shows their relationships), and the plot is full of threatened and actual violence. The villain Tiridate, King of Armenia, is married to Radamisto's sister Polissena but lusts after his sister-in-law Zenobia, Radamisto's wife. In order to gain his desires he makes war on his father-in-law Farasmane, King of Thrace, conquers all his dominions except the capital city in which Radamisto and Zenobia are besieged, captures the old king himself, and tries to blackmail Radamisto into surrender by threatening to kill his father before his eyes and put the city's whole population to the sword. Among Tiridate's allies are two other princes: Tigrane, who loves Polissena but tries to win her by persuasion rather than force, and Tiridate's brother Fraarte, who in Handel's first version also loves Zenobia. The events of the opera include Tiridate's capture of the city, the escape of Radamisto and Zenobia, her attempted suicide by jumping into the river Araxes, the faithful Polissena's denunciation of her husband when he refuses to pardon her brother, and a revolution led by Tigrane and Fraarte who, sick-

3 The others are *Almira, Ottone, Riccardo Primo* and *Poro*.

171

Table 1. Cast changes for Radamisto–Zenobia productions

| | Radamisto | | | | Zenobia |
	April 1720	December 1720	November 1721	January 1728	Hamburg, January 1722
Male					
Radamisto	Durastanti (soprano)	Senesino (alto castrato)	Senesino	Senesino	Bass
Tigrane	Galerati (soprano)	Berselli (soprano castrato)	? Baldassari (soprano castrato)	Baldi (alto castrato)	Tenor
Fraarte	Baldassari (soprano castrato)	Galerati (soprano)	—	—	Tenor
Tiridate	Gordon (tenor)	Boschi (bass)	Boschi	Boschi	Bass
Farasmane	Lagarde (bass)	Lagarde	? Lagarde	Palmerini (bass)	Tenor
Female					
Zenobia	Anastasia Robinson (contralto)	Durastanti (soprano)	? Anastasia Robinson	Faustina Bordoni (soprano)	Soprano
Polissena	Ann Turner Robinson (soprano)	Salvai (soprano)	Salvai	Cuzzoni (soprano)	Soprano
Version of score	1	2	3	4	5

ened by Tiridate's cruelty, bring the tyrant to his knees. He confesses and, to his surprise, is forgiven. This ensures the statutory happy end.

By the time of the Hamburg production Handel had performed the opera in three London seasons, in April 1720, December 1720, and November 1721, and he was to revive it again in January 1728. Each production saw changes in the music and the cast, and the first two – in April and December 1720 – were radically different. Even the plot was altered: In December Fraarte was no longer Tiridate's brother but his minister, his love for Zenobia was cut out, and the action of the third act was greatly tightened up. The casts are listed in Table 1. It will be seen that of the seven singers in April only one, the bass Lagarde in the small role of Farasmane, retained the same part in December. Two others, the sopranos Durastanti and Galerati, were still in the cast but sang different roles. Three important characters had a new vocal pitch: Radamisto, composed for a woman soprano, was sung by an alto castrato; Zenobia, a contralto, by a soprano; and Tiridate, a tenor, by a bass. It is worth noting, as typical of Handel's practice, that during the year 1720 all three male soprano roles were sung both by women and by castratos.[4]

To accommodate the new singers in December 1720 Handel was not content simply to transpose the old arias; he rewrote many of them, and composed twelve new pieces, including a magnificent quartet, one of the most elaborate ensembles in any of his operas. But the matter is more complicated than that. There are five, not four, versions of *Radamisto*, quite apart from changes made before performance, and no accurate printed score of any of them. The version staged in April 1720, representing Handel's original conception, which includes three ballet suites, has not been published at all.[5] Chrysander's first version is based on Hamburg MS MA/1044, which he assumed to be the April performing score. It is not a performing score, it is not the April version, and it is not a Smith copy. It was written by another copyist[6] about 1721, apparently because Handel wished to preserve a clean pre-December score for his library. It reflects not what was performed in April but the score as altered

---

4 O. E. Deutsch (*Handel: A Documentary Biography*, London, 1955) is wrong in listing Baldassari and Berselli as tenors, and in doubting whether the 1728 revival took place. Chrysander (in the Preface to the Händel-Gesellschaft score) is wrong in saying that Fraarte was cut in December 1720.
5 It survives complete in a single manuscript in the possession of the Earl of Malmesbury.
6 Hl in the enumeration of H. D. Clausen, *Händels Direktionspartituren ("Handexemplare")* (Hamburg, 1972), 202. Chrysander used this manuscript as copy for his edition.

either during the original run or a little later, but before December 1720. These alterations included the omission of the ballet suites and a number of modifications both to words and to music. Most unusually Handel entered some of these in the original authograph; but the survival of material canceled there both in the first printed score and in a number of early copies proves that he must have done this after the April production.

Chrysander's first version is thus no. 2 in Table 1, and corresponds to no known performance. His *Seconda e Terza Versione* is a confusing jumble of nos. 3, 4, and 5 – the versions performed in Handel's three revivals – none of them printed or indicated in full. Moreover Chrysander also backdated into his first version – no. 2 – some minor changes that belong to Handel's later productions.

Mattheson's Hamburg score, now in the Berlin Staatsbibliothek (Mus. MS 9051), differs from all of Handel's. That almost certainly was not Mattheson's intention, apart of course from the recitatives and vocal transpositions. It can be shown that he obtained three separate sources from London: a manuscript full score of the April version, the printed libretto of the December 1720 revival, and a manuscript full score of Handel's twelve new pieces composed for that occasion. He must have obtained the music from Handel himself, or at least with his consent. He cannot have relied on the Meares printed scores of either April or December,[7] since as usual they were incomplete, omitting many of the orchestral parts, and Meares did not print the quartet at all. There is no evidence that Mattheson knew the November 1721 score (no. 4), which omitted Fraarte altogether.

What he tried to do was to reproduce Handel's December version by grafting the twelve new pieces on to the April score. He needed the December libretto to know where to place them – not at all a simple matter – and he did this correctly; Chrysander prints three of them in the wrong place. But Mattheson obviously knew nothing of the other alterations and revisions made by Handel in December; nor did he know Handel's transpositions of the arias he retained. None of these appears in his *Zenobia* score, which (apart from the twelve new pieces and the recitatives) follows the April version without the ballet suites. One of Polissena's arias in Act II, "Non sarà quest'alma mia," received a new and stronger text in Handel's December revival, beginning "Che farà quest'alma mia." Mattheson realized that it was essentially the same piece, so he fitted the December words to the

7 Published in December 1720 and March 1721 respectively.

April music, unaware that in the meantime Handel had rewritten and improved the aria, especially the orchestration.

Table 1 shows that Mattheson gave six of the seven characters a different voice from Handel's April score, only Polissena retaining her original pitch. She remained a soprano in all Handel's versions too, though he lowered the tessitura a little for Salvai and raised it again later for Cuzzoni. Mattheson set about his task in a rather strange manner. The three high male parts – Radamisto, Tigrane, and Fraarte – were all put down an octave, though Radamisto now had five arias and one duet from the soprano version of April, and two arias, one duet, and the quartet from the alto version of December. Farasmane's single aria, for bass, had its voice part adjusted for tenor in the original key. Zenobia's six alto arias were simply written out at the same pitch in the soprano clef; she also had one soprano aria, "Fatemi, O cieli," the only new one composed for her in December, and incidentally the only aria of hers in that revival whose exact pitch we know. All Zenobia's other arias in Chrysander's *Seconda e Terza Versione* are adaptations for Faustina Bordoni in 1728 (version 5). For Tiridate, Mattheson had one bass aria from December and two tenor arias from April, both of which Handel had since rewritten with more elaborate scoring and striking improvements. Mattheson could not know this; he simply retained the tenor versions, and his copyist put the voice part of one into the bass clef, but for some obscure reason not the other.

This resulted in some odd inconsistencies of tessitura. Occasionally another hand made adjustments in the manuscript, generally shifting phrases at either end of the vocal compass up or down an octave, which does not improve the vocal line. One of Zenobia's April arias, the fiery "Già che morir non posso," is very awkward for a soprano at the original pitch, so many phrases in both sections were put in the higher octave. One of Tiridate's, "Si che ti renderai," and one of Radamisto's, "Vanne sorella ingrata," underwent the opposite procedure, their highest phrases going down an octave. Others, on the face of it equally uncomfortable for the singers, remained untouched. If the opera was sung as it stands in the score, some of the voices must have been subjected to considerable strain. This is particularly true of Radamisto's part, which veers between a high baritone and a bass. It is not at all clear why Mattheson did not have some arias transposed into more convenient keys before the score was copied. He may not have known who was to sing in the opera. He may even have delegated the whole job of reconciling the scores to the copyist and

175

confined himself to translating and setting the recitatives. Unfortunately we know nothing of the Hamburg casts, except that Signora Stradiotti, a soprano who had sung in London (though not under Handel), appeared in *Zenobia* in 1724.

Apart from annotations for revivals and the tessitura changes just mentioned, Mus. MS 9051 is in the hand of a single theater copyist. The bass is fully figured. On one page of Fraarte's first aria, "Deh! fuggi un traditore," the copyist forgot to alter the voice clef from soprano to tenor, and no one bothered to correct the mistake. Another aria for Fraarte, in the first scene of Act III, is in the soprano clef throughout. Apart from the recitatives, it is the only music in the manuscript not by Handel. Fraarte had an aria here in the April version, "S'adopri il braccio armato," but not in December. Mattheson decided to give him one, but instead of restoring Handel's he chose a piece very similar in style and mood both to "S'adopri" and to "Deh! fuggi un traditore," which Reinhard Strohm has identified as from Bononcini's *Etearco*. However, Mattheson then thought better of this, for the copyist never supplied the words, and the aria was apparently concealed or pasted down before the performance and not sung.

The modifications made for later Hamburg revivals include the omission of Farasmane's single aria, two of Tigrane's, and the remaining two of Fraarte's, though all seem to have been subsequently restored. The 1726 edition of the libretto omits Fraarte's first two arias but includes "S'adopri"; this may be a mistake, or the aria may have been inserted on loose pages and subsequently lost. Three of Tigrane's arias were marked for transposition, "L'ingrato non amar" from G minor to C minor, "Vuol ch'io serva" (which has a high tessitura) from G to A, and "La sorte, il ciel" from B-flat to F, either for an alto or a bass. The magnificent aria "Barbaro, partirò," in which Polissena finally denounces her brutal husband, copied in its December 1720 key of A major (not Chrysander's B-flat, which belongs to Cuzzoni in 1728), may on some occasion have been replaced by the original April aria, "Sposo ingrato," a much weaker piece; someone wrote those words in the margin, but the music is not in the manuscript. Another revival change was the raising of two of Zenobia's arias, "Fatemi, O cieli" and "Empio perverso cor," by a third. Handel himself made these transpositions, but not until 1728, when he transferred "Fatemi, O cieli" to Polissena.

The manuscript also contains the first words – not the music – of several arias that do not belong to any version of Handel's opera. They come from Zeno's *Caio Fabrizio*, first set by Caldara for Venice in

1729, and can only apply to the last revival of *Zenobia* in 1736, turning it into a pasticcio. Whether Mattheson was concerned with this performance we cannot tell; but his 1722 copy was still in use, though the inserted music has been lost.

Mattheson's recitatives are considerably longer than Handel's both in the words and in the music. The first of all, after Polissena's cavatina "Sommi Dei," has twenty-six bars in Handel's April score, twenty-eight in December, and thirty-eight in Mattheson's. Over the whole opera, on a rough estimate, Mattheson's recitatives exceed Handel's by at least twenty percent. Their actual performance time must have been longer still. Apart from the fact that the German language does not trip so lightly off the tongue as the Italian, much of the tessitura of Mattheson's recitatives is pitched very high, especially for the basses Tiridate and Radamisto, who often go up to top F-sharp and G. This would require a more declamatory delivery than the quick parlando of the Italian style that Handel always adopted in his operas. Mattheson's recitatives are also slower in harmonic movement and less bold in their progressions, with little of the rapid cut and thrust characteristic of Handel's. This is perhaps what we should expect; no one has claimed that Mattheson possessed Handel's dramatic genius. But it means that the pacing of the opera, the fine balance between the lyrical and the dramatic sections, is seriously disturbed.

Mattheson clearly tried to reproduce Handel's December 1720 score as accurately as possible from the resources at his disposal; he preserved its serious heroic tone and did not dilute it with comic subplots or extraneous spectacle, as Telemann did with *Tamerlano* and *Riccardo primo*. He may have grasped the grandeur of Handel's conception in one of the noblest of all Baroque operas. But here we must consider the effect of the vocal transpositions. One thing that modern revivals have proved beyond all dispute is that Handel's extraordinarily subtle insight into character and his acute feeling for the balance of vocal and instrumental texture – qualities in which he has had few rivals in any age – can be appreciated at their full value only if the original voice pitches are retained. In the nature of things that was impossible at Hamburg. By making Radamisto's old father a tenor and Radamisto himself, the young and vulnerable hero, a bass, Mattheson subverted their entire relationship as depicted in the music. The two Senesino arias in particular, with their very long low-lying coloratura divisions, lose all their brilliance when sung by a bass in the lower octave; they sound more like a man with a sore throat gargling in a bathroom. In the beautiful duet at the end of Act II

Radamisto is the soprano, Zenobia the alto, in Handel's April score that Mattheson was using. In his *Zenobia* manuscript Radamisto's part is in the bass clef, Zenobia's in the soprano, so that all the intervals between them are inverted. Someone later changed the names round, giving Zenobia's original part to the bass. This makes little dramatic difference, since both are uttering the same sentiments, but it sometimes places the voices more than two octaves apart and carries the lower one below the written bass line.

The purpose this inquiry is not to decry Mattheson or his Hamburg colleagues, but to discover how he set about adapting an Italian *opera seria* composed for London to the conditions of performance in Hamburg. He turned it into a different kind of opera, a hybrid neither Italian nor quite German, like the other Hamburg arrangements. The use of two languages made this inevitable, and the more deliberate pacing of the recitatives and the vocal transpositions accentuated it, though Mattheson was more faithful to Handel than Telemann was. His arrangement served its purpose by making some magnificent music familiar to German audiences. But *Radamisto*, whether in its April or its December version, is much more than a collection of fine arias. It is a closely organized masterpiece in its own right. We should be doing little service to Mattheson, and none at all to Handel, if we were to revive this version of *Zenobia* today.

8

Mattheson als Begründer der ersten Musikzeitschrift (*Critica musica*)
IMOGEN FELLINGER
Berlin, West

Bei Matthesons *Critica musica* handelt es sich nicht nur, wie vielfach angegeben wird, um die erste in Deutschland erschienene Musikzeitschrift, sondern um die früheste musikalische Zeitschrift im eigentlichen Sinne überhaupt, die zugleich die erste Fachzeitschrift auf künstlerischem Gebiet darstellt. Theaterzeitschriften und -almanache folgten seit 1750[1] und in den siebziger Jahren des achtzehnten Jahrhunderts entstanden die ersten Zeitschriften für bildende Künste[2]. Läßt sich aus dieser Tatsache allein bereits schließen, daß Mattheson von einem gewissen Pioniergeist beseelt gewesen sein muß, so kann dies noch weiterhin dadurch bekräftigt werden, daß er vor der Herausgabe der *Critica musica* auch als Begründer der ersten moralischen Wochenschrift in Deutschland zu gelten hat,[3] Zwar bringt diese Zeitschrift, die unter dem Titel *Der Vernünfftler* (1713/14) erschien, nur sporadische Angaben zur Musik; vielmehr wurden in ihr – gemäß dem von England ausgehenden Typus von Zeitschriften – in der Hauptsache Fragen von Sitte und Moral im menschlichen Dasein behandelt. Doch ist sie für Matthesons allgemeine Geisteshaltung von Interesse, worauf im Folgenden noch näher eingegangen sei, und auch für die Tatsache von Bedeutung, daß er nicht nur mit dem Zeitschriftenwesen seiner Zeit bestens vertraut

---

1 *Beyträge zur Historie und Aufnahme des Theaters.* Herausgeber: G. E. Lessing und Chr. Mylius, 1.-4. Stück (Stuttgart, 1750); *Calendrier historique des théâtres de l'opéra et des comédies . . . , ab 1752: Almanach historique et chronologique de tous les spectacles,* voll. 1–46 (Paris, 1751–93/4, 1800–1801, 1815); *Theatralische Bibliothek.* Herausgeber: G. E. Lessing, 1.-4. Stück (Berlin, 1754–8).
2 *Kunstzeitung der Kayserl. Akademie zu Augsburg.* Herausgeber: H. A. Mertens, Jg. 1–3 (Augsburg, 1770–2); *Journal zur Kunstgeschichte und zur allgemeinen Litteratur.* Herausgeber: Chr. G. von Murr, Tomus 1–17 (Nürnberg, 1775–89).
3 Siehe K. Jacoby, "Die ersten moralischen Wochenschriften Hamburgs am Anfange des 18. Jahrhunderts", in: *Oster-Programm des Wilhelms-Gymnasiums in Hamburg,* Programm Nr. 687 (Hamburg, 1888), 3–5.

war, sondern sich bereits darin aktiv betätigt hatte, als er daran ging, die erste Zeitschrift auf musikalischem Gebiet im Jahre 1722 ins Leben zu rufen. Ihr ließ er, wie bekannt, eine zweite mit dem Titel *Der musicalische Patriot* (1728) folgen, bevor andere Musikgelehrte und Musiktheoretiker in Deutschland, wie Mizler, Scheibe und Marpurg, sich dazu verstanden, einen solchen Weg zu beschreiten.

Es ist zunächst nach den Voraussetzungen zu fragen, die Mattheson im Zeitungs- und Zeitschriftenwesen seiner Zeit vorfand, bevor auf dessen Beweggründe, eine Musikzeitschrift herauszubringen, im einzelnen eingegangen sei. Welche Typen periodischer Veröffentlichungen bestanden zu jener Zeit im allgemeinen und im Zusammenhang mit Musik im besonderen? Auf welchen Voraussetzungen vornehmlich geistesgeschichtlicher Art konnten musikalische Zeitschriften überhaupt entstehen?

Zum einen sind periodische Musikpublikationen, die ausschließlich Kompositionen enthalten und – mit Ausnahme von Deutschland und Österreich, in denen zuerst musikalische Gelehrten-Zeitschriften erschienen[4] – in allen Ländern den aus Abhandlungen, Berichten, Kritiken, Nachrichten und Anzeigen bestehenden Musikzeitschriften im engeren Sinne zeitlich vorangingen, für die Entstehung von Musikzeitschriften bedeutungsvoll gewesen. Läßt sich in den Neujahrsblättern der "Musikgesellschaft ab dem Musiksaal" (Zürich, 1685–1812), die Zitate aus der Bibel, den Klassikern und neueren Dichtern zusammen mit Vokal- und Instrumentalkompositionen brachten[5], eine gewisse Vorform solcher periodischer Musikausgaben erblicken, so entstand diese Publikationsform im eigentlichen Sinne zu Beginn der neunziger Jahre in Frankreich. Es war der Pariser Verleger Christophe Ballard, der als erster, soweit nachweisbar, derartige Periodica mit der im Abstand von drei Monaten herausgegebenen Sammlung *Airs sérieux et à boire* (livres I–XVIII) von Jean Baptiste de Bousset (Paris, 1690–4) ins Leben rief. Ihr ließ er weitere Ausgaben dieser Art, wie *Recueil d'Airs sérieux et à boire de différents autheurs pour l'année 1695* (– 1724) (Paris) mit Generalbaß, folgen. Die erste englische Ausgabe war *Mercurius Musicus or, the Monthly Collection of New Teaching Songs, compos'd for the Theatres, and other Occasions. . .* (London, 1699–1702). Ihr folgte in den Niederlanden die periodische Samm-

---

4 Die erste Musikzeitschrift Österreichs, *Der musikalische Dilettante* (Wien, 1770–1, 1773) von J. Fr. Daube, besteht in der Hauptsache aus einer Kompositions- und Generalbaßlehre sowie einigen Kompositionen von Daube und anderen.

5 Siehe [H. Stierlin], "Die Neujahrstücke der frühern Musikgesellschaften bis 1812", in: *Neujahrstücke der Allgemeinen Musikgesellschaft* 45 (Zürich, 1857).

lung *Les Airs sérieux et à boire des mois de Janvier, Février, Mars*. . .
(Amsterdam, 1701–23) des Verlegers französischer Herkunft Estienne Roger und als erste periodische Musikpublikation in Deutschland Telemanns Ausgabe *Der getreue Music-Meister* (Hamburg, 1728)[6]. Diese Gruppe von Periodica beeinflußte die allgemeine Entwicklung musikalischer Zeitschriften nachhaltig. So ist wohl die Gepflogenheit, jede Nummer oder jeden Jahrgang einer Musikzeitschrift oder eines Almanachs mit Musikbeilagen oder einem musikalischen Anhang auszustatten, auf sie zurückzuführen, wie auch der Typ musikalischer Zeitschriften, die gleichgewichtig aus einem theoretischen und einem praktischen Teil bestehen, so die in Speyer bei Bossler herausgekommene *Musikalische Real-Zeitung* mit dem praktischen Teil: *Musikalische Anthologie für Kenner und Liebhaber* (1788–90)[7]. Andererseits wurden in der zweiten Hälfte des achtzehnten und der ersten Hälfte des neunzehnten Jahrhunderts in periodische Musikpublikationen Beilagen mit musiktheoretischen Darlegungen und Besprechungen von neuen Büchern und musikalischen Werken aufgenommen, aus denen sich etwa in England[8], Russland[9] und der Tschechoslowakei[10] die Musikzeitschriften im engeren Sinne herausgebildet zu haben scheinen. War diese Kategorie von musikalischen Periodica indes auch nicht unmittelbar von Bedeutung für Matthesons Zeitschriften-Gründungen, so scheinen diese in einer Art von Wechselwirkung zur ersten Ausgabe innerhalb dieser Publikationsform in Deutschland gestanden zu haben, nämlich zu Telemanns Publikation *Der getreue Music-Meister* (Hamburg, 1728). Eine in dessen Vorwort gebrachte Bemerkung scheint hierauf hinzudeuten. Telemann betont,

daß es ein musicalisches Journal sey, und . . . das erste, so, vermittelst wirklicher Music, in Teutschland, zum Vorschein kommt. Haben sonst die so genannten monatliche, oder solche, Schriften, die zu gewissen Zeiten Stückweise herauskommen, vielfältig ihre Liebhaber gefunden, so solte ich

---

6 Siehe I. Fellinger, *Periodica musicalia (1789–1830)*, vol. I: *Historischer Überblick* (Regensburg, 1983) (= Studien zur Musikgeschichte des 19. Jahrhunderts, vol. 55)

7 Fortgesetzt als: *Anthologie zur musikalischen Realzeitung für 1790*; seit 1790 unter dem Titel: *Musikalische Korrespondenz der Teutschen Filarmonischen Gesellschaft* mit dem praktischen Teil: *Notenblätter zur musikalischen Korrespondenz* . . . (Speyer, 1790–2).

8 *The Literary Part of the Musical Magazine* [i.e., der periodischen Musikpublikation *The New Musical and Universal Magazine*] (London, 1774–5).

9 *Literaturnoe pribavlemi k "Nuvellistu"* (1844–74) [i.e., Die literarische Beilage zu *Le Nouvelliste*] (St. Petersburg, 1840–1906).

10 *Literární příloha k Věnci* [i.e. Literarische Beilage zu der Liedsammlung *Věnec*] (Prag, 1843).

glauben, es werde auch diese nicht gar verworfen werden, da sie, mit jenen, den Zweck hat, zu nutzen und zu belustigen[11].

Mit diesen Worten, die auf Matthesons Zeitschriften gemünzt gewesen zu sein scheinen, wollte Telemann offensichtlich zum Ausdruck bringen, daß dessen Periodica zwar von Musik handelten, es aber ihm vorbehalten geblieben war, als erster in Deutschland ein Journal mit "wirklicher Musik" herauszugeben. Diese bewußte Betonung der praktischen Seite der Musik äußerte sich in Telemanns periodischer Ausgabe gegenüber den in Frankreich, England und den Niederlanden vorangegangenen Periodica in einer ungleich größeren Vielfalt in der instrumentalen Besetzung und den vertretenen Gattungen der dargebotenen Kompositionen, die er "nach und nach alle 14. Tage in einer Lection vorzutragen" gedachte gemäß seiner im Titel niedergelegten Absicht[12].

Neben den periodischen Musikausgaben spielten für die Entstehung musikalischer Zeitschriften noch andere Faktoren eine wesentliche Rolle. So sind gelegentliche Notizen über musikalische Ereignisse, Buchbesprechungen und Anzeigen von Druckwerken in Tageszeitungen als Vorläufer von Musikzeitschriften zu betrachten, etwa der *Hamburger Relations-Courier*, der seit 1708 Hinweise auf das Hamburger Musikleben, aber auch über das in Berlin, Leipzig und Dresden sowie in London, Paris und Wien, brachte[13]. Ähnliches gilt für den *Hollsteinischen unparteyischen Correspondenten* (seit 1712)[14], sowie für zahlreiche andere in- und ausländische Zeitungen dieser Epoche.

Beiträge über musikalische Fragen in allgemeinen Zeitschriften bildeten eine weitere Vorstufe zur Gründung von Musikzeitschriften. In Frankreich brachte die 1672 von dem Schriftsteller Donneau de

---

11 Vorwort zu *Der getreue Music-Meister. Fotomechanischer Neudruck der Originalausgabe von 1728* (Leipzig, 1980).
12 Offensichtlich hierauf gegen Telemann gerichtet sind Matthesons Worte im *Vorbericht* (p. 7) zum *Musicalischen Patrioten*: "Denn ob gleich einige in dem Wahn stehen, sie hätten die *Praxin* allein gepachtet: und das unstreitige *monopolium* an sich gebracht, so will ich mir doch, mit hoher Vergünstigung, noch ein kleines Eckgen davon ausbedungen haben, und meine *Theoriam* niemahls ohne *Praxi* treiben".
13 H. Becker, "Die frühe hamburgische Tagespresse als musikgeschichtliche Quelle", in: *Beiträge zur hamburgischen Musikgeschichte*, herausgegeben von H. Husmann (Hamburg, 1956), 22–45, hier: 22.
14 Ibid. Bei den auf p. 22, Fußnote 2 genannten "englischen Zeitungen" handelt es sich nur beim *Daily Courant* (seit 1702) um eine Tageszeitung. *The Gentleman's Magazine*, das 1731–1833 erschien, und *The London Magazine*, das 1732–79 herauskam, sind literarische Zeitschriften. *The Spectator* ist eine moralische Wochenschrift.

Visé begründete vornehmlich literarisch-politisch ausgerichtete Zeitschrift *Mercure galant* (seit 1724 unter dem Titel *Mercure de France* fortgeführt) wesentliche Hinweise zu musikalischen Ereignissen, vor allem zur Pflege der französischen Oper am Hofe Ludwigs XIV.[15] In England wurden in der von Peter Motteux monatlich herausgegebenen allgemein kulturellen Zeitschrift *The Gentleman's Journal: or the Monthly Miscellany. By Way of Letter to a Gentleman in the Country. Consisting of News, History, Philosophy, Poetry, Musick, Translations, &c.* (London 1691/2–4) wertvolle Angaben zu Komponisten wie Henry Purcell oder Johann Wolfgang Franck gemacht sowie in jeder Nummer ein Bericht über musikalische Ereignisse und Musikbeilagen mit zwei oder drei "Songs" von John Blow, Franck, Purcell und anderen Komponisten vorgelegt[16].

Als weitere Gruppe von Zeitschriften, die vor dem Jahr 1722 bestand, sind die von England überkommenen sogenannten moralischen Wochenschriften zu nennen, die der Erziehung und der Hebung der Sitten galten. Vorbilder waren hauptsächlich der von Richard Steele (1672–1729) dreimal wöchentlich herausgegebene *Tatler* (1709–10/11) und der von Joseph Addison (1672–1719) schließlich täglich edierte *Spectator* (1711–12, 1714), die bald großen Erfolg erlangten und zahlreiche Nachahmungen erlebten. Für die Musik wesentlich waren etwa drei von Addison 1711 im *Spectator* veröffentlichte satirisch-kritische Aufsätze über die italienische Oper in England[17]. Es war Mattheson, der – wie bereits anfänglich erwähnt – diese Gattung der moralischen Wochenschriften in Deutschland mit der Zeitschrift *Der Vernünfftler* (1713/14) eingeführt hat. Wie aus der Formulierung des vollständigen Titels, der der Zeitschrift 1721 vorangestellt wurde, *Der / Vernünfftler. / Das ist: / Ein teutscher Auszug / Aus den Engeländischen Moral-Schrifften / Des / TATLER / Und / SPECTATOR, / Vormahls verfertiget; / Mit etlichen Zugaben versehen / Und auf Ort und Zeit gerichtet / Von / JOANNE MATTHE-*

---

15 Siehe G. de Courcel, "Mémoire historique sur le Mercure de France", *Bulletin de bibliographie* (Paris, 1902), und E. Deville, *Index du Mercure de France 1672 à 1832* (Paris, 1910).

16 Siehe "Index to the Songs and Musical Allusions in 'The Gentleman's Journal', 1692–4", in: *The Musical Antiquary* II (1910/11), 225–34. Eine Übersicht über hauptsächlich literarische englische Zeitschriften mit Musikbeilagen bietet Fr. Kidson, "English Magazines containing Music before the Early Part of the Nineteenth Century", in: *The Musical Antiquary* III (1911–12), 99–102, und eine solche über die in *Exshaw's London Magazine* enthaltenen Gesänge W. J. Lawrence, "Eighteenth Century Magazine Music", ibid., 18–39.

17 G. Calmus, "Drei satirisch-kritische Aufsätze von Addison über die italienische Oper in England (London, 1710 [recte: 1711]). Übersetzt, mit Anmerkungen versehen und besprochen", in: *SIMG* IX (1907/8), 131–45.

SON und aus dem in der ersten Nummer vom 31. Mai 1713[18] abgedruckten "Vorbericht des Übersetzers dieser gelehrten Grillen" hervorgeht, handelt es sich nicht lediglich um eine Übersetzung von Teilen des *Tatler* und *Spectator* ins Deutsche, sondern um eine teilweise Übertragung englischer auf deutsche und von Londoner auf Hamburger Verhältnisse[19]. Von den insgesamt 100 erschienenen Nummern der Zeitschrift, die zunächst wöchentlich, ab Nr. 6 vom 1. Juli 1713 dann zweimal wöchentlich (mittwochs und sonnabends) erschien, und deren letzte am 26. Mai 1714 herauskam,[20] haben sieben Nummern (14, 15, 21, 22, 24, 75, 76) Mattheson zum Verfasser[21]. Die Musik angehend führt Mattheson im "Vorbericht" aus, daß die Autoren der englischen Zeitschriften zwar "viele nützliche Reflexiones auf die Schau-Spiele" machen, "weil sie sich aber alle auff die dortigen Comoedien, zu einigem Nachtheil der Opern oder Sing-Spiele beziehen", er "solche auch deswegen è Regione zu seyn erachtet, und gehet sie mit stillschweigen vorbey". Doch will er, wenn "dergleichen Theatralische Remarques geschicklich angebracht werden können", diese berücksichtigen[22]. In Nr. 23 wird *Thalestris*[23], in Nr. 78 *Julius Cäsar*[24], und in Nr. 66 *Iphigenia*[25] erwähnt, deren Übersetzung ins Englische Mattheson in Nr. 70 unter Zitierung einiger deutscher Stellen anführt. Offenbar kam Mattheson nicht mehr dazu, weitere Teile des *Spectator*, in denen sehr ausführlich auf die Oper eingegangen wird, zu übersetzen, wie auch seiner Anmerkung in der *Grundlage einer Ehren-Pforte* (Hamburg, 1740) zu entnehmen ist. In ihr führt er aus, daß er

18 Exemplar in der Staats- und Universitätsbibliothek Hamburg. Der von Cannon, *Mattheson*, 76, angegebene Beginn der Zeitschrift von "June 21, 1713" stellt bereits das Datum der Nr. 4 dar. Offenbar lag Cannon ein anderes Exemplar vor, bei dem die ersten drei Nummern undatiert geblieben waren.
19 Fol. A [1ʳ].
20 Siehe Matthesons Angaben in seiner *Ehrenpforte*, 199, die nicht in allem zutreffend sind: "Die Übersetzung des Tatlers, erschien dabey wöchentlich auf einem halben Bogen und verursachte vieles Aufsehen. Der Anfang mit diesen fliegenden Blättern wurde den 13. [recte: 31.] May gemacht, und der zu Ende des Jahrs, nehmlich den 26. May 1714. . .".
21 Siehe Jacoby, "Die ersten moralischen Wochenschriften", 7. Diesem hat auch noch eine Nr. 101 vom 30. Mai 1714 handschriftlich, vermutlich aus Matthesons Nachlaß, vorgelegen.
22 Fol. A [1ᵛ].
23 J. Ph. Förtsch: *Die grossmächtige Thalestris oder letzte Königin der Amazonen* (Chr. H. Postel) (Hamburg, 1690).
24 R. Keiser: *Der durch den Fall des grossen Pompeius erhöhete Julius Caesar* (B. Feind) (Hamburg, 1710).
25 Keiser: *Die wunderbahr errettete Iphigenia* (Postel, nach Euripides) (Hamburg, 1699).

der allererste gewesen, den des Steels [sic] Schrifften zur Übersetzung an-
gelocket, und der andern hernach Appetit gemacht hat, weiter zu gehen;
welches seiner häuffigen Geschäffte halber nicht [habe] geschehen können.
Vielleicht mögte er noch dereinst die in der frantzösischen und deutschen
Übersetzung des Zusehers, unerlaubter Weise, übergangene 206. Stücke,
worin vieles von Opern und theatralischen Dingen enthalten, nachholen und
sich weiter erklähren; falls ihm keiner zuvor kömt[26].

Hierin ist ihm in der Tat die Übersetzung der Patriotischen
Gesellschaft in Hamburg zuvorgekommen[27]. Aus dieser Tatsache
wird deutlich, daß es Mattheson bei der Herausgabe seines *Ver-
nünfftlers* nicht so sehr darum ging, die Musik betreffenden Teile in
Übersetzung vorzulegen, als vielmehr, wie aus einem Brief vom 26.
Dezember 1713 an Richard Steele hervorgeht, seinen Landsleuten,
besonders den "stubborn Hamburghers", eine Vorstellung von eng-
lischem Humor und Witz zu vermitteln[28]. Im Register zu Band I der
Critica musica bezeichnet er den *Vernünfftler* denn auch als "ein
Scriptum satyricum"[29].

Indes haben die moralischen Wochenschriften darüber hinaus
einen starken Einfluß auf die frühen Musikzeitschriften gehabt, la-
tent, wie noch zu zeigen sein wird, sogar auf Matthesons *Critica
musica*, vor allem aber auf dessen zweite Zeitschrift *Der musicalische
Patriot* (Hamburg, 1728)[30], in der er bei der Verteidigung der Musik
gegen Verfallserscheinungen und gegen die Anwendung veralteter
Kompositionstechniken, etwa in der Kirchenmusik, anging und vor
allem die von ihm hinsichtlich des Theaters vertretenen Ansichten
noch eindringlicher weiteren Kreisen von Lesern zu vermitteln
gedachte. Ein moralisierender Ton, schon im Titel und in der Vorrede

26 *Ehrenpforte*, 199, Fußnote. Hier verwahrt sich Mattheson auch energisch gegen die
   von Bodmer erhobene Behauptung, die von Leipziger Zeitungen aufgegriffen
   wurde, daß "dieser Vernünfftler obrigkeitlich wäre verboten worden", was demnach nicht der Fall war.
27 Sie erschien unter dem Titel: *Der Zuschauer, aus dem Englischen von Gottsched
   und den Seinigen*, Theil 1–9 (Leipzig, 1739–44).
28 Ein Entwurf dieses Briefes, von dem nicht überliefert ist, ob er den Adressaten je
   erreicht hat, abgedruckt bei Cannon, *Mattheson*, 76–8, hier 77: ". . . to gratify my
   contrymen with a Translation of some of the choicest Pieces, and give 'em a Taste of
   the true English humour & Witt".
29 Eine Wendung, die zumeist als Gattungsbegriff für moralische Wochenschriften
   angewandt wurde.
30 *Ehrenpforte*, 211: "An. 1728 kam der musikalische Patriot, eine Wochenschrifft, in
   4to, zum Vorschein" mit der Fußnote: "Er hat bisher, die Verlags=Kosten
   abgerechnet, 454 Marck 3. ß. eingebracht, und es ist nur noch ein eintziges
   Exemplar übrig".

zum Ausdruck gebracht, ist hierbei unüberhörbar[31]. Den moralischen Wochenschriften zuzurechnen sind sodann Johann Adolph Scheibes *Critischer Musicus* (1737/8–39/40), in dem es vornehmlich um den Einfluß auf die Geschmacksbildung geht, Friedrich Wilhelm Marpurgs *Der critische Musicus an der Spree* (1749/50) mit belehrenden Abhandlungen in Form fingierter Briefe und dessen *Kritische Briefe über die Tonkunst* (1759/60–4).

Neben den hauptsächlich der Belehrung und Erbauung dienenden moralischen Wochenschriften bildeten die gelehrten Zeitschriften enzyklopädischen Charakters eine weitere wichtige Voraussetzung für die Gründung von Musikzeitschriften. Zwar gehen die ersten universal-wissenschaftlichen Zeitschriften, die reine Gelehrten-Zeitschriften darstellten, wie das 1665 in Paris begründete *Journal des sçavans*, die im gleichen Jahr in London zu erscheinen beginnenden *Philosophical Transactions*, die von 1682 an in Leipzig herauskommenden *Acta eruditorum* und die 1688 von Christian Thomasius herausgegebenen *Monatsgespräche*, kaum je auf musikalische Fragen und Ereignisse ein, sind jedoch für die weitere Entwicklung des Zeitschriftenwesens, wie für das Entstehen musikalischer Zeitschriften von grundlegender Bedeutung. Deutsche Gelehrten-Zeitschriften enthalten gelegentlich Beiträge über Musik, so die *Monathlichen Unterredungen* von Ernst Wilhelm Tentzel (1689–98, 1704–7) etwa eine Abhandlung mit Hinweisen auf Kompositionen und einen Artikel über den Gebrauch von Musikinstrumenten im Gottesdienst[32] und die *Historischen Remarques der neuesten Sachen in Europa des 1699ten Jahrs* einen Beitrag über das Musikleben der Italiener[33].

---

31 *Der Musicalische Patriot, Welcher seine gründliche Betrachtungen, über Geist- und Weltl. Harmonien, samt dem, was durchgehends davon abhänget, In angenehmer Abwechselung zu solchem Ende mittheilet, Daß Gottes Ehre, das gemeine Beste, und eines jeden Lesers besondere Erbauung dadurch befördert werde. Ans Licht gestellet,* "Vorbericht", 5–6: "Wenn es übrigens außer Streit ist, daß einer jeden menschlichen Gesellschafft Vergnügung hauptsächlich auf der Tugend, den Sitten und der Gemüths-Beschaffenheit ihrer Mit-Glieder beruhet; so kömmt die Moral allerdings mit in unser Spiel: maßen eines Theils keiner im Grunde ein guter Musicus seyn kann, der nicht zugleich ein tugendhaffter, wolgesitteter Mann oder ethicus ist".

32 *Monatliche Unterredungen Einiger Guten Freunde Von Allerhand Büchern und andern annemlichen Geschichten. Allen Liebhabern Der Curiositäten Zur Ergetzlichkeit und Nachsinnen heraus gegeben. September* 1692, 709–27; p. 709 siehe I. Fellinger, "Zeitschriften", in: MGG 14 (1968), Abbildung 57, 1.

33 *Historische Remarques Der Neuesten Sachen In Europa Des M.D.C.IC. Jahres Wie solche nicht allein mit allen Fleiß zusammen getragen, sondern auch aus der Geographie, Genealogie, Historie, &c. erläutert, und dabey jederzeit, die so wohl in Franckreich, Engelland, Italien, Holland als Deutschland, in Druck gekommene*

Geistesgeschichtlich gesehen von entscheidender Bedeutung waren für Matthesons Zeitschriften-Gründung vornehmlich die Gelehrten-Zeitschriften universal-wissenschaftlichen Inhalts, daneben auch die der Belehrung und Erbauung dienenden moralischen Wochenschriften. Welches waren die Beweggründe, die Mattheson dazu bestimmten, eine ausschließlich der Musik gewidmete Zeitschrift herauszubringen? In der *Grundlage einer Ehren-Pforte* führt er darüber aus: ". . . was nun zu thun? Eine Critick schien nöthig zu seyn. Er schrieb sie, und gab monathlich ein Stück davon heraus. Das Werck bestehet in einer Untersuchung und Beurtheilung musicalischer Schrifften &c. und führt den Nahmen: Critica musica, 4to"[34]. Dieser sehr allgemein gehaltenen Schilderung ist zu entnehmen, daß es nach Ansicht von Mattheson vor allem die damalige Situation der Musik war, die Anlaß dazu bot, eine derartige Publikation ins Leben zu rufen. Ihr lag die Absicht zugrunde, durch Kritiken von älteren und neueren musikalischen Schriften zu belehren und vor allem das Gedeihen einer musikalischen Wissenschaft zu fördern, wie der Titel der *Critica musica* deutlich erkennen läßt[35], und ihr damit zu allgemeiner Anerkennung zu verhelfen. Im "Vortrab" zu seiner Zeitschrift gibt Mattheson eine Begründung dafür, weshalb er für seine kritischen Auseinandersetzungen diese Art einer sukzessiven Erscheinungsform wählte:

Weil ich denn nun sehe, daß dieses Ding nicht auf einmahl, oder mit einem einzigen Werke, zu heben ist: so habe ich mich entschlossen, die Arbeit per intervalla vorzunehmen, ob vieleicht dadurch was bessers auszurichten sey. Ich zweifle daran um so viel weniger, weil bey heutiger Mode, gar selten ein ganzes Buch; leicht aber ein paar monathliche Bogen, aus, und recht zu Ende gelesen werden. Auf diese Art ist auch der Angrif immer neu, und dürffte fast, wie ein steter Tropfen-Fall, endlich hie und da die Steine löchericht machen[36].

Die periodische Erscheinungsform sollte also Mattheson gleichsam als ein Instrument dazu dienen, seine kritischen Darlegungen immer wieder und dergestalt mit einer um so stärker wirksamen Eindringlichkeit verkünden zu können, mehr und nachhaltiger, als er

---

Bücher angeführet worden (Hamburg, 1699); Register I: "Music der Italiäner, wie sie beschaffen. 66.", speziell die Oper in Venedig angehend.

34 P. 208.

35 *Critica Musica. d.i. Grundrichtige Untersuch- und Beurtheilung, Vieler, theils vorgefaßten, theils einfältigen Meinungen, Argumenten und Einwürffe, so in alten und neuen, gedruckten und ungedruckten, Musicalischen Schrifften zu finden. Zur müglichsten Ausräutung aller groben Irrthümer, und zur Beförderung eines bessern Wachsthums der reinen harmonischen Wissenschaft, . . .*

36 "Vortrab". [3].

es bis dahin mit seinen Büchern, etwa mit *Das neu-eröffnete Orchestre* (1713), *Das beschützte Orchestre* (1717) und *Das forschende Orchestre* (1721) vermocht hatte.

Als Vorbild für die *Critica musica* beruft sich Mattheson in seinem Vorwort auf die erste deutsche Gelehrten-Zeitschrift *Acta eruditorum* (Leipzig, 1682–1776/82), begründet von Otto Mencke, deren bedeutendster Mitarbeiter Leibniz war, mit den Worten:

> Die Haupt-Absicht wird aber diese seyn und bleiben, allerhand musicalische Schrifften und Sachen, so wohl alte als neue, gedruckte und ungedruckte, einheimische und ausländische, Teutsche, Französische, Italiänische, Lateinische, Engelländische &c. auf solche Art und Weise, wie es die Acta eruditorum etwa machen, ja wohl noch ein wenig genauer, vor die Hand zu nehmen, und von einer jeden solchen (theils gar raren) Schrifft, nicht nur so viel Nachricht, und eine solche Recension zu geben, daß ein jeder, ohne das Buch zu kauffen, wissen möge, was der Kern desselben sey[37].

Inwieweit hat sich Mattheson an das Vorbild der *Acta eruditorum* gehalten? Die *Acta eruditorum* wurden im Jahre 1682 von einem Kreise Leipziger Gelehrter nach Art des französischen *Journal des sçavans* (1665–), der englischen *Philosphical Transactions* (1665–1886) und des italienischen *Giornale de letterati* (1668–81) begründet und in lateinischer Sprache monatlich mit wissenschaftlichen Abhandlungen und Buchbesprechungen herausgegeben. Wohl um die von vornherein angestrebte Internationalität der Zeitschrift zu sichern, bediente man sich der lateinischen Sprache[38]. Im Gegensatz zu den frühen Bänden weisen die vor 1722 erschienenen Jahrgänge keine wissenschaftlichen Beiträge mehr auf, sondern ausschließlich Rezensionen und zwar theologischer, kirchenhistorischer, juristischer, medizinischer, physikalischer, mathematischer, historischer, geographischer und vermischter Werke ("Libri miscellanei"), das heißt, philosophischer und philologischer Art hauptsächlich. Die Rezensionen bestehen aus einer Einordnung des zu besprechenden Werkes in den Zusammenhang der betreffenden Fach-Disziplin und aus einer dessen wesentliche Abschnitte charakterisierenden Inhaltsangabe. Jeder Jahrgang wird durch einen nach wissenschaftlichen Disziplinen angeordneten "Index Autorum, Quorum Libri aut Inventa hoc Volumine recensentur" und einen

---

37 Ibid., [4].
38 Siehe J. Kirchner, "Zur Entstehungs- und Redaktionsgeschichte der Acta Eruditorum", in: *Archiv für Buchgewerbe und Gebrauchsgraphik* 4 (Sonderheft Pressa Leipzig, 1928), 75–81.

"Index Rerum Notabiliorum in hoc Volumen obviarum" abgeschlossen[39].

Auf diese bis zum Jahre 1722 erschienenen Jahrgänge der *Acta eruditorum* dürfte sich Mattheson bei seiner Angabe im "Vortrab" zum ersten Stück der *Critica musica* vom "May 1722" bezogen haben. Doch weist er bereits hier darauf hin, daß er über eine Besprechung der wesentlichen Gesichtspunkte einer Publikation hinaus, "darinn enthaltene gute Sachen anzupreisen, die bösen Irrthümer aber auszumustern, und gesundere Lehren, an deren statt, vorzutragen" gedächte[40]. Zwar ist das Vorbild der *Critica musica* in erster Linie die Gelehrten-Zeitschrift universal-wissenschaftlichen Charakters. Jedoch geht Mattheson über deren damals herrschenden Status weit hinaus, indem er mit der Besprechung von Werken auf musikalischem Gebiet zugleich eine Wertung und Nutzanwendung im pädagogischen Sinne – er spricht hier von "sattsamem Unterricht"[41] – verbindet. Der Begriff der musikalischen Kritik umfaßt demnach in Matthesons Auffassung, so können wir aus der im "Vortrab" niedergelegten Absicht schließen, nicht nur eine Kritisierung musikalischer Schriften als solche, sondern darüber hinaus auch die Aufgabe, falsche Lehren anzuprangern, ad absurdum zu führen und durch bessere zu ersetzen. In diese Richtung geht auch, daß er, je nach Absatz des Werkes, "mit der Zeit, auch einige Didactica und Compositions-Gedanken, zu jedermañs Erbauung, auf eine unsträffliche critische Art" anbringen will[42]. Hiermit wendet Mattheson im Rahmen seiner in der Tradition der Gelehrten-Zeitschriften stehenden *Critica musica* ein moralisierendes Moment an, das ihn offensichtlich den moralischen Wochenschriften verpflichtet zeigt. Dieses zielt gleichsam auf eine Hebung musikalischer Sitten hin, soll aber letztlich wiederum einem gelehrten Zweck, nämlich der "Beförderung eines bessern Wachsthums der reinen harmonischen Wissenschaft" entsprechend der Titelformulierung, dienen.

Zwei Fragen haben uns zu beschäftigen: (1) Kann Matthesons *Critica musica* als Musikzeitschrift und damit als erste ihrer Art bezeichnet werden oder handelt es sich bei ihr mehr um ein in Lieferungen erschienenes Buch? (2) Inwieweit hat Mattheson die im Titel und im "Vortrab" verkündeten Pläne, die er mit der Herausgabe dieser Publikation verband, realisieren können?

Die *Critica musica* besteht aus zwei Bänden zu acht Teilen und

---

39 Siehe etwa *Acta Eruditorum Anno MDCCXX (–MDCCXXII)*.
40 "Vortrab", [4].   41 Ibid.   42 Ibid.

vierundzwanzig Stücken. Der Begriff "Band" steht, wie häufig bei Zeitschriften dieser Epoche, für den Begriff "Jahrgang". Der adäquate Ausdruck für "Stück" ist nicht "Lieferung", sondern in der damals üblichen Terminologie "Nummer". Die Auffassung, Matthesons *Critica musica* als ein in Lieferungen erschienenes Buch zu werten, scheint vor allem die unrichtige Deutung des Begriffes "Stück" als "Lieferung" verursacht zu haben. Noch in den ersten Dezennien des neunzehnten Jahrhunderts war dieser Terminus bei Zeitschriften in Gebrauch, wie etwa der Definition des Begriffes "Zeitschrift" von Joachim Heinrich Campe als "eine Schrift, welche zu gewissen bestimmten Zeiten herauskömt" und "in auf einander folgenden Stücken ausgegeben wird" zu entnehmen ist[43]. Die acht jeweils unter einer einheitlichen Thematik stehenden Hauptbeiträge der *Critica musica*, die als Teile bezeichnet sind, wurden in Fortsetzungen – je nach Umfang – in zwei bis vier monatlichen Stücken vorgelegt. Nachrichten, biographische Notizen, Nekrologe etc., die unter der Rubrik "Neues / Von Musicalischen Sachen und Personen" und ähnlich formulierten Überschriften gebracht werden, folgen jeweils am Ende der Stücke. Der Umfang der Stücke betrug in der Regel zweiunddreißig Seiten, in vier Fällen vierundzwanzig Seiten[44], in drei Fällen achtundvierzig Seiten[45] und beim vierundzwanzigsten Stück zwölf Seiten. Jeder Band wird durch ein "Register der fürnehmsten Personen und Sachen, so in diesem I. (II.) Tomo der Criticae Musicae vorkommen" abgeschlossen. Die zwölf Stücke des ersten Bandes weisen eine durchgehende monatliche Erscheinungsfolge von Mai 1722 bis April 1723 von insgesamt 368 Seiten Umfang auf. Ob diese Stücke tatsächlich mit solcher Regelmäßigkeit erschienen sind oder zum Teil auch verspätet, läßt sich im einzelnen nicht mehr nachweisen. Denn nach Matthesons Angabe wurde dieser Band erst im November 1724 fertiggestellt: "Der musikalischen Critik erster Band wurde im November fertig; alsofort muste der zweete daran"[46]. Die Datierung des zweiten Bandes, dessen Stücke im Gegensatz zum ersten Band keine Daten aufweisen, bereitete bisher Schwierigkeiten und führte zu keinem zufriedenstellenden Ergebnis. Jedoch sind die in diesen Stücken enthaltenen Nachrichten – entgegen dem ersten Band – zumeist mit exakten Daten versehen. Sie können daher für eine zumindest annähernde Datierung herangezogen werden. Die von Ferdinand Krome vorgenommene

---

43 *Wörterbuch der deutschen Sprache*, V. Theil (Braunschweig, 1811), 836.
44 1., 7., 22. und 23. Stück.   45 12., 17. und 19. Stück.
46 *Ehrenpforte*, 209.

Datierung des vierzehnten Stückes auf "Juli 1724"[47] aufgrund des darin abgedruckten Nachrufs auf Johann Theile, der am Johannistage (= 24. Juni) 1724 verstarb[48], ist von späteren Autoren, soweit sie die Frage der Datierung überhaupt berührten, übernommen worden[49]. Kromes zeitliche Zuweisung des vierzehnten Stückes auf Juli 1724 und entsprechend des dreizehnten Stückes auf Juni 1724 widerspricht nicht nur Matthesons bereits erwähnter Aussage, sondern läßt sich auch sonst nicht aufrecht erhalten. Da das vierzehnte Stück neben dem Nachruf auf Theile auch eine Nachricht vom 10. November 1724 aus London bringt und das dreizehnte Stück datierte Notizen vom 27. und 29. Oktober 1724 aus London und vom 6. November 1724 aus Wolfenbüttel aufweist[50], was Krome offenbar entgangen ist, könnte das dreizehnte Stück frühestens Ende November 1724, was Matthesons Angabe entsprechen würde, und das vierzehnte Stück dann im Dezember 1724 erschienen sein. Auch die folgenden Stücke lassen sich dieserart sukzessive monatlich zuordnen, so das fünfzehnte Stück dem Januar 1725, das sechzehnte Stück dem Februar 1725 und das siebzehnte Stück, das einen Nachruf auf Johann Philipp Krieger (gestorben 6. Februar 1725) enthält[51], auf März 1725. Hingegen dürfte die Auslieferung der Stücke 18 bis 24 nach den wenigen greifbaren Daten zu schließen, verzögert erfolgt sein. So ist anzunehmen, daß das achtzehnte Stück, das eine Nachricht vom 13. Mai 1725 aus Rom aufweist[52], im Juni 1725, vielleicht zusammen mit dem neunzehnten Stück, ausgefolgert worden ist. Das zwanzigste Stück dürfte im Verlauf des Juli gefolgt sein. Es hat den Anschein, daß der achte Teil (ein- bis vierundzwanzigstes Stück) als Ganzes konzipiert und Ende September 1725 zusammenhängend herausgegeben wurde, gemäß Matthesons Angabe: "und endigte hernach den zweeten Band seiner Critick am 28. Sept. mit einem reinen Gewinn von 200. Reichsthl., eignen Verlags"[53].

Eine anfänglich regelmäßig erfolgende Periodizität, die dann in eine zwanglosere übergeht, ist im Rahmen von Musikzeitschriften nichts Außergewöhnliches. Hierin ist noch kein Indiz dafür zu sehen,

---

47 F. Krome, *Die Anfänge des musikalischen Journalismus in Deutschland* (Diss. Leipzig, 1896), 10.
48 "Zeitungen von musicalischen Personen und Sachen. Naumburg", *Critica musica* II, 57–8.
49 So von K. Dolinski, *Die Anfänge der musikalischen Fachpresse in Deutschland. Geschichtliche Grundlagen,* phil. Diss. (Berlin, 1940), 85.
50 Siehe "Zeitungen von musicalischen Sachen und Personen", *Critica musica* II, 29–30.
51 "Musicalische Merkwürdigkeiten. Weissenfels", ibid., 169–74.
52 "Musicalische Merckwürdigkeiten", ibid., 208. 53 *Ehrenpforte,* 209.

Matthesons *Critica musica* als ein in Lieferungen herausgegebenes Buch, nicht als Zeitschrift zu betrachten; ebenso nicht in dem Umstand, daß die einzelnen Stücke teilweise unterschiedlichen Umfang aufweisen. Indes mögen einige Hinweise auf den Inhalt der *Critica musica* deren Klassifizierung als gelehrte Musikzeitschrift weiter rechtfertigen. Neben den Hauptbeiträgen, die in Fortsetzungen gebracht werden, und bei denen es sich um groß angelegte Polemiken gegen Franz Xaver Murschhauser, hauptsächlich um Solmisation und Modi (erster Theil), und gegen den Erfurter Organisten Buttstedt (sechster Theil), um eine Auseinandersetzung um das Schreiben von Kanons mit dem Wolfenbütteler Organisten Heinrich Bokemeyer (vierter Theil), um den Abdruck der theoretischen Abhandlung in Französisch und in deutscher Übersetzung des Abbé Raguenet (zweiter Theil) mit der Lecerf de la Viéville zugeschriebenen Erwiderung (dritter Theil) sowie etwa um den Abdruck von Bokemeyers *Versuch von der Melodica* mit Kommentaren von Mattheson (achter Theil) handelt, kommt vor allem den unter der Rubrik "Neues / Von Musicalischen Sachen und Personen" gebrachten Nachrichten und Mitteilungen vom Standpunkt einer Zeitschrift her gesehen besondere Bedeutung zu[54]. Mattheson folgte hierin dem Vorbild einiger deutscher Gelehrten-Zeitschriften, in denen Notizen über verschiedene Begebenheiten sowie auch Anzeigen von Büchern mit kürzeren Rezensionen hin und wieder größeren Abhandlungen angeschlossen wurden, so etwa in den *Historischen Remarques der neuesten Sachen in Europa* (Hamburg, 1699)[55]. Jedoch hat Mattheson diese Rubrik im Rahmen der *Critica musica* wesentlich vielfältiger ausgestattet. Hierbei handelt es sich um Musikberichte und Nachrichten aus verschiedenen in Deutschland und im europäischen Ausland gelegenen Städten, so um Aufführungen von Opern wie Telemanns *Gensericus* in Hamburg[56], Reinhard Keisers *Ulysses* in Kopenhagen[57] und dessen *Ariadne* in Hamburg[58], Pietro Torri's *Adelaide* in München[59], Francesco Brusa's *L'Amore eroico* in Venedig[60] oder

54 Zum Teil unter wechselnden Überschriften wie "Zeitungen von musicalischen Sachen und Personen", "Musicalische Merkwürdigkeiten", "Zeitungen", "Musicalische Zeitungen". Der Begriff "Zeitung" ist hier im Sinne von "Nachricht" zu verstehen.
55 Etwa P. 64: "Zu Paris hat Jean Guignard Ao. 1698 Ferdinandi Alvarez Hertzogs von Alba Lebens Historie in Frantzösischer Sprache drucken lassen. Solches ist auch zu bekommen bey Henry des Bordes zu Amsterd." mit nachfolgender kurzer Besprechung des Werkes, dem sich auf der gleichen Seite unten ein meteorologischer Bericht über ein ungewöhnliches Gewitter anschließt.
56 *Critica musica* I, 87–8.   57 Ibid., 208.   58 Ibid., 231–2.
59 Ibid., 254–5: "Auszug eines Briefes von Regenspurg".
60 *Critica musica* II, 286–8.

Händels *Tamerlane* in London[61]. Daneben werden Anzeigen musikalischer und musiktheoretischer Werke mit kurzen Inhaltsangaben, Nachrichten über aufgefundene Quellen und Rezensionen von Büchern und Ausgaben gebracht. Eine ausführliche Besprechung etwa widmete Mattheson den ersten drei Bänden des *Estro poetico-harmonico* von Benedetto Marcello (Venedig, 1724)[62]. Außerdem weist diese Rubrik zahlreiche biographische Notizen und Nachrichten sowie einige Nekrologe über namhafte Komponisten und Interpreten auf[63]. Auch Erfindungen und Verbesserungen auf dem Gebiet des Instrumentenbaus begegnen gelegentlich und betreffen etwa die "Claviatura" von Hänfling[64] oder die Entwicklung einer "Clavier-Gamba" durch Johann Georg Gleichmann[65]. Schließlich finden sich auch Stellungnahmen und Rechtfertigungen Matthesons. Dem an ihn aus Kassel gelangten Vorwurf der "gecommunicirten Tractätgens (Critica musica)" begegnete er beispielsweise mit einer Erwiderung, in der er die Nützlichkeit von "Opponenten" in der Wissenschaft betont, ohne die "man lange nicht so viel Gelegenheit haben würde, der Sache nachzudenken, und etwas nützliches hervorzubringen"[66].

Mit den groß angelegten, in Fortsetzungen gebrachten Beiträgen und einer Fülle verschiedenartigster Mitteilungen und Berichte aus unterschiedlichen Bereichen der Musik und des Musiklebens jener Zeit erfüllt dieses erste Periodicum auf musikalischem Gebiet die Aufgabe einer gelehrten Musikzeitschrift bereits in einem umfassenden Sinne.

Mattheson ist von dem Bestreben geleitet, das wird aus seinen Darlegungen im Rahmen der *Critica musica* immer wieder deutlich, dafür einzutreten, daß die Musik nicht nur als Handwerk, sondern vor allem als Kunst und Wissenschaft zu begreifen sei. Eine kurze Besprechung der von Ernst Wilhelm Herzog verfaßten Biographie über Johannes Kuhnau nimmt er zum Anlaß, darüber näher auszuführen:

Es wäre zu wünschen, daß diejenigen, so der Music obliegen, sich dergleichen Ehrwürdige Exempel anreitzen liessen, diese Hoch-Edle Profession nicht als ein blosses, und von aller gründlichen Gelehrsamkeit entfernetes Handwerk, sondern als ein Haupt-Studium, mit Zuziehung andrer

---

61 Ibid., 29: "Tamerlanes, und soll den 11 Nov. auf dem hiesigen Heumarktischen Schau-Platz zum ersten mal vorgestellet werden".
62 Ibid., 58–64 und 126–7.
63 So etwa auch Nekrologe auf J. Kuhnau, *Critica musica* I, 86, und J. A. Reincken, ibid., 255–6.
64 Ibid., 51–3.   65 Ibid., 254.   66 Ibid., 54–6.

Wissenschafften, die demselben, als ansae und adminicula, grosse Dienste leisten können, auf die Art, wie Sethus Calvisius, Zarlinus, Bononcini und Kuhnau gethan, zu treiben, und alles Ernstes fortzupflanzen⁶⁷.

Mattheson sieht sich in dieser Beziehung in einer Tradition stehen, die er fortgesetzt sehen möchte. Darum ist er auch bemüht, den jeweiligen Stand der Musik als wissenschaftliche Disziplin in seinem Periodicum sichtbar zu machen. Obwohl ein Periodicum, fügt sich die *Critica musica* in die Reihe der vorangegangenen und nachfolgenden Veröffentlichungen Matthesons organisch ein. Mattheson greift in ihr auf frühere Publikationen zurück und weist auf später geplante Vorhaben hin. So bezog er sich etwa auf die von ihm im *Neu-eröffneten Orchestre* (1713) erwähnte Erwiderung des "Sieur de Vieuville" auf das Werk von Abbé Raguenet⁶⁸, als er daran ging, die in der Zwischenzeit aufgefundenen Schriften beider Autoren in der *Critica musica* zum Abdruck zu bringen⁶⁹. Auch legte er in der *Critica musica* Entgegnungen und Verteidigungen vorher erschienener Publikationen vor, so Berichtigungen kritischer Anmerkungen eines schwedischen Organisten zu seiner *Exemplarischen Organisten-Probe* (1719)⁷⁰. Wie im zweiten Stück (Junio 1722) angekündigt, da die "Antwort zum besten der Kirchen-Music gereichet"⁷¹, rückte er im sechsten Stück (October 1722) "Christoph Raupachs abgenöthigte Beantwortung der beyden Fragen" ein, worin Raupach ein Kapitel seiner im Jahre 1717 von Mattheson mit einer Vorrede herausgegebenen Schrift *Veritophili deutliche Beweiß-Gründe der Music* verteidigte⁷².

Im "Vorbericht" zum zweiten Band deutete er in verklausulierter Form den Plan des *Musicalischen Patrioten* (1728) an: "Ich hätte Materien genug, schöne *Anecdotes theatrales*, oder eine geheime

---

67 Ibid., 118.
68 Ibid., 91. Er berief sich hier auf P. 231 (Pars Tertia. Caput Primum. Vom Unterscheid der heutigen Italiänischen, Frantzösischen, Englischen und Teutschen Music, §. 18), wo es heißt: "Ein Frantzose, Nahmens le Sieur de Vieuville soll zwar an dē Abbé Raguenet Antworten geschrieben haben, so er nennet: Comparaison de la Musique Francoise & Italienne; alleine ich habe biß dato noch nichts davon auffstäubern können."
69 "Der musicalischen Parallele Erster (– Dritter) Abriß", *Critica musica* I, 105–18, 121–47, 153–66, und "Des Französischen Anwalds Erste (– Zweyte) Supplic", ibid., 189–207, 209–30.
70 Ibid., 320.   71 Ibid., 53.
72 Ibid., 167–77. Die beiden Fragen lauten: "1) Ob das Wort Psalmodia, apud Patres, qui ante Nazianzenum vixere, ein blosses Singen, oder ein Singen zum musicalischen Instrument, bedeute? 2) Ob so wohl das Spielen auf musicalischen Instrumenten, als Singen, unter den ersten Christen, bey ihren geistlichen Versammlungen, manches mahl im Gebrauch gewesen?"

Opern-Historie zu schreiben; allein, es mag noch eine Weile anstehen: zumal da der Haupt-Zweck dieses Werks mehr dahin gehet,
gute *Musicos,* als gute Satyren, zu machen" und fährt weiter unten
fort, "daß es nicht übel gethan seyn würde, dereinst *Musicam mora-
lem* zu schreiben", zu der "in der Vorrede des brauchbaren Virtuosen" und "in *Praefatione Veritophili* der Anfang gemacht worden" sei[73]. Mattheson hat sich demnach bereits im November 1724
mit dem Gedanken an die Herausgabe einer weiteren Zeitschrift nach
dem Vorbild der moralischen Wochenschriften getragen, also
während des ersten Erscheinungsjahres des Organs der Patriotischen
Gesellschaft in Hamburg *Der Patriot* (1724–8), dessen Titel er nach-
mals entlehnte. Ein anderer zukünftiger Plan betraf die *Grundlage
einer Ehren-Pforte.* Als Vorlage für eine Biographie druckte er in der
Critica musica einen Auszug über Lully aus *Lettres historiques sur
tous les spectacles de Paris* (Paris, 1718) in geänderter Anordnung
unter dem Titel "Leben und Tod des weltberühmten Jean Baptiste de
Lully" ab, "damit ein deutliches Model gegeben werde, wie etwan
eine Lebens-Beschreibung einzurichten sey, die in der Ehren-Pforte
Platz finden will", wobei er einer sehr ins einzelne gehenden
Aufgliederung von Gesichtspunkten zuneigte[74]. Außerdem sind
zahlreiche biographische Angaben der *Critica musica* nicht nur in
das *Musicalische Lexicon* von Johann Gottfried Walther (Leipzig,
1732)[75], sondern gerade auch in dieses Werk übergegangen[76].

Vor allem bildete Matthesons *Critica musica* Grundlage und Ausgangspunkt für die weitere Entwicklung von Musikzeitschriften im
achtzehnten Jahrhundert. In einer Linie mit Matthesons Zeitschrift ist
Lorenz Mizlers *Musikalische Bibliothek oder Gründliche Nachricht
nebst unparteyischem Urtheil von Musikalischen Schrifften und
Büchern* (Leipzig, 1736–54) zu sehen, die ähnlich wie diese den
Typus der Gelehrten-Zeitschrift verkörpert[77]. Mizler beabsichtigte in
seiner Zeitschrift neben der Historie die Musik in akustisch-mathe-

---

73 *Vorbericht,* Fol. 3.   74 *Critica musica* I, 178–84.
75 Mattheson weist zuweilen selbst auf solche Übernahmen hin, etwa den Artikel
   "Theile" angehend: "Das meiste was von diesem braven Manne zu sagen ist, stehet
   bereits in meiner musicalischen Critik, T. II. p. 57. 282. sqq. und aus derselben im
   waltherischen Wörterbuche, p. 602. col. 2. sqq.", *Ehrenpforte,* 369, Ähnliches gilt
   für Raupach, ibid., 289.
76 Da die beiden von Theile in der *Critica musica* II, 282–4, abgedruckten Briefe im
   Lexikon von Walther unberücksichtigt geblieben waren, fügte sie Mattheson auszugsweise im Artikel "Theile" der *Ehrenpforte,* 369–70, ein.
77 Diese Zeitschrift wurde 1738 das Organ der von Mizler gemeinsam mit Graf G. de
   Lucchesini und G. H. Bümler begründeten Correspondirenden Societät der Musikalischen Wissenschaften in Deutschland.

matischer, physiologischer sowie praktischer und theoretischer Hinsicht zu erforschen, um dieserart vornehmlich die Erkenntnis ihrer naturwissenschaftlichen Seite zu vertiefen. Als Ergänzung in praktischer Beziehung zu seiner ersten Zeitschrift brachte Mizler das Periodicum *Musikalischer Staarstecher* (1739–40) heraus. In der Tradition der musikalischen Gelehrten-Zeitschrift Matthesons und Mizlers stehen vor allem Friedrich Wilhelm Marpurgs *Historisch-Kritische Beyträge zur Aufnahme der Musik* (Berlin, 1754–62 und 1778), in denen Marpurg gegenüber Mizler mehr den "practischen als theoretischen Theil der Kunst" zu betonen trachtete[78]. Enthalten sind kleinere Abhandlungen, Rezensionen historischer, kritischer und didaktischer Schriften, biographische Mitteilungen über berühmte Musiker, Nachrichten über bekannte Hofkapellen, Theater und musikalische Gesellschaften. Diese Gelehrten-Zeitschrift ist ihrerseits für die Weiterentwicklung des musikalischen Zeitschriftenwesens in Richtung auf eine alle Bereiche der Musik umfassenden Zeitschrift von grundlegender Bedeutung gewesen. In der Tradition eines Mattheson sind außerhalb Deutschlands etwa die erste in Frankreich erschienene Musikzeitschrift *Sentiment d'un harmoniphile, sur différens Ouvrages de Musique*, herausgegeben von A. J. Labbet, Abbé de Morambert und A. Léris (Paris, 1756), und das im gleichen Jahr als erste niederländische Musikzeitschrift in Amsterdam in acht Stücken herausgekommene Werk *Samenspraaken over Muzikaale Beginselen* von Jakob Wilhelm Lustig (1706–96), einem Schüler Matthesons, zu sehen.

Mattheson verband mit der Gründung der *Critica musica* letzlich die Absicht, "die Music, als einen fast rar gewordenen Theil der Gelehrsamkeit, der gesunden Welt-Weißheit und edleren Literatur"[79] vorzunehmen mit dem Ziel, ihr als eigenständiger Wissenschaft zu allgemeiner Geltung und entsprechendem Ansehen innerhalb der innerhalb der anderen wissenschaftlichen Disziplinen zu verhelfen. Daß gerade diese im Rahmen der Musikzeitschriften verfolgten Bestrebungen zum Erfolg führten, geht aus Johann Adam Hillers *Kritischem Entwurf einer musikalischen Bibliothek* (1768) deutlich hervor: "Diese periodischen Schriften haben in der That das gute gestiftet, daß man die Musik wieder als eine Wissenschaft, wovon sich eben so wie von allen andern Wissenschaften urtheilen läßt, anzusehen anfängt. Man giebt ihr in den kritischen Journalen und

78 "Vorbericht", XIV.
79 Widmung, Fol. [A 1^{r-v}], die am Ende das Datum "Am grossen Neu-Jahrs-Tage 1726." aufweist.

gelehrten Zeitungen mit Vergnügen den Platz, der ihr neben andern wissenschaftlichen Dingen gehört"[80]. In der Tatsache, diese Entwicklung eingeleitet und entscheidend bestimmt zu haben, liegt die besondere Bedeutung von Matthesons *Critica musica*.

---

80 *Wöchentliche Nachrichten und Anmerkungen die Musik betreffend* III (Leipzig, 1768), 7.

9

Polemik als Erkenntnisform:
Bemerkungen zu den Schriften Matthesons
ARNO FORCHERT
Detmold

Wenn man, in Anlehnung an Kant, das achtzehnte Jahrhundert als das "eigentliche Zeitalter der Kritik, der sich alles unterwerfen muß", bezeichnen will[1], so wird man auch sagen dürfen, daß es Johann Mattheson war, der dieses Zeitalter in der deutschen Musikliteratur recht eigentlich erst heraufgeführt hat. Schon vom Anfang seiner Tätigkeit als Musikschriftsteller an tritt er für die Überzeugung ein, daß musikalische Autoritäten und die von ihnen überlieferten Regeln nicht mehr ausreichten, um die Musik seiner Zeit erklären und begreifen zu können. Statt die Beurteilung der musikalischen Praxis auf unantastbare, durch die Tradition geheiligte Principien zu stützen, ist Mattheson der Ansicht, daß nur der umgekehrte Weg, der empirisch-induktive, für die Betrachtung der Musik angemessen sei. "Von solchen praetendirten luminibus Mundi, die da meinen / es müsse sich die Music nach ihren Reguln / und sich nicht vielmehr ihre Reguln / nach der Music richten", so schreibt er schon in der Einleitung zum *Neu-eröffneten Orchestre* von 1713,

mag man wol mit Recht sagen: Faciunt intelligendo ut nihil intelligant . . . Sie möchten sich aber bescheiden . . . daß die Music an ihr selbst keiner Regeln bedürffe / sondern daß wir vielmehr / unsers Unvermögens wegen der selbigen benöthiget sind / um einiger massen einen irdischen Begriff von diesem himmlischen Wesen zu erlangen / und daß dannenhero alle die unzehlige Reguln sich nach der Zeit / darinnen wir leben / auch nach den Umständen und Manieren / die in der Music eben so veränderlich als die Constellationes am Himmel sind / ändern und accomodiren müssen / weil nicht allein in den Sinnen selbst der eigentliche Ursprung aller Wissenschafft steckt / nam nihil est in intellectu, quod non prius fuit in sensu; sondern weil noch keine Regul noch Thesis in der Welt so beschaffen, die sich nicht / zu

---

1 I. Kant, *Kritik der reinen Vernunft*, Vorrede zur ersten Auflage 1781.

Folge den obhandenen Conjuncturen und Circumstantien / woraus sie eigentlich fliesset / richten / ändern und Abfälle leiden müsse[2].

Aus diesen Sätzen läßt sich die Rolle ableiten, die Mattheson sich selbst zuerkennt. Er sieht seine Aufgabe nicht als die eines musicus theoricus, der Kompositionsregeln, die dem schaffenden Musiker die Richtung weisen sollen, aus unwandelbaren, aller Musik in gleicher Weise zugrundeliegenden Axiomen ableitet und begründet, sondern als Musikkenner, der dank eigener Einsicht und Urteilskraft zur musikalischen Urteilsbildung seiner Zeitgenossen beitragen möchte. Der Verzicht auf die Begründung des eigenen Standpunktes durch den Rückgriff auf allgemeine Prinzipien wirft allerdings die Frage auf, wie unter solchen Bedingungen Aussagen möglich sein sollen, die mehr als lediglich subjektive Gültigkeit für sich beanspruchen kön-nen. Anders als später Kant, der das Problem in der Kritik der Urteilskraft grundsätzlich zu lösen versuchte, begegnet Mattheson dieser Schwierigkeit, indem er sich überwiegend einer Argumenta-tion bedient, die weit eher als die Begründung des eigenen die Entkräftung entgegengesetzter Standpunkte zum Ziel hat. Was man im allgemeinen vorwiegend als Charaktereigenschaft Matthesons anzusehen gesonnen ist, seine Neigung zu polemischen Auseinan-dersetzungen, zu Kontroversen von teilweise verletzender Schärfe, hat mithin auch einen durchaus sachlichen Hintergrund: Wenn nicht die Autorität traditionell verbürgter Regeln, sondern der Geschmack des auf der Höhe seiner Zeit stehenden Individuums den Maßstab der Urteilsbildung abgibt, dann kann sich die Richtigkeit solcher Urteile nur in der Konkurrenz mit anderen, abweichenden Urteilen behaupten.

So ist es denn auch kein Zufall, daß schon Matthesons erste musikalische Schrift, das *Neu-eröffnete Orchestre*, mit einer Polemik beginnt[3]. Sie gilt allen denen, die nach seiner Ansicht den Verfall der Musik in der Gegenwart bewirkt und damit – indirekt – das Erscheinen seines Buches notwendig gemacht haben: zuerst den-jenigen, die, ohne sich in der Musikausübung der Gegenwart aus-zukennen, aus der Musik eine Wissenschaft machen möchten, dann den oberflächlichen und eitlen Virtuosen und schließlich den un-gebildeten Musikanten, die sich mit der Musik nur um des Profites willen beschäftigen. Mit anderen Worten: Mattheson wendet sich gegen Theorie ohne Praxis, Ästhetik ohne Handwerk und Handwerk

2 *Orchestre* I. Für die ausführlichen Titel der Schriften Matthesons sei auf die Bibliographie bei Cannon, *Mattheson*, 146 ss. verwiesen.
3 Einleitung, "Vom Verfall der Music und dessen Ursachen", *Orchestre* I, 1 ss.

ohne Ästhetik. Dabei ist jedoch nicht zu übersehen, daß es ihm im Grunde allein um die Auseinandersetzung mit der älteren Musiktheorie zu tun ist – das seichte Virtuosentum erscheint demgegenüber nur als kleineres und zudem korrigierbares Übel, und die Unbildung und Rohheit vieler Musikanten wird von Mattheson zwar als ein Mißstand beklagt, aber als einer, der kaum zu ändern ist und daher eine eingehendere Auseinandersetzung nicht lohnt. Der Angriff auf die ältere Musiktheorie und ihre zeitgenössischen Vertreter hingegen ist prinzipieller und persönlicher Art. Denn er gilt der Verteidigung und Rechtfertigung eines musikalischen Bildungsweges, durch den sich Mattheson – und mit ihm auch Männer wie etwa Telemann oder Heinichen – nicht nur von seinen deutschen Vorgängern, sondern auch von den meisten seiner Zeitgenossen unterschied. Die entscheidenden musikalischen Eindrücke nämlich – seine eigentliche musikalische Lehrzeit, wie er später immer wieder betont hat – verdankte er der frühen Bekanntschaft mit der Oper[4], und damit dem Umgang mit einer ganz anderen Art von Musik als der, die in den traditionellen Musiklehren behandelt wurde. Und es ist die Erfahrung dieser Diskrepanz, die ihn im *Neu-eröffneten Orchestre* dazu veranlaßt, den "chimärischen Antiquitäten" der älteren Musiktheorie den Kampf anzusagen. Daß die Rede vom "Verfall der Musik", die sein Buch angeblich notwendig gemacht habe, in Wahrheit ein Vorwand ist, der ihm lediglich als Begründung für seine Polemik dienen muß, wird übrigens auch dadurch bestätigt, daß kein geringerer als Reinhard Keiser, Matthesons verehrtes Vorbild, sie in seinen "Kurtzen Anmerckungen" am Schluß des *Neu-eröffneten Orchestres* nicht nur ausdrücklich zurückweist, sondern im Gegenteil behauptet, daß die Musik eine gerade "anjetzo . . . hochgebrachte Science" sei[5], zu deren "Lustre" auch Mattheson durch seine Schrift beigetragen habe.

Wenn schon Matthesons musiktheoretischer Erstling mit lebhaftem Widerspruch aufgenommen wurde, so lag das freilich weniger an dem, was er hier inhaltlich zu seinen Lehrgegenständen zu sagen hatte. Denn die Hauptpunkte, denen dann Buttstetts Gegenschrift[6] galt, die Verwerfung der alten Solmisationspraxis und die Behandlung der Modi unter dem Aspekt ihrer Auflösung in verschiedene Transpositionen der Dur- bzw. Moll-Skala, waren bei

---

4 "Opern stehen bey mir, NB. quoad Musicam, in eben dem praedicato, als Universitäten, quoad caetera Studia", *Musicalischer Patriot*, 141.
5 *Orchestre* I, 330.
6 J. H. Buttstett, *Ut Re Mi Fa Sol La, Tota Musica et Harmonia Aeterna* (Erfurt, ca. 1716).

anderen Autoren – auch bei deutschen – zum Teil schon lange vorher in ganz ähnlicher Weise dargestellt worden[7]. Buttstetts Widerspruch entzündete sich denn auch wohl weniger an solchen sachlichen Problemen als vielmehr an der Art ihrer Behandlung, daran, daß, wie er schreibt, "der Herr Author des Orchestre die Antiquité, welche man doch veneriren soll / allzu hart angegriffen" habe[8]. Genau das aber ist das wirklich Neue, von dem sich die meisten seiner Zeitgenossen herausgefordert fühlten: eine Darstellung, in der nicht länger die Kontinuität der Überlieferung, nicht der Zusammenhang mit der älteren Literatur, sondern der Bruch mit ihr in den Vordergrund gestellt wurde. Da Mattheson aber, obwohl er sich mit starken Worten gegen diejenigen wandte, die die Musik in eine Wissenschaft verwandelt hätten, dennoch auf die Bestätigung seiner Ansichten durch anerkannte Autoritäten nicht meinte verzichten zu können, kommt es dazu, daß er als Kronzeugen im Neu-eröffneten Orchestre hauptsächlich französische Autoren wie Brossard, Boivin oder Jean Rousseau heranzieht, während er die deutschen Autoren, auch wenn sie, wie beispielsweise Niedt, Fuhrmann oder Heinichen, in sachlichen Fragen weitgehend mit ihm übereinstimmten, übergeht oder nur am Rande erwähnt[9].

Während aber das Neue in Neu-eröffneten Orchestre noch weit mehr in der Art der Darstellung als im sachlichen Gehalt lag, hat Buttstetts Angriff zur Folge, daß Mattheson nun zum ersten Mal zur Entwicklung wirklich eigener Gedanken provoziert wird. Zwar besteht ein großer Teil des Beschützten Orchestres[10], der Erwiderung auf Buttstetts Schrift, aus mehr oder minder kleinlichen Streitereien um vergleichsweise geringfügige Einzelheiten. Jedoch veranlassen einige Punkte in Buttstetts Gegenschrift Mattheson zu längeren Ausführungen von grundsätzlichem Charakter. So geht aus der Gegenüberstellung der Stilbegriffe Kirchers, auf den sich Buttstett beruft, und Brossards, des Gewährsmanns Matthesons, der Abschnitt "De stylis

7 Die Kritik an Solmisationspraxis und Moduslehre zieht sich durch die Musikliteratur des ganzen siebzehnten Jahrhunderts.
8 Buttstett, Ut Re Mi, Vorrede.
9 Siehe dazu A. Forchert, "Französische Autoren in den Schriften Johann Matthesons", in: Festschrift Heinz Becker (Laaber, 1982), 382 ss. Bei den einschlägigen Schriften der deutschen Autoren handelt es sich um Fr. E. Niedt, Musikalische Handleitung (Hamburg, 1700–1706); M. H. Fuhrmann, Musicalischer Trichter (Berlin, 1706); J. D. Heinichen, Neu erfundene und gründliche Anweisung . . . zu vollkommener Erlernung des General-Baßes (Hamburg, 1711). Die Tatsache, daß die Schriften Niedts und Heinichens wie die Matthesons in Hamburg erschienen, einer Stadt, deren Musikleben entscheidend durch die Existenz eines ständigen Operntheaters geprägt wurde, ist kein Zufall.
10 Orchestre II.

musicis" hervor[11], in dem Mattheson, herausgefordert durch Buttstetts Behauptung, daß zwischen den einzelnen Stilen in der gegenwärtigen Musik überhaupt kein Unterschied mehr gemacht werde[12],
zum ersten Mal versucht, sein Verständnis des Kirchenstils genauer
darzulegen. Damit aber und mit der sich anschließenden Frage nach
dem Wesen der "wahren" Kirchenmusik ist ein Thema angeschlagen,
das Mattheson späterhin nicht allein in der Kontroverse mit Joachim
Meyer, dem Göttingischen Ephorus[13], und nicht nur im *Musicalischen Patrioten*[14] zum Hauptgegenstand erhoben hat, sondern
das schließlich zum zentralen Bezugspunkt aller seiner nach dem
Vollkommenen Capellmeister[15] entstandenen musikalischen Spätschriften wird[16].

Ähnlich weitgehende Konsequenzen hat Buttstetts Kritik an Matthesons Behandlung der Frage, ob die Quart als konsonantes oder als
dissonantes Intervall anzusehen sei. Mattheson, der die Frage, dem
Gehör folgend, zugunsten des überwiegenden Dissonanzcharakters
der Quart entschieden hatte[17], mußte sich von Buttstett mit dem
Argument widersprechen lassen, daß das Gehör kein objektiver Richter sein könne. Entscheidend seien hier letztlich die vom subjektiven
Urteil unabhängigen, objektiv gegebenen Zahlenverhältnisse, und sie
entschieden weitgehend zugunsten ihres Konsonanzcharakters[18].
Die Frage, die nichts weniger als das Fundament von Matthesons musikalischer Grundanschauung, den Wert der Erfahrung nämlich, betraf, war ihm zu wichtig, um sie nur beiläufig in einer schnell
hingeworfenen Entgegnung zu behandeln. So kündigt er schon im
Beschützten Orchestre an: "Von der Quarta will ich / mit Gottes
Hülffe anderswo / nemlich in der dritten Eröffnung des Orchstre
handeln". Und nachdem er festgestellt hat, daß auch "Kunst-Sätze" –
d.h. allgemeine Regeln – die Bestätigung ihrer Gültigkeit allemal
allein durch das Gehör erhalten könnten, fährt er fort: "Ich will aber
nicht nur von der Quarta, sondern auch vom Sinne des
Gehörs / geliebts Gott / in besagtem dritten Theil / etwas recht aus-
führliches ans Licht geben / weil meines Erachtens / alle Zwistigkeiten in der Music / zusammen genommen / lange nicht von solcher

11 *Orchestre* II, 115 ss.   12 Buttstett, *Ut Re Mi*, 81 s.
13 *Göttingischer Ephorus*. Zur Kontroverse mit J. Meyer siehe A. Forchert, "Mattheson
   und die Kirchenmusik", in: *Gattung und Werk in der Musikgeschichte Norddeutschlands und Skandinaviens* (=Kieler Schriften zur Musikwissenschaft, vol.
   26), (Kassel, 1982), 114 ss.
14 Hamburg, 1728.   15 Hamburg, 1739.
16 Forchert, "Mattheson und die Kirchenmusik", 118 ss.
17 *Orchestre* I, 126 ss.   18 *Ut Re Mi*, 71 ss.

Wichtigkeit seyn können / als diese beyde Haupt-Stücke"[19]. Aber
auch mit diesem dritten Teil, dem *Forschenden Orchestre*[20], findet
der Streit darüber, ob Musik ratione oder sensu zu beurteilen sei,
noch lange kein Ende. In der modifizierten Form einer Frage nach
dem Nutzen der Mathematik für die musikalische Komposition[21]
liegt er noch der Auseinandersetzung mit Mizler zugrunde, die sich
ebenfalls bis in die Spätschriften fortsetzt.

Die Polemik, die durch das *Neu-eröffnete Orchestre* entfacht
wurde, hat aber schließlich für Mattheson noch die weitere Folge, daß
er gezwungen wird, sein Verhältnis zur älteren Musiktheorie still-
schweigend zu revidieren. Wenn er dort noch glaubte, seine musikalischen Ansichten vertreten zu können, ohne sie vor der Tradition rechtfertigen zu müssen, so wird er durch Buttstetts Angriff nun
selber genötigt, sich zur Verteidigung seiner Positionen auf die Autorität älterer Musiktheoretiker zu stützen. Der Rückgriff auf die
Geschichte, im *Neu-eröffneten Orchestre* noch dem Verdacht aus-
gesetzt, den Verfall der Musik mitverschuldet zu haben, muß nun
dazu dienen, Buttstetts Festhalten an der Solmisationspraxis und an
der Lehre von den alten Kirchentonarten ad absurdum zu führen.
Matthesons historischer Exkurs, in dem er unter Heranziehung älterer
Musiktheoretiker von Puteanus über Calvisius, Lippius, Profe, Mat-
thaei und anderen bis zu Printz und Werckmeister nachweist, daß die
Zweckmäßigkeit der guidonischen Silben für die Praxis schon seit eh
und je in Zweifel gezogen wurde[22], bezeichnet bereits jene Wende
vom Leitbild des musikalisch interessierten Galanthomme zum Ideal
des Musicus eruditus, die dann in den auf das *Beschützte Orchestre*
folgenden Schriften, in der *Exemplarischen Organisten-Probe*[23] und
vor allem im *Forschenden Orchestre*, vollends manifest werden
sollte[24]. Man wird freilich die Veränderung von Matthesons
Einstellung der Tradition gegenüber nicht erst auf den Zeitpunkt des
Erscheinens von Buttstetts Schrift, also um 1716–17, datieren dürfen.
Denn da Mattheson, wie er im "Vorspiel" zum *Beschützten Orchestre*
berichtet, schon seit langem bekannt war, daß eine Gegenschrift
vorbereitet wurde, und da ihm auch klar sein mußte, gegen welche
seiner Ansichten sie sich vornehmlich richten würde, hatte er längst

---

19 *Orchestre* II, 174 s.   20 Hamburg, 1731.
21 *Capellmeister*, 16 ss.   22 *Orchestre* II, 325 ss.
23 Hamburg, 1719. Die achtundvierzig Prob-Stücke dieses Bandes werden eingeleitet
   durch eine "Theoretische Vorbereitung / über verschiedene musicalische Merckwürdigkeiten".
24 Bezeichnend ist in diesem Zusammenhang auch Matthesons Schrift *De eruditione
   musica* (Hamburg, 1732).

Vorkehrungen treffen können, um seinen Widersachern zum gegebenen Zeitpunkt gerüstet gegenüberzutreten[25]. Die profunde Literaturkenntnis, mit der er Buttstetts Angriff zurückwies, war ohnehin nicht, wie uns Mattheson glauben machen möchte, in wenigen Wochen zu erwerben. Seine Behauptung, er habe "keine 4 Wochen in blossen Neben-Stunden mit der gantzen Sache zugebracht", da er Buttstetts Refutationsschrift erst am 24. Januar 1717 erhalten habe und bereits am 21. Februar mit der Verteidigung seiner Ansichten fertig gewesen sei[26], kann sich, wenn sie überhaupt ernst zu nehmen sein sollte, allenfalls auf die Schreibarbeit an den mehr als fünfhundert Seiten des *Beschützten Orchestre* beziehen. Sicher dürfte indessen sein, daß gerade die Aussicht, sich gegen Angriffe zur Wehr setzen zu müssen, Mattheson nicht nur dazu brachte, sich über die Positionen, die er im *Neu-eröffneten Orchestre* noch vergleichsweise ungeschützt vertreten hatte, ernsthaft Rechenschaft zu geben, sondern daß sie auch seine Produktivität anregte, indem sie ihn zwang, den eigenen Standpunkt weiter zu entwickeln und fester zu begründen.

Im Grunde ist Matthesons Polemik allerdings viel weniger persönlich, als es bei der Lektüre des *Beschützten Orchestre* vielleicht erscheinen könnte. Denn die ausführliche Begründung und Entwicklung der umstrittenen Kernpunkte des *Neu-eröffneten Orchestre* erfolgt ja nicht nur hier, in der unmittelbaren Entgegnung auf Buttstett und seine Hintermänner, sondern auch in den bereits erwähnten später erschienenen Schriften, also der *Organisten-Probe* und dem *Forschenden Orchestre*, deren Entstehung, wie Mattheson selbst bezeugt, bereits in die Zeit um 1716–17 fällt[27]. Der im *Forschenden Orchestre* behandelten Frage nach dem Vorrang der Sinne oder des Verstandes bei der Beurteilung der Musik fügt Mattheson in der *Exemplarischen Organisten-Probe* eine Verteidigung des "modernen" Systems der je zwölf Dur- bzw. Molltonarten gegen die alten Kirchentonarten hinzu. Damit wird hier der Streit um die Gültigkeit der Solmisation auf anderer Ebene fortgeführt, da sich selbstverständlich mit der Entscheidung über Beibehaltung oder Verwerfung der traditionellen Modi auch die über die Solmisationspraxis verbindet. Daß die *Exemplarische Organisten-Probe* vor allem die Durchsetzung des modernen Tonartensystems zum Ziel hat und erst in zweiter Linie, wie ihr Titel nahelegt[28], die Einführung neuer Methoden des Generalbaß-Unterrichts oder neuer Techniken des Ak-

25 *Orchestre* II, 1.   26 *Orchestre* II, 53.   27 *Orchestre* II, 501 s.
28 *Exemplarische Organisten-Probe im Artikel vom General-Baß.*

kompagnements, bezeugen auch die zweimal vierundzwanzig Prob-Stücke, die der ausführlichen "Theoretischen Vorbereitung" angefügt sind. In ihnen geht es Mattheson hauptsächlich darum, die Spieler an den vollständigen Zyklus der Dur- und Molltonarten zu gewöhnen und den Anhängern des traditionellen Systems der Kirchentonarten zu demonstrieren, daß im Hinblick auf musikalische Darstellungsmöglichkeiten und spieltechnische Anforderungen und im Gegensatz zu den begrenzten Transpositionsmöglichkeiten der alten Modi nun alle vierundzwanzig Tonarten prinzipiell gleichberechtigt seien[29].

Daß Matthesons Tätigkeit als Musikschriftsteller durch die polemische Auseinandersetzung stimuliert wird, ja daß er diese Auseinandersetzung geradezu sucht, um im Widerspruch seine eigenen Vorstellungen besser begründen, einleuchtender darlegen, wenn nicht sogar überhaupt erst entwickeln zu können, zeigt sich deutlicher noch als in der Polemik um das *Neu-eröffnete Orchestre* in den beiden Teilen der *Critica musica*[30], denen die Gegenüberstellung von Rede und Widerrede fast durchweg als Darstellungsprinzip zugrundeliegt. Von besonderem Interesse ist in diesem Zusammenhang die Auseinandersetzung mit Franz Xaver Murschhausers *Academia musico-poetica bipartita*[31]. Man hat Matthesons Polemik gegen den fast um zwanzig Jahre älteren Münchener Kirchenmusiker bislang meist nur als gereizte Reaktion auf den Titel des Werkes angesehen, in dem bekanntlich – vermutlich auf Initiative des Verlegers hin – angekündigt wird, der Traktat sei geeignet, dem "vortrefflichen Herrn Mattheson ein mehrers Licht zu geben". In der Tat bringt ja Matthesons "Melopoetische Licht-Scheere"[32] im Vergleich zu seiner Auseinandersetzung mit Buttstett sachlich kaum etwas Neues. Auch Murschhauser ist ein Vertreter der alten Generation, für die Solmisation und Kirchentonarten noch zu den unerläßlichen Requisita jeder Musiklehre gehören, auch sein Denken bewegt sich noch völlig – und sogar mehr noch als das Buttstetts – in den Bahnen einer an der Kirchenmusik des vorangehenden Jahrhunderts sich orientierenden Tradition. Entscheidend für Matthesons Widerspruch scheint aber hier etwas anderes zu sein, nämlich die Tatsache, daß Murschhauser mit seiner Schrift eine "Hohe Schul der musicalischen Composition . . . mit emsiger Untersuchung aller / zu dieser hohen Wissen-

29 So hat übrigens auch J. D. Heinichen die *Exemplarische Organisten-Probe* verstanden, der sie in seinem *General-Baß in der Composition* (Dresden, 1728), 582, vor allem deshalb empfahl, weil sie dazu dienen könne, Anfänger in den "Schwührigkeiten aller Modorum Musicorum" sattelfest zu machen.
30 Hamburg, 1722–5.   31 Nürnberg, 1721.   32 *Critica musica* I, 5 ss.

schaft dienlichen / Materien und Umstände"[33] versprochen hatte. Denn zur gleichen Zeit als Murschhausers Schrift erschien, hatte Mattheson selbst den Plan gefaßt, eine umfassende Kompositionslehre in Angriff zu nehmen. "Ich will mir nun", so schreibt er in der Nachlese zum *Forschenden Orchestre*[34],

ein Manuale machen von lauter weissem Papier / ein Album, ungefehr auf 2.Bogen groß / und das will ich alle Monath erneuern. In demselben Büchlein / welches zuletzt auf ein Buch hinaus lauffen wird / will ich meine Compositions-Gedanken schreiben / nicht eben allein / wie man diese oder jene Con- oder Dissonantiam hanthieren u. resolviren soll; sondern wie man mehr gout, als Kunst; mehr Melodie / als Weber-Streiche; mehr natürliches und vernünfftiges / als brodirtes und galonnirtes gebrauchen soll. Artem, non artificium, docebo.

Es spricht vieles dafür, daß Mattheson, veranlaßt durch Murschhausers Traktat und in ausdrücklichem Gegensatz zu ihm, nun mit dem Dispositionsentwurf seiner eigenen Kompositionslehre beginnt. Denn gegen Schluß der dritten und letzten "Schneuzung" der "Melopoetischen Licht-Scheere" kommt Mattheson auf die Frage zu sprechen, ob denn die Gegenstände, die Murschhauser in seinem Traktat behandelt hatte, ausreichten, um den Anspruch einer "Hohen Schule der Music" zu rechtfertigen. Dabei führt er die Versäumnisse Murschhausers in einem siebzehn Punkte umfassenden Katalog alles dessen auf, was seiner Meinung nach unumgänglich in einer solchen Kompositionslehre ebenfalls hätte abgehandelt werden müssen[35]. Vergleicht man nun Inhalt und Reihenfolge dieser siebzehn Punkte mit der Kapiteleinteilung des *Vollkommenen Capellmeisters,* so kann man feststellen, daß ihnen eine Disposition zugrundeliegt, in der sich in großen Zügen bereits die Kapitelanordnung von Matthesons Hauptwerk abzeichnet. So entsprechen die Punkte 1–4 sämtlich Gegenständen, die später im ersten Teil des *Vollkommenen Capellmeisters* abgehandelt werden, die Punkte 5–10 beziehen sich auf Lehrgegenstände aus dem zweiten, die Punkte 11–14 auf solche aus dem dritten Teil des späteren Werkes. Darüber hinaus ist in vielen Fällen auch die Reihenfolge innerhalb der einzelnen Teile schon vorweggenommen, wenn auch die Kapiteleinteilung des *Vollkommenen Capellmeisters* verständlicherweise sehr viel differenzierter ist. Sicher ist jedenfalls, daß durch die Auseinandersetzung mit Murschhauser seine eigene Idee einer umfassenden Kompositionslehre eine entschieden konkretere Gestalt angenommen hat.

---

33 So die Formulierung im Titel der *Academia musico-poetica.*
34 P. 766 s.   35 *Critica musica* I, 74 s.

Und so dürfte es denn auch kein Zufall sein, daß Mattheson nur kurze Zeit nach seiner kritischen Beschäftigung mit einer Schrift, die nach seinem Dafürhalten ihrem hohen Anspruch in nur höchst unvollkommener Weise gerecht geworden war, beschließt, seinem geplanten Werk den Titel *Der vollkommene Capellmeister* zu geben[36]. Daß er, diesem Titel entsprechend, hier die resümierende Zusammenfassung aller seiner musikalisch-praktischen und theoretischen Erfahrungen vorzulegen beabsichtigte, darauf deutet nicht nur der Hinweis, er werde bis zur Fertigstellung des Buches noch etwa neun Jahre benötigen, sondern auch seine Bemerkung, er stelle sich vor, der *Vollkommene Capellmeister* werde seine letzte Arbeit sein[37].

Im Lichte dieser Konzeption stellen sich denn auch die Themen, die von Mattheson in den folgenden Teilen der *Critica musica* behandelt werden, ihrem eigentlichen Sinn nach als in Form von Kontroversen durchgeführte Studien zu dem geplanten Werk dar. So dient ihm etwa die kommentierte Übersetzung der Auseinandersetzung zwischen Raguenet als Befürworter der italienischen Musik und jenem anonymen Anhänger der französischen Opernpraxis, den Mattheson fälschlich für Le Cerf de la Viéville hielt[38], zur Klärung des Problems der Nationalstile, während die in der "Canonischen Anatomie"[39] und im "Melodischen Vorhof"[40] ausgetragene Disputation über Bokemeyers Ansichten vom Nutzen der kanonischen Schreibweise offensichtlich von dem Bestreben geleitet ist, die Prinzipien der Melodielehre, die Mattheson gerade in diesen Jahren zunächst in der Unterrichtspraxis erprobt hatte[41], gegen mögliche Einwände zu sichern. Auch der im "Fragenden Componisten"[42] vorgetragene Angriff auf Händels *Johannes-Passion*, ein Werk, dessen Entstehung nahezu zwanzig Jahre zurücklag, läßt sich nicht allein daraus erklären, daß Mattheson das Bedürfnis haben mochte, die Wahl des gleichen Textes in seinem 1723 komponierten Passionsoratorium *Das Lied des Lammes*[43] zu rechtfertigen. Wichtiger für ihn mochte die

---

36 Die Auseinandersetzung mit Murschhausers Traktat fällt in die Zeit zwischen Mai und Juli 1722. Von einem künftigen Buch mit dem Titel *Vollenkommener Capellmeister / Teutsch und Lateinisch* ist erstmals im Januar 1723 die Rede; siehe *Critica musica* I, 240.

37 Ibid.

38 *Critica musica* I, 91 ss. Zur Frage der Autorschaft Viévilles siehe R. Wangermée, "Lecerf de la Viéville, Bonnet-Bourdelot et l'Essai sur le bon goust en musique de Nicolas Grandval", in: *RBM* 5 (1951), 132 ss.

39 *Critica musica* I, 289 ss.   40 *Critica musica* II, 291 ss.

41 Cf. die mehrfachen Hinweise auf seine Unterrichtstätigkeit in der Autobiographie, *Ehrenpforte*, 187 ss, z.B. die Erwähnung eines 1724 gehaltenen "Collegium de Melodica", ibid., 209.

42 *Critica musica* II, 1 ss.   43 Herausgegeben von B. C. Cannon (Madison, 1971).

Tatsache sein, daß er in der Konfrontation mit dem älteren Werk die Gelegenheit erhielt, seine Prinzipien der Textbehandlung und Affektdarstellung einleuchtend zu begründen – so einleuchtend, daß ihm Marpurg noch fast vierzig Jahre danach bestätigen konnte, seine kritischen Anmerkungen seien nach wie vor für Singekomponisten "wichtig und nöthig"[44]. Selbst die Auseinandersetzung mit Johann Georg Linike, dem ungenannten "guten Freunde" im sechsten Teil der *Critica musica*, der "Lehr-reichen Meister-Schule"[45], dürfte kaum anders zu erklären sein, als damit, daß es Mattheson drängte, nachdem der Plan zu einer umfassenden Kompositionslehre einmal Gestalt angenommen hatte, sich zunächst Rechenschaft über die Werke seiner Vorgänger auf diesem Gebiet zu geben. Dazu bot die Korrespondenz mit Linike willkommenen Anlaß, da die hier vorgebrachten Einwendungen und Ergänzungswünsche zu einigen Stellen in den beiden ersten Eröffnungen des Orchestres sich vorwiegend auf historische Sachverhalte und Fragen der traditionellen Kontrapunktlehre bezogen. Obwohl der letzte Kontakt zu seinem Kontrahenten zu diesem Zeitpunkt bereits mehr als vier Jahre zurücklag[46], so ergriff Mattheson daher nun die Gelegenheit, sich ausführlicher mit den von Linike genannten Schriften Beers, Scacchis, Zacconis und Donis zu beschäftigen, eine umfassende Ergänzung zu Brossards Register musikalischer Scribenten auszuarbeiten[47], historisch-biographische Exkurse über Orlando di Lasso und Lully einzuschalten, sowie kontrapunktische Fragen unter Berufung auf alt-ehrwürdige Autoritäten wie Gafurius, Salinas, Zarlino und selbst Kircher – den er im *Beschützten Orchestre* noch kräftig geschmäht hatte – zu behandeln.

Während man davon ausgehen darf, daß durch die polemischen Auseinandersetzungen in der *Critica musica* wesentliche Vorarbeiten für Teile des *Vollkommenen Capellmeisters* geleistet wurden, ja daß manche dieser Polemiken geradezu die Funktion hatten, solche Vorarbeiten überhaupt erst in Gang zu bringen, ist die Kontroverse mit Joachim Meyer, dem Göttingischen Ephorus, die vordergründig als Streit um die Verwendung von Kantaten im Gottesdienst ausgefochten wird, ganz anderer Art[48]. Kontroversen um Wesen, Wert

44 Fr. W. Marpurg, *Kritische Briefe über die Tonkunst*, vol. 1 (Berlin, 1760), 56.
45 *Critica musica* II, 67 ss. Daß die Polemik der "Lehr-reichen Meister-Schule" dem zu dieser Zeit als Geiger im Hamburgischen Opernorchester wirkenden Johann Georg Linike gilt, wird aus Matthesons Kritik der ihm eingesandten Lully-Biographie, *Critica musica* II, 117, deutlich. Daß ihm diese von Linike zugänglich gemacht wurde, berichtet er an anderer Stelle, *Critica musica* I, 178.
46 *Critica musica* II, 67.   47 *Critica musica* II, 109 ss.
48 Siehe dazu A. Forchert, "Mattheson und die Kirchenmusik", 117 ss.

und Nutzen der protestantischen Kirchenmusik gab es schon seit geraumer Zeit[49], sie waren im Grunde nur ein Anzeichen dafür, daß die Stellung der Kirchenmusik im Zeitalter des Rationalismus und der Aufklärung zunehmend problematischer und schwieriger geworden war. Meyers *Unvorgreiffliche Gedancken über die neulich eingerissene theatralische Kirchenmusik*[50], in denen Mattheson weder angegriffen noch überhaupt nur erwähnt wurde, waren nur ein Glied in dieser nicht abreißenden Kette beständiger Polemiken und galten dazu noch einer musikalischen Gattung, für die Mattheson bis dahin keineswegs eine besondere Vorliebe gezeigt hatte[51]. Wenn Mattheson gleichwohl sofort reagierte und in einer gereizten, auch vor persönlichen Angriffen nicht halt machenden Gegenschrift[52] die "theatralische" Kirchenmusik vehement verteidigte, so hatte das Gründe, die mit individuellen Erfahrungen zusammenhingen, die er seit dem Anfang der zwanziger Jahre in Hamburg hatte machen müssen. Denn nach dem Niedergang der Hamburger Oper, an deren Musikideal er sich gebildet hatte und das er nach wie vor für das einzig wahre hielt, schienen für ihn die stilistischen Errungenschaften der Oper nur dann zu retten zu sein, wenn es gelang, ihnen im institutionellen Rahmen der Kirche eine dauernde Heimstätte zu sichern. Meyers *Unvorgreiffliche Gedancken*, die in einem Augenblick ans Licht traten, als Mattheson gerade an einer Veröffentlichung – dem *Ehrwürdigen Theatrum*[53] – arbeitete, die der Rechtfertigung und Verherrlichung solcher "theatralischen" Kirchenmusik dienen sollte, mußten ihm deshalb geradezu als Bedrohung des Fortbestandes der Musik überhaupt erscheinen. Der Angriff Meyers auf die "theatralische" Kirchenmusik stützte sich auf Zeugnisse antiker und christlicher Schriftsteller, sowie vor allem auf die Bibel – die gleichen Quellen, die Mattheson bereits für den entgegengesetzten Zweck ausgiebig herangezogen hatte. Unter solchen Umständen konnte ihm die Entgegnung nicht schwer fallen. Sie blieb indessen auch diesmal nicht ohne Rückwirkungen auf sein eigenes Schaffen und seine eigenen Überzeugungen. Zunächst hatte die – von Meyer in seinem *Criticus sine crisi*[54] noch fortgesetzte – Kontroverse die Folge, daß Mattheson den Plan einer selbständigen

---

49 Eine ausführliche Darstellung dieser Kontroversen findet sich bei D. Beck, *Krise und Verfall der protestantischen Kirchenmusik im 18. Jahrhundert*, phil. Diss. (Halle-Wittenberg, 1952).
50 S. l., 1726.
51 A. Forchert, "Mattheson und die Kirchenmusik", 118 s.
52 *Göttingischer Ephorus.*   53 Ibid., Vorbericht.
54 J. Meyer, *Der anmaßliche Hamburgische Criticus sine crisi* (Lemgo, 1728).

Veröffentlichung des *Ehrwürdigen Theatrum* fallen ließ. An seine Stelle trat der als Wochenschrift herausgegebene *Musicalische Patriot*[55], in dem die Diskussion um die "theatralische" Kirchenmusik zwar weitergeführt, gleichzeitig jedoch um eine Reihe anderer Themen erweitert wurde. Wichtiger als diese äußerlichen Folgen ist freilich eine andere Konsequenz des Streites für Mattheson gewesen. Denn die im Ton so scharfe Auseinandersetzung kann nicht darüber hinwegtäuschen, daß Mattheson, indem er den Begriff des "Theatralischen" allmählich so stark erweitert, daß schließlich alles, was eine starke Wirkung erzielt, unter ihn fällt, sich den konservativen Ansichten der Verteidiger der traditionellen Kirchenmusik immer mehr annähert[56].

Matthesons Streit mit Meyer um die "threatralische" Kirchenmusik ist nicht sein letzter. Auch sein späteres Leben ist angefüllt mit Kontroversen und Auseinandersetzungen der verschiedensten Art: mit Rameaus *Traité de l'harmonie* um den Primat von Melodie oder Harmonie[57], mit Mizler um den Nutzen der Mathematik für die Musik[58], mit Scheibe um kleinliche Prioritätsfragen[59], mit Gottsched um den Gebrauch der deutschen Sprache[60], mit Biedermann um die Rolle der Musik in den Schulen[61] und mit vielen anderen mehr. Indessen sind Matthesons Überzeugungen durch diese späten Polemiken nicht mehr verändert, ist die Art und Richtung seines Erkenntnisstrebens durch sie nicht mehr entscheidend beeinflußt worden. Gerade das aber ist der Fall in den Auseinandersetzungen der Jahre zwischen *Neu-eröffnetem Orchestre* und *Musicalischem Patrioten*. Gewiß wird man nicht übersehen können, daß Matthesons polemisches Naturell in vielen Fällen auch da Streit und Auseinandersetzung sucht, wo es keineswegs in erster Linie um Erkenntnis, sondern vorwiegend nur um Eitelkeit und Rechthaberei geht. Aber in einer Zeit, in der das im Geschmacksurteil auf sich selbst gestellte Individuum sich seiner Maßstäbe allenthalben durch Vergleiche,

---

55 Hamburg, 1728.
56 A. Forchert, "Mattheson und die Kirchenmusik", 119 s.
57 Die Auseinandersetzung mit Rameau beginnt in *Critica musica* I, 7 ss., und zieht sich durch fast alle späteren Schriften.
58 Der Beginn dieser lang anhaltenden Kontroverse reicht bis auf den Abschnitt "Von der musikalischen Mathematik" aus der Vorrede zum *Capellmeister* zurück, obwohl der Name Mizlers bei dieser Gelegenheit noch nicht genannt wird. Jedoch bezieht sich Mattheson hier eindeutig auf die Besprechung seines *Kern melodischer Wissenschafft* (Hamburg, 1737) in Mizlers *Neu eröffneter musicalischer Bibliothek*, vol. 1, 6. Theil (Leipzig, 1738), und zwar speziell auf die Ausführungen über die Zahlenverhältnisse der Intervalle und deren Bedeutung für eine gute Melodie (ibid., 25 ss.); Siehe später auch *Plus ultra*, 301 ss., u.a.
59 *Capellmeister*, 9 s.   60 *Tresespiel*.   61 *Panacea* I, 41 ss.

Diskussionen oder mehr oder minder polemische Argumentation zu versichern suchen mußte, bedeutete der Verzicht auf Auseinandersetzung letztlich auch den Verzicht auf Erkenntnis. Von der Bemühung jedoch um die Erkenntnis des jeweils Richtigen und Wahren und dem Versuch seiner Durchsetzung in der Musikpraxis seiner Zeit hat Mattheson sein Leben lang nicht abgelassen.

10

Unbekannte Kompositionen aus Johann Matthesons Nachlaß

HANS JOACHIM MARX

Hamburg

Matthesons musikhistorische Leistung wird heute noch (wie schon im neunzehnten Jahrhundert) in der theoretischen Durchdringung und der systematischen Beschreibung der Musik seiner Zeit gesehen. Seine Schriften vom *Neueröffneten Orchestre* (1713) bis zum *Vollkommenen Capellmeister* (1739) gelten als sein Hauptwerk. Dabei wird übersehen, daß sein umfangreiches kompositorisches Werk, seine Opern und Oratorien, seine Kammer- und Klaviermusik nicht nur einen erfindungsreichen Komponisten erkennen läßt, sondern einen musikalisch umfassend gebildeten "musicus poeticus", der theoretisch beschrieb, was er kompositorisch erprobt hatte.

Daß Mattheson als Komponist völlig der Vergessenheit anheimgefallen ist, hat zwei Ursachen: einmal hat die Musikforschung des vorigen Jahrhunderts (besonders Winterfeld, Chrysander und Bitter[1]) keinen Zweifel daran gelassen, daß Matthesons Musik im Vergleich mit der Händels und Bachs von außerordentlich geringer Bedeutung sei. Dieses Verdikt hatte Folgen: solange einige Kompositionen des Hamburgers als Werke Händels[2], Bononcinis und Zianis[3] bekannt waren, wurden sie geschätzt und positiv beurteilt. Nachdem sie aber Mattheson zugeschrieben worden waren, fanden sie kein Interesse mehr: die Musik des "Theoretikers" schien blutleer, schematisch, uninspiriert. Andererseits stand die Überlieferung des kompositorischen Werkes einer intensiven wissenschaftlichen Be-

---

1 C. von Winterfeld, *Der evangelische Kirchengesang*, vol. 3, (Leipzig, 1847), 184; Fr. Chrysander, *G. F. Händel*, vol. 1 (Leipzig, 1858), 448; C. H. Bitter, *Beiträge zu einer Geschichte des Oratoriums* (Berlin, 1872), 168.
2 W. Braun, "Drei deutsche Arien – ein Jugendwerk Händels?", in: *AMl* 42 (1970), 248–51, Die beiden Arien aus Matthesons Oper *Henrico IV.*, die Dr. Hermann Moeck (Celle) im Manuskript besitzt, sind zeitgenössische Abschriften, kein Autograph Matthesons.
3 H. Schmidt, *Johann Mattheson, ein Förderer der deutschen Tonkunst, im Lichte seiner Werke* (Leipzig, 1897), 4.

schäftigung im Wege: zwar hatte Beekman C. Cannon[4] den von Mattheson der Johanneum-Bibliothek (der späteren Stadtbibliothek) vermachten handschriftlichen Nachlaß in den späten dreißiger Jahren noch durcharbeiten und bibliographisch erfassen können, und auch Hellmuth Christian Wolff[5] hat die autographen Partituren für seine Studien über die Hamburger Barockoper noch einsehen können. Seit der Zerstörung der Stadtbibliothek im Jahre 1943 gilt der Nachlaß Matthesons aber als verbrannt. Jüngere Arbeiten wie die von George J. Buelow über die Oper *Cleopatra* und von Henning Frederichs über die Brockes-Passion[6] konnten nur auf Sekundärquellen zurückgreifen.

Die Annahme, Matthesons autographe Partituren seien 1943 während der Bombenangriffe auf Hamburg vernichtet worden, läßt sich heute nicht mehr aufrecht erhalten[7]. Vor kurzem konnte anhand von Archivmaterial der Staats- und Universitätsbibliothek nachgewiesen werden, daß der vollständige Nachlaß des Komponisten (zusammen mit einem großen Teil der alten Musiksammlung der früheren Stadtbibliothek) wenige Wochen vor der Zerstörung der Bibliothek ausgelagert worden ist[8]. Da der Auslagerungsort, das Schloß Lauenstein bei Dresden, nach Kriegsende aber auf dem Gebiet der sowjetisch besetzten Zone lag, war es nicht möglich, die Quellen nach Hamburg zurückzuführen. Einem Briefwechsel zwischen der Staats- und Universitätsbibliothek Hamburg und dem Verwalter des Schlosses Lauenstein ist zu entnehmen, daß die Sowjetarmee im Februar 1946 das Hamburger Auslagerungsgut (287 Kisten voll Handschriften und Frühdrucken) an einen unbekannten Ort transportiert hat. Nachdem in den fünfziger Jahren ein Bibliothekar der Deutschen Staatsbibliothek in Berlin (-Ost) zufällig in einem Moskauer Magazin Handschriften mit dem Siegel der Hamburger Staats- und Universitätsbibliothek entdeckt hatte, übergab die Sowjetunion 1958 der Ostberliner Staatsbibliothek etwa 1850 Handschriften Hamburger

4 Cannon, *Mattheson.*
5 H. Chr. Wolff, *Die Barockoper in Hamburg (1678–1738)*, vol. 1: *Textband* (Wolfenbüttel, 1957), Kapitel "Mattheson", 284–99.
6 G. J. Buelow, "An Evaluation of Johann Mattheson's Opera *Cleopatra* (Hamburg, 1704)", in: *Studies in Eighteenth-Century Music. A Tribute to Karl Geiringer* (New York und London, 1970), 92–107; H. Frederichs, *Das Verhältnis von Text und Musik in den Brockespassionen Keisers, Händels, Telemanns und Matthesons* (=Musikwissenschaftliche Schriften 9) (München und Salzburg, 1975).
7 Siehe jüngstens den Artikel "Hamburg" in: *New Grove* 8 (1980), 68.
8 Hierüber hat der Verfasser in zwei Artikeln berichtet: "Johann Mattheson's Bequest", in: *Early Music* 10 (July 1982), 365–7, und "Johann Matthesons Nachlaß. Zum Schicksal der Musiksammlung der alten Stadtbibliothek Hamburg", in: *AMl* 55 (1983), 108–24.

Provenienz, wo sie bis heute, der Öffentlichkeit unzugänglich, treuhänderisch verwahrt werden.

Unter diesen Beständen befinden sich nun auch vier Bände bzw. Konvolute, die ehemals zum Nachlaß Matthesons gehörten (Cod.hans.IV.39–42, heute Berlin-Mappe 7–11). Die Bände enthalten auf etwa tausend, meistens von Mattheson selbst geschriebenen Seiten neben philosophischen, moralischen, theologischen und musikhistorischen Aufzeichnungen, auch zehn Kompositionen, die im folgenden kurz vorgestellt werden sollen[9].

Die Kompositionen, die in dem Konvolut Cod.hans.IV.42 enthalten[10] sind, sind Gelegenheitsarbeiten, die Mattheson für Schüler oder Freunde geschrieben hat. Sie stammen zum größten Teil aus dem ersten Jahrzehnt des achtzehnten Jahrhunderts, mit Ausnahme des "Melos exequiale"-Fragments von 1756, das Mattheson für sein eigenes Begräbnis komponiert hat.

Zu den frühesten, etwa um 1708 entstandenen Kompositionen gehören fünf Sätze für zwei Cembali (eine Sonata und eine Suite[11]), die Mattheson für sich und seinen Schüler Cyril Wich (1695–1756) geschrieben hat (Abbildung 1). Cyril Wich war der Sohn des in Hamburg akkreditierten Gesandten von Großbritannien, der zuvor bekanntlich bei Händel Unterricht hatte.

Gattungsgeschichtlich gehören die fünf Sätze zu den frühesten Beispielen von Kompositionen für zwei "Clavierinstrumente". Im *Vollkommenen Capellmeister* schreibt Mattheson etwa dreißig Jahre später, seit einigen Jahren habe man angefangen, "Sonaten fürs Clavier mit gutem Beifall zu setzen" (und damit schließt er Sonaten für zwei Claviere mit ein): "bisher haben sie noch die rechte Gestalt nicht, und wollen mehr gerührt werden als rühren, d. i. sie zielen mehr auf die Bewegung der Finger als die der Hertzen"[12]. Hinter der

---

9 Für die Einsichtnahme in die Originale danke ich der Staats-und Universitätsbibliothek Hamburg ebenso wie der Deutschen Staatsbibliothek Berlin (-Ost).

10 Das Konvolut besteht aus einer in braunes Leder bezogenen Mappe im Folio-Format (35, 5 × 22, 5 cm). Beschreibung des Inhalts auch in dem handschriftlichen Realkatalog der früheren Stadtbibliothek (heute in der Staats- und Universitätsbibliothek): "Manuscripte die Hansestädte betreffend", vol. IV, 42. Der Seitenzahl des entsprechenden Katalogs entspricht die Signatur "Cod. hans. IV. 42".

11 Die beiden Stimmen (Cembalo I und II) sind jeweils auf ein Blatt im Folio-Format (30 × 39 cm) notiert. Das Papier (Wasserzeichen: holländisches Wappen mit Krone, Name "M.^{E} BONNEAU") wird Mattheson von seiner Hollandreise 1704 mitgebracht haben. Die Cembalo II-Stimme der Allemande aus der Suite enthält außerdem ein Wappen, in dessen unterer Hälfte sich zwei gekreuzte Hämmer befinden. Die Sonate mit nachfolgender Suite hat B. C. Cannon in der Edition Hinrichsen (London und New York, 1960) herausgegeben.

12 *Capellmeister*, 233.

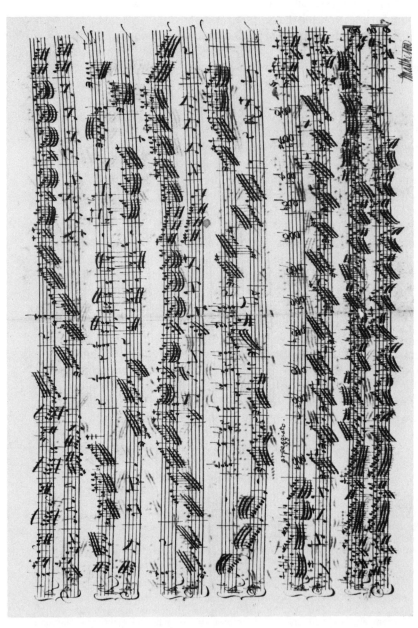

Abbildung 1. Letzte Seite der "Sonata à due Cembali", Cembalo I, Autograph Matthesons (früher Stadtbibliothek Hamburg, Cod. hans. IV 42, heute treuhänderisch in der Deutschen Staatsbibliothek Berlin [Ost])

einsätzigen, im Vergleich etwa zu Händels Suite für zwei Cembali[13] erstaunlich großangelegten (neunundachtzig Takte) und virtuosen Komposition steckt mehr als nur ein spieltechnisches Problem. Mattheson versucht nämlich, der Sonata eine "rechte Gestalt" zu geben, das heißt, sie einer bestimmten "inventio" zu unterwerfen. Diese formale Gestaltung erreicht er ansatzweise dadurch, daß er der Komposition in Anlehnung an die instrumentale Chaconne[14] ein Ostinato-Gerüst zugrundelegt, das er aber nicht streng beibehält. Im *Vollkommenen Capellmeister* beschreibt er dieses Verfahren als ein durchaus legitimes: In einer Chaconne könne man aus Gründen der Abwechslung von einem basso ostinato "bisweilen . . . abgeh[en]", diesen aber "bald wieder zum Vorschein" kommen "und seinen Posten behaupt[en]" lassen[15].

Mattheson stellt in der Sonata das Thema (g-Moll) expositionsartig auf (Takt 1–5 im I. Cembalo, siehe Beispiel 1), variiert es und schließt diesen Teil (Takt 10) in F-Dur, bevor er die gesamte "Exposition" im II. Cembalo, diesmal in d-Moll, wiederholt (Takt 11–14). Nach diesem Einleitungsteil, dessen thematische Wiederholung sich gattungsgeschichtlich zum Seitenthema der Sonatensatzform entwickelt, verändert er das melodische Material auf unterschiedliche Weise. Dabei verdeckt das figurative Spiel der beiden Cembali, das auf dem Prinzip des Manualwechsels beruht, das Baßgerüst teilweise bis zur Unkenntlichkeit (Beispiel 2). Andererseits variiert er nur die Oberstimmenmelodik der "Exposition", ohne deren harmonische Korrelation zu berücksichtigen (cf. Abbildung 1, 1.–4. Takt).

Die Suite erscheint gegenüber der Sonata in ihrer Satzfolge (Allemande, Courante, Sarabande, Gigue) und in ihrer kompositorischen Anlage weitaus konventioneller. Satztechnisch stehen sowohl die Sonata als auch die Suite in der französischen Tradition der Kompositionen für zwei Claviere, die Mattheson während oder kurz nach seiner Hollandreise durch die Drucke von Gaspard le Roux und Francois Couperin kennengelernt haben wird[16] (siehe Beispiel 3).

Etwa zur gleichen Zeit wie die Sätze für zwei Cembali entstanden die beiden italienischen Kantaten für Singstimme, Solo-Violine und

---

13 Suite c-Moll, herausgegeben von Th. Dart, Oxford University Press (London, 1951). Den Part von Cembalo II hat der Herausgeber ergänzt.
14 Cannon, *Mattheson*, 149, meinte in der Sonata eine Art Konzertform erkennen zu können.
15 *Capellmeister*, 233.
16 Cf. etwa von Le Roux die *Pièces de clavecin* (Paris, 1705) (-RISM A/I/5,L 2040) sowie die 1717 publizierte *Allemande à deux clavecins* von Fr. Couperin (-RISM A/I/2, C 4288).

Cembalo I

Cembalo II

Beispiel 1. Sonata à due cembali

Beispiel 2. Sonata à due cembali

218

Beispiel 2. (fortsetzung)

Basso continuo: einmal die "Cantata a voce sola con Violini soli Del
Sigr. Mattheson" überschriebene Komposition *Amorosa violetta*
(Satzfolge: Arie–Rezitativ–Arie), die Mattheson wahrscheinlich für
den Countertenor John Abell (1653 – nach 1716) geschrieben hat, mit
dem er im Oktober 1708 im Hamburger Drillhaus konzertierte. Abell

Beispiel 3. Suite à due cembali, Allemande

soll, wie Mattheson im *Vollkommenen Capellmeister* berichtet, eine "zärtliche und natürliche Alt-Stimme" besessen haben, die er "auf das reinste bis ins späte Alter" zu bewahren wußte[17].

17 *Capellmeister*, 95.

Beispiel 4. Kantate ohne Titel, Aria "Dove sei"

Die andere Kantate ist ohne Titel überliefert, beginnt mit den Worten "Il caro foco di tue pupille" und ist schon durch ihre Kürze (Arie–Arie) als Fragment bzw. als ein Teil einer größeren Komposition erkennbar[18].

Beiden Kantaten liegen weltliche Texte arkadisch-amourösen Inhalts zugrunde. Kompositorisch fordert Mattheson von solchen Kammerkantaten "mehr nettes und künstliches", als es in der theatralischen Arbeit möglich sei. Sie müßten "einen sauberen, ausnehmend merkwürdigen Generalbaß führen, lauter ausgesuchte nachdenkliche Erfindungen aufweisen und nicht zu lange währen"[19].

Dieser Beschreibung entsprechen Matthesons Kompositionen dadurch, daß er den Kantatentypus Alessandro Scarlattis (Arie–Rezitative–Arie) mit den von Kusser auch in der Theater- und Kammermusik eingesetzten kontrapunktischen Satztechniken verbindet. Auffallend ist nicht so sehr ihr devisenartig konzertierender Anfang, nicht die basso ostinato-Technik oder die instrumentale Kantabilität der Vokalstimme, – auffallend ist an den da capo-Arien vielmehr die "inventio", die Anlage des Mittelteils. Dieser Arienteil steht nicht, wie oft noch bei Händel, in einem affektiven und damit kompositorischen Gegensatz zum Anfangsteil. Mattheson bindet den Mittelteil vielmehr thematisch an den ersten Teil der Arie, indem er die beiden Oberstimmen (Violine und Singstimme) austauscht: Die Violin-Stimme des *A*-Teils wird (um eine Quarte nach oben transponiert) zur Vokalstimme des *B*-Teils und umgekehrt (Beispiel 4).

In der Kantate *Amorosa violetta* verfährt er sogar so, daß er im Mittelteil der ersten Arie die Solo-Violine der Vokalstimme kanonisch folgen läßt (Beispiel 5).

Mit dieser, von Kusser beeinflußten Kompositionsweise, in der sich kontrapunktische Techniken und sangliche Themenbildungen und -verarbeitungen verbinden, hat Mattheson "in Deutschland eine Norm aufgestellt, der seine Zeitgenossen Johann Sebastian Bach und Georg Philipp Telemann an der Spitze, und noch die nächsten Generationen folgten"[20].

Im ersten Jahrzehnt des achtzehnten Jahrhunderts ist auch die Ouverture mit nachfolgender Suite entstanden, die Mattheson für Blasinstrumente geschrieben und einem "General de Schoulen-

18 Die Handschriften der beiden Kantaten (bzw. des Kantatenfragments) umfassen jeweils vier Blätter im Quer-Folio-Format (21, 5 × 29 cm) mit dem Wasserzeichen: fleur-de-lis. Das Fragment ist unsigniert.
19 *Capellmeister*, 214.
20 Zitiert nach Wolff, *Barockoper in Hamburg*, vol. 1, 293.

B - Teil

Beispiel 5. Kantate *Amorosa violetta*, Aria "Tu sei vaga"

bourg" gewidmet hat[21]. Mattheson war 1706 in diplomatischer Tätigkeit in Hannover, wo er die "auserlesenste Bande Hoboisten" gehört hat, für die das Werk bestimmt war. Der Auftraggeber könnte also der von 1705 bis 1713 in Hannoverschen Diensten gestandene Adolf Friedrich von Schulenburg gewesen sein, der 1685 in Wolfenbüttel geboren worden war[22]. Es ist aber nicht auszuschließen, daß ein nicht näher bekannter G. E. Schoulenbourg die Komposition in Auftrag gegeben hat, von dem heute noch in der Hannoverschen Stadtbibliothek ein Notenbuch aufbewahrt wird ("Livre de Notte pour G. E. de Schoulenbourg")[23].

Wie aus der Besetzung hervorgeht, ist die Suite mit einleitender Ouverture als Freiluftmusik konzipiert: Die Partitur sieht zwei Cornetti (nach Walther: Quartzinken)[24], drei Oboen und einen "Basso" vor, der sicher von einem Fagott gespielt wurde, weil eine Generalbaß-Bezifferung fehlt. Der zweiteiligen Ouverture (Abbildung 2) folgen fünf stilisierte Tanzsätze (Marche, Angloise, Polonoise, Aria und Menuet), deren Melodik den begrenzten Spielmöglichkeiten der Cornetti entspricht. Die einzelnen Sätze, in denen sowohl die Zinken als auch eine Oboe solistisch auftreten, könnten durch ihre ausgeprägte Rhythmik als Musterbeispiele für die im *Vollkommenen Capellmeister* beschriebenen Tanzarten gelten.

In dem Konvolut des Matthesonschen Nachlasses befinden sich auch zwei autographe Stimmensätze, von denen einer mit *Carillons* überschrieben ist (Abbildung 3). Dem Papier nach zu urteilen werden sie um 1736 von Mattheson geschrieben worden sein. Beide Stimmensätze gehören, wie aus den Textincipits geschlossen werden kann, zu einzelnen Nummern der Brockes-Passion, die Mattheson 1718 für den Dom geschrieben hat. Die etwa achtzehn Jahre später geschriebenen Stimmen werden für eine Wiederholung der Passion vorgesehen gewesen sein.

Merkwürdigerweise enthält der eine Stimmen-Satz eine zweistimmige Fassung, der andere nur eine einstimmige, vereinfachte Version der betreffenden Passions-Sätze (bei den Sätzen handelt es sich um die Aria "Gott selbst, du Brunnenquell", den Choral "Ach Gott und Herr" und den Schlußchoral "Mein Sünd mich werden kränken

---

21 Die Partitur umfaßt vier Blätter im Hoch- Folio-Format (32, 5 × 21 cm) mit den Wasserzeichen: holländisches Wappen mit Krone und Gegenmarke: "M.ᴱ BONNEAU".

22 Siehe *Meyers Konversations-Lexicon* (³1878), vol. 14, 415.

23 Hinweis bei H. Sievers, *Hannoversche Musikgeschichte. Dokumente,Kritiken, Meinungen*, vol. 1 (Tutzing, 1979), 168.

24 *Musicalisches Lexicon oder Musicalische Bibliothec* (Leipzig, 1732); Facsimile-Druck (Kassel und Basel, 1953), 186.

Abbildung 2. "Ouverture avec sa Suite" für Blasinstrumente, Autograph Matthesons (früher Stadtbibliothek Hamburg, Cod.hans.IV.42, heute treuhänderisch in der Deutschen Staatsbibliothek Berlin [-Ost])

Abbildung 3. Carillons-Stimmensatz zur Aria "Gott selbst" aus der Brockes-Passion, Autograph Matthesons (früher Stadtbibliothek Hamburg, Cod.hans.IV.42, heute treuhänderisch in der Deutschen Staatsbibliothek Berlin [-Ost])

227

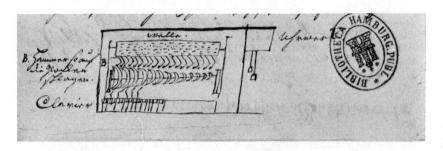

Abbildung 4. Zeichnung des "Glockenwerks" von J. Krieger; oben ist das
Uhrwerk, unten die Claviatur abgebildet, durch die die Glocken angeschlagen werden konnten (früher Stadtbibliothek Hamburg, Cod.
hans.IV.40, heute treuhänderisch in der Deutschen Staatsbibliothek
Berlin [-Ost])

sehr"). Frederichs hat in seiner Arbeit über die Vertonungen der
Brockespassion von Keiser, Händel, Telemann und Mattheson
wahrscheinlich gemacht, daß es sich bei den in der Berliner Partitur[25]
angegebenen *Carillons* nicht um ein Orgelregister, sondern um ein
Glockenklavier gehandelt haben muß[26]. Zufälligerweise befindet
sich in einem anderen Konvolut des Matthesonschen Nachlasses
(Cod.hans.IV.40) eine kleine Handschrift, auf der ein solches "Glockenklavier", hier als "Glockenwerk" bezeichnet, beschrieben und
abgebildet ist.

Bei dem "Glockenwerk" handelt es sich um ein Instrument von
siebenunddreißig Glocken, die sowohl von einem Uhrwerk mit Walze
als auch von einem "ordentlichem Clavier" angeschlagen werden
konnten (Abbildung 4). Als Erfinder dieses Instruments wird in der
Beschreibung der Zittauer Musikdirektor Johann Krieger genannt,
von dem in den dreißiger Jahren ein Sohn in Hamburg lebte. Er wird
der Vermittler dieses offensichtlich neuen Instruments zwischen
seinem Vater und Mattheson gewesen sein. Der Umfang des Glockenwerks betrug drei Oktaven (A bis a''); er stimmt genau mit dem

---

25 Eine zeitgenössische Partitur der Brockes-Passion in der Staatsbibliothek Preus-
sischer Kulturbesitz, Sign.Mus.ms.13 900. Die autographe Partitur Matthesons
befand sich nicht, wie Frederichs in *Text und Musik in den Brockespassionen*
vermutet, in den "Miscellanea Matthesoniana" der früheren Hamburger Stadtbibliothek, sondern, wie das Nachlaßverzeichnis zeigt, als gebundene Partitur mit
der Signatur ND.IV.130 im Nachlaß. Das Autograph befand sich nach dem II.
Weltkrieg noch in Schloß Lauenstein bei Dresden (siehe Marx, "Johann Matthesons
Nachlaß").
26 Siehe Frederichs, *Text und Musik in den Brockespassionen*, 194.

Tonumfang der einstimmigen "Carillon-Sätze" überein. Der Ambitus der zweistimmigen Fassung geht aber in der Tiefe über A hinaus, weshalb anzunehmen ist, daß diese Fassung für ein anderes Instrument gedacht war.

Als Beispiel für die spieltechnisch nicht leichten Carillon-Sätze sei der Anfang der zweiten Strophe der Arie "Gott selbst, du Brunnenquell" angeführt (Beispiel 6):

Beispiel 6. Aria "Gott selbst"

Die späteste Komposition Matthesons, die sich im Nachlaß erhalten hat, ist das Oratorium *Das fröhliche Sterbelied*. Mattheson hat es für sein Begräbnis geschrieben. Es wurde am 25. April 1764 während der Trauer-Feier in der St. Michaeliskirche aufgeführt[27]. Die vollständige Partitur des "Epicediums", wie Mattheson das Oratorium, oder genauer gesagt: die poetische Vorlage des Oratoriums literarischem Brauch folgend nennt, ist verschollen. Da sie auch nicht im Nachlaßverzeichnis aufgeführt wird, ist anzunehmen, daß die Komposition bei seinem Tod unvollständig war und erst vom Dirigenten der Aufführung vervollständigt worden ist. Erhalten ist lediglich eine Reihe von Entwürfen und einzelnen, vollständig instrumentierten Sätzen. Einige der Sätze sind mit "1756" datiert. Wie aus der unten mitgeteilten Tabelle zu ersehen ist, sind gerade diese Teile des Oratoriums nicht in die endgültige Fassung die im gedruckten Textbuch vorliegt, übernommen worden.

27 Ob Telemann die Aufführung des *Fröhlichen Sterbeliedes* leitete, wie Cannon, p. 107, vermutet, ist fraglich. Nach Menke (*Das Vokalwerk Georg Philipp Telemanns. Überlieferung und Zeitfolge* [Kassel, 1942], 92) hat Telemann die letzte größere Aufführung am 19. Oktober 1762 geleitet, als er bei der Einweihung der neugebauten St. Michaelis-Kirche sein Oratorium *Komm wieder, Herr* dirigierte. Wahrscheinlich hat der Organist der Michaelis-Kirche, Anton Altzen, Matthesons Partitur vervollständigt, einstudiert und aufgeführt.

Mattheson hat also nicht erst, wie er in seiner Autobiographie schreibt, 1760 mit der Komposition seiner Begräbnismusik begonnen[28], sondern schon vier Jahre früher, zu einer Zeit, als er schwer erkrankt war und den Tod vor Augen hatte. Offensichtlich hat sich der über siebzigjährige, durch seine Taubheit vereinsamte, aber "niehmals müssige" Mattheson in seinen späten Jahren ausschließlich mit dem Bibellesen und mit der Abfassung seines "Epicediums" beschäftigt.

In Konvolut Cod.hans.IV.42 des Nachlasses befinden sich außer der Musik auch Textentwürfe zum *Fröhlichen Sterbelied*, die größtenteils Strophen aus dem *Neu-vermehrten hamburgischen Gesang-Buch* von 1754 und freie Dichtungen enthalten. Der Titel des "Epicediums" lautet nach dem Autograph: "Matthesonii Melos exequiale oder Grablied, Text und Ton von ihm selbst" (siehe Abbildung 5a). Die Textentwürfe, die wahrscheinlich auch um 1756 geschrieben worden sind, würden aber keine mit den erhaltenen Kompositionsfragmenten und vollständigen Einzelsätzen übereinstimmende Ordnung ergeben, wenn nicht das gedruckte Textbuch zu Hilfe genommen werden könnte, das erst jüngst wieder zu Tage getreten ist[29]. Diesem Textbuch zufolge hatte das "Epicedium" eine oratorienartige Anlage, bei der die Einbeziehung des Gemeindechorals auffällt (siehe unten Tabelle 1).

Der von Mattheson zusammengestellte und teilweise auch von ihm selbst gedichtete Text bezieht sich auf ein Wort Luthers, das mottoartig auf dem Titelblatt des Librettos angegeben ist ("Wenns zum Sterben komt, so stirbt Johannes, Petrus, Paulus dahin; aber ein Christ stirbt nicht"). Diesem Glaubensbekenntnis entsprechen auch die "Interlocutori" des Oratoriums, die Stimmen ("voces") von Christus (im Textbuch bezeichnet als "S.S." = Sancti Sanctorum), Hiob, Paulus und Bernhardus. Die Gemeinde setzt er mit den "voces Sanctorum Omnium" gleich. Ihnen sind in der Regel die Choralstrophen des Oratoriums zugedacht. Mattheson selbst identifiziert sich mit der Gestalt des Timotheus ("vox ipsius Theotimi"), von dem im 1. Paulus-Brief gesagt wird, daß er ein "rechtschaffener Sohn im Glauben" gewesen sei.

Die fragmentarische Gestalt der Komposition, wie sie aus der

---

28 Siehe die vom Verfasser neu herausgegebene und kommentierte Autobiographie Matthesons, *Lebensbeschreibung des Hamburger Musikers, Schriftstellers und Diplomaten Johann Mattheson (1681–1764)* (Hamburg, 1982).

29 Auf das im StA Hbg, Sign. A 710/85, liegende Textbuch hat mich freundlicherweise Herr cand. phil. Walter Stephani aufmerksam gemacht.

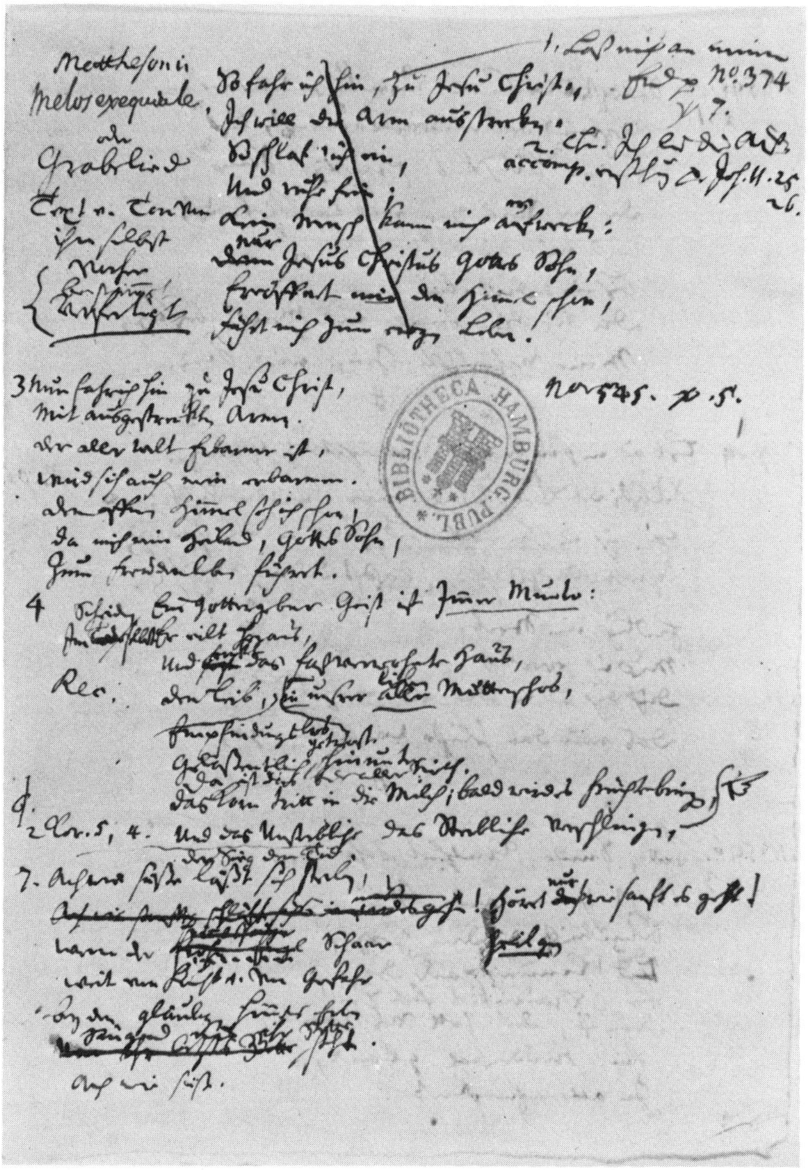

a

Abbildung 5. (a) Erste Seite des Textentwurfes, (b) erste Seite der Partitur von Matthesons eigener Begräbnismusik, "Das fröhliche Sterbelied" (früher Stadtbibliothek Hamburg, Cod.hans.IV.42, heute treuhänderisch in der Deutschen Staatsbibliothek Berlin [-Ost])

231

b

Tabelle 1. *Inhaltsangabe des Trauer-Oratoriums "Das fröhliche Sterbelied", das Mattheson für sein eigenes Begräbnis geschrieben hat*

Libretto (1764)		Erhaltene Musik (1756)
1. S.O.	"Wer weiß, wie nahe mir mein Ende?" [HGB Nr. 581]	[Gemeinde-Choral]
2. S.S.	"Ich bin die Auferstehung und das Leben" [Joh. 11, 25–6]	Recitativo accompagnato (T, Streicher)
3. S.B.	"Cum me mori sit necesse"	Strophenarie (S, Vl, Bc), überschrieben "Pro morte beata", datiert 10.III.1756
4. Th.	"Es bleibt ein Gott ergebner Geist im Scheiden" [2. Kor. 5, 4]	Recitativo secco (A), größtenteils untextiert
5. Th.	"Schau an, Bild Gottes" [Joh. 14, 2]	Arie (S, Vl, Bc), notiert sind 8 Takte Vorspiel und die Vokalstimme
6. S.O.	"So fährt er hin zu Jesu Christ" [HGB Nr. 555, V.5]	[Gemeinde-Choral]
7. S.P.	"Ich werde in keinerley Stück zu Schanden werden" [Philip. 1, 20–1]	nicht erhalten
8. Th.	"O, wie süsse läßt sichs sterben"	nicht erhalten
9. S.S.	"Freude wird seyn unter den Engeln Gottes" [Luk. 15]	Recitativo secco (B)
10. S.O.	"Der Engel Chor wird singen" [HGB Nr. 598, V. 17]	[Gemeinde-Choral]
11. Th.	"Zur Freude die Fülle"	Arioso (T, Bc)
12. S.P.	"Wir wissen, so unser irdisch Haus" [2. Kor. 5, 1]	Recitativo secco (A)
13. S.O.	"Seligstes Wesen, unendliche Wonne" [HGB Nr. 595, V. 1]	Arioso (?) (S), notiert nur Vokalstimme
14. Th.	"Auf, auf! Zum Kleinod"	Recitativo secco (B)
15. S.O.	cum Chorago "Kommt, ihr gott-ergebenen Seelen"	nicht erhalten
16. S.S.	"Das ist der Wille des Vaters" [Joh. 6, 40]	Recitativo accompagnato (B, Streicher)
17. S.P.	"Es wird gesäet verweslich" [1. Kor. 15, 43–4]	Recitativo accompagnato (A, Streicher), unvollständig
18. S.S.	"Ich lebe, und ihr sollt auch leben" [Joh. 14, 19]	nicht erhalten
19. S.I.	"Ich weiß, daß mein Erlöser lebt" [Hiob 19, 25]	Arie (B, 2 Vl, Bc), vollständig skizziert:vivace–adagio–vivace
20.	"Auf diesen Glauben bin ich sanft gestorben" [Hiob 30, 31]	Recitativo secco (B), untextiert

233

Tabelle 1 *(fortsetzung)*

Libretto (1764)	Erhaltene Musik (1756)
21. S.P. "Gekrönt, nicht mehr gebunden"	Cavata (A, 2 Fl, 2 Vl, Bc), siehe die Edition im Anhang dieses Beitrages
22. S.S. "Ich mach es alles neu" [Offenb. 1]	Recitativo secco (B), untextiert
23. S.O. "Weil du vom Tod erstanden bist" [HGB Nr. 555, V. 4]	[Gemeinde-Choral]

Außerdem sind folgende Sätze in Partitur oder Skizzen erhalten, die Mattheson 1756 konzipiert hat, die aber nicht in die endgültige Fassung des Oratoriums eingegangen sind:

a. "Laß mich an meinem Ende" [HGB Nr. 374, V. 7]	Chorsatz (SATB) mit Orchester (Ob, 2 Vl, Vla, Vlc, Vlone, Bc) in Partitur
b. "Ach, ach betrübte Zeiten"	Arioso (S, Bc). Instrumentales Nachspiel in Anlehnung an (a).
c. "Gelobet sey der Herr, mein Hort" [Ps. 144, 1–2]	Arietta (S), nur Vokalstimme notiert. Zusammen mit (d) und (e) datiert "1. Octr. 1756"
d. "Herr, was ist der Mensch" [Ps. 144, 3–5]	Recitativo secco (S), nur Vokalstimme notiert
e. "Sende deine Hand von der Höhe" [Ps. 144, 6–11]	da capo-Arie (S), nur Vokalstimme notiert
f. "Gott sey uns gnädig" [Ps. 67, 1]	Chorsatz (SATB) mit Orchester (Streicher, Bc). Überschrift: "De vultu illuminato", datiert "Mars 7, 1756".

Tabelle ersichtlich ist[30], läßt sich mit Matthesons ästhetischer Vorstellung vom zeitgemäßen Gout einer Komposition erklären. In seiner Autobiographie schreibt er im Abschnitt über das Jahr 1760, er habe die musikalische Ausarbeitung "mit Fleiß noch eine kleine vergönnte Weile" verschoben, "aus Beysorge, sie mögte, vor der Aufführung, einigermaßen aus der Mode kommen"[31]. Aus diesem Grunde hat er einige der 1756 konzipierten oder vollendeten Sätze nicht mit in die endgültige Fassung des Oratoriums aufgenommen (in der Tabelle die am Schluß angegebenen Nummern [a] bis [f]).

Der Vorstellung, in seiner Begräbnismusik den musikalischen Geschmack der sechziger Jahre zu entsprechen, war für den fast

---

30 Die in der Tabelle in eckige Klammern gesetzten Angaben [] sind Zusätze des Verfassers; HGB - *Hamburgisches Gesang-Buch* von 1754.

31 Marx, *Lebensbeschreibung Matthesons*.

achtzigjährigen Komponisten so kühn wie undurchführbar. Charakteristisch für die Fragmente ist aber, daß in ihnen, den vorgesehenen Arien, Ariosi und Rezitativen größtenteils nur die Melodiestimme notiert ist. Ihm ging es nicht mehr wie in den frühen, von Kusser beeinflußten Kompositionen, um einen gleichsam "gearbeiteten Stil", sondern um einen dem Text adäquaten Melodiestil, der sich durch "Leichtigkeit", "Deutlichkeit", "fließendes Wesen" und "Lieblichkeit" auszeichnete[32]. Diesem Melodiestil ordnet er das harmonische Geschehen ebenso wie die instrumentale Gestaltung der einzelnen Sätze unter. Deutlich ist die primäre Bedeutung des Melodischen in den Choralsätzen zu erkennen. In dem nicht in die Endfassung aufgenommenen Chorsatz "Laß mich an meinem End" (siehe [a]) verzichtet Mattheson auf ein Vorspiel und instrumentiert stattdessen lediglich den Dreiklang der Grundtonart (c-Moll), den er klanglich von unten nach oben aufbaut (Beispiel 7). Die Choralweise

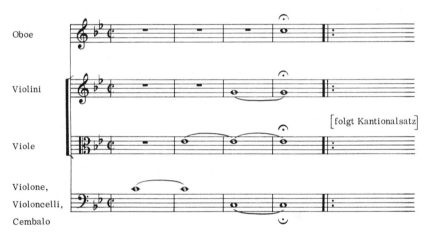

Beispiel 7. Vorspiel zum Choral "Laß mich an meinem End"

liegt im Sopran und wird Note gegen Note als Kantionalsatz vorgetragen. Die Instrumente (Oboe, Violine, Viola, Violoncello und Violone) gehen colla parte mit den Singstimmen mit, die Streicher spielen pizzicato.

Ein Musterbeispiel Matthesonscher Kompositionsweise aus der Spätzeit ist die Cavata "Gekrönt, nicht mehr gebunden" (Nr. 21), die vollständig im Anhang mitgeteilt ist. Mattheson beschreibt die Cavata im *Vollkommenen Capellmeister* als einen "Gesang mit Instru-

32 *Capellmeister*, 140.

menten, der . . . mehr auf eine scharfsinnige Betrachtung, als [auf] einen starcken Affect" angelegt ist[33]. Auch müsse er "ausgearbeitet" sein, was sich wohl besonders auf das Melodische bezieht. An den einzelnen Fassungen dieser Cavata (melodische Skizze [a], Entwurf des Satzes [b], Endfassung [c]) läßt sich ablesen, wie sehr es Mattheson um die melodische Gestalt der beiden Cavata-Strophen gegangen ist (Beispiel 8).

Die "Ausarbeitung" des Satzes bezieht sich primär auf die Vokalstimme. Mattheson gestaltet die beiden siebenzeiligen Strophen nach einem harmonischen Grundriß (erste Strophe: vier Zeilen - sechzehn Takte in g-Moll; drei Zeilen - zwölf Takte in B-Dur; zweite Strophe: drei Zeilen - sechzehn Takte in d-Moll; vier Zeilen - einundzwanzig Takte in g-Moll). Durch die Wiederholung der einzelnen Abschnitte und die doppelte Wiederholung der Schlußzeile, die er im Vollkommenen Capellmeister als "scharffsinnigsten Ausspruch" apostrophiert[34], rückt die inhaltliche Aussage der Cavata in den Mittelpunkt der Aufmerksamkeit des Hörers: sie will als Glaubensverkündigung verstanden werden. Insgesamt hat Mattheson mit dieser Komposition einen fast schon empfindsamen Melodiestil gefunden, der den Zeitgenossen der sechziger Jahre durchaus nicht fremd gewesen sein wird.

Das Konvolut Cod.hans.IV.42 enthält auch drei Kompositionen die Mattheson zwar geschrieben, aber nicht selber komponiert hat. Eine dieser Kompositionen ist mit "Sinfonia" überschrieben und trägt das Datum "25. Nov. 1704" sowie ein Monogramm, das man als "JM" lesen könnte (Abbildung 6). Mattheson hat aber seine Kompositionen grundsätzlich mit vollem Namen gezeichnet, was eine Autorschaft fraglich macht. Gegen eine Verfasserschaft Matthesons spricht auch die Tatsache, daß die ersten sechs Takte der "Sinfonia" im Vollkommenen Capellmeister als Beispiel einer "Opern-Intrada" abgedruckt sind und die Komposition ausdrücklich Reinhard Keiser zugeschrieben wird[35]. Auffallend an dem Manuskript ist außerdem, daß Mattheson nur einen Teil der Partitur geschrieben hat. Die durch Korrekturen und durch einen ganz andern Schreibduktus gekennzeichneten Unterstimmen sind wahrscheinlich von einem Schüler Matthesons geschrieben, der sich im Aussetzen von Mittel- und Unterstimmen üben sollte[36]. Sollte die von Mattheson selbst

---

33 Ibid., 213.   34 Ibid.   35 Ibid., 85. Hier auf drei Systemen notiert.
36 Matthesons Schrift ist in dunkler Tinte ausgeführt und betrifft die Violino I-Stimme, den Anfang des zweiten Teils der "Sinfonia", die Besetzungsangaben und verschiedene Korrekturen. Der Schreiber der übrigen Partien unterscheidet sich von Matthesons Schrift durch hellere Tinte und durch andere Schlüssel- und Notenformen.

Beispiel 8a. Cavata "Gekrönt, nicht mehr gebunden", melodische Skizze

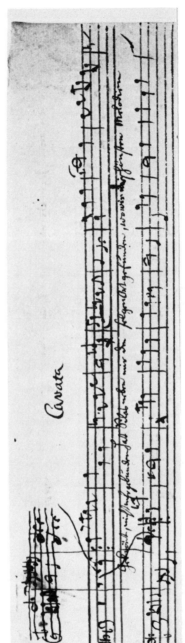

Beispiel 8b. Cavata "Gekrönt, nicht mehr gebunden", Entwurf des Satzes mit Vorspiel

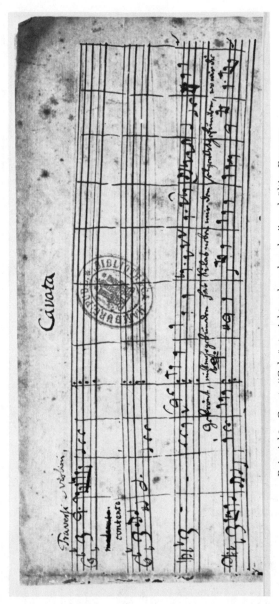

Beispiel 8c. Cavata "Gekrönt, nicht mehr gebunden", endgültige Fassung, Reinschrift

Abbildung 6. Erste Seite einer "Sinfonia" nach einem Thema von Reinhard Keiser. Erstes System und die Oberstimme Autograph Matthesons (früher Stadtbibliothek Hamburg, Cod. hans.IV.42, heute treuhänderisch in der Deutschen Staatsbibliothek Berlin [-Ost])

239

geschriebene Violino I-Stimme einem Werk Keisers angehören, könnte man an die beiden 1704 in der Gänsemarkt-Oper aufgeführten Opern *Nebucadnezar* oder *Almira* denken.

Dem Papier nach zu urteilen gehört auch eine vierstimmige Fuge in die Jahre um 1704–5, die (wie die "Sinfonia") ohne Verfassernamen überliefert ist[37]. Daß sie von Mattheson geschrieben worden ist, steht außer Zweifel. Seine Autorschaft scheint aber schon auf den ersten Blick deshalb unwahrscheinlich zu sein, weil die außerordentlich umfangreiche Fuge (dreiundsechzig Takte) ihrem Aufbau nach kaum mit den Fugen aus Matthesons *Wol-klingender Finger-Sprache* übereinstimmt. Vergleiche mit Fugen von Matthesons Zeitgenossen haben ergeben, daß die in c-dorisch notierte "Fuga sciolta" mit einer c-Moll-Fuge identisch ist, die der Londoner Verleger Walsh 1735 mit fünf anderen Fugen als "troisième ouvrage" Händels veröffentlicht hat[38]. Das Interessante an der Kopie Matthesons ist, daß sie ziemlich genau zu datieren ist (um 1704) und damit als ein Werk aus Händels Hamburger Zeit nachgewiesen werden kann.

Eine weitere Kopie in der Handschrift Matthesons liegt mit der in Partitur geschriebenen "Aria aus der Einweyhungs Musik zu St. Michaelis" vor (siehe Abbildung 7). Bisher hat man angenommen, Mattheson habe die Musik zu seiner eigenen *Recreation des Gemüts* komponiert, weil für die Einweihungszeremonie der neuaufgebauten St. Michaelis-Kirche im Jahr 1762 keine Komposition Matthesons aufgeführt worden ist[39]. Tatsächlich erklang aber ein Oratorium Telemanns, *Komm wieder, Herr*, von dem es in einer Rezension in der *Staats- und Gelehrte Zeitung* vom 20. Oktober des Jahres heißt, "der berühmte alte Herr Telemann" habe das Oratorium selbst geleitet[40]. Da Mattheson seiner Taubheit wegen das Oratorium nicht gehört hat (sein Bericht in der Autobiographie geht fast wörtlich auf die oben genannte Rezension zurück), ihn aber die Musik seines gleichaltrigen Freundes Telemann offenkundig interessierte, hat er sich die Arie "So waren Gnad und Zorn vereint" abgeschrieben.

Matthesons Kopie hat vor dem eher skizzierten Autograph Telemanns[41] den Vorzug der vollständigen Instrumentierung, ohne

---

37 Ein Blatt. Das Papier ist mit dem identisch, auf das die "Ouverture avec sa Suite" und die Sätze für zwei Cembali notiert sind. Wasserzeichen: holländisches Wappen mit Krone und der Gegenmarke "M.E BONNEAU".
38 L. Hoffmann-Erbrecht datiert die Fuge in seiner Arbeit: *Deutsche und italienische Klaviermusik zur Bachzeit. Studien zur Thematik und Themenverarbeitung in der Zeit von 1720–1760* (Leipzig, 1954), 28, mit "um oder vor 1720".
39 Siehe Cannon, *Mattheson*, 215.
40 Zitiert nach Menke, *Das Vokalwerk Telemanns*, Anhang 49.
41 Berlin, Staatsbibliothek Preußischer Kulturbesitz, Mus. ms. autogr. Telemann 8.

Abbildung 7. Erste Seite der Aria "So waren Gnad und Zorn vereint" aus dem Oratorium "Komm wieder Herr" (1762) von G. Ph. Telemann, autographe Abschrift Matthesons (früher Stadtbibliothek Hamburg, Cod.hans.IV.42, heute treuhänderisch in der Deutschen Staatsbibliothek Berlin [-Ost]

daß er auch nur eine Note hinzugefügt hätte. Außerdem enthält seine Kopie interessante Randbemerkungen, die sich auf die Deklamation des Textes beziehen. Matthesons kritische Bemerkungen[42] wollen nach allem, was wir über den Zweck seiner Kritik wissen, nicht Telemanns Kompositionsweise kritisieren, sondern darauf aufmerksam machen, daß erst die richtige Textdeklamation den Hörer "bewegen und belehren" kann[43].

Die wenigen Kompositionen Johann Matthesons, die hier erstmals besprochen wurden, widerlegen ohne Zweifel die negativen Urteile, die im neunzehnten Jahrhundert über die Musik des Hamburgers gefällt wurden. Sie bestätigen, wie mir scheint, in vielem die Beobachtungen Frederichs, daß es gerade Mattheson war, der in seiner musikalischen Erfindung weit in Neuland vorstieß.

Faßt man die stilistischen Beobachtungen, die wir an den unbekannten Kompositionen des Nachlasses gewonnen haben, zusammen, so läßt sich folgendes festhalten: Mit seinen frühen Kompositionen für zwei Cembali führt er nicht nur die französische Gattung der "Pièce à deux clavecins" in Deutschland ein, sondern unternimmt auch den Versuch, der "Sonata" eine rechte Gestalt zu geben: Als Chaconne angelegt, stellt er eine Art "Exposition" auf, deren Melodiestimme oder Baß er zehnmal verändert oder wiederholt, bevor er die "Sonata" mit einer Art "Reprise" abschließt. Dadurch erreicht Mattheson eine (wenn auch nicht vollständig gelungene) thematisch bezogene Struktur, die in der sogenannten Vorklassik vollausgeprägt als Sonatensatzform normativen Charakter erhält.

Auch in den frühen Kantaten ist ein kompositorisches Denken erkennbar, das auf Erneuerung überlieferter Formen zielt. Durch die thematische Verknüpfung einzelner Sätze gelangt er zu größeren, der Opernszene entlehnten Komplexen auch in der Kammermusik. In den da capo-Arien bricht er schließlich den Affektgegensatz zwischen Vorder- und Mittelteil, der besonders im Melodischen deutlich hervortritt, zugunsten einer "einthematischen" Form auf.

In der Einbeziehung von *Carillons*, also Glockenklavieren, in die

42 Auf Seite [2] seiner Partitur schreibt er beispielsweise am unteren Rand über eine Koloratur der Arie auf das Wort "Dank": "Der modulus auf dem Wort Dank, wenn es nicht schon vorher vernommen wäre, würde solches unverständlich machen: denn das k könnte dabey gar nicht zur Aussprache kommen, absonderlich da die dreyfache Unterbrechung des Läuffers mehr Seuffzendes, als Dankendes anzeiget".
43 Siehe hierzu die Einleitung ("Johann Mattheson – Künstler und Schriftsteller in galanter Zeit") in Marx, *Lebensbeschreibung Matthesons*.

Brockespassion von 1718 weitet Mattheson die Instrumentierung, die bei ihm immer textausdeutende Funktion hat, auf bisher ungewöhnliche Instrumente aus. Damit steht er zwar in einer gewissen Tradition der Hamburger Gänsemarkt-Oper[44], seine Charakterisierung bestimmter dramaturgischer Situationen durch bewußt gewählte Klangfarben dürfte aber bei keinem anderen Hamburger Komponisten der Zeit in dieser Prägnanz zu finden sein. Beispiele aus seinen Opern bestätigen diese Beobachtung nachdrücklich (es sei nur an die scordierenden Violinen und die Corni da caccia in seiner letzten Oper, *Henrico IV.* von 1711, erinnert!)[45].

Daß Mattheson in seiner spätesten Komposition, dem *Fröhlichen Sterbelied*, auf die traditionelle Gattung des Oratoriums zurückgriff, hängt wahrscheinlich mit seiner Vorstellung vom Sinn und vom Zweck einer geistlichen Komposition zusammen. Das Oratorium, das er schließlich in den zehn Jahren seiner Tätigkeit als Domkapellmeister in Hamburg und damit in Norddeutschland heimisch gemacht hat, erschien ihm als die geeignetste Form geistlicher Erbauung.

Im ganzen gesehen erscheint uns der Komponist Mattheson – den zugänglichen Quellen nach zu urteilen – durchaus als ein Neuerer. Satztechnisch zweifellos auf der Höhe der Zeit stehend hat er versucht, die überlieferten musikalischen Formen durch neue Ausdrucksmittel weiterzuentwickeln. Dabei lag sein Augenmerk vor allem auf den textausdeutenden Gattungen der Vokalmusik. Entgegen der weitverbreiteten Meinung, seine Kompositionen seien in ihrer Zeitgebundenheit kaum mehr als uninspirierte Gebrauchsmusik, beginnt sich heute die Vorstellung durchzusetzen, daß Mattheson als "musicus poeticus" seinen Zeitgenossen Kusser, Keiser und Telemann durchaus ebenbürtig war.

Anhang

Johann Mattheson, Cavata "Gekrönt, nicht mehr gebunden" für Alt (Vox Sancti Pauli), Traversi, Violini und Basso aus dem Trauer-Oratorium *Das fröhliche Sterbelied* (1760?), "womit ihm selbst, harmonisch und poetisch, im 83sten Jahre seines Alters zu Grabe gesungen" (Textbuch).
Partitur: früher Stadtbibliothek Hamburg, Cod. hans.IV.42, heute treuhänderisch in der Deutschen Staatsbibliothek Berlin (-Ost).
Libretto: Staatsarchiv Hamburg, Sign. A 710/85.

44 A. D. McCredie, *Instrumentarium and Instrumentation in the North German Baroque Opera*, phil. Diss. (Hamburg, 1964), besonders 100ss.
45 Wolff, *Barockoper in Hamburg*, vol. 1, 295–6.

1. Strophe

Gekrönt, nicht mehr gebunden,
Hat Silas neben mir den selgen Ort gefunden,
Wo wir die schönsten Melodien singen,
Und wo die reinsten Harmonien klingen[1];
Wo man der Mitternacht vergißt[2],
Bey heller Morgenröthe[3],
Wo Licht von Licht aus Gott geboren ist[4].

2. Strophe

Da können wir erst deutlich wissen,
Welch einen Himmelston Posaune, Harfe, Flöte[5],
Zu Gottes Ehren geben müssen.
Wir hören schon vom treusten Menschenfreunde
Ein göttlichs Blasen[6], Saitenzwingen,
Ein Danken, Rühmen, Preisen und Lobsingen[7],
Recht mitten in der seligsten Gemeinde.

Anmerkungen Matthesons (Ziffern 1–7 vom Herausgeber):
1 Offenb. 14, 2–3; 15, 3–4; 19, 1–7 etc.
2 Ap. Gesch. 16, 25
3 Es. 8, 20
4 Ps. 36, 10; Es. 10, 17; Mal. 4, 2–5; Joh. 14, 10; 1 Tim. 6, 16; Hebr. 1, 3
5 1 Kor. 14, 7–8
6 Zach. 9, 10; 1 Thess. 4, 16
7 Ps. 22, 23–26; 35, 18; 40, 10; Hebr. 2, 12; 2 Sam. 22, 50; Röm. 15, 11.

Me - lo - di - en sin - gen, und wo die rein - sten

Har - mo - ni - en klin - gen;

ge - krönt, nicht mehr ge - bun - den hat

Si – las ne-ben mir den sel – gen Ort ge-fun – den,

wo wir die schön – sten Me-lo-di – en sin-gen,

und wo die rein – sten Har-mo-ni – en klin-gen wo

247

man die Mit – ter-nacht ver – gisst, bey hel – ler Mor – gen –

– rö – the, wo Licht von Licht aus Gott ge – bo – ren

ist. Wo man der

Mit - ter-nacht ver - gisst, bey hel - ler Mor - gen - rö -the, wo

Licht von Licht aus Gott ge - bo - ren ist,

[2.Strophe]

Da kön - nen wir erst deut - lich wis - sen, welch ei - nen

249

Him — mels — ton Po — sau — ne,

col arco
[*f*]

Har — fe, Flö — te zu Got — tes Eh — ren

[*p*]

ge — ben müs — sen.

Da kön - nen wir erst deut - lich wis - sen

[*p*]

85

welch ei - nen Him - mels - ton Po - sau - ne,

6

90

Har - fe, Flö - te zu

Got — tes Eh — ren ge — ben müs — sen.

Wir hö — ren schon vom treu — sten Men — schen-

- freun — de ein Meis — ter-li-ches Bla — sen, gött — lichs

Klin – gen, ein Dan — — ken, Rüh — men,

Prei - - sen und Lob - sin - gen, recht mit-ten

in der se - lig - sten Ge - mein - de. Wir hö - ren

schon vom treu - sten Men - schen - freun - de ein

meis - ter-li-ches Bla - sen, gött - lichs Klin - gen,

ein Dan - - ken, Rüh - men,

Prei - - sen und Lob - sin - gen,

recht mit – ten   in   der   se – lig – sten   Ge – mein – de,

recht mit – ten   in   der   se – lig – sten   Ge – mein – de.

Mattheson on performance practice

FREDERICK NEUMANN
Richmond, Virginia

Apart from being a prolific composer, a singer, keyboard player, conductor, and diplomat, Mattheson was an indefatigable writer whose literary output exceeded 130 items. Even if we allow for some overlapping and repetition, the sheer quantity of that production is awe-inspiring. Reflecting his wide-ranging interests, his erudition and knowledge, his topics ranged well beyond music, though that remained his principal concern.

His theoretical works on music were greatly admired in his time and his forward-looking ideas on composition, style, and aesthetics strongly affected German musical thought and development in the eighteenth century and beyond. Today they are, for his epoch, a treasure trove of information on music theory, on the sociology of music, and on the life and works of the composers, while his incisive criticisms of his contemporaries are invariably revealing and arresting even if today we should not subscribe to all of his views.

Unfortunately, his otherwise encyclopedic coverage of the musical scene has, in the light of today's concerns, one weak spot: His writings deal, if at all, only peripherally with questions of performance practice. True, he wrote two books on the thorough-bass (the second an elaboration on the first), but this topic is confined to one specialized skill, however important. The lamented meager pickings concern the wide spectrum of elements that enter into the interpretation of any piece that we attempt to perform according to the composer's conception. Some of these elements are tempo, dynamics, rhythm, phrasing, articulation, and ornamentation. Having examined a considerable number of tracts by Mattheson, I found only two chapters that focus on such problems. Both are in *Der vollkommene Capellmeister*, his most important theoretical work. The chapters, to be discussed later, concern ornamentation and conducting. Apart from these two chapters we have to resort to garnering chance remarks that bear on

257

performance and to scanning the remarks addressed to the composer for their possible implications for interpreters. I shall start by registering some of these scattered observations, a number of which contain striking statements, and reserve for the end a report on the two chapters mentioned.

One of Mattheson's most original, forceful, and important pronouncements expresses his low opinion of rules – a theme to which he returns on various occasions. He ridicules the pedants who look to rules as supreme authority: "Concerning such would-be luminaries who believe that music has to follow their rules, when in truth their rules have to follow the music, one can rightly say 'Faciunt intelligendo ut nihil intelligant' " (roughly: They manage in their thinking to understand nothing). Elsewhere he says: "Rules are valid as long as I consider it well and sensible to abide by them. They are valid no longer than that," and later: "The rule of nature, in music, is nothing but the ear" (*Critica musica* I, 338 n. Z). It seems self-evident that such sentiment about the supremacy of the ear has validity for the performer as well as for the composer. Mattheson sees another reason for the relativity of rules in changing taste. Rules are based on aural perceptions ("observations aurium") of what produces euphony and what discordancy, and he notes that the ideas of what sounds well, and what not, differ with time and taste. In this connection he cites Werckmeister, who allows ornaments an average time span of only twenty to thirty years before their appeal fades and they become outdated (*Orchestre* II, 98).

Another of his general principles, insistently repeated, is the primacy of the voice over instruments: "The former is so to speak the mother, the latter the daughter." Instrumental music, he says, should emulate the voice in aiming at songfulness and smoothness ("alles fein singbar und fließend zu machen"; *Capellmeister*, 204, §4). Yet, aware of the vast difference between the two media, Mattheson in his methodical way lists no fewer than seventeen points of contrast between the two. The most interesting is perhaps the observation that vocal melody does not admit the same sharp and dotted character as does instrumental writing (*Capellmeister*, 206, §20). This tells us clearly that composers who wrote a voice part in a milder, a unison melody part in a sharper, rhythm did so not as a shorthand device that calls for rhythmic assimilation, but in acknowledgment of the difference between the idiomatic characteristics of the two media.

Another point he makes refers to balance. When voices are combined with instruments, the latter must not dominate; instead they should lower their dynamics by one degree in order to let the voices be properly heard (*Capellmeister*, 207, §28).

Mattheson admires the performance of the Italians, who owe much of their excellence to their singers. The Italians, he says, cultivate their best voices with the greatest care, in monasteries, churches, and hospices. By contrast, the Germans, with the exception of a few courts, do not train such voices when they happen to have them. They treat their singers as nonentities ("en bagatelle") and let them perish like animals ("crepiren" *Orchestre* I, 205–6). He has a comparable admiration for French instrumental and choral performance and is particularly impressed by their overtures and orchestral suites. The execution of the latter is "so admirable, so unified [unie], and so compact [fermé]" that nothing surpasses it. They learn the music by heart and are not ashamed, as the Germans are, to rehearse a piece a hundred times to achieve perfection (*Orchestre* I, 226). The Germans, he writes, try to combine Italian and French styles; the English look only to Italy for guidance.

Mattheson's discussion of the various meters and different musical forms is, as usual, addressed to the composer, but yields here and there some items of interest to the performer. The thorough cataloging of the meters and their use is notable by its failure to mention *notes inégales*, though he was familiar with French treatises, which never failed to include *inégalité* in a discussion of meter.

A remark in a later tract illuminates the still-prevailing link between meter, denominations, and absolute note values. Mattheson asks why a 9/16 meter is needed, since one could write 9/8 and "allegro"? The answer is that in order properly to express fast pieces, we need fast meters and fast notes so that there shall be agreement between symbols and their meaning (*General-Baß-Schule* I, 374–5).

Of the various instrumental forms the French overture is his unquestioned favorite: Beautiful as are the Italian symphonies and concertos, he says, "a fresh French overture is preferable to all of them . . . one can hear nothing more exhilarating than a fine overture" (*Orchestre* I, 226–7). Its first part, he writes earlier (ibid., 171), "has a fresh, gay, but also uplifting character" ("ein etwas frisches, ermunterndes und auch zugleich *elevirtes* Wesen"). It is interesting to use the difference of this characterization from the widely held modern idea of the overture's "majestic" pomp.

Another interesting vignette concerns dynamics and the newly invented fortepiano. Mattheson translates an Italian essay by Marchese Scipio Maffei about this innovative instrument, and does so with obvious approval of its contents (*Critica musica* II, 335–8). Its author extols the joys of dynamic shading in music. He speaks of the gradual swelling and tapering of the sound, occasionally mixed with sudden dynamic contrasts – "a feat much in use in the great concerts in Rome" that gives connoisseurs "incredible and wondrous delight." Then he proceeds to praise the great advance of the new invention in matters of dynamics and defends it against its critics who find its sound dull and too weak.

In *Capellmeister* (Part II, chap. 13) Mattheson reviews, extends and elaborates on the description given in *Orchestre* I of the various musical forms in a survey that yields some points of interest for our subject. In a note about Italian, and Italian-style German, recitative, Mattheson remarks that it has a meter but that the singer must not be bound by it. In the accompanied type that involves the whole orchestra more attention has to be paid to the beat in order to hold the instrumentalists together, but the vocal delivery should not betray such dependence.

In his review of the various dance forms Mattheson makes a clear distinction, notably for the menuet, gavotte, rigaudon, sarabande, and courante, between those that were meant to be played and those intended to be sung or danced. In order to distinguish these three types, Mattheson advises, one should look at a menuet by Kuhnau, Handel, or Graupner and ponder whether the piece is suitable for dancing or singing. A first glance, he says, will elicit a negative answer (*Capellmeister*, 225, §85). The differentiation he makes is significant because some scholars have tried to establish the tempo of instrumental "play" dances by gathering clues from dance treatises and other dance-derived evidence. Mattheson's typology should discourage this line of research. Concerning the much-debated differences between the chaconne and the passacaglia, Mattheson declares the tempo of the chaconne to be more deliberate than that of the passacaglia and not, as some maintain, the other way around. (ibid., 233, §135). He ends this section on musical forms with a new tribute to his favorite one, the overture, "whose character expresses nobility" (§141).

The two above-mentioned chapters, which alone seem to focus specifically on performance, do give us some enlightening information. Mattheson attaches much importance to the discussion of conducting in the very last chapter of *Capellmeister* (Part III, chap. 26; the paragraph numbers in the following section refer to this chapter, entitled "Von der Regierung, An- Auf- und Ausführung einer Musik"). Nobody, he says, has so far written anything useful on the subject.

In a previous chapter Mattheson had quoted Jean Rousseau about both the need to search for, and the difficulty of clarifying, the composer's intentions when performing his works (173, §26). Now, in the closing paragraph of the whole book, he returns to the same idea and stresses the need for a judiciousness that will lead to correct interpretation of the composer's thoughts concerning his works.

His own experience in directing a vocal work has taught him that it is best to do so from the harpischord while playing and singing, rather than just standing about and beating time (§16). He castigates as mischievous the habits of some conductors of beating loudly with a stick or with keys, or by stamping their feet. Provided the performers keep their eyes on the director, a small wave of the hand or a wink can achieve the best results without resort to ostentatious display ("ohne großes Federfechten," §14). This remark is noteworthy because it reveals that the good directors of the time used some of the subtlest of modern conducting techniques, and that the "Tact-Prügler" (time-threshers) mocked by Mattheson may have been numerous but were not the norm.

For the chorus he considers women's voices indispensable. Boys are of little use, he says: before they have achieved a tolerable skill their soprano voices are gone (§§19–20). As early as *Orchestre I* (p. 206) he wrote that it was "ridiculous" to prevent women from singing in church. In Hamburg he had great difficulty introducing them in the cathedral: First he had to hide them from view, but in the end everybody wanted to see and hear them.

The best arrangement of the performers is different in church, chamber, theater, and orchestra and has often to be adapted to the locale. If the bass voices are weak, they should be placed in the middle; if strong and at least six in number, they may be divided, and half placed on either side (§28). A harpischord is far preferable to the "rattling, annoying regale." In churches one can use a clean and quickly responding positive without a *Schnarrwerk* (a rattling stop that Mattheson despises) or, when the chorus is strong, two harpsichords (§29). Singers must always be in front except in operas, where the orchestra is closer to the public but on a lower level. Here the director has to see to it that the instruments do not overpower the voices (§30).

Mattheson gives some psychological advice that many a tyrant-conductor of today would do well to take to heart. The director of a chorus, he says, should be generous with praise as often as he finds occasion for it. Whenever he has to criticize he should do so with seriousness, but as gently and politely as possible. He gives an interesting account of J. S. Kusser (or Cousser), a well-known composer who was for a few years director of the Hamburg Opera. He was indefatigable in instruction; he let everybody under his supervision, from the highest to the lowest, come to his house, where he sang and played every note just as he wanted it to sound. He did so with gentleness and grace. In public rehearsals and performances, however, he was a tyrant and everybody trembled before him, but afterwards he unfailingly made up for his severity by extraordinary politeness. By these methods he accomplished things as no one had before. "He can serve as a model" (§8).

In performance the main responsibility of the director is the establishment of the proper tempo. It should be steady but also flexible enough to accommodate by slight slowing down a soloist's tastefully executed ornament, or by slight speeding up (and presumably also by slowing down) to respond to the demands of expression (§13).

Finally, an amusing piece of practical advice is worth recording. Since accidents can happen in any performance, the director of the choir will do well to prearrange spots where, at an agreed sign, everybody can meet and continue without obvious interruption (§32).

The penultimate chapter (Part III, chap. 25) addresses itself mainly to the organist's art of improvising for the church service the necessary preludes, fugues, chorale accompaniments, and postludes, with emphasis on the compositional aspects of these pieces. Preceding this discussion, however, are a few remarks more directly pertinent to performance practice. Mattheson distinguishes the role of the organist when playing with the trained singers of the church from his role when accompanying the congregation. In the former case the organist should use the powers of his instrument with modesty and always adapt the loudness of his playing to the number of singers so that the voices predominate (471, §10). Only in a work involving two or three choruses may he play with full power; in such cases there will have to be a special conductor whose direction and tempo the organist has to adopt without resentment. By contrast, when playing with the congregation the organist must play loudly (more or less so according to the numbers present) so as to carry the lay singers along. It will then be best to place next to him one lead singer ("Vorsänger") who acts as liaison, carefully listening to the congregation and helping the organist to keep pace with it (471, §15).

Turning now to the chapter on graceful singing and playing ("Von der Kunst zierlich zu singen und zu spielen," Part II, chap. 3; paragraph numbers in the following refer to this chapter), we encounter again at its outset the proposition that the voice is the fountainhead of music making, hence should serve as model for instrumental performance. But to serve properly as model, the voice has to be treated correctly. We gain insight into some objectionable vocal practices of the day from Mattheson's listing of common faults (§§10–16). He sees as the worst offense incorrect breathing: Breathing either too frequently or in the wrong places will ruin proper phrasing. Reprehensible too are: to slur what should be detached, and vice versa; poor intonation and poor diction; singing through the nose or with closed teeth or too widely opened mouth; using wrong dynamics; failing to heed the old, wise principle of easing the sound with rising pitch and reinforcing it when descending to the lower register. The florid, improvised ornamentation, be it for voice or instruments, can create confusion if it does not fit in with the other parts or if it is, "in corrupt Italian manner," so extravagant as to demolish the melody.

At various points Mattheson expresses his disapproval of immoderate ornamentation. "One has to add some embellishments to a melody, but by no means too much. . . . The so-called *Manieren* [meaning here coloratura] spoil many a good aria and I can't forgive the French when they embroider their *doubles* excessively and embellish, or rather disfigure, them with a thousand little curlicues that prevent us from perceiving anything of the original melody."[1] He then proceeds with the interesting but surprising statement that today's Italian singers, in contrast to their recent predecessors, prefer a simple style to the highly embellished one, and leave the decorations to the instruments "as is only fitting." He quotes in this connection Bononcini's operas and concludes that the florid embellishments ("Decorationes") belong more to instrumental than to vocal music (§11).

A few years earlier, in *Orchestre* I (p. 229), he wrote differently and, it would seem, with more pertinence that the French singers use few coloraturas because their voices are not suited to them; exceptions occur for words such as "gloire" or "victoire" which they often drag in by force. The Italians, he then wrote, use coloraturas almost to excess. It would seem that he must have heard different styles of both

---

1 *Melotheta* (dated Hamburg, 1721; autograph MS, Deutsche Staatsbibliothek, East Berlin), Part IV, sec. iii, §9.

French and Italian vocal performances to give, within about eight years, such contradictory accounts.

Concerning the "small" graces – those that are often indicated by symbol – Mattheson, with his aversion to strict rules, quotes approvingly Hermann Finck and Heinichen who, over a gap of one hundred eighty years, agree that what matters for questions of ornaments are not rules but usage, much practice, and experience (§§18–19). Mattheson recommends to follow the best Italians but without exaggeration or rigor. Though ornaments change with taste and style, a few have managed, he says, to maintain their hold on musical practice, and they are the ones that he deals with in the following pages of the chapter.

First he lists the *Accent* (otherwise *Vorschlag* or *port de voix*), which is done by touching very gently and "quasi-twice" the upper or lower neighbor pitch before sounding the principal tone (§20). A "single" *Accent* is very short and takes up only very little, a "double" *Accent* one-half, of the length of the following tone. The vocal *Accent* must be so gently executed and slurred that the two pitches seem to blend into one (§22). This explanation does not seem to favor a distinct, accented-downbeat execution since in that case the two pitches would be clearly distinguishable. For such a stepwise-moving *Accent* Mattheson refers to plentiful examples in textbooks, but he offers "approximate" models for leaping ones. Thus Example 1a may

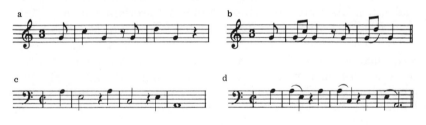

Example 1.

be rendered as in 1b, and 1c as in 1d, but only approximately ("ungefehr") since ornaments "can hardly be expressed by notation." He then gives a specimen of a *Nachschlag* that he calls "Ueberschlag" where the written Example 2a is sung as 2b.

In discussing vibrato, Mattheson mistakenly believes that it involves oscillations only of intensity ((§§27–9). Such is certainly the case with the tremulant stop of the organ, which he cites as proof, and with bow vibrato of strings and *Bebung* on the clavichord; but the

a

b   sung:

Ich will mich dem Schick-sal beu-gen   Ich will mich dem Schick-sal beu-gen

Example 2.

string vibrato produced by shaking the finger of the left hand on the string, and the common vocal vibrato, are (as is easily verified today by electronic means) primarily oscillations of pitch.

Mattheson defines the trill (*trillo* for the long, *trilletto* for the short type) in the usual way as fast alternations of two neighbor tones (§30). He gives no model because, he says, the grace is well known (§41).[2] French singers, he tells us, use slow alternations, the Italians very fast ones (§30). Either will occasionally start the trill with a long held one on either pitch (a *tenuta* or *tenue* respectively) and hence prepare the trill with either a long appoggiatura or a sustained main tone. He further illustrates ascending trill chains and expresses pleasure at having devised this term ("cadena di trilli" or "Trill-Kette"). His explanation that the individual links of the chain must connect so as to sound like one continuous trill (§37) that rises several degrees makes it clear that the trills have to start with their main tones because only then can the effect of a continuous trill be achieved. A *tenuta* on the main tone, as shown in Example 3a, can be modified into the *ribattuta* of 3b, whose gradual acceleration leads into a long trill.

Tenuta   Ribattuta   *tr*

Example 3.

Mattheson further lists the *groppo* and illustrates it in rising and falling form as shown in Examples 4a and 4b. Some Italians called this grace a *circolo*, some Germans a *Kugel* (ball) because it could be made to roll like a ball. The *circolo mezzo* or "Halb-Circkel" shown in Example 4c is closely related, except that in Mattheson's models it moves two pitches up or down before turning around to form the half circle. This grace, he says, is best used on a cadence or phrase ending.

2 Mattheson's criticism of Printz for defining the *trillo* as tone repetition is unjustified; use of the term in this meaning was frequent among seventeenth-century theorists and was usually contrasted with *tremolo* for the regular trill.

Example 4.

The *tirata* is a fast, scalewise – interbeat – connection between two pitches from a fifth to an octave apart. Mattheson stresses the need for speed and considers the term ill used by Brossard for a liesurely progression. Specimens are shown in Examples 5a and 5b. Furthermore he shows the slide ("Schleuffer") as a "small *tirata*" from the third above or below and illustrates it as in Examples 5c and 5d. In contrast to the interbeat *tirata* the grace is placed on the beat.

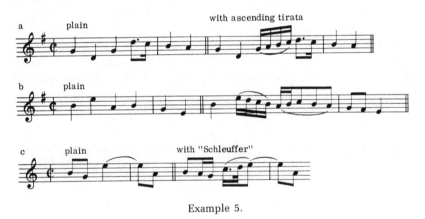

Example 5.

What he calls "Durchgänge" are *Nachschlag*-type pitches added as suffixes to a note as shown in Example 6.

Example 6.

For the vocal mordent Mattheson explains and illustrates the single-alternation type and stresses the need for the utmost speed, which will give the impression of the three pitches merging into a single sound. The speed is the reason why he makes no attempt to divide the two ornamental notes into the measure. Example 7 shows two distinct types: one at the start of a note, and the other as a *Nachschlag*-type suffix to an ascending appoggiatura (a *port de voix*). Again he stresses the inadequacy of notation for suggesting ornament execution.

Example 7.

Finally he mentions the acciaccatura, as explained by Gasparini and Heinichen: the simultaneous striking but quick release of a pitch one step below that of the principal tone. Mattheson has little use for it. It occurs, he says, only on the keyboard, in thorough-bass accompaniment, and causes many an impurity of harmony.

Mattheson passed in review most of the "small" ornaments that he felt had more than temporary significance. He showed symbols only for the trill and the *accent*. For the other ornaments the printer may have lacked the necessary types or, more likely, Mattheson expected them to be improvised. In a later (the penultimate) chapter he touches briefly upon the arpeggio, *passaggi*, and diminutions (p. 477, §§56–9).

The importance of Mattheson's writings on performance lies less in the illumination of specific details, however enlightening some of these glimpses are, but in his basic aesthetic posture of opposing the tyranny of rules. Much stiffness and outright unmusicality in today's performances of early music is due to a far too literal interpretation of rules found in old treatises. Most of their authors probably never meant to be interpreted so literally and with so little imagination, but they mostly failed to say so, and this failure opened the door to widespread modern misinterpretations. Mattheson did say so, and again and again he returned with the refrain that rules are relative, not absolute, that interpretation is a matter of taste and thus subject to change, and that models of ornaments are only very inadequate

267

approximations. In thus articulating what others left unsaid, he made what may be his greatest contribution to our quest for historical correctness. It behooves all modern theorists and practitioners of historical performance to engrave in their consciousness Mattheson's words: "The rule of nature, in music, is nothing but the ear."

12

Die Verzierungskunst aus Matthesons Sicht

HANS TURNOW
Höxter

Die s t i l g e r e c h t e Interpretation alter Musik stellt die heutigen Sänger, Instrumentalisten, Dirigenten und Editoren immer wieder vor Schwierigkeiten. Dies gilt besonders auch im Hinblick auf die Verzierungskunst. Spezielle Angaben zu den Notentexten vonseiten des jeweiligen Komponisten oder kompetenter Personen seiner Umgebung (z.B. seiner Lehrer bzw. Schüler), außerdem Traktate zeitgenössischer Theoretiker, können gegebenenfalls eine unschätzbare Hilfe bedeuten. Mattheson hat zwar bewußt darauf verzichtet, eine Abhandlung ausschließlich der vorliegenden Thematik zu widmen[1]; an verschiedenen Stellen seiner Werke äußerte er sich jedoch näher hierüber, so vor allem im *Vollkommenen Capellmeister* (zweiter Theil, drittes Haupt-Stück: "Von der Kunst, zierlich zu singen und zu spielen", p. 109ss.[2], und vierzehntes Haupt-Stück: "Von der Melodien Einrichtung, Ausarbeitung und Zierde", p. 242ss.)[3].

In der Terminologie Matthesons werden die Verzierungen – dem Sprachgebrauch seiner Zeit entsprechend – meist als "Manieren"[4] und "Zier[r]athen" benannt. Als synonyme Allgemeinbegriffe erscheinen bei Mattheson auch: "Ausschmückung[en]" (*Melodische Wissenschaft*, 139; *Capellmeister*, 115, 242), "Decoration[es]" (*Kelter-Treter*, §8; *Melotheta*, 165; *Melodische Wissenschaft*, 139),

---

1 Der Verzicht ist begründet in dem von Mattheson 1737 (*Melodische Wissenschaft*, 143), 1739 (*Capellmeister*, 244) und davor schon 1721–2 (*Melotheta*, 165) erwähnten schnellen, "fast jährlich" [*Melotheta*: "fast alle Jahre"] sich vollziehenden Wandel auf diesem Gebiet.

2 In Anlehnung an W. C. Printz (*Compendium musicae*, 1689, p. 34) spricht Mattheson auch von einer "Modulatoria vocalis & instrumentalis" (*Capellmeister*, 109 und Register).

3 Besonderen Wert soll ebenso den Äußerungen beigemessen werden, die die betreffenden Texte des *Capellmeisters* zeitlich vorwegnehmen, durch Übereinstimmungen bestätigen (bzw. durch interessante Varianten ergänzen.)

4 Die Schreibweise "Mannieren" gebrauchte Mattheson am Anfang seines musiktheoretischen Schaffens (*Orchestre* I, 269, 285).

"Schmuck" (*Kelter-Treter*, §13; *Melodische Wissenschaft*, 141; *Capellmeister*, 110), "Schmückungen" (*Capellmeister*, 242), "Ausputzungen" (*Melodische Wissenschaft*, 141; *Capellmeister*, 243), "Schnörkel" (*Plus ultra* I, 70). Den Ausdruck "Variation" für die Diminutio Notarum, d.h. für eine Verzierung wie [z.B.] den "Halb-Circkel", sieht Mattheson in der "Pöbel-Sprache" beheimatet (siehe *Capellmeister*, 116, Anmerkung). Obwohl er die Bezeichnungen "Coloraturen" und "Figuren" im *Capellmeister* (p. 110, Anmerkung) als überholte Kunstnamen für die "Manieren" abstempelt, verwendet er namentlich den Terminus "Figur" weiterhin, wenn auch in unterschiedlicher Bedeutung, sehr häufig (*Capellmeister*, 111, 116[5]; siehe ferner 242ss.[6]).

Die "Decoration" der Notentexte macht Mattheson in erster Linie von dem gesangs- und spieltechnischen Können und dem Urteilsvermögen der Interpreten abhängig; d.h. er schaut, wie er sich im *Melotheta* (p. 165) ausdrückt, "mehr auff die Adresse und das geschickte Judicium eines Sängers oder Symphonisten, als auff die Vorschrifft des Componisten"[7]. Im nachfolgenden Text fügt Mattheson jedoch hinzu: "Etwas Zierrath muß man einer Melodie beylegen, bey Leibe aber nicht zu viel"[8]. Die Auswahl und Anwendung der Manieren trifft Mattheson u.a. nach Regeln der Affektenlehre[9], der Lehre von den musikalischen Stilen, der Melodie- und Satzlehre und der Gesangslehre[10].

Auf unterschiedliche und mehr oder weniger begrenzte Möglich-

---

5 Auf p. 116 des *Capellmeisters* bemerkt Mattheson beiläufig, daß die "meisten Ausschmückungen des Gesanges" zu seiner Zeit ("noch [!] heutiges Tages") an den Schlüssen der Kompositionen angebracht und daher "Vorzugs-Weise" dann als "Cadentzen" bezeichnet würden.

6 Unter dem Terminus "Figurae cantionis" versteht Mattheson die "Sing-Manieren", kurz: die "Manieren". Dagegen faßt er in dem Oberbegriff "Figurae cantus" die "Figurae dictionis" (auch: "Wörter-Figuren") und die "Figurae sententiae" (auch: "Spruch-Figuren") zusammen. Näheres über die "Figurae cantus" findet sich in den Ausführungen über "Mattheson und die Rhetorik" von F. Feldmann (*Kongreß-Bericht Hamburg 1956*, 99–103).

7 Dieses Urteil über die Komponisten gilt für Mattheson selbstverständlich nicht, wenn sie gleichzeitig geschickte Sänger und Spieler sind.

8 Die beiden hier zitierten Stellen aus *Melotheta*, 165, kehren in sinngemäßer, zum Teil wortgetreuer Übereinstimmung inder *Melodischen Wissenschaft*, 139, und im *Capellmeister*, 242, wieder.

9 Siehe H.-P. Schmitz, *Die Kunst der Verzierung im 18. Jahrhundert* (Kassel, 1955), 12.

10 Die vokale Verzierungskunst betrachtet Mattheson bis zu einem gewissen Grad auch für den instrumentalen Bereich als verbindlich und spricht von der "Nachahmung der Menschenstimme". Andrerseits gesteht er aber zu: ". . . es läßt sich . . . vieles gar füglich spielen, das im Singen nicht die geringste gute Art haben würde" (*Capellmeister*, 109).

keiten, die im Bereich der instrumentalen Verzierungskunst bestehen und unter anderen durch divergierende Klangqualitäten und spieltechnische Schwierigkeiten einzelner Instrumente bzw. Instrumentengruppen bedingt sind, macht Mattheson wiederholt aufmerksam[11]. Dennoch ist es ihm unverständlich, daß seine Zeitgenossen beim Generalbaß-Spiel "wenig manierliches" anbringen, "da doch die gröste Douceur [*General-Baß-Schule* I: "Anmuth"] darinn[12], und nicht so wohl in der Faust-fertigkeit, beruhet" (*Organisten-Probe*, 142; *General-Baß-Schule* I, 330)[13]. Immer wieder warnt Mattheson vor Mißbrauch, vor Übertreibungen im Verzierungswesen. Demgegenüber fordert er "wohlangebrachte[14] Manieren" (*Melodische Wissenschaft*, 140; *Capellmeister*, 242, und *Melotheta*, 165), das heißt Verzierungen "zu rechter Zeit, am rechten Ort, und in gehöriger Maße" (*Collegium Hudemanno*, 12)[15]. Bisweilen verwendet Mattheson Manieren, um etwaige Mängel einer Melodie zu beheben bzw. abzuschwächen; z.B. läßt er im Beispiel 1 "zur Bedeckung" der verminderten Quarte vom Interpreten einen "Schleuffer" anbringen (cf. *Melodische Wissenschaft*, 50, und *Capellmeister*, 153s.).

Beispiel 1.

11 Cf. in diesem Zusammenhang folgende Gegenüberstellungen: Clavichord–Clavicymbel, Hautbois–Basson, "kleine Baß-Geigen" im Vergleich zuden "grossen Maschinen" (gemeint sind "Grosse Baß-Geigen"); siehe *Orchestre* I, 264, 268s. und 285s.

12 Ähnlich äußert sich J. D. Heinichen (*Der General-Baß in der Composition*, 1728, 521) Er sagt, daß durch den "manierlichen Generalbaß" dem Spiel "mehr Grace" gegeben werde.

13 Besonderes Gewicht legt Mattheson auch auf die Ausschmückung der Baßstimme und bedauert den bestehenden "Mangel" auf diesem Gebiet. Als Verzierungen, die hier in Betracht kommen, nennt er den "Schleuffer", der in diesem Fall "kurz und etwas vehement" gespielt werden soll, ferner: "gute scharffe Trilli, Vorschläge, Accente und dergleichen" (*Organisten-Probe*, 207; *General-Baß-Schule* I, 395). N.B.: Mattheson heißt es gut, wenn außer dem variirten Baß zugleich noch die ursprüngliche Baßstimme auf einem besonderen Instrument [bzw. auf mehreren Instrumenten] erklingt (*Critica musica* I, 201s. mit Anmerkung).

14 Verschiedene Schreibweisen kommen in den drei Werken vor: "Wohlangebrachte" (*Melodische Wissenschaft*), "Wolangebrachte" (*Capellmeister*) und "wohl angebrachte" (*Melotheta*).

15 So verurteilt Mattheson es, wenn die Manieren "mit den andern Stimmen gantz uneins sind; oder auch, nach der verdorbenen Welschen Zwang-Art, dergestalt ausschweifen, daß sie die Melodie im Grunde zerrütten" (*Capellmeister*, 111). Dagegen lobt er (*Melodische Wissenschaft*, 141; *Capellmeister*, 243) die gescheitesten von den "ächten, Welschen Setzern", voran Giovanni Battista Bononcini.

Daß Mattheson bei dem vorangegangenen Notenbeispiel nur die Tonhöhen der betreffenden Verzierung (durch Punkte) fixiert hat, unterstreicht seine an anderer Stelle (*Capellmeister*, 113) geäußerte Ansicht: ". . . so eigentlich lassen sich die Manieren mit Noten[16] schwerlich ausdrücken"[17]. Mit dem – von Mattheson beobachteten – steten Wandel des musikalischen Geschmacks und einer damit verbundenen deutlichen Änderung innerhalb der Verzierungskunst[18] stellt er gleichzeitig einen regionalen Unterschied heraus (*Capellmeister*, 110): "Es sind dergleichen Zierrathen nicht nur grössesten Theils mancher Veränderung, Mode und Neuerung unterworffen; sondern auch, nach dieser oder jener Landes-Art . . . an sich selbst sehr verschieden".

Nach Angaben im *Vollkommenen Capellmeister* und teilweise im *Collegium Hudemanno*, die wichtige Übereinstimmungen aufweisen, sollen im folgenden die Manieren speziell behandelt werden, "die noch[19] so ziemlich Stand halten, und eben nicht auf eines jedweden eigene Erfahrung und Geschmack lediglich ankommen" (*Collegium Hudemanno*, 12: "etliche der gebräuchlichen und beständigsten Manieren"; cf. *Capellmeister*, 112ss.).

"Accent"

Im *Vollkommenen Capellmeister* nimmt Mattheson den Terminus "Accent" (innerhalb der Verzierungslehre) als Oberbegriff für die

---

16 Gemeint sind die Notenwerte.

17 Hier sei ein Satz aus Scheibes (*Critischem Musicus* ²1745, 6. Stück, 62) erwähnt: "Alle Manieren, alle kleine Auszierungen, und alles, was man unter der Methode zu spielen versteht, drücket er [= J. S. Bach] mit eigentlichen Noten aus, und das entzieht seinen Stücken nicht nur die Schönheit der Harmonie, sondern es machet auch den Gesang durchaus unvernehmlich".

18 In der *Critica musica* II, 11, bemerkt er "eine merkliche Aenderung in den Zierrathen".

19 D.h. als er das dritte Haupt-Stück zum zweiten Theil des *Capellmeisters* schrieb. (Im Widerspruch hierzu steht u.a. schon das vierzehnte Haupt-Stück zum zweiten Theil des *Capellmeister*, §51, p. 244: Er sagt, daß "die alten [!] Manieren nicht mehr Stand halten wollen, eine andre Gestalt gewinnen, oder auch neuern Moden Platz machen". Deshalb trägt er Bedenken, (hierüber) "Vorschrifften" zu entwerfen. An der Parallelstelle in der *Melodischen Wissenschaft* (p. 143) nennt er die Manieren, die er zu den "alten" zählt: "tremoli, groppi, circoli, tirate &c." Ohne das Zeichen "&c." sind aber bereits im *Melotheta* an der Parallelstelle zu diesem Text diese Verzierungen als "die alten" angeführt worden (*Melotheta*, p. 165). Dagegen als Manieren "von ziemlicher vorwährenden Dauer" bezeichnet er im *Capellmeister* und in der *Melodischen Wissenschaft* "z.E. die Accente, die Schleuffer [*Melodische Wissenschaft*: "Schleifer"], die Vorschläge x.", während er im *Melotheta* nur namentlich hier "die Accentus, und [die] so genañten Schleiffer von zieml. Dauer" anführt.)

"Vorschläge"[20] und für die von ihm als "Überschläge"[21] bezeichneten Manieren[22]. Die Vorschläge unterteilt er in "Stuffen-Accente" und "Sprung-Accente"[23]. Beide Arten können sowohl eine Aufwärts-als auch Abwärtsrichtung einnehmen[24]. Die "accentirende Note" liegt bei den Stuffen-Accenten eine Sekunde über bzw. unter der "accentuirten"[25] und soll "gantz sanfft, und gleichsam zweimahl sehr hurtig berührt [werden]"[26]. Bei den Sprung-Accenten kann das betreffende Intervall – nach Matthesons Angaben – eine Quarte bis Oktave betragen[27].

Im Hinblick auf die Notenwerte unterscheidet er die "einfachen" von den "doppelten [Accenten]": "Bey den einfachen wird von der nächstfolgenden [=accentuirten] Note nur ein weniges, bey den doppelten aber die Helffte der Geltung genommen, so daß die accentirende Note desto länger, und mit einer angenehmen Verzögerung gehöret wird, als worin offt die beste Lust bestehet". Über die Anwendung der doppelten Accente bei Clavier-Kompositionen bringt Mattheson folgende Regel: "In Clavier-Sachen erfordert überdis die Verdoppelung der Accente zwo Stimmen oder zween Finger, die beide zu gleicher Zeit diese Manier anbringen"[28].

Ganz allgemein bemerkt Mattheson über die Ausführung der Vorschläge (vor allem als Gesangsmanieren), "daß die beiden Klänge . . . gantz genau an einander hängen, und fast wie ein eintziger Klang herauskommen mögen". Um dies zu erreichen, soll der Accent "gelinde gezogen[29] und geschleiffet werden". Hinsichtlich der Affekte kennzeichnet Mattheson die Stuffen-Accente

20 Außerdem erwähnt er im *Capellmeister* die französiscbe Bezeichnung "le port de voix".
21 R. Haas (*Aufführungspraxis der Musik* [=Handbuch der Musikwissenschaft], Potsdam, 1931, 191) schreibt fälschlicherweise: "Rückschlag" bzw. "Rückschläge".
22 Das *Collegium Hudemanno* enthält noch keine Beschreibung der Überschläge: Hier wird der Terminus "Accent" ausschließlich anstelle von "Vorschlag" gebraucht. Über die Terminologie anderer Autoren (z.E. sind Walther, F. Couperin [le Grand], J. S. Bach, Majer und Spiess angeführt) unterrichtet kurz Tabelle 1.
23 Im *Capellmeister* wird von einem "heutiges Tages starck eingeführten Gebrauch" der Sprung-Accente gesprochen.
24 "Im Singen wird fast kein eintziger Accent aufwärts gemacht, dabey nicht zugleich ein kleiner Mordant mit vorkömmt" (*Capellmeister*, 119s.).
25 Die erste Note eines Intervalls, bei dem ein Accent angebracht wird, nennt Mattheson "accentirende Note", die zweite "accentuirte".
26 Diese Regel dürfte nicht nur im vokalen, sondern auch (soweit es möglich ist) im instrumentalen Bereich gültig sein.
27 Heinichen (*Der General-Baß*, 525) schließt die Terz nicht aus.
28 G. Falck (*Idea boni cantoris*, 1688, 98) warnt vor fehlerhaften Parallelen, wenn diese Manier gleichzeitig in zwei Stimmen angebracht wird.
29 Auch M. Praetorius (*Syntagma musicum* III, 1619, 232) schreibt, daß diese Verzierung "im Halse gezogen" werden müsse.

nicht, dagegen aber die Sprung-Accente: Nach seiner Ansicht können sie "insonderheit etwas spöttisches, sprödes, freches und hochmüthiges"[30] ausdrücken. (Beispiel 2; cf. *Capellmeister*, 112s., und *Collegium Hudemanno*, 13.)

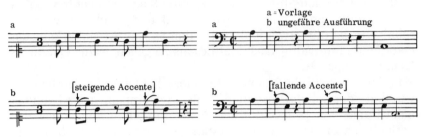

Beispiel 2.

Die Überschläge unterteilt Mattheson nicht weiter. Diese Art der Accente sollen besonders in den Kompositionen angebracht werden, "die was klagendes oder demüthiges haben", und zwar bei abwärtsgerichteten Sprüngen, die größer als eine Terz sind. Wie Mattheson sich ausdrückt, bekommt "das erste Ende solcher Intervalle einen feinen und kurtzen Anhang oder Zusatz von dem nächst überliegenden Klange" (cf. *Capellmeister*, 1135.; Beispiel 3.).

Beispiel 3.

Anmerkungen. Während bei Mattheson die Termini "einfache Accente" bzw. "doppelte Accente" sich auf die Notenwerte beziehen,

30 Im *Collegium Hudemanno* sind nur die beiden letztgenannten Eigenschaften erwähnt.

Tabelle 1.

J. G. Walther, *Praecepta der musicalischen Composition* (1708); Ausgabe von P. Benary, Leipzig 1955, 38s. und 152s.	A. I. *"Accentus simplex ascendens"* (="der einfache aufsteigende Accent") a) "Accentus major" (Intervall: gr. Sekunde) b) "Accentus minor" (Intervall: kl. Sekunde) II. *"Accentus simplex descendens"* (="der einfach[e] herabsteigende Accent") a) "Accentus major" (Intervall: gr. Sekunde) b) "Accentus minor" (Intervall: kl. Sekunde) B. *"gedoppelter [bzw. "doppelter"] Accent"* C. *"Superjectio"* ("Insgemein Accentus genennet")
François Couperin, *L'art de toucher le clavecin* (Paris, ²1717); *NA*, p. 16f. und Anhang* J. S. Bach, Clavier-Büchlein vor W. Fr. Bach (1720); Ausgabe von H. Keller, (Kassel, 1927), 14	A. "Port de voix (coulé)" "Port de voix simple" "Port de voix double" B. "Accent" I. "accent steigend" (Intervall: Sekunde) II. "accent fallend" (Intervall: Sekunde) "accent und mordant" "accent und trillo"
J. G. Walther, *Musicalisches Lexicon* (1732)	"Accento (ital.) Accent (gall.) Accentus (lat.) sc. musicus" (= "ein musicalischer Accent") A. *"Accentus simplices"* (="einfache Accente") I. *"Accentus descendens, oder remittens"* (="der Absteigende Accent") a) "Accentus major" (Intervall: gr. Sekunde) b) "Accentus minor" (Intervall: kl. Sekunde) II. *"Accentus ascendens oder intendens"* (="der Aufsteigende Accent") a) "Accentus major" (Intervall: gr. Sekunde) b) "Accentus minor" (Intervall: kl. Sekunde) "Port de Voix", "Vorschlag" ("[ist] eben was Accento") B. *"Accento doppio (ital.) Accent double (gall.) Accentus duplex (lat.)* (="ein doppelter Accent") C. *"Superjectio"* (="ein Uberwurff oder Accent")
J. Fr. B. C. Majer, *Museum musicum* (1732), 85	"Accento, Accentus Musicus" (="ein musicalischer Accent")

Tabelle 1 (fortsetzung)

M. Spiess, *Tractatus musicus* (1746), 155ss.	A.	"*Accentus Musicus*" (="Stimm-Einfall", "Vorschlag")
	I.	"*Accentus Descendens, oder Remittens*" (="der absteigende Accent [oder Vorschlag]")
	II.	"*Accentus Ascendens, oder Intendens*" (="der aufsteigende Accent oder Vorschlag")
	B.	"*Superjectio*" (="Uberschlag")

*Die im Anhang der *NA* veröffentlichten Verzierungstabelle ist folgendem Werk Couperins entnommen: *Pièces de Clavecin*, Livre Ier. (Paris, 1713).

bedeuten die entsprechenden Bezeichnungen bei Walther und Couperin etwas andres.

Walther versteht unter "Accentus simplex", "Port de Voix" bzw. "Vorschlag" die Art der Manier, die Mattheson "Stuffen-Accent" nennt. Der "gedoppelte [bzw. "doppelte"] Accent" ("Accentus duplex") ist bei Walther quasi eine Antizipation. Unter dem Stichwort "Anticipatione della Nota" schreibt er in seinem *Lexicon* (1732): "Diese Figur ist von dem Accentu duplici nur in so weit unterschieden, daß solcher auch springend angebracht wird, welches die Anticipatio . . . nicht thun kan".

Bei Couperin (siehe Tabelle 1) dagegen besteht der "Port de voix simple" aus "Port de voix (coulé)" + "Pincé-simple" und der "Port de voix double" aus "Port de voix (coulé)" + "Pincé-double".

Mit Ausnahme von Spiess bringen die in der Tabelle 1 genannten Autoren keine Beschreibungen der Sprung-Accente (in Matthesons Sinn). Spiess aber erfaßt diese Accente mit unter den Termini "Accentus Descendens, oder Remittens" bzw. "Accentus Ascendens, oder Intendens": "Beyde diese Vorschläg oder Accentus werden auch, in Sprüngen (Saltibus) in der Terz, Quart, Quint, Sext, Sept und Octav angebracht" (p. 155). Im Gegensatz zu Mattheson läßt also Spiess (wie auch Heinichen) den Terzsprung nicht außer acht.

Die bei Walther (1708 und 1732) und bei Spiess (1746) angeführte "Superjectio" (auch: "Uberwurff', [1732] bzw. "Uberschlag" [1746]) kommt dem "Uberschlag" bei Mattheson in gewissem Grade gleich. Ein Unterschied besteht in den Intervallen, bei denen diese Figur angewendet werden kann: Walther und Spiess schließen die kleinen Intervalle nicht aus und bevorzugen sogar den Sekundschritt. Dies bestätigen Notenbeispiele (1708, Ausgabe Benary, p. 152, und 1746,

p. 159) und folgender Text bei Spiess (p. 156): "Superjectio, der Uberschlag, ist eine kleine, jedoch gratieuse Manier; geschiehet sonderheitlich bey aufsteigender [recte: absteigender] Secund". Ein weiterer Unterschied (gegenüber Mattheson) wird hier deutlich: Da Mattheson den Uberschlag vor allem in Kompositionen anbringen läßt, "die was klagendes oder demüthiges haben", müßte auch die Eigenschaft dieser Verzierung den eben genannten Affekten ungefähr entsprechen. Spiess aber bezeichnet die Superjectio bzw. den Uberschlag als eine "gratieuse Manier".

"Tremolo"[31]

Nach Matthesons Definition (*Capellmeister*, 114) ist ein Tremolo "die allergelindeste Schwebung auf einem eintzigen festgesetzten Ton[32], dabey meines [=Matthesons] Erachtens das Oberzünglein des Halses (epiglottis)[33], durch eine gar sanffte Bewegung oder Mäßigung des Athems, das meiste thun muß: so wie auf Instrumenten die blosse Lenckung der Fingerspitzen, ohne von der Stelle zu weichen, gewisser maassen eben das [gleiche] ausrichtet, absonderlich auf Lauten, Geigen und Clavichordien". Einige Zeilen weiter bemerkt Mattheson im Hinblick auf die Streichinstrumente ("Geigen") noch folgendes: "Auf Geigen kan dergleichen Zittern auch mit den Bögen in einem Strich, auf einem Ton bewerckstelliget werden".

Mit Nachdruck weist Mattheson darauf hin, daß es unmöglich sei, diese Manier genau auszuschreiben: "Man kan wol andeuten, an welchem Orte ein solches Zittern oder Schweben geschehen soll, aber wie es eigentlich damit zugehe, kan weder Feder noch Circkel zeigen: das Ohr muß es lehren". So erinnert Mattheson z.E. an die Tremulanten in den Orgeln, die "ein Schweben im Spielen" bewirken. (cf. *Capellmeister*, 114, und *Collegium Hudemanno*, 13).

31 Die bei J. G. Walther (*Musicalisches Lexicon*, 1732, Stichwort: "Tremolo") zitierte Diminutivform "Tremoletto" erwähnt Mattheson nicht.
32 Folglich lehnt Mattheson (*Capellmeister* und *Collegium Hudemanno*) den Terminus "Tremolo" für jede "aus zween Klängen bestehende Figur" ab. Umgekehrt läßt er keine andern Bezeichnungen für die von ihm als "Tremolo" definierte Manier gelten. Von den Theoretikern, deren Terminologie Mattheson in diesem Punkt kritisiert, sind namentlich Printz (1678, siehe p. 46f.) und Falck zu nennen. Falck (*Idea boni cantoris*, 99) schreibt: "Tremulus ist ein Zittern der Stimm über einer Noten, auf zweyen Clavibus; die Organisten nennen es Mordanten, Beisser". Diese Definition hat Falck nahezu wörtlich von Praetorius (*Syntagma musicum* III, 235) übernommen: "Tremolo, vel Tremulo: Ist nichts anders, alß ein Zittern der Stimme uber einer Noten: die Organisten nennen es Mordanten oder Moderanten". Walther (*Lexicon*) faßt den Terminus "Tremolo" im modernen Sinn (wie Mattheson) auf, führt aber auch die andere Bedeutung an. Er betrachtet jedoch diese Verzierung als eine spezielle Manier für Streichinstrumente.
33 In der neueren Literatur heißt die Epiglottis "Kehldeckel".

"Trillo" (= "Triller")[34] und "Trilletto"

Der Unterschied zwischen einem Trillo und einem Trilletto beruht – wie Mattheson sich ausdrückt – "in der Länge und Kürtze ihrer Dauer"; d.h. die "Dauer" ist bei dem Trilletto "sehr klein"[35]. Die gemeinsamen Merkmale dieser Verzierungen sieht er "in einem scharffen und deutlichen Schlagen zweener zusammenliegender oder benachbarter[36], und mit einander auf das hurtigste[37] unverwechselnder Klänge". Mit diesen Worten legt Mattheson die für ihn geltende Norm fest. Außerdem zeigt er gewisse nationale Differenzierungen auf: "Die Frantzösischen Sänger, sonderlich die Sängerinnen, lieben ein etwas langsames Anschlagen der beeden zum Triller gehörigen unwechselnden Klänge". Mattheson beurteilt diese Ausführung folgendermaßen: ". . . es klingt vernehmlich und rein, obwol etwas matt". Über die Italiener schreibt er in diesem Zusammenhang: "Die Welschen hergegen schlagen ihre g e m e i n e Triller sehr geschwind, starck und kurtz, fast wie Trilletten".

Eine Ausnahme bildet der "auf" einer T e n u t a (frz. tenuë)[38]

---

34 Die bei Walther, Couperin, Majer und anderen vorkommenden Bezeichnungen "Tremblement" und "trille" verwendet Mattheson nicht.

35 Walther (Lexicon): "Trilletto, pl. trilletti (ital.) ist das Diminutivum von trillo, und bedeutet: daß es kurtz gemacht werden soll".

36 D.h. das betreffende Intervall ist eine große bzw. kleine Sekunde. Entsprechend gebraucht Walther (Praecepta, Ausgabe Benary, p. 38) die Termini "Trilla major" bzw. "Trilla minor". Die oben erwähnten Bezeichnungen lehnt Mattheson für die aus Tonrepetitionen bestehende Manier (=Temolo) ab. Er wendet sich deshalb gegen "fast alle alte Lehrer", u.a. auch gegen Printz und Falck. Demgegenüber hat bereits Cavalieri (Rappresentazione, 1600) den Terminus "Trillo" im heutigen [=Matthesons] Sinn appliziert, wie Haas (Aufführungspraxis, 145) bemerkt.

37 J. J. Quantz (Versuch einer Anweisung die Flöte traversière zu spielen, 1752, p. 83s.) verlangt dagegen ausdrücklich, daß die "Geschwindigkeit", mit der die Klänge aufeinander folgen, nach dem Aufführungsort und nach den Affekten der Kompositionen variiert wird: "Nicht alle Triller dürfen in einerley Geschwindigkeit geschlagen werden: sondern man muß sich hierinne so wohl nach dem Orte wo man spielet, als nach der Sache selbst, die man auszuführen hat, richten. Spielet man an einem großen Orte, wo es sehr schallet; so wird ein etwas langsamer Triller bessere Wirkung thun, als ein geschwinder. Denn durch den Wiederschall geräth die allzugeschwinde Bewegung der Töne in eine Verwirrung, und folglich wird der geschwinde Triller undeutlich. Spielet man hingegen in einem kleinen oder tapezirten Zimmer, wo die Zuhörer nahe dabey stehen: so wird ein geschwinder Triller besser seyn, als ein langsamer. Man muß ferner zu unterscheiden wissen, was für Stücke man spielet; damit man nicht, wie viele thun, eine Sache mit der andern vermenge. In traurigen Stücken muß der Triller langsamer; in lustigen aber geschwinder geschlagen werden".

38 Die Termini "Tenuta" und "tenuë" bedeuten nach Matthesons Definition: "wenn etwa auf einem oder andern Ton lange auszuhalten ist". (Walther, Lexicon: "Tenuë [gall.] die Haltung eines Klanges"; Spiess, Tractatus musicus, 156: "Tenuta, Aushaltung, ist, wann eine Stimm lang in einem Ton aushalten muß. . .")

angebrachte Triller[39]. In diesem Fall stellt Mattheson bei den italienischen Sängern eine langsamere Aufeinanderfolge der betreffenden
Klänge fest und führt diese Besonderheit auf die Atemtechnik
zurück[40]. Während es sich hierbei um gleiche Notenwerte handeln
dürfte – Mattheson erwähnt dies nicht extra –, schildert er ferner[41]
eine Möglichkeit, bei der auf einer Tenuta langsame und schnelle
Triller abwechseln. Für die letztgenannte Ausführung verlangt Mattheson "eine mehr als gemeine Geschicklichkeit und biegsame oder
geschmeidige Beschaffenheit der Werckzeuge im Halse".

Mattheson liebt zwar "ein wolangebrachtes[42] Trillo, das von
ziemlicher Geschwindigkeit und gehöriger Länge ist", und räumt ihm
sogar den Vorrang in der Verzierungskunst ein, er kritisiert aber eine
zu häufige Anwendung (cf. *Capellmeister*, 114s., und *Collegium
Hudemanno*, 13s.). Die Bezeichnungen "Cadena di Trilli" und "Trill-
Kette" gebraucht Mattheson für eine zur Zeit des *Capellmeisters* (p.
115) "nicht selten" angewandte Folge von Trillern. Nach seinem
Bericht wird hierbei auf jeder Note der betreffenden *aufsteigenden*
Sekunden[43] ein Triller angebracht. Mattheson fordert, daß diese
Triller sich "ohne Unterbrechung, an einander schliessen müssen,
als wäre es nur ein eintziger, der offt fünf, sechs, oder mehr Grade
fortwähret"[44] (Beispiel 4). Nach Moser ([4]1955, Lexikon, Stichwort:

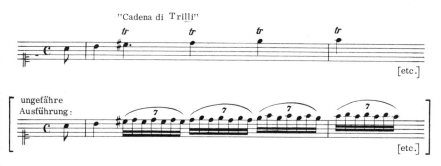

Beispiel 4.

39 Mattheson meint (*Critica musica* I, p. 198, Anmerkung), daß den Franzosen hierfür
die notwendige "disposition des Athems" fehle.
40 "Alsdenn müssen sie nothwendig ein wenig bedächtlicher und nicht so schnell zu
Wercke gehen, um den Athem zu sparen".
41 Von dieser Möglichkeit wird nicht im *Collegium Hudemanno*, sondern ausschließlich im *Capellmeister* gesprochen.
42 D.h. die Triller sollen nur dort angebracht werden, wo sie nach der Affektenlehre zu
rechtfertigen sind.
43 Eine Cadena di Trilli bei absteigenden Sekunden ist Mattheson unbekannt.
44 Die Notenwerte müssen demnach alle gleich sein. (Siehe dagegen Moser.)

Beispiel 5.

"Triller") führt man "Trillerketten" am besten wie im Beispiel 5 aus. Bei dieser Ausführung wird der Übergang von einem Triller zum andern etwas verzögert, da jeweils die letzte Note des ersten, zweiten und dritten Trillers einen relativ längeren Wert aufweist.

"Ribattuta"

Die Ribattuta unterscheidet sich vom Triller durch ihren punktierten Rhythmus. Mattheson definiert diese Verzierung folgendermaßen: ". . . sie bestehet in einer punctirten und bedächtlich-abgestossenen Umwechselung [*Collegium Hudemanno*: "in einer langsamen und punctirten Abwechselung"][45] zweener neben einander liegenden Klänge, dabey man immer auf den untersten, und längsten, als einen Ruhe-Punct, wiederkehret und Fuß fasset. Das Wort bedeutet eine Zurückschlagung"[46]. (cf. *Capellmeister*, 118, und *Collegium Hudemanno*, 16).

Mattheson sieht es als "gar füglich" an, wenn auf einer Tenuta mit

Beispiel 6.

45 Man beachte die Nuance, durch die sich die Parallelstellen ("bedächtlich" – "langsamen") hier inhaltlich voneinander unterscheiden.

46 Im *Collegium Hudemanno* wird der Terminus "Ribattuta" noch nicht verdeutscht. Spiess spricht von einer "wieder Zuruckschlagung" und verwendet für "Ribattuta" auch den Ausdruck "Repercussion" (cf. Anmerkung 47). Mattheson vermißt in den musiktheoretischen Publikationen die Beschreibung der Ribattuta und greift deshalb indirekt u.a. Walther an.

einer Ribattuta begonnen wird[47] und diese Manier schließlich in einen Triller mündet. Da hierbei die Notenwerte der Ribattuta "allmählig" immer kleiner werden, verwischt sich der Übergang zum Triller. (Beispiel 6).

"Groppo"

Mattheson berichtet lediglich über den Gebrauch und die Etymologie[48] dieser Verzierung. Auf speziellere Angaben verzichtet er und verweist im *Vollkommenen Capellmeister* auf seine Notenbeispiele[49] (Beispiel 7): Nach diesen Exempeln besteht ein Groppo aus acht Tönen[50]. Auch Mattheson unterteilt diese Manier

Beispiel 7.

47 Spiess (*Tractatus musicus*, 156) betont, daß dies "gemeiniglich" geschähe: "Tenuta . . . fanget gemeiniglich an mit einer Ribattuta, Repercussion, oder wieder Zuruckschlagung, und endiget sich gar wohl mit einem Trillo". Das Notenbeispiel (p. 159) stimmt mit Matthesons Exempel überein.

48 Den Terminus "Groppo" leitet Mattheson im *Capellmeister* von "Grappo" (= "Traube") her und übersetzt ihn mit "Knauff in Trauben-Gestalt". Im *Collegium Hudemanno* wird "Groppo" noch mit "Waltzung" verdeutscht. Demgegenüber bemerkt Mattheson im *Capellmeister*: "Ich kan nicht begreiffen, wie es möglich sey, daß dieses Wort, Groppo, im Welschen eine Waltze oder Kugel bedeuten könne; ob es gleich Printz, Walther und viele andre in ihren Büchern so auslegen". In Walthers *Praecepta* (Ausgabe Benary, p. 48) werden für "Groppo" auch die deutschen Ausdrücke "Knoten" und "Knopf" genannt.

49 Die Beispiele fehlen im *Collegium Hudemanno*.

50 Nur für diese – aus acht Noten bestehende – auf- bzw. absteigende Figur läßt Walther (*Lexicon*) die Ausdrücke "Kugel" und "Waltze" gelten. Er betont jedoch, daß ein Groppo sich gewöhnlich aus vier Noten zusammensetze: "Groppo, oder Gruppo, . . . bestehet ordinairement aus vier Achteln oder Sechzehntheilen, deren erstes und drittes in einerley Tone, das zweyte und vierdte aber in verschiedenen Tonen sich befinden". Die betreffenden Notenbeispiele in Walthers *Praecepta* (Ausgabe Benary, p. 120s.) bestätigen diese Regel. Walther hat die Exempel von J. G. Ahle (*Musicalisches Herbst-Gespräch*, 1699, p. 9ss.) übernommen. Auch Printz (*Musica modulatoria*, 1678, 48, und Compedium musicae, 1689, 48) sicht als Charakteristikum dieser Manier die aus 4 Noten bestehende Figur an. Häufig heißt

zweifach[51]: Im ersten Fall ("Mit einem Groppo hinauf") folgen auf
eine absteigende Sekunde zwei aufsteigende Sekunden; eine Sequenz
dieser Figur im Terzabstand schließt sich an. Der zweite Fall ("Mit
einem Groppo herunter") stellt die Umkehrung des ersten dar.

Zur Zeit des *Collegium Hudemanno* und des *Vollkommenen Capellmeisters* hatte diese Verzierung nicht mehr die frühere Bedeutung, wie aus den beiden Werken deutlich hervorgeht. Mattheson
äußert sich jedoch nicht negativ über die "Groppen", sondern wendet
sich nur dagegen, wenn sie fast ausschließlich als "Cadentzen"[52]
erscheinen[53]: "Wir dürffen uns in diesem Stücke eben an den Ort
nicht binden, sondern können die Groppen theils ausserordentlich,
als einen blossen zufälligen Zierrath, theils förmlich oder wesentlich
gar wol mit in die Melodie bringen, und gantze Läuffe daraus bilden:
welche keinen geringen Wol-Laut mit sich führen, falls die
Leidenschafft, so man ausdrücken will, dergleichen Dreh- und Wendungen vergönnet"[54] (cf. *Capellmeister*, 115s., und *Collegium
Hudemanno*, 14s.).

"Circolo mezzo"

Unter einem "Circolo mezzo", auch: "Halb-Circkel"[55], versteht Mattheson eine Manier, die "etwa um die Helffte kleiner, als der Groppo"
ist. Während andere Autoren diese Verzierung als eine viertönige
Figur darstellen[56], legt Mattheson sich in dieser Weise nicht genau
fest. (Notenbeispiel 8.)

Im Beispiel 8a setzt der Halbcirckel sich aus zwei absteigenden
Sekunden und einer aufsteigenden Sekunde zusammen. Die

---

aber die von Mattheson und anderen als "Circolo mezzo" bezeichnete Manier
"Groppo" oder "Gruppo": bei G. Caccini (*Le nuove musiche*, 1601), Praetorius
(*Syntagma musicum* III, 236) oder bei Falck (*Idea boni cantoris*, 100s.).

51 Die Bezeichnungen "Groppo ascendente" und "Groppo descendente" (cf. Walther,
Lexicon) oder "Groppo. Ascendens" und "Groppo. Remittens" (cf. Spiess, *Tractatus musicus*, 159) verwendet Mattheson nicht.

52 D.h. als Verzierungen an den Schlüssen der Kompositionen (*Capellmeister*, p. 116).

53 Mattheson kritisiert in diesem Punkt namentlich die früheren Sänger, wie man aus
dem *Collegium Hudemanno* ersehen kann.

54 Auch hier unterstreicht Mattheson die Abhängigkeit der Verzierungskunst von der
Affektenlehre.

55 Ferner kommt die Schreibweise "Halbcirckel" vor.

56 Cf. etwa Printz (*Musica modulatoria*, 49), Ahle (*Musicalisches Herbst-Gespräch*),
Walther (*Lexicon*) und Spiess (*Tractatus musicus*, 156, 159, Beispiel 11). Für diese
Verzierung werden auch folgende Bezeichnungen gebraucht: "Groppo" bzw.
"Gruppo" (cf. Fußn.50), "Double" (cf. Couperin), "cadence" (cf. J. S. Bach, *Clavier-
Büchlein vor W. Fr. Bach*, 1720).

Beispiel 8.

Halbcirckel im Beispiel 8b bestehen jeweils aus zwei auf- und zwei absteigenden Sekunden.

Nach Matthesons Auffassung wird ein Circolo mezzo am besten bei den Kadenzen angebracht[57]; außerdem kann diese Verzierung aber auch an andern Stellen einer Komposition erscheinen[58], dann vor allem bei mehreren Tonrepetitionen[59], wie er ausdrücklich bemerkt (*Capellmeister*, 116s.)[60].

"Tirata"

Der Terminus "Tirata" bedeutet nach Matthesons Ansicht "Schuß oder Pfeilwurff" und nicht "Zug oder Strich[61] . . ., weil die Stimme nicht bloßhin gezogen oder gestrichen wird, sondern mit Macht herauf oder herunter schiesset, und ein gar schnelles Schleuffen, gemeiniglich in Pans Quint, auch wol in die Octav, doch seltener[,] anstellet"[62]. Mattheson beschreibt demnach die Tirata als eine Manier, bei der die Töne in gleicher Richtung relativ schnell aufeinanderfolgen[63]. (Beispiel 9.)

---

57 Beispiel 8a.   58 Beispiel 9b.   59 Beispiel 8b.
60 Über den "Circolo mezzo" fehlen im *Collegium Hudemanno* präzise Angaben.
61 Walther (*Lexicon*: "Tirata . . . bedeutet einen Zug oder Strich".)
62 An der Parallelstelle des *Collegium Hudemanno* wird ausschließlich ein Intervall genannt: die Quinte (auf- und abwärts).
63 Bereits Praetorius (*Syntagma musicum* III, 236) bemerkt: "Je geschwinder und schärffer nun diese Läufflein gemacht werden, doch also das man eine jede Noten recht rein hören und fast vernemen kan: Je besser und anmütiger es sein wird". Falck (*Idea boni cantoris*, 101) hat diesen Satz fast wörtlich übernommen. Auch T. B. Janowka (*Clavis ad thesaurum magnae artis musicae*, 1701, 286) bezeichnet die Tiraten als schnelle Läufe: "Tiratae dicuntur longi, ac celeres gradatim per claves sursum, aut deorsum facti cursus". In den *Praecepta* (p. 55 der Ausgabe von Benary) äußert Walther sich in gleicher Weise: "Tirate, Pfeile, sind lange und geschwinde Läufflein, welche gradatim auf und niederwarts gemachet werden". Dagegen finden sich in Walthers *Lexicon melodisch* entsprechende Figuren, die er trotz

Beispiel 9.

Wie Mattheson im *Vollkommenen Capellmeister* hervorhebt, wurde die Tirata "bey itzigen Zeiten" häufiger als der Halbcirckel angebracht. Die Wahl, ob und wann diese Verzierung angewendet werden kann, überläßt er den Interpreten. Vor einem Mißbrauch warnt Mattheson. In diesem Zusammenhang erwähnt er, daß die Komponisten "Vor kurtzer Zeit [*Collegium Hudemanno*: "Vor einiger Zeit"]" in die Tirata sehr "verliebt" gewesen seien und diese Manier oft notiert hätten (Beispiel 10.) (*Capellmeister*, 117, und *Collegium Hudemanno*, 15s.).

Beispiel 10.

Als "Tirate maggiori oder grosse Tiraten" bezeichnet Mattheson die Tiraten, die das Intervall einer Oktave ausfüllen[64]. Tirate piccole" bzw. "kleine Tiraten" nennt er die "Schleuffer", d.h. die Verzierungen, "welche aus der Tertz entweder hinauf oder herunter gezogen werden"; er beschreibt sie auch als "kleine Schüsse oder Tertzen-Würffe". (Beispiel 11.)

relativ großer Notenwerte ebenfalls zu den Tiraten zählt: "Tirata di Semiminime" (Notenanhang, Tab. XX, F. 8, A) und "Tirata di legature" (Notenanhang, Tab. XX, F. 8, B). Spiess (*Tractatus musicus*, 159, Notenbeispiele 12–14) unterteilt die Tiraten u.a. folgendermaßen: "Tirata. Tarda", "Tirate velocior", "Tirata velocissima". Die "Tirata, Tarda" und überhaupt alle sogenannten Tiraten, die aus verhältnismäßig großen Notenwerten bestehen, widersprechen der Mattthesonschen Definition dieser Manier.

64 Siehe unten Anmerkung 65.

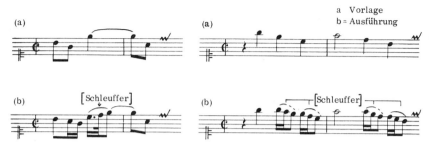

Beispiel 11.

Außer den eben erwähnten Termini für zwei Arten der Tirata begnügt Mattheson sich im übrigen mit einer Intervallangabe: z.B. "Tirata per 7" (Beispiel 13) (*Capellmeister*, 117f.)[65].

"Transitus" ("Durchgang")

In seiner Verzierungslehre beschränkt Mattheson die Termini "Transitus" und "Durchgang" auf die unbetonten Noten einer "aufgeschriebenen . . . einstimmigen Melodie"[66], die mit einem Sekundschritt erreicht und – in gleicher Richtung – wieder mit einem Sekundschritt verlassen werden[67]. Die Durchgänge sind in diesem Fall also bereits Bestandteile der Komposition. Aufgabe der Interpreten ist es, die Transitus entsprechend zu verzieren. Dies soll (nach Mattheson) bei einer Aufwärtsrichtung der betreffenden Sekunden ausschließlich "mit einem schnellen Triller und einer hurtigen Drehung [=Nachschlag]" geschehen. Wie wichtig diese Verzierung ist, unterstreicht Mattheson mit folgenden Worten: "Es ist ein solcher unentbehrlicher Zierrath, daß man ohne denselben schier keine Melodie annehmlich spielen oder singen kan". (Beispiel 12.)

---

65 Mattheson verzichtet in seinen Traktaten unter anderm auf folgende Termini, die bei Walther (*Lexicon*, hier abgekürzt: W) und Spiess (*Tractatus musicus*, 156, 159, Notenbeispiele 13 und 14, hier abgekürzt: S) vorkommen:
W: "Tirata mezza, oder mezza Tirata" (Intervalle: Quarte u. Quinte); S: "Tirata Mezza" (Intervall: ausschließlich Quinte).
W: "Tirata defectiva [lat.], Tirade defectueuse [gall.]" (Intervalle: Sexte u. Septime); S: keine Angaben.
W: "Tirata perfecta" (Intervall: Oktave); S: "Tirata perfetta" (Intervall: Oktave).
W: "Tirata aucta oder excedens" ("überschreitet die Grentzen der Octav um einige Noten"); S: keine Angaben.
66 Es erübrigt sich demnach, Dissonanzverhältnisse zwischen zwei oder mehreren Stimmen zu beachten. Cf. dagegen z.B. Walther (*Lexicon*): "Transitus [lat.], ein Durchgang; wenn nemlich die in arsi stehende Noten dissoniren."
67 Die Intervallangaben resultieren aus den Notenbeispielen.

"So genannter Durchgang"

"Dessen Trillender Zierrath"

Beispiel 12.

Bei den Durchgängen "herunterwärts" verlangt Mattheson keine
Triller. An ihrer Stelle bringt er in den ersten beiden Takten des
Beispiels 13b je einen "Vorschlag"[68] an, d.h. eine Manier, die er hier
für wirkungsvoller hält. (Capellmeister, 118f.; Beispiel 13.)

(a) "Grund-Noten vermeinter Durchgänge"[69]

(b) "Ihr Schmuck ohne Triller, herunterwärts"[70]

"Tirata per 7"

(a)

(b)

Halbcirckel

Beispiel 13.

68 Als "Vorschlag" bezeichnet Mattheson hier die Antizipation der Durchgangsnote.
69 "Da denn hiebey zu mercken stehet, daß es in den beiden ersten Täcten des
schlechten Ganges oder blossen Satzes der Grund-Noten allerdings nöthig sey,
kurtze Triller auf die mit dem obstehenden Sternlein bezeichneten durchgehenden
Klänge anzubringen; welches aber bey der Schmückung überflüßig fallen dürffte,
weil ein kleiner Vorschlag daselbst bessere Wirckung thut" (Capellmeister, 119).
70 Der letzte Takt (Beispiel 13b) ist nach Matthesons Angaben ergänzt worden.

"Mordant"[71]

Mattheson kennt von dieser Verzierung zwar verschiedene Spezies, beschreibt aber außer der "Acciacatur(a)" lediglich die Gesangsmanier[72].

Nach Matthesons Definition kann der Mordant nur so g e s u n g e n werden, "indem man den vorgeschriebenen Klang zwar erst, den unterliegenden halben oder gantzen Grad aber, nach Maaßgebung der Ton-Art, auf das schnelleste hernach, als obs zu einer Zeit geschähe, berühret, und darauf mit eben solcher äussersten Geschwindigkeit wieder empor kömmt, so, daß diese drey Anschläge gleichsam einen eintzigen Schall verursachen, der sich nur ein klein wenig zu zögern, an etwas aufzuhalten, oder sanfft zu stossen scheinet".

Mattheson betont, daß man diese Verzierung "ziemlich unvollkommen" in Noten[werten] ausdrücken könne: In seinen Beispielen wählt er für die ersten beiden Noten dieser Manier Vierundsechzigstel; sie stehen aber ebensowenig auf der "Tact-Rech-

Beispiel 14.

71 In der musikalischen Terminologie wird unter "Mordant" (bzw. "Beisser", "Moderant", "Mordens", "Mordentia") nicht nur eine dem Triller ähnliche Manier verstanden, sondern auch der Triller selbst. Cf. außer Praetorius, *Syntagma musicum* III, und Falck, *Idea boni cantoris*, auch Kuhnau (*Neue Clavier-Ubung* I, 1689, Vorrede). Janowka (*Clavis*, 78: "Mordens, vel mordentia est certa ludentis aut canentis trillae persimilis manira ac modus, excepto, quod mordens ad sui factionem, inferiorem vocem aut sonum adhibeat, cum ut contra trilla superiorem requirat." Den Kern dieser Definition bringt auch Walther (*Praecepta*, Ausgabe Benary, p. 38): "Mordens oder Mordentia . . .; welche Figur der Trillen fast ähnlich ist; außer, daß die Mordant zu ihrer expression allemahl ein Semitonium, oder einen gantzen Thon unterwarts haben will". Der Mordant bei Mattheson entspricht dem "pincé-simple" bei Couperin (*L'art de toucher le clavecin*, ²1717, Neuausgabe p. 15).
72 Auch nach Spiess (*Tractatus musicus*, 157) gehört der "Mordant" zu den "sowohl im Singen, als auf Instrumenten übliche[n] Manieren". Die meisten Theoretiker betrachten diese Verzierung nur als eine Instrumentalmanier. So sagt z.B. Majer

nung"[73] wie die hier vorkommenden Accente (*Capellmeister*, 119s.; Beispiel 14.).

"Acciacatur(a)"[74]

Im Gegensatz zu andern Theoretikern (z.B. Gasparini und Heinichen[75]) behandelt Mattheson diese Verzierung relativ kurz und beurteilt sie recht abfällig. Nach Mattheson (*Capellmeister*, 120) bedeutet "Acciacatura" nicht "Zerquetschung"[76] oder "Überfluß"[77], sondern "Verbindung". (Er leitet den Terminus her von "Accia" – "Bindfaden".) Wie Mattheson betont, ist die Acciacatur ein "Mordant im gantzen Grad". Er berichtet, daß (zur Zeit des *Capellmeisters*) diese Manier ausschließlich "auf dem Clavier im General-Baß bey vollen Griffen gebräuchlich" sei[78]. Mattheson macht auf folgendes besonders aufmerksam: Die Acciacatur verbindet zwar die Töne eines

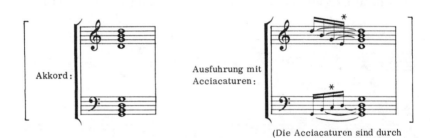

Akkord:

Ausfuhrung mit
Acciacaturen:

(Die Acciacaturen sind durch
Sterne ✳ gekennzeichnet.)

Beispiel 15.

(*Museum musicum*, 94): "Mordant. Eine auf Instrumenten gebräuchliche Manier". Die gleiche Aussage findet sich auch zu Beginn des Artikels "Mordant" in Walthers *Lexicon*: "Mordant [gall.], eine auf Instrumenten gebräuchliche Manier". In den *Praecepta* berührt Walther diesen Punkt dagegen nicht.

73 Die Autoren gehen hierbei nicht einheitlich vor: Die einen verfahren wie Mattheson und klammern die Werte der ersten beiden Noten dieser Verzierung aus der "Tact-Rechnung" aus (zum Beispiel Couperin, *L'art de toucher le clavecin*, Neuausgabe, p. 15), die anderen beziehen die betreffenden ersten beiden Notenwerte mit ein (etwa J. S. Bach, *Clavier- Büchlein vor W. Fr. Bach*, 1720).

74 Matthesons Schreibweise "Acciacatur" bzw. "Acciacatura" ist beibehalten worden, da die sonst übliche Form "Acciaccatura" bei ihm nicht vorkommt.

75 F. Gasparini, *L'armonico pratico al cimbalo*, 1708, 6. und 9. Kapitel; Heinichen, *Der General-Baß*, 535ss.

76 Cf. Heinichen, *Der General-Baß*, 535.

77 Cf. Walther (*Lexicon*, Stichwort: "Acciaccatura").

78 Demgegenüber nennt W. Georgii (*Die Verzierungen in der Musik*, 1957, 60) auch die Manier eine "Acciaccatura", die früher "Coulé" (Walther) oder "Tierce coulée" (Couperin) hieß.

Akkordes[79] enger miteinander, zwischen die sie eingeschoben wird, aber sie ist "offt an vieler Unreinigkeit in der Harmonie des Spielens Ursache"[80] (Capellmeister, 120; Beispiel 15.)

Schlußwort

Wie schon am Anfang dieses Beitrages hervorgehoben wurde, verfaßte Mattheson keinen ausschließlich der musikalischen Verzierungskunst gewidmeten Traktat, da er gerade in diesem Bereich einen zu schnellen Wandel registrierte. Er begnügte sich – abgesehen von seinen verstreuten Äußerungen über die Manieren – damit, in zwei Haupt-Stücken des *Vollkammenen Capellmeisters* und an den Parallelstellen der Vorläufer näher hierauf einzugehen. Durch Vergleiche dieser Texte konnten interessante wörtliche und inhaltliche Übereinstimmungen aufgezeigt, aber gelegentlich auch nicht unbedeutende Divergenzen festgehalten und Ergänzungen vorgenommen werden. Dabei wurden – sogar innerhalb des *Vollkommenen Capellmeisters* – Unterschiede deutlich, die durch eine zeitlich differierende Entstehung zu erklären ist. Auf die einschlägige Literatur einiger anderer Musiktheoretiker konnte in diesem Rahmen nur am Rande eingegangen werden.

Abschließend sei nochmals vermerkt: Mattheson achtete besonders darauf, daß geeignete (bzw. zu dem jeweiligen Zeitpunkt noch geeignete) Manieren maßvoll und "wohl" (gut) angebracht wurden. Weil aber das Idealbild, das Mattheson entwarf, nicht oder nur selten realisiert wurde, übte er auch auf diesem Gebiet immer wieder Kritik. So verurteilte er z.B. in seinem Spätwerk *Plus ultra* I, p. 70s) "die unmäßigen Schnörkel, à la moderne, die erzwungenen Cadenzen, all' italiana, und kurz, alle am unrechten Orte angebrachte überhäuffte kleine und große Künsteleyen der Kehle und der Instrumente, sowohl in Concerten, als auf Schaubühnen". Die damals "herrschende Mode" und "der alles bewundernde Unverstand" waren – nach Matthesons Ansicht – der Grund hierfür und für die dadurch hervorgerufenen negativen Gemütsbewegungen.

In diesem Zusammenhang kann noch ein Satz aus der Vorrede zu Matthesons Passionsoratorium *Der Blut-rünstige Kelter-Treter* (1721, §13) angefügt werden: "Schmuck muß die Music haben; aber keine Schmincke".

---

79 Mattheson sagt: "die Vollstimmigkeit der Clavier-Griffe".
80 Mattheson bringt kein Notenbeispiel.

PART III

Mattheson and his contemporaries

13

Der vollkommene Capellmeister as a stimulus to J. S. Bach's late fugal writing

GREGORY G. BUTLER

Vancouver, British Columbia

In Part Six of the first volume of Lorenz Christoph Mizler's *Musikalische Bibliothek*,[1] which can be dated between October and the middle of November 1738,[2] the following announcement appears under the heading "Musikalische Neuigkeiten":

HAMBURG

Herr Mattheson's Vollkommener Capellmeister, a writing which a great many people discerning in music have been awaiting eagerly for quite some time, is now actually "under the press" in Leipzig, and will make its appearance for the coming Easter fair without fail for the delight and profit of music lovers.

It has naturally been assumed that Johann Mattheson's *Vollkommener Capellmeister*, because it was published by Christian Herold in Hamburg, was also printed there. However, it is clear from the above announcement that the crowning achievement of Germany's leading music theorist was being printed in Leipzig to appear for the Easter Fair of 1739.[3]

Mizler was not exaggerating when he stated that the work was "eagerly awaited," for it was generally felt that this latest treatise of the Hamburg music theorist would be the most important theoretical work to appear in Germany in its time. The interest in Leipzig, where the work was in press, must have been particularly keen, for the

1 *Neu eröffnete Musikalische Bibliothek* I 6 (Leipzig, 1738), 97–8.
2 Part Five is dated October 1738; the preface to Volume One, of which Part Six is the last part, is dated 14 November 1738.
3 The anonymous printer in question may well be Adam Heinrich Holle (b. 1710), who had learned the printing trade from his father in Hamburg. Holle had set up his own shop in Leipzig in 1736 next door to the Breitkopf establishment, The Golden Bear, and married into the Breitkopf family in 1737. Mattheson may have known Holle from his Hamburg days. At any rate, Holle, if not the actual printer of Mattheson's treatise, could certainly have been the intermediary contact between Mattheson and other Leipzig printers, foremost among them Bernhard Christoph Breitkopf, with whom Holle had a close relationship. See O. von Hase, *Breitkopf und Härtel*, 5th ed. (Wiesbaden, 1968) I, 65.

review by the Societät der Musicalischen Wissenschaften of the first chapter, which had been published in advance, appeared immediately upon its publication (Mizler, I/6, 76–85). J. S. Bach was eventually to become a member of the society and was very close to its activities (Mizler, who founded it, was a pupil of his), and he must to some degree have shared this interest, particularly in light of Mattheson's treatment of him in print during the 1730s.

Up until 1731, Mattheson's few references in his treatises to Bach (with the exception of his celebrated criticism of Bach's declamation in 1725; *Critica musica* II, 368) had been favorable, if not actually laudatory. In 1730, Mattheson's positive disposition toward Bach suffered a shock, administered not by Bach himself but by one Gottfried Benjamin Hancke. In passing judgment on Mattheson's ability as a keyboard player, Hancke let slip the unfortunate comment that "Bach will play Mattheson into a sack and out again."[4] Now Mattheson was not without his share of vanity and this ill-judged comment must have rankled with him. Beginning in 1731, Mattheson leveled his vindictive pen at Bach. In his *Große General-Baß-Schule* (I, 344–5) he criticized the recently published Partitas for their difficulty and compared Bach's "künstliches Setzen" unfavorably with his own "singbare Sachen." In the same treatise, Mattheson had also made his third and last call to Bach for biographical information for his *Ehrenpforte*.[5] That both his previous appeals had met with silence must have irked Mattheson further. Six years later, in his *Kern melodische Wissenschafft*, Mattheson, in much the same vein, referred to "der künstliche Bach" (p. 147). This line of criticism is remarkably similar in nature to that of Bach's former pupil Johann Adolph Scheibe, and it is perhaps not surprising that it was with this same treatise that Mattheson became involved in the Scheibe–Bach controversy by publishing as a supplement[6] to the treatise a letter of Scheibe's continuing the attack on Bach. It is doubtful that before this time Bach took much notice of Mattheson's criticisms, but his hostility must surely have been aroused by Mattheson's apparent collusion with Scheibe and his further publicizing of the whole issue.

Being on close terms with both Mizler and the Leipzig printers Krügner and Breitkopf, Bach must have been aware that Mattheson's latest treatise was in press in Leipzig in the fall of 1738, and he would

---

4 *Poetischer Staarstecher* (Breslau and Leipzig, 1730), 111 f. Mattheson counterattacked in his *General-Baß-Schule* I, 444.
5 *General-Baß-Schule* I, 167. The first two appeals had been made in 1717 and 1719.
6 *Gültige Zeugnisse über die jüngste Matthesonische-musikalische Kern-schrifft* (Hamburg, 1738), 11.

probably have been kept informed by Mizler of references to him in the treatise. In fact, I would suggest that Bach himself read certain chapters of *Der vollkommene Capellmeister*, namely those on counterpoint, as early as fall of 1738. In the following study I shall present evidence that supports this suggestion.

Above all, the direct appeal made to him by Mattheson in the section of the treatise on counterpoint (p. 441) must have caught Bach's attention:

Of double fugues with three subjects, there is, as far as I know, nothing else in print but my own work under the name, *Die wolklingende Fingersprache*, Parts one and two (1735, 1737), which I, out of modesty, would commend to no one. On the contrary, I would much rather see something of the same sort published by the famed Herr Bach in Leipzig, who is a great master of the fugue. In the meantime, this lack exposes abundantly, not only the weakened state and the decline of well-grounded contrapuntists on the one hand, but on the other hand, the lack of concern of today's ignorant organists and composers about such instructive matters.

In order to appreciate the effect such a passage would have had on Bach, we must place it in the context of what was, by this time, the fairly intense musical rivalry between Hamburg and Leipzig – theoretically, between the "Ms of the North and South," Mattheson and Mizler, and compositionally, between Scheibe and Bach. In light of the Mattheson–Scheibe alliance, Bach, in his somewhat beleaguered state, can be expected to have taken Mattheson's appellation for him of "Fugenmeister" as epithetical in intent. Whether he had seen Mattheson's published keyboard collections or not, the show of false modesty over them and the obituary for counterpoint by this (as far as Bach was concerned) undistinguished composer of keyboard music must have rankled with Bach. Both of Mattheson's derogatory references to "today's ignorant organists" and to "the weakened state and the decline of well-grounded contrapuntists," in this context, would surely have been taken as insults by Bach and his circle. Bach must have felt compelled to respond to Mattheson's almost taunting call. In the fall of 1738 when he would have read this passage, Bach had a ready-made opportunity to expose Mattheson's death knell for counterpoint as premature and presumptuous. Bach's *Clavier-übung* III, for which the engraving was nearing completion, could serve both as a published musical rebuttal to Scheibe's criticisms[7] and as a response to Mattheson's call.

7 That this was, in fact, the case is clear from Mizler's defense of Bach in the first written review of the work, in Mizler, *Musikalische Bibliothek* II 1–2 (Leipzig, 1740), 156 f.

GREGORY G. BUTLER

My recent research on the original print of *Clavier-Übung* III[8] has brought to light evidence[9] that points to the concluding Fuga *a* 5, BWV 552/2, as having been among the last pieces in the collection to be completed, and there is good reason to believe that this fugue, along with the other works in this last compositional layer, may have been composed as late as spring of 1739. No other fugue of Bach's quite resembles this one in its structure, and it is not surprising that its classification has, for many years, been a source of contention. Is it a double or a triple fugue? In fact, it is a double fugue with three subjects as specified by Mattheson, that is, a fugue in which there are three distinct subjects and in which the first subject combines in double counterpoint with each of the two other subjects but never with both. I am suggesting, then, that the final form of this fugue and specific contrapuntal combinative procedures employed in it are a direct consequence of Mattheson's call to Bach.

Are there aspects of Mattheson's contrapuntal theory itself which may have exerted a demonstrable influence on Bach's subsequent fugal writing in the early 1740s? In a comparative stylistic analysis of certain of the fugues in strict style from *Das wohltemperirte Clavier* II and the first five Contrapuncti from *Die Kunst der Fuge*, one particularly striking feature is Bach's use of various contrapuntal *oblighi*, which help to impart to these fugues their characteristic severity. There is a notable similarity between the examples in Mattheson's lengthy discussion of contrapuntal oblighi in Chapter 22 of *Der vollkommene Capellmeister* and Bach's treatment of the same oblighi in the group of fugues mentioned above. Mattheson's discussion is derived almost verbatim from Part One of Angelo Berardi's *Documenti armonici* (1687), a borrowing that Mattheson readily acknowledges in his treatise. The only major differences are Mattheson's inclusion of a number of oblighi additional to Berardi's original list and his supplying of his own musical examples. In Examples 1 through 6 are given in each instance Mattheson's musical examples for seven of the oblighi followed by parallel examples selected from the fugal sample of Bach's referred to above.

In *contrapunto alla zoppa*,[10] a rhythmic obligo, the counterpoint to the subject limps, that is, is syncopated, employing the same rhyth-

---

8 "New Research on J. S. Bach's *Dritter Teil der Klavierübung*," read at the national meeting of the American Musicological Society, Minneapolis, 1978. An expanded version of this paper as a monograph is in preparation.
9 Briefly stated, this evidence is based on paper studies and studies of the engraving.
10 *Capellmeister*, 417. Mattheson comments here that this obligo is "considered to be artful in the so-called alla breve style." This is important, for the works in the fugal

296

mic figure repeatedly. The counterpoint in the example taken from the Bach fugue differs rhythmically only in that Mattheson's quarter notes have become pairs of eighth notes, thus emphasizing the long-held syncopated notes. These syncopated notes are further highlighted because of the dissonances they create with the notes of the subject. (Example 1.)

Example 1a. Mattheson, *Contrapunto alla zoppa*, p. 417

Example 1b. Bach, *WTC* II, Fuga XXIII, mm. 5–7

Two of Mattheson's oblighi, *contrapunto alla diritta* and *di salto* (*Capellmeister*, 417–18), in which the notes of the counterpoint move exclusively by step and by leap respectively, are problematic, since, especially in the case of the former, they are contrapuntal commonplaces and so their deliberate use as oblighi is difficult to substantiate. Furthermore, compositionally they are excessively limiting since a good counterpoint should employ a judicious and tasteful mixture of both steps and leaps. Nevertheless, I have given what appears to be a deliberate use of *contrapunto alla diritta* in a fugue of Bach's. Here Bach stresses the obligo by further restricting himself almost exclusively to melodic progression by half step. Notice that Bach, never slavish, does not adhere to the excessive stricture of this

sample I refer to are written almost exclusively in the *alla breve* style or *stile antico*. It is significant in this regard that Christoph Wolff considers counterpoint *per syncopationes* as one of the stylistic determinants of *stile antico* writing. See his *Der stile antico in der Musik Johann Sebastian Bachs* (Wiesbaden, 1968), 126.

obligo throughout but slips in the one leap at the beginning of
measure 8. (Example 2.)

Example 2a. Mattheson, *Contrapunto alla diritta*, p. 418

Example 2b. Bach, *KdF*, Contrapunctus 3, mm. 5–8

In the case of *contrapunto puntato* (ibid., 418–19), the adherence to
the same dotted-note figure in the counterpoint, the example gives
only the first appearance of this obligo in Bach's *Kunst der Fuge* but it
appears subsequently as a sort of pervasive obligo. (Example 3.)

Example 3a. Mattheson, *Contrapunto puntato*, p. 418

Example 3b. Bach, *KdF*, Contrapunctus 2, mm. 5–8

In *contrapunto fugato* (*Capellmeister*, 420) the same melodic fragment, often derived from the subject, is separated by rests and

repeated over and over at different pitch levels so as to simulate fugal entries. Notice how complex the example taken from the Bach fugue is. The repeated fragment (in this case the first three notes of the subject) appears syncopated in a second counterpoint and inverted in the answer form. (Example 4.)

Example 4a. Mattheson, *Contrapunto fugato*, p. 420

Example 4b. Bach, WTC II, Fuga XIV, mm. 8–11

Contrapunto d'un sol passo (ibid., 420), like *contrapunto fugato*, is a melodic obligo in which the same melodic fragment is repeated at the same pitch. Notice how similar the treatment of this obligo is in the two examples from Bach fugues. Particularly in the second example, the pervasive use of this obligo adds to the almost mesmeric static quality so characteristic of the piece. (Example 5.)

Example 5a. Mattheson, *Contrapunto d'un sol passo*, p. 420

299

Example 5b. Bach, WTC II, Fuga XXII, mm. 67–8

Example 5c. Bach, KdF, Contrapunctus 4, mm. 108–9.

Contrapunto sincopato (ibid., 422) is really a type of close canon with the entry of the comes at a time interval such that it is syncopated with the dux. The striking example from Contrapunctus 5 of Die Kunst der Fuge is, in some respects, very similar to Mattheson's example. (Example 6.)

It is interesting that the occurrence of these contrapuntal oblighi[11] in fugues by Bach is limited to a fairly small fugal sample. A logical explanation for this state of affairs may be that for Bach the overt use of these devices took the form of a limited experiment undertaken in a relatively short period soon after his encounter with Mattheson's chapter on double counterpoint in Der vollkommene Capellmeister.

Example 6a. Mattheson, Contrapunto sincopato, p. 422

11 Unlike Berardi, Mattheson also includes augmentation and diminution of the subject as oblighi. Capellmeister, 417.

Example 6b. Bach, *KdF, Contrapunctus* 4, mm. 107–14

The date of composition of the fugues in this sample from *Das wohltemperirte Clavier* II might then be clarified on the basis of the stylistic evidence presented above, which would argue for a date not before 1739 and probably not after 1740, with 1739 being the more likely date – a date not inconsistent with Breckoff's findings.[12] As for the early *Contrapuncti* of *Die Kunst der Fuge*, watermark dating of the autograph (Berlin, Deutsche Staatsbibliothek, Bach Mus. ms. P 200) has already pushed the date of the earliest compositions back possibly to the mid-1740s.[13] My hypothesis of a relatively short period of experimentation with contrapuntal *oblighi* would push this earliest date back even further to the period 1739–40. This dating would certainly influence our thinking about the early composition on *Die Kunst der Fuge* and raises interesting speculation concerning the interrelationship of the early *Contrapuncti* and the latest compositions in *Das wohltemperirte Clavier* II.

One might argue in response that Bach arrived at these contrapuntal *oblighi* independently as a consequence of his preoccupation with strict fugal writing at this time. Or, if one accepts the basic premise

---

12 For the dating of these pieces, see W. Breckoff, *Zur Entstehungsgeschichte des zweiten Wohltemperierten Klaviers von Johann Sebastian Bach* (Ph.D. diss., University of Tübingen, 1965), 74, 77, 81, 82, and 84–92.

13 See D. Seaton, "The Autograph: An Early Version of the 'Art of Fugue' ", in "Bach's 'Art of Fugue': An Examination of the Sources," in: *Current Musicology* 19 (1975), 47–77, on p. 55.

posed above, one might also argue that it was Berardi[14] and not Mattheson who was Bach's source. However, it can hardly be sheer coincidence that these contrapuntal constructs appear for the first time[15] in fugues from *Das wohltemperirte Clavier* II, written in all likelihood just at the time when Bach would have encountered them in Mattheson's treatise. Further, there is no proof whatsoever that Bach had read Berardi's work, whereas it seems more than likely, given the circumstances outlined at the beginning of this study, that he did read the Mattheson treatise, or parts of it, sometime in the fall of 1738.

A close study of the subjects used by Mattheson in his chapters on double counterpoint and multiple fugue suggests another intriguing stimulus for *Die Kunst der Fuge*. Example 7 gives three incipits from Mattheson subjects from these two chapters. Their strong resemblance to various versions of the principal subject of *Die Kunst der Fuge* is certainly striking. I believe Bach's subject, although it clearly exhibits ingenious adaptation on Bach's part, to be at least in part derivative. Although I would be the last to claim that the Mattheson subjects are the sole source for the subject from *Die Kunst der Fuge*,[16] I would suggest that the Mattheson subjects could well have been an important contributing stimulus.

Example 7a. Mattheson, p. 418

Example 7b. Mattheson, p. 428

14 J. G. Walther, Bach's cousin and close friend, is known to have had theoretical works by Berardi in his collection. See Wolff, 29, n. 35.

15 There would seem to be similar contrapuntal constructs in earlier compositions by Bach. One occurrence that immediately comes to mind is the counterpoint to the last two statements of the ground bass in the Passacaglia and Fugue BWV 582, which by all accounts would seem to constitute *contrapunto d'un sol passo*. However, here we are dealing not with an obligo but rather with an elaborated multiple pedal point used to create a climactic effect at a specific point calling for its use, at the conclusion of the passacaglia.

16 This is also a fairly common incipit in many keyboard ricercars in earlier, mainly Italian, sources.

Example 7c. Mattheson, p. 429

Now let us turn to what seems to be a further important stimulus of Mattheson's treatise for Bach, musical terminology. In particular, two terms occurring in Bach sources that are also found in Mattheson's treatise suggest themselves, namely "contrapunctus" and "evolutio." The latter occurs in the tenth of the fourteen *Verschiedene Canones*, BWV 1087[17] (the so-called Goldberg canons), and the former, of course, in *Die Kunst der Fuge*. It is interesting that both terms appear as titles in Dietrich Buxtehude's two settings of the chorale *Mit Fried und Freud ich fahr' dahin* in his *Fried- und Freudenreiche Hinfahrt*, BuxWV 76, published in 1674.[18] In the Buxtehude print we have Contrapunctus I and Contrapunctus II, each followed by its Evolutio in which all parts are inverted contrapuntally and, in Evolutio II, melodically as well. Understandably, it has been argued that this print is the source for Bach's use of the term "contrapunctus" in *Die Kunst der Fuge*, yet there is no evidence that Bach ever encountered the Buxtehude print, although it is not impossible.[19] However, as yet no one has ever considered a theoretical treatise on music as a possible source for these terms. It is significant that both appear in Mattheson's chapter on double counterpoint and elsewhere in *Der vollkommene Capellmeister* (p. 124, 246, and 415 ff.) although Mattheson most often employs the German and Italian equivalents.

In the case of contrapunctus, one can certainly not claim Mattheson as the source in which Bach first encountered this term. He must have come across it earlier in Fux's *Gradus ad Parnassum* (1725), of which he owned a copy. In Fux, however, it is employed in conjunction with cantus firmus as subject whereas Mattheson applies it exclusively to fugues. I believe therefore that it was not the term but Mattheson's fugal application and his concept of it that aroused Bach's interest.

In this connection, the definition of the term "contrapunctus" as understood by Bach must be reexamined and reassessed. Mattheson

---

17 See J. S. Bach, *Clavier-übung II und IV, Vierzehn Kanons*, Neue Ausgabe sämtlicher Werke, Serie V2 (Kassel, 1977), 120.

18 For the latest discussion of this source, see K. J. Snyder, "Dietrich Buxtehude's Studies in Learned Counterpoint," in: *JAMS* 33 (1980), 544–64, on p. 547ff.

19 Walther knew of and had probably seen the print. See his *Musicalisches Lexicon* (Leipzig, 1732), 123.

defines it quite literally as *Gegensatz* (*Capellmeister*, 422), a melody set against the *Punkt* or *Satz*, ideally in invertible counterpoint so as to constitute a *Doppelcontrapunkt*. Musicologists have tended to view the term "contrapunctus" as it applies to *Die Kunst der Fuge* in a rather narrow, purely generic manner to refer to a strict fugal type. Is it not possible, however, that Bach viewed it essentially in the same light as Mattheson, that is, as a contrapuntal procedure in which the dominant elements are the contrapunctus – the melody which is set against the punctus or principal subject – and, just as important, the inversions in double counterpoint at various intervals that arise from these combinations? In the first four Contrapuncti of *Die Kunst der Fuge*, various oblighi are featured as contrapuncti. In the next three we have further oblighi involving the subject itself as contrapunctus (stretto, diminution, and augmentation). In the multiple fugues, new subjects are featured as contrapuncti. In the mirror fugues, the contrapunctus expands to include all voices, extending the length of the piece, since the entire fugue in all voices is invertible. Finally, the quadruple fugue is in some ways a summation as well as a culmination, for it features a number of the preceding interpretations of contrapunctus. It is significant that both of the above-mentioned terms appear for the first time in works by Bach that stem from the early to mid-1740s, just after he would have read the chapters where they are discussed in the Mattheson treatise. It seems likely that Mattheson is Bach's source, certainly for the term "evolutio" and for his concept of the term "contrapunctus."

Thus far this study has pointed to what I believe to be specific and fairly immediate stimuli from Mattheson's treatise for particular fugal works of Bach. Are there other, more general and long-range, effects of the treatise on Bach's late fugal writing?

First, Mattheson puts great emphasis on multiple fugues in his direct appeal to Bach and, as has been suggested, this had an immediate effect on Bach. However, it is interesting to note that of the settings composed for *Clavier-Übung* III from the final layer, settings which must date from late 1738, three take the form of multiple fugues – the *Fuga a 5*, BWV 552/2, already referred to, the *Fuga super Jesus Christus unser Heiland*, BWV 689, and the *Fughetta super Allein Gott in der Höh sei Ehr'*, BWV 677. Among the late fugues in *Das wohltemperirte Clavier* II, two, those in F-sharp minor and B major, are multiple fugues exhibiting widely differing treatments. Five Contrapuncti from *Die Kunst der Fuge* are multiple fugues. Bach seems not to have occupied himself unduly before that time with the writing of multiple fugues for the keyboard. In the same context, could it not have been Mattheson's discussion of Johann Krieger's quadruple fugue (*Capellmeister*, 444) that suggested to Bach the inclusion of a fugue with four subjects, the "unfinished" quadruple fugue from *Die Kunst der Fuge*?

Further, we know that at just that time Bach was compiling preludes and fugues. Could this not have been a response to Mattheson's strong public indictment of the state of the art of counterpoint in Germany at the time with its attendant appeal to Bach, and also a spur contributing to Bach's completion of his second set of twenty-four preludes and fugues in all the major and minor keys soon after? Could it not also possibly have been one of the considerations prompting Bach's projection of a published collection exploring all aspects of fugal treatment, his *Die Kunst der Fuge*, which he began soon after?[20]

In conclusion, then, I believe that Johann Mattheson's *Vollkommener Capellmeister* acted as an important stimulus for Bach's fugal writing in the period around 1740 and served as a source for contrapuntal techniques, terminology, and concepts. There is a tendency, especially when considering the highly abstract contrapuntal works of Bach's last decade, to see these works as highly personal and internalized creations and therefore as products relying little on external stimuli. This is a distorted view. Bach continued to be open to diverse external influences not only through the music of other composers but also through the writing of music theorists such as Mattheson. Bach scholars have interpreted far too rigidly the statement that appears in his obituary that he did not "occupy himself with deep theoretical speculations on music, but was all the stronger in the practice of the art."[21] The key words here are surely "speculations" and "practice." This dichotomy would suggest that Bach did not reject theoretical discussions focusing on practical aspects of composition. It is precisely such practicality that informs almost all of Mattheson's *Vollkommene Capellmeister*, certainly those chapters dealing with counterpoint, fugue, and canon, the chapters which would have caught and held Bach's interest.

20 It is interesting that Mattheson presents and discusses a canon of Bach's (the *Canon à 4. dédié à Monsieur Houdemann*, BWV 1074, see *Capellmeister*, 412–13) in his chapter on canon, and it seems likely that Bach would have read this chapter as well. Again, could it not have been a contributing factor to Bach's growing interest in canon, which gave rise to a host of canonic compositions in the 1740s?
21 This translation in *The Bach Reader*, ed. H. T. David and A. Mendel (New York, 1966), 224.

14

Mattheson and Handel: their musical relations in Hamburg
J. MERRILL KNAPP
Princeton, New Jersey

The subject of the musical influence of one composer upon another is fraught with danger because, unless there are specific models to point to, comments end up by being generalities that cannot easily be proved. Yet the history of music and the biographies of great composers would be greatly reduced in size and importance if there were no reference to "influences" from one generation to the next. The best historians do try to back up their allegations with points of substance: the shape of melodies, harmonic structure, similar rhythmic figures, fondness for certain cadences, text settings that match each other, prevalence of formal patterns, and many other musical matters. But there is always uneasiness because if a composer has marked originality and genius he is really a law unto himself and his individuality is generally stamped on his best pages, no matter what the similarities in style and substance from teachers and older contemporaries may be.

Thoughts of this nature inevitably come to mind when we consider the musical relationship of Mattheson to Handel. The facts about their association in Hamburg are probably about as clear as they ever will be, admittedly as told by Mattheson himself[1] but substantiated to some extent in Mainwaring's biography of Handel, which Mattheson translated into German in 1761 at the age of eighty, with caustic comments and footnotes concerning Mainwaring's veracity and judgment.[2]

For the most part, what Mattheson writes rings true even if he did get mixed up in later life about some dates. Yet in order to remember with such exactitude that he and Handel went "out on the water"

---

1 *Ehrenpforte*, 93–101; 190–3.
2 J. Mainwaring, *G. F. Händel*, ed. B. Paumgartner (Zürich, 1947), after J. Mattheson's German ed. (Hamburg, 1761).

together (the Elbe or the Alster?) on 15 July 1703 and that they went to Lübeck on 17 August 1703 must indicate that he kept a diary and referred to it for at least some of these dates. He also had a right, even though his ego was always well developed, to react angrily to Mainwaring's slighting remarks about his abilities as a singer and his career in the Hamburg Opera. He did have a prominent and influential part in its development and spoke from personal knowledge, though many years later.

But the important thing for the purpose at hand is what he wrote about Handel the musician and what influence, he, Mattheson, four years Handel's senior, had upon the younger man. The well-known lines from the *Ehrenpforte* (1740) have been quoted often enough, but they must be repeated once again:

> He composed at that time very long, long arias and almost endless cantatas, poorly conceived and lacking in taste, though harmonically perfect; but soon his style took shape quite differently through the high school of opera.
>
> The organ was his strong point – he was better than Kuhnau at fugue and counterpoint, especially when improvising; but he knew very little about melody before he came to the Hamburg Opera. All of his pieces written in the style of Kuhnau, however, were highly melodic and singable, even those intended for instrumental performance. In the last century hardly anybody thought about melody; harmony was the only goal.
>
> At that time he took most of he meals at my dear father's house, and he gave me many hints on counterpoint. Since I rendered him no small service as regards the dramatic style, each hand may be said to have washed the other.[3]

There are also the comments Mattheson made about Handel in *Critica musica* (1722), which pertain more directly because they were written earlier:

> There is a world-famous man who, when he first came to Hamburg, knew almost nothing except how to compose fugues according to rules; imitations were as new to him as a foreign language, and as difficult. No one knows better

---

3 "Er setzte zu der Zeit sehr lange, lange Arien, und schier unendliche Cantaten, die doch nicht das rechte Geschicke oder den rechten Geschmack, ob wohl eine vollkommene Harmonie hatten; wurde aber bald, durch die hohe Schule der Oper, gantz anders zugestutzet.

Er war starck auf der Orgel; stärcker, als *Kuhnau*, in Fugen und Contrapuncten, absonderlich *ex tempore*; aber er wuste sehr wenig von der Melodie, ehe er in die Hamburgische Opern kam. Hergegen waren alle kuhnauische Sätze überaus melodisch und singbar; auch die zum Spielen eingerichtete. Es wurde im vorigen Seculo fast von keinem Menschen an die Melodie gedacht; sondern alles zielte auf die bloße Harmonie.

Die meiste Zeit ging er damahls bey meinem seligen Vater zu freiem Tische, und eröffnete mir dafür einige besondere Contrapunct-Griffe. Da ich ihm hergegen im dramatischen Styl keine geringe Dienste that, und eine Hand die andre wusch." *Ehrenpforte*, 93–4.

than I how he used to bring me his earliest opera scenes every evening for my opinion – and the trouble he had to conceal the pedant in himself.

Let no one be surprised that I learned from him just as he learned from me. *Docendo enim dicimus.*[4]

The emphasis here, if one may interpret, is that Handel, still inexperienced, was conservative in his style and had been taught by Zachau to write chiefly church cantatas. But he knew his counterpoint and his harmony. His melodies were not yet dramatically suitable for an opera, nor was his general style apt for the stage.

But Mattheson speaking is the young progressive, the man who had distinct ideas about what good melody should be and would expound his philosophy later in *Der vollkommene Capellmeister*. These included such guidelines as that melody must have something familiar in it for everyone and be limited in range (the singer speaks here); the French should be imitated more than the Italians; technical dexterity should be disguised; and conciseness is preferable to prolixity. With these points in mind, it is particularly interesting to compare the two closest sources that now exist for the two men's few years of association in Hamburg, namely the operas *Cleopatra* (1704)[5] and *Almira* (1705),[6] to see if Mattheson carried out his ideas as a young composer and whether Handel was influenced by them.

Before doing so it is best to review again the circumstances surrounding the two operas, particularly *Cleopatra*. Although we do not know how many times *Cleopatra* was performed during October, November, and December 1704, we know that it opened on 20 October; that the famous duel between Mattheson and Handel took place after the performance on 5 December; and that they were reconciled by 30 December when Mattheson attended a rehearsal of *Almira*. We know also, according to Mattheson, that he became tutor on 7 November to Cyril Wich, to whom Handel had been giving music lessons. Moreover, Handel, who had been playing second violin in the orchestra before this, became the harpsichord player for the opera

---

4 "Wie ein gewisser Weltberühmter Mann zum ersten mahl hier in Hamburg kam / wuste er fast nichts / als lauter regelmäßige Fugen / zu machen / und waren ihm die *Imitationes* so neu / als eine fremde Sprach / wurden ihm auch eben so saur. Mir ist es am besten bewust / wie er seine allererste Opera Scenen / weiß zu mir brachte / und alle Abend meine Gedanken darüber vernehmen wollte / welche Mühe es ihm gekostet / den Pedanten zu verbergen.

Hierüber darff sich niemand wundern Ich lernte von ihm; so wie er von mir. *Docendo enim dicimus. Critica musica* I, 243.

5 *Cleopatra*, ed. G. J. Buelow, in: *Das Erbe deutscher Musik* 69 (Mainz, 1975).

6 *Almira*, ed. F. Chrysander, in: *Ausgabe der Deutschen Händel Gesellschaft* (Leipzig, 1873).

while Mattheson, who sang the leading role of Antony, was onstage. After the death of Antony in the latter half of Act III, Mattheson was evidently accustomed to resuming his seat at the harpsichord as conductor and composer since there was about a half hour of playing time left in the opera.

While the quarrel between the two young men is not directly relevant to the topic (Mainwaring and Chrysander certainly distorted it), it might be said in passing and in defense of Mattheson that he had a perfect right to resume his position at the keyboard and had been doing so without incident during the previous run of the opera; Handel was probably jealous about Mattheson's having to a certain extent supplanted him with the Wich family in November; Handel had a temper; Mattheson was evidently already showing some signs of deafness, and a remark made by Handel to him during the performance may have been misunderstood; the theatrical atmosphere was an argumentative and quarrelsome one (Cannon emphasizes this point in his book)[7] – aside from the literary squabbles among the librettists; and Mattheson admits to having already had a duel with another musician who became an organist in London and then went off to America.[8]

The connection, then, between the two composers in *Cleopatra* was a close one. We know of very few other public performances by Handel in England when he was not directing or playing his own works, some opera pasticcios and perhaps an occasional anthem being the only ones. By virtue of his keyboard responsibility, he must have learned the work intimately, almost more than he would have, playing in the string section, for a Keiser opera.

Before embarking on musical comparisons, it is well to emphasize that both operas had similarities that were common to Hamburg opera of that period. The most striking element is the mixture of styles: French instrumental dances, Italian *da capo* arias, and German popular songs. For Mattheson in *Cleopatra* there is much less of the Italian element, largely because he was attempting to create a unified German style and because his libretto, by Feustking, was entirely in German. With *Almira*, which probably started as an Italian libretto by Pancieri for Venice in 1691 and went through several versions in Braunschweig and Weissenfels – largely for Keiser and then for Handel[9] – the text was macaronic in Italian and German, much more

7 Cannon, *Mattheson*, 27–8.   8 *Ehrenpforte*, 192.
9 R. Strohm, "Händel und seine italienischen Operntexte," in: *Händel Jahrbuch* (1975–6), 105.

like *Claudius*, Keiser's opera of 1703. The second factor is the prevalence of French dance movements, which had probably been introduced to Hamburg by Johann Kusser and others in the 1690s. Although there are more of these in *Cleopatra* than in *Almira*, the presence of dances in *Almira* – courante, bourrée, sarabande, minuet, rigaudon, rondeau in Act I and ballet in Act III – show the importance Handel also attached to this element in his score. The third common characteristic is the presence of a comic character who, as a servant, mocks his elders. In *Cleopatra* Dercetaeus, who is more cynical than comic, rushes in to retrieve Antony's sword after his suicide in Act III so that he can get a reward from Augustus, the emperor. He also nearly wrecks the tragic mood toward the end of the opera after Cleopatra's body has been found by Augustus and others, and Augustus asks if a physician might be called on to draw out the asp's poison so that she can be revived. Dercetaeus then sings a vulgar little song about knowing a good cathartic ("ein gut Clystier") that will purge the body when wives are sick. Perhaps this was thought necessary to relieve the tension and act as a transition to the happy last scene where the various lovers are united, but it is a violent and abrupt change from Cleopatra's moving death music. Tabarco in *Almira* has a less prominent role, but he mocks the fashionable French taste of playing cards and gambling. He also derides the older man, Consalvo, for lusting after a young woman, and his sardonic comments on the intrigues and love affairs of court actually end Act II.

Both operas are exceedingly long – fifty-six arias, eight duets, two trios, two quartets, and two choruses plus recitative (*accompagnato* and regular) for *Cleopatra*; fifty-three arias, three duets, and one chorus plus recitative for *Almira*. The choruses in both works are almost negligible, and each ends with a *coro* sung by the soloists. Both contain various kinds of arias: strophic, binary, quasi, and straight *da capo* (more of these in Handel than in Mattheson). With Mattheson, scoring for continuo is much more prominent: thirty-one arias, five duets, two trios, and one quartet. These may be with or without final instrumental ritornello. With Handel, only twenty-one arias are for continuo alone, the rest being instrumentally accompanied. The makeup of the orchestras is similar, though the instruments are used differently; trumpets and timpani for the few marches and triumphal entries; recorders, oboes, and strings for the basic group. Two of the leading roles in both operas were sung by the same people: Mattheson (Antony and Fernando) and Conradin (Cleopatra and Almira). Mattheson described Conradin's voice and person as follows: "Conradin had an individual, almost consummate beauty and an extraordinarily

311

splendid voice besides, which ranged with equal strength from a to d''. Thus she was the most eminent singer."[10] This would account for some of the high notes and generally high tessitura that both composers wrote for her. If notes are any criterion, Mattheson's tenor range was altogether more modest. He apparently excelled in the slower, more deliberate arias where his diction and acting abilities came to the fore – a fine example is his last aria before suicide in Cleopatra, "Jetzt will ich bei dir sein." But he also could sing the more virtuoso pieces – "Will denn von oben der zornige Himmel" in Cleopatra, and especially "Ob dein Mund" of Almira, which demands controlled breath and articulation of no mean order.

While there is comment in various Handel biographies about Mattheson's friendship and association with the younger composer in Hamburg and Mattheson's abilities as theorist, critic, and writer,[11] there is almost none about the musical relationship of the two men because almost none of Mattheson's music had been really studied, and after World War II, as we know, most of it was presumably destroyed in Hamburg. Thus it is particularly fortunate that George Buelow edited Cleopatra from the Library of Congress copy and that we have it today for reference and comparison.

Presumably the most direct relationship between Cleopatra and Handel's work is the fact, pointed out first by Hellmuth Christian Wolff[12] ("fast notentreu") and reasserted by Buelow[13] and Dean,[14] that Handel borrowed the closing coro of Cleopatra, "So wird nach den Thränengüssen" for the final coro ("Lieto il Tebro") of Agrippina – and previously for a minuet in Rodrigo, which is obviously a model for the Agrippina coro. I cannot wholly agree with my colleagues on this point. There is admittedly a certain similarity in the opening phrases – both pieces are 3/4 minuets in B-flat with the first-half cadence on the dominant – but thereafter they differ in harmony, phrase length, and accentuation. Handel's complete phrase is eight

10 "Die Conradin . . . besaß eine fast vollkommene, persönliche Schönheit, und hatte dabei eine außerordentlich herrliche Stimme, die sich vom bloßen a, in gleicher Stärke, bis ins dreygestrichene d erstreckte. Das machte sie zur vornehmsten Sängerinn." Mainwaring, Händel, 41.
11 See R. Rolland, Handel, trans. A. Eaglefield Hull (London, 1920), 23–33; and P. H. Lang, Handel (New York, 1966), 31–3.
12 H. C. Wolff, Die Barockoper in Hamburg (Wolfenbüttel, 1957), vol. 1, 289.
13 G. J. Buelow, "An Evaluation of Johann Mattheson's Opera, Cleopatra (Hamburg, 1704)," in: Studies in Eighteenth-Century Music: A Tribute to Karl Geiringer, ed. H. C. Robbins Landon and R. E. Chapman (New York and London, 1970), 92–107; see also Buelow's Vorwort to his ed. of Cleopatra, 6.
14 W. Dean, review of Mattheson's Cleopatra, ed. G. J. Buelow, in: M&L 67 (1976), 212–14.

measures long, Mattheson's ten, and they go off in different directions. As is well known, even Mattheson accused Handel of borrowing his ideas (although he disavowed any kind of plagiarism) by taking a theme from a *Porsenna* aria ("Diese Wangen will ich küssen") and using it in *Agrippina* ("Sotto il lauro") and *Muzio Scevola* ("A chi vive di speranza").[15] Since Mattheson's music does not survive,[16] there is no way of proving this point. What few people have noticed, however, is Mattheson's footnoted paragraph to this allegation, saying, in effect, that some composers have prodigious memories and recall musical ideas without being aware of having heard them before. They elaborate this material to their own satisfaction, paying taxes on it but not intentionally taking it from another person. This comment can certainly be applied to Handel and is an instance of Mattheson's broad-minded attitude in this respect.

The most detailed discussion of *Cleopatra* so far has come from Wolff,[17] who begins by pointing out in an exemplary fashion some of Mattheson's pertinent musical characteristics: his emphasis on song-like melody in conjunct motion, which is quite different from Keiser's more disjunct motion; his strict, symmetrical melodic formation with many sequences; his use of ostinato and quasi-ostinato basses for many continuo pieces; his suspensions and passing notes on strong beats of the measures to create temporary dissonances; his somewhat free voice-leading creating parallel ninths and fourths; this use of small motives in both voice and instruments for structural purposes; and the formation of scene complexes for the more dramatic moments (e.g., Cleopatra's death scene and the final dénouement, which is a variation suite). However, he then unaccountably states that Handel's style was much influenced by Mattheson — yet the only evidence he gives is the so-called borrowings already mentioned, with no further elaboration.

Earlier, in comparing Handel's and Keiser's *Almira* settings, Wolff had emphasized the qualities in Handel's opera that were distinctive to it: strong participation of the instruments in the accompaniments to the arias, vocal lines that were more instrumental than vocal, and the enlargement and expansion of the arias by the use of coloratura, concerto elements, and numerous repetitions. But these are hardly characteristic of *Cleopatra* or Mattheson's style.

Further examination of the scores leads one firmly to believe that Handel's model, if any, was not Mattheson but Keiser. Keiser was

15 *Critica musica* I, 71–2.
16 A few excerpts are in L. Schiedermair, *Die deutsche Oper* (Leipzig, 1930), 84–5.
17 Wolff, *Barockoper*, vol. 1, 286–90.

much more similar in temperament to Handel and was more eclectic in taste than Mattheson, utilizing every style at hand rather than trying to create a specific German model. Keiser's surviving operas[18] have many qualities in common with *Almira* (wide vocal leaps, use of solo instruments, much coloratura); and we know that if borrowing is a criterion, Handel found his chief source for later ideas in Keiser's *Octavia*, where, as Max Seiffert[19] demonstrated long ago, there are more or less direct correspondences with *Rodrigo, Agrippina, Il trionfo del tempo, Amadigi*, and various chamber works written by Handel in Italy. Mattheson may have tamed Handel's counterpoint, shown him the value of more conciseness, and demonstrated the value of the grand scena in opera, but he hardly had much influence on his basic style. In fact, the more one looks at the music, the more one sees each composer to be individual and independent in his own way. Keiser is by far the most florid, the most experimental, the most lavish in musical ideas. Handel is more controlled but less sure of himself, more uneven, as one would expect for a young composer embarking on his first opera. Mattheson is the most controlled, the most unified in style, the one who writes the clearest and best German recitative. His arias are very correct (they always abide by the poetic meter) and do not overflow with exaggerated effects (e.g., long melismas), but unfortunately, as a result, they sometimes become rather dull. One has the feeling that he is proving an aesthetic point or pointing out a moral rather than losing himself in a full-blooded musical drama – with some notable exceptions. Yet he can write a good tune when he wishes, and he knows what is theatrically effective. Antony's and Cleopatra's death scenes have already been mentioned, but there is also Cleopatra's "Gute Nacht" (No. 16) in Act I – a moving Adagio over a steady eighth-note bass figure that hovers between A minor and C major and has the result of winning Antony back again after his firm resolve to see Cleopatra no more as a result of the battle of Actium, in which the Egyptian ships, at Cleopatra's command, deserted Antony's forces (this from Plutarch, Shakespeare, and the *Argomento*).[20]

Two fine scenes are Act II Scene 9 and 10. In the former, set during the siege of Alexandria, the Roman general Proculejus, Augustus's

18 K. Zelm, *Die Opern Reinhard Keisers* (Munich and Salzburg, 1975).
19 Supplement, vol. 6: Reinhard Keiser, *Octavia*, in: *Händel Werke*, ed. F. Chrysander (Leipzig, 1902).
20 Printed in its entirety in Buelow, "An Evaluation of . . . *Cleopatra*," 105–6. See also Mattheson, *Cleopatra*, ed. G. J. Buelow, No. 16, 48.

emissary, comes with an offer to Antony, saying that if he will give up Cleopatra and marry Augustus's sister Octavia, Augustus will treat him like a brother and there will be peace again. In a D-minor aria (No. 36) with a continuing sixteenth-note motive in the violins and partly in the bass, Antony expresses his indignant refusal to waver from constancy: "Ach, ich kann unmöglich wanken / Phoebus wird eh stille stehn und das Meer aus seinem Schranker über Berg und Täler gehn / Ja, ich will eh selbst erblassen als das, was ich liebe, lassen," after which he angrily walks off (Example 1).[21] Proculejus then tries his wiles on Cleopatra (Scene 10). At first she is unimpressed by the flattering words that Augustus secretly loves her and wants to make her Empress of Rome. She asks for more concrete evidence, and Proculejus produces a letter from Augustus, presumably making his offer. As she reads it, Proculejus sings a continuo aria in D major (no. 38), evidently an aside) on a quasi-ostinato bass, showing obsession, that speaks of her ability to draw "honey from poison and nectar from gall" – in other words, to interpret what is in fact a trap as being to her advantage: "Leset, ihr Augen, nur Honig aus Gift / sauget den Nektar aus bitteren Gallen, / deutet die Worte nach euren Gefallen, / leset noch einmal die dunkele Schrift" (Example 2; Feustking must have liked this image because one of the arias in *Almira* reads: "Leset, ihr funkelnden Augen mit Fleiß"). As she realizes that Antony must die if she gives in, she gradually weakens, finally assents, and gives Proculejus a ring for Augustus as a token of her promise (recitative). Left alone, she sings a D-minor siciliano (No. 40) with violins and recorders in unison. It is a moving lament for what she has done and gives a human dimension to her treachery. Repeated several times are the words: "Ach, wo bleibet Lieb und Treue? / Armes Herz, du gehst zu weit" (the final cadence to this line is given a Neapolitan-second coloring). The three parts (strings and recordings, voice, and bass) exchange thematic material, built on the first phrase, that is quite similar, but different enough in combination to give the impression of separate lines. By varying his placement of the chief melodic idea, Mattheson achieves variety but adheres to a fundamental pattern (Example 3).

There is nothing quite like these scenes in Handel's *Almira*, largely because they are not provided for in the libretto, which is, on the whole, far inferior to the one Feustking did for *Cleopatra*, and on a

21 This and the following examples from Mattheson's *Cleopatra* are printed in their entirety in the edition by G. J. Buelow.

Example 1. *Cleopatra*, Act II Scene 9, "Ach, ich kann unmöglich wanken"
(No. 36)

Example 2. *Cleopatra,* Act II Scene 10, "Leset, ihr Augen" (No. 38)

very different kind of subject. For the purpose of comparison, Act I Scene 5, involving Fernando (Mattheson) and Almira (Conradin), may be selected. Fernando, who secretly loves Almira, the queen of Castile, is alone in a rural setting. His heart is heavy, but he hopes the woods and fields will grant him peace ("Liebliche Wälder, schattige Felder, kühlet des Herzens unnennbare Qual"). His *da capo* aria is a 3/4 D-minor pastoral, scored for two recorders and four-part strings. All the parts are largely independent (six instruments and voice). Nothing as instrumentally elaborate appears in *Cleopatra.* Handel takes an introductory motive in the ritornello and imitates it throughout most of the parts, including the vocal line. It acts as a kind of echo, as does another descending figure for the second half of the phrase period. The process continues in the middle ritornello after the intermediate cadence of the *A* part of the aria in the relative major.

317

Example 3. *Cleopatra*, Act II Scene 10, "Ach, wo bleibet Lieb und Treue"
(No. 40)

The *B* part has more of the same with the texture lightened and some new, but similar, ideas (Example 4).[22]

In his recitative, Fernando (an orphan adopted by Consalvo, senior counselor to the queen) hopes that Almira will pass through the area and see the message he will write on the bark of a tree: "Ich liebe die ich nicht darf nennen" (I love her whom I may not name). Almira, who also loves Fernando but has not openly confessed it, sees Fernando writing the inscription and sings a brief one-part continuo aria, built on a rapidly moving sixteenth-note quasi-ostinato bass, which could just have been written by Mattheson but for its irregularity. It goes in overlapping five-measure phrases, not the usual four, and the vocal line jumps around considerably, going up to b'' three times (Example 5). Almira asks that Fernando's "immaculate hands" be bound and made to heal the pain he has caused her ("Vollkommene Hände, wie wollt ihr stets schneiden, und blutig verwunden? / ihr seid ja verbunden, ohn' alles Verweilen zu heilen des Quälen der Seelen, mein heimliches Leiden"). In recitative Fernando then starts to cut into the bark, getting as far as "Ich liebe di–" when he is interrupted by Almira, who interprets the words to be "Ich lieb' Edi . . ." because of the irregular spacing between the letters and thinks it is going to mean "Ich lieb' Edilia," another royal princess. She breaks into a fury at the bewildered Fernando and banishes him from her presence. She then realizes that her infatuation has caused this outburst and sings another elaborate aria on an Italian text, declaring that jealousy torments and corrodes her heart ("Geloso tormento mi va rodendo il cor"). This aria, which ends the scene, is scored for solo oboe and four-part strings and is notable for alternating measures of *piano* and *forte* (eighths versus sixteenths), with the oboe pitted against the strings and voice in an almost concerto-like texture. The prominence given to the oboe – it becomes a second vocal line – against the alternating mood of the strings is highly sophisticated and Italianate and again there is no equivalent in the *Cleopatra* score. The voice has a number of octave and ninth leaps that make it appear almost like another instrumental part. The *B* section continues the mood of the *A* section with alternating dynamics and more solo writing for the oboe (Example 6).

While a few examples can hardly be totally convincing, they are nevertheless representative of these two operas and show that the two composers were different in their style and execution. Although both

22 The examples from *Almira* are found in their entirety in the *Händel Werke* edition.

Example 4. *Almira*, Act I Scene 5, "Liebliche Wälder, schattige Felder"

Fel - der küh - let des Her - zens un - nenn - ba - re Qual,

Lieb - li - che

Wäl - der schat - ti - ge Fel - der, küh - let des Her - zens un -

speak the same general language, *Cleopatra* and *Almira* are essentially quite far apart, and one could never confuse, through a long operatic evening, one with the other. It is not a question of quality or superiority but of individual utterance – each man saying something in his own way and hoping it will reach his particular public.

Example 5. *Almira*, Act I Scene 6, "Vollkommene Hände"

Almira

Bassi

Voll-kom - me -ne

Hän - de, wie wollt ihr stets schnei - den!

Voll - kom - me - ne

5

Hän - de, wie wollt ihr stets schnei - den, und blu - tig ver-

6
5

- wun - den? ihr seid ja ver - bun - den,

Example 6. *Almira*, Act I Scene 6, "Geloso tormento"

- men - to   mi   va   ro - den - do il cor,   ge -

lo -   -   so   tor - men - to   ge - lo - so   tor -

- men   -   to   mi   va   ro - den - do il cor, ro - den - do il

cor,   ge - lo - so tor - men - to,   ge-lo - so tor-

- men - to mi va ____ ro-den-do il cor, ro - den - do il cor

15

Mattheson und Gottsched

SIEGFRIED KROSS
Bonn

Matthesons öffentliche Auseinandersetzung mit dem bedeutendsten
Vetreter aufklärerischer deutscher Literatur-Kritik und -Wissenschaft
manifestiert sich in drei Schriften und wurde ausgelöst durch einen
scheinbar weit hergeholten Anlaß, auf den noch zurückzukommen
ist: Gottsched hatte in einer Rezension des ersten Teils von Johann
Adolph Scheibes *Critischem Musikus* in der dreiundzwanzigsten
Ausgabe[1] seiner *Beyträge zur critischen Historie der Deutschen
Sprache, Poesie und Beredsamkeit* auch Matthesons positives Urteil
über Scheibe aus dem *Vollkommenen Capellmeister*[2] zitiert, das sich
freilich auf eine andere Publikation Scheibes bezog. Mattheson
erkannte sogleich und durchaus zu Recht die Doppelbödigkeit dieser
Berufung auf den *Vollkommenen Capellmeister* und reagierte mit
einer kurzen Stellungnahme, die Gottsched in der fünfund-
zwanzigsten Ausgabe der *Beyträge*[3] zwar abdruckte, zugleich jedoch
nicht ohne Häme in dreizehn Anmerkungen glossierte. Damit war die
offene Fehde erklärt. Mattheson entwarf eine Antwort, ließ sich mit
ihrer Publikation jedoch elf Jahre Zeit, auch dann noch räumte er ein:
"Mit Vorsatz, oder ex professo, gerathe ich nicht in diesen Text
hinein. Man hat mich vorlängst dazu gehöthiget. Es geschiehet fast
wieder meinen Willen, daß ich dergleichen Ahndungen, absonderlich wegen des Gesindels, vornehme: Daher habe auch eine
Zeitlang damit hinter dem Berge gehalten, und mache mir endlich
itzo nur ein Spiel daraus": das *Philologische Trese*[= Treize]*spiel*[4],
das er sich gleichwohl nicht enthalten konnte, wenigstens im Unter-
titel als Gegenstück zu Gottscheds Publikation zu kennzeichnen:
"kleiner Beytrag zur kritischen Geschichte der deutschen Sprache".

---

1 Kapitel VIII, p. 453; Nachdruck (Hildesheim, 1970), vol. VI.
2 P. 463; *Capellmeister*, P.S.   3 Vol. VII, 25. Stück, Kapitel II, p. 8–28.
4 Hamburg, 1752; Nachdruck (Leipzig, 1975).

Während also Matthesons 1752 zum *Tresespiel* ausgearbeitete Replik zunächst ausblieb, eröffnete sich Anfang der vierziger Jahre ein weiterer Kriegsschauplatz, auf dem die Auseinandersetzung zugleich an Heftigkeit zunahm bis hin zu persönlichen Invektiven. Gottsched hatte nämlich im dreiundzwanzigsten Stück der *Beyträge* das fünfte Kapitel des dritten Bandes von Lodovico Antonio Muratoris[5] *Della perfetta poesia Italiana*[6] abgedruckt, das sich sehr kritisch mit der Ästhetik der Oper auseinandersetzt. Mattheson hatte sogleich reagiert, eine Erwiderung zur Verteidigung der Oper geschrieben und am 13. Juli 1743 abgesandt[7] aber Gottsched hatte sie weder beantwortet, noch abgedruckt. Die Angelegenheit erhielt zusätzliche Brisanz und Aktualität, als Mizler 1742 im zweiten Band der *Musikalischen Bibliothek* den Artikel erneut abdruckte[8], und damit aus dem Bereich der Literarwissenschaft in den der Musikliteratur überführte, diesmal als Teil einer Zusammenstellung von Schriften gegen die Oper, die aus Gottscheds *Beyträgen* auch noch den *Versuch eines Beweises, daß ein Singspiel oder eine Oper nicht gut sein könne*[9] von dem Leipziger Mediziner Dr. Chr. G. Ludwig übernahm, und das Opernkapitel[10] aus Gottscheds *Versuch einer critischen Dichtkunst vor die Deutschen* anschloß mit dem ausdrücklichen Hinweis, "wie Herr Muratori im vorhergehenden Theil und unser Herr Prof. Gottsched hier einerley Gedanken haben"[11]. So sah es auch Mattheson, wenn er seine Replik ganz auf Muratori abstellte, aber offensichtlich damit eigentlich auf Gottsched zielte. Überdies erschien im gleichen Jahr 1742 die *Critische Dichtkunst* Gottscheds in erweiterter Neuauflage, nachdem schon die Erstausgabe von 1730 die Oper in einer für den Opernkomponisten und Musikschriftsteller Mattheson unerträglichen Weise abgewertet hatte, zu einem Zeitpunkt also, von dem Mattheson unwidersprochen öffentlich behaupten konnte, Gottsched habe damals "Zeit seines Lebens noch keine gute Oper gesehen oder gehöret" gehabt[12].

Es gab also tatsächlich in dieser Zeit eine besorgniserregende Häufung von Anti-Opern-Schriften, und dies allein war eine Herausforderung für Mattheson, der sich seit dem *Vollkommenen Capellmeister* mit Recht immer noch als den führenden deutschen Musikschriftsteller ansehen konnte. Nun zeigte sich Gottsched an-

---

5 1672–1750.
6 Modena, 1706.   7 *Singspiele*, p. 2, §4; Nachdruck (Leipzig, 1975).
8 *Musicalische Bibliothek* II/2, p. 161.
9 *Beyträge* VIII; Mizler, *Musicalische Bibliothek* II/1, p. 1.
10 XII. Hauptstück.   11 *Musicalische Bibliothek* II/3, p. 1.
12 *Singspiele*, p. 107, §205.

dererseits keineswegs gewillt, Gegenargumenten Raum zu geben, zumindest in den damals nur noch von ihm allein redigierten, von der Deutschen Gesellschaft abgelösten *Beyträgen*. So forderte und erhielt Mattheson im Dezember 1743 sein Manuskript zurück, allerdings in einer Form, welche die titelsüchtige und etikettebewußte Zeit nur als gezielte Beleidigung auffassen konnte. Gottsched gab Mattheson sein Manuskript zwar mit einigen kritischen Ausrufezeichen, doch ohne jedes Anschreiben zurück und unterließ in der Adresse überdies die ihm zukommenden Titel eines Legationssecretaires oder zumindest eines *Director musices*, sondern schrieb statt Titel oder Berufsangabe schlicht "Musicien"[13], was angesichts des diplomatischen Status und der doch unbestreitbaren wissenschaftlichen Meriten Matthesons und der gesellschaftlichen Inferiorität des bloßen praktischen Musikers nun in der Tat eine Provokation war, deren sich auch Gottsched bewußt sein mußte; leider haben wir Grund zu der Annahme, daß sie kalkuliert war. Nicht ganz zu Unrecht warf mithin Mattheson die rhetorische Frage auf, wie wohl die wissenschaftliche Öffentlichkeit und Gottsched selbst reagiert hätten, wenn er seinerseits an den Rector magnificus adressiert hätte "A. Mr. Gottsched, fameux Grammarien"[14].

Was Mattheson zu seiner ersten, noch mehr ergänzenden als replizierenden Zuschrift an Gottsched[15] veranlaßt hat, bekannte er später unumwunden: "Die Absicht der . . . Gedancken, ging eigentlich und vornehmlich dahin: daß denen, die was Merkliches zur Reinlichkeit der deutschen Sprache, so wohl in musikalischen, als andern Dingen, nach Vermögen beytragen," – dieses Verdienst nahm er für sich in Anspruch – "ihr Recht wiederfahren; andern aber, die doch nur auf unsern Achseln stehen, und uns gern zu Kopfe wachsen wollen," – damit sind fraglos Johann Adolph Scheibe und sein *Critischer Musikus* gemeint – "nicht so partheischer Weise der ganze Verdienst allein zugeschrieben werden möge"[16]. Dies zielt auf Gottscheds Bemerkung, Scheibe habe seinen *Critischen Musikus* in der "reinen und unvermengten Muttersprache abgehandelt", woran er den Seitenhieb geknüpft hatte, es habe zwar auch vor Scheibe "in unserer Sprache schon musikalische Bücher" gegeben, "alleine sie sind mehrentheils von einer anderen Art gewesen". Was Gottsched darunter verstanden wissen wollte, steht einige Zeilen später: die Bücher über Musik seien "wegen der besonderen Schreibart, in

13 Ibid., p. 16–17.   14 Ibid.
15 "Matthesons Gedanken über einige Artikel des drey und zwanzigsten Stücks der Beyträge," vol. VII, 25, II, p. 8–28.
16 *Tresespiel*, S. 2–3.

welche sie meistentheils, wo nicht alle eingehüllet sind, dunkel, wo nicht gar unverständlich"[17]. Wenn Gottsched seiner Freude darüber Ausdruck gab, daß sich "heute zu Tage" – offenbar seit Scheibe – "der gute Geschmack und sonderlich die Reinigkeit der deutschen Schreibart auch in der Musik stark ausbreitet habe"[18], so bekommt dieses Lob einen merkwürdigen Aspekt, wenn es mit den Äußerungen Matthesons über eine ganz andere Schrift·Scheibes in dieser Weise kombiniert wird. Das ist schon ein beeindruckendes Stück suggestiver Textkombination, die dem Leser konkrete Assoziationen vermittelt, aber zugleich dem Autor den Rückzug offenläßt, er habe dies ja nicht wörtlich gesagt.

Genau das aber machte Gottsched, als Mattheson tatsächlich monierte, das Urteil über Dunkelheit und Unverständlichkeit der bisherigen Musikliteratur könne "unmöglich so durchgehends, ohne besondere Ausnahme [lies: Mattheson] gelten"[19]. Er druckte zwar die Ausstellung Matthesons ab, versah sie jedoch mit einer Anmerkung, dies habe er schließlich auch nicht behauptet, doch fehlen in seinem Selbstzitat aus der Scheibe-Rezension die drei entscheidenden Wörter "wo nicht alle", außerdem relativierte er seine Kritik insofern, als dies ja durch die vielen fachbedingten Fremdwörter unausbleiblich sei. Auch das war dem ursprünglichen Text nicht zu entnehmen gewesen. Der scheinbare Rückzug diente mithin lediglich dazu, Mattheson weiter ins Unrecht zu setzen. Anspruch und Wirklichkeit waren also auch bei Gottsched zwei verschiedene Größen.

Genau genommen hatte Gottsched die Rezension des *Critischen Musikus* gar nicht aus eigenem Antrieb unternommen: "Bishero hat es nicht den geringsten Schein gehabt, als ob uns die Musik etwas angienge"[20]. Wie wir aus der dreiundvierzigsten Ausgabe des *Critischen Musikus* vom 23. Juni 1739[21] wissen, war es zwischen Mattheson und Scheibe zu Differenzen um Titel und Zielsetzung von Scheibes Publikation gekommen, die Mattheson als Nachahmung seiner *Critica musica* von 1722–5 ansah, obwohl sich Scheibe doch ausdrücklich auf Gottsched und seine *Critische Dichtkunst* berief[22]. Mattheson hatte der Affäre eher beiläufig witzig in der Vorrede des *Vollkommenen Capellmeisters* Erwähnung getan. Scheibe aber hatte seinen streitbaren Lehrer und Mentor am 10. Juni 1739 brieflich um

---

17 *Beyträge* 23, VIII, p. 453.
18 Ibid., p. 465.
19 *Beyträge* 25, II, p. 9.
20 Ibid. 23, VIII, p. 453.
21 Buchausgabe, p. 402.
22 Cf. etwa *Critischer Musikus* 40 (2.6.1739), Buch-Ausgabe p. 375.

publizistische Schützenhilfe angegangen[23] und sie ja auch rasch und gründlich erhalten. Anschließend ging nicht nur ein Dankbrief nach Leipzig, sondern auch die "unter der Hand" besorgte Vollzugsmeldung, daß Mattheson "eben nicht allzu wohl mit den Anmerkungen zu frieden seyn mag". Und dann folgt in beinahe byzantinischer Devotion: "Die Wahrheit und Vernunft begleiten Ew: Magnif: Anmerkungen und der Herr Mattheson ist Denenselben noch Dank schuldig, daß Sie seiner Schrift [des *Vollkommenen Capellmeisters*] so viel Ehre angethan haben"[24].

Ob nun Mattheson diese Hintergründe gekannt hat, oder nicht: Seine Einschätzung, daß Gottscheds Elogen auf ihn falsch seien und es hier weniger pro Scheibe, als contra Mattheson ging, war ebenso realistisch wie zutreffend. Es gab also eine konkrete persönliche Herausforderung durch die Gefälligkeitsrezension, die in einem bereits abklingenden Streit Partei ergriff und bei der Gottsched mit seinem hohen wissenschaftsethischen Anspruch gar nicht gut aussah, zumal er seiner persönlichen Aversion gegen Musiker freien Lauf gelassen hatte unter Hinweis auf die von Livius[25] überlieferte Geschichte, daß man in Rom streikende Tempelmusiker durch Ausnutzung ihrer Schwäche für den Alkohol zur Raison gebracht hatte, indem man sie vorsätzlich trunken machte und dann zwangsweise in den Tempel zurückverfrachtete. Man habe in Rom von Schmarotzern und Schnorrern gesagt, sie "lebten musice" (was ein Schlaglicht auf die Anschrift "Mr. Mattheson, Musicien" wirft) und schließlich brachte er gleich doppelt, lateinisch und deutsch, die Geschichte von dem seinerzeit berühmten sardischen Sänger Tigell, der sich Horaz durch Kritik an der Sangbarkeit seiner Oden zum Feind gemacht hatte und dafür in dessen Satiren büßen mußte[26]:

> Das ist der Sänger Art, daß sie durchaus nicht singen,
> Wenn ihre Freunde sie auch noch so sehnlich bitten;
> Doch niemals stille sind, wenn sie kein Mensch ersucht.

Das Fazit dieser Schilderung lautet dann: "Kurz, niemals war ein Mensch so uneins mit sich selbst". Daß Mattheson sich in seinem jahrzehntelangen Bemühen um soziale Aufwertung des Musiker-

---

23 Die Briefe Gottscheds an Scheibe waren Bestandteil der Dissertation von Eugen Rosenkaimer, *Adolph Scheibe als Verfasser seines "Critischen Musicus"* (Bonn, 1923), von der lediglich ein Teildruck erschien. Die Übertragung der Briefe hat sich nicht erhalten; sie werden daher neu ediert in einer in Entstehung befindlichen Dissertation von Anneli Steil.
24 Brief Scheibes an Gottsched vom 21.8.1741.
25 IX. Band, Cap. 30; *Beyträge* 23, VIII, p. 458.
26 *Satiren*, 1. Buch, III, Vers 1–19.

standes betroffen fühlen mußte, auch in seinem Bestreben, den Rang der Musik als einer Wissenschaft außerhalb des Quadriviums unter den Bedingungen des aufklärerischen Wissenschaftsbegriffs zu behaupten[27], liegt auf der Hand. Kein Wunder also, daß er diese Spitze sogleich umkehrte:

Wie viele alte Dichter sind entsetzliche Tellerlecker gewesen, und haben ungemein musice gelebt; ich finde aber nirgend, daß die Unart ihres Betragens etwas anders, als ihre Person, nicht aber ihre Kunst und Wissenschaft, in Verfall gebracht habe, bey denen, die das Gute einer Sache überhaupt von dem Bösen eines Menschen insbesondere zu unterscheiden wissen[28].

Der letztere Seitenhieb zielte natürlich auf Gottscheds undifferenzierte und unzulässige Identifikation von Person und Sache, was diesen aber keineswegs hinderte, in einer Anmerkung nun gerade von Musikern schlechthin als "Tigelliern" zu reden: "Für solche Besoldungen, als diese Leute kriegen, müssen ja wohl Staatsmänner, und geheime Räthe, die ganzer Länder Wohlfahrt befördern, ihrem Fürsten Tag und Nacht zu Diensten stehen. Was bilden sich also solche Tigellier ein? Doch die großen Herren machen dieses Gesindel selbst so stolz"[29]. Es ging mithin bei dieser moralisch-sozialen Abwertung einwandfrei um die Gagen der Spitzenkräfte, nicht um den ungebildeten kleinen Dorfmusikanten.

Historisch und wissenschaftlich wesentlich wichtiger und ertragreicher als diese mehr mit Ressentiments als Argumenten geführte Zänkerei ist natürlich die Auseinandersetzung um die Opernästhetik. Mattheson hatte sie zu einer eigenständigen Schrift (Singspiele, p. 2, §4) ausgebaut, nachdem Gottsched die ursprünglich kürzere Fassung annähernd ein halbes Jahr hatte liegen lassen. Das muß nicht unbedingt persönliche Gründe gehabt haben, denn der Höhepunkt seines Einflusses war ja bereits überschritten, die Beyträge konnten nach dem Bruch mit der Deutschen Gesellschaft nur noch unregelmäßig in immer größer werdenden Abständen erscheinen, bevor sie 1744 ganz eingingen. Den wichtigsten Grund jedoch nennt Mattheson selbst: "hauptsächlich die hitzigen, schweizerischen Zänkereyen"[30], die Auseinandersetzungen mit Bodmer und Breitinger[31], die den Niedergang von Gottscheds Vorrangstellung signalisierten. Im Grunde ging es in der Konfrontation

27 Cf. etwa seinen "Entwurff der vorhabenden philologisch-musicalischen Wissenschafft", *Capellmeister*, 21.
28 *Beyträge* 25, II, p. 13.
29 Anmerkung 8; *Beyträge* 25, II, p. 22.   30 *Singspiele*, p. 2, §4.
31 Siehe J. J. Bodmer, *Critische Abhandlung von dem Wunderbaren in der Poesie*, *Beyträge* 24, IV.

mit Mattheson um die gleiche Sache, die *Critische Abhandlung von dem Wunderbaren in der Poesie* (und im dramatischen Wort-Ton-Kunstwerk), um den Titel Bodmers zur Charakterisierung zu zitieren.

An der Darstellung Matthesons fällt zunächst auf, daß er wie seine Kontrahenten, welche die Oper grundsätzlich ablehnten, von "der Singbühne Verfall"[32] spricht und das Argument vom "musikalischen Verderben"[33] übernimmt, einmal spricht er sogar von "verderbten Notenwerken und ihrer kurzen Dauer"[34], obwohl diese Perspektive ja eigentlich impliziert, daß es irgendwann in der Vergangenheit einmal einen Hochstand dieser Kunst gegeben habe, von dem die derzeitige Dekadenz beurteilt werden müsse. In Wirklichkeit ist natürlich die Diskrepanz zwischen Ideal oder Anspruch und der Realität keine historische Dimension. Tatsächlich formulierte er an anderer Stelle vorsichtiger aber präziser vom Mißbrauch der Künste[35]. Wirklich auch aus historischer Perspektive exakt bezeichnet wird der "grösseste Wiederspruch zwischen Notenwerken und Unterweisungsschriften unserer berühmtesten, gescheutesten und allerneuesten Tonkünstler"[36] nur einmal als Diskrepanz zwischen Ideal und Wirklichkeit oder historisch als Widerspruch zwischen der fortgeschrittenen aufklärerischen Ästhetik und Theorie einerseits und der nachhinkenden musikalischen Praxis andererseits.

Acht Gründe sehr unterschiedlicher Herkunft und Gewichtigkeit führt Mattheson für diese Diskrepanz an. Er hat sie selbst am Ende noch einmal zusammengefaßt[37], doch kann wohl auch hier die Kenntnis der historischen Entwicklung zur terminologischen Präzisierung beitragen. Als erste Ursache für das Auseinanderklaffen von Anspruch und Wirklichkeit des Operntheaters seiner Zeit nennt Mattheson "der meisten Zuhörer verwehnten Geschmack", es werde "die Musik im Grunde verdorben: weit mehr von den Zuhörern, als von den Componisten oder Sängern, deren vornehmste und vernünftigste in ihrem Herzen oft viel bessere Absichten führen, als sie öffentlich ins Werk stellen dürfen"[38], die theatersoziologische Situation im Spannungsfeld zwischen Hofoper absolutistischer Herrscher und bürgerlichem Unterhaltungsbedürfnis. Daß eine Verurteilung "dieses tyrannischherrschenden Geschmacks" als Ursache des künstlerischen Tiefstandes der Oper weitere Konflikte mit Scheibe vorprogrammierte, ergibt sich allein daraus, daß dieser ja, über Matthesons sensualistischen Ansatz[39] hinausgehend, mit dem aus-

---

32 *Singspiele*, p. 87, §170.   33 Ibid., p. 13, 27, 31, 33.
34 Ibid., p. 112.   35 Ibid., p. 118, §225.   36 Ibid., p. 9, §18.
37 Ibid., p. 119, §226.   38 Ibid., p. 8, §17.
39 Cf. dazu Scheibe: *Critischer Musikus* I, 9, p. 90.

drücklichen Anspruch auftrat, "den guten Geschmack auch in der Musik einzuführen" (Gottsched)[40]. Scheibe nahm den Fehdehandschuh selbstverständlich auf: "Herr Mattheson wird inzwischen die Ehre haben, eine Sache zuerst zu verwerfen", die von "gesunder Vernunft und reifer Beurtheilungskraft"[41] angenommen wurde, welche beide er damit Mattheson absprach: "Man kann inzwischen aus dem ersten Anblicke seiner Schrift erkennen, mit welchem Geiste er geschrieben hat, und welche Achtung seine Sätze bey vernünftigen Leuten verdienen"[42].

Als zweiten Grund für die von Muratori diagnostizierte Weichlichkeit der "weibischen" Opernmusik, für die er aus Überbewertung eines nebulösen Idealbildes der antiken Tragödie die Mehrstimmigkeit verantwortlich machen zu können glaubte[43], will Mattheson statt der "zu vielen Kunst des Contrapunktes" eher die moderne Verflachung der Satztechnik verantwortlich machen, denn vieler moderner, insbesondere italienischer, Opernkomponisten "Kopf ist viel zu leer und galant zu mehrern Mittelstimmen"[44]. Der dritte Grund, den Mattheson anführt, bezieht sich eigentlich gar nicht auf die Probleme der damaligen Opernbühne, sondern auf die Motive derjenigen Schriftsteller, welche – wie Muratori und Gottsched, aber zum Teil auch Scheibe – nach dem Zerbrechen des mathematisch begründeten, theozentrischen quadrivialen Musikbildes, an dessen Ablösung Mattheson ja entscheidend mit beteiligt war, nun aus historischer Sicht ein fraglos überbewertetes Idealbild der Antike entwarfen, an dem sie die Gegenwart maßen. Mattheson vermutete nun, daß in Wirklichkeit die Antike bereits dieselben Mißstände auf dem Theater gekannt habe, wie sie zu seiner Zeit angeprangert wurden, daß es daher in Wahrheit "blos um Verkleinerung der itztlebenden Künstler"[45] gehe, konkret: die Leugnung des Wissenschaftscharakters moderner Musik, den wieder zu begründen, ja Matthesons Hauptbestreben war. Vielleicht ist hier ein Zusammenhang zu sehen mit der von Gottsched benutzten Titulatur "Musicien" für Mattheson und dessen scharfe Reaktion darauf.

Der vierte Angriffspunkt Matthesons betrifft sozusagen einen Nebenschauplatz der literarästhetischen Opernkritik. Da das Oratorium sich derselben musikalischen Formen und Ausdrucksmittel bediente wie die Oper, hatte Muratori seinen Vorwurf, diese Musik

---

40 Rezension des Critischen Musikus, Beyträge 23, VIII, p. 454; cf. Scheibe, Critischer Musikus, Vorrede der Buchausgabe, p. 9–17 und 750.
41 Critischer Musikus, Vorrede der Buch-Ausgabe, p. 16.
42 Ibid., p. 17.   43 Beyträge 23, X, p. 487.
44 Singspiele, p. 12, §23.   45 Ibid., p. 16, §31.

sei insgesamt "weibisch und weichlich, leichtfertig und ver-
führerisch für das Volk" oder gar "wollüstig"[46], ebenso pauschal auf
die geistliche Musik, vor allem das Oratorium, übertragen und
wiederum seinem überhöhten Bild der Antike und ihrer Götterkulte
gegenübergestellt. "Das weibt sich und weibt sich immer fort!"[47],
glossierte Mattheson und fragte sich, was Muratori wohl für ein
Mensch sei, "daß er immer auf die armen Weiber stichelt". In
Wirklichkeit treffe seine Zustands-Diagnose weder die derzeitigen
Verhältnisse, noch stimme die Vergleichsbasis zur Antike; im übrigen
handele es sich wieder um einen unzulässigen Schluß von der Person
auf die Sache: Nicht "daß eine theatralische Musik die Oratorien
vergiften sollte", sei das Problem, vielmehr: "Ungeistliche Dichter
und seichte Notenklecker vergiften die Musik, sowohl auf dem
Schauplatze, als beym Gottesdienste"[48]. Zumindest betrifft das Problem Literatur und Musik gleichermaßen. Mit dem unstreitig zu
geringen Persönlichkeitsniveau und der mangelnden Bildung vieler
Künstler als Ursache der Diskrepanz zwischen Theorie und Praxis
des Theaters beschäftigt sich auch der fünfte und kürzeste Punkt von
Matthesons Kritik, da Muratori wiederum zu Unrecht die Sache statt
der Personen treffe.

In der textgebundenen Musik des Theaters wie der Kirche, hier in
erster Linie bei den zeitgenössischen Neudichtungen des Oratoriums,
ist der Musiker naturgemäß von der Beschaffenheit seiner Text-
vorlage abhängig. Soweit sich die aufklärerische Opernkritik gegen
inhaltliche Fragen richtete, war sie von der Musikliteratur leicht auf
die Dichtung selbst zurückzulenken. In seinem sechsten, ebenfalls
recht kurz gehaltenen Punkt konnte Mattheson denn auch nicht ohne
Genugtuung konstatieren: "Da lassen wir einem jeden freye Hände.
Die Herren Dichter mögen sich selbst verantworten"[49]. Dann aber
konnte er sich doch nicht enthalten, mit zwei Zitaten gerade aus
Gottscheds eigenen *Beyträgen* zu demonstrieren, wie wider-
sprüchlich in sich auch jetzt noch die zeitgenössische Literaturkritik
war, wenn dem von Gottsched so hochgelobten Johann Valentin
Pietsch in derselben literaturwissenschaftlichen Zeitung die
Fähigkeit der (musik-) dramatischen Dichtung schlechthin ebenso
abgesprochen wurde wie die Fähigkeit zu vertonungsgeeigneter
Lyrik[50]. Unausgesprochen steht dahinter natürlich die Frage, woran
sich denn bei einem derartigen Stand literaturästhetischer Kritik der

---

46 *Beyträge* 23, X, p. 490s.
47 *Singspiele*, p. 25, §47.   48 Ibid., p. 27, §53.
49 Ibid., p. 31, §60.   50 Ibid., p. 33–4, §65–6.

Musiker halten solle, zumal letztlich ja der Komponist auf Text-
vorlagen angewiesen ist, die sich sprachlich und inhaltlich zur
Vertonung eignen.

So wie die Kritiker der Oper Theater- und Kirchenmusik miteinander in Verbindung brachten und daraus eine moralische Frage
machten, weil die hauptsächliche Unwahrscheinlichkeit des Musiktheaters darin bestehe, daß im wirklichen Leben bei ernsten
Vorgängen niemals gesungen werde und folglich das Musikdrama
wie das Oratorium keine ernsten Themen zum Gegenstand haben und
daher nicht zur Tugend anleiten könne, was doch Aufgabe ernster
dramatischer wie kirchlicher Kunst sei, so bedient sich Mattheson in
seiner siebten Untersuchung zwar der gleichen Argumente, aber in
umgekehrter Stoßrichtung. Dann aber zeigt sich deutlich, wie stark er
eben doch noch in einer Übergangssituation steht, in der zwar eine
historische, (sozial-)psychologisch abgesicherte Musikwissenschaft
bereits gefordert wird, aber im Einzelfall doch noch auf die Bibel als
Offenbarungsquelle zurückgegriffen und ihr historischer Quellen-
charakter substituiert wird.

So wie er im *Vollkommenen Capellmeister* mit ausführlichen
Literaturangaben Ursprung und Alter der Musik aus der Schöp-
fungsgeschichte zu bestimmen suchte und dazu tiefsinnige Betrachtungen über die Dauer des Zustands der Unschuld im Paradies
angestellt hatte[51], so begründete er hier die Ernsthaftigkeit von Musik
aus zahlreichen Bibelstellen ohne Rücksicht auf die Reaktion des
bereits durchaus geschichtsbewußten Rationalismus. Dabei ist seine
theologische Kritik sehr wohl berechtigt, "daß in unsrer deutschen
Bibel ... der eigentliche Ausdruck des Singens mit Fleiß, und
gleichsam aus, ich weiß nicht, was für Beysorge, so wie das Wort
Vernunft, vermieden wird"[52], durchaus im Gegensatz zum Origi-
naltext und zu Übersetzungen in andere moderne Sprachen.

Der Kampf gegen das Musiktheater sei zugleich ein Anschlag auf
die Kirchenmusik und dies widerspreche eindeutig dem geoffen-
barten Willen Gottes. Das Spannungsverhältnis von Aufklärung und
traditionell theozentrischem Musikverständnis bei Mattheson wird
selten so deutlich wie in dem engen Nebeneinander von ra-
tionalistischer Bibelkritik, da mit der Übersetzung zugleich ten-
denziell Exegetik betrieben werde, und dem deutlichen Versuch,
seine Gegner in einer wissenschaftlichen Kontroverse als Leugner
von Gottes geoffenbartem Willen in die Defensive zu treiben: "Wer
die Musik erst aus den Schauspielen wegschafft, der kann sie desto

---

51 *Capellmeister*, 11–12. 52 *Singspiele*, p. 42, §81.

leichter aus der Kirche verbannen. Und das ist, so wahr Gott lebet! meines Erachtens, die rechte heimliche Absicht der meisten Verächter und Spötter"[53]. Für den Fall eines Erfolges der rationalistischen Kritik am Musiktheater fürchtete er darum sehr viel weiterreichende Folgen: "Der Singbühne Verfall ziehet den Verfall des ganzen musikalischen Wesens nach sich: worunter Gottes Lob and Ehre denn auch leidet, welches viel wichtiger ist als alles andere"[54]. Das erklärt über die persönliche Betroffenheit von den Angriffen hinaus die Heftigkeit seines Einsatzes.

Der achte und letzte Grund der Diskrepanz zwischen Anspruch und Wirklichkeit des Musiktheaters, die Mattheson keineswegs wegdisputieren wollte, erforderte schon vom Umfang her die längste Darstellung, fast die Hälfte der Seitenzahl der vorhergehenden sieben Abschnitte zusammengenommen, erweist sich auch historisch als der gewichtigste und wurde zudem schon im voraufgehenden siebten Teil angerissen. Er enthält nämlich Matthesons Auseinandersetzung mit der Nachahmungsästhetik, der Tradition der vera similanza, die zwei Jahre später von Batteux verabsolutiert wurde: *Les beaux-arts réduits à un même principe*[55] ein Werk, das Gottsched so wichtig war, daß er es trotz Vorliegens zweier vollständiger Übersetzungen[56] noch einmal auszugsweise übertrug. In der Musikliteratur der Zeit vertrat der Gottsched-Schüler Scheibe am konsequentesten die Ästhetik der Nachahmung, wenn er in der Buchfassung des *Critischen Musikus* ohne Umschweife konstatierte: "So bestehet denn die Wahre Kunst in der Musik bloß allein in der Nachahmung der Natur. Je genauer wir nun dieselbe erreichen, desto regelmäßiger und künstlicher werden wir auch seyn. Je weiter wir uns aber davon entfernen, desto verworrener und unnatürlicher werden wir auch unsere Stücke machen"[57]. Dagegen spielt bei Mattheson in allen seinen Schriften die Nachahmung der Natur lediglich eine nachgeordnete Rolle, die durch seinen sensualistischen Ansatz zum Teil unter direkter Berufung auf Locke[58] bestimmt ist. Er akzeptierte sie als durchgehendes Grundprinzip eigentlich nur für die bildende Kunst[59]. Selbst da aber betonte er stärker die Grenzen der Nachahmung[60] und die Notwendigkeit, die bloße Natur durch Ver-

---

53 Ibid., p. 64, §125.   54 Ibid., p. 87, §170.   55 Paris, 1746.
56 *Die schönen Künste, aus einem Grundsatz hergeleitet von P. E. B. [ertram]* (Gotha, 1751) und *Einschränkung der schönen Künste auf einen einzigen Grundsatz von Johann Adolph Schlegel* (Leipzig, 1752).
57 *Critischer Musikus* IV, 773; cf. auch u.a. III/60, p. 555–6 oder IV, p. 890.
58 *Orchestre* I/1, §6, p. 32–3 u.a.
59 *Orchestre*, Vorw. XII; auch *Critica Musica* II, p. 99.
60 *Orchestre* I, II/4, §20, p. 166–7.

ständnis und rationale Überformung erst zur Kunst zu machen[61] allerdings auch die Grenzen, die zur Verformung hin zu beachten sind[62]; in diesem Verständnis vermag dann tatsächlich keine Kunst so viel wie die Musik[63]. Im übrigen jedoch orientierte er sich stärker an einem sensualistischen Verständnis der Natur, das man getrost als psychologisch bezeichnen kann[64].

Auch in seiner Antikritik gegen Muratori und Gottsched blieb Mattheson bei der Position seiner früheren Schriften; es ist festzuhalten, daß er sie nicht erst hier ausgebildet hat. Er forderte geradezu, daß Kunst grundsätzlich über das natürliche Vorbild hinausgehen müsse, "nothwendig" etwas aufweisen müsse, "welches sonst bey dem Original weder gebräuchlich, noch vorhanden ist"[65]. Die Kunst müsse stets eine überhöhte, idealisierte Wirklichkeit wiedergeben[66]. Damit relativiert sich entscheidend der Vorwurf der Unwahrscheinlichkeit, der wegen des Gesangs von den Kritikern der Musikbühne und dem ihr daher eigenen Mangel an Nachahmung von Natur erhoben wurde. Wenn Gesang das Wort um eine zusätzliche Dimension bereichere und im Sinne einer idealisierenden Nachahmung überhöhe, müsse, wer das Singen von der Bühne verbannen wolle, konsequenterweise eben auch die anderen Mittel kunstvoller Sprachstilisierung auf dem Theater verbieten, also vor allem Vers und Reim[67]. Theateraufführungen bei Lampenlicht unter Hintansetzung der dargestellten Zeit seien im Prinzip ebenso eine Entfernung vom Grundsatz strikter Naturnachahmung[68] wie die Sprachbehandlung der Schauspieler, die Dramaturgie der Auftritte und schließlich die aristotelischen Einheiten insgesamt[69].

Stattdessen möchte Mattheson die Nachahmung der Natur dem Satz vom zureichenden Grunde unterworfen wissen: "Art und Weise, . . . wie und wo man die Natur und Gestalt von Dingen nachahmen will, ist durchaus willkürlich, und . . . eine Nachahmung darf nur so viele Aehnlichkeit mit dem Urbilde aufweisen, als zu dessen augenblicklicher Erkennung genug ist. Sie ist alsdenn zureichend gegründet"[70]. Eine so begründete Nachahmung der Natur wird dann auch integrierbar in seinen sensualistischen Ansatz:

---

61 Siehe etwa *Critica musica* I, 331.
62 Siehe etwa *Capellmeister*, II/5, §64, p. 143, und II/5, §15–16, p. 135–6.
63 *General-Baß-Schule* I, p. 374, §1.
64 Cf. dazu u.a. *Orchestre* III, I/3, §69, p. 367, und *Critica musica* I, 248.
65 *Singspiele*, p. 88, §172, und 90, §174.
66 Ibid., p. 91, §176.   67 Ibid., p. 69–71, §137–40.
68 Ibid., p. 92, §177.   69 Ibid., p. 71, §140.   70 Ibid., p. 72, §143.

Da nun das Vergnügen, welches man aus geschickter Nachahmung emp-
findet, der wahre Endzweck und die einzige Ursache ist, warum wir die Natur
nachahmen; so verfehlet man dieses Zwecks den Augenblick, da das Vergnügen aufhöret. Alles Vergnügen aber entstehet aus Bemerkung einer angenehmen Verschiedenheit gewisser Ordnung und Verhältnisse. Durch
sothane Ordnung, welche eine Verschiedenheit und Veränderung nothwendig erfordert, vergnügt uns auch die Nachahmung[71].

Daraus ergibt sich als Umkehrschluß: "Nimmermehr kann ein solches Wohlgefallen in uns erwecket werden, wenn das Urbild mit der
Abbildung just einerley . . . Alsdenn höret, mit der Verhältnisse Verschiedenheit, auch zugleich das Vergnügen auf . . . Man soll in den-
jenigen Dingen, welche nachgeahmet werden das Abgebildete,
seinem vorgesetzten Muster niemals so ähnlich machen, daß kein
merklicher Unterschied dazwischen sey"[72]
Historisch interessant ist, daß Mattheson in einer Zeit der Vorherrschaft französischer Ästhetik im deutschen Geistesleben (vor allem
Batteux und Boileau) sich auch in dieser Frage an der englischen
Literaturkritik, in diesem Fall Alexander Pope[73], orientierte, wie er
sich mit dem *Vernünfftler* an Steeles und Addisons *Spectator*
gehalten hatte, der auch in seinen musiktheoretischen Schriften
mehrfach angezogen wird[74], und sich immer wieder auf Lockes *Essay
on Human Understanding* berief[75]. Hier faßte er seine Überzeugungen zusammen: "Natur ohne Kunst [ist] wie ein Diamant, der nicht
geschliffen; doch aber edel und kostbar bleibt. Pope hat längst
gewiesen, daß, was wir oft für künstlich oder gekünstelt halten, nichts
anders sey, als die von uns nicht gnugsam verstandene und erkannte
Natur selbst. Der Diamant gehet doch dem Schleifen vor"[76]. Nach
einer Welle der Nachahmungseuphorie, auf deren Höhepunkt
Charles Batteux und seine deutschen Nachfolger sogar geglaubt hatten, die Künste insgesamt auf dieses einzige Prinzip zurückführen zu
können, machte sich, zeitgleich mit diesem Höhepunkt, Er-
nüchterung breit. Sie drückte sich aus in einem Titel wie *Abhandlung, daß die Nachahmung der Sache, der man nachahmt,
zuweilen unähnlich werden müsse* von Johann Elias Schlegel, von

71 Ibid., p. 73, §144.
72 Ibid., p. 73s., §145. Der Gottsched-Schüler vertrat eine genau entgegengesetzte
   Position: "Die Kunst muß der Natur nachahmen. So bald aber diese Nachahmung
   die Natur überschreitet, so bald ist sie auch verwerflich, und der Natur selbst
   zuwider". *Critischer Musikus* IV, 890.
73 Wahrscheinlich *An Essay on Criticism*, 1711.
74 U.a. *Capellmeister*, 10.
75 U.a. *General-Baß-Schule* I, Vorwort, 4; *Orchestre* III, 32, 83, 97, 112.
76 *Singspiele*, p. 102, §194.

dem auch der Hinweis auf Shakespeare ausging, der die Abkehr vom Ideal der klassischen französischen Tragödie einleitete und vor allem vom Sturm und Drang aufgenommen wurde. Wie sehr die Dinge hier zeitgleich ineinandergreifen, mag man daran ablesen, daß Johann Elias Schlegels jüngerer Bruder, der zum Kreis der Bremer Beiträger gehörte, einer der Batteux-Übersetzer war.

Soweit diese geistesgeschichtlich höchst komplexe Gemengelage der Argumente und wechselseitigen Einflüsse derzeit zu übersehen ist, behauptete Mattheson eine durchaus eigenständige Position in dieser Auseinandersetzung. Das schließt andererseits nicht aus, daß sie in einer Kontroverse mit Gottsched allein durch den Zeitpunkt, zu dem diese geführt wurde, in einen bestimmten Kontext geriet, der sich seinem Einfluß entzog: das, was er selbst "die hitzigen schweizerischen Zänkereyen" (Singspiele, p. 2, §4) genannt hatte, die ab 1740 Gottscheds Stellung so unterminierten daß er innerhalb weniger Jahre zum verspotteten Buhmann der Literaturwissenschaft abgewertet wurde. So steht Mattheson, obwohl in der ganzen Frage offenbar sehr wohl eigenständig und von seinem durch die englische Aufklärung bestimmten sensualistischen Ansatz herkommend, inhaltlich nahe bei Positionen, wie sie gegen Gottscheds dominierenden Einfluß vor allem durch Bodmer und Breitinger aufgebaut wurden. Folgender gegen Muratori und Gottsched gerichtete Satz Matthesons findet sich in anderen Wendungen inhaltlich ähnlich in Breitingers *Critischer Dichtkunst*[77] von 1740: "Wahr und wahrscheinlich muß man in den Nachahmungen keineswegs miteinander vertauschen. Wir haben wohlgegründete, vernünftige, natürliche Ursachen, uns mit dem Wahrscheinlichen, wenn solches nur in den vornehmsten Stücken kenntlich zutrifft, groß und neu ist, völlig zu vergnügen"[78]. Weitere Parallelen, etwa mit den *Discoursen der Mahlern*[79], ließen sich unschwer beibringen.

---

77 Cf. dort den dritten Abschnitt: "Denn es giebt zwo Gattungen des Wahren in der Natur, eines hat allein in der gegenwärtigen Welt Platz, das andere aber findet sich nur in der Welt der möglichen Dinge; jenes können wir das historische, und dieses das poetische Wahre nennen". ". . . ist dieses die erste und Grund-Regel, nach welcher sich alle Künste, hiermit auch die Künste des Mahlers und des Poeten achten und richten sollen, daß sie in ihrer Nachahmung alleine auf die Kräfte der Natur sehen, ihre Materie, Muster, und Urbilder von derselben entlehnen, und hiermit ihre Arbeit auf das Wahre oder Wahrscheinliche gründen . . . Die Kunst suchet ihren Ruhm nicht darinnen, daß sie mit der Natur um den Vorzug eifere, sondern ihr Ruhm-Eifer bestrebet sich allein durch die Nachahmung und den angenommenen Schein des Wahren in der Art und Gleichheit ihrer Würckungen zu erreichen". Daraus folgt: "Die [künstlerische] Copie ziehet uns stärcker an sich, als das Original [der Natur]".
78 *Singspiele*, p. 104s, §199.   79 1721–3; cf. etwa I. Theil, XIX. und XX. Discours.

Es war Mattheson bewußt, daß nicht nur sein eigenes Temperament, seine Vorliebe für eine deutliche Sprache die Operndiskussion so verschärft hatte, sondern daß der Zeitpunkt, zu dem sie geführt wurde, der konzentrierte Beschluß, unter den Gottscheds Absolutheitsanspruch durch die Schweizer und die jetzt mehr und mehr sich zu Wort meldende jüngere Generation der deutschen Literatur geraten war, rationalen Erwägungen nicht eben förderlich war. Es war daher ebenso realistisch wie deutlich, wenn er die Situation so einschätzte: "Wer weiß, ob nicht die critische Klapper, nach wie vor, vermeynen wird, in dem musikalischen Garten, den sie selbst nicht kennet, sondern ein heterogeneum darinn ist, das Amt einer Vogelscheue verwalten zu müssen? Große Weisen geben ungern zu, daß ihnen von ihrer Universalität etwas abgedungen werde"[80]. Und auch mit dieser Einschätzung hatte er gewiß zeitübergreifend recht: "die wenigsten Kunstrichter bleiben in den Schranken einer bescheidenen Beurtheilung"[81], das galt freilich auch für ihn selbst.

Der kritischen Abhandlung fügte Mattheson noch die beißende Satire einer "Musikalischen Geschmacksprobe, worin die heutigen allergalantesten Mittel und Wege zur Niedlichkeit des Gesanges und Klanges nachdrücklichst" und ganz im Sinne von Benedetto Marcellos *Teatro alla moda* dargestellt wurden. Gegen Scheibes ausdrücklich auf die Identität mit der Dichtungstheorie (sprich: Gottsched) gegründeten[82] und sichtlich gegen Matthesons sensualistisches Konzept gerichteten Anspruch:

Ein bloßer sinnlicher Geschmack in Wissenschaften und Künsten würde lächerlich seyn; noch lächerlicher aber wäre es, wenn man gar vorgeben wollte, man brauche zur Erkenntniß des Guten und Schönen in den Wissenschaften und Künsten keine Fähigkeit des Verstandes, sondern nur eine bloße Empfindung der Sinne. Wenn wir aber die Empfindung gesunder Sinne mit der Fähigkeit des Verstandes verbinden: so werden wir dasjenige Urtheil, welches, hieraus entsteht, den guten Geschmack nennen können[83].

setzt Mattheson entgegen:

Der Geschmack untersuchet und urtheilet zwar; aber endliche [= engültige] Schlüsse kann er nimmer machen. Er stellet gleichsam ein bequemes Fuhrwerk vor, zum rechten Zwecke zu gelangen. Doch wenn ein Wagen noch so gemächlich ist, kann er umwerfen[84].

Das Urteil des Geschmacks läßt sich seiner Meinung nach nicht so verabsolutieren; er relativiert es entgegen der rationalistischen Eu-

80 *Singspiele*, p. 112s., §214.
81 Ibid., p. 114, §218.   82 *Critischer Musikus* IV, 758.
83 Ibid., I 21, p. 201; siehe auch Vorrede, 9, und IV, 769.
84 *Singspiele*, p. 123, Geschmacksprobe §3.

phorie Gottscheds und Scheibes zu einer historisch bedingten Größe und meint ironisch: "Das ist die Mode. Das ist ein Stück des herrlichen Geschmacks unserer Zeiten"[85]. Auf die Persiflage des rationalistischen Anspruchs, zeitunabhängig wahre ästhetische Urteile kraft entwickelten Verstandes fällen zu können, braucht hier nicht mehr ausführlich eingegangen zu werden. Zu ihrer Charakterisierung möge die Forderung genügen: "Doch muß, bey, aller dieser Galanterie, ein heutiger Capellmeister etwas lesen können", und die ironische Empfehlung an den Leser: "Sollte aber jemand in gegenwärtiger Geschmacksprobe einige Schreibrichtigkeit antreffen, so halte er es nur frey für Druckfehler, die von einer sehr gelehrten Unwissenheit herrühren"[86].

Das *Philologische Tresespiel*, das als Nachzügler der Auseinandersetzung mit Gottsched 1752 erschien, rankt sich einmal um Fragen der Orthographie, deren Bedeutung Mattheson auch vor den Angriffen Gottscheds schon sehr wohl gesehen hatte: "Nun nähme man es zwar wohl so genau nicht mit der Recht-schreibung; wenn nicht eine Zweydeutigkeit daraus erfolgte"[87]. Daß auch er mit boshaften Bemerkungen zu treffen verstand, bewies Mattheson ein weiteres Mal, wenn er Gottsched ankreidete, er ziehe sich einmal darauf zurück, was er anderen anmahne, sei eine regionale Schreibform, ein andermal sei eine Frage noch nicht spruchreif. Wenn Gottsched die Frage, ob "mögte" oder "möchte" zu schreiben sei, offenhalten wollte, so empfahl er ihm, mit "ich tauge, er tauchte" ebenso zu verfahren[88]. Mit ein auslösender Faktor für die Wiederaufnahme einer überflüssigen und überholten Fehde mit Gottsched scheint das Bekanntwerden der *Lehre deutscher Vorwörter* des Professors am Collegium Carolinum zu Braunschweig, Elias Caspar Reichard, zu sein, weil Mattheson einige seiner Positionen darin bestätigt fand, so was er über die Verwechslung von "vor" und "für" schreibt[89]. Was dagegen über den Vorzug des Niederdeutschen vor dem schon durch Luthers Bibelübersetzung zur Grundlage des Schriftdeutschen gewordenen Obersächsischen gesagt wird, was zur Etymologie des Wortes "Namen" von nehmen oder zur Rückführung sowohl des Griechischen als des Lateinischen auf das Altsächsische vorgetragen wird, ist so unhaltbar und überholt, war es wohl auch schon zu seiner Zeit, daß man darüber kein Wort mehr zu verlieren braucht.

Interessanter wird es, wenn er in die alte Sachauseinandersetzung

85 Ibid., p. 125, Geschmacksprobe §9.
86 Ibid., p. 127, Geschmacksprobe §13.
87 *Critica musica* II, 148.   88 *Tresespiel*, 16.
89 Gottscheds *Critische Dichtkunst* war ja v o r die Deutschen bestimmt.

mit Gottsched wieder eintritt. Dabei sind die Herleitung des Oden-
begriffs von Horaz und die Annahme, daß Ode prinzipiell ein zur
Vertonung bestimmtes Gedicht sei[90], ein spezielles Problem deutscher Literaturästhetik und Dichtungsgeschichte[91], ein historischer
Irrtum, dem Mattheson in gleicher Weise wie Gottsched aufgesessen
ist. Erneut wird Gottscheds Bezeichnung aller Musiker als Tigellier
(Anmerkung 8; Beyträge 25, II, p. 22) auf das zurückgeführt, was sie ja
in der Tat war, eine pauschale Verunglimpfung des Musiker-
standes[92].

Konkret wird Mattheson in der Nr. X des *Tresepiels*, wenn er im
Einzelnen nachweist, daß Horaz sich eben keineswegs besonders zur
Vertonung eigne und somit eigentlich der von ihm verspottete Tigell
aller deutschen Antiken-, Altphilologen- und besonders in der
Aufklärung verbreiteten Horaz-Verehrung zum Trotz ein wohl be-
gründetes ästhetisches Urteil abgegeben hatte. Dies war natürlich ein
entscheidender Schlag gegen den rationalistischen Anspruch über
den Aussagecharakter ästhetischer Urteile. Auch Gottscheds Vorein-
genommenheit gegen importierte, insbesondere aus Italien importierte, Musikkultur, ging es nicht besser: nicht nur weil Gottsched über
Grauns Bemühungen, für die neue Berliner Oper Friedrichs II. italienische Kräfte anzuwerben, so offensichtlich und wohl auch noch
bewußt falsche Angaben gemacht hatte[93], sondern weil es ein histo-
risches Faktum ist, daß die musikalische Kultur des gesamten
Abendlandes mediterraner Prägung ist[94]. Es war eben eine unbestreit-
bare Tatsache, daß die gesamte europäische Musik der ersten Hälfte
des achtzehnten Jahrhunderts einschließlich der französischen –
denn auch Lully war Italiener – von Italien beeinflußt war[95].

Zwar räumte Mattheson durchaus ein, "daß es uns Deutschen sehr
wohl möglich sey, mittelst gesunder Urtheilskraft, den Ausländern
ihre Künste nicht nur richtig abzulernen; sondern dieselben auch von
allem Zwange zu befreyen, zu reinigen, und in eine viel bessere
Verfassung zu setzen"[96]. Aber was die Realisation solcher
Möglichkeiten anging, blieb er voller Skepsis: "Die heutige Schacher-
und Schindewelt, die trotzige und kriechende Lebensart der meisten
Menschen läßt bey uns nicht die geringste Hoffnung übrig, einen
solchen musikalischen Pflanzgarten in Deutschland, als in Welschland, anzulegen"[97]. Im Gegenteil: Gottscheds Vorstellungen einer

---

90 *Tresespiel*, 16.
91 Siehe dazu S. Kross: "Telemann und die Liedästhetik seiner Zeit", in: *Konferenzbericht Magdeburg 1981*.
92 *Tresespiel*, 60–5.   93 Ibid., 82–3.   94 Ibid., 89–94.
95 Ibid., 97.   96 Ibid., 100.   97 Ibid., 102.

Reform von oben, die ihn ja letztlich am Prinzip der Großschreibung von Substantiven mit der ausdrücklichen Begründung festhalten ließ, daß so die Beherrschung der Orthographie nicht zum Gemeingut verkommen könne, setzte Mattheson eine Begründung seiner Vorbehalte entgegen, die man fast schon als empirische Musiksoziologie, getragen von seiner sensualistischen Grundkonzeption, bezeichnen kann:

Wir haben hier in Hamburg ein grosses Haus voll etlicher hundert Waisenkinder: ich untersuchete ihre Eigenschaften vor einigen Jahren; fand aber lauter entsetzliche Schreyhälse, keine einzige gute Stimme bey ihnen. Die Buben hatten mehr Geschmack an den verworffensten Handwerken; die Mädgen zum Waschen, Scheuren und Platten, nebst andrer groben Hausarbeit; als zum Gesange und Klange; sie schämten sich fast, wenn man nur davon sagte; es war ihnen so lächerlich . . . ; sie hatten auch nimmer etwas dergleichen von ihren Vorgesetzten vernommen, und schüttelten die Köpfe einmüthlich[98].

Auf die Einschätzung der Musikalität seiner Landsleute verzichtet so gut wie keine Mattheson-Darstellung, und sei sie noch so kurz. Nur die soziologische Begründung wird nirgends angeführt, geschweige denn deren entmutigende, aber realistische Verallgemeinerung:

Bürgerleute, ja sogar einige, die in dieser Stadt kümmerlich auf Salen und in Kellern wohnen, würden . . . mit vollem Halse schreyen: . . . unsre Knaben und junge Mädgens sollen lieber Katundrucker, Zuckerbäcker, Färber, Weinmischer, oder auch, wenn sie auf kein Comptoir kommen können, nur Knöpf- und Sammitmacher werden: denn bey dieser letzten Weberey gibts noch wohl Mützen oder Kappen . . . Vornehme Kinder aber sollen und müssen nothwendig studirn! studirn! studiren[99].

Ungeachtet seines ausgeprägten Selbstbewußtseins hatte Mattheson schon früher von sich gesagt: "Ich bin ein Musicus eclecticus, und kehre mich an keine autorité, . . . wenns wieder Sinnen, und Vernunfft streitet . . . In Wissenschafften gilt die autorité einer Meynung von tausend Leuten nicht so viel, als ein Füncklein Vernunfft eines einzigen"[100]. Er hat danach gehandelt, selbst gegenüber dem Absolutheitsanspruch der rationalistischen Literaturkritik seiner Zeit.

98 Ibid., 120.   99 Ibid., 104.
100 *Critica musica* I, 48.

16

Mattheson as biographer of Handel

ALFRED MANN

Rochester, New York

It is one of the striking tributes to Handel's artistic personality that the first biography of a composer ever issued was devoted to him. This, the *Memoirs of the Life of the Late George Frederick Handel,* was published anonymously in 1760, within a year of his death. Within another year it appeared in a German translation by Johann Mattheson, Handel's erstwhile colleague and friend. As is noted on the title page, the translator published the translation at his own expense, and he added a number of annotations "primarily concerned with the section about Hamburg" that provide such extensive comment and correction that they turn the original text into a veritable autobiography of the translator. Mattheson speaks with unquestionable authority, for he had known Handel for more than half a century before the time at which the anonymous biographer, identified by later generations as the Reverend John Mainwaring, fellow of St. John's College, Cambridge, took on his task. Moreover, Mattheson's earlier publications had dealt again and again with Handel, and not without justification Mattheson points out that his *Critica musica* of 1722, his *Musicalischer Patriot* of 1728, and his *Grundlage einer Ehren-Pforte* of 1740 might have been consulted. There are two sides to this argument, as one realizes upon checking the beginning of the list. Mattheson's *Critica musica* was the first music periodical published in German, and it is an interesting fact in itself that, as a matter of course, its discussions refer to Handel's works; but the references once more deal not so much with these as with Mattheson's own — they are concerned with Handel's alleged borrowings of Mattheson's melodies.

The earliest appraisal of Handel's stature made by a contemporary composer is Georg Philipp Telemann's brief statement to the effect that in the year 1701, traveling from Magdeburg to Leipzig, he met the "damals schon wichtigen Hrn. Georg Friedr. Händel." He adds the

footnote "Dieser war damals kaum sechzehn Jahre alt." This statement, however, was contained in Telemann's autobiography written
at the request of Mattheson for inclusion in the Ehrenpforte. Similarly, the entry devoted to Handel in J. G. Walther's Musicalisches
Lexicon (1732), the first German dictionary of music, was written – as
Walther expressly remarks – in preparation for Mattheson's more
exhaustive account in the Ehrenpforte. Whereas Walther's text consists of one short paragraph, Mattheson's article in his Ehrenpforte is
of sizable length; and Mattheson's acquaintance "mit dem
weltberühmten Händel" is given further attention in the largest
article of the same work, dealing, naively though understandably,
with Mattheson himself. Thus Handelian biography begins, in fact,
with Mattheson, and if the picture of Handel arises in the mirror of
Mattheson's own career, the critical reader cannot fail to be grateful
for an eyewitness account that offers fascinating detail.

In order to appreciate the originality of Mattheson's remarks, it is
necessary to obtain a wider view of the sources of Handel biography.
Mainwaring's book was "written under the inspection of Mr. Smith,"
as we learn from another early biographical account, the Anecdotes of
George Frederick Handel and John Christopher Smith. Printed in
1799, this work, like Mainwaring's, was published anonymously, but
its provenance is clear: It is based entirely on the report of John
Christpher Smith, Handel's pupil, assistant conductor, and eventual
successor as director of the London oratorio seasons and Royal Music
Master. Having shared the major part of Handel's professional life,
Smith was more intimately acquainted with its course than any other
musician of Handel's time. He is an obscure figure, not only because
we have apparently no written account from his own hand but also
because his working association with Handel is easily confused with
that of his father owing to their identical names. While the elder J. C.
Smith acted as Handel's principal copyist, his relationship with the
composer was essentially that of business manager. It was the younger Smith who assisted Handel as a professional musician and who
became the chief source of information when the interest in Handelian biography began to grow.

This becomes especially apparent from a further early biographical
work, the sensitively written "Sketch of the Life of Handel," which
forms the introduction to Charles Burney's detailed report of the
London Handel Commemoration of 1784 (An Account of the Musical
Performances in Westminster Abbey). In comparing Burney's Sketch
with Mainwaring's Memoirs and with the Anecdotes – both of which
are patently based on information obtained from Smith – we recog-

nize Smith's narration again. But Burney approached his task with the attitude of the experienced historian; thus he was keenly aware of the importance of Mattheson's role as an earlier Handel biographer, a role that is lightly treated in the *Memoirs* and ignored altogether in the *Anecdotes*. Burney logically concludes that "Mattheson was never so abandoned a writer as to invent or disguise facts, which he knew the whole city of Hamburg, and even Handel himself, who was living within five years of this author's death, could refute"; and he adds to this statement a highly interesting note:

> When I first began this *Sketch*, several of Mattheson's Musical Tracts in my possession having been mislaid, I was unable to consult them; but being since found, respect for my readers, and for truth, have induced me to cancel several leaves that were already printed, and to new write this part of HANDEL's Life, in order not only to correct the mistakes into which I had been led by trusting to his former English Biographers, but to insert from German writers such other incidents as concern HANDEL's younger years, of which, as we know but little in England, the admirers of this venerable master will be more particularly curious (*Sketch*, p. 7).

What do Mattheson's reminiscences tell us? The image of the great man rises before us in the reflections of youthful encounters, and it gains definition through that very reluctance on Mattheson's part to relinquish the spirit of *Burschenherrlichkeit* that informed their association. Handel had not answered Mattheson's request to contribute an autobiographical article for the *Ehrenpforte*, as Mattheson relates with evident annoyance. Thus the Handel entry was by necessity marked "ex liter. & familiar." – it was based solely on correspondence and recollection. In vain Mattheson tries to recapture a modicum of communication by alluding to memories of no interest other than the purely personal – the mail-coach ride shared with the pigeon dealer and the services of the pastrycook's son as bellows blower – and he remarks: "I am sure he will laugh in his heart when he reads this; for outwardly he rarely laughs." Yet the biographer caught Handel's wry humor at the crucial point. It is through Mattheson that we learn of Handel's initial observation hideout in the second-violin section of the Hamburg Opera orchestra "as if he could not count to five" and of his sudden emergence when a harpsichordist – that is, a conductor – was needed. The promotion from the ranks that Mattheson describes was more than a prank. It was only a few years later that, in an argument over the performance of a French overture, the ripienist from the Hamburg Opera took the violin out of Corelli's hand, as we know from the *Memoirs*. What a sure violinistic training Handel must have acquired during his apprenticeship as cantor and organist; and Mattheson's account shows how well Handel knew that true access to opera required orchestral experience and command.

Mattheson tells us that he met Handel when the latter was 19¼ years old, on 9 July 1703 at the organ bench of St. Mary Magdalen's in Hamburg. "Er war starck auf der Orgel"; that is the first impression Mattheson gained, and it refers to both Handel's brilliance in performance and his polyphonic improvisation. Mattheson places the fugal art of the young Handel above that of Kuhnau, whom he elsewhere praises as unequaled. The description of Handel's introduction into Mattheson's home and into the Hamburg aristocracy suggests the picture we know from other phases of Handel's life: His upbringing had placed him securely in the upper strata of society, whatever struggles the maintaining of this status entailed; but Mattheson does not fail to lend the personal favors a shrewd turn. Free fare at father Mattheson's table had assured the son expert contrapuntal advice; he in turn offered advice in the dramatic style, "and one hand washed the other." It is obvious that Mattheson would like to take credit for the transformation of Handel's writing in this style. "He wrote very long, long arias at this time and well-nigh endless cantatas, harmonically perfect but poorly thought out and lacking proper taste." But Mattheson's report is fair in that he points out that Handel's compositions after the manner of Kuhnau were always melodically conceived and singable, even when they were meant for instrumental performance, and that it was, of course, the "hohe Schule" – the refining experience – of opera that shaped Handel's vocal style.

The cordial relationship between the two young composers must have reached its highest point with the famous day excursion they took to Lübeck on 17 August 1703, passing the time in the coach by inventing double fugues "da mente, non da penna." The comparison with Bach's extended journey on foot three years later remains forever touching, and once again we appreciate Mattheson's service to posterity in portraying the circumstances. He had been invited, as he writes, by the president of the city council to consider the succession of Buxtehude in office and "took Handel along." The usual circumstances of a formal audition, however, were reversed: Mattheson goes on to say that they tested almost all the organs and harpischords there, reaching in a friendly contest of their own the conclusion that Handel's overriding interest was in the organ and Mattheson's in the harpsichord (an observation which runs parallel to Mainwaring's account of the contest between Handel and Domenico Scarlatti). The two visitors paid their "attentive respects" to Buxtehude at St. Mary's. "Since, however, a marriage clause [involving Buxtehude's daughter] was proposed in connection with the matter, which was of no interest whatsoever to either of us, we took our leave, having received and delighted in many honors and favors." One senses the first suggestion of rivalry here. Though the memory of the occasion is so obviously enjoyed by the author, it is written between the lines that the sovereign role he played was decidedly aided by the fact that he presented Handel to his hosts; and it was Handel who carried the day as far as the qualification in question, namely excellence at the organ, was concerned.

The first open rift was all the more dramatic. As we know, Mattheson attempted the impossible in a performance of his opera *Cleopatra* on 5 December 1704, acting in the triple function of composer, conductor, and principal soloist. While onstage, he left the direction of the work to his friend, but – his part as Antony ending in suicide about half an hour before the end of the last act – he returned afterward to the conductor's harpsichord. The professional conflict flared up. In a manner worthy of early opera, the drama moved from the proscenium into the market square, and, true to aristocratic fashion, the comrades took up arms against each other. Mattheson pursues his role to the last; as he explains, he would have won the duel save for the metal button on his opponent's coat that diverted the deathly blow. (Mainwaring, in his recounting of the incident, confuses the button with a scroll of music in Handel's pocket and the role of Handel with that of Reinhard Keiser.) The reconciliation, brought about by several dignitaries, was marked by a dinner in Mattheson's home after which the two, "better friends than ever," attended a rehearsal of Handel's first Hamburg opera, *Almira*. The première performance of *Almira* took place on 8 January 1705; that of Handel's *Nero*, on 8 February. Mattheson completes his account by saying that he played the main roles in both, with considerable success, after which he retired from his stage career. The dates he gives for Handel's next two operas, *Florindo* and *Dafne*, seem uncertain, and his date for Handel's departure to Italy is undoubtedly wrong; the personal contact had ceased.

Almost exactly midway between the date of the journey to Lübeck and that of the clash and appeasement in Hamburg is the date of Handel's first recorded letter. It is a communication from Handel to Mattheson, and their correspondence forms a new and fairly clearly delineated phase of the Mattheson–Handel memoirs. Three letters from Handel to Mattheson have been preserved, dating from 1704, 1719, and 1735, respectively. So far as we know, the autographs are lost; all three have come down to us as quoted in Mattheson's writings, and in spite of Deutsch's understandable warning[1] that details of wording may not be reliable, the letters convey a convincing impression of the unfolding of two totally different careers as well as of the eventual estrangement of the two artists.

The first letter, written in Hamburg on 18 March 1704, and contained in Mattheson's Handel article in the *Ehrenpforte*, reflects the situation at the Hamburg Opera, placing Mattheson's position in a most favorable light. Mattheson had embarked on a journey intended to take him to several countries, but he had gotten only as far as Holland when Handel informed him that his extended absence would severely threaten the opera season, and that assurance of his return was eagerly awaited by himself and others.

The second letter, by far the longest, was dated 24 February 1719 in London. It deals with two issues, both of which throw light on Handel's reserved attitude. Mattheson had attempted to involve him in his polemic discussion of solmization and of the abolition of the modal system. Handel's answer, which, as we gather from the letter, was given after repeated urging, is thorough; it conveys agreement with Mattheson's stand but, in describing the advantages of this stand as self-explanatory, dismisses the argument. It is interesting that Handel later reversed his opinion by working out a collection of fugal studies covering the entire range of the modes; but this was not known to Mattheson. The other part of this letter represents a first answer to Mattheson's request for an autobiographical sketch. Handel writes that to comply with such a request would obviously take a considerable amount of sifting, and that with so many more urgent tasks at hand the matter will have to be postponed to a more leisurely moment. Not surprisingly, the latter point formed the basis for further correspondence, though the third Handel letter preserved by Mattheson is separated from the second by sixteen years; it is dated 29/18 July in London.[2]

Apparently it had taken repeated reminders to produce an answer from Handel. The opening of this third letter refers to an earlier communication from Mattheson, which had been followed by his sending a copy of his newly published *Wol-klingende Finger-Sprache*, a series of double and triple fugues dedicated to "the noble-born, learned, and world-renowned Mr. Georg Friedrich Händel." The dedication and the presentation are gratefully acknowledged

1 O. E. Deutsch, *Handel: A Documentary Biography* (London, 1955).
2 The duality of dates results from the fact that the Gregorian calendar had not yet been adopted in England.

with Handel's regrets for not having been able to be of service. He states that the work is worthy of the attention of connoisseurs, and he assures the author that, for his part, he wishes to do justice to the undertaking – a curious reminiscence of their fugal explorations of former days. But the central question is answered quite specifically: Handel says that collecting autobiographical material has proved to be impossible because of his obligations to court and nobility. From the pages of the *Ehrenpforte* we learn that Mattheson pleaded with Handel again in a letter barely antedating the appearance of the work – Mattheson quotes the date 10 November 1739 and says he tried to break Handel's silence with the argument that court and nobility must have been preoccupied at the time with the Spanish War rather than with musical entertainment. He never received an answer.

This end of a written exchange between Handel and Mattheson is all the more striking when viewed against the correspondence between Handel and Telemann, which extends to the last years of their lives and abounds with the warmest expressions of Handel's esteem and personal concern for his colleague and friend. It shows, above all, that they had maintained a vital exchange of matters professional. In a letter dated 25/14 December 1750, Handel thanks Telemann for a message he received at The Hague immediately before his departure for London and says that in spite of the pressure of time he was able to hear a singer whom Telemann had recommended – Christina Passerini, who was to appear in the *Messiah* performance of 1754. Comparison of the two associations may offer the key to an understanding of the erosion of one marked initially by such high spirits and promise: The roads of artistic commitment had parted.

Thus there is a certain poignant element in the continued Handel references appearing in Mattheson's writings. Whereas Mattheson's account of the twenty months of their alliance at the Hamburg Opera resulted in a unique and invaluable portrayal of the young Handel to which every Handel biography since has been indebted, anything dealing with the remaining half century of Handel's life – and Mattheson outlived him by five years – was written from a distance that could not be bridged.

A typical example is Mattheson's mention of Handel's mastery of double fugue – a point of such particular personal interest for the author – in *Der vollkommene Capellmeister*, where he quotes the two themes of the fugue in Handel's second suite from the Harpsichord Lessons of 1720 as the supreme example of dual thematic design. What he did not realize, having known only the printed edition, was that the second theme was an afterthought through which the fugue, originally written on a single theme, had been revised measure by measure. What a fascinating opportunity for discussion the work would have offered to the two former friends, had an exchange *viva voce* still been possible!

The saddest document is Mattheson's edition of Mainwaring's work, the last book he published. Understandably piqued at the unfavorable account of his share of events and, moreover, the misspelling of his name, the octogenarian wished to set the facts straight − a task that his failing memory was unable to accomplish and one that has been taken up anew in a number of modern reissues, notably the annotated editions by Bernhard Paumgartner (published in 1947) and Walther Siegmund-Schultze (published in 1976), the latter offering Mattheson's text in facsimile.

There is some historic justice in the fact that the first to undertake a defense of Mattheson was an English writer, Burney. This defense is all the more impressive since it is not offered without frank critique. And there seems to be justice, too, in the fact that the occasion of Burney's writing, the first great Handel commemoration, which took place twenty years after Mattheson's death, served also as the first occasion for an appraisal of Mattheson's role as biographer of Handel.

17

Johann Mattheson and J. S. Bach: the Hamburg connection

GEORGE B. STAUFFER
New York City, New York

The relationship between Johann Mattheson and Johann Sebastian Bach is an intriguing one. Mattheson, the most prolific theorist in eighteenth-century Germany, often cited Bach's works and helped to spread the fame of the venerable Thomaskantor to areas outside of Thuringia. Bach, acknowledged to be one of the most gifted keyboard players of his time, was acquainted with Mattheson's publications and on at least one occasion cited them to defend his own views.

But what were the personal ties between the two men? To what degree did Mattheson, the pundit living in the progressive, cosmopolitan city of Hamburg, know Bach and his compositions? To what degree did Bach, living in the more conservative, parochial town of Leipzig, react to Mattheson's printed criticisms and challenges? In recent years scholars involved with *Bach-Forschung* have probed deeply into Bach's activities and have reconsidered many aspects of his life. Still, they seem to have overlooked what appears to have been an eventful exchange of ideas between Bach and his prolix contemporary Mattheson — an exchange we might term the "Hamburg connection."

Mattheson's aquaintance with Bach and his music

Certainly no one could easily surpass Handel in organ playing, unless it be Bach in Leipzig. For this reason these two must be placed at the top of the list, out of alphabetical order. I have heard them in their prime, and have performed with the former many times in Hamburg as well as Lübeck.[1]

I am indebted to Hans-Joachim Schulze of the Bach-Archiv, Leipzig, for reading the final draft of this article and offering helpful advice on various points.

1 *Capellmeister*, 479: "Insbesondere gehet wol Händeln so leicht keiner im Orgelspielen über; es müste Bach in Leipzig seyn: Darum auch diese beyde, ausser der Alphabetischen Ordnung, oben an stehen sollen. Ich habe sie in ihre Stärcke gehöret, und mit dem ersten manchesmahl sowol in Hamburg, als Lübeck, certiret."

Thus spoke Mattheson in 1739 of his acquaintance with Bach. He had heard the famous organist "in his prime," most probably during the auditions for the Jakobikirche post that took place in Hamburg in the fall of 1720. Bach, then thirty-five, was indeed at the height of his powers, and his performances received considerable approbation. Nevertheless, as Mattheson later reported in *Der musicalische Patriot*, Bach was passed over in favor of "an untalented Journeyman, the son of a well-to-do artisan, who could prelude better with his talers than with his fingers."[2] In the rest of his writings Mattheson alluded to no other encounters with Bach, and it is possible that his personal tie with the great organist was limited to hearing him on this one occasion.

Consider for a moment Mattheson's repeated entreaties for biographical information. Initially, in *Das beschützte Orchestre* (1717), Mattheson asked Bach to clarify a point of genealogy.[3] Later, in the *Exemplarische Organisten-Probe* (1719) and the *Große General-Baß-Schule* (1731), he appealed for a full résumé, to be used in the forthcoming *Grundlage einer Ehren-Pforte*.[4] When the *Ehrenpforte* finally appeared in 1740, it did not contain an entry for Bach. We must assume, then, that Mattheson's solicitations went unanswered, and that he never enjoyed the opportunity to interview the composer himself.[5]

Mattheson's knowledge of Bach probably stemmed from mutual friends such as Johann Gottfried Walther or Georg Philipp Telemann. Walther, Bach's close associate in Weimar, sought Mattheson's counsel for the *Musicalisches Lexicon*.[6] Telemann, godfather to C. P. E.

---

2 *Musicalischer Patriot*, 316. The position was awarded to Johann Joachim Heitmann, who contributed 4,000 marks to the church treasury. See M. Seiffert, "Sebastian Bach's Bewerbung um die Organistenstelle an St. Jakobi in Hamburg in 1720," in: *AfMw* 3 (1921), 123–7.

3 Mattheson wondered aloud whether or not Bach was related to Johann Michael Bach, author of the celebrated work (now lost) *J. M. Bachs Revange*. The two Bachs were related: Johann Michael was Johann Sebastian's father-in-law.

4 *Organisten-Probe*, 120–1; *General-Baß-Schule* I, 167.

5 At the beginning of each biographical entry in the *Ehrenpforte* Mattheson cited the sources of his information. These included personal acquaintance, autograph letters, diaries, and existing documents and works.

6 Walther drew heavily on Mattheson's publications for the *Lexicon*, which appeared in 1732. In the fall of 1729 Walther sent Mattheson an advance copy of the opening section (letter "A") of the *Lexicon* in the hope of receiving a review from the Hamburg theorist. Mattheson became annoyed when he did not receive further installments of the book. He apparently forgave Walther, however, for he eventually reviewed the *Lexicon* favorably in the *Niedersächsische Nachrichten*. This story is related in the correspondence between Walther and Heinrich Bokemeyer preserved in the Deutsche Staatsbibliothek, East Berlin. See G. Schünemann, "J. G. Walther und H.

Bach and a frequent visitor to the Bach household, worked with Mattheson in Hamburg. In addition, several students at the university in Leipzig may have kept Mattheson posted on Bach's activities. Ludwig Friedrich Hudemann, who matriculated at the university in 1727 and later became the dedicatee of the enigmatic canon BWV 1074, attended Mattheson's "melopoetisches Collegium" in Hamburg.[7] Johann Adolph Scheibe, Bach's famous nemesis, attended the university from 1725 to 1729. A decade later he voiced some of his criticisms of Bach's cantata style to Mattheson, who published them in the *Gültige Zeugnisse über die jüngste Matthesonisch-musicalische Kern-Schrifft.*[8] And in the late 1740s Georg Friedrich Einicke, a cantor in Frankenhausen, made his personal correspondence with Bach available to Mattheson for perusal.[9] Mattheson's acquaintance with the events in Bach's life seems to have come from intermediaries such as these.

We wonder, of course, how many of Bach's works Mattheson knew. His first allusion to Bach's compositions is the famous remark that appeared in *Das beschützte Orchestre* of 1717: "I have seen things by the famous organist of Weimar, Herr Johann Sebastian Bach, both for the church and for the keyboard, which are so well written that one must certainly rate this man highly."[10] This comment, the first mention of Bach in print, stirs our curiosity, for it indicates that Mattheson had seen Bach cantatas and keyboard compositions at a very early date, almost a full decade before any of his works became more readily available through the initiation of the *Clavier-Übung* publications in 1726.

Mattheson's later references are more specific. In 1725, in *Critica musica*, he criticized the repetitious text of Cantata 21, *Ich hatte viel Bekümmernis.* In the *Große General-Baß-Schule* of 1731 he alluded to the use of the subjects from the Organ Fugue in G Minor, BWV 542/2, and the Unaccompanied Violin Sonata in C Major, BWV 1005, for *Organistenproben* in Hamburg. He also mentioned the technical difficulties of the partitas of *Clavier-Übung* I. In *Kern melodischer*

Bokemeyer," in: *B-J* 30 (1933), 86–118, which contains excerpts from the letters in question. The entire Walther–Bokemeyer correspondence is presently being edited for publication by Hans-Joachim Schulze and Klaus Beckmann.

7 *Capellmeister*, 412.
8 (Hamburg, 1738), 11. See also n. 20.
9 Mattheson published excerpts from the letters in *Sieben Gespräche der Weisheit und Musik* (Hamburg, 1751), 183.
10 *Orchestre* II, 222: "Ich habe von dem berühmten Organisten zu Weimar, Hrn. Joh. Sebastian Bach, Sachen gesehen, so wohl vor die Kirche als vor die Faust, die gewiß so beschaffen sind, daß man den Mann hoch aestimiren muß."

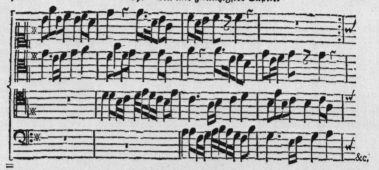

§. 48.

Es ist sonst ein ziemlicher Vorrath von dergleichen Seltenheiten bey mir vorhanden. Aber sie finden hier keinen Raum. Thun es doch diese kaum.

§. 49.

Der berühmte Bach, dessen ich so wie vormahls *), also auch itzo, absonderlich wegen seiner Faustfertigkeit in allen Ehren erwehne, hat noch vor einigen Jahren ein solches Kunst-Stück verfertiget und in Kupffer stechen lassen, auch einem grossen Kenner und Könner der Music, einem wircklich hochgelahrten Lehrer der Rechten, der mir die Ehre gethan hat, mein Zuhörer im melopoetischen Collegio zu seyn, solches zugeschrieben hat. So siehet es aus!

Canon a 4.

dedié

A Monsieur Houdemann

et
composé
par J. S. Bach.

§. 50.

Das ist eine Rätzel-mässige Kreis-Fuge, auf Welsch: Canone enimmatico, auf Lateinisch Canon ænigmaticus: in welchem zwar mehr, als ein Schlüssel, hinten und vorn angeschrieben stehen, und hergegen bey keinem Zeichen. §. §. §. zu erkennen ist, in welcher Ordnung die 4 Stimmen eintreten sollen; doch eben darum, weil solches von dem Componisten verschwiegen worden, wird in demselben Satze den Ausführern das Errathen desto schwerer gemacht. Man hat dergleichen Canones, die bey ihrer Runde mit allen Stimmen einen Ton tiefer eintreten müssen. Ach! welche Künste!

§. 51.

Weil das obige Rätzel nun eben von Leipzig kam den 18 Aug. 1727, wie wir in unsern Lehr-Stunden begriffen waren, so muste sich ein iedes Mitglied der anwesenden Gesellschafft darüber machen, und die Auflösung suchen und versuchen. Denn es waren, wie ieder siehet, verschlossene Thüren, und ein mit Recht so genannter Canon clausus.

§. 52.

Dem einen gerieth diese Auflösung so; dem andern so: bis endlich ihrer zween, deren einer itzo den

*) II. Orch. p. 222.

Plate 1. Mattheson's reproduction and discussion of Bach's "Hudemann" canon, BWV 1074, in *Der vollkommene Capellmeister*

Table 1. *Citations of Bach's works in Mattheson's writings*

Bach work	Location of Mattheson's citation	Additional citations (if any)
Cantata 21, *Ich hatte viel Bekümmernis*	*Critica musica* II, 368	—
Fugue in G Minor, BWV 542/2	*General-Baß-Schule* I, 34–5	—
Partitas from *Clavier-Übung* I, BWV 825–30	*General-Baß-Schule* I, 344–5	*Capellmeister*, 144–5
Sonata in C Major for Unaccompanied Violin, BWV 1005	*General-Baß-Schule* I, 36	*Melodischer Wissen-schaft*, 146 *Capellmeister*, 368
Sonata in A Minor for Unaccompanied Violin, BWV 1003	*Melodische Wissenschaft*, 147	*Capellmeister*, 369
"Hudemann" Canon, BWV 1074	*Capellmeister*, 412–13	—
Die Kunst der Fuge, BWV 1080	*Tresespiel*, 98	—

Wissenschafft of 1737 he pointed out Bach's ingenious treatment of a short fugue theme in the Unaccompanied Violin Sonata in A Minor, BWV 1003. In *Der vollkommene Capellmeister* of 1739 he reproduced the "Hudemann" canon, BWV 1074, and described how years earlier he and his seminar students worked out solutions to it (see Plate 1). And in the *Philologisches Tresespiel* of 1752 he applauded the high achievement of *Die Kunst der Fuge*, BWV 1080. In short, Mattheson knew at least seven Bach compositions: Cantata 21, the Organ Fugue in G Minor, the unaccompanied violin sonatas in C major and A minor, the partitas of *Clavier-Übung* I, the "Hudemann" canon, and *Die Kunst der Fuge* (summarized in Table 1).

How did Mattheson obtain these pieces if, as it seems, he did not know Bach personally? The works which were published during Bach's lifetime were available in cities outside Leipzig. The partitas could be purchased from Bach's "agents" in Dresden, Halle, Lüneburg, Wolfenbüttel, Nürnberg, and Augsburg. *Die Kunst der Fuge* was sold in Halle, Berlin, and Naumburg. The "Hudemann" canon, engraved on a single sheet of paper, was undoubtedly distributed on a more private basis. According to his own account, Mattheson first saw the canon on 18 August 1727, when it was presented to him during one of his seminars by someone who had brought it directly from Leipzig. The unnamed courier may have been Hudemann himself.[11]

More obscure are the routes from Bach to Mattheson of the unprinted works. Mattheson probably heard Cantata 21 as well as the Organ Fugue in G Minor during Bach's 1720 concerts in Hamburg. This hypothesis, initially proposed by Philipp Spitta,[12] seems to be the most logical explanation for Mattheson's familiarity with the two pieces. Moreover, additional evidence supporting Bach's use of Cantata 21 as part of the Hamburg audition has been presented by Hans-Joachim Schulze.[13] Using watermarks and scribal evidence, Schulze demonstrates that D-minor parts for the cantata were written out sometime during the fall or winter of 1720–1. The temporal proximity of Bach's audition, the use of *Kammerton* pitch in Hamburg, and Mattheson's later citation of the Cantata 21 test all suggest that the copying of the parts was undertaken for the Hamburg *Probe*.

But there are other possibilities. As Paul Brainard has shown, Cantata 21 may have been performed and submitted as part of Bach's audition in Halle in 1713.[14] Mattheson may have obtained a copy of the work from the church's archives or from someone involved with the test. Although it seems less likely that Mattheson encountered Cantata 21 through Halle than Hamburg, it is still a possibility. With regard to the Fugue in G Minor, the surviving source material suggests that the work was widely circulated in manuscript during Bach's lifetime. Thus Mattheson may have procured a copy of the piece from a Bach student or friend by chance rather than by hearing it at a Bach performance in Hamburg.

As for the violin sonatas, Schulze has demonstrated that Anna Magdalena Bach helped to make a copy of the collection for Georg Heinrich Ludwig Schwanberg, who served as the Wolfenbüttel agent for *Clavier-Übung* I.[15] It would be too brash to suggest that Mattheson traveled to Wolfenbüttel and purchased the keyboard partitas and violin sonatas from Schwanberg. Schwanberg's known possession of

11 Mattheson describes the momentous arrival of the canon in the midst of his seminar in *Capellmeister*, 412.
12 P. Spitta, *Johann Sebastian Bach* (Leipzig, 1873–9); ed. and trs. C. Bell and J. A. Fuller-Maitland (London, 1889; repr., New York, 1951), vol. 1, p. 535; vol. 2, p. 23.
13 H.-J. Schulze, Foreword to the facsimile edition of Johann Sebastian Bach: *Brandenburgisches Konzert Nr. 5 D-dur, BWV 1050* (Leipzig, 1975).
14 P. Brainard, "Cantata 21 Revisited," in: *Studies in Renaissance and Baroque Music in Honor of Arthur Mendel*, ed. R. L. Marshall (Kassel and Hackensack, 1974), 231–42.
15 J.-J. Schulze, "Ein 'Dresdner Menuett' im zweiten Klavierbüchlein der Anna Magdalena Bach, nebst Hinweisen zur Überlieferung einiger Kammermusikwerke Bachs," in: *B-J* 65 (1979), 45–64.

the partitas and sonatas simply demonstrates the availability of both works outside Leipzig.

The most likely source of Bach manuscripts in Hamburg was Telemann, whose ties with the Bach family were close. Wilhelm Friedemann entered Telemann's Suite in A Major into his own *Clavier-Büchlein vor Wilhelm Friedemann Bach* of 1720. Johann Sebastian regarded Telemann's works highly and performed his cantata *Machet die Tor weit* and passion *Seliges Erwägen* in Leipzig in the 1730s.[16] He also subscribed to the "Paris" Quartets of 1738.[17] It seems safe to assume that works flowed in more than one direction: Telemann must have obtained Bach compositions in exchange for his own. He was acquainted with the "Hudemann" canon, for he published it in *Der getreue Music-Meister* of 1728. He must surely have possessed additional Bach pieces, and may have made them available to Mattheson.

How many other Bach works did Mattheson know? One cannot provide a conclusive anwer to this question, of course, but one can speculate from the existing facts. It is curious that in his twenty-four publications, which include over two dozen references to Bach, Mattheson mentions only seven pieces. Moreover, he cites several of them, the partitas and the violin sonatas, more than once (see Table 1). If Mattheson had access to a large store of Bach compositions, why did he not quote other works for sake of variety?

Also telling is his use of Bach fugue subjects. For the *Organistenprobe* of 1725 he adopted the theme from Bach's Organ Fugue in G Minor. For the *Organistenprobe* of 1727, however, he used the theme from the C-Major Violin Sonata. If Mattheson owned a sizable collection of Bach organ and clavier fugues, why did he not draw on these works instead? The subjects of such pieces were specially designed for the keyboard, and would have been more appropriate for a test of keyboard skill than the C-major violin fugue theme, which was tailor-made for a string instrument. Mattheson's decision to cross media and use the violin subject may well indicate that he had no other Bach keyboard themes to hand.

In all likelihood Mattheson's knowledge of Bach's works mirrored that of other musicians outside the Bach circle. They knew Bach from reputation and from an occasional performance, but their acquaintance with his compositions was slight. Acquisition of manuscript

16 A. Dürr, *Zur Chronologie der Leipziger Vokalwerke J. S. Bachs* (2d ed., Kassel, 1976), 109 and 113 (n. 29).
17 *Bach-Dokumente*, ed. W. Neumann and H.-J. Schulze (Kassel and Leipzig, 1963–), vol. 2, No. 425.

copies was a difficult matter. While Bach's own students, Agricola, Kirnberger, Kittel, and others, obtained unprinted pieces such as the free organ works, the Inventions and Sinfonias, or *Das wohltemperirte Clavier* as a normal part of their studies, outsiders had to rely on chance encounters with those who owned a Bach manuscript or two. Perhaps that explains, in part, why so many composers and students undertook the trip to Leipzig to meet or study with Bach, making his house "hum with activity like a beehive," as C. P. E. Bach put it.[18] The visitors wished to learn, but they also wished to gain copies of pieces unavailable elsewhere.[19] Mattheson's hubris, clearly evident in his publications, would have prevented him from making such a pilgrimage.

Bach's acquaintance with Mattheson's publications and his response to the criticisms and challenges issued in them

To what extent, if any, did Mattheson influence Bach? To answer that question we must first consider whether or not Bach was acquainted with Mattheson's treatises. It is clear that Mattheson's books were available in Leipzig, one of the centers of the German publishing industry. In 1729 Martin Heinrich Fuhrmann described his recent visit to the Leipzig Easter fair, where he heard Bach perform. In the same account Fuhrmann mentioned that the current publications of Mattheson and Heinichen (*Der musicalische Patriot* and *Der General-Baß in der Composition*) were being sold at the fair. According to Fuhrmann, the volumes were judged by one musician to be "somewhat heavy reading, but quite accurate nevertheless." The musician went on: "Whoever fails to learn from Mattheson's and Heinichen's writings is a blockhead!"[20] Who was the anonymous critic quoted by Fuhrmann? Perhaps Bach. More important is the fact that Mattheson's books were on sale at the Leipzig fairs and were a popular topic of conversation.

They were also the focus of a series of lectures given in Leipzig by Lorenz Christoph Mizler. Mizler, who frequently discussed Mattheson's treatises in the *Musikalische Bibliothek*, spoke on *Das neu-*

---

18 *Bach-Dokumente*, vol. 3, No. 803.
19 This can be observed in the remarks of Bach student Philipp David Kräuter, who pleaded with the church boards of Augsburg to extend his stay in Weimar in 1713 because he wished to attend Bach's forthcoming concerts and "see, hear, and obtain copies of a great deal." See *Bach-Dokumente*, vol. 2, New Document No. 58a.
20 M. H. Fuhrmann, *Die an der Kirchen Gottes gebauete Satans-Capelle* (Cologne, 1729), 32. Fuhrmann used the pseudonym Marco Hilario Frischmuth.

eröffnete Orchestre at the university in 1737. While Bach himself may not have attended the talks, it seems probable that his son Carl Philipp Emanuel – enrolled at the university between 1731 and 1738 – would have been present. Mizler later founded the Societät der Musi-calischen Wissenschaften, which Bach was invited to join in 1747. As Carl Philipp Emanuel remarked, "My father was no admirer of dry mathematical stuff."[21] But his attention must have been aroused by Mattheson's discussions of the practical aspects of music making. If Bach did not have time to read Mattheson's wordy volumes, then he probably received summaries of them from friends with a literary bent – Walther, Kirnberger, or Mizler.

Several events link Bach with Mattheson's publications. In the famous Scheibe–Birnbaum imbroglio, Mattheson fanned the fires of controversy by printing one of Scheibe's letters criticizing Bach's cantata writing.[22] The next year Bach's defender and mouthpiece, Johann Abraham Birnbaum, quoted Mattheson's *Neu-eröffnetes Orchestre* in justifying Bach's style.[23] Birnbaum may have done this at the urging of Bach himself, who undoubtedly provided the Leipzig *Dozent* with musical advice.

In 1747 Mizler reviewed *Der vollkommene Capellmeister* in the *Musikalische Bibliothek* and gave additional solutions to the "Hudemann" canon that Mattheson had solved.[24] Again we can see Bach standing in the wings, giving cues to Mizler, his colleague and fellow member of the Societät der Musicalischen Wissenschaften. Finally, in *Sieben Gespräche der Weisheit und Musik*, Mattheson aired the Schröter–Biedermann controversy, quoting directly from Bach letters sent to G. F. Einicke.[25] Thanks to Mattheson we are treated to a rare glimpse of Bach's personality. We see the Thom-askantor in the last two years of his life, seeking vindication of his own church program by attacking the curriculum recently proposed by the rector, Johann Gottlieb Biedermann. Biedermann scorned the role of music in church scbools, a view diametrically opposed to Bach's. In this case as in others, Bach did not pick up the standard himself, but worked behind the scenes, asking Christoph Gottlieb Schröter, another member of the Societät der Musicalischen

21 *Bach-Dokumente*, vol. 3, No. 803.
22 Mattheson published the letter in *Gültige Zeugnisse*, 11. In it Scheibe remarked: "Bach's church works are always more artificial and tedious and by no means as full of impressive conviction and intelligent reflection as those of Telemann and Graun."
23 *Critischer Musikus* (Leipzig, 1747), 978.
24 L. C. Mizler, *Musikalische Bibliothek* (Leipzig, 1739–54), III/3 (1747), 484–8.
25 *Sieben Gespräche*, 183.

Wissenschaften, to defend him. In a letter to Schröter Bach ridiculed Biedermann, saying the "*Rec*-tor" had a "*Dreck*-ohr." This pun was so scandalous that Mattheson, who published the remark, felt obliged to explain it to his readers in French. When Schröter's defense of Bach eventually appeared in print, it was so heavily edited that the author complained bitterly. Schröter blamed the changes on Bach. An embarrassed Bach blamed them on the printer – an unlikely explanation. Here we see Bach the culpable, behind-the-scenes manipulator, willing to voice his opinion through the writings of others but unwilling to keep his hands off the copy. In this light we can more easily understand his tampering with his librettists' cantata texts.[26] For this look inside Bach's psyche, we are indebted to Mattheson.

Turning to another aspect of Bach's personality, we may ponder why he never responded to Mattheson's requests for biographical information. Several factors seem to be involved. First, Mattheson was an imposing literary figure. He was secretary to the British ambassador in Hamburg and corresponded in German, English, and French. By 1740, the year the *Ehrenpforte* appeared, he had written fifteen books. Bach, by contrast, was a reluctant correspondent. If the poems "Erbauliche Gedanken eines Tobackrauchers" or "Durchlauchtigst zarter Prinz den zwar die Windeln decken" are any indication of his literary tastes, it is understandable that he might feel intimidated by Mattheson's polished style.[27] In matters of public debate Bach consistently voiced his opinions through others of greater literary expertise: Birnbaum, a rhetorician at the university in Leipzig, or Schröter, a contributor to Mizler's *Musikalische Bibliothek*. Second, there is the matter of Bach's modest education. Handel, Telemann, Graupner, Walther, Heinichen, and Mizler had university training. Bach's formal education went no further than the Michaelis-Schule in Lüneburg. This deficiency would have become painfully evident in a published biography. Bach probably preferred to be judged by his works and his performances rather than by his academic credentials. If Mattheson was disappointed by Bach's silence, he did not show it in print. He repeatedly classified Bach as one of the best practicioners of the modern cantata style (despite his

---

26 See the foreword to *Sämtliche von Johann Sebastian Bach vertonte Texte*, ed. W. Neumann (Leipzig, 1974).

27 The "Erbauliche Gedanken eines Tobackrauchers" was written into the *Clavierbüchlein für Anna Magdalena Bach* of 1725. "Durchlauchtigst Zarter Prinz den zwar die Windeln decken" was entered into a copy of the Partita in B-flat Major, BWV 825, presented to Emanuel Ludwig, the son of Prince Leopold of Anhalt-Cöthen.

contrived treatment of texts), as one of the greatest representatives of German composition, and as one of the finest masters of the fugue.

We must also ask what effect Mattheson's publications might have had on Bach's compositional output. As Robert Marshall and Gerhard Herz have already observed, Bach's vocal writing in the 1730s and 1740s underwent a noticeable stylistic change, not in one direction but in two: Balancing the movement toward the *stile antico* was a movement toward the *style galant*.[28] The retrospective *antico* style of private works such as the B-Minor Mass was matched by the progressive, *galant* features of public pieces such as the *Coffee Cantata* and the *Peasant Cantata*. What caused Bach to turn to the more forward-looking style? Surely the criticisms leveled by Scheibe and promulgated by Mattheson pushed Bach in that direction. In addition, the pointed observations of Mattheson himself must have found their mark on Bach's sensitive pride. Mattheson's satirical remarks of 1725 about the repetitious text of Cantata 21 undoubtedly did not fall on deaf ears. Mattheson made his point by quoting the lines of Bach's cantata word for word:

> So that the honorable Zachau (Handel's teacher) might have company and not stand completely alone, let us place next to him an otherwise upright practicing musician of today, who for a long time does nothing but repeat:
> "I, I, I, I had much grief. I had much grief, in my heart, in my heart, in my heart. I had much grief ‖ in my heart ‖ ‖ I had much grief ‖ in my heart ‖ I had much grief ‖ in my heart ‖ ‖ ‖ ‖ ‖ I had much grief ‖ in my heart ‖" etc.
> And then:
> "Sighs, tears, grief, misery (pause) sighs, tears, anxious longing, fear and death (pause) gnaw at my oppressed heart," etc.
> And in a similar manner:
> "Come, my Jesus, and refresh (pause) and refresh with thy glance (pause) come, my Jesus (pause) come, my Jesus, and refresh, and rejoice . . . with thy glance this soul," etc.[29]

28 R. Marshall, "Bach the Progressive: Observations on his Late Works," in: *MQ* 62 (1976), 313–57; G. Herz, "Der lombardische Rhythmus im 'Domine Deus' der h-Moll Messe J. S. Bachs," in: *B-J* 60 (1974), 90–7. Bach's latest interest in the *stile antico* is discussed in C. Wolff, *Der stile antico in der Musik Johann Sebastian Bachs* (Wiesbaden, 1968).

29 *Critica musica* II, 368: "Damit der ehrliche Zachau (Händels Lehrmeister) Gesellschafft habe, und nichts so gar allein da stehe, soll ihm ein sonst braver *Practicus hodiernus* zur Seiten gesetzt werde, der repetirt nicht für die lange Weile also: 'Ich, ich, ich, ich hatte viel Bekümmerniß, ich hatte viel Bekümmernß, in meinem Hertzen, in meinem Hertzen. Ich hatte viel Bekümmerniß ‖ in meinem Hertzen ‖ ‖ Ich hatte viel Bekümmerniß ‖ in meinem Hertzen ‖ Ich hatte viel Bekümmerniß ‖ in meinem Hertzen ‖ ‖ ‖ ‖ ‖ Ich hatte viel Bekümmerniß ‖ in meinem Hertzen' ‖ etc. Hernachmahl so: 'Seufzer, Thränen, Kummer, Noth (Pause) Seufzer, Thränen, ängstlichs Sehnen, Furcht und Tod (Pause) nagen mein beklemm-

Nor does it seem likely that Mattheson's comment in the *Große General-Baß-Schule* that Bach's works were "unsingable" went unheard. Bach was probably piqued by these public criticisms, launched by so esteemed a man as Mattheson, and his efforts to "update" his cantata writing in his later years may have resulted from the barbs. Elements of the *galant* style – lyrical melodies, transparent textures, uncomplicated harmonies, light dance meters, and folk idioms – can be perceived not only in secular compositions written for the Collegium Musicum such as Cantata 201, *Geschwinde, ihr wir – belnden Winde* (ca. 1729)[30] Cantata 209, *Non sa che siá dolore* (ca. 1734), Cantata 211, *Schweigt stille, plaudert nicht* (ca. 1732–5), and Cantata 212, *Mer hahn en neue Oberkeet* (1742), but also in the few sacred works written after 1730 such as Cantata 195, *Dem Gerechten muss das Licht* (after 1737?), and Cantata 200, *Bekennen will ich seinen Namen* (after 1742?). The declamation in these cantatas continues to be repetitious, but the repeated sections of the text are arranged in more orderly, balanced phrases.

Finally, there is the challenge Mattheson issued in 1739 in *Der vollkommene Capellmeister*:

> With regard to double fugues with three subjects there is, as far as I know, nothing in print other than my own work, published under the title *Die wolklingende Fingersprache* (Parts I and II, 1735 and 1737). Out of modesty I would not recommend this collection to anyone. Rather I would hope to see something similar brought forth by the famous Herr Bach in Leipzig, who is a great master of fugue. Meanwhile, this lack exposes not only the negligence and decline of well-grounded contrapuntists, but also the lack of inquisitiveness of today's ignorant organists and composers about such instructive things.[31]

Would Bach, whose skills as a contrapuntist far exceeded Mattheson's, have ignored this request?

As the title page of *Die wol-klingende Finger-Sprache* shows (see Plate 2), Mattheson proudly proclaimed – in contrast to his feigned

---

tes Hertz etc.& it. 'Komm, mein JEsu, und erquicke (Pause) und erfreu mit deinem Blicke (Pause) komm, mein JEsu, (Pause) komm, mein JEsu, und erquicke, und erfreu . . . mit deinem Blicke diese Seele, etc.'"

30 The dates for the cantatas are those proposed by Dürr in *Zur Chronologie*.

31 *Capellmeister*, 441: "Von Doppelfugen, mit dreien Subjecten ist, so viel man weiß, nichts anders im Kupffer-Druck herausgekommen, als mein eignes Werck, unter dem Nahmen: Der wolklingenden Fingersprache. Erster und zweiter Theil, 1735, 1737, welches ich, aus Bescheidenheit niemand anpreisen mag; sondern vielmehr wünschen mögte, etwas dergleichen von dem berühmten Herrn Bach in Leipzig, der ein grosser Fugenmeister ist, ans Licht gestellet zu sehen. Indessen legt dieser Mangel einer Seits die Nachlässigkeit und den Abgang gründlicher Contrapunctisten, andern Theils aber auch die geringe Nachfrage heutiger unwissenden Organisten und Setzer nach solchen lehrreichen Sachen, gnugsam vor Augen."

Die

wol-klingende

Finger=Sprache,

in

Zwölff Fugen,

mit

zwey biß drey Subjecten,

entworffen;

und dem

Hoch=Edel=Gebohrnen, Hochgelahrten und

Weltberühmten Herrn,

Herrn Georg Friedrich Händel,

Königl. Groß-Br. und Churfürstl. Braunschw. Lüneb.

Capellmeister,

als ein Merckmahl sonderbarer Ehrbezeigung,

zugeeignet

von

Mattheson.

Erster Theil.

HAMBURG, 1735. im Verlage des Verfassers.

Plate 2. The title page of Mattheson's *Wol-klingende Finger-sprache*, with
dedication to Handel

modesty in *Der vollkommene Capellmeister* – that his fugues were composed "with two to three subjects." Moreover, he dedicated the collection to Handel, Bach's principal rival in the field of fugue writing. These gestures must have stirred the Thomaskantor's competitive spirit. If Christoph Wolff is correct in his assessment that *Die Kunst der Fuge* was started in the early 1740s,[32] then we have reason to believe that Bach's unusual fugal compendium may have been a direct response to Mattheson's challenge.

In addition, Mattheson may have had some effect on Bach's organizational plan and choice of fugue types. In its initial form, that conveyed in the manuscript Berlin, Deutsche Staatsbibliothek, Bach Mus. ms. P 200,[33] *Die Kunst der Fuge* closely resembles *Die wol-klingende Finger-Sprache* in its design. Like Mattheson's collection, the early version of *Die Kunst der Fuge* contains a dozen fugues, employing one, two, and three subjects. Bach supplemented the fugues with two canons, not unlike the way Mattheson provided an extra fughetta and dance movements in *Die wol-klingende Finger-Sprache* (see Table 2). Bach even bridged the second and third simple fugues (BWV 1080/3 and BWV 1080/2) with a half cadence, the device employed by Mattheson to join the sections of his largest piece.

Bach was probably unimpressed with the *galant* writing of *Die wol-klingende Finger-Sprache*. He was undoubtedly interested in more "instructive things" (to use Mattheson's term) – fugues that would display to the full the dying art of counterpoint. Bach's methodical use of the most sophisticated contrapuntal procedures in *Die Kunst der Fuge* may have had its foundation in *Der vollkommene Capellmeister* itself. In the chapters on double counterpoint and double fugue,[34] Mattheson discusses *contrapunto alla zoppa, contrapunto alla diritta, contrapunto sincopato*, and other recherché devices that received their most systematic application in *Die Kunst der Fuge*.[35] That is not to imply, of course, that Bach needed Mattheson's advice, for he had employed sophisticated contrapuntal techniques much earlier, in the fugues of the free organ works, the violin sonatas, and

---

32 Communications with the author. See also Wolff's section 10 of the article "Bach, §III:(7) Johann Sebastian," in: *New Grove*, vol. 1, 803.

33 The *P 200* version of *Die Kunst der Fuge* is discussed in Christoph Wolff et al., "Bach's 'Art of Fugue': An Examination of the Sources," in: *Current Musicology* 19 (1975), 47–77.

34 *Capellmeister*, 415–57.

35 The possible influence of *Der vollkommene Capellmeister* on Bach's late fugue writing is discussed in G. G. Butler's article, "*Der vollkommene Capellmeister* as a stimulus on J. S. Bach's late fugal writing," Chapter 13 of this volume.

Table 2. *Similarities in fugue types found in Mattheson's Wol-klingende Finger-Sprache and Bach's Kunst der Fuge*

Die wol-klingende Finger-Sprache (1735–7)	Die Kunst der Fuge, manuscript version (early 1740s)
Fugue I: one subject	Fugue I: one subject (BWV 1080/1)
Fugue II: one subject	Fugue II: one subject (BWV 1080/3)
Fugue III: one subject	Fugue III: one subject (BWV 1080/2)
Fugue IV: one subject	Fugue IV: one subject, in contrary motion
Allemanda	(BWV 1080/5)
Corrente	Fugue V: two subjects (BWV 1080/9)
Gavotta	Fugue VI: two subjects (BWV 1080/10a)
Fugue V: one subject	Fugue VII: one subject, in contrary mo-
Fugue VI: two subjects	tion (BWV 1080/6)
Fughetta	Fugue VIII: one subject, in contrary mo-
Fugue VII: one subject	tion (BWV 1080/7)
Fugue VIII: two subjects, prefaced	Canon (BWV 1080/15)
by a Sinfonia	Fugue IX: three subjects (BWV 1080/8)
Fugue IX: one subject	Fugue X: three subjects (BWV 1080/11)
Burla	Canon (BWV 1080/14)
Fugue X: three subjects	Fugue XI: mirror fugue (BWV 1080/12,1)
Seriosita	Inversa (BWV 1080/12,2)
Fugue XI: one subject	Fugue XII: mirror fugue (BWV 1080/13,1)
Fugue XII: two subjects	Inversa (BWV 1080/13,2)

Das wohltemperirte Clavier, vol. I. But Mattheson may have given him the idea of exploring the methods of fugue in a single, unified collection – an idea imperfectly realized in *Die wol-klingende Finger-Sprache*.

As Mattheson properly noted, *Die wol-klingende Finger-Sprache* contained some of the first double fugues in print. Bach may have wished to surpass this publication, just as he earlier exceeded J. C. F. Fischer's *Ariadne musicae* in *Das Wohltemperirte Clavier* or Johann Kuhnau's *Neue Clavier-Übung* in *Clavier-Übung* I. If so, he created a contrapuntal tour de force that went well beyond Mattheson's modest model. The cyclical treatment of themes, the thorough exploration of contrapuntal genera, the sophisticated organizational design, and the later expansion of the *P 200* format characterize the high standard Bach upheld for *Die Kunst der Fuge*.

When *Die Kunst der Fuge* appeared in print after Bach's death, Mattheson was extravagant in his praise:

Johann Sebastian Bach's so-called Art of Fugue, a practical and splendid work of seventy plates in folio, will one day astonish all the French and Italian fugue writers – at least to the extent that they can really penetrate and understand it, to say nothing of playing it. How would it be then if every foreigner and compatriot risked his *louis d'or* on this rarity? Germany is and will most certainly remain the true land of the organ and the fugue.[36]

The publication of *Die Kunst der Fuge* fulfilled the wish that Mattheson had expressed earlier in *Der vollkommene Capellmeister*: the collection demonstrated that contrapuntal writing remained a vital compositional skill in Germany.

We can regret that Bach did not provide Mattheson with a *curriculum vitae* for the *Ehrenpforte*. But if Bach felt, as he seemed to, that works speak louder than words, then it is a consoling thought to imagine that he responded to the Hamburg theorist with progressive vocal pieces and a contrapuntal compendium rather than a dry autobiography. If the late cantatas and *Die Kunst der Fuge* are the legacy of Mattheson's prodding, then for Bach – and for posterity – the "Hamburg connection" was a fruitful connection indeed.

---

36 *Tresespiel*, 98: "Joh. Sebast. Bachs so genannte Kunst der Fuge, ein praktisches und prächtiges Werk von 70 Kupfern in Folio, wird alle französische und welsche Fugenmacher dereinst in Erstaunen setzen; dafern sie es nur recht einsehen und wohl verstehen, will nicht sagen, spielen können. Wie wäre es denn, wenn ein jeder Aus- und Einländer an diese Seltenheit seinen *Louis d'or* wagte? Deutschland ist und bleibet doch ganz gewiß das wahre Orgel- und Fugenland."

PART IV

Mattheson and the music theory and aesthetics of the eighteenth century

18

Zur Handhabung der "inventio" in der deutschen Musiklehre des frühen achtzehnten Jahrhunderts

WULF ARLT

Basel

Die Diskussion darüber, was eine Interpretation musikalischer Sachverhalte des siebzehnten und achtzehnten Jahrhunderts aus den Fragestellungen und mit den Verfahren der Rhetorik zu leisten vermag, scheint zur Ruhe gekommen. Der weitreichende hermeneutische Anspruch, der in den Arbeiten eines Arnold Schering, Wilibald Gurlitt oder auch Arnold Schmitz mit der Wiederentdeckung der "Figurenlehre" als Teil einer umgreifenderen "musikalischen Rhetorik" bzw. "musikalischen Oratorie" verbunden war, klingt in den neueren Beiträgen zum Thema kaum mehr an. Die einschlägigen Aussagen der Musiklehre sind zumindest soweit erfaßt und geklärt, daß ihre pragmatische Anwendung in der Interpretation musikalischer Texte keine grundsätzlichen Probleme mehr aufgibt. Das gilt vor allem für die einzelnen "Figuren" und zumal dann, wenn es sich um Komponisten des deutschen Sprachbereichs handelt, auf dessen Lehrschriften sich die Vorstellung von einer spezifischen "musikalischen Rhetorik" stützt[1]. Die weitgehende Ausklammerung jener grundsätzlichen Frage nach dem, was der Rückgriff auf die Rhetorik zum Verständnis musikalischer Sinngebung beitragen kann, ist aus zwei Gründen verständlich: zum einen, weil ihre

---

1 In diesem Sinne faßte jetzt G. J. Buelow die Ergebnisse der Forschung unter dem nüchternen Stichwort "Rhetoric and music" zusammen: *New Grove* 15 (1980), 793–802, mit Hinweis auf weitere Arbeiten. Eine dort noch nicht erfaßte Untersuchung, die den Figuren Christoph Bernhards in seinen eigenen Kompositionen nachgeht, bietet die Hamburger Dissertation von F. Fiebig, *Christoph Bernhard und der stile moderno. Untersuchungen zu Leben und Werk* (Hamburg, 1980) (=Hamburger Beiträge zur Musikwissenschaft 22). Eine kritische Haltung gegenüber der "zu einer Methode wissenschaftlicher Hermeneutik erhobenen Lehre von den musikalisch-rhetorischen Figuren" forderte Carl Dahlhaus bereits 1953 mit generellen Beobachtungen zum Verhältnis zwischen Musik und Rhetorik: "Die Figurae superficiales in den Traktaten Christoph Bernhards", in: *Kongreß-Bericht Bamberg 1953* (Kassel und Basel, 1954), 135–8.

Berücksichtigung allenthalben auf Probleme führt, die weit über die Analyse eines konkreten kompositorischen Sachverhalts hinausreichen; zum anderen, weil die Musiklehre selber in ihren Exempla, die zu einem guten Teil Kompositionen entnommen sind, zur unmittelbaren, analogen Erklärung kompositorischer Sachverhalte geradezu herausfordert. Nur provoziert die bloße Bestandsaufnahme und Einordnung einzelner kompositorischer Aspekte gemäß dem Vorgehen der Lehrschriften gerade bei diesem Erklärungsmodell immer wieder die Frage, was denn letztlich mit einer solchen "Applicatio" gewonnen, ja was mit ihr überhaupt zu leisten sei. Und das umso entschiedener, je konsequenter sich die analytische Untersuchung auf die Anwendung dessen beschränkt, was an Fragestellungen und einzelnen technischen Verfahren in einer bestimmten Lehrschrift vorliegt.

Die Schriften Johann Matthesons zählen zu den wichtigsten Quellen einer umgreifenderen "musikalischen Rhetorik". Das gilt vor allem für den *Vollkommenen Capellmeister*, der weithin durch die Auseinandersetzung mit den Fragen und Verfahren der Rhetorik geprägt ist. Wie sich denn Mattheson im hohen Alter nicht ohne Grund zugute hielt, das Gefüge einer "musikalischen" Rhetorik wesentlich mit ausgebaut zu haben. In der Rhetorik hat die "Ars inveniendi" ihren festen Platz. Sie behandelt die Möglichkeiten, dem Einfall mit bestimmten Techniken nachzuhelfen: von der allgemeinen "Amplificatio" über die "Ars combinatoria" bis hin zu den "loci topici", die mit stereotypen Verfahren beim Namen der Sache einsetzen, um die es geht, bei deren Definition, bei den Gründen, warum etwas geschieht, bei den "Umständen", bei der "Wirkung" und so fort.

Nun besteht – und diese Beobachtung hat den hier vorgelegten Beitrag provoziert – ein schroffer Gegensatz in der Einstellung zur "inventio" und insbesondere zur "Findelehre" der "loci topici" zwischen dem *Vollkommenen Capellmeister* des Jahres 1739 und der rund fünfundzwanzig Jahre früher entstandenen ersten Lehrschrift Matthesons, dem *Neu-eröffneten Orchestre*. Der Vergleich der beiden Texte führte zu der Frage, wieweit es überhaupt möglich und sinnvoll sei, fürs siebzehnte und frühe achtzehnte Jahrhundert von einer eigentlichen "musikalischen Inventionslehre" zu sprechen, und damit auf das übergeordnete Problem der Rekonstruktion eines umgreifenderen Lehrgebäudes der "musikalischen Rhetorik" bzw. "musikalischen Oratorie" aus dem Rückgriff der Musiklehre auf die Fragen und Verfahren der Rhetorik. Die drei Aspekte hängen, wie der erste Teil des Beitrags verdeutlicht, eng miteinander zusammen. Das zeigt die Notwendigkeit einer Interpretation der Lehrschriften, die diese nicht von vornherein als Zeugnisse derselben rhetorischen Lehrtradition ansieht, sondern bei den je anderen Haltungen der Autoren, ihren unterschiedlichen Absichten, Voraussetzungen und Konsequenzen ansetzt. Denn abzuklären ist bereits, wieweit die Texte im einzelnen des Ansatzes wie der Argumente tatsächlich einem gleichen Lehrzusammenhang zuzuordnen sind, wo und in welcher Weise sie aufeinander Bezug nehmen und wieweit die Gemeinsamkeiten zwischen ihnen gegebenenfalls bereits aus dem je eigenen Rückgriff auf die Fragestellungen und Verfahren der Rhetorik resultieren, an welcher Lehre der Rhetorik sich die einzelnen Autoren orientieren und so fort. Zu prüfen ist schließlich, ob und wieweit die verschiedenen Arten des Rückgriffs auf die Rhetorik unterschiedliche Konsequenzen für die musikalische Analyse mit sich bringen, und damit, wieweit die Unterschiede der Haltungen jener Tage Anregungen für den heutigen Umgang mit diesem Erklärungsmodell bieten. Zu diesen Fragen legt der zweite Teil dieser Studie einige Beobachtungen und Überlegungen vor, in denen es insbesondere um den Gegensatz zwischen der Position Heinichens und derjenigen Matthesons im Umgang mit der "inventio" geht.

I

1. In seiner programmatischen ersten Lehrschrift des Jahres 1713 distanziert sich Mattheson eindeutig und spöttisch von jeglicher Möglichkeit, die "inventio" zu lehren. Er verweist dabei ausdrücklich auf die nur vermeintlichen "Wunder-Wercke", die den "bekannten loci Topici" und der "mächtigen Ars combinatoria" zugeschrieben würden. Die Aussage findet sich am Anfang des zweiten Teils, "Von der musicalischen Composition und dem Contra-Punct an sich selbst", und sie steht zwischen der Definition des Kontrapunkts und den "General-Reguln der Composition". Dieser Kontext aber folgt, wenn auch mit einigen Umstellungen und Ergänzungen, weithin wörtlich den beiden ersten Kapiteln des *Tractatus compositionis augmentatus* von Christoph Bernhard, dessen systematische Verbindung der Figurenlehre mit der Dissonanzbehandlung für die Frage nach einem fachlichen Lehrzusammenhang in der Erklärung musikalischer Sachverhalte aus dem Ansatz und mit den Verfahren der Rhetorik schulebildend war[2]. Zwischen die still-

2 Der Text Bernhards bei J. Müller-Blattau, *Die Kompositionslehre Heinrich Schützens in der Fassung seines Schülers Christoph Bernhard* (Leipzig, 1926). Das erste Kapitel

schweigend übernommenen Bestimmungen Bernhards ist im *Neu-eröffneten Orchestre* ein Abschnitt eingefügt, der mit einer generellen Feststellung über die enge "Verwandtschaft" zwischen Komposition und Redekunst beginnt: "Es gehören sonst zu einer Composition dreyerley: Inventio, (Die Erfindung) Elaboratio, (Die Ausarbeitung) Executio, (die Ausführung oder Aufführung) welches eine ziemliche nahe Verwandschafft mit der Oratorie oder Rhetorique (Rede-Kunst) an den Tag leget". Es folgt die Einschränkung, daß zwar "Die beyden letzten Stücke ... erlernet werden" könnten, daß sich aber "zum ersten", also zur Inventio, "noch kein tüchtiger Maitre" habe "finden wollen", da diese "keine zu erlangende / sondern eine angebohrne gute Eigenschafft" erfordere: "qualitatem innatam non verò acquisitam"[3]. Nun gehört der Hinweis auf das notwendige "ingenium", auf die Naturanlage als Voraussetzung einer handwerklichen Schulung, zum festen Gut der Rhetorik wie der Poetik. Doch lehnt eben Mattheson in dieser frühen Schrift die Schulung der Inventio im Rahmen einer Ars schlechthin und mit einer offenkundigen An-spielung auf die rhetorisch untermauerte Predigtlehre ab, wenn er forfährt: "daß also einer / der eine Invention zu suchen / eine Kunst nennet / eben so sehr irret / als der einen habilen Pastorem vor einen kunstreichen Prediger schelten wollte". Es folgt die Abqualifizierung der "loci Topici", der "Ars combinatoria" sowie des "barm-hertzigen" Verses "Quis, quid, ubi, quibus auxiliis, cur, quomodo, quando", als eines Leitverses der "Amplificatio". Diese Zurück-weisung einer Lehrbarkeit der Findekunst ist umso auffälliger, als sie mit dem Hinweis auf die generelle Verwandtschaft zwischen Kom-position und Rhetorik übereingeht und an einer zentralen Stelle in die Darstellung Bernhards eingefügt ist, an die sich Mattheson auch im weiteren und mit ergänzenden Hinweisen unter anderem auf die "musicalische Rhetoric" anlehnt[4].

handelt "Vom Contrapuncte insgemein" (p. 40), das zweite "Von denen General Regeln des Contrapuncts" (p. 40–2).
3 *Das Neu-Eröffnete Orchestre, Oder Universelle und gründliche Anleitung / Wie ein GalantHomme einen vollkommnen Begriff von der Hoheit und Würde der edlen Music erlangen / seinen Gout darnach formiren / die Terminos technicos verstehen und geschicklich von dieser vortrefflichen Wissenschaft raisonniren möge* (Hamburg, 1713), 104; dort und auf der folgenden Seite auch die weiteren Zitate.
4 So ist die zweite der "General Regeln" Bernhards, in der die in der ersten geforderte Kantabilität mit den Worten präzisiert wird "Zu solchem Ende dienet vornehmlich, daß Text und Noten sich wohl zusammen reimen", bei Mattheson folgendermaßen erweitert: "Daß sich in der Vocal-Music Text und Noten vor allen Dingen wol zusammen reimen / und die in den Worten steckende Emphasis, nebst den Distinc-tionen / als Comma, Colon &c. wol in acht genommen werden. Als worinn mit Recht die musicalische Rhetoric stecket" (105–6). Der präzisierende Hinweis auf die

Rund fünfundzwanzig Jahre später legte Mattheson selber im *Vollkommenen Capellmeister* ein umfangreiches Kapitel "Von der Erfindung" vor[5]. Es bietet die eingehendste Behandlung der "inventio" im Bereich der Musiklehre überhaupt. Zwar findet sich auch in diesem Text eingangs der Hinweis auf die zur Erfindung notwendigen "natürlichen Eigenschafften" und wird im folgenden mehrfach betont, daß den erörterten Verfahren nur eine Hilfsfunktion zukomme; im Vordergrund aber steht hier eine handfest an Beispielen verdeutlichte Inventionslehre, die eben das aufnimmt, was Mattheson 1713 ausdrücklich abgelehnt hatte. So greift er auf die Verfahren der "Ars combinatoria" zurück und behandelt er in fünfundsechzig der fünfundachtzig Paragraphen ausführlich die einst zurückgewiesenen "loci topici". Mattheson betonte, daß er in seiner Erfindungslehre weiter gegangen sei als andere. Tatsächlich bietet dieses Kapitel – nach der älteren, nicht mit der Rhetorik verbundenen Anwendung einer "Ars combinatoria", etwa bei Athanasius Kircher, oder auch der Zusammenstellung von "loci communes" des Kontrapunkts, wie sie Andreas Herbst nach Giovanni Battista Chiodino wiedergab – den ersten systematischen Versuch, die Fragestellungen und Verfahren der "inventio" nicht nur zum Verständnis eines zu vertonenden Textes und im Sinne einer Anregung für die musikalische Gestaltung heranzuziehen, sondern unmittelbar in die "musicalische Setz-Kunst" zu übertragen und damit auf die Gegebenheiten der Musik hin umzudeuten[6]. Das ist vor zwei Voraussetzungen zu sehen: Zum einen

---

Vokalmusik entspricht einer Erweiterung der ersten Regel: Aus Bernhards Formulierung "Die erste Regel, und aus der die andern alle herfließen, ist, daß eine jede Stimme des Contrapuncts sich wohl singen lasse" wird bei Mattheson "So ist die erste und vornehmste: Daß man Cantable setze h.e. daß sich alles / was man machet / es sey vocal- oder Instrumental-Music wohl singen lasse". Mattheson besaß, wie er im *Orchestre* III vermerkt (p. 48–9), eine Kopie der ungedruckten Abhandlung Bernhards. Der von ihm genannte Titel stimmt mit demjenigen in einer der beiden erhaltenen Fassungen überein, doch ist eine Einordnung der Zitate Matthesons in die Überlieferung des *Tractatus* aufgrund der Umformulierungen problematisch; vgl. die Angaben zur Überlieferung bei K. Deggeller, "Materialien zu den Musiktraktaten Christoph Bernhards" in: *Basler Studien zur Interpretation der alten Musik* (Winterthur, 1980), 141–68 (=Forum Musicologicum 2). Herrn Deggeller, der an einer Studie zu den Traktaten Bernhards arbeitet, danke ich für diesen und weitere Hinweise.

5 So die Formulierung des Kolumnentitels. Die Kapitelüberschrift lautet "Von der melodischen Erfindung", *Capellmeister*, 121–32.

6 In diesem Sinne heißt es in §24 von den "loci": "Ob nun gleich mancher dencken dürffte, es würde großen Zwang erfordern, alle diese Dinge zur musicalischen Setz-Kunst hinzuziehen; so wird doch die Folge einen ieden überführen, daß solches nicht nur gantz natürlicher Weise geschehen könne, sondern daß es auch in der That bey der Erfindungs-Lehre so seyn müsse: ungeachtet es noch von niemand ordentlich versuchet worden" (124). Athanasius Kircher verweist in den Aus-

war dem späten Mattheson die Analogie zwischen Musik und Sprache so fraglos, daß er die "singende und [die] sprechende Beredtsamkeit" mühelos nebeneinander stellen und betrachten konnte – "wie sie da, an und für sich selbst, abgemessen, eingetheilet, hingesetzt und geschrieben werden" –, entsprechend dem Stichwort der "Klangrede", das dann eben auch die Instrumentalmusik einschloß. Die zweite Voraussetzung liegt in dem älteren enzyklopädischen Ansatz des *Capellmeisters*. Ihm entspricht die umgreifende, kompilatorische Behandlung seines Gegenstandes, dessen Verankerung in einem hierarchischen, wenn auch nur mehr mühsam zusammengehaltenen Wissenschaftsgebäude, und im einzelnen das Klassifizieren als ein leitendes Prinzip gemäß der Maxime "Wer wohl unterscheidet, lehret wohl". Als gliedernde Gesichtspunkte nannte er vier allgemeine "Verhältnisse": "natürliche, moralische, rhetorische und mathematische"[7]. Nun erstreckte sich die Anwendung der Rhetorik gerade im deutschen Sprachbereich und mit den Schriften Christian Weises aus dem letzten Viertel des siebzehnten Jahrhunderts auf die verschiedensten Bereiche; zur Sprache gebracht aber wurde sie selbst in der allgemeinen Redelehre insbesondere am Beispiel der "Dichtkunst", die ein Stück weit zur allgemeinen Bildung gehörte[8]. So verband sich Matthesons Rückgriff auf die Rhetorik mit der im *Capellmeister* allenthalben greifbaren, ausdrücklichen und vielfältigen Anwendung des Ansatzes sowie der

führungen "De partibus rhetoricae musurgicae" für die "inventio" allein auf den Zusammenhang zwischen Musik und Text (*Musurgia universalis* II. [Rom, 1650], 143). Das steht im achten Kapitel ("Musurgia rhetorica") des zweiten Teils des achten Buches, in dem es um die "Musurgia rhythmica sive poetica" geht (27ss.). Der erste Teil dieses Buches handelt von der "Musurgia combinatoria" (3–27). Andreas Herbst bringt in der *Musica poetica* nach den Generalregeln "dreyßig Loci communes Musicales, pro Tyronibus Oder kurtze Exempel für die Anfahenden / so mit zweyen Stimmen contrapunctweiß componiret und gesetzet seyn. Autore Giov. Battist. Chiodino" (Nürnberg, 1643, 115–19). Ein zweites Mal veröffentlichte er diese "loci" im Kontext seiner Übersetzung der Abhandlung Chiodinos, *Arte prattica & poetica* (Frankfurt, 1653), 26–32. Zur Sammlung solcher "Gemeinstellen" als ein Aspekt der rhetorischen Inventionslehre in der deutschen Poetik jener Zeit: J. Dyck, *Ticht-Kunst – Deutsche Barockpoetik und rhetorische Tradition* (Bad Homburg etc., 1966), 59–63 (=Ars Poetica 1).

7 So in den grundsätzlichen Bemerkungen der "Vorrede" des *Capellmeisters* zur "musikalischen Mathematik" (p. 16); dort und auf der folgenden Seite auch die vorangehenden Zitate. Zum Stichwort der "Klang-Rede" (Vorrede, p. 26, Haupttext, p. 82 et alia): C. Dahlhaus, *Musikästhetik* (Köln, 1967), 39 ss., sowie die Beobachtungen und Überlegungen in der eingehenden Untersuchung von Fr. Reckow über "Sprachähnlichkeit" der Musik als terminologisches Problem. *Zur Geschichte des Topos Tonsprache*, Habilschrift (Freiburg i. Br., 1977), 49–52 et alia (Druck in Vorbereitung als Band 4 der Neuen Studien zur Musikwissenschaft).

8 Dazu im einzelnen die breit angelegte Studie von W. Barner, *Barockrhetorik. Untersuchungen zu ihren geschichtlichen Grundlagen* (Tübingen, 1970).

Verfahren der Sprach- und Dichtungslehre. Das bestimmte weithin die Anlage und die Darstellung des Buches. In diesem Sinne hielt sich dann Mattheson eben 1754 rückblickend zugute, mehr als jeder andere zum Ausbau der "musikalischen Rhetorik" beigetragen zu haben[9]

2. Die deutsche Musiklehre des frühen achtzehnten Jahrhunderts ging in zahlreichen Texten auf den Problemkreis der "inventio" ein. Das betrifft neben den erwähnten Beiträgen Matthesons vor allem Kuhnaus *Texte zur Leipziger Kirchen-Music* (1709), Heinichens *General-Baß in der Composition* (1728) oder Niedts *Musicalische Handleitung*, aber auch kürzere Hinweise, wie in Scheibes *Compendium musices* aus der Zeit um 1730. Von einer "ausgedehnten musikalischen Inventionslehre" dieser Zeit läßt sich freilich mit Hans Heinrich Eggebrecht nur insofern sprechen, als die "inventio" seit dem ausgehenden siebzehnten Jahrhundert und bis zu Matthesons *Capellmeister* im Musikschrifttum öfters, ausführlicher und unter mehr Gesichtspunkten zur Sprache kam als je zuvor[10]. So ist den erwähnten Texten nicht einmal der Rückgriff auf eine Fragestellung der Rhetorik gemeinsam. Und dort, wo sie diesen Ansatz aufnehmen, geschieht das in je anderer Weise. Das gilt für die Verankerung der "inventio" in den verschiedenen Schemata, von denen in der Musiklehre vor allem die Reihung *inventio–dispositio–elocutio* mit unterschiedlichen Umformulierungen aufgenommen wird (so als *inventio–elaboratio–executio* neben der längeren Gliederung in *inventio–dispositio–elaboratio–decoratio–executio*), das schließt die Abgrenzung zwischen Naturgabe und Kunstlehre ein, bringt die "Ars combinatoria" wie die "loci topici" als Verfahren der Findelehre ins Spiel und das hat je nach Vorlage gegebenenfalls Gemeinsamkeiten bis ins einzelne der Formulierung zur Folge. Bezeichnenderweise nehmen die erwähnten Texte der Musiklehre bei dieser Frage kaum aufeinander Bezug. Symptomatisch für die je andere Zielsetzung und das unterschiedliche Vorgehen ist der Unterschied zwischen den Ausführungen des späteren Mattheson einerseits und andererseits den erwähnten Abhandlungen Kuhnaus und Heinichens, aber auch zwischen diesen beiden Texten. So geht es Kuhnau und Heinichen beim Rückgriff auf die "inventio" traditionellerweise um die Aufbereitung eines Textes unter dem Aspekt

9 Auf den Rückblick Matthesons in der 1754 erschienenen *Plus ultra* verwies Fr. Feldmann, "Mattheson und die Rhetorik", in: *Kongreß-Bericht Hamburg 1956* (Kassel und Basel, 1957), 103.
10 Die Formulierung Eggebrechts im Artikel "Invention", in: *Riemann-Musiklexikon. Sachteil* (Mainz, 1967), 416.

der musikalischen Vertonung, und überdies bei beiden unter je anderen Gesichtspunkten: Kuhnau erläutert die philologische Auseinandersetzung mit einem Bibeltext im Rückgriff aufs Hebräische und aus der Aufgabe des Kantors, einen Text gleich einem "Prediger von Gottes Wort . . . in allen Stücken zu exhauriren" und "den rechten Sensum und Scopum der Worte" zu erfassen[11]; Heinichen hingegen greift mit der Frage nach den "Antecedentia, Concomitantia & Consequentia Textus" einen bestimmten Gesichtspunkt der "loci topici" heraus, um am Beispiel "etlicher seichter [Opern-]Texte" zu verdeutlichen, wie sich aus den "dabey concurrirenden Umständen der Person / der Sache / des Wesens / des Uhrsprungs / der Arth und Weise / des Endzwecks / der Zeit / des Ortes etc." vielfältige Anregungen für die kompositorische Gestaltung gewinnen lassen, insbesondere hinsichtlich der Affekte[12]. Dem steht Matthesons faustfertige Übertragung der Inventionslehre ins Musikalische gegenüber, wie sie anschaulich der "locus notationis" zeigt, der seit Christian Weise als erster und wichtigster genannt wird[13]. Hier geht die Lehre der Rhetorik von der Bezeichnung, vom Namen der behandelten Sache aus. Mattheson überträgt das Stichwort unmittelbar auf die Musik. Er gelangt vom "bezeichnen" als "notare" zur Notation, von den "Buchstaben eines Nahmens oder Dings" zu den einzelnen Notenzeichen als "Klang-Buchstaben", und er bringt unter dem auf diese Weise mehr vage umschriebenen als präzise abgegrenzten Gesichtspunkt verschiedenste Möglichkeiten der "Erfindung" mit Tönen zur Sprache. Dabei greift er aus den "schier unzehligen Veränderungen" mittels "der Gestalt und Stelle" der Noten vier – wie er es nennt – "Wege" heraus, vier Verfahren der "Veränderung", die je andere Aspekte der Melodieformulierung, der Satztechnik und des Vortrages betreffen. Sie lassen sich insofern mehr oder weniger

11 Zitiert nach B. Fr. Richter, "Eine Abhandlung Joh. Kuhnau's" in: *Monatshefte für Musikgeschichte* 34 (1902), 153–4, 150. Bezeichnenderweise hebt Kuhnau die hermeneutische Frage dieses Textes von der "Art und Weise zu variiren und inventiren" ab, die er "an einem andern Orte" bereits nach den mathematischen "Praeceptis artis combinatoriae" behandelt habe (p. 150). Die entsprechende Lehrschrift ist offensichtlich verloren – siehe O. Wessely, "Zur Ars inveniendi im Zeitalter des Barock", in: *Orbis musicae* 1 (1971–2), 122–3.
12 *Der General-Baß in der Composition* (Dresden, 1728), 31, 30; cf. G. J. Buelow, "The Loci Topici and Affect in Late Baroque Music: Heinichen's Practical Demonstration", in: *MR* 27 (1966), 161–75.
13 Chr. Weises *Politischer Redner* erschien erstmals 1677. Mir liegt die fünfte Auflage vor (Leipzig, 1688) mit der Behandlung der "loci" auf den Seiten 115 ss. Seiner Aufzählung entspricht – wenn auch mit zum Teil anderen Bezeichnungen – diejenige Chr. Weissenborns, auf den sich Mattheson in §23 des Kapitels "Von der melodischen Erfindung" beruft (*Capellmeister*, 123–4).

plausibel diesem Stichwort zuordnen, als es bei allen in irgendeiner Weise um ein" 'Spiel' mit den Noten" geht[14]: "Veränderungen . . . 1) durch die Geltung der Noten [mit Länge und Kürze, aber auch obligaten Wendungen]; 2) durch die Verkehr- oder Verwechselung; 3) durch die Wiederholung oder den Wiederschlag; und 4) durch die canonischen Gänge". Wie hier beim "locus notationis", so sind auch im weiteren die Termini der Rhetorik, wo immer möglich, unmittelbar ins Musikalische übertragen, so beim "locus generis et speciei" mit dem "Contrapunct" als "genus" und der Fuge als "species", mit dem "solo" als "genus" sowie dem "Violino solo" als "species" und so fort[15]. Eine Ausnahme bilden die Stichwörter der Findelehre, die auch Mattheson auf einen der Komposition zugrundeliegenden Text bzw. auf die Darstellung der "Affecten" schlechthin bezieht. Das gilt vor allem für den "locus descriptionis", den er als "die reichste Quelle, ja gar . . . die sicherste und wesentlichste Handleitung zur Invention" bezeichnet, aber auch für die "causa materialis" und insbesondere für die "Materia in qua"[16]. Nur war es ihm eben gerade bei diesen Gesichtspunkten "wegen der Menge und Beschaffenheit solcher vielfältigen und vermischten Leidenschafften" nicht möglich," so viele deutliche und besondere Regeln" zu geben als etwa beim "locus notationis".

Das Vorgehen Matthesons verdeutlicht, daß die meisten Stichworte der "Findelehre" auf die skizzierte Weise unmittelbar ins Musikalische zu übertragen sind. Ausgespart aber bleibt die Frage, was denn letztlich mit solchen Übertragungen geleistet bzw. zu leisten ist. So bietet dieses Kapitel in der Sammlung unterschiedlichster Beobachtungen, die sich mit den Fragestellungen und Begriffen der Lehre von der "inventio" verbinden lassen, die Einlösung eines Stücks rhetorischer Theorie im Bereich der Musik, bei der dann für die einzelnen Hinweise die Frage nach deren Stellenwert, nach deren Funktion im musikalischen Kontext wie im Kontext der musikalischen Lehre unberücksichtigt bleibt. Das läßt sich in seinen Konsequenzen bezeichnenderweise gerade am "locus notationis" als "*fast* der reichsten Quelle" beobachten[17]. So verweist Mattheson unter den Beispielen seines zweiten "Weges", bei dem es um die

---

14 So H.-H. Unger in Anlehnung an eine Formulierung von Weise, *Die Beziehungen zwischen Musik und Rhetorik im 16.–18. Jahrhundert* (Würzburg, 1941), 43 (=Musik und Geistesgeschichte. Berliner Studien zur Musikwissenschaft 4); die Zitate Matthesons aus dem §24 (p. 124).
15 §50 (p. 128).   16 §43 ss. bzw. 54 und 60 (p. 127–9).
17 §24 (p. 124), dort ohne Hervorhebung; die Einschränkung bezieht sich auf den "locus descriptionis". Die folgenden Zitate aus dem §28.

"Verkehr- oder Verwechselung" geht, auf die "evolutio" als eine Bezeichnung für die "Umkehrung", bei der "man die aufgehenden Noten zu heruntersteigenden, die sinckenden zu erhebenden, die rechtgängigen zu rückgängigen u.s.w. mache". Als "Umkehrung der Gänge" war ihm dieser Begriff aus der Ausgabe der *Musicalischen Handleitung* von Friedrich Erhard Niedt vertraut, die er seit 1710 in Hamburg besorgt hatte. Bei Niedt findet sich das Stichwort im fünften Kapitel des zweiten Teils, der den Schritt von der akkordischen Realisierung eines Generalbasses zum *ex tempore*-Spiel bzw. zur Ausführung von Tanzsätzen auf der Grundlage eines rhythmisch variierten Basses lehrt, und zwar anhand der "Variationes" des Basses selber (von der diminuierenden Veränderung bis eben zu den "Verkehrungen") sowie der freien Veränderung der Akkorde in der rechten Hand[18]. Wenn Niedt im elften Kapitel dieses Teils, "Von Praeludiis und Ciaconen", eine dann in immer wieder anderer Weise veränderte Tonfolge mit den Worten einführt "Ich setze also diesen Baß zum Grunde meiner Invention", so entspricht das der Tatsache, daß seine Abhandlung weithin eine eingehende und in sich schlüssige "Findelehre" im Rahmen einer musikalischen Lehrtradition darstellt, die weder in der Anlage noch im einzelnen der Darstellung auf die Rhetorik zurückgreift; so wie das Stichwort der "inventio" hier nicht als Terminus der Rhetorik, sondern in seiner allgemeinen, vokabularen Bedeutung, also im Sinne von "Erfinden" bzw. Erfindung verwendet ist[19]. Hier hatte die "evolutio" ihren sinnvollen Ort im Kontext der musikalischen Handwerkslehre. Bei

18 Friederich Erhard Niedtens Musikalischer Handleitung Anderer Theil / Von der Variation Des General-Basses, Samt einer Anweisung / Wie man aus einem schlechten General-Baß allerley Sachen / als Praeludia, Ciaconen, Allemanden, &c. erfinden könne, herausgegeben von Mattheson (Hamburg,² 1721), (Facs, Buren, 1976 [Bibliotheca Organologica 32]) 43. Zu Niedts Kompositionsbergriff die Beobachtungen von W. Heimann: *Der Generalbaß-Satz und seine Rolle in Bachs Choral-Satz* (München, 1973), 35–41 (=Freiburger Schriften zur Musikwissenschaft 5); doch scheint mit die Eingrenzung der Zielrichtung Niedts "auf die Berufspraxis speziell des Organisten" (ibid., p. 37) zumal im Blick auf den ersten Teil zu eng. Daß sich Niedt vom ersten zum dritten Teil zunehmend auf das Handwerk des Organisten konzentriert, schließt die Wendung an ein weiteres Publikum nicht aus, die im Titel des ersten Teils mit den Worten angesprochen ist: "Oder Gründlicher Unterricht Vermittels welchen ein Liebhaber der Edlen Music in kurtzer Zeit sich so weit perfectioniren kan / daß Er nicht allein den General-Baß nach denen gesetzten deutlichen und wenigen Regeln fertig spielen / sondern auch folglich allerley Sachen selbst componiren / und ein rechtschaffener Organiste und Musicus heissen könne".

19 *Musicalische Handleitung* II (Matthesons Ausgabe), 117; dazu die Beobachtungen und Überlegungen von H. H. Eggebrecht, *Studien zur musikalischen Terminologie* (Wiesbaden, 1955), 72–82 (=Abhandlungen der Akademie der Wissenschaften und der Literatur in Mainz, geistes- und sozialwissenschaftliche Klasse 1955 10).

Mattheson hingegen erscheint die "evolutio oder eversio" als eine von unzähligen Möglichkeiten des "Spiels mit den Noten", die sich unter der vagen Bestimmung des übergeordneten Stichworts der Rhetorik beliebig sammeln und aufzählen lassen. Daß aber die unterschiedlichen Verfahren eines Kuhnau, Heinichen oder Mattheson in der Musikgeschichtsschreibung unter das Stichwort einer eigentlichen "Inventionslehre" zusammengefaßt werden konnten, ist nur aus deren vermeintlicher Verankerung in einem übergeordneten Lehrgebäude der "musikalischen Rhetorik" verständlich.

3. Sicher gab es nie einen Lehrzusammenhang der "musikalischen Rhetorik", der auch nur annähernd mit der Anwendung der Rhetorik in der Predigtlehre oder in der Poetik zu vergleichen wäre, obschon die Texte der Musikgeschichte gelegentlich so vorgehen, als wollten und könnten sie aus der partiellen Information der einzelnen Traktate einer *musica poetica* und deren Fortführung sowie Erweiterung im Schrifttum des achtzehnten Jahrhunderts so etwas wie ein Lehrgebäude der "musikalischen Rhetorik" rekonstruieren, dessen Kernstück die sogenannte "Figurenlehre" wäre; ein Lehrgebäude, dessen Applikation dann eine sinnvolle und historisch legitimierte Interpretation der Musik jener Zeit gewährleisten würde. Doch ist die Problematik dieser übergeordneten Fragestellung ohne Zweifel vielschichtiger als beim Teilmoment der "inventio". Verantwortlich dafür ist zunächst die Tatsache, daß die beim späten Mattheson explizite Vorstellung von einer eigentlichen "musikalischen Rhetorik" ansatzweise auch schon aus älteren Texten herauszulesen ist, und sei es nur aufgrund einer verkürzenden Formulierung[20]. Bei den meisten Autoren jedoch geht es nur um den Vergleich mit der Dichtungslehre oder auch mit einer allgemeinen Rhetorik, so in Bernhards bekannter Feststellung, "daß . . . die Musica so hoch kommen . . . , daß sie wohl einer Rhetorica zu vergleichen" und entsprechend in Matthesons frühem Hinweis auf die "ziemlich nahe Verwandschafft" der Komposition "mit der Oratorie oder Rhetorique"[21]. Entscheidend aber war, daß die Interpretation musikalischer Sachverhalte im Sinne der "Tropen" im siebzehnten Jahrhundert in

20 In diesem Sinne heißt es etwa 1563 bei G. Dressler: "Sicut enim oratio habet octo partes orationis . . . , ita etiam concentus musicalis octo vel etiam plures habet tonos" und "Quod autem in oratione est periodus et comma, id in poetica musica sunt clausulae", zitiert nach M. Ruhnke, *Joachim Burmeister. Ein Beitrag zur Musiklehre um 1600* (Kassel und Basel, 1955), 137 (= Schriften des Landesinstituts für Musikforschung Kiel 5).

21 Das Zitat Bernhards aus dem "Ausführlichen Bericht vom Gebrauche der Con- und Dissonantien" (ed. Müller-Blattau, *Die Kompositionslehre Schützens*, 147); zu Mattheson siehe oben Abschnitt I/1.

die Kompositionslehre einging. Das gilt vor allem für Bernhards schulebildende systematische Integration des "Figurbegriffs" in die Darstellung der Dissonanzbehandlung. Denn dadurch wurde dieses Teilmoment der Rhetorik mit demjenigen Bereich der Musiklehre verbunden, der seit dem sechzehnten Jahrhundert – und stärker als jeder andere zuvor – eine eng umschriebene und außerordentlich stabile Lehrtradition aufweist. So überschneiden sich bei der "Figurenlehre" zwei Momente: einerseits der *ad hoc*-Rückgriff auf die Rhetorik als Teil der Dichtungslehre oder auch als ein allgemeines bzw. explizit der Musiklehre übergeordnetes Verfahren und andererseits ein fachspezifischer Lehrzusammenhang. Das zweite trug wesentlich zur skizzierten Vorstellung der Musikgeschichtsschreibung bei; das erste spiegelt sich in den bekannten Schwierigkeiten, die sich dem Versuch entgegenstellen, Sachbeschreibung und Namensgebung in der Rekonstruktion einer allgemeinen Figurenlehre miteinander zu verbinden[22].

II

Der Umgang mit der "musikalischen Rhetorik" läuft Gefahr, aus der Erwartung einer gefestigten Lehrtradition oder gar eines mehr oder weniger geschlossenen Lehrgebäudes den Zugang zu den historisch interessantesten Aspekten zu verstellen, die der Rückgriff auf die Rhetorik bietet. Damit wäre zugleich die spezifische Produktivität dieses Ansatzes für die musikalische Analyse zugunsten der Einlösung einzelner Gesichtspunkte einer Theorie preisgegeben. Die "inventio" verweist insofern besonders anschaulich auf diese Problematik, als hier offen zutage liegt, wie wenig mit dem generellen Hinweis auf diesen Gesichtspunkt sowie mit der Nennung einzelner Fragestellungen und Verfahren einer "Findekunst" gewonnen ist. Wie seitens der Germanistik und einer allgemeinen Rhetorikforschung in den letzten fünfzehn Jahren immer wieder betont wurde,

---

22 Daß es trotz der einschlägigen Hinweise der Musikgeschichtsschreibung für die Zeit vom sechzehnten bis achtzehnten Jahrhundert im Musikschrifttum keine systematische Figurenlehre gab, betonte im Sinne der generellen Überlegungen von Dahlhaus (siehe oben Anm. 1) jetzt auch Buelow ("Rhetoric and Music", 794); zur ähnlichen Problematik des älteren Rückgriffs auf die Rhetorik, der auch im ausgehenden vierzehnten und frühen fünfzehnten Jahrhundert bis zur Applikation einzelner Figuren reicht, jetzt Fr. Reckow, "Rectitudo–pulchritudo–enormitas. Spätmittelalterliche Erwägungen zum Verhältnis von materia und cantus", in: *Musik und Text in der Mehrstimmigkeit des 14. und 15. Jahrhunderts*, Bericht über ein Symposium der Herzog-August-Bibliothek Wolfenbüttel 1980 (Druck in Vorbereitung).

sind gerade in diesem Bereich die Unterschiede zwischen den Autoren vielfach aufschlußreicher als die Übereinstimmungen zwischen ihren Texten[23]. Das richtet den Blick auf die je anderen Voraussetzungen und den je anderen Kontext eines Rückgriffs auf die "inventio", auf das je andere Interesse der Autoren sowie dessen Konsequenzen für den Umgang mit diesem wie mit anderen Aspekten der Rhetorik. Selbst dort, wo eine weitergehende Übereinstimmung zwischen den Texten vorliegt, wie im Fall der "Figurenlehre", stellt sich im einzelnen die Frage nach symptomatischen Gewichtsverlagerungen in der Akzentsetzung bzw. Formulierung.

Kontext und Akzentverlagerung verdienen bei der "inventio" umso mehr Beachtung, als ja hier mit der Abgrenzung zwischen Naturgabe und Kunstlehre, zwischen "ingenium" und "inventio" bzw. "ingenium" und "ars", ein Problemkreis angesprochen ist, bei dem es im achtzehnten Jahrhundert zu einer bedeutsamen Gewichtsverlagerung mit einer Neubewertung des "ingenium" kam, die sich selbst in den Texten der deutschen Poetiken aus dem zweiten Drittel des Jahrhunderts oft nur in einer neuen Gewichtung älterer Begriffe und Formulierungen spiegelt[24]. Nicht weniger bedeutsam aber ist, daß die Auseinandersetzung der Musiklehre mit der "inventio" in eine Umbruchssituation fällt, in der der Geltungsbereich der Rhetorik aus der Gracian-Rezeption des deutschen Sprachbereichs erheblich ausgeweitet worden war. Das geschah vor allem durch Christian Weise. Sein 1677 erschienener *Politischer Redner* gab den "Anstoß zu einer wahren Flut deutschsprachiger Rhetoriken und Briefsteller", in denen die Redekunst, dem Stichwort des "Politischen" entsprechend, auf eine bestimmte Haltung und Form des "gemeinen Lebens" bezogen war[25]. Eine Gruppe dieser vielfach programmatisch modischen Texte griff in akzentuierter Form das Schlagwort des "Galanten" auf. Zu ihren Autoren gehört Christian Hunold, dessen 1707 in Hamburg unter dem Pseudonym Menantes erschienene *Allerneueste Art / Zur Reinen und Galanten Poesie zu gelangen* Erdmann Neumeisters Leipziger Poetikvorlesungen aufnahm.

Hunolds Text führt auf den Gegensatz zwischen dem frühen und dem späteren Mattheson zurück. So steht das *Neu-eröffnete Or-*

23 So schon L. Fischer, *Gebundene Rede. Dichtung und Rhetorik in der literarischen Theorie des Barock in Deutschland* (Tübingen, 1968), 3–6, 8 et alia (=Studien zur deutschen Literatur 10).
24 Dazu im einzelnen die Beobachtungen von H. P. Herrmann, *Naturnachahmung und Einbildungskraft. Zur Entwicklung der deutschen Poetik von 1670 bis 1740* (Bad Homburg etc., 1970) (=Ars poetica 8).
25 Barner, *Barockrhetorik*, 135, 181ss. et alia.

chestre, wie schon Beekman C. Cannon betonte, mit der programmatischen Wendung an den "galant homme" wie mit der Berufung auf "einen guten gout und gesundes Judicium" ganz im Gefolge dieser *a la mode*-Schriften[26]. Ihre Haltung ist eine wesentliche Voraussetzung für Matthesons Abgrenzung gegenüber der älteren Musiklehre. Es ist anzunehmen, daß Mattheson schon damals die *Allerneueste Art* kannte, und dort gibt es in den Ausführungen zur "Oratorie" ein eingehendes Kapitel auch über die "inventio"[27]. Daß Mattheson 1713 – im Gegensatz zu Hunold–Neumeister – die Lehre der "inventio" so scharf zurückwies, geht mit der Ablehnung alles "Schulfüchsigen" und mit der entschiedenen Berufung auf das Geschmacksurteil überein[28]. Das entspricht einer progressiven Haltung, die Reinhard Keiser in seinen "Kurtzen Anmerkungen" zum *Neu-eröffneten Orchestre* als "ein auf Experientz und beste Praxin gegründetes Raisonnement" charakterisierte[29]. Sie war zumindest im Ansatz gegenüber den Fragestellungen und Positionen der französischen Kunsttheorie offen, deren Rezeption – direkt oder mittelbar – die neuen instrumentalen Lehrschriften aus dem zweiten Drittel des Jahrhunderts prägte, denen dann eine weitgehende Vermittlung zwischen Geschmacksurteil und musikalischer Handwerkslehre gelang, wie sie insbesondere bei Quantz vorliegt.

Der Wandel in der Einstellung Matthesons zur "inventio" ist in zwei Bemerkungen greifbar. Die erste findet sich im *Beschützten Orchestre*, die zweite in der *Critica musica*. 1717 zeichnet sich insofern eine erste vorsichtige Öffnung gegenüber diesem Problemkreis ab, als der Erlernbarkeit und vor allem den Techniken der

26 Cannon, *Mattheson*, 115; cf. den Titel des *Orchestre* I (oben Anm. 3); das Zitat auf den Seiten 135–6.
27 pp. 540–58.
28 So heißt es etwa in der "Einleitung", daß "ein galant homme . . . vor allen Dingen sich wol fürzusehen" habe, "daß ihn kein Schulfuchs mit seiner eingebildeten Weißheit / kein wilder Fantaste / mit seiner Federfechterey; und kein Leyrmann . . . praeoccupire" (p. 20–1). Das geht mit der Feststellung überein, "daß dannenhero alle die unzehligen Regeln sich nach der Zeit / darinnen wir leben / auch nach den Umständen und Manieren / die in der Music eben so veränderlich als die Constellationes am Himmel sind / ändern und accomodiren müssen" (p. 3–4). Der generellen Ausrichtung auf die Schulung des "gout" im Titel (siehe oben Anm. 3) entspricht im einzelnen der häufige Hinweis auf den "gout" bzw. "gusto" als Instanz und die entsprechende Differenzierung nach Nationen, Orten und Stilbereichen in der "Pars tertia, iudicatoria" (p. 200 ss.). Oder wie eines und anderes in der Music zu beurtheilen" (p. 200 ss.). Nachdrücklich weist Mattheson noch im *Orchestre* III darauf hin, daß man sich "nach der Mode, dem gout und dem stylo . . . unauszetzlich richten / und nicht eigensinnig bey der alten Leyer bleiben" solle, "wenn dieselbe aus der Welt verbannet wird". (p. 369); cf. W. Braun, *Johann Mattheson und die Aufklärung*, phil. Diss. (Halle, 1951), 41 et alia.
29 *Orchestre* I, 336.

384

Inventionslehre die "Nachahmung" als eine legitime Hilfsfunktion gegenübergestellt ist: "Daß man der Invention nicht zu Hülffe kommen könne / streitet niemand; daß die invention aber erlernet werden möge / allerdings. Wenn man ihr zu Hülffe kommt per artem combinatoriam, so ist es armseelig und gezwungen Werck; geschieht es durch natürliche Dinge / so ist es eine Nachahmung / und das ist der beste Weg"[30]. Nur ist die "Nachahmung" hier nicht auf das zentrale Stichwort der Kunst- und Literaturtheorie jener Tage bezogen, sondern schlicht auf eine Anregung durch bestehende Kompositionen. So heißt es nach dem Hinweis darauf, daß Reinhard Keiser nur auf diesem Wege "67 Opern" habe schreiben können, präzisierend: "muß einer aber seine einzige Zuflucht zur Anhöhrung gut und inventieuser Musiquen nehmen/und hat sonst vor sich selbst nichts / so ists und wird es platterdings ein Plagium". Noch weiter geht 1722 die *Critica musica* in der polemischen Auseinandersetzung mit Murschhausers *Academia musico-poetica*, die mit dem Stichwort des Titels traditionellerweise die Kompositionslehre bezeichnet. Hier wird von Mattheson erstmals eine umgreifende Berücksichtigung der Fragen und Gesichtspunkte der Redekunst gefordert und dabei die programmatische Frage aufgeworfen: "Wo ist der Inventions-Kasten / und wie ist derselbe zu eröffnen?"[31] Diese Forderung ist dann im *Capellmeister* mit der eingehenden Behandlung des Gegenstandes eingelöst.

Nun findet sich in dem Kapitel "Von der melodischen Erfindung" des *Capellmeister* nach der eingehenden Behandlung der "loci topici" der Hinweis auf eine weitere, "besondre Erfindungs-Art . . ., welche man eine unvermuthete, unerwartete und gleichsam außerordentlich-eingegebene nennet, (inventio ex abrupto, inopinato, quasi ex enthusiasmo musico)"[32]. Das könnte man auf den ersten Blick hin und zumal im zweiten Drittel des Jahrhunderts im Sinne einer neuen Betonung der Eingebung lesen. Beim näheren Zusehen hingegen machen drei Momente stutzig: zunächst, daß auch dieser besonderen Eingebung handfest nachgeholfen werden kann, sodann, daß der zweite der dann folgenden Hinweise einen Gesichtspunkt aufnimmt, der schon vorher zur Sprache kam, und schließlich, daß der letzte Hinweis von etwas ganz anderem handelt. So heißt es erst:

denn dazu hilfft: 1) Wenn man eines vortrefflichen Componisten Arbeit, zumahl dafern derselbe etwa einerley Materie mit der unsrigen behandelt hat, vorher wol ein- und ansiehet. 2) Wenn man sich eine Leidenschafft fest

---

30 *Orchestre* II, 104; dort auch das folgende Zitat.
31 *Critica musica* I, 75.   32 §85 (p. 132).

eindrückt, und sich gleichsam darin vertiefft, als wäre man in der That andächtig, verliebt, zornig, hönisch, betrübt, erfreuet u.s.w. dieses ist gewiß der sicherste Weg zu gantz unvermutheten Erfindungen.

Unter (3) hingegen findet sich die Feststellung:

Kann man auch in einer eintzigen Melodie verschiedene Erfindungen anbringen, und so zu reden fast augenblicklich, auf unerwartete Art, mit denselben abwechseln: welches die Zuhörer vergnüglich überraschet; wenn nur sonst dem Zusammenhange oder der Haupt-Absicht dadurch nicht zu nahe geschiehet.

Die Widersprüche sind einfach zu erklären. Sie beruhen darauf, daß Mattheson an dieser Stelle grob verkürzend kompiliert und den zwei Begründungen seiner Vorlage einen dort klar abgesetzten Gesichtspunkt anreiht. Das läßt sich im *Capellmeister* noch öfters beobachten und ist für die Problematik gerade dieses Kapitels charakteristisch. Denn die Vorlage ist hier nichts anderes als der Schluß des erwähnten Kapitels über die "inventio" in der *Allerneuesten Art*. Eine zusätzliche Pointe besteht nun aber darin, daß dort die Eingebung ausdrücklich hervorgehoben wird. So heißt es bei Hunold–Neumeister nach der Behandlung der "loci" und vor den beiden von Mattheson weitgehend wörtlich übernommenen Begründungen: "Schließlich *gefällt mir* eine Invention ex abrupto & inopinato. Ich meine, welche uns am ersten, *ohne sonderbahre Praemediation und Zergrübelung* beyfällt, und gleichsam ex Enthusiasmo Poetico herfließet"[33]. Mattheson hingegen fügt diesen Aspekt als eine letzte Ergänzung mit den Worten an: "Doch ist noch eine besondre Erfindungs-Art übrig". Das wiederum ist verständlich, weil er schon eingangs einen entsprechenden Paragraphen hatte, in dem es zumindest hieß: "Hingegen kömmt bisweilen, ohne großes Nachsinnen, gantz unschuldiger und natürlicher Weise eine Einfall, der unvergleichlich ist", mit dem schulmeisterlichen Nachsatz: "Solchen Augenblick muß man alsdann nicht vergeblich vorbey streichen

---

33 P. 556 ohne Hervorhebung. Die beiden folgenden Punkte lauten dort: "LIV. Man wird einen mercklichen Vortheil hierinnen erlangen, wenn man vorher eine Passage aus einem guten Poeten lieset, welcher gleich Materie mit unsern conceptibus, die wir itzo zur Elaboration im Sinne haben, tractiret hat." "LV. Oder man imprimiret sich einen Affect wohl, ja man verstellet sich gleichsam gar in demselben, als ob man verliebt, zornig, höhnisch, betrübt etc. wäre, nachdem es die Beschaffenheit des Carminis erfordert". Nach einem weiteren Punkt folgt dann unter "LVII. Auch dieses solte ich nicht unberühret vorbey gehen lassen. Manchmal hat man in einer jedweden Strophe gleichsam eine neue Invention, welche aber alle in der Haupt-Invention oder Themate concentriren müssen . . . Doch müssen solche Realia oder Inventiones homogenae seyn, das ist, eine mit der andern einige Verwandschafft haben" (p. 557).

lassen, sondern sich denselben wol zu Nutz machen"[34]. Das steht in einem ganz merkwürdig zusammengewürfeltem Kontext verschiedenster Gründe für "gute Erfindungen", von "einer angebohrnen Gemüths-Beschaffenheit und glücklichen Einrichtung der Fächer im Gehirne" über die "Zeit" und "gute Laune" bis hin zu "Ehre, Lob, Liebe und Belohnungen"! So führt die kompilatorische Behandlung der "inventio" beim späten Mattheson in der Bewertung des "ingenium" nicht nur hinter die radikale Position seiner ersten Lehrschrift, sondern auch hinter die differenzierende Bewertung des Einfalls in seiner dreißig Jahre älteren Vorlage zurück.

Sicher sind die Konsequenzen des älteren enzyklopädischen Ansatzes, des kompilatorischen Verfahrens, der schulmeisterlichen Haltung und nicht zuletzt eines negativen Aspekts der "Polemik als Erkenntnisform", auf die Arno Forchert hinwies, in diesem Kapitel des *Capellmeisters* besonders deutlich zu greifen[35]. Bezeichnenderweise steht denn auch unmittelbar anschließend ein so wichtiger, eigenständiger und anregender Text wie der "Von der Kunst eine gute Melodie zu machen" – gleichsam als kreatives Gegenstück der Musiklehre zur wenig ergiebigen Einlösung eines Stücks rhetorischer Theorie im vorangehenden Kapitel[36]. Auch erschien das "inventio"-Kapitel Matthesons mit der Übertragung der "loci" ins Musikalische noch einem Johann Georg Sulzer als ein "Versuch", "den man nicht ohne Nutzen zum Grund einer nähern Ausführung legen könnte"[37]. Aber das ist dann eben für einen der traditionelleren Aspekte Sulzers charakteristisch. Er geht mit dem erstaunlich langen Fortwirken der Affektenlehre wie des Rückgriffs auf die Rhetorik überein, die dann im Musikschrifttum zu Forkels umgreifenden Entwurf einer "musikalischen Rhetorik" als "höherer und eigentlicher Theorie der Musik" führte[38]. Nur läßt sich ja die konservative Einengung einer dem

34 §5 (p. 121); dort in den Paragraphen 3 und 6 die folgenden Zitate.
35 Dazu der Beitrag Forcherts in diesem Band (Kapitel 9).
36 *Capellmeister*, 133–60. Die Bedeutung gerade dieses Kapitels für die deutsche Musiklehre des achtzehnten Jahrhunderts bis zu Koch bzw. Daube wäre im einzelnen noch zu untersuchen; dazu die Beobachtungen und Überlegungen von C. Dahlhaus in: L. U. Abraham und C. Dahlhaus, *Melodielehre* (Köln, 1972), 22–7, sowie das einschlägige Kapitel bei P. Benary, *Die deutsche Kompositionslehre des 18. Jahrhunderts* (Leipzig, 1961), 81–100 (=Jenaer Beiträge zur Musikforschung 3).
37 *Allgemeine Theorie der schönen Künste* 2 (Leipzig, ²1792), 90.
38 J. N. Forkel, *Allgemeine Geschichte der Musik* I (Leipzig, 1788), 37 et alia. Daß auch der ältere Ansatz einer nicht an die Rhetorik gebundenen "Ars combinatoria" im Musikschrifttum des weiteren achtzehnten Jahrhunderts in anregender Weise aufgenommen wurde, betonte L. G. Ratner, "Ars combinatoria. Chance and Choice in Eighteenth-Century Music", in: *Studies in Eighteenth-Century Music. A Tribute to Karl Geiringer*, herausgegeben von H. C. Robbins Landon und R. E. Chapman (New York und London, 1970), 343–63.

Neuen gegenüber offenen frühen Position Matthesons im *Capellmeis-ter* auch sonst beobachten[39]. Umso interessanter ist der Vergleich mit demjenigen Autor, den Mattheson indirekt kritisierte, wenn er schrieb, es sei "keine gute philosphische Lehr-Art", wenn man bei der Findekunst "die Notation und Description gar nicht anführe" und sich nur auf die "antecedentia, concomitantia & consequentia" beschränke[40]. Das ist eindeutig auf Heinichen gemünzt. Nur hatte dieser seine guten Gründe, es bei der Applikation dieser Gesichts-punkte auf den Text zu belassen und sich auf die Veranschaulichung der Konsequenzen am musikalischen Beispiel zu konzentrieren.

Heinichens *General-Baß in der Composition* geht auf seine sieb-zehn Jahre ältere *Neu erfundene und gründliche Anweisung* zurück, *wie ein Musicliebender auff gewisse vortheilhafte Arth könne zu vollkommener Erlernung des General-Basses . . . gelangen*, die im gleichen Verlag erschien wie das erste *Orchestre*. Ihre Position war nicht weniger aufgeschlossen als die des jungen Mattheson. Ja es ist, wie Arno Forchert betonte und schon der Titel nahelegt, anzuneh-men, daß die Vorrede von Heinichens Schrift des Jahres 1711 eine Anregung für Matthesons *Neu-eröffnetes Orchestre* bot[41]. Die Übereinstimmungen zwischen den Texten betreffen die Öffnung gegenüber dem Geschmacksurteil, den programmatischen Praxis-Bezug, die Berücksichtigung bestimmter Gesichtspunkte und nicht zuletzt die Berufung auf die *a la mode*-Schlagwörter der Kunsttheorie französischer Provenienz. Während sich aber Mattheson in der Aus-einandersetzung mit der älteren Lehre und mit seinen Kritikern immer weiter von seiner aufgeschlossenen frühen Position entfernte, setzte Heinichen in der wichtigen Einleitung des Jahres 1728 den einst eingeschlagenen Weg fort. Der Unterschied spiegelt sich etwa in den Anforderungen an einen Komponisten. Beide nennen drei Stich-wörter: Mattheson im *Capellmeister* "Naturell', "Lust" und "Fleiß", Heinichen im *General-Baß* "Talent", "Wissenschafft" und "Erfah-rung"[42]. "Naturell" und "Talent" sowie "Fleiß" und "Wissen-schafft" lassen sich einander zuordnen, auch wenn das Schwer-gewicht beim "Fleiß" für Mattheson bezeichnenderweise beim

39 Besonders scharf zu fassen ist dieser Wandel, wie jetzt A. Forchert zeigte, bezeich-nenderweise anhand von Matthesons Beschäftigung mit französischen Autoren und insbesondere mit den kunsttheoretischen Schriften: "Französische Autoren in den Schriften Matthesons", in: *Festschrift Heinz Becker* (Laaber, 1982), 382–91 und insbesondere die Zusammenfassung (p. 388).
40 §49 (p. 127).   41 "Französische Autoren", 382.
42 *Capellmeister*, p. 108, §61; *General-Baß* in der auf Seite 20 beginnenden langen Anmerkung (i), dort auf den anschließenden Seiten auch die folgenden Zitate.

"Schreiben" liegt ("es sey nun abschreiben, umschreiben, aufschreiben oder nachschreiben"), während Heinichen bei der "Wissenschafft" vor allem die Kompositionslehre der "musica poetica" im Auge hat. Umso stärker tritt der Gegensatz beim dritten Stichwort hervor: Dem blassen "Lust" bei Mattheson steht Heinichens Hinweis auf das "allerwichtigste requisitum compositoris moderni" gegenüber, auf die "Erfahrung", durch die der ganze Problemkreis des Geschmacks eingebracht ist. Der "Gout", "worinnen sich unsere 3. haupt requisita compositoris . . ., ja selbst der wahre finis Musices, gleichsam als in Centro terminiren", war und blieb für Heinichen ein leitender Gesichtspunkt – nicht nur in der Deklaration "a la moderne", sondern auch im Austragen der Konsequenzen[43]. Das ließ ihn die Auseinandersetzung mit dem unterschiedlichen "Gout" anderer Nationen fortführen und programmatisch eine "glückliche Melange vom Italienischen und Französischen Gout" fordern, die auf das Stichwort des "vermischten Geschmacks" vorweist[44]. Und das ließ ihn im Abwägen zwischen den einzelnen Kriterien des Urteils eine Position beibehalten, die in dem Leitsatz umrissen ist, "daß wir alle unsere Musicalische Regeln nach dem *Gehöre* einrichten sollen, und da findet gleichwol die Frau *Vernunfft*, (die super kluge ratio) alle Hände voll zu thun, ja mehr, als wir noch bey unsern Zeiten einsehen können"[45].

Auch Heinichen sprach 1728 von "dieser schönen musicalischen Rhetorica", aber nicht im Sinne eines Systementwurfs, sondern als eine "Materia", die "ad Praxin sublimiorem" abziele; "practice" galt es ihm vom "musicalischen Gout / Invention, Accompagnement, deren Natur / Unterscheid und Würckung" zu schreiben[46]. Auf die "musikalische Rhetorik" wie auf deren Teilbereich der "Inventio"

---

43 Von den "Sachen *a la moderne*" spricht Mattheson im *Orchestre* I etwa bei der Behandlung des 12/8-Taktes (p. 80).

44 Das Zitat in der Anmerkung auf den Seiten 10–11. Zum Stichwort des "vermischten Geschmacks" als "ein allgemeiner guter Geschmack in der Musik" aus der Verbindung der Nationalstile insbesondere J. J. Quantz, *Versuch einer Anweisung die Flöte traversiere zu spielen; mit verschiedenen, zur Beförderung des guten Geschmackes in der praktischen Musik dienlichen Anmerkungen* (Breslau,[3] 1789), 332–3 (Facs. als Documenta musicologica I/2). Den unterschiedlichen Haltungen Matthesons und Heinichens entspricht bezeichnenderweise auch eine je andere Einstellung zur Reise in die stilprägenden Länder. So bejaht der spätere Mattheson das "Reisen, und vor allen die Besuchung Italiens" nur mit erheblichen Vorbehalten (*Capellmeister*, p. 108, §62–3). Der Italienfahrer Heinichen hingegen unterstreicht den Sinn des Reisens "in andere Länder . . . umb unsern Gout zu reguliren" (p. 23, in der Anmerkung zu den Anforderungen an einen Komponisten).

45 Seite 4 in der auf Seite 2 beginnenden Anmerkung (a).

46 P. 25.

bezogen, ist damit bei Heinichen eine Position beibehalten, die im *ad hoc*-Zugriff die Fragestellungen der Redekunst unter den Aspekten aufnimmt, die sich fürs Komponieren wie für die Kompositionslehre als besonders tauglich erweisen. Das gilt für die Integration der "Figurenlehre" Bernhards in den Generalbaß wie für die ebenso hilfreiche wie anregende Anwendung der "inventio" in der Einleitung zur Vertonung "etlicher seichter [Opern-]Texte", auf die George J. Buelow wieder aufmerksam machte[47].

So stehen sich bei Mattheson und Heinichen in der Einstellung zur Rhetorik und insbesondere in der Auseinandersetzung mit der "Findekunst" der inventio zwei Haltungen gegenüber, die zugleich die Chancen und die Problematik des Umgangs mit diesen Fragen verdeutlichen. Um es pointiert zu formulieren: der produktive *ad hoc*-Rückgriff auf ein außerfachliches Erklärungsmodell, dessen man sich so lange bedient, wie es sich als tauglich erweist, und nur unter den Aspekten, die zum Verständnis musikalischer Sachverhalte beitragen, gegenüber der Einlösung eines Stücks Theorie. Daß Mattheson dabei für einmal in einem seiner schwächeren Aspekte zur Sprache kommt, gehört gewiß auch zu den Aufgaben einer Standortbestimmung anläßlich seines dreihundertsten Geburtstages. Zumal die Gegenüberstellung von Mattheson und Heinichen die Chance bietet, ein Stück Geschichte unserer Wissenschaft im Umgang mit der Rhetorik kritisch zu durchdenken und möglicherweise in einen Neusansatz zu überführen.

Der Umgang der Musikgeschichtsschreibung mit der "musikalischen Rhetorik" wie mit einzelnen ihrer Fragestellungen pendelte zwischen zwei Extremen: Auf der einen Seite stand die Feststellung Arnold Scherings, Heinichen und Kuhnau gäben "uns den Rechtsbrief in die Hand, *mit jeglichen* zur Verfügung stehenden *Mitteln* der musikalischen Hermeneutik" an die Werke Bachs und anderer Komponisten heranzugehen[48]. Die Gegenreaktion führte zu einer Einlösung, die sich auf das beschränkte, was sich, historisch absichernd, den Texten zu einer "musikalischen Rhetorik" an einzelnen Interpretationsverfahren entnehmen ließ. Die Grenzen beider Positionen liegen auf der Hand. Nun kann man über die Interpretation musikalischer Sachverhalte mit den Mitteln der Rhetorik mit guten Gründen unterschiedlicher Meinung sein. Läßt man sich aber auf diesen Problemkreis ein, so liegt eine Chance der

---

47 Siehe oben Abschnitt I/2 und Anm. 12.
48 "Geschichtliches zur 'ars inveniendi' in der Musik", in: *JbP* 32 (1926), 30, ohne Hervorhebung.

Vermittlung zwischen jenen extremen Positionen in einem Vorgehen, das die Haltung Heinichens aufnimmt. Das wäre eine Verfahren, das einerseits aus dem *ad hoc*-Rückgriff auf den Ansatz, die Fragestellungen und Verfahren der Rhetorik in der Erklärung zentraler Fragen des Komponierens (mit und ohne Text) ein breiteres Spektrum der Interpretationsmöglichkeiten gewinnt, als sie in den einzelnen Aspekten eines vermeintlichen Lehrgebäudes der "musikalischen Rhetorik" vorliegen, und das andererseits im Rückbezug auf ein umgreifendes Interpretationsverfahren jener Zeit unter Kontrolle bleibt.

19

Johann Mattheson and the invention of the *Affektenlehre*

GEORGE J. BUELOW

Bloomington, Indiana

Johann Mattheson, distinguished eighteenth-century composer, music theorist, diplomat, man of letters, and philosopher, was born in Hamburg on 28 September 1681. The tricentenary year of his birth presented a unique occasion to encourage a review of his legacy to the music historian in the vast assemblage of facts and opinions about music and musical thought during his lifetime: a crucial moment in music history, a stylistic crossroads witnessing the end of the German Baroque and the foundation of pan-Germanic Classicism.

Mattheson composed a large amount of music, mostly in the earlier part of his career, including operas, oratorios, and various kinds of vocal and instrumental pieces. The extant works reveal a composer of significant talent who was very much involved in the developing stages of musical change taking place in North Europe during the first decades of the eighteenth century. His major theoretical works number more than two dozen volumes, beginning in 1713 with *Das neueröffnete Orchestre*. The magnitude of Mattheson's collected writings has hampered our appreciation of their merit. Their individual size and difficult eighteenth-century German have proved to be especially problematical for English-language scholarship. We lack a useful summary of the rich and complex variety of materials contained in Mattheson's works, which consist of practical data, reports on contemporary musical issues, performances, personalities in the news, insight into contemporary performance practice, and much more. Beyond this, his works exhibit a panorama of statements about what music was and also what he thought it should be in his lifetime. In effect, he set out to re-formulate much of the theory and aesthetics of music, attempting to replace with new ideas the worn-out, irrelevant rules and principles of theory and composition which had hardly changed in the previous two hundred years. As a judge of the new, Mattheson invariably had disdain for the past. In a number of didactic works, he cast aside almost all of the theoretical-philosophical foundations of earlier musical thought. In attacking the past, he found himself committed to constructing a new musical order, a musical Rationalism, a new philosphical mode of thinking about how to judge music as an art.

Mattheson seldom worked out his ideas into fixed doctrines, but he did proclaim his conclusions as serious new approaches to the music of the eighteenth century. He found himself redefining the relationship between composer and listener. His approach was split between two poles: sensuousness and rationalism. As he stated: "Nothing can move [us] that cannot be understood." The substance – he called it the body – of all music was melody, and he was the first to attempt to create guidelines for composing good melodies. For Mattheson melody was the basis of everything meaningful and moving about music. Yet he was also a rationalist, a true participant in the Age of Enlightenment, looking for new ways by which a listener could be led to understand his feelings – his emotions – as they were stimulated by musical sounds. These facts bear remembering as we approach the topic of this discussion: the concept of the Affections and Mattheson's invention of the term "Affektenlehre."

II

One cannot for long read about the music of the seventeenth and eighteenth centuries without being confronted by the concept of the *Affektenlehre* – the Doctrine or Theory of the Affections. In running aground on this terminological reef for the first time, a reader normally turns to one of the standard music dictionaries or encyclopedias to find a definition. Unfortunately, most of these definitions are confused, frequently misleading, and at times grossly in error. For example, in the now obsolete fifth edition of *Grove's Dictionary of Music and Musicians,* Eric Blom gave the curious definition of *Affektenlehre* as a term "applied to the teaching of musical expression in 18th-century Germany, and especially to the work of Carl Philipp Emanuel Bach and the Mannheim School. It classifies musical effects used to express particular emotions, such as sorrow, joy, languor, passion, etc., and thus inevitably tends to freeze them into stereotyped forms" (vol. 1, 66). Willi Apel, in the second revised edition of the *Harvard Dictionary of Music* (Cambridge, Mass., 1969, 16), includes the following passage in his definition of "Affections, Doctrine of": "An aesthetic theory of the late baroque period . . . It was treated in greatest detail by Mattheson . . . , who enumerates more than twenty affections and describes how they should be expressed in music."

In Manfred Bukofzer's *Music in the Baroque Era* (New York, 1947, 388–90), there is a long passage concerning the Affections, including the following:

The technical aspects of the theory of composition must be complemented by the doctrine of the affections which set stringent rules to all composers. The wealth of baroque affections was stereotyped into an infinite number of "figures" . . . which "represented or depicted" the affections in music. The elaborate systematization of figures must be regarded as the main contribution of the baroque era to the doctrine of the affections.

Finally, a long article under the rubric "Affektenlehre" appears in *Die Musik in Geschichte und Gegenwart* (vol. 1, col. 116) and includes the following statement (in translation):

The seventeenth century is especially rich in discussions on the musical *Affektenlehre*. Not surprisingly too, it would be during this century that the systematic foundation of the entire theory [i.e., *Affektenlehre*] would be brought to conclusion.

Such citations from four of our most respected reference works would seem to leave no doubt in our minds: There existed in Baroque music a Doctrine of the Affections, which can be defined and described in considerable detail. Mattheson himself is credited with having best presented the theory at least to eighteenth-century readers. Unfortunately this conclusion has led students and musicologists to believe they can learn and then employ a unique and universal theory of analysis for the expressive content of Baroque music. To show the inaccuracy of this premise is the purpose of the following discussion. But first, it is important to sketch out briefly exactly what is meant by the concept of the Affections.

III

The Affections, as well as the closely related idea of musical figures, can be understood only in connection with their origins in the extensive literature on oratory and rhetoric formulated by Greek and Roman writers of antiquity, especially Aristotle, Cicero, and Quintilian. Quintilian, like Aristotle before him, stressed the similarities between music and oratory. The goal of Quintilian's work, the *Institutio oratoria*, as well as all other studies of oratory since ancient times, was the same: to instruct the speaker to learn how to control and direct the emotional responses of an audience or, in the language of Classical rhetoric, to enable the orator to move the Affections of his audience. Subsequent music theorists simply substituted "composer" or even "performer" for the orator; their goal was comparable: to move the Affections of an audience through the art of music.

The evidence of rhetorical influence on musical thought becomes unmistakable from the late fifteenth century, and to pursue this subject in depth would require the examination of works by authors as diverse as Burmeister, Lippius, Mersenne, Kircher, Heinichen, Walther, Werckmeister, Scheibe, and Johann Mattheson. What these writers and many others tell us is that Baroque composers assumed as music's primary expressive goal the achieving of a musical unity based on a rationalized concept of emotions called the Affections. At least this was the result of some one hundred years of musical and theoretical developments in the seventeenth century, for we find the logical outcome of the growing theory of expression only in eighteenth-century sources. The word "Affection" (*Affekt* in German, *pathos* in Greek, and *affectus* in Latin) stood for an idealized emotional state. During the Baroque the composer assumed the mantle of the orator, and as a general principle he believed music should arouse the listener to feel these idealized emotional states.

Based on these few facts of a complex subject[1], it should be evident that as an ideal the Affections were part of the aesthetic basis of music throughout the seventeenth century and much of the eighteenth. And these largely rhetorical ideas were greatly influenced by the equally important developments in philosophy led by such seminal figures as Descartes, Hobbes, Locke, and Shaftesbury, all of whom created an intellectual climate nurtured in their highly innovative studies of the emotions of man, leading to one of the foundations of the Age of Rationalism.

Music theorists and composers talked incessantly about expressing the Affections, although one finds little in the literature that is consistent as to what is meant or how the Affections were to be conveyed in practical, musical terms. Some writers suggested the Affections could be expressed by various gradations of pitches, or through types of rhythms, or by means of modal distinctions. But in no instance in the seventeenth century can one find any writer who advocates or establishes a doctrine – that is, a set of rules – for expressing the Affections. How curious then it is to read in light of this fact musicological testimonies stating, for example, that Mon-

---

1 For a detailed discussion of the relationship of music to rhetorical concepts see the author's "Rhetoric and Music," in: *New Grove*, vol. 15, 793–803.

teverdi employed the *Affektenlehre,* or, even stranger, that the *Affektenlehre* can be found in treatises as early as Zarlino.[2] These and similar statements in the literature can only be described as frivolous misuses of the term.

The circumstances hardly change in the eighteenth century. Although some writers are bolder in demanding attention to expressing the Affections and, at times, develop lists of common Affections they believe can be expressed in music, nevertheless none of them suggests either a method or methods for translating into musical sounds the various emotional states they identify.

The key to the problem can be identified in the very failure of any theorist of the Baroque, other than Mattheson, and also those of the subsequent *galant* and Classical periods, ever to employ the crucial term of *Affektenlehre.* This frequently misused word is apparently unknown in the musical literature of the Baroque and seems not to have had any common currency even through the nineteenth century. Clearly one must ask: If the terminology for a musical practice does not exist, how could the practice have been known as a general principle by composers? Even in Mattheson's unusual and inventive applications of the term we shall see that he too had no intention of associating it with a general theory of musical Affections. At this point we need to examine what the concept of the *Affektenlehre* meant to this important writer on music from the first half of the eighteenth century.

IV

Beginning with the term itself, although Mattheson was prolific as a writer on music, he devoted surprisingly little attention to the subject of the Affections; it appears in only three of his major works. In each of these the term "Affektenlehre" appears but once. The first usage is found in *Critica musica* (1722, 1725), the second in *Der musicalische Patriot* (1728), and the third in *Der vollkommene Capellmeister* (1739). It should be reiterated that these are the only instances of the employment of the term "Affektenlehre" in the Baroque and post-Baroque theoretical literature that this writer has been able to discover.

Critica musica II, 324:

(i) Pardon me! No contrary Affections come together in the words: The rich must suffer and be hungry, but those seeking the Lord will lack for nothing.

---

2 See H. Goldschmidt, *Die Musikästhetik des 18. Jahrhunderts* (Zürich, 1915), 51; and R. Dammann, *Der Musikbegriff im deutschen Barock* (Cologne, 1967), 218.

This is a simple consideration of the kindness of God and a satisfaction with his righteousness, that he allows the rich to go hungry and those fearing God to lack for nothing. These antitheses are good for double fugues because, while having different expressions, they still concur on one conclusion. Thus there must be first of all much greater insight into the *Affektenlehre* when one wishes to judge soundly about such matters.[3]

Here Mattheson has reprinted and then commented upon a passage in a treatise by Heinrich Bokemeyer entitled *Der melodische* Vorhoff. Mattheson, who was engaged at this time in planning his own theory of melody, found a great deal to criticize in the Wolfenbüttel cantor's recommendations. In the passage concerned (not quoted here), Bokemeyer had given examples of texts suitable to double fugues – in this instance, one from Psalm 34:10: "The rich must suffer and be hungry, but those who seek the Lord will lack no good things." To these words Bokemeyer adds the qualification: "Dieser Punct muß noch besser untersucht werden, weil zu weilen wiedrige Affection zusammen kommen, wie hier im letzten Exempel" (This point must be more carefully looked into, because at times contrary Affections come together, as in this last example). Mattheson disagrees, as the translation indicates.

The second appearance of the term, in *Der musicalische Patriot*, is imbedded in a different context. The passage comes from the introduction of the book and grows out of Mattheson's comments regarding what one must know in order to be a true patriot, a lover of one's country, or of the world. *Musicalischer Patriot*, 3:

Neither must the condition of the government and what occurs in its policies ever be left out of sight by one who contemplates, no matter by which method, creating benefits for the fatherland. And therefore in the following reports it will be necessary to include one or another of political, dramatic, and theatrical matters. Who would also speak well of sounds, or of the art of music, and would leave out entirely physical laws together with the *Affektenlehre*? Certainly no one except he who wished to be laughed at; thus we also find something of natural science before us.[4]

---

3 *Critica musica* II, 324: "(i) Um Vergebung! Es kommen keine wiedrige Affecten zusammen in den Worten: Die Reichen müssen darben und hungern; aber die den Herrn suchen, haben keinen Mangel. Es ist eine bloße Betrachtung der Freundlichkeit Gottes, und eine Vergnügen über seiner Gerechtigkeit, daß er die Reichen hungern, und es den Gottsfürchtigen an nichts fehlen, läßt. Diese antitheses geben gute Doppel-Fugen ab, weil sie, ob gleich mit verschiedenen Ausdrückungen, doch zu einerley Ende, concurriren. In der Affecten-Lehre muß also vorher eine viel grössere Insicht erhalten werden, wenn man hievon gesund urtheilen will."

4 *Musicalischer Patriot*, 3: "Den Zustand der Regierung, und was in der Policey vorfällt, muß ebenfalls niemand aus den Augen setzen, der dem Vaterlande, es sey auf welche Art es wolle, Vortheil zu schaffen gesinnet ist; und also wird in folgenden Vorträgen nothwendig ein und anderes politsches, dramatisches, theatralisches, u.

To understand what he means in these two passages by *Affektenlehre*, one must turn to the third passage.

This occurs in *Der vollkommene Capellmeister* and on first glance seems no less obscure. Mattheson concludes Chapter 3, entitled ". . . von der musicalischen Natur-Lehre," with the observation that he has brought together in the previous pages instructions in both physics (natural science) and the *Affektenlehre. Capellmeister*, 19:

My humble advice at the end of this chapter, which combines the physics of sound with the theory of emotions [*Affecten-Lehre*] to a certain and necessary extent, is stated: One should seek out some good, really good, work of poetry in which nature is vividly portrayed and should endeavor accurately to distinguish the passions contained therein, for many a composer and critic would undoubtedly succeed better if he himself knew, just occasionally, what he actually would like to do.[5]

It is clear from the content of this chapter that Mattheson means by *Affektenlehre* a concept parallel to *Natur-Lehre* (physics) and one which he was familiar with from his study of Descartes's famous treatise, *De passionibus animae* (1649). Descartes's work was often referred to as the *Traité des passions*, and it was among the first to describe a substantial theory explaining the physical bases of the emotions, a theory of the Passions, or in German a *Lehre de Affectibus*[6] or *Affektenlehre*. This treatise had a profound effect on developments in philosophy and music theory in the later seventeenth and the eighteenth centuries, and one finds in it lists of the Affections divided into classifications according to the humors of the body, where Descartes believed the Passions originated. It is to these, to us pseudoscientific explanations of the emotions, that Mattheson refers by coining a term of parallel structure and meaning to *Natur-Lehre*.

Therefore, by *Affektenlehre* Mattheson means in all three instances the Cartesian theory basing human emotions on physical laws for the

---

vorfallen. Wer wollte auch wol von Klange, oder von der Ton-Kunst reden, und die Natur-Kunde, samt der Affecten-Lehre, dabey gantz zurück lassen? Gewiß niemand, als der sich lächerlich zu machen gedächte; da finden wir also auch was physicalisches vor uns.

5 *Capellmeister*, 19: "Mein weniger Rath gehet zum Beschlusse dieses Haupt-Stückes, welches die Natur-Lehre des Klanges mit der Affecten-Lehre einiger und nöthiger Maassen verknüpffet, dahin: Man suche sich eine oder andre gute, recht gute poetische Arbeit aus, in welcher die Natur lebhafft abgemahlet ist, und trachte die darin enthaltene Leidenschafften genau zu unterscheiden. Denn, es würden manchem Setzer und Klang-Richter seine Sachen ohne Zweifel besser gerathen, wenn er nur bisweilen selbst wüste, was er eigentlich haben wollte."

6 In *Critica musica* II, 60, Mattheson does employ the expression "Lehre de Affectibus," the clearest reference to Descartes's Theory of the Passions.

body. Again, it is noteworthy that although *Der vollkommene Capellmeister* includes much more discussion concerning musical styles, forms, instruments, and so on, never again does the author use this term to suggest that he meant a musical application of the Doctrine of the Affections, nor does the word "Affektenlehre" appear in subsequent treatises by him or in the works of those writers upon whom he had a strong influence, such as Scheibe, Marpurg, and C. P. E. Bach.

Just as the major philosophers of the seventeenth and early eighteenth centuries – Spinoza, Descartes, Bacon, Locke, Shaftesbury, and numerous French writers – were immersed in formulating new theories of knowledge, of the Passions, of ethics, of education in the broadest sense, so too Mattheson's writings are often directed at three basic kinds of formulation: (1) a redefinition of the theory of musical composition, including the problems of joining theory with current practices, as with modes versus keys, the thorough-bass, melodic composition versus multilinear textures; (2) redefining the nature of music as an expressive (i.e., sensuous) art of the emotions, but also as an equally rational art perceived and interpreted by the mind; (3) redefining the relationship of music to ethics, and ultimately to religion, a broadly developed philosophy that preoccupied Mattheson in his later works.

What becomes clear throughout Mattheson's many works is the essential dichotomy of his theoretical ideas: Music was first and foremost an expressive, sensuous art. The ear determined all aspects of musical excellence, and no rules were valid if they were contrary to this fact. Yet music, to be understood and appreciated on an intellectual and ethical level, was also a rational art. To be moved by music is to understand music. He could issue the stirring proclamation that "everything that occurs without laudable Affections [in music] can be considered nothing, does nothing, and means nothing,"[7] but the problem remained as to how an audience comprehended which Affection the music was supposed to express. Mattheson believed the listener was involved in a four-part aesthetic experience. First, he heard the music; second, apperception occurred when the listener interpreted the various musical symbols (hermeneutical interpretation) leading to a recognition of an Affection; third, the listener perceived the emotion; and fourth, through reflection on the experience, he would enjoy moral improvement and, when appropriate, a

---

7 *Capellmeister*, 146: ". . . alles was ohne löbliche Affecten geschiehet, heißt nichts, thut nichts, gilt nichts."

religious edification. Like Descartes and other contemporary philosophers, Mattheson thought the Affections existed either as virtues or as
vices. Both types were capable of musical expression, but only
through the virtuous Affections could the soul be healed.

Therefore, the identification of the Affections in music became the
crucial element in Mattheson's rationalistic philosophy of musical
expression, and the Affections played a role far exceeding anything
implied or stated by earlier writers on music. Mattheson's views also
influenced a number of subsequent writers of the eighteenth century.
But the question remains: How exact were his descriptions of the
musical means for expressing an Affection? Can we agree with
Bukofzer, for example, that in Mattheson composers found a "stringent set of rules" for expressing emotions?

V

Probably the most frequently quoted of all the statements by Mattheson on the Affections occurs in *Das neu-eröffnete Orchestre* (1713),
where he describes characteristic Affections for the seventeen most
practical keys. This entire passage has been translated elsewhere,[8] but
here the material has been reduced to Mattheson's basic descriptive
words:

Orchestre I, 231–53.
1. C: = rude, bold, also tender
2. c: = sweet, sad
3. D: = sharp, headstrong, for warlike and merry things
4. d: = devout, tranquil, also grand; devotion in church music,
amusing, flowing
5. E♭ = pathos, serious, sad, hostile to all sensuality
6. E: = despair, fatal sadness, hopelessness of extreme love, piercing,
painful
7. e: = pensive, profound, grieved, sad
8. F: = most beautiful sentiments, generosity, constancy, love
9. f: = tender, calm, profound, weighty, a fatal mental anxiety,
exceedingly moving
10. f♯ = languishing, amorous, unrestrained, strange, misanthropic
11. G: = suggestive and rhetorical, for serious as well as gay things
12. g: = almost the most beautiful, graceful, agreeable, tender,
yearning, diverting, for moderate complaints, tempered
joyfulness

8 In the author's article, "An Evaluation of Johann Mattheson's Opera, *Cleopatra*
(Hamburg, 1704)," in: *Studies in Eighteenth-Century Music: A Tribute to Karl
Geiringer*, ed. H. C. Robbins Landon and R. E. Chapman (New York and London,
1970), 92–107.

13. A: = affecting and brilliant, inclined to complaining, sad passions
14. a: = plaintive, decorous, resigned, inviting sleep
15. B♭: = diverting, magnificent, but also dainty
16. B: = offensive, harsh, unpleasant, desperate character
17. b: = bizarre, morose, melancholic

This important document has sent several musicologists off on fishing expeditions into the music of the Baroque, where they have hoped to find that many if not all Baroque composers of the eighteenth century knew these same key Affections, either by acquaintance with Mattheson's treatise, or because they were in fact common knowledge. There is the famous case, for example, of Rudolf Wustman's application of these key Affections to Bach's *Wohltemperirtes Clavier*.[9]

Despite such musicological determination, it is clear that Mattheson never intended such willful applications of his comments. Although it seems likely that he followed his own ideas to some extent in his own music, that is quite different from making his personal ideas into a universal Doctrine of Key Affections for the eighteenth century. And it is remarkable that no one who has written on the subject seems to have noted Mattheson's own warning on the subject. Concluding his remarks, he says that he could continue with a much more extensive discussion, for, he observes, if everything that needed to be said for it were said, each key would require a chapter to itself. Then he continues:

Besides, the more one tries to postulate something positive about them, the more one finds contradictory things, because the beliefs about this material are almost numberless. For this I know no other reason than that based on the differences of human constitutions [*Complexionen*], according to which for someone with a sanguine temperament a key may seem lively and merry, but for someone who is phlegmatic, it will seem complaining and troubled, etc. And therefore we shall not say more about the subject, but give willingly to everyone the freedom that they choose for this or that key the characteristics that best correspond to their own temperamental tendencies.

In other words, Mattheson's list is at best a table of key Affections corresponding to his own temperament, and he wisely admits that its relevance to other composers is small if at all valid.

At the conclusion of this article is appended a translation of the passage frequently referred to in the literature as Mattheson's prescriptions for writing music with affective expression. It is based almost entirely on Descartes's classification of the Passions. In many

9 "Tonartsymbolik in Bachs Zeit," in: *B-J* 8 (1911).

of the details it reads like a summary of Descartes's own treatise. Mattheson gives little instruction beyond general and vague advice as to how a composer can turn an Affection into a musical idea. This passage cannot be described as a Doctrine of the Affections in a musical sense and was never intended to serve that purpose. Yet it is this passage that led Blom in *Grove's Dictionary* to say that the *Affektenlehre* "classifies *musical effects* [my italics] used to express particular emotions, such as sorrow, joy, languor, passion, etc., and thus inevitably tends to freeze them into stereotyped forms." It also led Apel to the incorrect conclusion that Mattheson "enumerates more than twenty affections and describes how they should be expressed in music," and Bukofzer to say that Mattheson's *Vollkommener Capellmeister* "contains the most lucid and musically most fruitful account of the subject." Nothing in Mattheson's own words justifies any of these conclusions.

Also at the end of this article are listed Mattheson's general emotional characteristics for common dance forms, and the equally vague affective indications for tempo markings. Mattheson also described musical instruments as having basic affective connotations. But again we need to remember the author's own words regarding key Affections. In essence any of these affective descriptions is personal, and Mattheson surely would have agreed that another individual's response might not correspond to his interpretation. This places convincing doubt on the universality of these ideas. And it proves the error in believing that Mattheson created a musical *Affektenlehre* as the basis of musical composition in the late Baroque.

Exactly how musicology created this error of understanding about a basic principle of Baroque music remains to be fully investigated. It is clear, however, that the modern usage of the term "Affektenlehre" is an invention, not of Mattheson, but of early twentieth-century German musicology. It seems to occur first in 1907 in an article by Arnold Schering,[10] and then five years later was made an immutable theoretical concept by Hermann Kretzschmar, in his article, "Allgemeines und Besonderes zur Affektenlehre."[11] Kretzschmar was followed by numerous German and, not long afterward, non-German scholars all of whom have helped to create a false impression that a rigid system of rules for composing music in the Baroque could be applied to such diverse styles as those by J. S. Bach and C. P. E. Bach, Monteverdi,

---

10 "Die Musikästhetik der deutschen Aufklärung," in: *ZIMG* 8 (1907), 263–71, 316–22.
11 *JbP* 18 (1911), 63–77, and 19 (1912), 65–78.

Alessandro Scarlatti, Keiser, Handel, Vivaldi, and many more. Distinguished scholars and students alike have been caught up in a web of manufactured conclusions that have frequently blocked out original thought about the analysis and understanding of music in the Baroque.

Throughout the Baroque, musical expression was certainly associated with the Affections. But how composers viewed this association, how they composed with affective considerations in mind, and indeed when they ignored that whole question, are questions as diverse and as different as are the musical outcomes of the Baroque. What is needed is to comprehend more exactly how composers understood their own principles of musical expression, and the answers will not come from assuming *a priori* an aesthetic straitjacket called the *Affektenlehre,* invented by musicologists in our own century. Mattheson in his own case is rather specific about what he thought the general nature of musical expression should be. His vivid insights into how a composer *might* employ the Affections as an aspect of compositional craft suggest to us a valuable avenue of investigation.

Many German Baroque writers on music were fond of saying that the expression of the Affections in music was a subject as vast as the bottomless ocean. We shall not come closer to understanding this important aspect of Baroque music if we insist, like so many writers of the past and present, in condensing the uncharted, watery expanses of Baroque expressivity into a single raindrop labeled the *Affektenlehre.* The answers lie in a much more careful reading of the sources, truly an avalanche of words from the Baroque itself, and equally important, in the music, in all of its varied forms and styles. We have frequently looked at it with the wrong lenses. Baroque music, in its multiplicity of stylistic achievements, contains the answers to questions about musical expression, and we can undoubtedly find better lenses for our examination if we will eliminate the *Affektenlehre* from our prescription.

Appendix: Johann Mattheson's Definitions of the Affections

Excerpts from *Der vollkommene Capellmeister* (Hamburg, 1739),[12] (Part I, Chapter 3), §53 et seq.:

Where there is no passion, no affection, neither is there virtue. If our passions are sick, then they must be healed, not murdered.

12 These translations have been adapted from the English version of *Capellmeister* by E. C. Harriss (Ann Arbor, 1981).

The experts in the natural sciences know how to describe the way in which our emotions actually and, so to speak, physically function, and it is to a composer's great advantage when he is not inexperienced in this [knowledge].

[1.] Since, for example, JOY is an expansion of our vital spirits, it follows reasonably and naturally that I can best express this Affection by large and enlarged intervals.

[2.] Contrarily, if one knows that SADNESS is a contraction of these subtle parts of our body, then it is easy to see that the small and smallest intervals are the most suitable for this emotion.

[3.] HOPE is a raising of the spirits.

[4.] DESPAIR, however, is a depression of the same. All of which are things that can very naturally be represented with sounds, especially when the other circumstances (tempo in particular) contribute their part. . . .

Describing each and every emotion here would clearly be too tedious; only the most important ones must we not leave untouched here. And LOVE clearly among all of them belongs at the top, as it occupies far greater space in musical works than the other passions.

[5.] LUST cannot be separated from LOVE; however, the difference between the two is that the latter is concerned with the present but the former looks to the future and as a rule is intrinsically more violent and impatient. ALL YEARNING, all LONGING, all WISHING, all STRIVING, and CRAVING, whether tempered or violent, belong here.

[6.] SADNESS plays no small role among the Affections. In sacred works where this emotion is most moving and beneficial, it belongs to all these: PENANCE, REMORSE, SORROW, CONTRITION, PLAINT, and the recognition of our misery. With such conditions, sorrow is better than laughter (Eccles. 7). A writer we have already mentioned [La Mothe le Vayer] also gives a good reason why most people prefer to hear sad rather than happy music, namely: "because almost everybody is unhappy."

[7.] PRIDE, HAUGHTINESS, ARROGANCE, and the like are also usually depicted or expressed with their special musical colors, for which purpose the composer draws primarily upon a bold, pompous style. One has in this way opportunity to use all sorts of majestic-sounding figures which require a special seriousness and grandiloquent motion, but one must never allow a hasty or falling motion, but always one that ascends.

[8.] The opposites of these emotions are HUMILITY, PATIENCE, etc., which one handles with a descending form of sounds, and never allows the insertion of something rising.

[9.] STUBBORNNESS deserves its own place among the Affections appropriate to music and helpful in invention. It can be represented by means of so-called capricci or strange passages, for example when one brings such peculiar passages into one or another part which one is resolved not to alter, come what may. The Italians know a form of counterpoint which they call *perfidia*, and which to some extent belongs here . . .

[10.] ANGER, ARDOR, VENGEANCE, RAGE, FURY, and all other such violent emotions are actually far better at making available all sorts of musical inventions than the gentle and pleasant passions which are handled with much more refinement . . .

[11.] Music, like poetry, nearly always deals greatly with JEALOUSY, because this emotional state is a combination of seven other passions, namely, MISTRUST, DESIRE, REVENGE, SADNESS, FEAR, SHAME, which are secondary to the main emotion, ARDENT LOVE. Thus one can easily see that numerous inventions can be led out of these. These, however, according to their nature, must aim in the end at something restless, vexatious, angry, and distressing.

[12.] HOPE is a pleasant and caressing matter. It consists of a joyful longing which fills the spirit with a certain courage; thus this Affection is served by the loveliest use of the voice and the sweetest combinations of sounds in the world . . .

[13.] What to a certain extent is to be placed in opposition to hope, and thus gives rise to a contrasting arrangement of sounds, is called FEAR, DEJECTION, TIMIDITY, etc. Here belong also FRIGHT and HORROR, which, if one thinks of them correctly and has a good mental picture of their natural character, produce very suitable musical passages which correspond with the condition of the emotions.

[14.] DESPAIR is the furthest degree and extent to which terrible fear can drive us; therefore, it is easy to see that this passion can lead us to unusual extremes of all kinds in our music, indeed to the most extreme in order to express it naturally in sounds, and hence it can bring about unusual passages and strange, absurd, disordered sequences of notes.

[15.] PITY remains to be considered. It is of no small impact in music because it is composed of two main Affections, namely, LOVE and SADNESS, one of which suffices for us to contrive our notes most movingly.

Der vollkommene Capellmeister, Part II, Chapter 13, §81 et seq.:

I. Menuet:	No other Affection other than MODERATE GAIETY.
II. Gavotte:	The Affection is a true EXULTING JOY.
III. Bourrée:	Its true character is CONTENTMENT and PLEASANTNESS, and at the same time somewhat UNTROUBLED or CALM, a little slow, easygoing, and yet not unpleasant.
IV. Rigaudon:	Its character consists of a somewhat TRIFLING JOCULARITY.
V. March:	Its true character is something HEROIC and FEARLESS, yet not wild or running.
VI. Entrée:	Here certainly the NOBLE and MAJESTIC nature must occur; however, it must not move along too pompously.
VII. Gigue Loure Canarie Giga:	The common or English gigues have as a character a PASSIONATE and VOLATILE ARDOR, a rage that soon subsides. The loure, which is slow and punctuated, on the other hand, reveals a PROUD, ARROGANT nature. The canarie must have great EAGERNESS and SWIFTNESS, the Italian giga the greatest QUICKNESS and NIMBLENESS.
VIII. Polonaise:	If I had to compose something to words in which a special FRANKNESS and FREE MANNER prevailed, I would choose no other melodic type.
IX. Angloise:	The principal character is STUBBORNNESS.
X. Passepied:	Its nature is quite close to FRIVOLITY.

XI. Rondeau:	In my opinion a good rondeau contains a certain FIRMNESS or rather a firm CONFIDENCE.
XII. Sarabande:	This has no other emotion to express but AMBITION [Ehrsucht].
XIII. Courante:	The Affection which should be brought out of a courante is SWEET HOPEFULNESS, for there is something stouthearted, something longing, and something delightful in this melody.
XIV. Allemande:	The allemande . . . has the image of a CONTENTED or SATISFIED SPIRIT which takes pleasure in good order and peace.

Der vollkommene Capellmeister, Part II, Chapter 12, 208:

In examining large and important instrumental pieces we see that the composer can make much clearer the variety of expressions of the Affections as well as the observation of each and every division of the musical oration [Klang-Rede] if he finds the right tempo; Where, for example,

[1.] ADAGIO	distinguishes	GRIEF [Betrübniβ]
[2.] LAMENTO	distinguishes	LAMENTATION [Wehklagen]
[3.] LENTO	distinguishes	ALLEVIATION [Erleichterung]
[4.] ANDANTE	distinguishes	HOPE [Hoffnung]
[5.] AFFETTUOSO	distinguishes	LOVE [Liebe]
[6.] ALLEGRO	distinguishes	COMFORT [Trost]
[7.] PRESTO	distinguishes	DESIRE [Begierde]

Whether the composer has thought on this or not, it can occur when his genius is truly effective; this may very often happen without our knowledge or cooperation.

20

The genesis of Mattheson's style classification

CLAUDE V. PALISCA

New Haven, Connecticut

The search for the origins of Johann Mattheson's scheme of style classification leads us in two directions. Its emergence over a period of twenty-six years, observable through two of his *Orchestres*, the *Kern melodischer Wissenschafft*, and the *Vollkommener Capellmeister*,[1] traces one path. The other is the genesis of the systems upon which Mattheson founded his own. It is with this that I shall be most concerned.

First I should briefly survey the evolution of Mattheson's own thinking about style.[2] Mattheson's theories of style were tempered in the heat of polemics. After he published his first thoughts in the *Neueröffnetes Orchestre* of 1713 in a chapter entitled "Von der Composition unterschiedenen Arten und Sorten,"[3] his approach was attacked by Johann Heinrich Buttstett[4] – on good grounds, because Mattheson's treatment of the subject was disorganized and primitive.

According to Mattheson, the *styli musici* were "Ecclesiae, Theatri, & Camerae"[5] (of the church, of the theater, and of the chamber). It is not clear at first if these are places in which a variety of styles found a home, or whether Mattheson is saying that there are three fundamental styles, church, theater, and chamber. Having proposed the three

---

This paper is dedicated to Beekman C. Cannon on the occasion of his retirement from Yale University.

1 The four works in which Mattheson developed his style theory are: *Das neu-eröffnete Orchestre* (Hamburg, 1713), *Das beschützte Orchestre* (Hamburg, 1717), *Kern melodischer Wissenschafft* (Hamburg, 1737), and *Der vollkommene Capellmeister* (Hamburg, 1739). I used copies in Yale University Music Library, which has an almost complete collection of Mattheson's publications.

2 In so doing I shall have to repeat some of what E. Katz reported in his excellent inaugural dissertation of 1926, *Die musikalischen Stilbegriffe des 17. Jahrhunderts* (Freiburg im Breisgau, 1926).

3 Part II, chap. 4.

4 *Ut, mi, sol, re, fa, la, tota musica et harmonia aeterna* (Leipzig, [ca. 1717]).

5 *Orchestre* I, Part II, chap. 4, §2.

categories, he proceeds to describe various *Arten* of composition. The first, the *Choral* (that is, polyphonic music for voices), is, of course, a church manner. But in recent times, he says, vocal music is written for the church with greater freedom for a single voice with bass, as in passions and oratorios, in the form of arias and recitatives. These genres, which originated in the chamber and theater, are treated with more seriousness and are more studiedly worked out when intended for the church.

Mattheson goes on to speak of various kinds of theater works – operas, pastorals, little operas (*operetgen*), and ballets – and some of the types of pieces found in them, such as overtures, symphonies, and intradas. Without ceremony, he tumbles onto concertos and cantatas. The latter brings him to definitions of aria, arietta, recitative, cavata, ritornello, and so on. Are these substyles, one wants to ask, or are they genres within the theater style? In defense of Mattheson's vagueness, it must be pointed out that he wrote this book for the *galant homme*, to improve his taste and technical vocabulary, and only secondarily for musicians or critics.

Buttstett, nevertheless, took him seriously and challenged the division into three *stylos*, church, theater, chamber. Buttstett would have preferred to see some difference, in practice, among the three, but despaired of the modern tendency to mix them up. Here is the real objection to Mattheson's threefold division. By admitting the mixing of church, theatrical, and chamber genres, Mattheson blurs whatever distinction there may be. Buttstett asks, "What difference is there today between church, theater, and chamber music? One is pretty much the same as the other. Nearly every kind of songful stuff is presently brought into the church along with the *stylus recitativus theatralis*, and the more merrily and dancingly it goes, the better it pleases most people."[6]

Against Mattheson's simplistic threefold division Buttstett sets Kircher's nine styles of the *stylus expressus*. Buttstett quotes Kircher's entire chapter in Andreas Hirsch's German translation.[7]

Kircher's categories, it should be recalled, were the following. The *stylus ecclesiasticus* is divided into *stylus ligatus* (with cantus fir-

---

6 "Und was ist heut zu tage zwischen Kirchen- *Theatral* und Cammer-Musique für ein Unterschied? es ist ja fast eine wie die andere. Bringet man doch jetzo nebst dem *Stylo recitativo Theatrali* fasst allen liederlichen Krahm in die Kirche / und je lustiger und tantzlicher es gehet / je besser gefallet es theils Personen." Buttstett, *Ut, mi, sol,* 64.

7 A. Hirsch, *Kircherus jesuita germanus Germaniae redonatus: sive artis magnae* (Schwäbisch Hall, 1662).

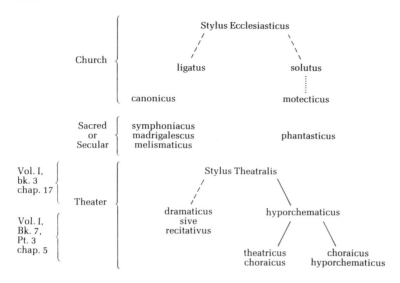

Figure 1. Kircher's style categories (adapted from Katz)

mus) and *stylus solutus* (without). The categories of the next group are undivided: *stylus canonicus, stylus motecticus, stylus phantasticus* (that is, free composition for instruments), *stylus madrigalescus,* and *stylus melismaticus* – this last is a style of simple homophonic vocal music such as the villanella. The *stylus hyporchematicus* is divided into *theatralis* (conventional music for plays and the like) and *choraicus. Stylus symphoniacus* is ensemble instrumental music.[8] (See Figure 1.) Mattheson took Buttstett's criticism to heart, and in the *Beschütztes Orchestre* (1717) he not only adopted some of Kircher's categories advocated by his opponent, but he began to extend his research beyond Kircher to other authors. He discovered that Sébastien de Brossard had incorporated a somewhat modernized version of Kircher's style scheme into his article "Stilo" in the *Dictionaire.*[9] Mattheson at the outset of his discussion translates Brossard's definition of style:

8 A. Kircher, *Musurgia universalis* (Rome, 1650), Vol. I, Book 7, Part 3, chapt. 5, 581–97. Kircher discusses styles also in Vol. I, Book 3, chap. 17, 309ff., and here *stylus theatralis* is divided into *dramaticus sive recitativus* and *hyporchematicus.* In Book 7 he does not have a *stylus theatralis* as such.
9 "Stylus in der Music wird von der Art und Weise verstanden / welche eine jede Person vor sich zu *componiren* / zu *executiren* und zu *informiren* hat; und alles dieses ist sehr unterschieden nach Maßgebung des *Genii* der Verfasser / des Landes

Style in music is understood to be the type of manner that each person uses to compose, to perform, and to communicate. All this is very different according to the mode of operation of the genius of the author, of the nation, and of the people, according also to what the material, the place, the time, the subjects, the expressions demand.

Mattheson goes on to quote Brossard's enumeration of different epithets for style – ancient, modern; Italian, French, German; ecclesiastical, dramatic, chamber; grave, serious, majestic, grand, high, *galant*; familiar, popular, low, servile (*kriechend*), and so on. He also follows Brossard in citing Kircher's categories, placing the dramatic and recitative first and omitting altogether the *canonicus*. Brossard also overlooked Kircher's split of the ecclesiastical into *ligatus* and *solutus*, and simply repeated his qualification of it as a grave, majestic, serious style able to inspire devotion, and Mattheson follows suit. He invites the reader to compare Brossard's treatment with the *Verteutschung* of Kircher, sure that everyone will find Brossard's characterizations more apropos.[10]

Mattheson entered the final stage of his style criticism with *Kern melodischer Wissenschafft* (1737).[11] Here his system appears essentially as it is in the *Vollkommener Capellmeister* of two years later, with one important difference. The very year Mattheson published his book on melody, Scheibe in *Der critische Musicus* (13. Stück, 20 August 1737) introduced the division of styles or *Schreibarten* into *hoh*, *mittler*, and *niedrig*,[12] following those of Johann Christoph Gottsched in *Versuch einer critischen Dichtkunst* (1730).[13] One of the new features of Mattheson's style system in his 1739 book is such a division of all styles into high, middle, and low species, as it were, of the genre "style." The question of priority naturally arises. It appears that neither Scheibe nor Mattheson was the first to apply Gottsched's rhetorical levels to music. Scheibe at the end of his piece on the

und des Volckes; ingleichen / die Zeit / die Subjecta, die Expressiones & c. es. erfordern." S. de Brossard, "Stilo," in: *Dictionaire des termes grecs, latins et italiens, dont on se sert fréquemment dans toutes sortes de musique* (Paris, 1701); 2d ed., 1705, repr. ed. H. Heckmann (Hilversum, 1965). For the passage in German, see Mattheson, *Orchestre* II, 115.

10 Buttstett used the German translation of selected parts of *Musurgia universalis* published by A. Hirsch (see above, n. 8).

11 Zweytes Haupt-Stück, "Von der Componisten Schreib-Art." Most of the sections in this discussion parallel those in *Capellmeister*, Part I, chap. 10, 68–93. However, *Capellmeister*, §§6–33, 35–6, 60–2, 76–8, 109, and 116 are not in the 1737 book. Some of the chapters of 1739, besides, expand parallel chapters of 1737.

12 J. A. Scheibe, *Der critische Musicus* (Hamburg, 1738–40).

13 J. C. Gottsched, *Versuch einer critischen Dichtkunst für die Deutschen* (Leipzig, 1730).

Schreibarten quotes a passage from a letter in which Heinrich Bokemeyer proposes applying to music the three styles *niedrig, mittelmäßig,* and *hoh;*[14] it is likely that Mattheson as well as Scheibe benefited from this initiative of Bokemeyer's.

The introduction of the three rhetorical levels into Mattheson's already eclectic system called for some criteria of combinatoriality of high–middle–low with church–theater–chamber. The passion of a text will dictate the style level, but it will not determine the style itself. Splendor and majesty can be expressed in noble dances as well as in church music, for example. Pomposity, fear, rage deserve a low style, while diligence is suited to the middle style. What is important is that the expression be "natural." Naturalness can be measured by whether an elevated piece is properly majestic, whether a middle-style piece flows easily as it should, and whether a lowly piece is simple, unelaborated and uncluttered by ornament.

Other new elements in this last stage of Mattheson's style theory derive from Italian authors. Marco Scacchi is now identified as the inventor of the church–theatrical–chamber triad.[15] Scacchi is cited also for his distinctions between the older and modern motet styles.[16] Giovanni Battista Doni is credited with having clarified the history and character of the madrigal style.[17] And in this new synthesis Kircher's categories also find a place.

In the *Vollkommener Capellmeister* Mattheson germanizes Kircher's categories, which in the book on melody were still couched in Kircher's Latin. But every one of the categories themselves is retained: *Motetten-Styl, Madrigal-Styl, melismatische Schreib-Art, hyporchematischer Styl, phantastische Schreib-Art, canonischer Styl.* Only *stylus symphoniacus* retains its Latin form. From the earlier terminological focus Mattheson now shifts toward compositional procedures. He is now writing for the musician, initiating him into unfamiliar styles in which he needs to become proficient as a listener, performer, and composer. Style is now almost infinitely

---

14 "Der Styl ist eine gewisse Manier des musikalischen Vortrags, und gehöret hauptsächlich zur Ausdrückung Betrachtet man solche insgemein so findern wir, wie in der Redekunst und Poesie, drey Arten desselben, nämlich den niedrigen, mittelmäßigen und hohen Styl, nachdem die vorkommenden Personen, Sachen und Verrichtungen beschaffen sind, die dadurch vorgestellet werden sollen." Scheibe, *Critischer musicus,* 14. Stück, 20 August 1737, 139. Mattheson and Bokemeyer exchanged numerous letters, and Mattheson printed some of these in *Critica musica* I.

15 *Capellmeister,* I, chap. 10, §4.   16 Ibid., §43.

17 Ibid., §§54–5. G. B. Doni, *Compendio del trattato de' generi e de' modi della musica* (Rome, 1635), 100–116.

Table 1. *Mattheson's style classifications*

Church (geistlich) high–middle–low		
gebunden	*ungebunden*	Madrigal
Capell-Styl	Motet-style	Melismatic
	4–8 v. no organ	Symphonic
	polychoral	
	sacred concerto	
	modern motet	
Chamber (häuslich) high–middle–low		
Canonic	Madrigal	
	cantata	
	Melismatic	
	Instrumental	
	sonata, concerto, etc.	
	hyporchematic	
	choraic	
	Fantastic	
Theater (weltlich) high–middle–low		
Dramatic	Madrigal	
recitative	Singspiele	
chorus	cavata	
Instrumental	continuo-madrigal	
aria	Melismatic	
Canonic	Instrumental	
Fantastic	hyporchematic	
	choraic	

divisible. In elaborating upon the *stylus symphoniacus*, he drops the remark that "this style is divided into almost as many subordinate kinds as there are instrumental media" ("so theilet sich dieser Styl fast in eben so viele Neben-Arten, als es Werckzeuge gibt"[18]). A composer writes quite differently for violins from the way he writes for lutes or flutes or trumpets. Throughout his chapter Mattheson strives to instill a sensitivity to stylistic propriety and decorum with verbal characterizations that are more evocative than scientific.

The multilevel style distinctions in the *Vollkommener Capellmeister* defy graphic schematization, as was possible with Kircher's system, for example (see Figure 1). No grid or lattice will adequately represent it. Mattheson's complex web or network refuses to be reduced to a neat checkerboard format. Table 1 is a feeble attempt to give a picture of this complexity and interdependence of parts.

18 Ibid., §64.

After this brief account of Mattheson's nonsystem of musical style, I come to my main purpose, to investigate the little-understood genesis of certain strands of this web.

Although Mattheson would probably have been well advised to discard his original triad, church–theater–chamber, after Buttstett's first challenge, he held fast to it throughout his spirals of rising style consciousness, and these three categories continue to be the backbone of his theory. What is the origin of this triad? Katz was content to verify that it existed in Scacchi and Bernhard, investigating no farther back. However, Mattheson apparently did not know Scacchi's or Bernhard's writings in 1713 when he first broached the subject of style in *Das neu-eröffnete Orchestre.*[19]

The path of transmission of this threefold scheme leads back through Angelo Berardi and Marco Scacchi to its eventual scource. That source, for at least two of the three components, is Claudio Monteverdi. In the foreword to the eighth book of madrigals, *Madrigali guerrieri ed amorosi* (1638), in explaining why he characterized the madrigals of that collection diversely as warlike (*guerrieri*), amorous (*amorosi*), and representational (*rappresentativi*), Monteverdi proposes that there are three styles (*modi*) of music used in the royal chambers of great princes to please their refined tastes: music of the theater, of the chamber, and of the dance. The context of the remark is the following:[20]

Therefore I give notice that in this genre the basso continuo must be played with its accompaniments in the manner and form as written. Similarly found written is every other indication to be observed in other compositions of other

---

19 Mattheson's *Forschendes Orchestre* (Hamburg, 1721), his most scholarly (also most pedantic) work, is a good guide to his reading. In it he cites Marco Scacchi's *Cribrum musicum* (Venice, 1643) but not his letter to Werner. He also by this time had become acquainted with Christoph Bernhard's unpublished *Tractatus compositionis augmentatus*. He also cites Berardi's *Documenti armonici* (Bologna, 1687) but not his *Ragionamenti musicali* (Bologna, 1681) or *Miscellanea musicale* (Bologna, 1689), both important for their discussions of styles.
20 Monteverdi, *Opere*, ed. G. F. Malipiero (rev. ed., Vienna, 1967), Vol. 8, "A chi legge": Perciò auiso douer essere sonato il basso continuo con gli suoi compagnamenti, nel modo & forma in tal genere che sta scritto, nel quale si troua parimente ogni altro ordine che s'ha da tenere nelle altre compositioni d'altro genere; perche le maniere di sonare deuono essere di tre sorti, oratoria, Armonicha, & Rethmicha; la ritrouata da me del qual genere da guerra, mi hà datto occasione di scriuere alcuni Madrig[ali] da me intitolati Guerrieri; & perche la Musica de Gran Prencipi viene adoperata nelle loro Regie Camere in tre modi per loro delicati gusti; da Teatro, da camera, & da ballo; perciò nella present mia opera, hò accennato gli detti tre generi con la intitulatione Guerriera, Amorosa & rapresentativa; sò che sarà imperfetta, perche poco vaglio in tutto, in particolare nel genere Guerriero per essere nouo & perche *omne principum est debile.*

genres. For the manners of playing must be of three kinds, oratorical, harmonic, and rhythmic. That discovered by me, the genre of war, has given me the opportunity to write various madrigals entitled by me "warlike." Since the music of great princes is employed in their royal chambers for their refined tastes in three styles, music of the theater, of the chamber, and of the dance, I have identified the said three genres with the labels "warlike," "amorous," and "representational" in my present work. I know that it will be imperfect, because I am not worth much at all, particularly in the warlike genre, since it is new, and because *omne prinum est debile* [every beginning is weak].

This statement suggests the following grid:

method of performance	oratorical	harmonic	rhythmic
style	theater	chamber	dance
genre	warlike	amorous	representational

When set opposite the works themselves as labeled by the composer, the neat correspondences are valid only to a point. Several of the warlike "madrigals" are theater pieces and require oratorical (speechlike) delivery. The amorous pieces are mostly chamber ensemble vocal works, therefore in "harmonic" performance medium. The balli are meant to be "represented," that is, danced in rhythmic performance with mimed gestures on a stage.[21] But not every piece in each genre fits the scheme, and one should not take Monteverdi too literally.

Scacchi saw that the scheme did not really work, and he telescoped it into two categories, theater and chamber, to which he added an obvious third, church music. Scacchi's clearest formulation of the tripartite scheme is in his letter to Christoph Werner[22] of approximately 1646, and this may be outlined as follows:

Stylus Ecclesiasticus	Stylus Cubicularis	Stylus Theatralis seu Scenica Musica
1. Missae, motettae et similes cantilenae 4, 5, 6, 8 vocum absque organo.	1. Madrigales exclusis instrumentis: da tavolino.	1. Unico contenta stylo, ut cantus colloquendo, et colloquia canendo perficiantur.
2. Eaedem cantilenae adiuncto organo; plures etiam chori pleni	2. Cantilenae cum basso generali.	

21 The only madrigals that contain stage directions in the score are two warlike balli, *Combattimento di Tancredi e Clorinda*, *Ballo delle ingrate*, and *Non havea Febo ancora*. The last, marked "rapresentativo," is not a ballo, however.
22 Printed in Katz, *Stilbegriffe*, 83; Mattheson, *Capellmeister*, I, Chap. 10, §45.

3. Similes cantilenae in concerto	3. Admittit omnia instrumenta.
4. Motetta juxta usum modernum.	

At the very outset of the discussion in *Kern melodischer Wissenschafft* and *Vollkommener Capellmeister* Mattheson introduces Scacchi's three classes (*Classen*), the church, theatrical, and chamber styles.[23] This division, he proclaims, is not only right but necessary: ". . . nicht nur ihre völlige Richtigkeit habe; sondern auch nothwendig also, und auf keine andre Haupt-Weise, gemacht werden könne noch müsse, ungeachtet man dieselbe drey Schreib-Arten wol auf verschiedene Neben-Arten ausdehnen und betrachten möge."[24] Mattheson then goes on (without, however, attributing a further division to Scacchi) to say that "at that time" the church style had four different categories, the chamber style, three, and the theatrical style, only one. But since that time other substyles have developed and more undoubtedly will; even so, the three primary styles will maintain their fundamental distinctions.[25]

Mattheson, if he accepted the basic premises of this partition of styles, was not uncritical of Scacchi. In section 45, he quotes Scacchi (omitting quotation marks), but then adds his own dismissal of the ideas quoted.

Sacchi, Letter to Werner:	*Capellmeister*, I, Chapter 10, Section 45:
I. Ecclesiasticus in quatuor iterum stylus dividitur. Primusque comprehendit Missas, Motetta, et similes Cantilenas 4. 5. 6. 8. vocum, absque Organo. Secundus easdem Cantilenas, adiuncto Organo, ita, ut plures etiam chori pleni possint constitui. Tertius similes Cantilenas in concerto. Quartus demun Motetta juxta usum modernum.	Nach damahliger Eintheilung des gesammten Kirchen-Styls machten die Missen, Moteten und dergleichen Gesänge von 4, 5, 6 bis 8 Stimmen, ohne Orgel, die erste Gattung desselben aus; die zweite bestund in eben denselben Stücken mit der Orgel und verschiedenen abwechselnden Chören: die dritte lieferte geistliche Concerten, und die vierte eine damahls neue Art der lieben Moteten. Schlechter Unterschied!

Where did Sacchi's style consciousness come from? Its origins predated Monteverdi's 1638 preface, even Monteverdi's distinction

---

23 §§ 4 and 5 in both books. Mattheson gives Scacchi's Latin text in a footonte.
24 *Capellmeister*, I, chap. 10, §4.   25 Ibid., §5.

between the two practices, which Scacchi helped to keep alive. Scacchi in his *Breve discorso* (1649) states:

Ancient music consists in one practice and almost in one and the same style of employing consonances and dissonances. But the modern consists of two practices and three styles, namely, the church, chamber, and theater styles. The practices are: the first, which is *ut Harmonia sit Domina Orationis*, and the second, which is *ut Oratio sit Domina Harmoniae*. Each of these three styles contains very great variations, novelties, and inventions of extraordinary dimension.[26]

Although Monteverdi was the first to speak of the two practices, there was growing recognition in the last decade of the sixteenth century and the first of the seventeenth of stylistic diversity and of a double standard of counterpoint, one strict, the other free.

Girolamo Diruta clearly saw that there were two kinds of counterpoint, *contrapunto osservato* and *contrapunto commune*. The second, he says, is much easier, because one has to observe hardly any rule except that of avoiding consecutive perfect consonances of the same species.[27] Adriano Banchieri in an essay dated 1613, "Moderna pratica musicale," was more articulate about the difference. The *contrapunto osservato*, he recalls, was explained with erudition by Gioseffo Zarlino and Giovanni Maria Artusi. But of the *contrapunto misto* or *commune*, no one has written, nor is it susceptible of description, "since it does not have in my opinion other rational principles than that the sense of hearing should be pleased by it" ("non havendosi (a mio giuditio) altre ragioni, solo che il senso dell'udito se ne compiace"). No one has been able, he goes on, to produce a single rule of how "to accommodate with imitated affections any genre of words, whether Latin or vernacular, and particularly words that express pain, passion, sighing, weeping, laughing, interrogation, error, or any other circumstance" ("che mostri in-pratica accommodare con imitati affetti le parole in qual si voglia genere o sia latino, over volgare, & in particolare alle parole ch'esprimono, dolore, passione, sospiro, pianto, riso, interrogativo? errore o qual sia si altro accidente").[28]

---

26 Marco Scacchi, *Breve discorso sopra la musica moderna* (Warsaw 1649), fol. C3v–C4r. For an English translation of the entire little book, see C. Palisca, "Marco Scacchi's Defense of Modern Music (1649)," in: *Words and Music: The Scholar's View, A Medley . . . in Honor of A. Tillman Merritt*, ed. L. Berman (Cambridge, Mass., 1972), 189–208. The above passage is on p. 204.

27 Girolamo Diruta, *Seconda parte del Transilvano dialogo* (Venice, 1609); 2d ed., 1622, facs. ed., Bibliotheca musica Bononiensis, II, 132 (Bologna, 1969), Libro II, 15–16.

28 Adriano Banchieri, *Cartella musicale* (Venice, 1614), 165.

Actually, someone had attempted to develop such a theory. Vincenzo Galilei in his manuscript counterpoint treatise of 1589–91 in the volume on dissonance distinguishes between composers who were *osservatori* and wrote *cantilene osservate* and those who, like Cipriano de Rore, felt free to follow their own judgment, independent of all rules.[29]

Mattheson still recalls this distinction but gives the impression that the modern composer has liberated himself from the *osservato* style – from the *gefesselte Setz-Art*, the *gebunden*, or *Capell-Styl*.[30] Now the same kinds of texts once set in these stricter manners are set in the melismatic style, in other words, the *contrapunto commune*. But what this melismatic style is remains in Mattheson's books almost as vague as in Banchieri and Diruta. It was Kircher's term, and he had a rather restrictive view of it, as sweet melody set to metrical verses that allowed for musical repetition, as in strophic songs. Kircher's musical examples by Hieronymus Kapsberger were homophonic part-songs.[31] Mattheson cites several generic examples that point in the same direction: chorales, strophic ariettas, canzonette in Italian intermezzi, and German odes.

Another important early manifestation of style consciousness is Pietro Pontio's *Ragionamento di musica* (1588). In a remarkable section of the *Quarto ragionamento* he sets out to demonstrate "the mode or style, as I might call it, to make a motet or a mass or other compositions, which come out of that florid counterpoint" – the florid counterpoint that the disciple in this dialogue had been previously taught.[32] Pontio here prescribes the proper style that should be maintained in each common type of composition: mass, motet, psalm, Magnificat, ricercar, and madrigal. The instructions embrace considerations of note values, texture, text underlay, length of syncopated dissonances, length of melodic subjects, invention or borrowing of subjects, imitation or note-against-note technique, dissonance, and text expression.

Mattheson probably did not know Pontio's work directly, or even through Pietro Cerone's paraphrases and glosses of this section of the

---

29 Vincenzo Galilei, *Discorso intorno alle dissonanze*, Florence, Biblioteca nazionale centrale, MS Galilei 1, fol. 142v.
30 *Capellmeister*, I, chap. 10, §§38–9.
31 Kircher, *Musurgia*, 586–8.
32 ". . . il modo, o stile, che vogliamo dire, per far vn Motetto; ouer vna Messa; & altre compositioni, quale vengono da quel contrapunto florido." P. Pontio, *Ragionamento di musica* (Parma, 1588; facs. ed. S. Clercx, Kassel, 1959), 153.

dialogue,[33] but he felt the influence through Kircher. Particularly important is Pontio's definition of what he called the *stile grave*.[34] Most essential for Pontio in maintaining this style was the control of note values, so that gravity of motion, yet variety, is achieved. This style should reign in the mass and motet. Pontio's characterization is echoed in Kircher's statement about the *stylus motecticus*, which he qualifies as a "processus harmonicus, grauis, maiestate plenus, summa varietate floridus, nullo subiecto adstrictus,"[35] all points that were covered by Pontio. By the time of the *Vollkommener Capellmeister* Mattheson had rejected the old motet style as a viable medium for expressing the affections.[36]

Mattheson was indebted to the Italians also for certain of the descriptions of the secular media. He made a point of acknowledging some but not all. For the early history of the madrigal and the derivation of the word he relies upon Doni (*Compendio del trattato de' generi e de' modi*), thanks to whom he could discard the fanciful story of Kircher's that the form was invented by a certain Madrigallus. Doni's etymology is through *materialis*, because at first they dealt with commonplace and coarse subjects (*Materien*).[37] For a description of the madrigal with basso continuo Mattheson goes to Scacchi's *Cribrum musicum* and includes excerpts from two concertato madrigals by Scacchi published there, *Questa nuova Angioletta* and *Ah! dolente partita*, both for four voices with basso continuo.[38] To describe the styles of the two, Mattheson again borrows from Scacchi.[39]

Scacchi, Cribrum, 184:

Dictum est supra, in stylo hoc recentiori orationem esse dominam, et non ancillam ipsius harmoniae. Recentiorumque; Compositiones considerandes esse non quoad verba tantum, sed et cumprimis quoad ipsum loquendi modum, qui juxta diversas animi affectiones subinde variatur.

Capellmeister, I, chapter 10, section 61:

Scacchi . . . nennet diesen Styl einen neuern (*recentiorem*) und unterscheidet ihn vornehmlich von der Motetischen Schreib-Art auch dadruch, daß, in den Madrigalen, die Worte Herren und keine Knechte sind, d.i. man müsse darin mehr auf den Inhalt des Wort-Verstandes, und der Affecten, als auf das künstliche Klang-Gewebe der Noten sehen; welches bey dem Moteten-Styl just umgekehrt war.

33 D. P. Cerone, *El Melopeo y Maestro* (Naples, 1613), Book 12, chap. 12ff. See the partial translation in O. Strunk, *Source Readings in Music History* (New York, 1950), 236–73.
34 Pontio, *Ragionamento*, 154.   35 Kircher, *Musurgia*, 585.
36 *Capellmeister*, I, chap. 10, §§48–50.   37 Doni, *Compendio del Trattato*, 113.
38 They are published in full in C. Palisca, "Marco Scacchi's Defense," 211–30.
39 Trans. into Eng. in ibid., 209, from *Cribrum*, 184.

Although the German *Wort* is neuter (*oratio* is feminine), Mattheson turns Monteverdi's Mistress into a Lord, and her maid becomes a male servant (male chauvinism on his part?) Mattheson also reports Scacchi's wish in these madrigals to avoid the excessive liveliness of the Italian style current in his time:[40]

. . . sine nimia alacritate, quae alias hodie Italis in ejus modi cantionum generibus imprimis approbatur, componere volui siquidem satis scio, stylum illum nimis alacrem atque affectatum ob omnibus aegue comprehendi non posse.	. . . er habe darin die bey seinen Lands-Leuten Beifall-findende gar zu große Munterkeit mit Fleiß vermieden, weil ihm wol bekannt, daß nicht iedermann fähig, von dergleichen allzufrischen und hurtigen Gesängen ein bescheidenes Urtheil zu fällen.

More debts of this kind could be pointed out; it is clear that Mattheson's chapter on styles is an eclectic and composite work. And this may be its chief virtue, if a source of confusion.

Grafting together several style systems confounds the issues, because four levels of style division are at work: Scacchi's sociologically or functionally determined tripartite division, Kircher's nine categories of *stylus expressus*, Gottsched's rhetorical levels, and the *gebunden–ungebunden* dichotomy in compositional technique (see Figure 2). Not altogether compatible sets of criteria – functional, expressive, rhetorical, and technical – thus converge and compete, scattering the focus, tangling lines of demarcation.

Mattheson's is not a rational system. In coming to this conclusion I part with Katz, who found in it a rationalistic manifestation of the Enlightenment. Katz's characterization may well apply to other chapters of the *Vollkommener Capellmeister*, but the chapter on style is not systematic; it is exploratory, pragmatic, and garrulous. It occasionally strikes a scholarly tone, but as a whole it is too casual and diffuse for a scientific treatise. As acute an observer of the current musical scene as this Spectator in Music was could have developed a much better organized and logical style classification, if that had been what he set out to do. Instead, we have something that grew plantlike into a creeping, climbing organism that clings to the earliest triple trunk, while branching off into Kircher's nine-stemmed system, pruned by Brossard's sharp lexicographic shears, and finally domesticated to thrive in Gottsched's triple-tiered garden. Mattheson's understanding of style distinctions never stopped growing and maturing, but in the *Vollkommener Capellmeister* it had not crystallized into a truly integrated, rational system.

40 Ibid., 209, trans. from *Cribrum*, 169; *Capellmeister*, I, chap. 10, §62.

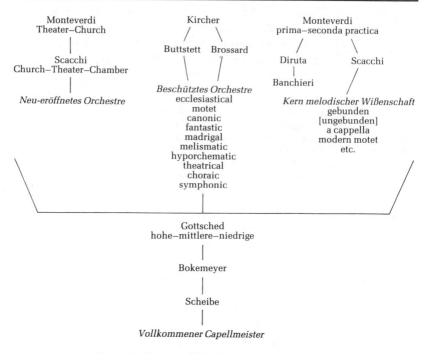

Figure 2. Genesis of Mattheson's style categories

Moreover his treatment lacks temporal definition, of a moment in the flux of stylistic change that would circumscribe the musical reality against which it is to be judged. Pseudotheoretical, vaguely historical, it sums up, really, a personal philosophy. The moral is clear: No style should be ruled out of any of the three spheres, and, in particular, all styles can serve church and private devotions. This for Mattheson remains music's noblest mission. Mingling styles on one level, while distinguishing function and genre on another, is a consequence of this philosophy.

Mattheson's eclecticism and confusion of styles thus has a positive side. By borrowing from a multitude of traditions, his style system is rooted in history. Through his reading and his well-traveled ear Mattheson was steeped in the ideas and sounds of the past and present and could arrange them, as few others could, from some chronological perspective. It was apparent to him, as it is to us, that Baroque music was a rich tapestry of characteristic genres and styles, some projecting into the future, others retreating into the past. These diverse styles invited the composer to explore their delights and constraints. Nothing was more crucial to the *vollkommener Capellmeister* of the Baroque than an acute sense of style. The master composer faced no more formidable challenge than to match his wits and talent against the best exemplars of the discrete styles. His response to function, occasion, level, technical demands, and expressive intent – the parameters of Mattheson's critique – were all put to a supreme test in this exercise.

21

Mattheson und die französische Musik

HERBERT SCHNEIDER
Bayreuth

In seiner Gegenüberstellung der Vorzüge des italienischen, französischen, englischen und deutschen Nationalstils kommt Mattheson 1713 zum Ergebnis, die Franzosen "divertirten" am besten, sie machten sich bei den Zuhörern "aimables", sie seien "spirituels", ihre Musik belebe die Anwesenden, aber die Komponisten wendeten "ihren Fleiß nicht zum besten"[1] an. Damit löst er sich von älteren Erklärungen stilistischer Differenzen, die von der "constitutio temperamenti" und der "constitutio regionis" ausgingen. Kennzeichnend für die uns wie ein Klischee erscheinende Mentalitätsskizze des Vorberichtes der *Grundlage einer Ehren-Pforte*[2] ist ein Zitat aus den *Mémoires* von Roger Comte de Bussy-Rabutin, in dem die Nationaleigenschaften Ungeduld, Oberflächlichkeit und Mangel an Ausdauer genannt sind, die dafür verantwortlich seien, daß Franzosen zwar über jedes Thema eine Konversation führen, aber in keiner Wissenschaft zur Vollkommenheit gelangen könnten. Mattheson nimmt im *Philologischen Tresespiel* die ihm seit langem bekannte Bemerkung von Le Cerf de la Viéville, "Les Allemands dont la réputation n'est pas grande en Musique"[3], zum Anlaß, polemisch gegen die französische Musik auszuholen. Der deutsche Ruhm

bei itzigen Zeiten in der Musik zum wenigsten viermal größer zu seyn verdienet, und zwar wegen der Gründlichkeit, als der Franzosen sogenannte Reputation: denn gegen einen einzigen, sehr mittelmäßig fruchtbaren Lulli[4] und seiner eingebildeten Nachahmer, den affektierten, pedantischen Rameau, können wir jederzeit vier aufweisen, die nicht nur in Deutschland, sondern auch in Frankreich und England, ja, selbst mitten in dem anitzo sehr

---

1 Orchestre I, 219.   2 Siehe *Ehrenpforte*, XVII–XVIII.
3 Mattheson zitiert P. Bonnets *Histoire de la musique*, III, 95, cf. *Tresespiel*, 94.
4 Mattheson beruft sich hier auf Le Cerf de la Viéville, der an dem angegebenen Ort, Bonnet, *Histoire de la musique*, III, 131, aber gerade die kompositorische Fruchtbarkeit Lullys und Campras betont.

vermischten Italien, den größesten musikalischen Ruhm davon getragen haben[5].

So viel der Polemik von Mattheson, die jedoch entscheidend dazu beigetragen hat, ein in Frankreich von Gegnern des großen Rameau verbreitetes Negativbild in Deutschland bekannt zu machen. Mattheson beschränkt sich in seinem musiktheoretischen Oeuvre keineswegs auf solche Allgemeinheiten. Aus seinen Mitteilungen läßt sich die Rezeption französischer Musik, Musiktheorie und Musikauffassung im norddeutschen Raum und die sich verändernde Einschätzung ihrer Bedeutung für deutsche Komponisten ablesen[6]. Alle bibliographischen Angaben Matthesons machen deutlich, daß die in Holland bei Roger, Mortier und Le Cène erschienenen Theoretiker und Musikalien französicher Herkunft bekannt waren. In Hamburg gab es eine Auslieferung des Verlages Roger, die von Johann Christian Schickhardt geleitet wurde. Im Gegensatz dazu war die Beschaffung von musikalischen Quellen und Informationen aus Paris offensichtlich wesentlich schwieriger. Zwar setzte sich Mattheson bereits im zweiten Band der *Critica musica* von 1725 mit Rameaus *Traité de l'harmonie* von 1722 auseinander, aber noch 1739 konnte er nicht ermitteln[7], wer die Teile II bis IV von Bonnets *Histoire de la musique* geschrieben hatte. Die *Défense du Parallèle* Raguenets aus dem Jahre 1705 will sich Mattheson 1722 "aus Paris bringen"[8] lassen.

I

In seiner "Judicatoria" überschriebenen "Pars tertia" des *Neu-eröffneten Orchestre* kommt Mattheson zu einer klaren Präferenz der italienischen gegenüber der französischen Musik:

Man streitet hierbey nicht / daß nicht so wohl die Frantzösische Composition als Exccution, in ihrer Art / ihr eigenes Lob verdiene / und vielleicht der Italiänischen nicht viel nachgiebet; allen weil ein großes Theil in solchen Sachen von dem Gout dependiret / und aber die Frantzosen noch keine solche generale Approbation ihrer Music, als wol ihrer Sprache / in der Welt erhalten habe / so wird sich vermuthlich das davon etwa zu machende Elogium hauptsächlich intra, und nicht gar weit extra fines Galliae erstrecken können. So viel muß man gerne gestehen: In der Instrumental, insonderheit

5 *Tresespiel*, 94–5.
6 Den Einfluß der französischen Musiktheorie und -ästhetik auf Mattheson stellt A. Forchert in seinem Aufsatz "Französische Autoren in den Schriften Johann Matthesons", in: *Festschrift Heinz Becker* (Laaber, 1982), 382–91 dar.
7 Siehe *Capellmeister*, 22 und 480.
8 Siehe *Critica musica* I, 231.

aber in der Choraischen oder Tantz-Music sind die Frantzosen Meister / und werden überall / ohne imitiret zu werden / imitiret[9].

Nur die italienische und die französische Musik werde als stilistisch eigenständig angesehen, jedoch prahlten die Franzosen ständig, sie "haben auch sonst wenig aufzuweisen"[10]. Mit außerordentlicher Scharfsinnigkeit hat Mattheson die von Lully in besonderem Maße herbeigeführte Stilisierung der französischen Gattungen sowie die Typisierung der Melodik und des Satzes charakterisiert: "Chorda aberrant eadem, es ist immer die alte Leyer. Sie würden nicht übel thun / wenn sie eine universelle Melodie verfertigten / darauf mit weniger Veränderung / alle ihre Chansons gesungen werden könten; es wäre practicable, denn sie sind der Unität ohne dem schon ziemlich nahe gekommen"[11]. Insbesondere die Gestaltung der melodischen Übergänge bei Absätzen und Schlüssen "vermittelst bequemer Zugänge und Fortschreitungen", d.h. die stilisierten "transitiones" kritisiert Mattheson, da die französischen Komponisten "dadurch ihren Melodien viel leyerhafftes" geben[12]. Mattheson war trotz dieser Kritik ein Freund der französischen "melodischen Leichtigkeit", so daß er sie noch 1737 zur Nachahmung empfiehlt[13]: "So kann man nicht besser thun, als des Lully Wercke, und einiger kurtz nach ihm berühmten Verfasser Arbeit vorzunehmen". Jedoch fordert er nicht nur ein schönes Thema, sondern die bei den Franzosen seltenere Ausarbeitung der Mittelstimmen "mit gleichem Fleiße"[14].

Spöttisch fordert er die Franzosen auf, ihm einen "universellen" Komponisten namhaft zu machen, der nicht lediglich "ein paar Ouvertürgen / oder ein Suitchen auff dem Clavier, mit einer großen Parisischen Überschrifft"[15] komponiert habe.

Im Kommentar zum zweiten Teil seiner Übersetzung aus *Parallèle des Italiens et des François* in der *Critica musica* erklärt sich Mattheson mit den Gedanken Raguenets einverstanden "weil alles mit der Wahrheit / Erfahrung und gesunden Vernunfft übereinkommt"[16]. Auch hier ist wieder von der starken Stilisierung und Typisierung die Rede, wenn Raguenet das Wesen der Franzosen als "ziemlich eng eingeschlossen" ansieht. Ihre Musik "wiege die Zuhörer ein", sie sei "sehr plat und ungeschmackt", "man findet nichts erhabnes und

---

9 *Orchestre* I, 208.   10 Ibid., 209.   11 Ibid., 209.
12 *Melodische Wissenschaft*, 47, und in fast wörtlicher Übereinstimmung im *Capellmeister*, 151.
13 *Melodische Wissenschaft*, 38, und ähnlich im *Capellmeister*, 140 und 143.
14 *Critica musica* I, 132, Zitat aus Raguenets *Parallèle*.
15 *Orchestre* I, 209.   16 *Critica musica* I, 121.

gewagtes darinn; alles ist gleichförmig / alles ist von einer Art"[17]. Außerdem hielten die Franzosen zu streng am Kanon der Kompositionsregeln fest und mieden schärfere, ausdrucksstarke Dissonanzen. Die Beobachtung der Regelhaftigkeit der französischen Musik gipfelt schließlich in der Bemerkung: "Da höret man allemahl einerley Accords / einerley Fälle und Gänge / keine Veränderung / keine Überraschung / man siehet alles vorher / was kommen soll. Die Französ. Componisten bestehlen allenthalben einer den anderen / oder sie schreiben sich selber dergestalt aus / daß sich fast alle ihre Werke gleich sehen"[18]. Untermauert wird diese Argumentation mit Zitaten aus Dubos' *Réflexions critiques sur la poésie et sur la peinture* (1719)[19]. Auch Pierre Bonnet[20] wird als Kronzeuge bemüht, um festzustellen "wie ungesalzen und abgeschmackt dergleichen Leyerwerk und Monotonie, so wohl in den Französischen Opern / als in ihrer Kirchen-Music sey".

Dieser vernichtenden Kritik allzu stilisierter und typisierter Nachahmung unmittelbarer Vorbilder, die kaum Modifizierungen erfahren, steht aber andererseits die Wertschätzung französischer Eigenarten gegenüber: "Man gibt dem Frantzösischen Geschmack im Punct der Leichtigkeit darum den Vorzug, daß er einen aufgeräumten lebhafften Geist erfordert, der ein Freund wolanständigen Schertzes, und ein Feind alles dessen ist, was nach Mühe und Arbeit riecht"[21]. Bereits im *Neu-eröffneten Orchestre* hatte er im gleichen Sinn die "Facilität" betont, mit der sie "zum Zweck aller Studien gelangen / sie brauchen aber unsere amplissimam dominam methodum keineswegs"[22]. Durch sein *Neu-eröffnetes Orchestre* hatte Mattheson nicht nur die Kritik Buttstetts und Murschhausers provoziert, sondern auch einen ungenannten Verteidiger der französischen Musik zum Widerspruch herausgefordert, so daß Mattheson sich zu einer Richtigstellung im *Beschützten Orchestre*[23] veranlaßt sah:

Weil ich vernehme / daß ein gewisser großer Compositeur vermeinet / ich hätte in meinem Orchestre die Frantzosen ein bißgen zu viel herunter gemachet; so habe ich mich verbunden erachtet / diese Imputation von mir abzulehnen und zu versichern / daß solches gantz und gar meine Absicht nicht gewesen; sondern daß ich groß Egard für die Frantzösische / insonderheit Instrumental-Music trage. . . . So bemercke ich auch / daß die Herren Frantzosen neulich angefangen haben / viele Vocal-Sachen auf

---

17 Ibid., 122.   18 *Critica musica* I, 135.
19 Siehe ibid., 135 und 217.
20 Ibid., 217.   21 *Capellmeister*, 141.
22 *Orchestre* I, 198.   23 *Orchestre* II, 237.

Italiänische Art zu setzen / welche ich würcklich recht artig und wohlausgearbeitet befunden habe. Vormahls waren sie zu eigensinnig dazu / nun sie aber sehen / wie das Schwimmen gegen den Strohm nicht gut gehet / kommen sie zu bessern Gedanken. Ich gratulire und sehe es hertzlich gerne.

Das Verhältnis der französischen zur italienischen Musik, das in Frankreich seit der "Querelle des anciens et des modernes" die Musikliteratur entscheidend bestimmt hat, findet auch bei Mattheson starke Beachtung; insbesondere auch deswegen, weil er Zeuge des zunehmenden italienischen Einflusses in Frankreich wurde. Im *Neueröffneten Orchestre* bemerkt er dazu, Lully sei trotz seiner Bevorzugung der französischen Musik in der "Verknüpfung beyder Arten" am erfolgreichsten gewesen, mit ihm scheine "aber zugleich diese schöne Kunst / wenigstens in Franckreich / verstorben und begraben zu seyn"[24]. Im Jahre 1722 interpretiert er dann diese Auffassung: Lully habe "die wahren Zierrathen und das würcklich glänzende Wesen der Italiänischen Music wohl aufzusuchen / und am rechten Orte anzubringen gewußt: Dadurch er denn seinen Zweck / in Bewegung der Affecten / hauptsächlich erreichen können"[25].

In der *Großen General-Baß-Schule* bezeichnet Mattheson das "Welschland" "unstreitig das musicalische Eden / absonderlich des Geschmacks halber"[26]. Frankreich und England trügen "mehrenteils nur Zinsen von solchen Haupt-Stühlen / welche so wol die Welschen / als unsre teutsche Vorfahren / alda beleget haben / wie solches die Schuldner selbst hin und wieder nicht in Abrede seyn können". Diese Auffassung erscheint allerdings sehr gewagt, sind doch deutsche Einflüsse auf das französische Musikleben bis zur Zeit, als er seine *Große General-Baß-Schule* publizierte, kaum festzustellen.

Der *Critica musica* zufolge können französische Musiker, die in Italien gearbeitet haben, "die Französische / Art des Komponierens / gar nicht mehr leiden"[27]. Daher sei es besser für sie,

wenn sie den Italiänischen Styl hübsch mit Frieden liessen / und bey ihrer angeborenen Weise blieben. Die Cantaten / so neulich bey ihnen all'Italia zum Vorschein gekommen / sind (die Wahrheit zu sagen) rechte musicalische Zwitter / und ihr mehr zu wünschen als zu hoffen / daß es ein Franzose jemahls darinn hoch bringen werde. Da sie aber eine solche ursprüngliche und große Schönheit in ihrer Mutter-Music finden / wollte ich rathen / daß sie auch nicht ein Haar breit davon abweichen[28].

24 *Orchestre* I, 208.   25 *Critica musica* I, 213.
26 *General-Baß-Schule* I, 46.   27 *Critica musica* I, 166.   28 *Ibid.*, 204.

Noch 1737[29] wirft Mattheson, indem er sich auf Bonnet beruft, den jüngeren französischen Komponisten vor, die Italiener nachzuäffen und damit ihre gewohnte und angeborene Leichtigkeit aufzugeben.

II

Mattheson setzte sich in verschiedenen Traktaten mit der französischen Aufführungspraxis auseinander. In den frühen Publikationen hielt er sie in Ehren: "so wol die Frantzösische Composition als Execution" gebe der italienischen nicht viel nach[30]. Später kritisiert er bestimmte äußerliche Manieren, die offensichtlich mehr Anklang fanden als die von ihm geschätzten "Fleiß / ihre Nettigkeit / ihre Fertigkeit in den Schlüsseln / ihre Einigkeit im Spielen / und andere gute Eigenschafften"[31]. Die "übermäßige Tactierungslust", "die Lufftstreiche / das Aufheben / das Windfechten / die Verdrehungen / so ihrer etliche mit Händen und Füssen / mit Leib und Seele / bey ihrem Tactschlagen anbringen"[32], sind Mattheson verhaßt, weil sie in Deutschland auf Nachahmung stießen. Die affektierten Manieren französischer Geiger[33] stünden in großem Gegensatz zur Unsauberkeit ihres Spiels.

Das Aufstampfen mit dem großen Taktstock war in Deutschland wenig verbreitet, während die "übermäßige Tactierungs-Lust"[34] und der "dabey vermachte gottlose Ehr-Geitz" charakteristisch für die Franzosen sei[35]. Er berichtet auch von einer französischen Sängerin, die während einer Aufführung mit Hilfe des Kopfes, der Hände und Füße den Takt geschlagen habe, aber dabei "keine Note kannte"[36]. Mehrfach lobt er zwar die Delikatesse französischer Sängerinnen, denen aber die "Deutsche Force" abgehe[37].

Die Disziplin von Lullys Orchester imponierte noch Mattheson: "Da muß man den Franzosen ihre ungemein egale Execution lassen, darauff sie sich unermüdlich üben. Hingegen steht es gar fein / wenn

29 Siehe *Melodische Wissenschaft*, 38. 30 *Orchestre* I, 207.
31 *General-Baß-Schule* I, 384. 32 Ibid., 386.
33 "Welche gefährliche Striche fallen da nicht vor; alles muß unter seinen Füssen krachen / erzittern und erbeben: seine Ermel (sonderlich bey der aufschneiderischen Mode) lassen keine Fliege leben / und sind besser / als alle Wedel und Fechtel in der Welt", *General-Baß-Schule* I, 385.
34 Ibid., 386.
35 Mattheson teilt hierzu (ibid., 386) eine Anekdote aus Versailles mit, die den Streit eines Komponisten und eines Kapellmeisters um die Leitung einer Aufführung zum Inhalt hat.
36 Ibid., 385.
37 *Orchestre* I, 223, und *Critica musica* I, 143, besonders die französischen Sängerinnen seien "ohne Krafft und ohne Athem".

sich z. E. das Clavicimbel / bey ersehender Gelegenheit / mit einigen besonderen Zierrathen hören läßt / auch mit den andern Instrumenten in die Wette arbeitet"[38]. Die Franzosen seien in der Aufführungspraxis "wie in ihrer Regierungsform schrecklich gebunden".

Die Praxis französischer Musiker, das Cembalo in der Generalbaßbegleitung häufig pausieren zu lassen, lehnt er ab, da das "so nackend und kahl [klinge] / daß ein Kenner sich schämet / und ein Unkundiger offt in aller Welt nicht weiß / was dem Dinge fehlet"[39]. Auch die bereits von Lully unterbundene, willkürliche Auszierung der Melodie und die Double-Bildung in Tänzen und Vokalstücken, die "übermäßige Liebe zu Zierrathen und bunten Sachen"[40] verurteilt Mattheson, da man nichts mehr von der "wahren natürlichen Schönheit ihrer Sätze vernehmen" könne.

III

Die meiste Bewunderung bringt Mattheson von den frühesten Schriften an den französischen Instrumentalmusik entgegen, insbesondere der Ouvertüre[41]. "Unter allen Pieçen, die instrumentaliter executiret werden / behält ja wol per majora die so genandte Ouverture das Prae. Ihr eigentlicher Platz ist zu Anfang einer Opera, oder eines anderen Schau-Spiels / wiewol man sie auch vor Suiten und übrigen Cammer-Sachen setzet. Wir haben ihre Invention den Frantzosen zu dancken / die sie auch am allerbesten zu machen wissen". Mattheson, der den "Character des Edelmuth"[42] der Ouvertüre bewundert, hat selbst eine große Anzahl davon komponiert[43]:

In der That / hier fieng ich erst recht an fleißig zu seyn / und das / was zu Leipzig in Singe-Sachen gethan / allhier auch in der Instrumental-Music, besonders in Ouverturen / zu versuchen / weil Se. Excellence der Herr Graf kurtz zuvor aus Franckreich kommen waren / und also dieselben liebeten. Ich wurde des Lulli, Campra, und anderer guten Autoren Arbeit habhafft / und ob ich gleich in Hannover einen ziemlichen Vorschmack von dieser Art bekommen / so sahe ihr doch jetzo noch tieffer ein / und legte mich eigentlich gantz und gar / nicht ohne guten Succes, darauf / es ist mir auch der Trieb hierzu bey folgenden Zeiten immer geblieben / so daß ich biß 200 Ouverturen von meiner Feder wohl zusammen bringen könnte.

---

38 *Orchestre* I, 264.
39 *Ibid.*, 140.
40 *Orchestre* I, 170. Auch p. 226 betont Mattheson, allgemein habe "die Instrumental-Music der Frantzosen recht was sonderliches voraus".
41 *Orchestre* I, 170.
42 *Capellmeister*, 234.   43 *General-Baß-Schule* I, 174.

Mattheson weist auf das "Reißende, punctirte Wesen", die "geschärfften rhythmi" der französischen Instrumentalmusik hin, das jedoch mit dem Vokalstil unvereinbar sei, und bestätigt damit die heute noch gelegentlich umstrittene verschärfte Punktierung in der französischen Ouvertüre und in Entreen ähnlicher Faktur. "Wenn die Frantzosen, die ich für große Meister im Instrumenten-Styl halte, sich der Puncte bey den Noten begeben sollten, würden sie, wie Küche ohne Saltz, bestehen"[44].

Lullys "Instrumental-Styl" in den Opern sei "überaus fleißig und starck"[45] gewesen, ohne aber den Reichtum "noch die innerliche Wichtigkeit [zu] besitzen, welche dem Instrumental-Styl in Kirchen eigen sind"[46]. Insbesondere auf dem Gebiet der Tanzmusik, genannt werden Chaconnen, Passacaglien, Entreen und andere "große Täntze", sei die französische Schule der italienischen überlegen, "denn Franckreich ist und bleibet die rechte Tantz-Schule"[47]. Lully gilt noch 1737 als der große Lehrmeister, denn er habe "nicht nur Täntzern, sondern allen anderen Personen, taugliche Gesetze"[48] vorgeschrieben. In diesem Zusammenhang weist Mattheson auf die Partiturdrucke französischer Opern und die "gantz kleinen und gemeinen Bücher, worin die neuesten Frantzösischen Täntze heraus kommen, und in Holland nachgedruckt werden"[49]. Nur in der Critica musica[50] bleibt Raguenets Meinung, die Instrumentalsätze der Opern seien "an vielen Orten sehr trucken und verdrießlich zu hören", unwidersprochen.

Mattheson unterscheidet niedrige und hohe Tänze, zu denen er Chaconne, Passacaglia und Entreen rechnet[51]. Ouvertüren und Menuette erforderten einen eigenen Stil: "Man betrachte sie, sage ich, mit Fleiß, welche feine Ordnung, Gleichförmigkeit, große und kleine Abschnitte darin anzutreffen, ich weiß gewiß, man wird befinden, daß eben diese Tantz-Style (den Hyporchematischen mit eingeschlossen) von ungemeinem Reichthum sind, allerhand schöne

---

44 *Melodische Wissenschaft*, 64.   45 Ibid., 21.
46 Mit fast gleichen Worten wiederholt Mattheson diese Gedanken im *Capellmeister*, 86.
47 *Melodische Wissenschaft*, 22.
48 Ibid., 22, und fast identisch im *Capellmeister*, 86.
49 *Melodische Wissenschaft*, 23, und ähnlich im *Capellmeister*, 87, wo Lully-Drucke aus Paris (*Phaéton*, *Persée*, *Archille et Polixène*, *Proserpine*, *Amadis*, aber auch *Thétis et Pelée* von Collasse, *L'Europe galante* von Campra, *Le Triomphe des arts* von M. de La Barre) sowie Amsterdamer Suitendrucke von Lully erwähnt sind. Cf. dazu die Bibliographie der Amsterdamer Suitendrucke Lullys in: H. Schneider, *Die Rezeption der Opern Lullys im Frankreich des Ancien régime* (Tutzing, 1982), 333–5 (=Mainzer Studien zur Musikwissenschaft, vol. 16).
50 *Critica musica* I, 140–1.   51 *Melodische Wissenschaft*, 23 und 47.

Empfindungen im Setzen an die Hand geben"[52]. Die hohen Tänze des hyporchematischen Stils werden der französischen Praxis zufolge[53] getanzt, mit Texten versehen (parodiert) und auch vokal vorgetragen. "In Erkenntniß dieser Schreib-Art thun einige ausgesuchte Frantzösische Sachen mehr Dienste, als alle Welsche: denn Franckreich ist und bleibet doch die rechte Tantz-Schule und dessen, so dazu gehöret"[54]. Die hyporchematische Schreibart ist charakterisiert durch "eine mehr als gemeine Einförmigkeit in den ziemlich-starcken Gliedern der Melodie; eine genaue Abtheilung der Zeitmaaße; ein langsamer Rhythmus in richtigem Verhalt; eine ebenträchtige, ernsthaffte doch muntere Bewegung; eine gehörige Länge, und die möglichste Vereinigung oder Gleichheit aller Theile"[55].

Auch für die niedrigen[56] und hohen Tänze stellt Mattheson eine Poetik auf, die deutlich von französischen Vorstellungen geprägt ist:

Bey einer Chaconne ist der Affect schon viel erhabener und stoltzer als bey einer Passacaille; bey einer Courante ist das Gemüth auf eine zärtliche Hoffnung gerichtet; (ich meyne aber keine welsche Corrente) bey einer Sarabande auf lauter steiffe Ernsthaftigkeit; bey einer Entrée auf Pracht und Eitelkeit; bei einem Rigaudon auf angenehmen Schertz; bey einer Bourée auf Zufriedenheit und ein gefälliges Wesen; bey einem Rondeau auf Munterkeit; bey einem Passepié auf Wanckelmuth und Unbestand; bey einer Gigue auf Hitze und Eifer; bey einer Gavotte auf jauchzende Freude; bey einem Menuet auf mäßige Lustigkeit u.s.w.[57]

Zu den in der französischen Oper verbreiteten Märschen bzw. Aufzugsmusiken schreiten "die Personen nur gantz langsam und ehrbar nach dem Tact daher, ohne tantzen, hüpffen oder springen; doch figuriren sie unter einander, welches wohl zu sehen ist, absonderlich von Gewaffneten oder Kriegsleuten"[58]. Auch innerhalb ungeradtaktiger Märsche habe Lully "die prächtigen Abzeichen und das kriegerische Wesen angelegen seyn lassen"[59].

Neben Lully und Campra, die Mattheson als Vorbilder für die Tanzmusik nennt, werden im *Vollkommenen Kapellmeister* auch Rameaus *Indes galantes* erwähnt: "Ich habe noch schöne Ouvertüren-

---

52 Ibid., 26–7, ebenso im *Capellmeister*, 94.
53 Cf. dazu H. Schneider, *Rezeption der Opern Lullys*, 157ss.
54 *Capellmeister*, 86.   55 *Capellmeister*, 87.
56 Im *Capellmeister*, 92, als "gewöhnliche und gebräuchliche Tantz-Kunst" der Bälle, Maskeraden und Tanzübung oder als "chorische Schreib-Art" bezeichnet.
57 *Melodische Wissenschaft*, 66–7. In ähnlicher Formulierung auch im *Capellmeister*, 225–6. Ibid., 94, wird betont, daß alle französischen Tanzlieder ihre eigene "Schreib-Art" erforderten.
58 *Melodische Wissenschaft*, 113. In ähnlicher Formulierung auch im *Capellmeister*, 226.
59 Ibid., 113, ähnlich im *Capellmeister*, 227.

Sätze und Nachahmungen hinter der Hand von Mr. Rameau, aus seinem Balet: *Les Indes galantes* . . . Indessen sind die Sachen dieses berühmten Verfassers, wegen der gekünstelten Nachahmungen, iedem aufs beste anzupreisen"[60].

IV

Abgesehen von der Beschäftigung mit der Ästhetik der Oper ist Matthesons Stellung zum französischen Rezitativ, zur Ausstattung der Oper sowie zur Gattung des Balletts bzw. der Opéra-ballet aufschlußreich. Aus der Kritik an der italienischen Oper, die nicht "anderes sind / als ein Gewebe von lauter aufeinander folgenden Cantaten"[61], ist abzulesen, daß Mattheson gerade die Ausstattungsteile schätzte. Die Anzahl der Chöre in französischen Opern, die meist Tanzlieder seien, erscheint ihm aber zu hoch, zumal sie zu wenig konzertant und imitatorisch angelegt seien[62]. Sehr positiv bewertete er das Ballett, worunter er auch den Opéra-ballet und Gelegenheitskompositionen wie Lullys *L'Idylle sur la paix* subsumierte. Ihre Vokalteile sollen "nur galant und natürlich, nicht aber sehr künstlich und ausgearbeitet seyn dürffen"[63]. Das Ballett "will lauter Leben, Geist und Galanterie haben: ist also eben kein Werck eines gelehrten Componisten oder eines theoretischen Meisters . . . , sondern eines aufgeweckten Kopffes"[64]. Mattheson empfiehlt deutschen Komponisten daher Stücke wie Campras *Le Carnaval de Venise*, in Hamburg 1707 erfolgreich aufgeführt[65], zur Nachahmung. Aus der *Parallèle* Raguenets stammende Beurteilungen der französischen Oper läßt Mattheson unkommentiert, wodurch er sich mit ihnen einverstanden erklärt. Dies betrifft die Ausnahmestellung Lullys sowie die Kritik der kurzen vaudevilleartigen Arien als "ungeschmackte Liedergen . . . die niemand . . . das Herze rühren / noch im geringsten jemand gefallen können"[66].

In der *Critica musica*[67] bezeichnet er das französische Rezitativ als "liedermäßig", hebt die ständigen Taktwechsel hervor sowie die

60 *Capellmeister*, 337.   61 *Orchestre* I, 181.
62 Siehe *Capellmeister*, 216.   63 *Melodische Wissenschaft*, 102.
64 Ibid., 102. Im *Capellmeister*, 217, wird als einziger Sinn des Balletts "lauter Freud und Wonne" genannt.
65 Als weitere nachahmenswerte Muster nennt er Lullys *Triomphe de l'Amour* und *L'Idylle sur la paix*, das *Ballet des Saisons* von Collasse, Campras *L'Europe galante*, *Aréthuse*, *Les Muses*, *Les Fragments de M. de Lully*, Desmarets' *Les Fêtes galantes*, La Barres *Le Triomphe des Arts* und J.-B. Niels *Les Romans*.
66 *Critica musica* I, 138–9.
67 Ibid., 140, ebenso bereits im *Orchestre* I, 166: "Tact- und Liedermäßiges Recitativ".

Tatsache, daß es "nach Battut" zu singen sei. Das Rezitativ sei aber verfehlt, wenn es nicht der "Declamation, öffentlichen Rede oder Erzehlung"[68] nahe stehe, "wobey man folglich mehr Regard vor zu exprimirende Passiones hat / als vor die reguliere Observanz der Mensur"[69]. Am schärfsten fällt die Kritik des Rezitativs im *Kern melodischer Wissenschafft*[70] aus, jedoch wird er damit dem Rezitativ Lullys nicht gerecht, das erst nach dessen Lebzeiten zunehmend langsam und arios gesungen wurde.

Mattheson hat bereits die besondere Qualität des Rezitativs von Rameau erfaßt und sie prägnant formuliert: "Inzwischen haben die Frantzosen eine andre Art der Nachahmung in ihren Rezitativen. Wenn nehmlich die Singstimme vom Donner, Ungestüm und von der Verwirrung handelt, so erhebt sich alsofort im Baß ein Wesen, Poltern und Rollen; dadurch zwar jene Ausdrückungen ziemlich vorgestellet oder nachgeahmet werden; doch nur den Worten, nicht dem Gesange und Gedanken nach"[71].

Die Opéra comique der Jahrmarkttheater mit ihren teilweise obszönen Späßen war offensichtlich in Norddeutschland lange vor der "European vogue of Favart"[72] bekannt, wie Mattheson an einem typischen Beispiel deutlich macht[73]. Die Verspottung der ernsten Oper scheint er an dieser französischen Gattung ebenso geschätzt zu haben wie die Virtuosität ihrer Tanzsolisten[74], die sich vor ihren Kollegen vor der ernsten Oper kaum zu verstecken brauchten.

Die von Le Cerf de la Viéville so hochgeschätzte Kunst des Vaudevilles, die besonders in der Opéra comique gepflegt wurde, findet auch in Matthesons Schriften ihren Niederschlag. Er betont das "aufgeräumte Naturell" der Franzosen, die gerne und an allen Orten "lallen und singen"[75]. In Anlehnung an Le Cerf schätzt er zwar das französische Tanz- und Trinklied höher ein als das der Italiener, nicht aber die Fähigkeit, sie vorzutragen[76]. Vaudeville- und Kanonsingen als Gesellschaftskunst der Franzosen betont Mattheson mehrfach[77].

V

Die bislang in der Forschung noch weitgehend vernachlässigte französische Kammermusik hat nur wenig Resonanz in den Schriften

---

68 *Orchestre* I, 181.   69 *Ibid.*
70 *Melodische Wissenschaft*, 40 und 97.   71 *Capellmeister*, 334.
72 Siehe A. Jacuzzi, *The European Vogue of Favart* (New York, 1932).
73 *General-Baß-Schule* I, 228.   74 Siehe *Critica musica* I, 144.
75 *Ibid.*, 126.   76 *Ibid.*, 166.
77 Cf. *Melodische Wissenschaft*, 26. Hier spricht er von "auserlesener, musicalischer Gesellschaft". Cf. auch *Capellmeister*, 92, wo vom Singen von "Sitten-Sprüchen" im Kanon in "Lust-Versammlungen" die Rede ist.

Matthesons gefunden. Nach Vorstellungen, die zur Zeit Matthesons bereits verbreitet waren und bis zum klassischen Streichquartett nachwirkten, "fordert sonst dieser Styl in der Kammer weit mehr Fleiß und Ausarbeitung, als sonst, und will nette, reine Mittel-Partien haben, die mit den Oberstimmen beständig, und auf eine angenehme Art gleichsam um den Vorzug streiten. Bindungen, Rückungen, gebrochene Harmonien, Abwechslungen mit tutti und solo, mit adagio und allegro etc. sind ihm solche wesentliche und eigene Dinge"[78]. Diesen Forderungen entspricht das französische Kammertrio bzw. die Kammersuite kaum. Im kontrapunktisch geprägten Trio sind die Italiener sowie J. J. Fux führend, während Lully nur einige Trios "besagter Schönheit verfertiget"[79] habe. Es ist aber kaum anzunehmen, daß Mattheson die *Trios de la Chambre du Roi* von Lully kannte, in denen sich in der Tat relativ viele kontrapunktisch geführte Stücke befinden[80]. Noch im *Vollkommenen Capellmeister* wird Lully als der Meister des "ächten frantzösischen Trio"[81] bezeichnet, während unter den "jüngern Frantzmännern" "dermaaßen verwelschte Kräuseler" seien, die keiner Nachahmung wert seien. Telemann dagegen vereinige italienische Elemente mit dem "sehr natürlichen und altfranzösischen" Fließen, so daß sich selbst Lully dieser Trios von Telemann "keines weges zu schämen hätte"[82]. Es ist bemerkenswert, daß von den zahlreichen französischen Kammertrios, die bei Roger in Amsterdam erschienen[83] und somit bei Mattheson als bekannt vorausgesetzt werden können, nur die Trios von Michel de La Barre erwähnt sind. Die Triosonaten von François Couperin, die heute als die bekanntesten Werke dieser Gattung französischer Provenienz anzusehen sind, bleiben unerwähnt, wie man überhaupt Couperins Name bei Mattheson vergeblich sucht. Die Kritik an La Barres Trios bezieht sich auf die in Frankreich bis hin zu Couperin üblichen Wechsel der Schlüssel im Baß. Mattheson zufolge haben sie "einen verworrenen Baß", sind "so starck bezieffert" und "so voller Veränderungen der Schlüssel", "daß einer Haar auf den Zähnen haben muß / wer selbigen sogleich richtig wegspielen

78 *Capellmeister*, 91.
79 *Critica musica* I, 132, es handelt sich um die Übersetzung aus der *Parallèle* Raguenets.
80 H. Schneider, *Chronologisch-Thematisches Verzeichnis sämtlicher Kompositionen von J.-B. Lully* (Tutzing, 1981), LWV 35.
81 *Capellmeister*, 345.   82 Ibid., 345.
83 Den Roger-Katalogen zufolge erschienen Trios und Opernsuiten, die auch in Triobesetzung musiziert wurden, von Babel (*Trios de différents auteurs* in zwei Lieferungen), Bertin de la Doué, Campra, Desmarets, Destouches, Grandval, La Barre, La Coste, La Maillerie, Lambert, Le Quointe, Lully, Marais, Anne-D. Philidor und J.-B. Stuck.

will"[84]. Auch im *Musicalischen Patrioten* hat Mattheson auf die Trios des "wolbekannten Frantzösischen Autors" La Barre verwiesen mit Bässen, "bey welchen dem armen Medio die Haare zu Berge stehen würden"[85].

Die französische Cembalo- und Orgelmusik wird selten erwähnt. Im folgenden verspottet er die tonmalerischen und deskriptiven Stücke: "Hierher gehören alle sonst auf diesem edlen Instrument übel inventirte bizarre Stückgen / als Guckguck / Nachtigal / Bataillen und dergleichen Bagatellen / die aber bey Leuten von gutem Gout mehr vor ridicul als plaisant passiren"[86]. Die französische Cembalo-Courante bezeichnet er also "kahle und hackbrettische Klimperey" im Vergleich zur "tüchtigen, nerveusen, vollstimmig-gebrochenen teutschen Courante"[87]. An Komponisten nennt er nur J.-Ph. Rameau, dessen "Noten-Arbeit fürs Clavier"[88] ihn beeindruckt habe. Aus den Amsterdamer Katalogen dürfte er auch eine Reihe berühmter anderer französischer Cembalisten gekannt haben[89]. An Organisten erwähnt Mattheson im übrigen lediglich Clérambault und Rameau[90].

Skeptischer noch äußert er sich zur französischen Lautenmusik, von der er wenigstens die bei Roger erschienenen Lautenkompositionen von Charles Mouton gekannt haben dürfte: Er beklagt ihre "Pauvreté"[91] im allgemeinen. Zuerst erwähnt Mattheson im *Neu-Eröffneten Orchestre*, ohne Komponisten zu nennen, französische weltliche Kantaten, "die nicht übel von statten gehen"[92].

Später[93] nennt er weltliche Kantaten von Nicolas Bernier und André Campra, die er entweder aus Pariser Drucken oder aber aus Abschriften kennengelernt haben muß, da in Amsterdam keine Kantaten französischer Meister erschienen. Daß Abschriften französischer Kantaten in Deutschland verbreitet waren, beweisen z. B. die Kopien von sieben Kantaten Berniers in der Sächsischen Landesbibliothek in Dresden[94]. Bereits in der *Critica musica* werden Berniers Kantaten als Beispiele dafür angeführt, "daß die Welsche Art

---

84 *General-Baß-Schule* I, 232.
85 *Musicalischer Patriot*, 332.   86 *Orchestre* I, 176.
87 Ibid., 187.   88 *Capellmeister*, 133.
89 Bei Roger erschienen Cembalowerke von J.-H. d'Anglebert, Ch. Dieupart, N. Lebègue, G. Le Roux und L. Marchand. Während alle diese Namen in den Ergänzungen zum Brossardschen Register erscheinen, fehlen dort allerdings auch L. und F. Couperin, M.-A. Charpentier und M. Delalande, cf. *Critica Musica* II, 109–15.
90 *Capellmeister*, 479 und 133.
91 *Orchestre* I, 275.   92 *Orchestre* I, 178.
93 *General-Baß-Schule* I, 30.
94 Unter der Signatur Musica 1-C-504 sind folgende Kantaten erhalten: "Diane, L'inconstance, Vénus, Iris, Le Portrait d'Uranie, le Caffé, Hippolyte et Aricie".

bereits guten Fortgang habe"[95]. Die Auffassung Grandvals, die Kantaten von Jean-Baptiste Morin, der zum ersten Mal in Frankreich
Kantaten drucken ließ, und Bernier seien mit italienischen Kantaten
auf eine Stufe zu stellen, beurteilt Mattheson im Register als "französische Prahlerei"[96]. Die Mode, Kantaten zu komponieren und
stechen zu lassen, die Grandval in seiner "Dissertation" darstellt[97],
kommentiert Mattheson mit herber Kritik:

> Darinn hat der Autor ganz recht / daß die Französischen Cantaten / wenn die
> Componisten / ohne einzigen Dank / den Italiänern nach zu äffen affec-
> tiren / eine schreckliche Marter ihrer Sprache und Worte / ein großer Verdruß
> den Ohren / (zumahl bey angeführter übermäßigen Länge) und / in Wahrheit
> lauter fatras, lauter Lumperey sind . . . Messieurs, laßt die Italiänische Mu-
> sic / samt ihren Cantaten / ungeschoren! Sie geht euch von der Hand / wie
> Pech! bleibt bey eurer einländischen Weise[98].

VI

Die französische Kirchenmusik des Barock steht, abgesehen von
wenigen Kompositionen, heute in keinem hohen Ansehen und ist im
Gegensatz zur italienischen Kirchenmusik weitgehend unbekannt
geblieben[99]. Einige Abschriften von Motetten in deutschen Beständen aus dem achtzehnten Jahrhundert und die Überlieferung von
Drucken aus dem siebzehnten Jahrhundert zeigen jedoch, daß die
Komponisten des frühen achtzehnten Jahrhunderts in Deutschland
doch über die französische Kirchenmusik orientiert waren. Mattheson betont 1713 ihre Eigenständigkeit, aber auch ihre Unterlegenheit
gegenüber der italienischen und deutschen Kirchenmusik[100]. "Die
Frantzosen haben in diesem Stück einen zwar particulieren, aber
nicht gar zu glücklich- und regulieren Stylum; dennoch lassen sich
ihre Moteten gar wol anhören / ob sie gleich den Italiänischen nicht
beykommen / weil ihnen insonderheit die in den Kirchen so nöhtige
Gravité einiger maßen abgehen wil". Die wichtigsten Eigenschaften,
über die ein Komponist von Kirchenmusik verfügen müsse, "Elaboration" und "Vivacité", seien die Stärke der Deutschen, nicht aber der
Franzosen. Während in der italienischen und deutschen Kirchenmusik das solistische Singen neben dem Chor einen hervorragenden
Platz einnehme, "reflectierten" die Franzosen meist auf den Chor
und ließen Solisten kaum hervortreten[101].

95 *Critica musica* I, 165.   96 *Critica musica* I, 193.
97 Siehe *Critica musica* I, 209s.   98 Ibid., 210s.
99 Abschriften von Motetten Lullys gibt es in der Bibliothek Preußischer Kulturbesitz
   in Berlin sowie in Dresden.
100 *Orchestre* I, 222.   101 Ibid., 222.

Bereits die Bezeichnung "Motet" für alle "Kirchen-Stücke" ist Mattheson zufolge ein Indiz für die Unkenntnis der Franzosen auf dem Gebiet der Kirchenmusik: "Allein die Einrichtung ist doch etwas besser, als sie vor Alters war: denn es kommen gar offt Abwechslungen dabey vor, daß nehmlich eine oder andre ausnehmende Stimme sich etwa allein hören läßt, und concertiret"[102]. Im Gegensatz zu Deutschland habe sich aber der "Concerten-Art"[103] dort noch nicht genügend durchgesetzt. Offenbar waren, wie aus dieser Bemerkung zu schließen ist, die späten Motetten von M. Delalande in Deutschland noch nicht bekannt. Es ist bemerkenswert, daß trotz dieser geringen Einschätzung der französischen Kirchenmusik Mattheson der Ästhetik der Kirchenmusik von Le Cerf de la Viéville[104] so weitgehend zustimmt. Die wichtigsten Regeln, die im *Musicalischen Patrioten* wiedergegeben sind, stimmen mit jenen von Le Cerf überein[105]:

1. Die Kirchenmusik soll "nicht so wol schön von außen gleißen, als gründlichen, innerlichen Nachdruck haben".

2. "Die Worte einer geistlichen Music . . . müssen beweglich und abwechselnd seyn, voller Gemüths-Neigungen und Veränderungen".

3. "Da die Gedancken und Meynungen in unsern Kirchen-Stücken weit erheblicher sind, als in den Opern-Arien, . . . so erfordern sie auch eine weit stärckere Ausdrückung".

Mattheson scheint offenbar die *Leçons de ténèbres* nicht gekannt zu haben, obgleich sie in dem zitierten *Discours sur la musique d'eglise* von Le Cerf eine Rolle spielen, denn er bemerkt: "in Frankreich muß es um eine Passions-Music was rares seyn"[106]. Wie gut er in anderer Hinsicht orientiert war, zeigt die Erwähnung des Requiem von Jean Gilles, das am 23. August 1726 in Grenoble "in höchster Vollkommenheit" aufgeführt worden war und "man zu den schönsten Musicalischen Wercken" rechne[107]. das aber in Paris erst im Jahre 1760 nach Aufführungen im Concert spirituel eine bis heute andauernde Popularität erlangte. Bereits im *Musicalischen Patrioten* hatte Mattheson auf das besonders in Frankreich verbreitete Verfahren der geistlichen Umdichtung von Opernarien hingewiesen und manche dieser Parodien als "anstößig und ärgerlich"[108] befunden. Dennoch

102 *Melodische Wissenschaft*, 108. In fast gleicher Formulierung im *Capellmeister*, 223.
103 Ibid., 108.
104 *Discours sur la musique d'église*, in: Bonnet, *Histoire de la musique*, IV, 32ss. Zitiert werden insbesondere p. 58, 59 und 72ss.
105 *Musicalischer Patriot*, 105–6. Weitere Bemerkungen zur Interpretation ibid., 107 und 108, nach Le Cerf, p. 72–4.
106 *Critica musica* II, 53.　107 *Musicalischer Patriot*, 13.　108 Ibid., 109.

seien sie für den unbefangenen Hörer, der von der Oper und Parodie nichts wisse, durchaus nützlich. Anläßlich einer kritischen Besprechung der *Imitation de Jésus Christ,* einer von vielen Sammlungen von Cantiques spirituels nach Opernarien und Vaudevilles, von Simon-Joseph Pellegrin[109] aus dem Jahre 1727 zeigt sich Mattheson noch einmal als Gegner der geistlichen Parodie[110].

VII

Drei französische Komponisten hat Mattheson mit biographischen Artikeln bedacht, sofern man in dem Fall von Michel Delalande davon sprechen kann. Über Lully, der von allen französischen Komponisten am häufigsten von Mattheson im Munde geführt wird[111] und dessen gesellschaftlicher Aufstieg ungeheueren Eindruck auf ihn machte[112], verfaßte er zwei biographische Abrisse. Dem ersten der *Critica musica*[113] weist Mattheson besondere Bedeutung als Modellartikel zu: "Die Ordnung aber ist . . . deswegen so gemacht: damit ein deutliches Model gegeben werde / wie etwan eine Lebens-Beschreibung einzurichten sey / die in der Ehren Pforte Platz finden will"[114] Aus den ausgeworfenen Stichworten des Artikels ist die beabsichtigte Ordnung abzulesen, die er, wenn auch Ergänzungen aus der *Comparaison* von Le Cerf de la Viéville, aus Perraults *Hommes illustres* und aus La Fontaines satirischem Gedicht gegen Lully hinzugekommen sind, im Wortlaut in der *Ehrenpforte*[115] beibehielt. Zwischen den einzelnen Stationen der Karriere Lullys sind jeweils

---

109 Zum Problem der geistlichen Parodie siehe Schneider, *Rezeption der Opern Lullys,* 202–32.
110 "Das ist sehr übel gethan . . . Die Music ist so reich, man kann wol zu einer jeden Art war eignes und neues machen: Dannenhero diejenigen ärgerlich handeln, die da geistliche Worte mit einer bekannten weltlichen Melodie, vorsetzlicher Weise, zu schmücken vermeynen", *Musicalischer Patriot,* 15.
111 In der *Critica musica* I, 115, verteidigt er ihn gegen Heinichen, der in der Arie "C'est l'amour qui nous menace" aus *Roland* Quintenparallelen entdeckt hatte: "Wenn man dieses und dergleichen wahrhaftes Lob von den grossen Meriten des Lully lieset / so verschwindet dabey fast der kindische Vorwurff / daß er etwan bißweilen ein paar Quinten gesezet haben".
112 "Lully, Stephani, und tausend mehr / können Zeugnis geben / wie entrant die Music uns mache / und wie geschickt man zu allen Affairen sey / dafern man (exteris paribus) in derselben was rechtes gethan habe". *Orchestre* I, 40. Noch im *Tresespiel,* 98, erwähnt er die "Standeserhöhungen" hervorragender Tonkünstler als lobenswert.
113 *Critica musica* I, 178–84, und II, 116–19. Quellen sind Perraults *Hommes illustres,* Le Cerf de la Viévilles *Comparaison,* La Fontaines *Satire Le Florentin* und *Epître à M. de Nyert* und die *Lettres historiques sur l'Opéra de Paris.*
114 *Critica musica* I, 178.   115 *Ehrenpforte,* 174–83.

Mitteilungen über die charakterlichen Fähigkeiten, das gesellschaftliche Ansehen der Person und über seine Mitarbeiter eingeschoben.

In beiden Artikeln stellt Mattheson die Herkunft, den Wechsel nach Frankreich, seinen Aufstieg vom Küchenjungen zum Secrétaire du Roi, seine Begabung, die gesangs- und tanzpädagogischen Verdienste, sein Organisationstalent und seine Fähigkeit als Regisseur in den Vordergrund. Die Zusammenarbeit mit den Textdichtern, seine familiären Verhältnisse und seine tödliche Verletzung einschließlich der Anekdote mit dem Beichtvater bilden den zweiten Teil der Biographie-Skizze. Im Text ist zwar das *Te Deum* und *Le Bourgeois Gentilhomme* Lullys erwähnt, in der Übersicht über die Werke sind aber lediglich die Bühnenwerke mitgeteilt, die für die Académie royale seit 1672 komponiert wurden. Weder die Ballets de Cour noch die Comédies-ballets noch die Motetten sieht Mattheson als erwähnenswert an. Ebensowenig die Kammermusik, die in Le Cerfs *Comparaison* eine gewisse Rolle spielt. In der *Grundlage einer Ehren-Pforte* berichtet er nach Le Cerf auch über den Schaffensprozeß[116]. nach Perrault über die Stationen der Entstehung eines Librettos und über das auf dem Totenbett entstandene Sterbelied "Il faut mourir pécheur"[117] aus der *Comparaison*.

Der Artikel über Lully in der *Grundlage einer Ehren-Pforte* ist nach jenem über Mattheson selbst (mit einunddreißig Seiten) und Telemann (mit sechzehn Seiten) nicht nur der umfangreichste, sondern gleichzeitig auch einer der gelungensten und inhaltsreichsten biographischen Beiträge Matthesons überhaupt. Unter den 148 Personenartikeln befinden sich noch kurze Beiträge über Claude Goudimel und Michel Delalande, der nirgendwo sonst von Mattheson erwähnt wird. Er erhielt wohl nur aufgrund einer Meldung der *Gazette d'Amsterdam* über die in einer prunkvollen Ausgabe posthum erschienenen "grands motets" einen inhaltsarmen Artikel in der *Ehrenpforte*.

Im Zusammenhang mit der im Mattheson-Jahr legitimen Frage, ob denn auch sein Oeuvre im Frankreich des achtzehnten Jahrhunderts bekannt gewesen sei, ist lediglich von einem von Mattheson selbst erwähnten Detail zu berichten. Mattheson war ebensowenig wie Bach, auf dessen Einstellung zu Rameau wir aus Äußerungen C. Ph. E. Bachs Rückschlüsse ziehen können, ein Freund des Rameauschen *Traité de l'harmonie* – andere Traktate scheint er nicht kennengelernt zu haben. Im *Philologischen Tresespiel* berichtet er über eine Reaktion Rameaus auf Matthesons Kritik am *Traité de l'harmonie*[118]:

---

116 *Ehrenpforte*, 178.   117 Ibid., 183.   118 *Tresespiel*, 96.

Rameau hat gleichwohl dasjenige gelesen, was ich ehemals von ihm, aus prophetischem Geiste, über seinen Traité de l'Harmonie geschrieben habe. Zur Verantwortung sagte er zu einem gewissen charakterisirten Herrn, der mit ihm davon redete: Ich hätte ihn nur unrecht verstanden. Nun ist mirs doch sehr lieb, daß ihn seine Landsleute schon besser verstehen, als ich. "Rameaus Musik (so lautet es im Neuesten etc. p. 525) in der Opera Zoroaster, soll so elend seyn, daß man sie kaum anhören kann''.

Insgesamt macht die Auseinandersetzung Matthesons mit der französischen Musik den Wandel deutlich, der sich in der Einstellung zu ihr in der ersten Hälfte des achtzehnten Jahrhunderts vollzog. Bis 1720 nahm er alles Französische in der Musik begierig auf, studierte Schrifttum und Musik und eignete sich vieles davon an. Nach 1720 wandte er sich spürbar von der französischen Ästhetik und Musik ab, die zunehmend italienische Elemente aufnahm. Im Tresespiel[119] schließlich begnügt sich Mattheson damit, Polemiken gegen den bedeutendsten französischen Komponisten des achtzehnten Jahrhunderts, J.-Ph. Rameau, wiederzugeben.

119 Siehe ibid., 95.

22

Verwechselung, Vorausnehmung, and Verzögerung: important Mattheson contributions to eighteenth-century music theory

DAVID A. SHELDON
Kalamazoo, Michigan

Johann Mattheson's *Vollkommener Capellmeister* made several important contributions to later eighteenth-century music theory in Germany. Of particular interest are the concepts of the exchanged resolution (*Verwechselung*), anticipation (*Vorausnehmung*), and delay (*Verzögerung*), important analytical devices for explaining the irregular handling of dissonance. Although both the exchanged resolution and anticipation have their origins in musical-rhetorical figures of the seventeenth century, Johann David Heinichen's treatise of 1728, *Der General Baß in der Composition*, deserves most of the credit for establishing these concepts in the eighteenth-century theoretical literature.[1] Heinichen's influence was profound, and his concepts of exchange and anticipation, which he used to explain certain freedoms of the theatrical style, were taken up by succeeding generations of German writers as an important theoretical basis for definitions of the *galant* style. The role of Johann Mattheson regarding these concepts has been largely overlooked, and the importance of his own concept of irregular delay (*Verzögerung*) seems to be completely unknown.

The influence on Mattheson with regard to the exchanged resolution, or *Verwechselung*, comes not from Heinichen's *General-Baß* but apparently from Johann Walther's earlier treatise of 1708, the *Praecepta der musicalischen Composition*, a work that remained unpublished until the twentieth century.[2] Mattheson repeats almost

1 J. D. Heinichen, *Der General-Baß in der Composition* (Dresden, 1728). See also G. J. Buelow, "Heinichen's Treatment of Dissonance," in: *JMT* 6 (1962), 216–76.
2 See J. Walther, *Praecepta der musicalischen Composition* (Ms Weimar, 1708), ed. P. Benary, in: *Jenaer Beiträge zur Musikforschung* II (Leipzig, 1955), esp. 145, 155–6.

note for note both of the examples of exchange found in Walther's *Praecepta*. These are resolutions of the diminished fifth and augmented fourth to the octave. The exchanged resolution of augmented fourth to the octave is given in Example 1. Example 1a is Walther's

Example 1a. Walther, *Praecepta*, 144

Example 1b. Mattheson, *Capellmeister*, 316

version, and Example 1b, Mattheson's. Not only has Mattheson added two inner parts, but he has also provided the reader with a clear explanation that was lacking in the *Praecepta*. Mattheson states that the tenor voice, which he has added, and the soprano have exchanged (*vertauschet*) pitches. Interesting is the fact that Mattheson uses a vernacular designation for this phenomenon. Elsewhere, in addition to *Vertauschung*, he also uses *Verwechselung*, a term more common to Heinichen and to later German theorists. Moreover, Mattheson also continues the use of the Greek term, *heterolepsis*, for this device.[3] This is Walther's term, one established in the seventeenth century by Christoph Bernhard.[4] Despite the transitional nature of Mattheson's

---

3 *Capellmeister*, 322.
4 Discussed in Chap. 41 of Bernhard's *Tractatus compositionis augmentatus* and Chap. 20 of his *Ausführlicher Bericht von Gebrauche der Con- und Dissonantien*. See J. M. Müller-Blattau, *Die Kompositionslehre Heinrich Schützens in der Fassung seines Schülers Christoph Bernhard* (Leipzig, 1926), 87–9, 152.

terminology in this regard, he obviously clarifies and expands the usage of the concept as found in Walther. For example, he adds another exchanged resolution of augmented fourth to octave, this one with the bass skipping rather than the soprano. Neither of these resolutions of the augmented fourth is to be found in Heinichen's *General-Baß*, nor is the resolution of the diminished fifth to the octave mentioned earlier. Mattheson also adds several exchanged resolutions of the diminished seventh to the theoretical literature. Most of Mattheson's new examples are utilized by Friedrich Wilhelm Marpurg in his *Handbuch bey dem Generalbasse und der Composition* (1755–60).[5] This influence, together with that of Heinichen, helps to explain the diversity of Marpurg's discussion of *Verwechselung*. And it is Marpurg who specifically establishes the association between *Verwechselung* and the free or *galant* style.

Of greater impact on Marpurg and his followers is Mattheson's use of the anticipation concept. Here the possible influence of Walther on Mattheson is less certain. The clearest and most typical early example to cite, perhaps, involves the progression of perfect fourth to diminished fifth. Walther's explanation is given in Example 2a, Heinichen's in Example 2b, and Mattheson's in Example 2c. Typically, the bass is assumed to have anticipated its next pitch, thereby explaining the apparent resolution of one dissonance to another. As can be seen,

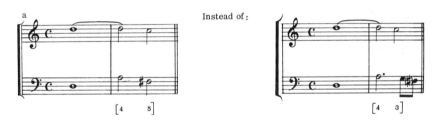

Example 2a. Walther, *Praecepta*, 143

Example 2b. Heinichen, *Der General-Baß*, 691–2

5 F. W. Marpurg, *Handbuch bey dem Generalbasse und der Composition* (Berlin, 1755–60; repr. Hildesheim, 1974).

445

Example 2c. Mattheson, *Capellmeister*, 309

there are strong similarities between all three examples. Those provided by Walther and Heinichen are identical except for their explanations. Heinichen's bass is shown merely to have progressed a beat too soon. This interpretation is typical of his many examples in that the anticipated bass almost always progresses by skip to the second dissonance. In this instance, therefore, Heinichen's interpretation might well be a simplification of Walther's earlier example, where in addition to an anticipated bass the omission of a passing tone is assumed. Mattheson's example, Example 2c, again seems to be an expansion of one drawn from an earlier source. Unfortunately, he does not provide an illustrated explanation. From his verbal description of this "Figur der Anticipation," however, it is clear that he prefers the simpler explanation such as provided by Heinichen. Mattheson refers to the resolution of the fourth to diminished fifth here as figural (*figürlich*), stating that the bass, instead of waiting as it should for the upper voice to progress to the third, skips down a third and thereby creates a diminished fifth. Although he goes on to add that the effect of such progressions can be concealed by filling in the skip of a third in the bass with a passing tone, it is obvious that he regards the essential progression here to be from fourth to third, as do Walther and Heinichen.

Mattheson includes among his examples of bass anticipation several progressions of the ninth, namely those to the diminished fifth, to the sixth, and to another ninth. His examples are almost identical with those in Walther's *Praecepta*, with some elaboration or extensions. Likewise, Mattheson's explanations are also basically Walther's. The main difference is that Walther only illustrates his explanations, whereas Mattheson only verbalizes his. Their handling of the progression of ninth to diminished fifth is typical. Example 3a gives Walther's example and explanation. Example 3b gives Mattheson's. Although Mattheson does not provide an illustrated explanation, he

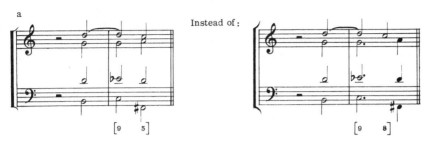

Example 3a. Walther, *Praecepta*, 148

Example 3b. Mattheson, *Capellmeister*, 324

does state that this is a case of *Vorausnahm*, or anticipation, because here the bass skips sooner than it should. The essential resolution in both examples, therefore, is interpreted as being to the octave. Very important is Mattheson's use of the vernacular "Vorausnahm" to designate the figure of anticipation, a designation that he uses frequently in the *Capellmeister*. Interestingly, Marpurg reprints Mattheson's example note for note in his *Handbuch*, and modifies its designation to *Vorausnehmung*. It should be added here that Walther's *Musicalisches Lexicon* of 1732 had already translated the seventeenth-century figure of *anticipatio notae* as "die Vorausnehmung einer Note."[6]

Walther's example of ninth progressing to ninth is not explained in the *Praecepta*. It is to Mattheson's credit that in borrowing this example he typically provided it with a rational explanation—that of bass anticipation.[7] A more important contribution made by Mattheson in this regard, however, is his explanation of the conjunct, downward progression of seventh to seventh, another progression not

6 J. G. Walther, *Musicalisches Lexicon* (Leipzig, 1732; repr. Kassel, 1953), 38.
7 Cf. Walther, *Praecepta*, 149, and Mattheson, *Capellmeister*, 326.

explained, to my knowledge, in any source[8] before the *Capellmeis-ter*.[9] In this instance the anticipated bass can move by conjunct motion rather than having to skip. This application of *Vor-ausnehmung* is fully utilized by Marpurg, not only in the progression of seventh to seventh, and seventh to diminished fifth, but also in their inversions – second to second, and second to augmented fourth. In the last progression cited, the anticipation is assumed in an upper part.[10] This innovative interpretation seems actually to have originated with Mattheson, who, to my knowledge, is the first to explain the progression of second to augmented fourth, as well as second to diminished fifth, in terms of assumed anticipation in an upper voice.[11] Example 4 gives Mattheson's example and clearly illustrated explanation of the progression of second to augmented fourth, both voices moving in conjunct motion. Example 4a is the figural version, Example 4b is the essential, or corrected, version. The essential resolution, therefore, is to the third. Although Mattheson's explanation is new, his procedure of offering two versions here is obviously modeled on that of Walther and other earlier writers.

Example 4a. Mattheson, *Capellmeister*, 305

Example 4b. Mattheson, *Capellmeister*, 306

8 Cited in *Praecepta*, 147, but not explained.   9 *Capellmeister*, 320.
10 See Marpurg, *Handbuch*, 102–3, 115–6; also, at the end of Part II, Table 4, figs, 16–18, and Table 5, figs. 19, 24–5.
11 *Capellmeister*, 305–6. The author also explains the progression of perfect fourth to perfect fourth (ibid., 309) in terms of upper-part anticipation.

In such situations where both voices move stepwise it would be just as feasible to regard either voice as anticipated. In fact, Marpurg chose to interpret the progression of second to second, an inversion of the progression seventh to seventh, in terms of bass anticipation rather than upper-voice anticipation.[12] Obviously, either interpretation can be regarded as correct, and also, therefore, as complementary. A concept more truly complementary to that of bass anticipation, however, and one more applicable to all such situations, is that of an assumed retardation in an upper voice. Mattheson, more clearly than in the case of anticipation, seems to be the first to have given this figure its vernacular designation, *Verzögerung*. Moreover, he also seems to be the one most responsible for establishing the concept of retardation in the theoretical literature. Nevertheless, it should be added that just as with exchange and anticipation, influence here from an earlier source is apparent. That source again is Walther's *Praecepta* of 1708.

Walther interprets the progressions of second to diminished fifth and second to augmented fourth as instances where the bass has been delayed, rather than upper voices anticipated. However, he speaks of the bass being *behält* or *nachgesetzt*, not *verzögert*. It might be pointed out, too, that Walther explains the progression of perfect to augmented fourth in terms of a *nachgesetzt* upper part, whereas Mattheson interprets it as an anticipated bass.[13] Perhaps the best example of Walther's influence on Mattheson in this regard, as well as the reciprocal relationship of anticipation and delay, involves the progression of ninth to tenth. Walther's example and notated explanation are given in Example 5a, Mattheson's example in Example 5b. As one can see, this is another of those ninth progressions that Mattheson seems to have borrowed from Walther with some elaboration. In this

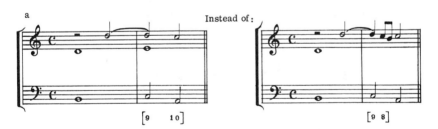

Example 5a. Walther, *Praecepta*, 148

12 Marpurg, *Handbuch*, 116, and Part II, Table 5, figs. 24–25. See n. 10.
13 Cf. Walther, *Praecepta*, 142–3, and Mattheson, *Capellmeister*, 309.

Example 5b. Mattheson, *Capellmeister*, 325

instance the two writers differ somewhat in their interpretations, although for both the essential resolution is to the octave. As in the case of the progression of perfect to augmented fourth, Walther illustrates this as a delayed upper voice, whereas Mattheson again speaks of "eine Vorausnahm in Baß."

Interestingly, the progression of ninth to seventh is explained both ways by Walther: as arising from either an anticipated bass or a delayed upper voice. Mattheson, in this instance, is in favor of the delayed upper voice explanation. His example, differing somewhat from Walther's, is given in Example 6a. Mattheson clearly states that if the second note of the soprano were changed to a quarter value and the third note to a half, then the *Figur der Verzögerung* would be eliminated and the resolution of the ninth would be made to the octave. Example 6b is a representation of what Mattheson describes. Mattheson's discussion here is important in that it is really his clearest association of *Verzögerung* with assumed rhythmic delay in a situation where dissonance appears to resolve to dissonance. It might be added, too, that Marpurg seems to repeat Mattheson's example, transposed up a minor third, and faithfully transcribes in his *Handbuch* Mattheson's verbal explanation into notation.

Example 6a. Mattheson, *Capellmeister*, 325

450

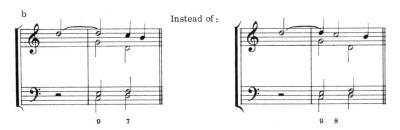

Example 6b. Cf. Marpurg, *Handbuch*, Part II, Table 6, Figs. 34, 35

For the progression of fourth to seventh, Mattheson himself provides such a notated explanation of assumed delay in the upper part. His figural example is given in Example 7a, his explanation in 7b.

Example 7a. Mattheson, *Capellmeister*, 311

Example 7b. "Unfigürlich," Mattheson, *Capellmeister*, 311

In his description Mattheson speaks of the unaccented sixth that would have resulted without the figure, which he designates not as Verzögerung but as an irregular passing tone ("transitum irregularem" and "nicht regelmäßigen Durchgang"). Such disparity of terminology exists throughout Mattheson's examples of similar situations, in which, in an attempt to explain dissonance resolving to dissonance, a voice is assumed to have been delayed from its regular resolution. For example, the progressions of ninth to perfect fourth and major seventh to perfect fourth are also explained by Mattheson in terms of an irregular passing tone. In the case of the latter progres-

451

sion, the upper voice is clearly illustrated as having been delayed.[14] This inconsistency regarding terminology possibly reflects Mattheson's new and somewhat uncertain grasp of the concept, or perhaps he is simply still searching for the most suitable designation for his newer conception of retardation. He seems to prefer, however, the literal translation of another seventeenth-century Latin designation, *retardatio*. Bernhard defines this figure of the theatrical style as "a lingering, when a note should climb a second but waits too long before climbing."[15] Although he seems merely to be describing the upward-resolving suspension, it was probably the element of irregular delay associated with this figure that prompted Mattheson to use it for his broader conception of delayed consonance. His translation of this term obviously gave him a more concise designation than "ein nicht regelmäßiger Durchgang." Interestingly, some later German writers continue the seventeenth-century meaning of *retardatio* by defining Verzögerung as an upward-resolving suspension.[16] The word, therefore, acquires two meanings.

Mattheson's concept of Verzögerung seems clear from most of his musical examples and discussions. The only real confusion lies in his introduction of the term, and in his initial use of it in discussing the augmented second and perfect fourth. He introduces the reader to Verzögerung in his discussion of the progression of augmented second to major third. Here it is defined as the counterpart (*Gegenspiel*) of *Vorausnahm*, or *anticipation*, a point he seems already to have made in his *Kleine General-Baß-Schule* (1735).[17] This definition is, as we have seen from the examples presented thus far, a very apt description. His augmented-second example, however, shows a normal, suspended-bass resolution to the major third. Mattheson goes on to use the term in conjunction with another augmented-second resolution to the third, one in which the upper voice resolves the dissonance. *Vorausnahm* and Verzögerung are then referred to not only as "extraordinary phrases" ("außerordentliche Sätze"), but also as "the strangest of all suspensions, in that the effect of a dissonance is actually only an *anticipatio* or *retardatio*, that is, a pleasant anticipation of passing tones or a clever holding back [Zurückhaltung] of the consonance."[18]

14 *Capellmeister*, 318.
15 ". . . eine Veräumung, wenn nehmlich eine Note eine Secunda steigen solte und sich zu lange vor dem Steigen aufhält." Bernhard, *Ausführlicher Bericht*, Chap. 19. See Müller-Blattau, *Kompositionslehre*, 151.
16 E.g., Heinichen, *Der General-Baß*, 702–5.
17 Cf. *Capellmeister*, 306, and *General-Baß-Schule* II, 228.
18 *Capellmeister*, 306–7.

The last portion of Mattheson's statement here seems to be not only a justification for these strange figures, but also a broad, theoretical explanation of the origin of all dissonance. As if to illustrate this association of *Verzögerung* with this broader conception, Mattheson applies his new term a few pages later to a discussion of perfect fourths progressing to thirds. His figural example given in Example 8a shows two such progressions. He describes them as "nothing but *retardationes* or *Verzögerungen,*" without which the passage would appear as in Example 8b, his version of the passage "sine figura." One

Example 8a. Mattheson, *Capellmeister,* 308

Example 8b. Mattheson, *Capellmeister,* 308

must laud Mattheson's attempt here to synthesize the ideas of his predecessors into a more unified conceptual framework, but censure his ambiguous terminology. Nevertheless, his other examples reveal his intent clearly enough. Marpurg especially profited from Mattheson's examples of *Verzögerung,* particularly those examples dealing with ninths. On the basis of these examples, Marpurg extends the application of this explanation to the progression of eleventh to sixth. The *Handbuch* also applies *Verzögerung* to the bass, as an alternate explanation of its inverted ninth and eleventh chords.[19] In fact, the term "Verzögerung" seems most often associated with the ninth chord by other German writers after Mattheson.

19 Part II, Table 7, fig. 17; and Table 9, figs. 20–5.

Although Verzögerung never becomes as important in German theory as the concepts of Verwechselung and Vorausnehmung, it did have a noticeable influence. It was used by Daniel Türk, for example, as an alternate explanation of the concept of the anticipated right-hand chord. In this usage, too, it realizes Mattheson's claim regarding its complementary relationship to anticipation.[20] Most interesting, however, is its use by Johann Philipp Kirnberger and J. A. P. Schulz to explain nonessential dissonance. Although only Schulz actually used the term "Verzögerung," the concept is clearly the same in the writing of both authors. This concept was particularly useful to them in explaining the nonessential seventh of the leading-tone seventh chord. Quite simply, the seventh is described as having been delayed from its normal resolution to the sixth, before the harmony resolves to the tonic chord. Therefore, the figural resolution is to the fifth, but the essential resolution to the sixth. The latter resolution implies, however, that the leading-tone seventh chord is really a dominant-ninth chord in first inversion, and that the seventh is really a nonessential ninth being delayed from its normal resolution to the true fundamental of the chord. Schulz's figural example of this progression is given in Example 9a, his notated explanation in Example 9b.[21] It should be pointed out that throughout his discussion in *Die wahren Grundsätze zum Gebrauche der Harmonie* (1773) Schulz is careful to distinguish between normal suspensions (*Vorhälte*) and those whose resolutions have been retarded (*verzögert*).[22]

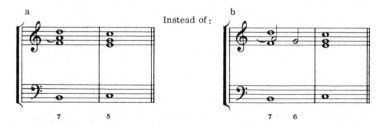

Example 9a. Kirnberger (Schulz), *Grundsätze*, 17–18

Example 9b. Kirnberger (Schulz), *Grundsätze*, 17–18

20 D. Türk, *Anweisung zum Generalbaßspielen* (Halle, 1824), 316–19.
21 See also J. P. Kirnberger, *Die Kunst des reinen Satzes in der Musik* (Berlin, 1776–9; repr. Hildesheim, 1968), I, esp. 68, 70, 79.
22 See J. A. P. Schulz [with J. P. Kirnberger], *Die wahren Grundsätze zum Gebrauche der Harmonie* (Berlin, 1773), esp. 17–20.

Also innovative is Schulz's use of both the anticipation and delay concepts to provide progressions of parallel sixth chords with root movements by fourths and sixths. Schulz's examples here can be said to illustrate perfectly Mattheson's conception of the complementary relationship between anticipation and retardation. Example 10a is intended to be figural, the result of a continually anticipated upper voice. The essential progression is given in Example 10b. Example 11a is another figural passage, almost identical with Example 10a. Schulz states, however, that it is the result of continually retarded lower voices, the unfigural examples given in Example 11b. It is particularly interesting to note that in this series of examples Schulz is using both anticipation and retardation to explain away consónance rather than dissonance. The descending sequences of sevenths are not only fully justified as essential dissonances but represent a basic, unembellished version of the harmony. One is tempted to speculate that it was because of Mattheson's broad conception of Verzögerung that Schulz was able to utilize it in the variety of ways he did.

Example 10a. Kirnberger (Schulz), *Grundsätze*, 45

Example 10b. Kirnberger (Schulz), *Grundsätze*, 45

455

Example 11a. Kirnberget (Schulz), *Grundsätze*, 46–7

Example 11b. Kirnberger (Schulz), *Grundsätze*, 46–7

To draw conclusions from such a narrow examination of Mattheson as a theorist is admittedly difficult and presumptuous. Any such conclusions must be tentative, and taken in the context of similarly close examinations of other areas of Mattheson's theoretical writings. What emerges from this study, however, does seem to correspond to a growing consensus among scholars regarding Mattheson's importance and contributions. This is a view of him not so much as a bold innovator, but as one who was highly receptive to the innovative ideas of others, and one who attempted to clarify and systematize these ideas into a broader conceptual framework. As the foremost musical spokesman of his age in Germany, Mattheson tried to explain new ideas and in the process to evaluate them in light of current practice and theoretical tradition. With regard to *Verwechselung* and *Vorausnahm* he must be regarded as an important clarifier and transmitter of these concepts to succeeding generations. These concepts were fairly well defined and established by others before him.

Mattheson elaborated upon them in *Der vollkommene Capellmeister*, adding some of his own examples. In so doing, he became an important source for Marpurg and others. Unlike the concepts of *Verwechselung* and *Vorausnehmung*, the conception of an assumed rhythmic retardation was not received by Mattheson in a well-formulated state. Nevertheless, he perceived its complementary relationship to anticipation and defined it accordingly. Without Mattheson's creative efforts in this regard, the concept of *Verzögerung* might well have died with Walther. With respect to all three of these concepts Mattheson's *Vollkommener Capellmeister* represents a rich repository, providing later writers with a wealth of material. Mattheson's definite views, together with his systematic mind, ensured that this work was not only remarkably comprehensive for his day, but also highly unified. One can conclude that, despite the diversity of information in *Der vollkommene Capellmeister*, this unique work stands as a monumental synthesis of all that was worth knowing about music during that time.

PART V

Mattheson bibliography: an evaluation

23

Johann Mattheson's historical significance: conflicting viewpoints

ERNEST HARRISS

Martin, Tennessee

Johann Mattheson was active in diplomatic service for half a century, a successful businessman, a central figure in Hamburg's rich cultural life, and indefatigable in the pursuit of his interests.[1] Though he was the leading advocate of English pragmatism in Hamburg,[2] he did not hesitate to use concepts from philosophies to which he was fundamentally opposed, if that was convenient and practical.[3] As a result, scholars seeking to categorize him have been led to different conclusions. A review of the Mattheson literature reveals just how varied the interpretations of his significance and perspective are.

One reason for the conflicting interpretations of Mattheson is to be found in the diversity of his works and the changing cultural climate in which they were produced. Some of the basic elements of the stylistic synthesis that evolved during the eighteenth century were emerging as Mattheson began his long career as an author on musical subjects in 1713.[4] By the time he put down his pen, about fifty years later, the essential elements of the new style had long been established. Although the complexities of this process are reflected in his books, Mattheson's basic philosophical posture remained the same during this entire period.[5]

Another source of divergent views is to be found in the perspectives of later writers. Their studies of Mattheson's contributions have yielded a wide range of conclusions. A number of these differences are revealed in the following discussion of the literature on Matthe-

---

1 See Cannon, *Mattheson*, especially the annotated bibliography. Bibliographical data for most items cited here are to be found in the annotated bibliography.
2 Flaherty, *Opera*, 81–92.
3 Hosler, *Changing Aesthetic Views*, 71–6.
4 With *Orchestre* I.
5 Flaherty, *Opera*, 81–92, traces this from 1713 to 1755. See also Braun, *Mattheson*, 115–17.

son. The reader finds that it is possible to think almost anything about Mattheson, as a person and as a scholar. Depending upon which authorities one chooses to believe, Mattheson can be considered a charlatan or one of the greatest music scholars who ever lived. He can be labeled a French rationalist or the leader of British pragmatism in Hamburg. Confounding this situation is the fact that there are so many misunderstandings to be found in the general literature on eighteenth-century music.[6]

The literature

Hirsching (1800–1) opens the nineteenth-century literature on Mattheson with a short, positive article on Mattheson's historical significance. Becker (1842) recognizes Mattheson's contributions but also notes that he knew how to make enemies. This last observation proves apocalyptic, as Winterfeld (1847) is very harsh. His study of Mattheson's Brockes Passion is a bitter commentary about Mattheson's supposed incompetence as a composer. Because Winterfeld finds him to be so inept, he regrets that Mattheson's scholarly works about music have received so much favorable attention. Winterfeld thus initiates a period of overt hostility toward Mattheson.

Chrysander (*G. F. Händel,* 1858) unmercifully attacks Mattheson, both as a person and as a musician. His view that Handel's experiences in Hamburg were essentially negative led him to question the personal and professional qualities of the musicians with whom Handel had worked, especially Keiser and Mattheson. Perhaps because Mattheson left considerable documentation that tends to contradict such an interpretation, Chrysander expended a great deal of energy assaulting his credibility. Even though Chrysander disseminated certain of Mattheson's contributions widely through a series of articles in the *Allgemeine musikalische Zeitung,* his views have tended to limit the interest of Handel scholars in his Hamburg years and in his colleagues there.[7] Later scholars have repeated his prejudices against Mattheson's ideas, sometimes with embellishments.

Von Dommer (1864, vols. 252–4, 273–4) projects the same perspective as Chrysander. Anti–eighteenth-century and anti-*galant* biases are strongly expressed. But Ungewitter (1868, p. 5) takes up Matthe-

6 "The music of the so-called Classic era is still among the least explored areas." P. H. Lang, "Musicology in the 1980s: Points of Arrival and Goals, Introduction," in: *The Journal of Musicology* 1 (1982), 3.
7 The situation seems to have been improving since the appearance of P. H. Lang's *George Frideric Handel* (New York, 1966).

son's defense, saying that he was as important for theory and aesthetics as were Bach and Handel for practice. Engel (1876, p. 26–7) presents a more balanced picture of Mattheson, but concludes by implicitly attacking Chrysander and other then-modern scholars, whom he found to be less competent as writers than Mattheson had been. While Meinardus (1879, p. 216–17) continues to defend Mattheson, Eitner (1884, p. 626) presents an evenhanded review of Mattheson's accomplishments, calling him a musical reformer who was in the right place at the right time.

Haberl (1885) essentially follows von Dommer's line of thinking, and Riehl (1886) entertains us with a novellike description of life in the eighteenth century.[8] While the latter is not free of errors, Mattheson is portrayed as a pathfinder for modern musical aesthetics. In his discussion of the beginnings of music journalism in Germany, Krome (1897) reviews Mattheson's role as an important innovator and outlines the contents of his journals. This dissertation is one of the first studies with sufficient depth to be of use to scholars interested in Mattheson.

Schmidt (1897) brings the Mattheson studies of the nineteenth century to a close with the first relatively thorough general study of Mattheson and his music. He had carefully reviewed the primary sources, including the items from Mattheson's own library that were in the Hamburg Staats- und Universitätsbibliothek until 1943. Though the intense nationalism with which Schmidt celebrates Mattheson's contributions may be offensive to some, his monograph stands as the best nineteenth-century study of Mattheson.

The overwhelmingly negative commentary from the mid-century writers such as Winterfeld and Chrysander was effectively countered by the time Schmidt's book appeared. Nevertheless, the anti-Mattheson position taken by those scholars has had impact upon the literature of this century. Some twentieth-century writers have recapitulated or expanded upon the hostile views found in this earlier literature, while others have felt constrained to defend Mattheson or to launch counterattacks.

A new and more insidious type of misunderstanding emerged during the early years of this century. The perception crystallized that, in the eighteenth century, formalistic *Affekten-*, *Figuren-*, and

---

8 Riehl, "Mattheson," 44, for example: "Sein Wirken war wie eines Märzsturmes, wie eines Aprilgewitters, das gewaltigen Lärm macht, viel Wasser ergießt, vielen Staub aufwirbeln läßt, mancherlei stört und schädigt, dennoch aber die Luft fegt und den Frühling vorverkündet. Ueber den nachfolgenden sonnigen Tagen vergißt man jenes heilsame Unwetter."

Rhetoriklehren evolved that had a pervasive and direct impact upon compositional processes in some conscious way. Mattheson is often cited as primarily responsible for the formulation of these theories. Such a rationalistic conceptualization of the compositional process is traced in his works, especially in Der vollkommene Capellmeister. This attribution is repeated in much of the pertinent literature.[9]

Schering (1907) was one of the first to develop the concept of an Affektenlehre and to suggest that Mattheson contributed significantly to its formal development.[10] Kretzschmar (1912–13) states that Mattheson was responsible for generating an Affektenlehre for music.[11] Goldschmidt (1915) goes further by indicating that Mattheson began his literary career in 1713 as a very practical person, but that he became thoroughly committed to French neoclassical ideals by the time he published his masterpiece, Der vollkommene Capellmeister, in 1739.[12] According to Goldschmidt, Mattheson fell totally under the sway of French ideas, became anti-German, and therefore was a corrupting influence upon the German national spirit and upon German music. Goldschmidt states that the fully developed Affektenlehre is to be found in the Capellmeister, indicating that this is a major flaw in the work. While Schering had been rather cautious in dealing with Mattheson's relationship to an Affektenlehre, Goldschmidt is unrestrained.

Schering (1911) expressed a very positive opinion of Mattheson as a composer.[13] His study of Mattheson's oratorios contrasts sharply with that of Winterfeld, not least by virtue of its greater thoroughness. He describes Mattheson as an innovative composer and his works as representing an important historical phase in the development of the oratorio.

Whereas Chybinski (1911, p. 60–3) maintains that Mattheson's

---

9 Buelow, "Mattheson and the invention of the Affektenlehre" (Chapter 19 of this volume) traces the process.
10 In "Musikästhetik," 318, he states, however: "Aber an einer wissenschaftlichen Begründung der Lehre, an einem festen Prinzip fehlte es [ca. 1740] noch immer."
11 "Affektenlehre I," 68: "Erst das achtzehnte, das große Jahrhundert einer auf Rationalismus und Philanthropie gegründeten Pädagogik, hat die Affektenlehre aus dem Bereich der Allgemeinheiten hinausgeführt. Ihr Hauptpionier ist da J o h a n n M a t t h e s o n."
12 Musikästhetik, 63: "'Der vollkommene Kapellmeister'. . . faßt alles das Angeführte zusammen, unterstreicht aber die rationalistische Neigung des Verfassers energisch. Der französische Einfluß ist auch äußerlich bemerkbar."
13 Geschichte des Oratoriums, 340: "So bilden denn Mattheson's Oratorien eine wichtige Entwicklungsstufe in der Geschichte der Gattung und sichern uns zugleich einen Standpunkt, von dem aus einzelne Züge Bach'scher und Händel'scher Oratorienkunst geschichtlich zu beurteilen sind."

writings have made a positive contribution to our understanding of Polish music of the eighteenth century, Torrefranca (1917–18) finds little good to say about the Germans. He uses Mattheson's words to attack German music and musical scholarship.[14] It is unfortunate that he chose to attack a German strength, musicology; he would have been more precise if he had indicated that German musicologists, as excellent as they have been, have not accurately reported the Italian influence upon the music of the eighteenth century.

Koch (1923, p. 5–8) studied the music periodicals of the eighteenth century, reviewing the contents of Mattheson's path-breaking contributions. However, he failed to recognize that Mattheson's models had influence upon later writers. Petzoldt (1931, p. 890) renews the counterattack against scholars hostile to Mattheson, giving a relatively favorable opinion of his abilities as a composer. Schäfke (1934) provides the first substantial response to those (e.g., Goldschmidt) who label Mattheson a neoclassicist and rationalist.[15] After a discussion of the *Affektenlehre* and the *Rhetoriklehre*, he concludes that Mattheson was much more intuitive and much less rationalistic than had been indicated by earlier writers. In stating that Mattheson was not really under the spell of French neoclassical thought, he anticipates the conclusions of several more recent authors.[16]

Andres (1938) and Stege (1939) consider Mattheson as a music critic. The former emphasizes Mattheson's role in arousing intellectual interest in music among dilettants and in establishing music as a scholarly discipline.[17] Though Stege considers Mattheson to have been a rationalist, he also states that he was unfairly attacked or suppressed during the nineteenth century by persons who did not share the aesthetic values of the *galant* period in the eighteenth century. Stege also asserts that Mattheson is a genuine hero who only during this century is beginning to receive a fair evaluation (p. 411).

These two studies prepared the way for the appearance of Cannon's work on Mattheson (1947). His monograph is the only one that

---

14 "La lotta," 358–78, has the subtitle: "Pregiudizi estetici dei tedeschi."
15 Schäfke, *Musikästhetik*, 306–7, discusses Mattheson's point of view, quoting Mattheson, and then notes: "Diese Worte Matthesons zeigen deutlich, daß Hugo Goldschmidts Kritik [1915], die er vom Standpunkt des 'konkreten Idealismus' Eduard von Hartmanns an der Affektentheorie des 18. Jahrhunderts übt, . . . nicht zutrifft."
16 Braun (1952), Flaherty (1978), and Hosler (1981).
17 *Musikkritik*, 9: "Die ersten Ansätze zu einer bewußten und gesellschaftsbildenden Musikkritik [Mattheson's *Critica musica*] . . . ist nicht nur als die erste musikalische Fachzeitschrift zu trachten, in ihr beginnt Musik in der öffentlichen Meinung eine Rolle zu spielen."

reflects a thorough study of all of the materials from Mattheson's library which were housed in the Hamburg library until 1943. Until these materials are again generally available to Western scholars, Cannon's study will stand as the only source for obtaining an adequate overview of their contents. Thus his critical bibliography (p. 146–217) is especially valuable. While Cannon's book marks the close of the period during which scholars had easy access to Mattheson's personal papers, it also initiates a period in which his ideas have received increasing attention. It has served as a catalyst, according to Blume (1948, p. 71), making more apparent the scope of the work yet to be done if we are to understand Mattheson adequately.

A major contribution to understanding Mattheson's part in philosophical and theoretical issues appeared in Braun's dissertation (1952). Braun systematically reviews the evolution of Mattheson's philosophical perspective and gives attention to the major musical issues that Mattheson had explored. Thus, this dissertation complements Cannon's biographical and cultural study. Had it been generally available, some of the confusions about Mattheson's philosophical-aesthetic point of view, so numerous in the scholarly literature since 1952, could have been avoided.

Wessel (1955), for example, continues to associate Mattheson with a formalistic *Affektenlehre,* even though his dissertation reveals that he is ambivalent about the formality of this "doctrine" as it relates to practice. While he fairly consistently follows the interpretation established by Schering, Kretzschmar, and Goldschmidt, he never seems to accept fully the view that Mattheson developed a formal *Affektenlehre.*

Further, Lenneberg (1958) continues to associate Mattheson with French neoclassical thought, providing a well-annotated translation of sections of the *Capellmeister* to demonstrate that Mattheson tended toward a rationalistic position.[18] Because the studies done by Wessel and Lenneberg have been easily accessible (while Braun's dissertation has not), their ideas have, until very recently, had considerably more impact upon the literature on Mattheson than have Braun's.

Hoffmann-Erbrecht (1954) published a brief study of Mattheson's keyboard music. Though he is less enthusiastic about Mattheson's music than Seiffert (1899), he states that his keyboard music has been

18 "Mattheson on Affect," 47–8: "In the course of his many writings . . . Mattheson became more and more specific . . . [until] he finally created a veritable catalogue of almost all that should be known by the composer in order to write affectingly." This is the point of Goldschmidt's discussion that leads up to his conclusion quoted in note 12.

unjustly ignored, placing it on a par with that of Kuhnau, Telemann, and Muffat. While Mattheson is characterized as a conservative composer, conforming to the German keyboard tradition, elements of his style reveal that he was aware of the innovations occurring in Italian instrumental music.[19]

Wolff (1957) supplies the only adequate survey of Mattheson's operas.[20] Having had access to the scores that were in the Hamburg library before 1943, Wolff finds that Mattheson was an individualistic and musically quite advanced composer. He traces Mattheson's efforts into the 1720s, when he "recomposed" an Italian opera in the modern "preclassical" Italian idiom. Wolff also offers a new assessment of Mattheson's relationship with Handel, indicating that Mattheson had in fact been a strong and positive influence upon his younger contemporary during the latter's years in Hamburg.

Buelow's study and edition of the opera *Cleopatra* (1970 and 1975) lead the list of analyses which make the past decade one of the most fruitful for gaining a clearer understanding of Mattheson. Buelow amplifies upon Wolff's view (p. 289) that Mattheson was a gifted composer who had a significant influence upon the younger Handel. He also demonstrates that Mattheson's theoretical observations were consistent with his practice as a composer. The interrelationship is so consistent as to cause Buelow to consider the theorist's writings to be practical guides to Mattheson's compositional practices.[21]

Frederichs (1975) provides one of the most thorough studies of Mattheson the composer. His detailed examination of the four settings of the Brockes Passion (by Keiser, Handel, Telemann, and Mattheson) reveals that Johann Mattheson was a skilled and innovative composer who bears comparison with his distinguished colleagues (p. 197). Frederichs devotes considerable attention to the treatment of the text and provides a careful analysis of the musical settings. Mattheson's version is shown to be equal to the others and, in a number of ways, considerably more advanced stylistically.

19 *Klaviermusik*, 34: "[Man muß feststellen,] . . . daß er sich, seinen musikalischen Qualitäten entsprechend, fast ebenbürtig in der Linie Kuhnau–Telemann–Muffat einorden läßt." P. 36: "In vielen kompositorischen Einzelheiten kündigt sich . . . unmißverständlich ein neues musikalisches Zeitalter an."
20 *Barockoper*, 293: "Trotz der verschiedensten italienischen, französischen und englischen Einflüsse schloß Mattheson sich im Wesen seiner Musik der deutschen Tradition an . . . Er richtete sich dabei niemals mechanisch nach den Schulregeln, sondern bildete diese im Stile des neuen Affektausdruckes und der 'gesanglichen' Melodiebildung um. So stellte er zum ersten Male mit aller Deutlichkeit in Deutschland eine Norm auf, der seine Zeitgenossen . . . und noch die nächsten Generationen folgten."
21 "An Evaluation of *Cleopatra*," 95–8.

Benary (1960, p. 69) states that Mattheson is a key figure in understanding the changes in musical style that occurred in mid-century. Mattheson's theories about melody are singled out as the basis for the *galant* aesthetic. Curiously, Benary asserts that those theories antedate *galant* practices. The reason for this conclusion is that Benary sought his models for innovative practices among German composers (e.g., C. P. E. Bach).[22] But, as indicated above, the Italian composers with whom Mattheson was familiar had moved toward the new "preclassical" style by the 1720s. His theories do not antedate practice, though they do reveal that he was aware of the latest stylistic developments.

Wessely (1964, p. 9–10) deals with the relationship between Mattheson and Fux.[23] After pointing out that Fux scholars have manifested a bias against Mattheson, as a rule, he states that the correspondence between these two important theorists had been distorted by historians. Neither man, as Wessely sees it, sustained either short- or long-term animosity toward the other. Indeed, he considers Mattheson to have been the winner in the dispute, and noble in victory. But Federhofer (1970) maintains that Mizler considered Mattheson less important than Fux. He focuses his attention upon theories of harmony and counterpoint, showing that Fux's influence is clearly superior to that of Mattheson. Federhofer suggests that Mattheson should have considered harmony and counterpoint important enough to spend more energy upon them.[24] He seems to overlook the fact that Mattheson would not have considered such an emphasis proper, for he considered melody, not harmony and counterpoint, the aspect of music of greatest interest.[25] Federhofer's view that Fux's theories of harmony and counterpoint were of greater importance than Matthe-

---

22 P. 81: "Johann Sebastian Bach, sein Sohn Philipp Emanuel und Mozart sind die entsprechenden Meilensteine. Auf sie stützt sich die musikgeschichtliche Darstellung . . . In der Melodielehre geht aber offensichtlich die theoretische Beschäftigung der kompositorischen Praxis voraus! . . . [mit] Johann Mattheson als vorangehender Theoretiker . . . " An even more curious situation is encountered in K. G. Fellerer, "Zur Melodielehre im 18. Jahrhundert," in: *Studia musicologica* 3 (1962), 109–15. Though Mattheson's writings establish the basis for a *Melodielehre* during that century, he is completely ignored.
23 "Überhaupt muß man sagen, daß Fux leider schlecht gerüstet in den Krieg gezogen ist . . . und schon die unmittelbar darauf folgenden Jahre haben Mattheson Recht und Fux unrecht gegeben. Daß der 'böse' Mattheson trotz dieser Sachlage ein nobler Sieger blieb, zeigt nicht nur sein letzter Brief an Fux, sondern die Art und Weise, wie er nach dieser kleinen Episode . . . über diesen geurteilt hat."
24 "Fux und Mattheson," 111, compares *Gradus ad Parnassum* and *Der vollkommene Capellmeister*, as seen by Mizler.
25 He devotes only about half a page to melody, p. 113–14.

son's theories to the emergence of the Classical Style indicates that his perspective is fundamentally different from Mattheson's.

Lester (1977) presents a different interpretation of his thoughtful analysis of the Fux–Mattheson correspondence, emphasizing Mattheson's efforts to rid music of outmoded practices. Lester (1978) also assigns to Mattheson a major role in consummating the change from a modal to a major-minor orientation in theoretical treatises. While he had traced this process to the late seventeenth century in an earlier article,[26] the central objective of this essay is to describe the final theoretical acceptance of the newer system. Though Heinichen is given a significant role in this process, Mattheson is clearly the central figure in the discussion.[27] At the end of the decade, Buelow (1978–9, p. 184), in his review of the evolution of the *Melodielehre* as it relates to Classical style, also considers Mattheson to have been a key figure in the development of the new musical synthesis of the eighteenth century.

Returning to the philosophical issues, Willheim (1963) focuses sharply on Mattheson in his dissertation on Scheibe.[28] He asserts that Mattheson had been a rationalist, heavily influenced by the ideas of the French neoclassicists. Scheibe, a student of the neoclassicist Gottsched, is said to have turned against the ideals of that teacher as well as those of Mattheson as he led the movement toward a pragmatic philosophical perspective, based upon British models, which became increasingly influential (p. 24, 95–6). Had Willheim shared Braun's insights into Mattheson's point of view, this dissertation would surely have painted a different picture of the relationship between these two important theorists. Indeed, it probably would have been clear to Willheim that the time Scheibe lived in Hamburg (1736–9) was critical to his change of philosophical orientation. Mattheson, an employee of the English Resident and an advocate of British ideas, would have been seen as a major influence.[29] Lindberg (1964, p. 148–58) does in fact quarrel with the view that Mattheson was in the French neoclassical camp. Taking a position which was to become more common during the 1970s, his specific observation is that Mattheson rejected neoclassical arguments relating to opera.

26 In: *JAMS* 30 (1977), 208–53; see Bibliography.
27 Of the twenty-one pages which make up the main body of this study, about six emphasize Heinichen's contributions whereas about thirteen focus upon Mattheson's ideas.
28 Willheim provides possibly the best illustration of how twentieth-century misunderstandings of Mattheson's perspective have led modern scholars to distort his relationship with his contemporaries.
29 Braun, *Mattheson*, 129–35.

On the other hand, Dahlhaus (1967, p. 507–8) finds that Mattheson's analogies between rhetoric and music are a basis for a rationalistic or neoclassical interpretation of his position similar to that found in Goldschmidt. But Ramirez (1967) never seems able to make up her mind on this critical question.[30] Her thesis on the *Affektenlehre*, Mattheson, and Rameau is filled with a sense of ambivalence toward the notion of a formal "doctrine" of the Affections. The nonspecific nature of the *Affekten*, and the important role which intuition plays for both theorists, conflict with rationalistic assumptions in a manner which is never fully resolved. While Brenner (1968, p. 49–52) is clearly torn by the same conflict, she ultimately comes to the position that there was in fact some quasi-formal doctrine which had a direct impact upon the compositional process during the eighteenth century.

Kivy (1973, p. 140) uses Lenneberg's translation (1958) as a basis for indicating that Mattheson's aesthetic is essentially the same as Susanne Langer's. Thus Mattheson is said to have anticipated the modern semantic-symbolic theory of music and to have been a pioneer in this area. Here again it is assumed that Mattheson was basically a neoclassicist. The same interpretation appears again in Ritzel's discussion (1974, p. 30–1) of the development of the sonata form. On the one hand he seems content to give Mattheson considerable credit for his role during the early evolutionary phases, but he seems unwilling to admit that Mattheson's ideas had practical implications as the century wore on. The assumption that Mattheson was a rationalist seems to prevent the author from dealing with his theoretical contributions in a practical manner. These two studies are the latest to be based upon the assumption that Mattheson's philosophical perspective derived from, or was based upon, French neoclassical models.

Two important works appeared in 1978 which brought into focus a perception of Mattheson's philosophical position that contrasts sharply with the view that Mattheson was a neoclassicist. As indicated above, such a view had been quite influential into the 1970s. Flaherty (1978), in her discussion of Hamburg as an important center for the development of German critical thought, shows that the true orientation of the "Hamburg School" was toward British pragmatism. Further, she selects Mattheson as the primary spokesman for this

30 P. 23: "Though there are treatises on symbolism in the Baroque (such as Mattheson's), the modern reseacher cannot know in what manner the composer applied these rules, or the degree to which he actually abided by them."

point of view, illustrating that he maintained such a perspective throughout his writings.

Hosler's dissertation (1978) is one of the most fascinating to have been transformed into a book for the UMI Research Press series (1981). Having reviewed the secondary literature and having found it extremely confusing and misleading, she turned directly to the primary sources for information. In her analysis of Mattheson's works, she finds that he was not in sympathy with the views of the French neoclassicists (p. 71). Her conclusions are similar to those of Flaherty, expanding upon ideas found in Schäfke (1934), Braun (1952), and Lindberg (1964). Flaherty's and Hosler's analyses provide a basis for questioning the assumptions of Schering, Kretzschmar, and Goldschmidt that are fundamental to much of the literature on Mattheson of this century.

Feldmann (1966) opens his discussion on Mattheson's *Ehrenpforte* with a lengthy assessment of Mattheson's historical significance.[31] In explicit terms, he states that Mattheson had been maligned by earlier historians, especially Chrysander, and that he had thus been denied his proper place in history. After mounting a forceful defense for this position, Feldmann provides a detailed study of the contents of the *Ehrenpforte*. Since this work is sometimes considered Mattheson's most important literary contribution,[32] and since this is the only detailed study devoted to it, Feldmann's essay is of special interest.

Reddick's dissertation (1956) provides the English-language reader with easy access to Mattheson's ideas on continuo performance. Harriss (1981) has provided a modern English translation of Mattheson's important work, *Der vollkommene Capellmeister*. Turnow's article for *Die Musik in Geschichte und Gegenwart* (1960) is the best general source available on Mattheson in German, and a parallel claim can be made for Buelow's English-language article for *The New Grove Dictionary*. Mattheson is seen by Buelow as the most foward-looking and the most representative theorist of his era. Marx's fine edition of Mattheson's autobiography (1982) and his article demonstrating that Mattheson's *Nachlaß* did not perish with the Hamburg library in 1943 (1983) are significant. The former provides the entire autobiography under one cover for the first time, and the latter reveals that primary source material thought lost is still extant. The signifi-

---

31 An important related publication is Max Schneider's edition of the *Ehrenpforte* (Berlin, 1910), which contains substantial additions from manuscript sources.
32 *Baker's Biographical Dictionary of Musicians*, 6th ed., s.v. "Mattheson, Johann."

cance of this last discovery will have its full impact only when Mattheson scholars again have access to these materials. Finally, Buelow (1983) rejects soundly the idea that Mattheson was the creator of a formal Doctrine of Affections. With this, scholars have come full circle in their fundamental perception of Mattheson during this century.[33]

Bibliography

Abraham, L. U., and C. Dahlhaus. *Melodielehre*. Cologne, 1972, 22–7.

> The authors depict Mattheson as the codifier of the concept of melody that was to prevail throughout the eighteenth and nineteenth centuries in vocal and instrumental music.

Andres, H. *Beiträge zur Geschichte der Musikkritik*. Ph.D. diss., Heidelberg University, 1938, 9–13.

> Andres provides insights into the general social conditions under which Mattheson worked and also emphasizes the significant role that he played in the development of nonmusic periodicals.

Becker, C. F. "Winke für allerlei Leser," in: *AmZ* 44 (1842), cols. 345–9.

> Mattheson is characterized as a most fertile writer about music, as richly entertaining, and as more feared than loved by his contemporaries.

Becker, H. "Johann Matthesons handschriftliche Einzeichnungen im 'Musicalischen Lexicon' Johann Gottfried Walthers," in: *Mf* 5 (1952), 346–50.

> Illustrates that Mattheson's annotations to Walther's *Lexicon* are extensive. As Walther had borrowed considerably from Mattheson's writings, the latter's corrections and additions are of particular interest.

Benary, P. *Die deutsche Kompositionslehre des 18. Jahrhunderts*. Leipzig, 1961, 49–61, 81–7.

> Mattheson is described as a mid-century figure. The author states that the *galant* style derived its impetus from Mattheson's

---

33 Buelow, "Mattheson and the invention of the *Affektenlehre*" (Chapter 19 in this volume), by rejecting the assumptions that there was a formalistic "Doctrine" used by composers and that Mattheson was primarily responsible for it, undermines the often-expressed view that Mattheson was an advocate of French neoclassical values.

theory of melody. He ignores the precedents to be found in Italian music and the fact that Mattheson was familiar with that music.

Blume, F. "Beekman C. Cannon, *Johann Mattheson, Spectator in Music*," reviewed in: *Mf* 1 (1948), 69–72.

The positive statements made about Mattheson's historical significance by Blume in this review, just as he was beginning the publication of *MGG*, no doubt contributed to an improved climate for Mattheson-related research.

Braun, W. "Bachs Stellung im Kanonstreit," in: *Bach-Interpretationen*, ed. M. Geck. Göttingen, 1969, 106–11.

This article is as much about Mattheson (and his role in the changes in style that were then occurring) as about Bach.

Braun, W. "Drei deutsche Arien – ein Jugendwerk Händels?" in: *AM1* 42 (1970), 248–51.

Corrects material appearing in the Handel *Forschungs-Bericht* by A. Mann and J. M. Knapp in *AM1* 41 (1969). Three arias that had been attributed to Handel are shown to be from an opera of Mattheson.

Braun, W. *Johann Mattheson und die Aufklärung*. Ph.D. diss., Martin Luther University, Halle-Wittenberg, 1952.

Braun deals with the philosophical crisis of music during the eighteenth century, Mattheson's philosophical and theoretical position, his musical perspective, and his position in relation to the younger generation of rationalists. Braun focuses on Mattheson's ideas and his impact upon musical scholarship. His work complements that of Cannon.

Braun, W. "Musiktheorie im 17./18. Jahrhundert als 'öffentliche' Angelegenheit," in: *Über Musiktheorie*, ed. F. Zaminer. Cologne, 1970, 37–47.

Deals with works intended for dilettantes and especially with Mattheson's *Orchestre* I (1713), the first such publication of significance.

Brenner, R. D. *The Operas of Reinhard Keiser and Their Relationship to the Affektenlehre*. Ph.D. diss., Brandeis University, 1968.

Part One uses Mattheson's ideas extensively. At times Mattheson is depicted as a rigid neoclassicist, and at other times shown to be flexible in considering the Affections beyond neatly rationalistic systems.

Buelow, G. J., ed. Johann Mattheson's *Cleopatra*, in: *Das Erbe deutscher Musik 69*, Mainz, 1975.

Buelow, G. J. "The Concept of 'Melodielehre': A Key to Classic Style," in: *Mozart-Jahrbuch* (1978–9), 182–95.
   Contains a summary of Mattheson's basic concepts on melody, noting that his ideas "foreshadow many of the elements of melodic style found in the music of Classic composers."

Buelow, G. J. "An Evaluation of Johann Mattheson's Opera, *Cleopatra* (Hamburg, 1704)," in: *Studies in Eighteenth-Century Music: A Tribute to Karl Geiringer*, ed. H. C. Robbins Landon and R. E. Chapman. New York and London, 1970, 92–107.

Buelow, G. J. "Mattheson, Johann," in: *New Grove*, vol. 11 (1980), 832–6.
   This most recent encyclopedia article has a good balance between biographical data, evaluation of his importance as a composer, and a commentary on his scholarly and theoretical contributions.

Butler, G. G. "Fugue and Rhetoric," in: *JMT* 21 (1977), 49–109.
   Discusses the relationship between music and rhetoric. Mattheson is cited as the leading German theorist who deals with this topic, and his ideas dominate large sections of the article.

Cannon, B. C., ed. Johann Mattheson's *Das Lied des Lammes*. Madison, 1971.
   In his foreword, Cannon summarizes Mattheson's historical position. The relationship between *Das Lied des Lammes* and Mattheson's critique, in *Critica musica*, of the so-called Handel *St. John Passion* is discussed in light of Chrysander's subsequent attacks on Mattheson.

Cannon, B. C. *Johann Mattheson, Spectator in Music*. New Haven, 1947.
   The most significant study of Mattheson, his life and times. A chapter entitled "The Enlightenment of the Musical Spectator" gives an introduction to Mattheson's intellectual development, with special attention devoted to *Das neu-eröffnete Orchestre*. The critical bibliography of Mattheson's works is particularly important. See Blume's review (1948).

Chrysander, F. "Die erste Periode der Hamburger Oper von 1678 bis 1681," in: *AmZ* 12 (1877), cols. 369–75, 385–91, 401–7, 417–24, 433–7, 449–53, 465–70, 481–6.

Chrysander, F. "Die zweite Periode der Hamburger Oper von 1682 bis 1694, oder vom Theaterstreit bis zur Direction Kusser's," in: *AmZ* 13 (1878), cols. 289–95, 305–12, 324–9, 340–6, 355–61, 371–6, 388–92, 405–10, 420–4, 439–42.

Chrysander, F. "Die Hamburger Oper unter der Direction von Joh. Sigmund Kusser, 1693–1696," in: AmZ 14 (1879), cols, 385–93, 401–8.

Chrysander, F. "Geschichte der Hamburger Oper vom Abgange Kusser's bis zum Tode Schott's (1695–1702)," in: AmZ 14 (1879), cols. 433–41, 449–59, 465–74, 479–83, 497–504, 513–21, 529–33.

Chrysander, F. "Geschichte der Hamburger Oper unter der Direction von Reinhard Keiser (1703–1706)," in: AmZ 15 (1880), cols. 17–25, 33–41, 49–55, 65–72, 81–8.

  Chrysander draws heavily upon Mattheson's writings for his information. His first significant comments about Mattheson occur in his discussion of Mattheson's first opera, *Die Plejades* (1699). More substantial statements on Mattheson in this article are found in the discussion of the Handel–Mattheson duel, and in his observations relating to Mattheson's involvement in the composition of Handel's first opera, *Almira*. Chrysander's personal copy of *AmZ*, now in the Hamburg Staats- und Universitätsbibliothek, has numerous handwritten corrections.

Chrysander, F. *G. F. Händel*. 3 vols., Leipzig, 1858–67, vol. 1, 72–146.

  Chrysander's examination of Handel's time in Hamburg deals equally with Mattheson. Not only are his writings extensively utilized, but his personality also receives considerable attention. Chrysander is especially harsh in his comments about Mattheson; his negative judgments have subsequently had a deleterious impact on Mattheson's reputation.

Chrysander, F. "Matthesons Verzeichniss hamburgischer Opern von 1678 bis 1728, gedruckt im 'Musikalischen Patrioten,' mit seinen handschriftlichen Fortsetzungen bis 1751, nebst Zusätzen und Berichtigungen," in: AmZ 12 (1877), cols. 198–200, 215–20, 234–6, 245–51, 261–6. 280–2.

  Chrysander provides a brief introduction and some annotations for Mattheson's chronicle of the Hamburg opera found in the *Musicalischer Patriot* and in related manuscript documents.

Chrysander, F. "Miscellanea Matthesoniana," in: AmZ 13 (1878), cols. 673–80, 691–6.

  A shortened version of a manuscript in Mattheson's hand in the collection of the Hamburg Staats- und Universitätsbibliothek (MS 1272/1). Chrysander adds brief comments to this listing of titles of texts that were set by Mattheson. Short essays are also listed.

Chybiński, A. "Die deutschen Musiktheoretiker im 16.–18. Jahrhundert und die polnische Musik," in: *ZIMG* 12 (1911), 55–65.

Comments upon German writers' observations about Polish music, especially dance forms. Mattheson is considered an important source in aesthetic and theoretical concerns.

Dahlhaus, C. "Gefühlsästhetik und musikalische Formenlehre," in: *Deutsche Vierteljahrsschrift für Literaturwissenschaft und Geistesgeschichte* 41 (1967), 505–16.

Mattheson's discussion relating musical form and rhetoric in his *Capellmeister* is cited as the last theory of composition that is not based in musical practice. Mattheson is also judged to have come at the end of an era.

Dommer, A. von. "Die deutsche Oper in Hamburg zu Ende des 17. und Anfang des 18. Jahrhunderts," in: *AmZ* 2 (1864), cols. 217–23, 233–54, 273–7.

A lecture presented in Hamburg exhibiting the anti-*galant*, pro-Handel tone so evident in Chrysander's *Händel*. Mattheson is not seen in a favorable light.

Eitner, R. "Mattheson, Johann," in: *Allgemeine deutsche Biographie,* vol. 20 (1884, 2d ed. 1970), 621–6.

In face of Chrysander's attack upon Mattheson in his Handel biography, Eitner strives to present a more balanced view. He bases his biographical information on Mattheson's *Ehrenpforte*.

Engel, C. "Mattheson on Handel," in: *Musical Myths and Facts,* vol. 2. London, 1876, 1–27.

The article centers primarily upon Mattheson's annotations to his translation of Mainwaring's biography of Handel.

Federhofer, H. "Johann Joseph Fux und Johann Mattheson im Urteil Lorenz Christoph Mizlers," in: *Speculum musicae artis: Festgabe für Heinrich Husmann,* ed. H. Becker and R. R. Gerlach. Munich, 1970, 111–23.

Federhofer discusses Mizler's sympathy for Fux's theories and his antipathy for those of Mattheson. Much of the article deals with Mattheson's theories of harmony and counterpoint found in Part III of the *Capellmeister*.

Feldmann, F. "Der Hamburger Johann Mattheson (1681–1764) und die Musik Mittel- und Ostdeutschlands," in: *Hamburger Mittel- und Ostdeutsche Forschungen,* vol. 5, ed. H. Pönicke. Hamburg, 1966, 41–113.

The first section of this article contains one of the most positive assessments of Mattheson's importance to have appeared up to that time. The remainder of the study is a narrative analysis, topographically organized, of the persons whose biographies appear in the *Ehrenpforte*, with particular focus upon middle and eastern Germany of the pre–World War II period.

Feldmann, F. "Mattheson und die Rhetorik," in: *Kongreß-Bericht Hamburg 1956*. Kassel, 1957, 99–103.

Emphasis is placed upon Mattheson's significant contributions in developing the relationship between musical and rhetorical structures.

Fellerer, K. G. "Sixteenth-Century Musicians in Mattheson's *Ehrenpforte*," in: *Studies in Musicology: Essays . . . in Memory of Glen Haydon*, ed. J. W. Pruett. Chapel Hill, 1969, 72–9.

The main thrust of this article is to show how little attention was afforded to sixteenth-century musicians during the eighteenth century.

Flaherty, G. *Opera in the Development of German Critical Thought*. Princeton, 1978, 81–92.

Flaherty establishes the fact that the bases for critical thought in Hamburg were pragmatic. Mattheson is singled out as the primary exponent of the Hamburg view, maintaining this position consistently as illustrated in his writings between 1713 and 1755.

Fortner, W. *Johann Matthesons Grosse General-Baß-Schule*. Mainz, 1956.

A greatly abridged version of Mattheson's much larger thorough-bass manual.

Frederichs, H. *Das Verhältnis von Text und Musik in den Brockespassionen Keisers, Händels, Telemanns und Matthesons*. Munich and Salzburg, 1975.

Frederichs provides the best recent analysis of Mattheson's abilities as a composer. The careful attention given to the text is noteworthy, as is Frederichs's systematic analysis of the four musical settings.

Goldschmidt, H. *Die Musikästhetik des 18. Jahrhunderts und ihre Beziehungen zu seinem Kunstschaffen*. Zürich and Leipzig, 1915, 58–68.

The development of Mattheson's aesthetic views is traced through his principal works to the *Capellmeister*. Goldschmidt contributes to the tradition, initiated by Schering (1907) and

Kretzschmar (1911/12), that one need only study the works of Mattheson to find the "Doctrine of the Affections" in its fully developed and definitive forms.

Haberl, F. X. "Johann Mattheson: Biographische Skizze zu dessen Porträt," in: *Caecilien-Kalender* 10 (1885), 53–60.

After reviewing the recent (in 1885) literature on Mattheson, most of which was negative in nature, the author quotes and annotates the sketch of Mattheson contained in von Dommer's *Handbuch der Musik-Geschichte* (1867, 2d ed. 1878).

Harriss, E. C. *Johann Mattheson's "Der vollkommene Capellmeister": A Revised Translation with Critical Commentary.* Ann Arbor, 1981.

Supersedes the original translation completed as a Ph.D. dissertation for George Peabody College for Teachers in 1969.

Hirsching, F. C. G. *Historisch-literarisches Handbuch berühmter und denkwürdiger Personen, welche in dem 18. Jahrhunderte gestorben sind.* Leipzig, 1800–1; repr. Graz, 1953, vol. 5, 85–8.

A biographical article based essentially upon Mattheson's *Ehrenpforte.* The tone is positive.

Hoffmann-Erbrecht, L. *Deutsche und italienische Klaviermusik zur Bachzeit,* in: *Jenaer Beiträge zur Musikforschung* 1 (Leipzig, 1954), 33–7.

The author maintains that Mattheson wrote keyboard music of the same quality as Kuhnau, Muffat, and Telemann. Although he demonstrates that Mattheson's music is conservative, he shows that certain elements of his style reflect an awareness of the latest innovations in Italian instrumental music.

Hosler, B. H. *Changing Aesthetic Views of Instrumental Music in 18th Century Germany.* Ann Arbor, 1981.

The ideas of Johann Mattheson are cited extensively in this work. Hosler's position is that Mattheson was not in sympathy with the principles of French rationalists, despite the fact that he used their ideas whenever they seemed appropriate.

Kivy, P. "What Mattheson Said," in *MR* 34 (1973), 132–40.

Susanne Langer's theory of music expression is compared by Kivy with Mattheson's theories found in the *Capellmeister.* Kivy maintains that Mattheson "deserves perhaps even more than Schopenhauer to be considered a pioneer, an unsung pioneer, in the semantic-symbolic theory of music."

Koch, H. *Die deutschen musikalischen Fachzeitschriften des achtzehnten Jahrhunderts.* Ph.D. diss., University of Halle, 1923.

The evolution of the music periodical is discussed.

Mattheson's role in establishing the first music periodicals and the purposes for such periodicals is outlined.

Kretzschmar, H. "Allegemeines und Besonderes zur Affektenlehre," Parts I and II, in: *JbP* 18 (1911), 63–77, and *JbP* 19 (1912), 65–78.

With Schering (1907), Kretzschmar is one of the first to link Mattheson with the Doctrine of the Affections. He calls Mattheson the "Hauptpionier" of the *Affektenlehre*.

Krome, F. *Die Anfänge des musikalischen Journalismus in Deutschland*. Leipzig, 1897, 9–22.

This dissertation reviews Mattheson's *Critica musica* and *Musicalischer Patriot* and his important contributions to musical journalism in the eighteenth century.

Lenneberg, H. H. "Johann Mattheson on Affect and Rhetoric in Music," in: *JMT* 2 (1958), 47–84, 193–236.

Consists of a well-annotated translation of a section of the *Capellmeister*, taken from Lenneberg's master's thesis (New York University, 1956).

Lester, Joel. "The Fux–Mattheson Correspondence: An Annotated Translation," in: *Current Musicology* 24 (1977), 37–62.

The introduction and annotations to this correspondence are useful. Mattheson leads the attack on outmoded theoretical concepts while Fux defends tradition.

Lester, Joel. "The Recognition of Major and Minor Keys in German Theory, 1680–1730," in: *JMT* 22 (1978), 65–103.

The companion article to Lester's "Major-minor Concepts and Modal Theory in Germany, 1592–1680," in: *JAMS* 30 (1977), 208–53. Lester emphasizes Heinichen's role, but gives greatest credit to Mattheson for consummating this change of theoretical perspective.

Lindberg, D. I. *Literary Aspects of German Baroque Opera: History, Theory, and Practice (Christian H. Postel and Barthold Feind)*. Ph.D. diss., University of California, Los Angeles, 1964.

Mattheson's chronicle of the Hamburg opera is frequently quoted. He is seen as rejecting the arguments of the rationalists relating to opera.

Marx, H. J., ed. *Johann Mattheson (1681–1764): Lebensbeschreibung des Hamburger Musikers, Schriftstellers und Diplomaten. Nach der "Grundlage einer Ehrenpforte" und den handschriftlichen Nachträgen des Verfassers herausgegeben und kommentiert*. Hamburg, 1982.

Mattheson's autobiography is presented under one cover for

the first time. A perceptive introduction, excellent annotations, and numerous photographic reproductions vivify the text.

Marx, H. J. "Johann Matthesons Nachlaß: Zum Schicksal der Musiksammlung der alten Stadtbibliothek Hamburg," in: *AML* 55 (1983), 108–24.

Mattheson's manuscripts and personal copies of his own publications were left to the Staats- und Universitätsbibliothek Hamburg. These items were thought lost during the bombings of 1943. Marx has traced their survival of the war and has demonstrated that most of these invaluable materials are probably now in Russian hands, except for a few items which have been returned to the Staatsbibliothek in East Berlin.

Meinardus, L. "Johann Mattheson und seine Verdienste um die deutsche Tonkunst," in: *Sammlung musikalischer Vorträge*, Series 1, ed. P. Graf Waldersee. Leipzig, 1879, 213–72.

A lecture presented in Dresden in 1874 and repeated in Hamburg a few years later. Meinardus is concerned that the attacks on Mattheson made by Köstlin and Chrysander are excessive and fears that Mattheson's true significance to music has gone unrecognized. The lecture is important primarily as a precursor to Schmidt's biography (1897).

Paumgartner, B., ed. J. Mainwaring's *G. F. Händel*, translated by Mattheson (1761). Zürich, 1947.

The introduction to this edition contains considerable information about Mattheson. Also, in the appendixes, the editor provides the observations made by Charles Burney on Mattheson.

Petzoldt, R. "Johann Mattheson (Zu seinem 250. Geburtstag am 28. September)," in: *Die Musik* 23 (1931), 887–90.

Petzoldt reviews the precarious nature of Mattheson's historical position.

Ramirez, C. J. *A Historical Study of the Doctrine of the Affections as Exemplified in the Theoretical Writings of Johann Mattheson and Jean-Philippe Rameau*. M.A. thesis, University of Oregon, 1967.

Ramirez deals with the nature of musical expression in the eighteenth century, with the physical and philosophical environment in relation to the Doctrine of the Affections, and with the nature of this doctrine in the writings of Rameau and Mattheson.

Reddick, H. P. *Johann Mattheson's Forty-Eight Thorough-Bass Test Pieces: Translation and Commentary*. Ph.D. diss.,

University of Michigan, 1956.

A translation of most of the *Grosse General-Baß-Schule*, and a transcription of the musical examples into modern notation.

Riehl, W. H. von. "Mattheson und seine Zeitgenossen," in: *Musikalische Charakterköpfe* I. Stuttgart, 1886, 37–72.

Written with no pretense to scholarship, Riehl portrays Mattheson as setting the direction for musical aesthetics down to the end of the nineteenth century.

Ritzel, F. *Die Entwicklung der "Sonatenform" im musiktheoretischen Schrifttum des 18. und 19. Jahrhunderts*, in: *Neue musikgeschichtliche Forschungen* I, ed. L. Hoffmann-Erbrecht. Wiesbaden, 3d ed. 1974, 23–55.

Mattheson receives credit for establishing most of the theoretical foundations for the development of the formal theory of instrumental music, but Goldschmidt's (1915) views apparently influence Ritzel's attitude toward Mattheson's later works, especially the *Capellmeister*.

Schäfke, R. *Geschichte der Musikästhetik in Umrissen*. Berlin, 1934, 300–21.

Schäfke illustrates Mattheson's view that the purpose of music is to move human emotions. After relating the *Affektenlehre* to the *Rhetoriklehre*, he uses Mattheson's words to prove that Goldschmidt (1915) is wrong in applying Eduard von Hartmann's "concrete idealism" to the *Affektenlehre*. Schäfke relates Mattheson's theories to the *galant* aesthetic.

Schenkman, W. "Portrait of Mattheson, the Editor, Together with His Correspondents," in: *Bach* 9 (Oct. 1978), 2–10; 10 (Jan. 1979), 3–12; 10 (April 1979), 2–8.

Special attention is given to the *Orchestre* controversies as they are discussed in the letters from famous musicians printed in the *Critica musica* together with Mattheson's commentary.

Schenkman, W. "Theory and Practice: Mattheson's Differing Key Arrangements," in: *Bach* 12 (July 1981), 2–10; 12 (Oct. 1981), 3–9.

In some respects a companion article to the previous one, this deals with issues raised in the Fux–Mattheson correspondence described in the earlier study.

Schering, A. *Geschichte des Oratoriums*. Leipzig, 1911; repr. Wiesbaden, 1966, 335–40.

Schering takes a generally positive view of Mattheson's music, stating that he introduced the oratorio to Hamburg in 1715, and pointing out that Mattheson was innovative in his use of instruments.

Schering, A. "Die Musikästhetik der deutschen Aufklärung," in: ZIMG 8 (1907), 263–71, 316–22.

An important article that establishes the concept of the *Affektenlehre* and Mattheson's relationship to the formal development of the doctrine.

Schmidt, H. *Johann Mattheson, ein Förderer der deutschen Tonkunst, im Lichte seiner Werke.* Leipzig, 1897.

An excellent survey of Mattheson's life and works, with biographical information based upon his autobiography, brought to life by Schmidt's stimulating insights. This study is the most useful work about Mattheson written in the nineteenth century.

Seiffert, M. *Geschichte der Klaviermusik.* Leipzig, 1899; repr. Hildesheim, 1966, 342–50.

As a composer of keyboard music, Mattheson borrowed the most advanced ideas from the Italians, Kuhnau, and Krieger, but he moved beyond them toward more modern harmonies and compositional techniques.

Steblin, R. K. *Key Characteristics in the 18th and Early 19th Centuries: A Historical Approach.* Ann Arbor, 1983.

The fourth chapter is called "Johann Mattheson and the Early 18th-Century German Approach to Key Characteristics" (p. 63–86). It reflects careful study of the primary and secondary literature. Mattheson's statements on this subject are depicted as significant but often contradictory.

Stege, F. "Johann Mattheson und die Musikkritik des 18. Jahrhunderts: Zur 175. Wiederkehr seines Todestages," in: *Zeitschrift für Musik* 106 (1939), 407–11.

Stege gives evidence that periodicals were the organs for change and that Hamburg was Germany's door to the Enlightenment. He sees Mattheson as a leader, with both nonmusical and musical periodicals, and as the father of music criticism.

Torrefranca, F. "La lotta per l'egemonia musicale nel settecento," in: *Rivista musicale italiana* 24 (1917), 343–78; 25 (1918), 1–28, 137–75.

Torrefranca asserts that historians have distorted the facts of the eighteenth century, making it appear that Germany was then in a position of musical leadership. He tries to prove that the Italians were the innovators. In his attacks on the Germans of that period, Mattheson is a primary source and target.

Turnow, H. "Mattheson, Johann," in: *MGG* 8 (1960), cols. 1795–1815.

The biographical information is based mainly on Mattheson's autobiography in the *Ehrenpforte* and on his manuscript continuations of that source. Considerable information from other sources is interpolated. Mattheson's literary works are described and illustrated, and his compositions discussed.

Ungewitter, O. *Johann Mattheson, ein Musiker mit "Zopf und Schwert."* Leipzig, 1868.

An interesting little book in which Mattheson is credited with developing the new aesthetic. He is seen to be as important for theory and aesthetics as Bach and Handel were for practice.

Wessel, F. T. *The "Affektenlehre" in the Eighteenth-Century.* Ph.D. diss., Indiana University, 1955.

Mattheson's ideas are used extensively in the section of this dissertation that focuses upon practical applications.

Wessely, O. "Johann Joseph Fux und Mattheson," in: *Jahresgabe der Johann Joseph Fux-Gesellschaft 1964.* Graz, 1965.

Portrays the literature on Fux as anti-Mattheson. Wessely sees this as basically a case of misunderstanding and unfairness. The focus of the discussion is on the Fux–Mattheson correspondence in *Critica musica.*

Willheim, I. *Johann Adolph Scheibe: German Musical Thought in Transition.* Ph.D. diss., University of Illinois, 1963.

Willheim describes Scheibe as primarily a spokesman for an intuitive, pragmatic philosophical outlook, based upon English models. Mattheson is depicted as an exponent of French neoclassical ideals. Because he places these two contemporaries on opposite sides of the philosophical debates of their time, he misses an opportunity to show how their ideas were interrelated, and does not recognize Scheibe's indebtedness to Mattheson.

Winterfeld, C. von. *Der evangelische Kirchengesang.* Leipzig, 1847, vol. 3, 177–85.

The only oratorio by Mattheson that Winterfeld had seen and studied was his setting of Brockes's version of the Passion. While critical of certain aspects of this composition, Winterfeld believes that the real problem is that Mattheson, here described as a bad composer, has been so influential through his writings.

Wolff, H. C. *Die Barockoper in Hamburg (1678–1738).* Wolfenbüttel, 1957, vol. 1, 284–99.

An especially valuable study of Mattheson's operas. Wolff

asserts that the attacks made upon Mattheson by historians, such as those of Chrysander, are unjust. He sees Mattheson's relationship with Handel as positive and substantial, and his music, though influenced by Keiser, as distinctive and musically advanced.

Zeifas, N. "Mattezon i Teoriia Orkestrovki" (Mattheson and the Theory of Orchestration), in: *Istoriia i sovremennost': Sbornik Statei (History and the Present: A Collection of Articles* [Festschrift Mikhail Druskin]), ed. A. I. Klimovitskii, L. G. Kovnatskaia, and M. D. Sabinina. Leningrad, 1981, 33–54.

Baroque developments in what is now called orchestration are discussed. The roles of individual instruments and types of instruments are discussed in some detail, as these were described in the literature on music of the seventeenth and eighteenth centuries. The ideas of Mattheson are interpolated and placed in their historical context.

Name index

493

Index of Mattheson's writings and compositions

494

Practica